INTEGRATED MARKETING COMMUNICATION

A Balanced Approach

INTEGRATED MARKETING COMMUNICATION
A Balanced Approach

Maxwell Winchester

Peter Ling

Lara Stocchi

May O. Lwin

Wonsun Shin

Hyunjin Kang

OXFORD

OXFORD
UNIVERSITY PRESS

Oxford University Press is a department of the University of Oxford.
It furthers the University's objective of excellence in research,
scholarship, and education by publishing worldwide. Oxford is a registered
trademark of Oxford University Press in the UK and in certain other countries.

Published in Australia by
Oxford University Press
Level 8, 737 Bourke Street, Docklands, Victoria 3008, Australia

A catalogue record for this
book is available from the
National Library of Australia

ISBN 9780195596717

Reproduction and communication for educational purposes

Edited by Sandra Balonyi
Typeset by Newgen KnowledgeWorks Pvt. Ltd., Chennai, India
Indexed by Jon Jermey
Printed in China by Golden Cup Printing Co. Ltd.

BRIEF CONTENTS

Expanded Contents	vi
Figures	xiii
Tables	xvii
About the Authors	xix
Acknowledgments	xxiii
Guided Tour	xxiv
Preface	xxvii
Chapter 1 Introduction to IMC and Communication Models and Processes	3
Chapter 2 Marketing Communication and Consumer Behaviour	35
Chapter 3 Marketing Communication Strategy and Planning	65
Chapter 4 Positioning and Objectives	97
Chapter 5 Advertising	123
Chapter 6 Public Relations	173
Chapter 7 Direct Marketing	219
Chapter 8 Sales Promotions	249
Chapter 9 Electronic and Social Media (ESM)	293
Chapter 10 Media Decisions	339
Chapter 11 Responsible Marketing Communication	371
Glossary	420
Index	434

EXPANDED CONTENTS

Figures   xiii

Tables   xvii

About the Authors   xix

Acknowledgments   xxiii

Guided Tour   xxiv

Preface   xxvii

Chapter 1 Introduction to IMC and Communication
              Models and Processes 3

Maxwell Winchester

Marketing and IMC   5

The marketing planning process   6

Aims of IMC   7

Components of IMC   7

    Advertising   8

    Public relations   8

    Sales promotion   8

    Direct marketing   8

    Personal selling   9

    Digital marketing   9

    Sponsorship   9

Communication models   9

    Traditional communication models   9

Memory processing   10

    Sensory store   11

    Working memory store   11

    Rehearsal   11

    Long-term store   11

    Retrieval   12

The role of memory in IMC   13

Attitudes and persuasion   13

Emotions and hedonism   17

Overview of approaches to IMC   17

    The Strong theory   18

    The Weak theory   18

Case study: Thinking outside the marketing box in the third sector:
A case of marketing the support of asylum seekers 21
Case study: Brown Brothers 'Colourful Conversations' 22
Practitioner profile: Sloane Orger 26

Chapter 2 Marketing Communication and Consumer Behaviour............. 35
Lara Stocchi and Maxwell Winchester
How IMC relates to consumer behaviour theories 37
Commonly prescribed cognitive models of consumer behaviour 37
Behaviourist models of consumer behaviour 39
Reinforcement model of consumer behaviour 40
Habit model of consumer behaviour 41
Learning theories 43
Memory 45
Empirical evidence 48
The Duplication of Purchase Law (DoPL) 49
Double Jeopardy Law (DJL) 50
Case study: Understanding Dior customers 52
Practitioner profile: Sonia Heinrich 55

Chapter 3 Marketing Communication Strategy and Planning.................... 65
Lara Stocchi
The different levels of strategy 68
Marketing planning and strategy 69
The IMC planning process 71
Market research 71
Target market 72
Product and brand positioning 72
Strategic brand development 72
IMC objectives 75
Strategy considerations 76
Setting IMC budgets 77
Successful IMC planning 79
Planning using relevant marketing metrics 80
Case study: *Game of Thrones* 83
Practitioner profile: Damien White 86

Chapter 4 Positioning and Objectives 97
Maxwell Winchester
Branding and IMC 99
Brand segmentation, targeting and positioning (STP) 100

Brand segmentation 100
Brand targeting 101
Brand positioning 101
  Positioning strategies 101
Measuring a brand's position 104
A critique of brand STP 105
  Critiquing segmentation 105
  Critiquing targeting 105
  Critiquing positioning 105
Alternative approaches to brand positioning and distinctive assets 106
IMC execution 107
  Informational appeals 107
  Emotional appeals 108
Case study: BMW changes campaign 111
Practitioner profile: Vicky Kalofolias 113

Chapter 5 Advertising 123
Peter Ling
What is advertising? 125
Who advertises? 126
  Individuals 126
  Home and small businesses 127
  Professional services 127
  Government 127
  Non-profit organisations 127
  Industry marketers 129
  Brand marketers 130
History of advertising 133
  Pre-seventeenth centuries 133
  Eighteenth and nineteenth centuries 133
  Twentieth century 134
  Twenty-first century 135
Creating advertising 136
  Strong/Weak or hard/soft sell? 136
  Left brain-right brain or whole brain? 137
  Big idea or execution? 137
Advertising effectiveness 142
  Best industry practices 142
  Advertising effectiveness research 147

Case study: P&G successfully sponsors mums! 150
Practitioner profile: Alicia Pridgeon 154

Chapter 6 Public Relations 173
Peter Ling
What is public relations? 175
History of public relations 176
    Communication timeline 177
    PR pioneers 182
    Industry associations 183
PR theories and models 185
    Theories 185
    Models 185
Public relations practice 187
    PR functions 187
    Industry associations 187
    PR consultancies 188
    Planning processes 191
    Media tools 191
    Codes of practice 193
Case study: Edward Bernays' PR campaigns (1920s–1930s) 200
Practitioner profile: Emily Tutt 204

Chapter 7 Direct Marketing 219
May O. Lwin
What is direct marketing? 220
History of direct marketing 221
The business of direct marketing 222
Databases and direct marketing 223
Direct-marketing strategies 224
    Setting an objective 224
    Selecting a medium 225
    Selecting an offer 225
    Selecting a message 225
    Managing customer relationships 226
    Responding to and fulfilling orders 227
Direct marketing platforms 227
    Online media 227
    Catalogues 228
    Direct mail 229
    Telemarketing 231

Direct advertising   231
   Direct advertising on the internet   232
   Direct advertising on print media   232
   Direct advertising on broadcast media   232
   Integrated direct marketing   234
Case study: Delightful direct campaign for the Arts Centre   237
Practitioner profile: Stephanie Swain   240

Chapter 8 Sales Promotions 249
Peter Ling
What is sales promotion?   250
Sales objectives   251
   Objectives for the sales force   251
   Objectives for retailers   252
   Objectives for consumers   252
Incentives for the sales force   252
   Incentive pay   252
   Sales contest   253
   Incentive travel   253
Incentives for business buyers   253
   Industrial goods and services   253
   Consumer goods and services   254
Incentives for consumers   255
   Delayed or immediate incentives   255
   Appropriateness of incentives   257
Exciting sales promotions   258
   Social causes   259
   Movie launches   259
   Television reality shows   260
   Global sports competitions   260
   Specially created events   263
Challenges in sales promotion   264
   Deceptive pricing   264
   Coupon redemption   264
   PR impact   265
   Sales promotion effectiveness   266
Case study: Inciting consumer feedback   270
Practitioner profile: Christopher Villani   276

Chapter 9 Electronic and Social Media (ESM) 293
Wonsun Shin and Hyunjin Kang

A paradigm shift in marketing communication   295
    Web 1.0, 2.0 and 3.0   296
How digital and social media shape consumer behaviour   299
ESM marketing communication options   301
    Brand websites   301
    Display advertising   302
    Native advertising   303
    Social media marketing   304
    Mobile marketing   307
Challenges in electronic and social media   309
Emerging trends   311
    Big data and data-driven marketing   311
    The Internet of Things   313
    Virtual reality   314
Case study: Marketing to digital kids   317
Case study: Hashtag #12banner – How to Develop a Supercharged
    Social Media Campaign   321
Case study: When I grow up, I want to be 'Instafamous'   324
Practitioner profile: Reese Masita   327

Chapter 10 Media Decisions 339
Maxwell Winchester

Mass media   340
    Broadcast media   341
    Print media   341
    Out Of Home (OOH)/outdoor   345
    Digital media   345
Media planning   349
    The ratings process   350
Is traditional media dead?   351
Media buying, targeting and consumption   353
    Media duplication   353
    Targeting heavy or high-value buyers   354
Case study: Targeting a high-value segment   357
Practitioner profile: Michael Laps   360

Chapter 11 Responsible Marketing Communication 371
Peter Ling

Regulatory frameworks   373
    The International Chamber of Commerce (ICC)   374
    Researchers   375
    Ayres & Braithwaite   377

Legislation and enforcement   383
    The ACCC & enforcement   384
    The ACMA & enforcement   385
    ASIC & enforcement   386
    The OAIC & enforcement   386
    The TGA & enforcement   386

Media-specific codes   387
    Complaints   387

Delivery-specific industry codes   388
    Outdoor advertising   388
    Direct marketing   389
    Digital advertising   389
    Native advertising   389

Product-specific industry codes   390
    Code focus   390
    Non-compliance   391

The AANA's codes   391
    The Advertising Standards Bureau (ASB)   391

Case study: AMI—'serial offender'   395
Practitioner profile: Chloe Neo   400

Glossary   420
Index   434

FIGURES

1.1	Marketing planning process	6
1.2	Components of IMC	8
1.3	Linear communication model	9
1.4	Memory processing model	10
1.5	Example of a newsletter's content for Katies, an Australian high-street retailer for affordable women's apparel	16
1.6	Elaboration likelihood model	17
1.7	Strong and Weak theories of advertising	19
1.8	Example of an IMC campaign based on the Strong advertising theory	19
1.9	Example of a campaign based on the Weak advertising theory	20
1.10	What kind of mood are you in?	22
2.1	A still from Air New Zealand's 'A better way to fly' advertising campaign	35
2.2	Stages of the high-involvement consumer decision-making process	37
2.3	Microsoft's Surface	38
2.4	An example of point-of-purchase advertising	39
2.5	Continuum of problem solving and information processing	40
2.6	The Ehrenberg and Goodhardt repeat purchase model	40
2.7	Examples of price promotions at a Coles supermarket	41
2.8	Baby Oleg from Compare the Market	42
2.9	Aleksandr from Compare the Market	42
2.10	Examples of classical conditioning via branding	44
2.11	Examples of instrumental conditioning using price promotions	44
2.12	Peter Alexander shopfront	45
2.13	An example of a memory network for McDonald's	46
2.14	Coca Cola's new, improved packaging	46
2.15	Commonwealth Bank's 'retail bank'	47
2.16	Dior fashion show at Musée Rodin	53
2.17	'Dior Eyes', a VR headset that lets you see what's going on backstage at Dior events	53
3.1	Airbnb's tagline reads: 'Don't just go there. Live there.'	65
3.2	Airbnb: a real home away from home	66
3.3	Different levels of strategy	68
3.4	Key brands owned by Mars Australia	68
3.5	Milestones of the marketing planning process	70
3.6	A formal marketing planning process	71
3.7	The IMC planning process	71

3.8	Keller's Customer Based Brand Equity (CBBE) framework	73
3.9	Samsung's ostrich commercial	74
3.10	IMC objectives	75
3.11	IMC choices	76
3.12	Booking.com's campaign	76
3.13	AirAsia's campaign for UK flights	77
3.14	*Game of Thrones* logo	83
3.15	Spotify's *Game of Thrones* service	83
4.1	'I Can't Believe It's Not Butter'—positioned against product class	102
4.2	M&M's new chocolate blocks	103
4.3	Bic's 'For her' range	103
4.4	Avis positions its brand against competitors	103
4.5	Example of a positioning map of fast food brands in Australia	104
4.6	BCAA breakdown insurance slice of life ad	108
4.7	Comparative Pepsi advertisement	108
4.8	Lavazza fantasy execution in coffee advertising	109
4.9	BMW 'Diesel gone good' advertisement	111
5.1	Rolex advertising in 1927	123
5.2	Building a successful Rolex brand	124
5.3	Australia's campaign to prevent skin cancer (1981)	129
5.4	Australia's campaign to prevent skin cancer (2017)	129
5.5	Volkswagen's apology advertisement	132
5.6	American Express and Superman webisode	136
5.7	#LikeAGirl	139
5.8	Fearless Girl	140
5.9	Sweetie	141
5.10	The Snickers campaign that started with Betty White	142
5.11	Volkswagen's 'Think small' advertisement	143
5.12	A Dove 'Campaign for Real Beauty' advertisement	144
5.13	American Legacy's 'Body Bags' advertising	145
5.14	P&G's 'Kids' tagline	150
5.15	P&G #MomsWisdom Mother's Day 2013 poster messages	152
6.1	Injured passenger Joseph Dao, who was dragged off a United Airlines flight in 2017	173
6.2	The packaging for Tylenol Extra-Strength capsules, which caused poisoning in 1982	181
6.3	Dove's campaign for Real Beauty	191
6.4	NHS Missing Type campaign: D WNING STREET	196
6.5	Tourism Australia's 'Missing Type' campaign	196
6.6	Freedom for women to smoke publicly in 1928	202

7.1	Daily Délifrance coupons	219
7.2	Coupon inserts reach readers in *The New Yorker*	222
7.3	A seasonal catalogue for *Gardener's Edge*	228
7.4	The annual IKEA catalogue	229
7.5	David Ogilvy's direct advertisement for an advertising agency	231
7.6	Coach sales coupons	234
7.7	*Sally Sees Her First Show* children's book	237
8.1	iPhone 7 Plus (RED)	259
8.2	The Beast Box Limited Edition grooming products	260
8.3	Budweiser World Cup promotion	262
8.4	Hoover's free flights advertising	265
9.1	The world's first banner advertisement	296
9.2	Social networking site usage in the US: 2005–2015	297
9.3	Doritos' 'Live the Flavor' Super Bowl 2007 advertisement	298
9.4	New communication paradigm	301
9.5	BMW's website	302
9.6	In-feed unit on Buzzfeed	303
9.7	Number of active users of key social media platforms	305
9.8	Gillette Venus 'Tag the Weather' campaign in Sweden	306
9.9	Smartphone penetration rate worldwide, 2015–2020	307
9.10	Geo-targeting, geofencing and beaconing	308
9.11	Band-Aid's Magic Vision campaign	309
9.12	Daily usage of multi screens	310
9.13	Marriott's 'Teleporter' booths	315
9.14	A Marriott Hotels VRoom set	315
9.15	ToyToyota's Backseat Driver app	317
9.16	Target's 'Holiday Wish List' app	318
9.17	#That'sGold's print advertisement	319
9.18	Australian social influencers Cody and Alli Simpson carried the Olympic torches	320
9.19	Chiara Ferragni and Fedez	324
9.20	The Pyramid of Influence	325
10.1	Victoria University advertisement	339
10.2	Rate card from Melbourne's *Age* newspaper	343
10.3	Rate card for South Africa's *Cape Times* newspaper	344
10.4	Examples of transit advertising (left) and own vehicle advertising	345
10.5	Example of behavioural targeting	346
10.6	Media scheduling	350
10.7	Adspend by medium, 2016–2019	352

10.8   Growth in adspend by medium   352

10.9   Radio penetration across countries, 2015   353

10.10   Kellogg's Special K buyers buying X times per annum   354

10.11   Take up of Pay TV   355

11.1   Australian Bananas' energy snack advertisement   371

11.2   The IFBA's framework for responsible marketing communication   375

11.3   Braithwaite's enforcement pyramid   376

11.4   FTC's consumer protection pyramid   377

11.5   Ayres & Braithwaite's enforcement pyramid   377

11.6   ACCC's enforcement pyramid   378

11.7   ACMA's enforcement pyramid   380

11.8   EASA's inverted enforcement pyramid   380

11.9   AANA's regulatory guide   381

11.10   Nurofen's range of pain products   385

11.11   The AMI's 'Censored' billboard   399

TABLES

2.1	Duplication of purchase in luxury fashion brands	49
2.2	Double Jeopardy—banks and credit cards	50
2.3	Simulated market statistics	54
3.1	Key empirical facts and relative implications for strategy and planning	69
4.1	The nine main styles of creative execution appeals, divided into 'informational' and 'emotional'	107
5.1	World's largest advertisers by category, 2015	130
5.2	Average advertising spend per category, 2015	131
5.3	World's five largest advertisers, 2015	131
5.4	Ad Age's top 10 ad campaigns of the twentieth century	143
5.5	Ad Age's top 10 ad campaigns of the twenty-first century	144
5.6	Cannes Lions Creative Effectiveness Winners, 2011–2017	146
6.1	Timeline of the different ages of communication	177
6.2	Characteristics of the four models of PR	186
6.3	Digital era and the four models of PR	187
6.4	Top 10 PR firms and their practices	189
6.5	The PESO model	192
6.6	Dell's usage of the PESO model	192
7.1	Advantages and disadvantages of catalogues and direct mail	230
7.2	Summary of three popular social media platforms	233
8.1	Push strategy incentives	254
8.2	Pull strategy incentives	256
8.3	Sales promotion incentives for various consumer goods and services	257
8.4	Popular consumer incentives—students' favourites	258
8.5	Popular consumer incentives—funeral services?	258
8.6	Rio Olympics Sales Promotion	261
8.7	FIFA World Cup sales promotion	262
9.1	Percentage of respondents who trust advertising format by region	300
9.2	Classification of social media by media richness and self-presentation	304
9.3	Relevant metrics for social media applications, organised by key social media objectives	312
10.1	Mass media benefits and disadvantages	341
10.2	Circulation of major Australian daily printed newspapers and YoY change	342
10.3	Circulation of digital major Australian daily newspapers with YoY change	342
10.4	Duplication of reading in women's magazines in New Zealand	354

10.5	Average circulation of competing major national South African weekly newspaper titles	358
10.6	Advertising rates for common format advertisements in leading national South African newspapers	358
10.7	Readership and LSM readership for national newspapers in South Africa	359
11.1	Australian legislation and enforcement authorities	384
11.2	Media-specific co-regulatory codes	387
11.3	Delivery-specific industry codes	389
11.4	Product-specific industry codes	390
11.5	The AANA's codes and guidelines	391
11.6	The ASB's top 10 most complained-about advertisements, 2016 and 2017	392
11.7	ASB cases against the Advanced Medical Institute, 2006–2015	395

ABOUT THE AUTHORS

Dr **Maxwell Winchester** is the Head of Scholarship and Professional Learning at Victoria University, and a Visiting Professor at the Copenhagen Business School. He has previously held the role of Discipline Leader, Marketing and Learning, and Teaching Leader in the School of International Business at Victoria University. Maxwell teaches postgraduate level units in consumer behaviour and marketing communications, and the undergraduate unit Introduction to Marketing. He holds a PhD in Marketing from the esteemed Ehrenberg-Bass Institute for Marketing Science.

Maxwell has consulting experience as a marketing researcher in Australia, Asia, North America and Europe. His clients have included Astra Motor Company, Cartier Asia, BHP, Pernod Ricard and a number of government agencies. He has also held a senior management position at one of Australia's largest companies, held political seats in the UK and had board positions at organisations including Shropshire and Wrekin Fire Authority, Tourism Shropshire, Tourism Macedon Ranges and Shropshire Business Enterprise.

In addition to his industry experience, Maxwell has many years of academic teaching experience globally, having held permanent faculty positions in Australia, Canada and the UK. He has also taught as a guest lecturer in Vietnam, Denmark, China, Singapore, Malaysia, Kuwait, France, Germany, the USA, Mexico and Austria.

His research interests include learning and teaching; reflective practice; qualitative and quantitative research methods; empirical generalisationalist research methods; and behaviourist consumer behaviour theories. He has published articles on student evaluations of teaching and reflective practice, as well as negative brand beliefs, luxury and premium brands, and wine marketing.

Peter Ling is lead author of *Consumer Behaviour in Action* and author of *Be the Innovators: How to Accelerate Team Creativity*, both published by Oxford University Press.

Since 2018, he has been Visiting Fellow at the Wee Kim Wee School of Communication and Information at Singapore's Nanyang Technological University.

From 2011–2017, he was Associate/Deputy Dean overseeing three portfolios in the School of Media and Communication at RMIT University Australia. He had previously worked with Edith Cowan University in Western Australia, where he won teaching and industry engagement awards, including supervising a team that became Asia Pacific winners in the 2010 Google Online Marketing Challenge.

His doctorate on accelerated adult creativity won the Fogarty Prize for Best Thesis in 2005 at the University of Western Australia.

Before academia, he worked in journalism, public relations, advertising, marketing communication and team creativity. His advertising agency career included Ogilvy & Mather, Leo Burnett, Young & Rubicam (where he helped to launch the Singapore office and was trained in New York) and Lintas (where he was attached to Sydney, worked in Taipei and wrote weekly newspaper columns that became two books on marketing insights and effective living).

He was Chairman of the Public Relations Sub-Committee for the 12th Asian Advertising Congress, where he edited the book *Communication towards Asia's 21st Century*. He was Vice President and then President of the Association of Accredited Advertising Agents (4As) and received the Max Lewis Silver Award and the 4As Excellence Award for his contribution to the Singapore industry.

Dr **Lara Stocchi** is Senior Lecturer in Marketing at the College of Business, Government and Law at Flinders University. Previously, she held a marketing lectureship at Loughborough University (UK), an associate lectureship at Nottingham University (UK) and an associate lectureship at Università Carlo Cattaneo LIUC (Italy). She has also lectured and tutored at the University of South Australia, where she completed her PhD in marketing at the Ehrenberg-Bass Institute for Marketing Science, one of the largest groups of marketing researchers in the world.

She is an experienced researcher in two key marketing fields: consumer buying behaviour and consumer memory. In the area of consumer buying behaviour, she has experience in modelling and anticipating patterns in purchases for different contexts (e.g. consumer packaged goods, as well as services). In the area of consumer memory, she has done research on memory associations, as well as examined the cognitive processes that characterise brand-information retrieval. Her work is published in the *European Journal of Marketing*, the *Journal of Advertising Research*, the *Journal of Marketing Management*, the *Journal of Product and Brand Management*, the *International Journal of Market Research*, the *Journal of Consumer Behaviour* and the *Australasian Marketing Journal*. Her work has also been presented at the European Marketing Academy (EMAC), the Australia and New Zealand Marketing Academy (ANZMAC), the Association for Consumer Research (ACR) and the Academy of Marketing (AM). Currently, she is associate editor for the *Journal of Consumer Behaviour*.

Other areas of research interest include branding and the measurement of brand performance, and digital marketing (consumer perceptions of mobile applications).

May O. Lwin is a Professor at Wee Kim Wee School of Communication and Information and a Professor (Joint) at the Lee Kong Chian School of Medicine, Nanyang Technological University (NTU), Singapore. May is Associate Dean (Special Projects) for the College of Humanities, Arts and Social Sciences and the Director of NTU's University Scholars Programme. She is also the Asia Scholar Professor, an honorary appointment at the University of Melbourne, Australia.

Professor Lwin specialises in strategic and health communication. Her research projects involve the development and assessment of health communications based on psycho-social theoretical frameworks to improve health outcomes of target audiences. She has conducted extensive research on Singaporean children and adolescents' health behaviours, investigating parental mediation, school environments and media messaging influences on children's health attitudes, intention and behaviour. May and colleagues have developed and validated a number of instruments to measure food label effects and examine child and family responses to food advertising.

Prior to academia, she worked at Ogilvy & Mather Singapore, an international advertising and public relations agency. Dr Lwin has won several research grants from prestigious institutes and academic bodies. She has conducted research on various facets of strategic communication and published in leading journals like the *Journal of Communication*, the *Journal of Consumer Research*, the *Journal of the Academy of Marketing Science*, the *Journal of Retailing* and the *Journal of Advertising Research*. She has also authored several books, book chapters and won numerous awards, including the Ogilvy Foundation Award and the Fulbright ASEAN Scholar Award.

Dr **Wonsun Shin** (PhD, University of Minnesota) is Senior Lecturer in Media and Communications and Co-Director of the Master of Marketing Communications program at the University of Melbourne, Australia. Before joining the University of Melbourne, she was Assistant Professor at the Wee Kim Wee School of Communication and Information, Nanyang Technological University, Singapore. Wonsun teaches advertising and marketing communications subjects for both undergraduate and postgraduate students. Prior to academia, she worked as Account Research Manager at Gallup & Robinson, Inc., an advertising and marketing research company in the USA.

Wonsun has extensive research experience in youth, digital media, and marketing communications. Her work has been published in top-tier, high-impact communication journals, including *New Media and Society*; *Communication Research*; the *International Journal of Advertising*; the *Journal of Computer-Mediated Communication*; *Computers in Human Behavior*; the *Journal of Broadcasting and Electronic Media*; *Cyberpsychology, Behavior, and Social Networking*; the *Journal of Health Communication*; and the *Journal of Children and Media*, among others. She has received multiple research awards and recognition from renowned international academic organisations, including four best paper awards at the International Communication Association

(2018), the International Conference on Research in Advertising (2018), and the Association for Education in Journalism and Mass Communication (2007 and 2015) conferences. She serves on the Editorial Review Board of the *Journal of Advertising* and the Global and Multicultural Committee of the American Academy of Advertising.

Hyunjin Kang, PhD (The Pennsylvania State University) is an Assistant Professor in the Wee Kim Wee School of Communication and Information at Nanyang Technological University, Singapore. She teaches Integrated Marketing Communication and Brand Management at NTU. Before joining NTU, she worked as a postdoctoral researcher in the School of Business at the George Washington University. She also has teaching experience in MBA programs at the George Washington University School of Business and the Faculty of Business at the University of Wollongong. Before entering academia, she worked as a PR practitioner in Samsung Card in South Korea. Her research investigates the effects of interactive communication technologies, ranging from websites to smart objects, on consumer psychology and behaviors. She is particularly interested in the psychology of 'self' underlying psychological and behavioural effects of using interactive media technologies. Her research has been published in *Media Psychology*, *Computers in Human Behavior*, *Mass Communication & Society*, and *Journalism & Mass Communication Quarterly*, among others.

ACKNOWLEDGMENTS

The author and the publisher wish to thank the following copyright holders for reproduction of their material.

AAP/The Advertising Archives, 98/AP, 169/PR Handout, 377; Advertising Archives, 42 (bottom); Reproduced by permission of Air Asia, 73; Alamy/The Advertising Archives, 20, 99 (bottom right), 105, 120, 139, 140, 187/Martin Berry, 41/B. Christopher, 198/Ian Dagnell Computing, 79 (top) /EBD Image, 49 (top)/Clive Sawyer, 337 (right)/Urbanbuzz, 254; Cancer Council Victoria, 125; Fairfax Photos/Anthony Johnson, 391; Getty Images/Buda Mendes, 312/Chestnot, 49 (bottom); Hort Innovation, 363; Reproduced by permission of IKEA 225; Articles courtesy of Marketing Mag, www.marketingmag.com.au, reproduced by permission, 22, 233; Shutterstock, back cover, 2, 30, 34, 35, 37, 40 (top), 43, 42 (top), 60, 92, 118, 168, 214, 241, 251, 284, 309, 330, 337 (left), 362; Image courtesy Victorian University 331.

Every effort has been made to trace the original source of copyright material contained in this book. The publisher will be pleased to hear from copyright holders to rectify any errors or omissions.

GUIDED TOUR

Opening Vignette: Each chapter opens with a contemporary and relevant example that introduces you to some of the key concepts covered within the chapter.

CHAPTER 2

Marketing Communication and Consumer Behaviour

Lara Stocchi and Maxwell Winchester

Air New Zealand: releasing our inner Dave

In its advertising campaign featuring 'Dave'—a migratory bird that has learnt the secrets to travelling with great comfort—Air New Zealand wants its Australian customers to know that there is a #BetterWaytoFly long haul. The company has used a similar marketing and communication approach in the past, but its #BetterWaytoFly campaign, featuring the voice of Australian actor Bryan Brown,

Learning Objectives: Clearly defined learning objectives at the beginning of each chapter will help you focus on the key points of the chapter, and highlight the abilities and skills you should be able to demonstrate after reading the chapter.

> **LEARNING OBJECTIVES**
>
> After reading this chapter you should be able to:
> 1. explain advertising
> 2. discuss the various sectors of advertising
> 3. discuss milestones in the history of advertising
> 4. discuss how advertising is created
> 5. discuss effective advertising from the perspectives of theories, best industry practices and key research studies.

Key Terms: To aid your understanding of important concepts, key terms are highlighted where they first appear in the text, as well as listed at the end of the chapter, and collated and defined in a complete glossary at the end of the book.

> ## Key terms
>
> | | | |
> |---|---|---|
> | behavioural segmentation | demographic segmentation | psychographic segmentation |
> | brand attributes | geographic segmentation | segmentation |
> | brand perception | IMC execution | targeting |
> | brand positioning | intention to buy | top of mind awareness |
> | brand salience | mass market | |
> | brand user profile | objectives | |

IMC in Action: 'IMC in Action' boxes are featured to contextualize concepts explained throughout the book, and to help you understand and apply theory to real-life examples.

IMC IN ACTION: COMPARETHEMARKET.COM

Aleksandr, Sergei, Yakov, Bogdan, Vassily and baby Oleg are meerkats and they help consumers comparing markets in essential services. The success of Compare the Market (playing on the similarity in sound between 'meerkats' and 'markets') is an example of brilliant, unique and distinctive branding that went viral, making the firm extremely popular in the UK and Australia.

Figure 2.8 Baby Oleg from Compare the Market

Case Studies: Real-life case studies will arm you with knowledge of the current climate, as well as important issues and innovations going on within the industry. This will help equip you with the skills and knowledge to deal with similar situations you may encounter as a marketing professional. Reflective revision questions will test your understanding of the issues and concepts explained in the case studies.

Case study: *Game of Thrones*

Lara Stocchi

Game of Thrones' marketing and communication strategy deeply involves the use of social media and social media marketing. When *Game of Thrones* was first being produced, it was announced on the HBO network, which promoted the show on all of its own social media platforms. Afterwards, *Game of Thrones* opened its own social media accounts.

Figure 3.14 *Game of Thrones* logo

Figure 3.15 Spotify's *Game of Thrones* playlist

Chapter Summary: A concise summary of key points is included at the end of each chapter, which will help you reinforce comprehension of the learning objectives and the fundamental themes explored.

■ CHAPTER SUMMARY

In this chapter we dealt with key concepts around the definition of 'public relations'; significant influences in public relations; theories and models of communication that guide professional practice; and public relations practice in terms of functions, planning processes, media tools and codes of practice.

We began with an explanation of the term 'public relations'. The various definitions from Bernays, Cutlip and Center, PRSA, CIPR and PRIA share a common understanding. PR is about mutual understanding or mutually beneficial relationships between an organisation and its various audiences. It is a management responsibility crossing internal and external stakeholders. It is a strategic, planned, integrated and sustained interactive process guided by research on public opinion. It uses two-way ethical communication that leads to organisations and audiences mutually changing their attitudes and behaviours to sustain goodwill and trust. It requires practitioners with knowledge of social science, professional communication skills and ethical standards to communicate effectively with diverse audiences and cultures.

Revision Questions: Carefully designed review questions have been included at the end of every chapter. These can be used to check your understanding of the key topics before moving on to the next chapter.

Revision questions

1. What is your own definition of sales promotion after reading this chapter?
2. What are similarities and differences in objectives for the sales force, retailers and consumers?
3. If you were starting as a sales person selling B2B or B2C household appliances, which incentives would appeal to you and why?
4. If you were a business buyer purchasing goods and services for your chain of retail outlets, what sales promotion incentives would you prefer and why?
5. Distinguish between push and pull strategies.

Practitioner Profiles: Profiles of marketing professionals are included throughout the book to provide you with informed and up-to-date perspectives on the industry, as well as showcase how IMC is used in various marketing roles.

Practitioner profile: Michael Laps

Co-Founder and Strategy Director, Yoghurt Digital

Michael is Co-Founder and Strategy Director at Yoghurt Digital, a digital marketing agency specialising in user behaviour research, customer data analysis and all things search.

After graduating from Monash University with a business degree and a double-major in marketing and management, Michael went on to work in the client services and strategy teams at both traditional advertising and digital agencies. Over the past 10 years, he has been privileged to design, build and execute digital strategies for household names such as ANZ Bank, H&R Block and Converse.

Michael is also a guest-lecturer at the University of NSW and was recently named the winner of the Australian Marketing Institute's 'Future Marketing Leader' award.

Further Reading and Notes: Further reading and references are placed at the end of each chapter to help reinforce and broaden your understanding of the topics covered in each chapter.

Further reading

Carolyn J. S. & Becker-Olsen, K. L. (2006). Achieving marketing objectives through social sponsorships. *Journal of Marketing*, *70*(4), 154–69.

Hoek, J. (2013). Sponsorship: an evaluation of management assumptions and practices. *Marketing Bulletin*, *10*, 1–10.

Hoek, J. et al. (1997). Sponsorship and advertising: a comparison of their effects. *Journal of Marketing Communications*, *3*(3), 21–32.

Mamic, L. I. & Almarez, I. A. (2013). How the larger corporations engage with stakeholders through Twitter. *International Journal of Market Research*, *55*(6), 851–72.

PREFACE

All organisations, whether private companies, public companies, not-for-profit organisations or government departments, need to communicate with their clients and the wider community. Integrated Marketing Communication (IMC) is the method used to achieve this.

Although books on advertising often use the term 'advertising' interchangeably with 'IMC', we use the term IMC in this book for good reason. IMC requires specific attention to the use of consistent messages and branding, and distinctive assets across all promotional tools. The trend towards IMC came about because many companies saw different marketing functions as separate and let them operate with relative autonomy.

This book is different from many IMC books you will read. It aims to provide an overview of IMC that compares and contrasts different theories of how IMC works and considers the empirical evidence available. In addition, it considers the practical implications of the evidence available, at times challenging the mainstream practices of marketers.

The authors of this book have endeavoured to differentiate it by taking a balanced approach. In particular, we do this with underlying beliefs about the way marketing communication works, as there is an inconsistency between how IMC is largely taught and practised, and the empirical evidence.

This 'balanced' theme will be present across the text through:
- both salience and persuasion (Strong and Weak) theories of advertising
- balancing IMC strategies with marketing needs
- balancing the IMC mix of traditional 'stars' (e.g. advertising and sales promotion) with the 'supporting cast' (e.g. direct marketing and personal selling)
- balancing traditional and new media
- integrating content other than B2C, such as B2B, social marketing and services
- balancing push/pull or pull/push strategies, depending on variables such as local/global marketing, immediate/delayed incentives in sales promotion
- balancing short-term/long-term or tactical/strategies needs
- balancing corporate needs and societal ethics/regulations
- balancing creativity and effectiveness in IMC.

As a result of this balanced approach, you may find that the conclusions in this book are in contrast to others you may read. We hope you find this approach refreshing and informative.

CHAPTER 1

Introduction to IMC and Communication Models and Processes

Maxwell Winchester

2XU: Australia's first global sportswear brand

Tiffany Winchester

If you are not familiar with the brand name 2XU, or how to pronounce it—'Two Times You'—you may at least be familiar with the branding. It's the distinctive silver 'X' logo transfer running down the outside leg of those enormously popular black compression tights that you've probably spotted on the running track, yoga mat or even just out and about in the street. 2XU was founded in 2005 by Australians Clyde Davenport, Jamie Hunt and Aidan Clarke. The company designs, develops and sells sporting apparel, including compression garments; triathlon, cycling, running and open-water swimming wear; and general fitness wear. The philosophy is simple: to create products that will advance human performance.

Since 2007, the company has grown at around 25 per cent a year, expanding from one retail store to 15 outlets across Australia and New Zealand. 2XU is now selling into markets in Asia, Central and South America, Europe, the US and Canada. In less than a decade, 2XU, based in Hawthorn, Melbourne, has become a global success, exporting 70 per cent of its products to 60 countries, and is celebrating its seventh year in Hong Kong.

2XU has the potential to be a billion-dollar operation. 'If we're truly going to be one of the global brands in this category, we look to $500 million to a billion dollars because that's the scale. If you take a brand like Adidas, I think they're about $14 billion. Nike are $25 to $30 billion,' Davenport says.

In December 2013, LVMH's (Moët Hennessy Louis Vuitton) Singapore-based private investment arm, L Catterton Asia, acquired a 40 per cent stake in 2XU for an estimated AU$75 million. 2XU's embrace by the LVMH luxury empire shows Australian design is racing around the world.

Target market

Aimed primarily at elite athletes, 2XU is best known for its compression tights, which it supplies to athletes at the Australian Institute of Sport. Fifty per cent of 2XU's sales come from its sports version

of 'couture': high-tech compression garments. But driving the biggest growth is its more recent expansion into mainstream consumer sportswear.

CEO Kevin Roberts and the company's co-founders feel they have positioned the brand as an item that serious athletes use and need to create a competitive advantage. This image and positioning will be used to attract more general-minded fitness seekers. According to Roberts, 2XU is presently attractive to the most serious athletes—people pursuing fitness with the intention of performance—a group that only represents about 20 per cent of the fitness market.

Promotion

'With 2XU, it's a global strategy, which comes with the problem of more competitors, with enormous marketing budgets. If we're going to be successful, we can't compete the way our larger competitors compete because they will smash us,' Davenport says. 'We have to be very clever—very tactical'.

Worn by multiple world champions, endorsed by sports institutions the world over and praised by professional athletes from all disciplines, 2XU understands what is needed to be the best. For example, it sponsors multiple sports teams and events including the 2XU Great Ocean and Otway Classic Ride.

Value for money, distribution, advertising and promotion are highly valued by 2XU, but its number-one priority is ensuring its product is right. The company relies heavily on email around the clock to conduct business nationally and internationally with its stores, distributors, and factories in Asia, and to communicate with staff on the road. It also has a presence across social media platforms such as Facebook, Twitter, YouTube and Instagram, where it runs contests and promotions and keeps its followers up to date on a daily basis.

In 2015 2XU launched a global campaign, 'Heart not Hype', focusing on athletes training in 2XU gear. Aiden Clarke noted that while 2XU is a household name in Australia, it still isn't as well known in other markets. 'We're a niche,' says Davenport. 'Australia isn't big enough for the niche we're in.' The 5-minute 'Heart not Hype' campaign focuses on emotion, featuring various athletes, including para-athletes. A voice-over says, 'I don't want to be famous for my face, I want to be famous for my heart'.

'Our job is to explain to the exercising public that this is not a fad,' Clarke says. 'And we're here today to begin that storytelling.'

Expansion

China is expected to become one of the major growth markets for compression gear in the coming years, fuelled by ongoing investments by the Chinese government in the development of sports infrastructure. Sure Step Asia Pacific is the sole distributor of 2XU in the Asia–Pacific region. Kirsty Hulme, director of Sure Step, says of the #HeartNotHype campaign, 'there is something in this film for all sports lovers, and members of Hong Kong's fitness communities will be able to find a story that resonates with their own personal experiences'. 2XU has grown very quickly in Hong Kong and in Singapore, but is still not a well-known brand across Asia and has yet to crack this lucrative market. 2XU is eying Asia's health-conscious middle-class, as well as the 'sportswear as fashion' trend that's seeing activewear shoot up from 6 to 28 per cent of teen apparel purchases. Thanks to the Chinese government's early promotion of the 2022 Winter Olympics in Beijing, extreme sports apparel and expensive activewear sales are booming.

Tiffany Winchester is a lecturer at the Monash Business School

■ INTRODUCTION

In this chapter we will explore the concept of Integrated Marketing Communication (IMC). Integrated Marketing Communication as a title is pretty self-explanatory. Let's start with the last word and work forwards. Communication is an important component of academic study in its own right as it considers how individuals or entities communicate with each other and, more importantly, why communication as a process may succeed or fail. The section of this chapter headed 'Communication models' reviews communication theory in some depth, including how people process information in their brain.

It is likely that, as you have picked up this book, you have an understanding of what marketing is, either by having taken a university course in it, or having worked in the industry. Marketing, as you are probably aware, is the facilitation of the exchange of goods and services in the economy. It involves in particular the consideration of 'the 4Ps' of marketing, also known as the marketing mix. In this book, we are particularly interested in how the product or service is promoted to the consumer or business we wish to market to.

Finally, let's consider the first word of the IMC acronym: integrated. 'Integrate what?' you may ask. The importance of integrating the marketing communication program can't be understated. Empirical research confirms that consumers need to see consistent branding of elements to help recall them, consistent messages in advertising and consistency across the 4Ps. This is a concept that will be emphasised in all chapters of this book.

How this occurs, however, is less clear. There are many ideas and limited clear empirical evidence on how IMC works. On the topic of advertising alone, researcher Simon Broadbent suggested there were 456 views of how advertising works.[1] Add to that the differing perspectives on how price promotions and other IMC tools might work, and it is easy to see how confusing it can be to come up with an IMC plan that is guaranteed to work effectively and efficiently.

LEARNING OBJECTIVES

After reading this chapter you should be able to:

1. discuss the connection between marketing and IMC
2. identify the components of the marketing mix
3. define the aims and components of IMC
4. identify the components of the communication process
5. evaluate the role of memory in marketing communication processing, retention and recall
6. evaluate the applicability of communication theories in IMC
7. distinguish between the basic premise of Strong and Weak theories of IMC.

Marketing and IMC

Fundamentally, marketing is an exchange process whereby a consumer is willing to part with their money in exchange for services or goods.[2] The importance of IMC in this process is that for a consumer to be aware of, or even want, goods or services, communication is necessary.

The marketing process can be much more varied than the example at the beginning of the chapter. It could relate to the communication of an idea, event or public service. Take, for example, a politician who is not seeking any money from constituents, but is seeking their vote. The politician is also not offering goods or services, but ideals about the way a community should be run. Such are the varied scenarios in which IMC can be applied.

There are many IMC roles in a range of organisations in which a graduate could find themselves: anything from an Internal Marketing Communication Manager/Director within a large company, to working in IMC strategy or research roles within a communication agency. There is no 'typical' day in the life of someone who works in IMC as there are so many varied roles out there. In this book, we have interviewed a number of IMC professionals in a range of roles so that you can get an understanding of the type of work done by people who work in IMC.

It should also not be assumed that graduates with IMC skills will work in a for-profit setting. As mentioned earlier, organisations need to be able to communicate with consumers, including not-for-profits. Given that graduates of an IMC course will not necessarily work for a large, for-profit company, we will consider a scenario in a not-for-profit organisation later in the chapter.

The marketing planning process

Regardless of whether you end up working for a large corporation, a small business, a charity or a government organisation, there's no doubt IMC is big business. Globally the industry is worth around half a trillion dollars.[3]

In your previous studies in marketing, it is likely you would have come across a chapter or topic on strategic marketing and marketing planning (the marketing and IMC planning processes are discussed in depth in Chapter 3). A summary of the marketing planning process is presented in Figure 1.1.

The business analysis process begins in the top box of Figure 1.1 with an environmental analysis (using tools such as SWOT and PEST or PESTEL) to understand the internal and external environments the organisation works within. A SWOT analysis is an analysis strategic managers do to determine the business's Strengths, Weaknesses, Opportunities and Threats. This is usually complemented by a PEST or PESTEL analysis,

Figure 1.1 Marketing planning process

which is an analysis that considers outside forces that might affect the company. These outside forces are:

- political
- economic
- social
- technological
- environmental
- legal.

Once the analyses are complete, the management team will create a series of objectives for the organisation from which a series of marketing-specific objectives will be developed. These objectives are usually further developed into a core marketing strategy from which marketing planning can take place.

The marketing planning process involves managing what are commonly known as the 4Ps or one of the many variants of these, such as 7Ps, 4Cs, 5Vs or MIXMAP.[4] It involves the consideration of how an item should be priced (Price); how it should be distributed (Place); how the product or service should perform (Product); and (of particular interest to us here) how it should be promoted (Promotion).

It should be obvious by now that IMC fits into the 'Promotion' part of the marketing planning process.[5] However, IMC does not work alone and must work in a complementary manner with the other parts of the marketing mix: 'IMC attempts to combine, integrate, and synergize elements of the communication mix'.[6] For example, there is no point promoting a product as a luxury product if the quality is not very good (Product), nor if it is distributed in discount outlets (Place), nor if it is priced lower than most competitors (Price). All elements of the marketing mix must complement each other.

Aims of IMC

For a consumer to buy a particular brand, two criteria must be met: physical availability and **mental availability**.[7] Physical availability is, as the term suggests, how available the product or service is physically. Questions such as 'Can it be bought?' and 'Is it in stock?' relate to physical availability. The marketing functions of logistics and supply chain relate to this criterion. This criterion has little direct relationship with IMC.

Mental availability, on the other hand, is how available the brand is in the consumer's mind. The purpose of IMC is to increase the mental availability of the target brand using a range of communication methods discussed later in the chapter.

Integrated Marketing Communication can have a number of aims. Chris Fill determined that there are four major aims that an IMC campaign can have: Differentiation, Reinforcement, Informing or **Persuasion**.[8]

- *Differentiation*: to ensure consumers perceive your brand as performing differently from other competitive brands
- *Reinforcement*: to remind and reinforce consumers to use your brand
- *Informing*: particularly with new brands, to notify consumers about your brand
- *Persuasion*: to persuade consumers to use your brand by convincing them your brand performs better on key performance attributes.

As we will see in coming chapters, there are differing views and conflicting evidence on the validity of each of these various aims of an IMC campaign.

Knowing that IMC is equivalent to the promotions 'P', it's now time to consider what elements make up the promotions (or communication) mix.

Components of IMC

Figure 1.2 proposes a range of key components of Integrated Marketing Communication, focusing on what is commonly referred to as the 'promotional mix' or the promotions part of the marketing mix.[9]

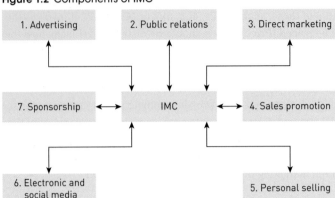

Figure 1.2 Components of IMC

Each of these is briefly described in the following paragraphs.

Advertising

Advertising is the part of the IMC mix most people will be familiar with. From billboards, to television or advertising on web pages, we are all regularly exposed to advertising.

Advertising is a one-way communication from the organisation to the consumer. Advertising generally reaches a large population of buyers and it allows for high message repetition and frequency, compared to say a targeted direct mail campaign.

Advertising is discussed in more detail in Chapter 5.

Public relations

Public relations (PR) is one of the most cost-effective IMC tools available. This is because the IMC tactic involves creating news in the media, which can be free (but usually isn't). It is also one of the more believable tools in the IMC mix because consumers see PR as news rather than another form of advertising or promotion. Because of this, it is possible to reach prospects who may avoid other IMC approaches.

Public relations is discussed in detail in Chapter 6.

Sales promotion

Sales promotion is an immediate attempt to get a consumer to purchase something at point of sale. No other part of the IMC mix has such immediacy. Sales promotions you may be familiar with include special offers such as two-for-one deals (also known as B1G1F and BOGOF—Buy One Get One Free) and price discounting. They are very common in businesses with fast-moving consumer goods (that is, FMCGs—the kinds of products you would find in a supermarket) but you will also see sales promotion used in high-value items such as new house and land packages.

Sales promotion is discussed in more depth in Chapter 8.

Direct marketing

Direct marketing involves directly contacting the consumer in some way. This can be via mail or email, by telephone or, less commonly nowadays, by fax machine. The communication is usually personalised to the recipient, meaning it can get more attention than other IMC tools.

Direct marketing will be discussed in more detail in Chapter 7.

Personal selling

Personal selling involves a staff member working on a personal level with a customer or potential customer. It is the most expensive option in the IMC or promotions mix as the company pays one person to deal directly with one customer at a time. The aim is to work with the customer or potential customer to provide a solution that is most suitable for the customer.

Personal selling will be discussed briefly in Chapter 8.

Digital marketing

As the name suggests, digital marketing is any form of promotion that involves electronic means such as the internet, apps, social media and so on.

This will be discussed in greater detail in Chapter 9.

Sponsorship

Sponsorship is the name given to any promotion that involves placing your brand on a person or organisation while providing them with financial compensation. In return, the person or organisation promotes your brand.

This will be discussed in Chapters 5, 6 and 8.

Communication models

The first step in understanding IMC is to appreciate how communication works more generally: marketers must know how consumers process the information received from them. This section of the chapter considers how communication between two people, two organisations or a person and an organisation may work.

Traditional communication models

Communication models are generally drawn from psychological literature. While there are many communications models, for simplicity we present the most common linear model. At one end of the model there is a 'sender' and at the other there is a 'receiver'. Between these two, there is a range of variables that can affect the success of communication efforts. A traditional linear communication model is illustrated in Figure 1.3.

Figure 1.3 Linear communication model

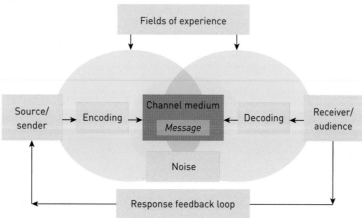

To understand the communication model presented in Figure 1.3, you should start with the sender/source. This is the person or organisation sending the message—that is, the source of the message.

The source encodes the message so that the receiver will hopefully understand it. In an IMC context, this might mean interpreting communication objectives into a storyboard for a television advertisement.

Next, the source of the message chooses the channel/medium of communication. In terms of IMC, you will be familiar with the term 'media', which is literally the plural of 'medium'. This is the form of exchange chosen by the sender, which may be a type of traditional mass media or digital media, for example. If the communication is person to person, the medium might be verbal. If the message is verbal, it is likely to be encoded by the sender as speech.

Finally, the receiver receives the message via the medium used by the sender and decodes it into an interpretation of the message. If all goes well, it will be very similar to the message the sender intended to communicate.

Separately from the communication process in the model you will notice the word 'noise'. This is anything that might interfere with or disturb the communication process. From an IMC perspective, there are many possible causes of noise during the communication process. Examples include:

- If the sender encoded a message that was sent through the medium of a television commercial, the receiver could, upon seeing there was a commercial break, turn to their partner and start talking about their day.
- There are times when an advertising agency attempts to engage the consumer with a complex message in a campaign. This assumes that the consumer will be motivated to interpret the content of an advertisement. If the consumer is not motivated to pay much attention to the campaign, it is likely they will not take the desired message out of the campaign.

Memory processing

Now that we have considered the communication process, the next part of this chapter considers how information is processed once it is received by the audience or recipient. Marketers need to understand how their communication efforts are received by consumers and how consumers process and store brand information.

This section will explore the memory processing model in Figure 1.4 from an information processing perspective.

Figure 1.4 Memory processing model

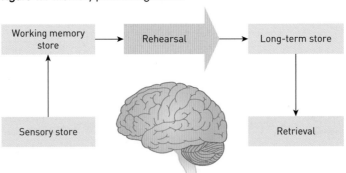

Sensory store

The **sensory store** is where information enters the brain. We need to keep in mind that communication is not just verbally based but can come from any of the five senses.

In terms of an IMC communication effort, the majority of what we are interested in will relate to visual and auditory information processing.

While much of what is involved in IMC relates to visual and auditory information, other sensory information may also be involved. For example, how will customers react to non-verbal body language or being touched by sales staff? Is this culturally defined?

Working memory store

Information from the sensory store is transferred to the working memory (also known as the 'short-term memory store') until it is either forgotten or coded into long-term memory.[10] This usually happens within a one-minute time frame.[11] You might be familiar with Miller's Law, which states that a person can only hold 7 ± 2 items in their working memory.[12] Consider the implications of this limitation. For example, we must consider how realistic it is for a consumer to process large amounts of information about competing brands if they are only able to work with 7 ± 2 items at any one time in their working memory.

From an IMC perspective, the types of communication that would be related to the **working memory store** that might be acted on are such things as price promotions or other in-store promotions. In addition, many IMC efforts at point of sale attempt to use cues (such as distinctive brand assets including logos, colours and shapes of packaging) to facilitate retrieval of other brand information from the **long-term store** back into their working memory.

Much of what we are trying to achieve with IMC programs relates to longer term memory rather than just point of sale communication such as sales promotions.

Rehearsal

Particular brand information and information on certain qualities of brands (referred to as 'attributes') are stored, for the most part, in the consumer's long-term memory and brought back into the consumer's working memory when required for purchases.[13] While it is suggested that the amount of storage space in the long-term memory is almost infinite, not all information available will be encoded into the long-term memory store, as much of it will be ignored.[14] Encoding brand information into permanent storage can take up to two years and is encoded through repetition of the information.[15] This repetition is known as **rehearsal**.

Long-term store

While the long-term memory store is virtually infinite in capacity, the retrieval process limits what is remembered about a concept. Much of the information in memory is available but not able to be retrieved on any one occasion and such memory must be retrieved in order to be able to utilise it to make a decision.[16] Until recently, many researchers assumed that the human brain could be paralleled with that of a computer hard drive.[17] For example, if you wanted to remember a home phone number, the node (we talk about nodes a bit further down) for home phone number would retrieve all the home phone numbers you ever had. A filtering process would then block out old phone numbers leaving only the current one. Such memory models are considered inaccurate because the human brain is much more complex than a computer and very rarely do humans make what would seem a rational decision in choice behaviour experiments.[18] Confounding mechanisms, including inhibition, adaptation and learning, all affect the way information is retrieved from the long-term memory store.[19]

Misunderstandings of human memory have resulted in misinterpretations in how marketing programs work.[20]

Next, information retrieval is considered in more depth to better understand how it is affected by mechanisms such as inhibition, adaptation, learning and the way information is organised in the memory store.

Retrieval

The information in long-term memory is said to be linked to other associated information in long-term memory through a series of networks.[21] Such networks are the result of neural connections that are 'fired' instantaneously, which ensures similar or related information comes to mind at the same time.[22]

Retrieving information from your long-term memory involves priming a particular cue (such as 'I am thirsty').[23] Such concepts are known as 'memory nodes' and each node is linked to other nodes in a network of nodes, which in turn are connected to other nodes again.[24] Such packets of information are known as 'schemas'.[25] Generally, only around six nodes are retrieved for each cue at any one point in time; however, different nodes are fired at different points in time, suggesting there can be more than six nodes associated with any particular schema.[26] This is consistent with Miller's Law, which suggests that people can only handle 7 ± 2 bits of information.[27]

An individual may retrieve the concept that they are thirsty, which then primes the **retrieval** of other concepts related to the initial concept.[28] The consumer could retrieve a product category node (say, beer or soft drinks) possibly primed by a relevant thought process (for example, 'I am thirsty'). This thought process is said to prime the retrieval of other related information through a spreading activation of recall of the related information, which would include other information about, say, cola soft drinks (such as 'effervescent', 'refreshing' and 'sweet') and also brands that would be related to these attributes (such as Coke, Pepsi or Virgin). The concept of being thirsty would be considered a node from a superordinate category with which the respondent may then prime the subordinate nodes.[29]

All of this suggests that there is no such thing as forgetting something, but rather that occasionally we fail to retrieve information. This is an often-misunderstood aspect of dementia—patients with dementia actually don't forget as such, but fail to recall things.[30]

From a practical IMC perspective, this could mean that while a brand is on a shelf in front of us at a supermarket, if cues are not available to recall that brand over other brands, we will not retrieve information about it, reducing the chance that we would consider it, or even notice it. Our IMC program plays a very important role in this process, in that it helps a consumer create the schema of memory associated with the brand, increases the probability of the brand being recalled in a purchase situation.

The role of memory in IMC

What we have just discussed suggests that brands are brought to mind through a cue of some sort that in turn triggers activation of linked nodes, which trigger other nodes and eventually a brand node. Nodes are simultaneously fired when they have something in common: 'the more properties two concepts have in common, the more links there are between the two nodes'.[31]

The mind is said to categorise items, including concepts and abstractions, in a structured, hierarchical manner.[32] This categorisation enables the mind to work efficiently.[33] For example, people develop a superordinate category for 'chair', which enables them to avoid storing a large amount of information on every type of chair they are aware of.[34] Under this superordinate category, they may have categories of types of chairs that would include kitchen chairs, lounge chairs and outdoor chairs, for example.

Typicality is how typical an item is to a category. For example, if a consumer were to see a new item that they had not seen before, but it had four legs, a large flat horizontal surface and was made of wood, chances are they would consider it a table. Just as we categorise everyday items based on how well they represent taxonomic categories, consumers are said to also categorise brands in a similar manner.[35]

In conducting brand image studies, market researchers are essentially testing to see how typical any particular brand is to any particular brand attribute. This means that any particular attribute's response level will be indicative of how closely associated respondents believe it is to any particular brand or set of brands.[36]

A study by Ward, Bitner and Barnes of fast food restaurants found that more typical fast food restaurants such as Burger King and McDonald's were better liked on average than those that were less typical.[37] More typical (that is, larger) brands were found to be more likely to come to mind during the recall process.[38] Such findings are not consistent with the marketing literature, which suggests it is unique brand positioning that attracts consumers to a given brand (Alpert 1971; Sampson 1993).[39] This aspect of brand perceptions and memory structure is discussed in more detail in Chapter 2.

Consider the implications of the above discussion to an IMC program. The next part of this chapter considers alternative ways marketing communication might work.

Attitudes and persuasion

Attitudes are lasting evaluations of a certain object or person (for example, a product or service, a brand, a firm, a cause, an idea, a celebrity or a politician).[40] Although they can be gauged via market research (for example, surveys conducted online or face to face) attitudes cannot be directly observed and are often inferred from their outcomes, such as specific actions undertaken or decisions made. This is why many marketing and communication managers (and marketing researchers), such as Bagozzi, consider attitudes as precursors of behaviour.[41]

In theory, attitudes comprise three different facets: a *cognitive* facet (a person's beliefs, knowledge or thoughts); an *affective* facet (positive or negative feelings); and a *conative* or *behavioural* facet (the underlying predisposition or behavioural tendency entrenched in the attitude itself and directed at the object). The 'tripartite' nature of attitudes yields implications for IMC because, depending on contingent factors, one facet may prevail, resulting in different chains of effect and different levels of consumer *involvement*—that is, varying levels of personal relevance.[42] In Chapter 2 we will explore the different consumer behaviour models that may result from different levels of involvement and relative implications for IMC tactics. Here we focus on understanding implications in relation to the communication process.

While it is widely accepted that cognition offers a 'platform' for the development of attitudes in most circumstances, the prevalence of the affective facet over the conative facet is primarily confined to *high involvement* consumption situations; for example, deciding which mortgage broker to use when buying property. In contrast, we see the prevalence of the conative facet over affect in *low involvement* consumption, whereby attitudes are typically considered to be the result of behaviour (and not the opposite way around). For instance, you may determine whether you are positively impressed with the service offered by a certain airline after using it.

Thinking about the key underlying goals of the IMC, it is desirable to positively impact consumers' attitudes. This can be done either by ensuring that they hold positive perceptions towards a certain product or service, or via changing perceptions with the hope of subsequently also influencing their behaviour (and decisions) as consumers. This process is commonly referred to as *persuasion* and, as mentioned earlier in the chapter, is a fundamental underlying aim of IMC. For example, many IMC campaigns tend to be tailored around messages framed as 'better than …[insert competitor's name here]' or to deploy specific communication tactics (discussed later in the chapter) to use emotional appeal in advertising, by leveraging values such as family, love or self-expression (see the example of Telstra's 'Thrive On' campaign in IMC in Action).

IMC IN ACTION: TELSTRA'S 'THRIVE ON' CAMPAIGN

Lara Stocchi

In recent years, it goes without saying that technology has become part of the lives of people around the world, permeating all sorts of aspects: professions and careers, social connections and family ties, ambition, art and creativity, and more. Firms involved in the provision of technology such as telecommunications have risen very quickly to the top of the charts of most valued brands and, contextually, have also become some of the heaviest investors in IMC tactics. With these natural and inevitable changes, standing out from the crowd and attracting the attention of millions of consumers has become increasingly challenging, especially in light of a steady commoditisation of portable digital technologies, allowing us all to carry the world in our hands and make the most of it in all aspects of life.

In light of these factors, many firms involved in telecommunications have strived for highly distinctive messages and communication approaches, filled with a broad range of unwritten meanings and metaphors, bouncing back to consumers a broad range of possible interpretations, as if they were invited to make what they want of it. The narrative leveraging 'endless opportunities' is therefore not particularly original anymore, yet various organisations have attempted to execute it in different ways within their communication approaches, with more or less successful outcomes.

Telstra (the 'most valuable Australian brand' for several years running—see *Business Insider*'s ranking from 2018) is no exception—its recent campaign, 'Thrive On', has been perceived particularly positively among Australian consumers, by bringing a little bit of 'magic' back into technology.[43] The campaign was conceived around the words of futurist Arthur C. Clarke: 'Any sufficiently advanced technology is indistinguishable from magic'. Accordingly, Telstra has launched a series of beautifully executed advertisements (television, radio, print, digital and outdoor) that showcase through vivid imagery how people, businesses and communities can thrive thanks to the many possibilities and telecommunication solutions that Telstra offers. The campaign has had a strong bearing in sustaining the re-affirmation of Telstra as the key player in its field and a reputable global brand, and continues to be used widely. The longevity of the campaign primarily results from the possibility of executing the main message through different yet coherent narratives and images, all revolving around the main catch phrase, 'What if I promised you the world, then could you believe in magic?'[44]

Source: www.youtube.com/watch?v=VW53n3e53Dk

Many IMC campaigns also straightforwardly encourage consumers to act in line with the key message communicated by the likes of direct marketing initiatives such as newsletters highlighting sales promotions offered for a very limited time (see Figure 1.5).

Besides a basic understanding of attitudes and persuasion, what marketing and communication managers really want to understand is *when* and *how* attitude changes might occur as a result of the communication process. The Elaboration Likelihood Model (ELM) by Petty and Cacioppo is a comprehensive framework that outlines the conceptual relationship between the communication process instigated by IMC tactics and changes in attitudes.[45] The model prescribes different 'routes' to the possibility of individuals engaging in any sort of cognitive activity as a result of exposure to a piece of communication (such as exposure to an advertisement) and to attitude change, pending on three important factors that 'filter' persuasion:

- *Motivation*—the presence of consumption-related goals
- *Opportunity*—the physical ability to process the message
- *Ability*—the underlying level of familiarity (or ease of comprehension) of the message.

To a great extent, these three factors (referred to as MOA for practical purposes) are partly out of the control of marketing and communication managers. However, specific IMC tactics such as a clever mix of

Figure 1.5 Example of a newsletter's content for Katies, an Australian high-street retailer for affordable women's apparel

promotional approaches and/or the distinctiveness of the message itself (e.g., through clear branding that facilitates recognition) can play a role. In fact, the assumption is that by enhancing motivation, opportunity and ability, it is possible to increase the likelihood of message elaboration and, as a result, the chance of persuasion in the form of lasting attitude change.

Figure 1.6 depicts the various 'routes' to persuasion and differences between them in a visual manner to further assist you with understanding this framework. In a nutshell, the assumption is that when the overall level of MOA is high (**central route** to persuasion) the consumer should be in the position to understand the main point of the communication (that is, the main argument or proposition, such as understanding which brand or product is being promoted and its main feature), which typically results in a lasting change in attitude. If the MOA level is low (**peripheral route** to persuasion) the consumer may only be able to pick up some details of the message (for example, the music in an advertisement), which are secondary to the main point of the communication, so the attitude change may not be lasting. Finally, when the MOA level is moderate (**dual route** to persuasion) consumers are typically in the position to absorb 'new' information and tend to be receptive to the main point of the communication as well as some secondary details. In this instance, the attitude change will be ongoing (that is, it will evolve on a continuum) thanks to the dual effect of peripheral and central references in the main message communicated.

While it is always best to 'handle with care' all conceptual models (something that we reflect upon extensively throughout this book) it is fair to say that the ELM offers a solid basis for understanding how the communication process works beyond the more simplistic views of meaning transfer and the rational encoding/decoding aspects discussed earlier in this chapter. However, it should be kept in mind that the ELM is a model based on a theory with limited empirical evidence to support it, and questions have been raised as to its validity.[46]

Figure 1.6 Elaboration likelihood model

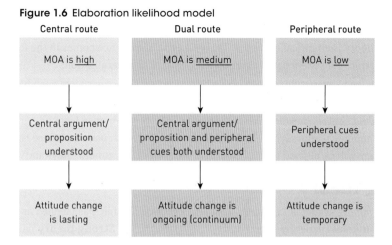

Emotions and hedonism

Aside from how consumers might process information received via marketing communication or change their attitudes over time, the effect of emotions needs to be acknowledged. Consumers can make some decisions on the basis of emotion and such decisions are not necessarily 'irrational'. Rather, individuals constantly try to maintain harmony between thoughts, feelings and actions, and can change any of these three elements to enable consistency. Interestingly, a great deal of the importance of emotions in consumption (and thus in the context of IMC) has been understood using the same communication models presented earlier in this chapter. For example, the way we feel about a certain brand may be used as a mental shortcut and key piece of information that is retrievable when facing a decision. Therefore, a great deal of the role that emotions and feelings might play in the way consumers react to the IMC can be understood using the same conceptual bases. Nonetheless, IMC tactics should take into consideration consumers' emotions and even play with emotions through clever campaigns, which is an approach very much aligned with hedonic consumption or **hedonism**. Holbrook & Hirschmann argued that experiential aspects of consumption such as hedonism, symbolism and aesthetics can be used in marketing communication to attract consumers to a brand.[47] A good example of this is in the marketing of prestige or luxury brands. Luxury brands are known to be used as symbols of social status but many consumers are also said to use luxury brands or products for the hedonistic benefits they bring.[48] For example, when communicating a high-end car, the strategy would not be to rationally argue to the consumer that the car is better, but to concentrate on a message that shows what a great experience it would be to drive this car. In Western markets, where hedonism is more valued, advertisements for prestige cars such as BMW often highlight the brand as being the 'ultimate driving machine'.

Overview of approaches to IMC

There are quite literally hundreds of theories about how IMC works. In fact, Simon Broadbent conducted a meta-analysis and suggested that he found more than 450 different theories about how advertising works.[49] Now try to imagine how many theories there are about how sales promotion or direct marketing works and you'll understand how difficult it is to know the right thing to do in IMC.

When there are so many different theories in a field, how do we work out what actually works in practice? After all, a theory is just that: a conceptual idea about how something might work. What is required after developing a theory is empirical evidence. The best type of evidence comes in the form of replicated studies that demonstrate consistent patterns, known as 'empirical generalisations'.[50]

In studies of IMC and advertising, many accepted theories and practices have been based on one study and not replicated—in fact, replication of results has been rare for decades in marketing studies.[51]

This section of the chapter considers the effect that an IMC program may have on consumers based on two very different theoretical approaches. You will find an in-depth discussion of these two approaches in Chapter 2, where they will be aligned with comparable theories of consumer behaviour.

The Strong theory

The majority of marketing academics and practitioners subscribe to what was labelled as the 'Strong' theory of advertising in the seminal paper by John Phillip Jones (1990).[52] The **Strong theory** has very few followers even though it appears the empirical evidence for this theory is very convincing.

The paper by John Phillip Jones makes the valid point that our knowledge of how advertising works is at best imperfect. While this paper may be decades old, it is as relevant today as ever and is a must-read for any student of IMC. Although the focus of the paper is on advertising, we can extend the assumptions being made more widely to all aspects of IMC.

Overall, the Strong theory assumes that advertising (or IMC) is persuasive in nature and that marketers need to use models to convince a consumer over time to use the brand.[53] Underlying such models is the assumption that consumers' attitudes drive their behaviour, which is an assumption that we already critically evaluated earlier in this chapter.

Jones summarises the approach of the Strong theory to assume that advertising (or IMC) changes people's attitudes, and therefore persuades them to buy a brand and convinces them that that brand is better suited to them than any other brands available.[54] The Strong advertising theory implies a chain of effects linking thoughts, emotions and behaviours, with the aim of getting consumers to think, feel and do, thereby linking the cognitive, affective and conative facets of consumer behaviour, which is supposed to initiate a process of transforming awareness into interest, desire and action (hence the use of the acronym AIDA—see Figure 1.7).

We can see that the Strong theory assumes that consumers are passive and can be convinced by advertising to change their behaviour. As marketers, we need to ask ourselves if this is how we believe advertising really works.

For example, do price promotions convince consumers to buy the brand while it is on sale and then remain loyal to the brand after it goes back to full price? Does an advertisement on a website engage and convince a consumer to click through to the advertiser's website? Does comparative advertising work? These are questions you will need to ask yourself as you make your way through this book. It takes a balanced approach and therefore presents alternative points of view. You will need to consider the evidence presented and then decide for yourself which way you believe IMC tactics work and consider what underlying assumptions are being made.

The Weak theory

Jones also presents a counter argument to the Strong theory, which was until recently largely underpinned by the research of marketing scientist Andrew Ehrenberg.[55] With many years of empirical evidence, Ehrenberg et al. (1988) argued that advertising has no persuasive effect.[56] He suggested that advertising has the effect of building brand knowledge, which increases the probability a brand will be bought in the future. In summary, the assumptions underlying the Weak theory suggest that advertising increases salience for a brand. They suggest that consumers are not particularly involved in a relationship with brands, and that brand purchases are trivial.

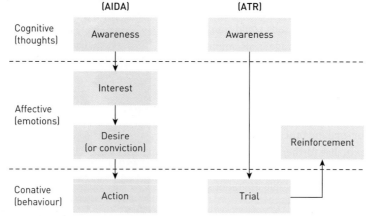

Figure 1.7 Strong and Weak theories of advertising

The Weak theory suggests that consumers are unlikely to be convinced or persuaded to buy a brand but that brand purchases are probabilistic in nature, as is brand recall. Accordingly, the Weak advertising theory conceives advertising as a way to create awareness and encourage trial, or to reinforce behaviour (hence the use of the acronym ATR—see Figure 1.7). The irony of the Weak view is that it is not popular among marketing practitioners or marketing academics globally but it actually has more robust empirical evidence supporting it.[57]

To understand how these two theories work, it is best to look at some examples. If we consider mortgages—which are an example of a financial product with which consumers are likely to be highly involved—it is very likely that individuals will engage in lengthy and complex decision making. In this instance, the Strong advertising theory offers a valuable and directly relevant framework for the IMC, useful to any firm operating in this market. Specifically, in order to influence consumers, the advertising campaigns put forward by firms in this market should a) deal with rational matters (for example, raising awareness of the fact that the firm is offering mortgages and what are the most distinctive features of the service provided); b) raise interest and desires by playing with emotions (for example, showing images of consumers accessing their new homes stress free and enjoying life); and c) include elements specifically directed at encouraging action (for example, 'Call us now for a free consultation' and similar claims—see Figure 1.8).

Conversely, if we consider products such as shampoos, it is

Figure 1.8 Example of an IMC campaign based on the Strong advertising theory

highly probable that consumers will approach purchase decisions with limited involvement, acting upon habits or past experience. Therefore, the Weak advertising theory provides a simple model for IMC that revolves around awareness raising and reinforcement of habits. This means IMC campaigns for brands could simply aim to raise awareness and encourage trials among new customers while reinforcing the behaviour of existing customers (see the example in Figure 1.9).

In Chapter 2, we will delve further into considering how IMC programs might influence consumer behaviour, including the decision-making process. Accordingly, we will be able to contextualise further these two theories, reflecting on how to determine which theory (Strong or Weak) should be used, and the possible limitations to what IMC tactics can actually achieve.

The approach taken in this book is balanced between two major paradigms of consumer behaviour: cognitive and behavioural approaches as defined by East et al.[58]

Figure 1.9 Example of a campaign based on the Weak advertising theory

■ CHAPTER SUMMARY

In this chapter we introduced you to the concept of Integrated Marketing Communication. We also clarified how IMC essentially extends and executes the meaning of the marketing function, resulting in a full-on program that facilitates communication and information processing between firms and consumers. In doing so, we drew a connection between the IMC and marketing planning process, which will be explored later on in this book.

We then outlined in a concise manner four key aims of the IMC: differentiation, reinforcement, information and persuasion. These four overarching aims will be explained and explored in far greater detail across the next few chapters, as your understanding of how IMC works deepens.

We also briefly described the various components of the IMC: advertising, public relations, direct marketing, sales promotion, personal selling, electronic and social media, and sponsorship. These will be described at length in later chapters.

Next, we offered you an overview of some key communication models, embracing relevant insights derived from psychology concerning traditional or linear communication models; memory and information-processing models; attitudes and persuasion models—with particular attention paid to the elaboration likelihood model—and emotions and hedonism.

Finally, we introduced you to two widely accepted (and contrasting) approaches to IMC—the Strong and Weak theories—which represent two rather contrasting takes on the inner 'power' of IMC in affecting consumers—with the Strong theory positing greater effects of the IMC on consumers, and the Weak theory assuming that the IMC is best deployed to 'nudge' consumption.

Case study: Thinking outside the marketing box in the third sector: A case of marketing the support of asylum seekers

Gabrielle Tong was very happy. She had just graduated from a marketing degree at Sunway University three months ago, and had received a letter from AsylumHelp, a not-for-profit organisation that aims to help asylum seekers in Malaysia. The letter offered her a position as a marketing coordinator based at the head office in Chow Kit, an inner suburb of Kuala Lumpur. She had called her new manager and had been asked to think about developing a marketing plan for the organisation.

Asylum seekers are common in Malaysia, as the country is both a final destination and a stop on the way to countries like Australia and New Zealand. There are few resources to help these asylum seekers, so AsylumHelp was set up to offer food supplies and temporary shelter.

Over the days following the job offer, Gabrielle's delight with her new job turned to concern, as she realised that all her training in marketing had been for profit oriented firms. She had always been trained that the marketing concept was *satisfying customer needs by providing them with products and services at a profit*. Gabrielle has turned to you, her long-time friend and fellow marketing graduate to help her think through marketing issues for this global not-for-profit organisation

---

Questions

1. Can you redefine the marketing concept for this not-for profit organisation?
2. What products and services does AsylumHelp provide and who is the market for these products and services?

Case study: Brown Brothers 'Colourful Conversations'

Background

Brown Brothers is one of Australia's most iconic family-owned wine companies. Founded in 1889 by John Francis Brown, it continues to be owned and run by members of the third and fourth generation of the family. In 2014, the company celebrated its 125th year in operation. To celebrate this milestone, it launched Colourful Conversations, a multifaceted campaign designed to showcase its full portfolio of wines.

Figure 1.10 What kind of mood are you in?

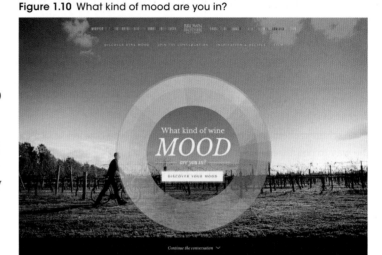

Market research had indicated that most consumers associated the brand with fruity wines. Also, while the much loved brand conjured up feelings of happy nostalgia for long-time advocates, it was struggling to attract new customers.

To really understand the mindset of the wine consumer, Brown Brothers engaged creative brand consultancy Flock of Starlings and embarked on a series of focus groups to better understand how to revitalise the brand. The results highlighted a disconnection between the way wine had traditionally been marketed and actual consumer sentiments.

Through these workshops and other market research conducted by Brown Brothers, the brand realised that typical connoisseur-style tasting notes were simply missing the mark. The everyday wine drinker was less interested in 'aromas of cherry and rose petal,' than the mood and occasion they associated with a particular wine.

Objectives

While the broader objectives of the campaign were to revitalise the brand and reconnect with consumers, on a more granular level it was designed to:

- Raise brand awareness,
- Increase the level of engagement on social channels, and
- Drive more traffic to the brand's online assets.

  The challenge was to achieve all of this in a way that would amplify a relatively modest budget.

Strategy

Brown Brothers realised that its strategy needed to be one that turned conventional wine wisdom on its head. It needed to help consumers select wine based on their mood and the nature of the occasion. The strategy needed to move away from traditional 'wine language' and inject a bit more emotion into the process of selecting wine. Above all, it needed to highlight the role that wine plays in bringing people together – to frame it as an integral part of the social experience, rather than just a product.

From these insights, Brown Brothers worked with Flock of Starlings to create a mood-based wine selection tool. The concept of a 'mood wheel' developed out of the idea that there is a Brown Brothers wine for every mood – and a colour to reflect that wine and mood. The mood wheel essentially formed the basis of the Colourful Conversations campaign.

Execution

Armed with the concept of the mood wheel, Brown Brothers brought together a group of experts – including its own PR, events and sponsorship and online teams, as well as designers, writers, a documentary filmmaker and a social media specialist – and got them to produce ideas around connecting people through wine and shared experiences.

The dinner party

From the brainstorming exercise, it was decided to create a dinner party event curated and attended by influential creatives or 'makers'. Ten makers were selected to take part, including stylists, florists, bakers, artists and chefs. The idea was that they would come together to connect over Brown Brothers' wine and 'colourful conversations'.

The mini film

The unscripted dinner party event was filmed and edited down into a two-minute film, uploaded to YouTube and played in Palace Cinemas. It was also used as the basis for an online behavioural marketing campaign. If people had visited a particular recipe site, for example, they would be served with a web banner that would expand with the film, to drive people to the campaign site.

The conversation starters

The concept of the conversation starters was originally conceived to facilitate conversation among the makers at the dinner party, but it quickly became an integral part of the campaign.

The central premise is that Brown Brothers is a company built on questions. 3,000 box sets of conversation starter question cards were created. Consumers could buy the box from the cellar door, or get it as part of a package when they purchased Brown Brothers' wines online.

The box reads: "With these cards, a glass of Brown Brothers wine in hand and your friends and family around you, you have the perfect elements for a lively, curious and meaningful time together."

The website

Central to the campaign has been its online hub, colourfulconversations.com.au. The site was designed and created by Get Started to bring Colourful Conversations to life digitally. The mood wheel – an interactive tool that allows the user to 'take the wine mood test' to see what sort of wine mood they're in and find a suitable Brown Brothers product to match it – forms the centrepiece of the site. In line with the campaign objectives, it was designed to be fun, engaging and easy to share. The mood wheel has been so well-received that it has now been integrated into Brown Brothers' main site.

Another key aspect of colourfulconversations.com.au is the digital extension of the conversation starters. Site visitors can view the questions and add their own answers, as well as read through some of the contributions that others have submitted.

Social

The Colourful Conversations concept has laid the foundations for an ongoing communications platform that Brown Brothers plans to use to launch new products.

Each of the makers had substantial social followings. The collaboration between Brown Brothers and the makers was not only to extend the reach of the brand into new consumer markets, but also to collectively create content that could be shared through various social media platforms. This content included photography, recipes and even a series of 'Make It' videos that were shared on Facebook and Instagram with useful tips to make an event special.

Print media advertising

Magazine advertising in home and lifestyle titles was also used to drive people to the campaign site. The ads, which appeared in publications such as Vogue Living, Belle and Home Beautiful, provided a cost-effective way for Brown Brothers to extend the reach of the campaign. Rather than producing ads, the company created executions that would integrate into the content of the magazines, including recipes and conversation starters.

Colourful Conversations was officially launched on 14 November 2014, to coincide with the reopening of the historic 125-year-old 'Barn' at Brown Brothers' Milawa vineyard. The concept continues to underpin the company's marketing initiatives and will do so for the foreseeable future.

Results

One of the key success metrics of this campaign has been social engagement. At the start of the campaign, Brown Brothers' Instagram following was sitting at 1500. 12 months on, it had grown to almost 22,000. The brand has also seen a rise in its Facebook following, up from 49,000 at the start of the campaign to 55,000.

Since its launch, the Colourful Conversations website has attracted over 140,000 visitors. It has also been a significant referrer of traffic to Brown Brothers' main website, with 44% of this traffic to date being new visitors to the main site. The campaign website also won Gold in the 2015 Melbourne Design Awards, and it took out the top gongs for both the Commercial and Innovation categories at the Australian Web Awards.

In terms of brand awareness, Colourful Conversations has enabled Brown Brothers to hold its ground in an extremely competitive and crowded market, while numerous competitor brands have declined on brand health measures.

In a broader sense, the Colourful Conversations concept has laid the foundations for an ongoing communications platform that Brown Brothers plans to use to launch new products and tell the brand's story into the future.

Questions

1. Outline which Components of IMC are used in this campaign. Which other Components of IMC could Brown Brothers have used?
2. Do you think this campaign sits better with the Strong theory of IMC or the Weak theory of IMC? Justify your position using material from the case.
3. Do you believe that this campaign is persuasive in its approach? Justify your position.

Adapted from and originally published 7 March 2016 on the Marketing Magazine website: https://www.marketingmag.com.au/hubs-c/case-study-brown-brothers-colourful-conversations/.

Practitioner profile: Sloane Orger

I graduated from VCE with hope to be a psychologist. After one year and six weeks struggling to understand statistics, I left to travel and find myself. During this time I fell into marketing by accepting a role promoting the launch of Pepsi Max. I consider myself a jack of most trades, master of none. That's what is great about marketing; it is always evolving and someone will always like your work and someone will not. My marketing career started in the early 2000s as a brand ambassador for various Fast-Moving Consumer Goods (FMCG) brands. I went on to be Campaign Manager for Victorian promotional campaigns and then embarked on formal studies at Victoria University. In 2012 I undertook a Masters of Business, Marketing degree, which included a minor thesis. It was challenging but a great way to solidify my professional experience with academic knowledge.

Describe your current role or previous roles and the organisation/s you've worked for, and give a brief account of what you do/did in your role on a day-to-day basis.

I've held a range of roles that involve elements of marketing, including Communications Officer, Campaign Manager, Product Coordinator, Account Manager and Media Buyer. I have worked across State (Department of Health and Human Services and Department of Premier and Cabinet) and Federal (Federal Magistrates Court) government as well as for a leading media agency, Mitchell & Partners and for media publishers, Val Morgan Outdoor and Authentic Entertainment. Most recently, I've worked as a Marketing Assistant for a property development company. The role was highly digital focused: updating their social media channels, working with digital and creative agencies, and developing and editing copy for both print and online collateral.

How important is Integrated Marketing Communication (IMC) to what you and your organisation do?

Having an understanding of Integrated Marketing Communication has been beneficial in all of my roles. As a marketer, developing strategies to effectively communicate a company message is vital. The rise of digital marketing has brought the world closer together, which means we can communicate with audiences previously out of reach but this also brings more competitors to the market. As marketers, we are faced with the challenge of designing marketing campaigns that reach consumers; this means you need to consider your creative, media types, timing and target audience.

What types of promotional tools do you use in your IMC campaigns? Please provide examples.

Promotions are a great way to increase awareness. As brand ambassadors we hit the streets to raise awareness of products but also drive sales. Promotional campaigns like these are a great way to communicate directly with consumers, but they can be expensive and not always relevant. I've also utilised events and advertising throughout my marketing career and most recently digital promotional tools. While at the property development company, we regularly used property insight nights to not only increase their client base, but also to reinforce their reputation as an expert in their field. Each campaign will require different promotional tools, so it is important to consider the marketing objective and use it accordingly. Direct mail and electronic direct mail (EDMs) to communicate to larger audiences have been effective as to sales offers.

What has been your favourite IMC project to work on and did it achieve its objective?

I've had the privilege to work on numerous media and marketing campaigns. There is no better feeling than planning a media or marketing strategy and seeing it executed. I've had fun delivering Below The Line (BTL) campaigns; the energy of promotions is addictive and a great way to start in marketing. Campaigns I've worked on included Pepsi Max keg racing and Solo 'Chest Testers', where we had members of the public race to drink a can of solo wearing a bib! I've also planned many media campaigns for multiple Victorian government departments. The main challenge when designing a media schedule for government is to ensure their creative is strategically placed to reach a wide number of Victorians within tight budgets. While at Val Morgan Outdoor, I worked on a project in partnership with Clemengers and Pedigree Petfoods to raise awareness for the website Pet Rescue. This was one of my favourite campaigns as to be part of something that helped animals find their forever home was something important to me.

How do you believe an IMC campaign affects the consumer decision-making process for your particular target audience?

If you can't reach your audience, you can't influence the consumer decision-making process. It is a competitive and cluttered market now and as marketers, we understand that consumers have a repertoire of brands to choose from. Advertising, promotions, price and availability can impact sales so an effective campaign can help keep your brand top of mind among current customers and potentially increase awareness to the broader public.

How has your application of IMC changed with the increase in digital marketing?

Digital marketing has allowed marketers to communicate to bigger and broader audiences, both domestically and globally. It has also given them tools to get to know consumers more than ever before. Marketers can now follow their target audiences around the web and gain insights into their interests, behaviours and lifestyles. This allows us to create and send tailored messages at the right time, which not only can positively impact the marketing budget, but can also reduce wastage by communicating on platforms relevant to your target. By attaching tags to creative, marketers can now track sales and where the consumer came from. This is valuable when measuring the success of a campaign or promotion and can then help with future planning. Another impact digital marketing has had on IMC is that as people tend to multi screen, marketers have had to come up with ways to grab attention, and shorter, snappier creative is emerging—known as 'snackable'—running for 5 to 10 seconds. It is a challenge to convey the brand message in such a short time but is also proving to be an appealing form of advertising. Having said that, longer creative is not dead—just look at the success of the Super Bowl ads each year. Digital marketing has also given marketers the opportunity to run multiple creatives and to swap creative at short notice should the need arise, compared to other forms of media, which need longer lead times.

What do you believe are some of the challenges to implementing an IMC campaign?

I believe there are no rules in marketing, which is so much fun! This can be powerful but can also be limiting. With such a suite of tools available to marketers it can be difficult to select the appropriate IMC. Furthermore, how do you stand out from your competitors? It's also important to be aware that consumers are becoming more savvy and aware of marketing and advertising so your campaign needs to be genuine, relevant and appealing to your target audience, otherwise they can quickly become negative spokespeople. Digital media channels have given consumers a voice they did not have previously and many are quick to voice their dislike of a product or brand. While you can't please everyone, consider your objectives when designing an IMC campaign.

What advice would you offer a student studying IMC?

Be creative! Have fun with the subject and be curious about IMC—ask why. Studying marketing only benefits you when you get involved. Debate and listen to each other's differences; don't be afraid to share your opinions. Remember, we are all consumers, so what you think—whether you like or dislike something—is relevant. For those of you passionate about marketing, consider a thesis. While I was hesitant at first, it proved to be rewarding and such a fun and challenging experience. Researching a subject you're interested in becomes addictive. Good luck!

Key terms

attitudes	long-term memory	sensory store
central route	peripheral route	Strong theory
dual route	persuasion	Weak theory
hedonism	rehearsal	working memory store
IMC	retrieval	

Revision questions

1. How would you define IMC?
2. What role does IMC play in an organisation's marketing plan?
3. What are the aims of IMC?
4. What are the components of IMC/the promotions mix?
5. Draw a linear communication model, outlining the elements of it.
6. Draw the memory processing model and describe each element of it.
7. What is the difference between the Strong and Weak theories?
8. As you are studying IMC, it is likely you have already completed an introductory marketing course. Thinking back to that course and the fundamental principles taught within it, how do you think Integrated Marketing Communication fits in with what you learnt?
9. How do you think 'noise' may affect an IMC campaign? Consider a television commercial (TVC). Give examples of noise and how it may affect the communication process.
10. Draw a diagram of how you think the communication process might work in IMC. Where in the process might there be miscommunication?
11. How should IMC programs be developed, given that coding brand information into permanent storage can take up to two years and repetition of the information helps encode the information? Consider the following questions when answering:
    a. Should we reposition our brands regularly to make them 'fresh'?
    b. Should we have consistency in branding elements such as colour and logos?
    c. What are the implications of changing logos or brand colours?
12. If only 7 ± 2 bits of information can be handled by the working memory at any one time, how might an IMC program work in comparison to consumer memory?
13. Consider the ideas that were presented in the discussion on communication and memory early in the chapter. Is the information presented more supportive of a Strong or Weak approach to IMC? Why? Why not?

Further reading

Belch, G. E., Belch, M. A., Kerr, G. F. and Powell, I. (2014). *Advertising: an integrated marketing communication perspective*. McGraw-Hill Education.

Blakeman, R. (2018). *Integrated marketing communication: creative strategy from idea to implementation*. Rowman & Littlefield.

Fill, C. (2000). Essentially a matter of consistency: integrated marketing communications. *The Marketing Review, 1*(4), 409–25.

Fill, C. & Turnbull, S.L. (2016). *Marketing communications: brands, experiences and participation*. Pearson.

Hutton, J. (1996). Integrated marketing communications and the evolution of marketing thought. *Journal of Business Research, 37*, 155–62.

Keller, K. L. (2016). Unlocking the power of integrated marketing communications: how integrated is your IMC program? *Journal of Advertising, 45*(3), 286–301.

Luxton, S., Reid, M. & Mavondo, F. (2015). Integrated marketing communication capability and brand performance. *Journal of Advertising, 44*(1), 37–46.

Notes

1 Broadbent, S., & Burnett, L. (1992). 456 views of how advertising works. *Admap*, *27*,17.

2 Sharp, B. (2017). *Marketing: theory, evidence, practice.* Oxford University Press: South Melbourne.

3 Handley, L. (2016). Global advertising spend to slow in 2017, while 2016 sales reached nearly $500bn: Research. CNBC. https://www.cnbc.com/2016/12/05/global-ad-spend-to-slow-in-2017-while-2016-sales-were-nearly-500bn.html.

4 Baker, M. & Hart, S. (2008). *The marketing book* (6th edn). London: Routledge; Constantinides, E. (2006). The marketing mix revisited: towards the 21st century marketing. *Journal of Marketing Management*, *22*(3–4), 407–38.

5 Hartley, B. & Pickton, D. (1999). Integrated marketing communications requires a new way of thinking. *Journal of Marketing Communications*, *5*(2), 97–106.

6 Kitchen, P. J., Brignell, J., Li, T. & Jones, G. S. (2004). The emergence of IMC: a theoretical perspective. *Journal of Advertising Research*, *44*(1), 19–30.

7 Sharp, op. cit.

8 Fill, C. (2005). *Marketing communications: engagements, strategies and practice.* Pearson Education.

9 Spotts, H. E., Lambert, D. R. & Joyce, M. L. (1998). Marketing déjà vu: the discovery of integrated marketing communications. *Journal of Marketing Education*, *20*(3), 210–18; Kitchen, op. cit.

10 Raaijmakers, J. G. W. & Shiffrin, R. M. (1981). Search of Associative Memory. *Psychological Review*, *88*(2), 93–134.

11 Craik, F. I. M. & Lockhart, R. S. (1972). Levels of processing: a framework for memory research. *Journal of Verbal Learning and Verbal Behavior*, 11, 671–84; Reed, S. K. (1996). *Cognition: Theory and Applications*. Pacific Grove: Brooks/Cole Publishing.

12 Miller, G. A. (1956). The magic number seven, plus or minus two: some limits on our capacity for processing information. *The Psychological Review*, *63*(2), 81–97.

13 Nedungadi, P. (1990). Recall and consumer consideration sets: influencing choice without altering brand evaluations. *Journal of Consumer Research*, *17*(3), 263–76; Franzen, G. & Bouwman, M. (2001). The mental world of brands: mind, memory and brand success. Henley-on-Thames, World Advertising Research Centre.

14 Bjork, R. A. & Vanhuele, M. (1992). Retrieval inhibition and related adaptive peculiarities of human memory. *Advances in Consumer Research*, *19*, 155–60; Franzen & Bouwman, op. cit.

15 Franzen & Bouwman, op. cit.

16 Tulving, E. & Pearlstone, Z. (1966). Availability versus accessibility of information in memory for words. *Journal of Verbal Learning and Verbal Behavior*, *5*(4), 381–91; Tulving, E. & Psotka, J. (1971). Retroactive inhibition in free recall: inaccessibility of information available in the memory store. *Journal of Experimental Psychology*, *87*(1), 1–8; Lynch, J. G. Jr & Srull, T. K. (1982). Memory and attentional factors in consumer choice: concepts and research methods. *Journal of Consumer Research*, *9*(1), 18–37.

17 Bjork & Vanhuele, op. cit.; Franzen & Bouwman, op. cit.

18 Anderson, J. R. (2013). *Learning, Memory and Thought*. New York: Psychology Press.

19 Bjork & Vanhuele, op. cit.

20 Bjork & Vanhuele, op. cit.

21 Raaijmakers & Shiffrin, op cit.; Anderson, op. cit.

22 Franzen & Bouwman, op. cit.

23 Collins, A. M. & Loftus, E. F. (1975). A spreading activation theory of semantic processing. *Psychological Review, 82*(6), 407–28; Raaijmakers & Shiffrin, op cit.

24 Collins & Loftus, op. cit.

25 Mitchell, A. A. (1982). Models of memory: implications for measuring knowledge structures. Advances in Consumer Research (US) Conference. Urbana, Illinois: Association for Consumer Research.

26 ibid.

27 Miller, op. cit.

28 Collins & Loftus, op. cit.

29 ibid.

30 Grober, E. & Buschke, H. (1987). Genuine memory deficits in dementia. *Developmental Neuropsychology, 3*(1), 13–36.

31 Collins & Loftus, op. cit., 411.

32 Franzen & Bouwman, op. cit.

33 Rosch, E. (1978). Principles of categorization. In E. Rosch & B. B. Lloyd (eds). *Cognition and Categorization*, 28–49.

34 Franzen & Bouwman, op. cit.

35 Ward, J. C. et al. (1992). Measuring the prototypicality and meaning of retail environments. *Journal of Retailing, 68*(2), 194–221.

36 Romaniuk, J. & Sharp, B. (2000). Using known patterns in image data to determine brand positioning. *International Journal of Market Research, 42*(2), 219–30.

37 Ward et al., op. cit.

38 ibid.

39 Ries, A. & Trout, J. (2001). Positioning: The Battle for Your Mind. NY: McGraw Hill; DiMingo, E. (1988). The fine art of positioning. The Journal of Business Strategy, 9(2), 34–8.

40 Petty, R. E. & Cacioppo, J. T. (1986). The elaboration likelihood model of persuasion. In L. Berkowitz (ed.), *Advances in Experimental Social Psychology, 19*, 123–205.

41 Bagozzi, R. P. (1982). A field investigation of causal relations among cognitions, affect, intentions, and behavior. *Journal of Marketing Research, 19*(November), 562–84.

42 Zaichkowsky, J. L. (1985). Measuring the involvement construct. *Journal of Consumer Research*, 12, 341–52.

43 www.businessinsider.com.au/australias-most-valuable-brands-2018-2

44 See also https://mumbrella.com.au/telstra-promises-the-world-new-brand-push-381288

45 Petty, R. E. & Cacioppo, J. T. (1983). Central and peripheral routes to persuasion: application to advertising. In L. Percy & A. G. Woodside (eds), *Advertising and Consumer Psychology*, 3–23; Petty, R. E. & Cacioppo, J. T. (1986). The elaboration likelihood model of persuasion. In L. Berkowitz (ed.), *Advances in Experimental Social Psychology*, 19, 123–205.

46 Kitchen, P., Kerr, G., Schultz, D., McColl, R. & Pals, H. (2014). The elaboration likelihood model: review, critique and research agenda. *European Journal of Marketing*, *48*(11/12), 2033–50.

47 Holbrook, M. B. & Hirschman, E.C. (1982). The experiential aspects of consumption: consumer fantasies, feelings, and fun. *Journal of Consumer Research*, *9*(2), 132–40.

48 Dubois, B. & Duquesne, P. (1993). The market for luxury goods: income versus culture. *European Journal of Marketing*, *27*(1), 35–44; O'Cass, A. & Frost, H. (2002). Status brands: examining the effects of non-product-related brand associations on status and conspicuous consumption. *Journal of Product and Brand Management*, *11*(2), 67–88; Kapferer, J. N. & Bastien, V. (2009). The specificity of luxury management: turning marketing upside down. *Journal of Brand Management*, *16*(5/6), 311–22.

49 Broadbent, op. cit.

50 Barwise, T. P. (1995). Good empirical generalizations. *Marketing Science*, *14*(3), Part 2 of 2, G29–G35; Bass, F. M. (1995). Empirical generalizations and marketing science: a personal view. *Marketing Science*, *14*(3), G6–G18.

51 Reid, L. N., Soley, L. C. & Wimmer, R. D. (1981). Replication in advertising research: 1977, 1978, 1979. *Journal of Advertising*, *10*(1), 3–13; Barwise, op. cit.

52 Jones, J. P. (1990). Advertising: strong force or weak force? Two views an ocean apart. *International Journal of Advertising*, *9*(3), 233–46.

53 Barry, T. E. & Howard, D. J. (1990). A review and critique of the hierarchy of effects in advertising. *International Journal of Advertising*, *9*(2), 121–35.

54 Jones, op. cit.

55 ibid.

56 Ehrenberg, A. S. C., Barnard, N. & Scriven, J. (1998). Advertising is publicity not persuasion. R&DI research report. London: South Bank University, p. 4.

57 Cierpicki, S., Wright, M. & Sharp, B. (2000). Managers' knowledge of marketing principles: the case of new product development. *Journal of Empirical Generalisations in Marketing Science*, *5*, 771–90; Binet, L. & Field, P. (2009). Empirical generalisations about advertising campaign success. *Journal of Advertising Research*, *49*(2), 130–3.

58 East, R., Wright, M. & Vanhuele, M. (eds). (2017). *Consumer Behaviour: Applications in Marketing*. (2nd edn). London: Sage.

CHAPTER 2

Marketing Communication and Consumer Behaviour

Lara Stocchi and Maxwell Winchester

Air New Zealand: releasing our inner Dave

In its advertising campaign featuring 'Dave'—a migratory bird that has learnt the secrets to travelling with great comfort—Air New Zealand wants its Australian customers to know that there is a #BetterWaytoFly long haul. The company has used a similar marketing and communication approach in the past, but its #BetterWaytoFly campaign, featuring the voice of Australian actor Bryan Brown, is specifically aimed at shifting the perceptions and behaviour of a large base of customers. The objective of the campaign is to ensure that Australians will consider Air New Zealand as an option for long-distance flights (especially to North and South America), as opposed to being 'just' their obvious choice for flying between Australia and New Zealand. However, in a market currently dominated by 'all time favourites' such as Qantas and new, highly compelling offers such as those of Emirates, can one very cool bird do the trick? For many consumers wanting to travel long haul from Australia, a flight purchase will most likely come down to a thorough price comparison at the touch of a button, rather than the impellent need to avoid 'sticking with the flock'. Therefore, although the airline is eager to be seen in a different light, it might be overly optimistic about its campaign's ability to cause such a drastic change in the perceptions and behaviour of many consumers.[1]

Figure 2.1 A still from Air New Zealand's 'A better way to fly' advertising campaign

■ INTRODUCTION

The example of Air New Zealand's #BetterWaytoFly campaign illustrates, in a nutshell, the relationship between the integrated marketing communication (IMC) process and consumer behaviour. The general belief is that all the tricks up the sleeve of marketing managers can be used to attract the attention of consumers—and change their perceptions, thoughts and feelings, ultimately influencing their behaviour. This belief determines how organisations strive to attain their market goals and is at the heart of theoretical frameworks explaining the mechanisms of advertising and communication effectiveness.

The key aims of this chapter are:

- to explore the tantalising idea that this might be, at times, harder than expected
- to discuss how the IMC process can (at least in theory) affect consumer behaviour.

Accordingly, we start by providing further details of how the IMC process relates to consumer behaviour and then introduce some foundations of consumer behaviour, such as commonly prescribed cognitive (decision-making) models and the reinforcement and habit behaviourist models.[2] To encourage further reflection and debate, we include relevant empirical evidence based on buying behaviour literature to further elucidate how fundamental aspects of the IMC process relate to consumer behaviour.

Consumer behaviour is an applied social science that focuses on understanding all of the processes involved in how individuals select, access, buy, use and dispose of all sorts of goods and services.[3] It is linked to other important knowledge fields, including psychology, sociology and economics; it is also pivotal to marketing because understanding of the consumer is a crucial ingredient to brand performance management and the attainment of a competitive advantage—that is, it is essential for creating and maintaining a strong brand and for outperforming rivals.[4]

In the specific context of designing and managing the IMC process, principles and theories of consumption are extremely important. Put simply, to identify a key message worth communicating and the right medium to use, organisations need a solid understanding of consumers: who they are; what they feel and think; what motivates them and why; what they buy and like, and so on. Nonetheless, existing academic and practical knowledge often only implicitly connects consumer behaviour and the IMC process. As a result, key theoretical frameworks in both areas are not often directly linked and/or compared. This chapter will take you on a journey that 'connects the dots', illustrating how IMC and consumer behaviour relate and the relative implications for marketing practices of all sorts of organisations.

LEARNING OBJECTIVES

After reading this chapter you should be able to:

1. explain the contextual relevance of the decision-making process and memory functions
2. illustrate the cognitive and behavioural learning theories, and their relative implications for explaining consumer behaviour
3. link consumer behaviour theories with IMC activities
4. describe the importance of empirical evidence when interpreting the link between IMC and consumer behaviour.

How IMC relates to consumer behaviour theories

From a basic theoretical perspective, **consumer behaviour** relies upon psychological principles regarding **decision-making**, **memory** and **learning**. Traditionally, marketers put a lot of emphasis on the rational decision-making process in consumer behaviour. This emphasis has greatly influenced the way marketers traditionally do IMC activities. Learning is particularly important because it explicates how individuals decode reality, 'making sense' of large amounts of stimuli and cutting through clutter on an ongoing basis. Therefore, 'borrowing' learning theories from consumer behaviour provides a simple platform of knowledge for explaining how communication and persuasion work (see Chapter 1), and how to improve the nuts and bolts of IMC. Similarly, understanding how memory works is essential to the effective and efficient management of IMC because it improves the understanding of how individuals process information and subsequently access this information when carrying out cognitive tasks such as purchase decisions. Combined, these insights provide a frame of reference for all IMC activities, since the underlying objective of marketing communication is to influence the choices of individuals before a decision is made; when a decision is made (e.g. at point of purchase); and even after a decision is made (e.g. through reinforcement of a behaviour). This section of the chapter covers all three key theoretical bases of consumer behaviour and illustrates in more detail their relevance to IMC.

Commonly prescribed cognitive models of consumer behaviour

Traditionally, decision making has been depicted as a series of subsequent stages (see Figure 2.2) according to which consumers first become aware of a certain need; then seek information and

alternatives likely to meet this need; compare and evaluate these alternatives; and ultimately reach a concluding decision, which provides feedback for future reference.[5] This way of conceptualising decision making is aligned with cognitive (decision-making) theories of learning and is more generally labelled as the **cognitive model of consumer behaviour**.

A key distinguishing aspect of the cognitive model is the fact that it considers consumers as **rational problem-solvers**, in line with the economic notion of **utility**; that is, individuals attempt to outweigh perceived losses with perceived benefits, and run decisions by considering the value that each alternative yields.[6] These assumptions can be challenged in many ways by current consumption contexts; yet, on a basic theoretical level the cognitive decision-making model offers a fundamental framework of reference to link consumer behaviour and IMC.

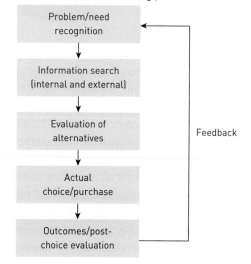

Figure 2.2 Stages of the high-involvement consumer decision-making process

During the **problem (or need) recognition** stage of decision making, consumers become aware of the existence of a gap between a desired status and their current status; clearly, many facets of the IMC are specifically aimed at raising this awareness and triggering consumer needs using various communication methods and promotional strategies (e.g. advertising, price promotions, direct marketing). Subsequently, the **information search** stage includes the more or less conscious search of relevant information internally (i.e. in memory) as well as externally (i.e. in the environment or context where the decision making is taking place). An effective management of all IMC-related activities is supposed to provide consumers with information about a certain product, service or organisation, and to ensure that such information is accessible during decision making; in fact, the whole idea of IMC is to persuade and inform consumers. Similarly, IMC can offer multiple opportunities for providing the information that decision makers will seek externally, via advertising, web-presence, social media activities, direct marketing initiatives, and so on. Moreover, when it comes down to the **evaluation of alternatives**, branding, market positioning and advertising strategies are specifically devised to influence consumers and to ensure that a certain offering is seen as somewhat superior to directly comparable alternatives. For example, the campaign for Microsoft's Surface products has been devised to highlight how the Surface is a more flexible and efficient machine than MacBook Pro laptops and other comparable devices by Apple, such as the iPad (see Figure 2.3).

Figure 2.3 Microsoft's Surface

Crucially, various elements of IMC can have a bearing on the evaluation of alternatives, influencing the stages of the decision-making process during which consumers systematically 'narrow down' brands for purchase. This typically occurs during the process of mentally downsizing the available options (the **universal set**) on the basis of the options that come to mind—the **evoked** (or **awareness**) **set**; the options that meet the consumers' needs more closely (the **consideration set**); and, importantly, most likely in line with the options that they have bought in the past (the **purchase repertoire**).[7] All IMC activities can alter this process, somewhat ensuring that a brand is also retained across sub-sets of alternatives and ultimately included in the portfolio of brands that consumers routinely purchase.

Lastly, when a decision is made, IMC tactics could still play a fundamental role via initiatives such as point-of-purchase advertising (see Figure 2.4), price promotions and direct marketing. Also, the **evaluation of outcomes** following the decision could be linked to IMC. For example, all activities linked to direct marketing, customer relationship management and other relationship-building initiatives such as interacting with consumers via social media are specifically conceived to ensure that the feedback that follows a decision is positive and lasting, possibly leading to outcomes such as customer retention and loyalty.

Figure 2.4 An example of point-of-purchase advertising

Although IMC has a strong bearing on the cognitive model of consumer behaviour, there are several reasons why the desired outcomes might not be obtained. These are:

1. Consumers might adopt specific decision-making strategies, which can reduce and/or override parts of the process; that is, consumers might rely upon **heuristics** or mental shortcuts to minimise the cognitive effort, deal with uncertainty and reduce risk.[8] For instance, consumers may use **compensatory decision-making rules**.[9] That is, instead of considering and comparing alternatives (and their features) thoroughly, they may simplify their choice by using simple 'rules of thumbs' such as always picking the cheapest product or service available to them.

2. Consumers might base their decisions on **hedonic factors**; that is, feelings and emotions, as opposed to rational thoughts.[10] For example, consumers may purchase certain items because they 'feel good' about them (e.g. going to a certain café because the atmosphere is enjoyable); change their thinking because of feelings and emotions (e.g. deciding to purchase some 'comfort food' as opposed to a healthy snack because of feeling stressed or tired); and base their decisions exclusively on feelings and emotions (e.g. buying a designer handbag primarily because of 'loving' the label).

3. The decision-making process might be altered and/or voided due to **external contingencies** out of the direct control of marketers, such as the influence of other consumers or the lack of **physical availability**[11], an issue linkable to sales and distribution instead.

4. The decision-making process might not be as formalised and some stages could be skipped or the whole decision could be performed with **limited information processing**.[12]

The last point is particularly relevant because it feeds into the discussion of other models of consumer behaviour, which theorise consumption as a response to environmental stimuli, discussed next.

Behaviourist models of consumer behaviour

Another way of looking at decision making implies considering all nuances of it in line with a **continuum of problem solving and information processing**, ranging from low to high.[13] Different decisions for different products and services will fall somewhere along the continuum, with many common purchase decisions made by consumers on a regular basis sitting at the lower end of the spectrum (see Figure 2.5).[14]

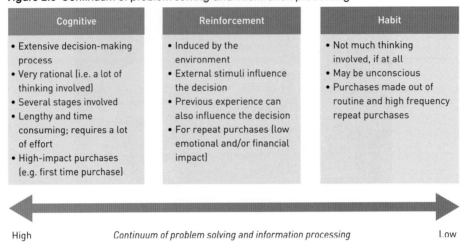

Figure 2.5 Continuum of problem solving and information processing

Cognitive	Reinforcement	Habit
• Extensive decision-making process • Very rational (i.e. a lot of thinking involved) • Several stages involved • Lengthy and time consuming; requires a lot of effort • High-impact purchases (e.g. first time purchase)	• Induced by the environment • External stimuli influence the decision • Previous experience can also influence the decision • For repeat purchases (low emotional and/or financial impact)	• Not much thinking involved, if at all • May be unconscious • Purchases made out of routine and high frequency repeat purchases

High   *Continuum of problem solving and information processing*   Low

The previous section discussed the top end of the continuum and the cognitive model of consumer behaviour. In reality, many purchase decisions fall under one of two models of consumer behaviour:

1. the reinforcement model of consumer behaviour
2. the habit model of consumer behaviour.

Reinforcement model of consumer behaviour

The **reinforcement model of consumer behaviour** theorises decision making in terms of limited problem solving and information processing, placing a lot of emphasis on the consumer's response to stimuli (i.e. behavioural learning, which is discussed later in this chapter) and the influence of past behaviour.[15] Accordingly, consumer behaviour can be explained through the analysis of repeat purchases; that is, acquisitions of products and services that are purchased from time to time as needs arise (e.g. groceries, car service, new pair of jeans). Importantly, this way of theorising consumer behaviour led to the development of formal models of buying behaviour, such as **Ehrenberg and Goodhardt's repeat purchase model**, illustrated in Figure 2.6.[16] The model fully embraces a behavioural view of consumer behaviour and defines purchases as 'as-if random' occurrences, determined, to a great extent, by past behaviour. As such, environmental stimuli can be used to 'nudge' pre-established **purchase propensities**; that is, the chance of buying something again in the near future, given the number of times that it was bought in the past.[17]

Figure 2.6 The Ehrenberg and Goodhardt repeat purchase model

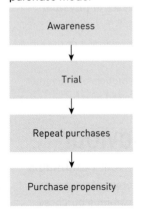

The reinforcement model of consumer behaviour therefore implies that, at best, IMC should be able to trigger a 'stimulus → response' chain of effects. While this most certainly challenges the hypothesis of a direct influence of IMC onto the decision-making process, it does not imply that all IMC activities are pointless; rather, it means that the most realistic outcome of marketing communication is to reinforce pre-established purchase propensities by raising awareness and encouraging trials until a purchase takes place, and subsequently maximising the chances of re-purchase.

To this end, certain IMC activities will be more effective than others, depending upon how likely it is that they can be deployed 'close enough' to the point of purchase. For instance, it is extremely hard to sync exposure to advertising to consumer decisions. Therefore, other strategies such as working on point-of-sale initiatives (e.g. price promotions, attractive packaging) could be much better options, especially because they can enhance physical availability.

Habit model of consumer behaviour

While the reinforcement model of consumer behaviour involves some degree of problem solving and information processing, the **habit model of consumer behaviour** sees decision making as the outcome— or as needing *very little* or *no cognitive effort at all*.[18] The automaticity arises from routine and habits of the consumers' daily lives, which are typical of many aspects of 'default' behaviours, including grabbing a coffee on the way to work, buying milk when it runs out and re-fuelling your car.

The development of such habits is, to a certain extent, a coping mechanism to minimise the time and effort put into decisions that are not that important to consumers. Intuitively, this way of looking at consumer behaviour implies an even more limited relevance of IMC than the reinforcement paradigm. However, such a conclusion is not entirely correct, due to two factors. First, habits must be established in the first place in order to recur routinely. Therefore, many aspects of IMC could be crucial in establishing such habits, especially if using simple approaches such as prominent branding, which could make a product or service very easy to find (and buy) even in the context of routine decisions. Second, priming is possible, especially given that habitual decisions are often, at least in part, unconscious. This is the case of specific IMC initiatives deployed at the point of purchase such as price promotions framed as simple and compelling 'grab and go' deals (see Figure 2.7).

Figure 2.7 Examples of price promotions at a Coles supermarket

Nonetheless, an important aspect that limits the influence of IMC on consumer behaviour in contexts relatable to the behavioural and habit models is the notion of **involvement**.[19] On a basic level, involvement is the personal relevance of a certain object, which can be a product or service, but also a piece of information such as one included in an advertisement and even the actual decision itself. It is determined by:

- *personal characteristics*—individual needs, values and interests
- *characteristics of the object itself*—novelty, complexity, and so on
- *situational factors*—for example, purchase occasion.[20]

Essentially, the reinforcement and habit models of consumer behaviour operate under the assumption that consumer involvement is generally low and individuals have little or no motivation to think about brands, marketing communication or making decisions, which is commonly referred to as **inertia**.[21] This makes it extremely hard for any element of IMC to have an impact. Again, this does not mean that it is not possible, but it is most likely more challenging. For example, it would require the use of novel and highly prominent stimuli, such as unique and distinctive branded elements (see IMC in Action: Comparethemarket. com). Interestingly, this links to the notion of mental availability (discussed more in this chapter), signalling that a key way that IMC can impact consumer behaviour is by making products and services easy to think of in buying situations and easy to come to mind as options to buy.

IMC IN ACTION: COMPARETHEMARKET.COM

Aleksandr, Sergei, Yakov, Bogdan, Vassily and baby Oleg are meerkats and they help consumers comparing markets in essential services. The success of Compare the Market (playing on the similarity in sound between 'meerkats' and 'markets') is an example of brilliant, unique and distinctive branding that went viral, making the firm extremely popular in the UK and Australia.

Figure 2.8 Baby Oleg from Compare the Market

As a basic service, Compare the Market deals with a simple consumer need: assisting with the confusion people are experiencing, and simplifying finding the right insurer. Their approach to IMC, in contrast, is incredibly original and made an insurance comparison brand one of the most memorable and top-of-mind brands, especially in the UK, where it created a fortune in excess of £420 million. You can read more about Compare the Market at www.comparethemarket.com.au.

Figure 2.9 Aleksandr from Compare the Market

Aleksandr Orlov

I am handsome and success businesskat and have many claws in many pies. Despite being talent singer and actorkat, I follow in footsteps of my ancestors, and take over family business of compare meerkats.

As founder of comparethemeerkat.com.au, I am help many peoples across Australia to compare meerkats through magic of the internets. I have valuable experience in compare over 400 different types of meerkat.

To understand in more detail how IMC tactics can work in light of the theories of consumer behaviour considered so far it is necessary to look into some details of the key learning theories that underpin information processing and utilisation; namely, the cognitive learning theory and behavioural learning theories, discussed next.

Learning theories

Learning causes a relatively permanent change in behaviour, and occurs either in the form of complex reasoning (e.g. building associations in your memory, or accessing and updating information) or as a near-default response to the environment.[22] The former is relevant to the **cognitive learning theory**; the latter is applicable to **behavioural learning theories**.

According to behavioural learning theories, the smell of freshly roasted coffee and the bright, warm colours in your local café are anything but random, and are deployed to draw you in on your way to work for an overpriced 'cuppa'. Similarly, 'On special' signs at the end of the aisle in the supermarket are cleverly positioned to grab your attention and remind you that, after all, you could stock a few extra tuna tins. This way of looking at consumption essentially comes down to a simple 'stimulus–response' chain of effects, and is at the heart of two behavioural learning theories widely used in marketing: classical conditioning and instrumental conditioning.

Classical conditioning is embedded in many aspects of IMC work because it assumes that repeated exposure to the same stimulus will induce a certain outcome behaviour; the more novel, exciting and distinct the stimulus used, the more likely the behavioural response.[23] Roughly all elements of the promotional mix, on a very basic level, work in this way:

- branding and the use of **distinctive branding elements**[24] (e.g. logos, jingles, characters, colours, fonts); see Figure 2.10 and the example of Peter Alexander in IMC in Action later in the chapter
- advertising
- price promotions
- PR and sponsorship
- web and social media presence.

These are all examples of stimuli that organisations repeatedly and consistently present to consumers to induce a behavioural response. In fact, the consumer differential response to marketing initiatives is the very essence of the concept of **brand equity**, discussed in Chapter 3.[25]

Instrumental conditioning works in a slightly more complex way because it presumes the use of specific approaches to trigger a behavioural response, as individuals instinctively engage in behaviours that produce positive outcomes and avoid the ones that yield negative consequences.[26] Specifically, instrumental conditioning can occur in three different ways:

1. *by using* **positive reinforcement**—that is, providing a reward (e.g. a free sample, voucher or coupon)
2. *by using* **negative reinforcement**—that is, by removing something negative (e.g. waiving sign-up fees) to strengthen behaviour
3. *by using* **punishment**—that is, the presentation of something negative (e.g. being charged a fee when withdrawing from another bank's ATM).

Figure 2.10 Examples of classical conditioning via branding

Many aspects of how IMC works are based on behavioural learning theories. For example, price promotions (see Figure 2.11) are often detailed in line with instrumental conditioning, offering 2×1 offers (positive reinforcement), price cuts (negative reinforcement) and making the unit price higher than bundle or multi-buy purchases (punishment). Similarly, advertising messages are often framed using these aspects in figurative or subliminal ways; for instance, advertisements for deodorants or detergents often show what would happen if consumers do not use the recommended products as a way to encourage buying decisions (punishment).

Figure 2.11 Examples of instrumental conditioning using price promotions

IMC IN ACTION: PETER ALEXANDER

I have always dreamt I can fly ... and those dreams have driven me to succeed.

Peter Alexander grew from humble beginnings; he fought through innumerable challenges and celebrated monumental triumphs. The pyjama game started on Peter's mum's dining-room table with a simple idea: embedding his passion for animals and childhood into pyjamas, dreaming of new designs every day. These unique collections are designed to delight women, men and children alike and are crafted from the most comfortable and luxurious fabrics. There's also loungewear, daywear, footwear and gifts. The Just Group acquired the business in 2000. Since then, Peter Alexander Sleepwear has grown in leaps and bounds from a pure catalogue-based business to a multi-channel business with 100 retail stores in Australia and New Zealand, with Peter Alexander himself as the Creative Director of the brand.[27]

A focal aspect of Peter Alexander is most certainly the clever use of marketing stimuli throughout its IMC. This includes a strong and consistent use of the colour pink and a particular font type; Peter's beloved dachshund as mascot; bedroom-like décor in the stores and the voluptuous smell of scented candles; iconic shopfronts and the recurring theme of dreams and fairytales; frequent co-branding with Disney; and celebrity endorsement.

Figure 2.12 Peter Alexander shopfront

The cognitive theory of learning does not discharge the relevance of the 'stimuli–response' chain of effects; rather, it assumes that the stimuli response is formalised via the establishment of links and associations in memory as a response to the environment; these links are retained over time and subsequently accessed as 'scripts' guiding behaviour.[28] For example, when considering IMC, over time, everything that a certain brand or product stands for (see the notion of **brand image** in Chapter 3) can also occur via processing complex information and seeking clarification during personal selling (and so on).

Therefore, an important aspect that contradistinguishes the cognitive theory of learning concerns the relevance of memory, regarded as the hub of all input and output information.

Memory

In Chapter 1, we discussed the role of memory in relation to information processing in detail. In this chapter, we need to further consider how information that consumers acquire and, at times, memorise as a result of IMC tactics might be used as reference to consumer behaviour.

Psychological theories such as the **Associative Network Theory (ANT) of memory**[29] provide marketing and communication managers with a valuable framework for understanding how individuals process information related to products and services; and how this information is accessed in the context of consumption (e.g. when a purchase decision is made). Specifically, the ANT framework is based on the assumption that individuals store information (and thus knowledge) in long-term memory in a network of inter-linked concepts (see Figure 2.13 for an example for the McDonald's brand). Within this structure of interlinked concepts, information processing and accessing occurs via the activation of neural pathways in a stimuli–response fashion, which is cue-based.

Figure 2.13 An example of a memory network for McDonald's

Marketing academics and practitioners have adopted these principles, motivated by the desire to make products and services mentally available to consumers.[30] For example, Coca-Cola often revised its cans' colouring after ascertaining that consumers struggled to recognise some of the different variants offered in different colours other than the iconic red, especially Coca-Cola Life, which was initially offered in a green can (see Figure 2.14).

Figure 2.14 Coca Cola's new, improved packaging

Through the range of tactics resulting from IMC, organisations can:

- expose consumers to a large amount of information that needs to be interpreted and memorised; so, to a great extent, IMC might influence the creation of meaning
- maintain and refresh memory associations and the meanings created; for example, via repetition of the same advertising message or memorable sponsorships and celebrity endorsement

- facilitate the recall of information about brands and of the brand itself at the point of purchase; for example, through price promotions or direct marketing initiatives.

The ANT theory mentioned earlier explains that these processes all depend on the concept of **familiarity** or strength of the associations retained in memory.[31] Accordingly, marketers assume that IMC should be aimed at establishing many strong links between a brand and a range of concepts (e.g. the benefits that it offers, its distinctive brand image and any secondary association with other ideas such as celebrities).[32] This is because large and strong networks of memory association facilitate brand recall, especially in buying situations.[33]

However, more recent advancements in memory theory superseded the ANT assumptions and clarified that, besides familiarity, it is also important to encourage the recollection (or reliving) of autobiographical episodes; that is, memories of episodes of personal experiences and related spatial and temporal details.[34] Unlike familiarity, recollection has a stronger bearing on human behaviour because it relates to goals attainment, self-expression and personhood.[35]

Recollection has been examined in regard to advertising effectiveness as a way of bolstering the consumer's emotional reaction to advertisements.[36] However, more recently, researchers started to explore the possibility of a more direct influence on purchase decisions.[37] The assumption is that many other aspects of IMC could trigger the recollection of autobiographical episodes, which consumers could relive at a later stage to guide decision making. For instance, reliving a positive customer experience in the context of direct marketing initiatives or personal selling could influence purchase decisions (see IMC in Action: Commonwealth Bank of Australia).

IMC IN ACTION: COMMONWEALTH BANK OF AUSTRALIA

The Commonwealth Bank's 'retail bank' is the public face delivering a seamless banking experience to 10 million+ personal and small business customers. They offer market-leading products and services, supported by some of the world's best systems and processes. The 'retail bank' has one of the largest branch and ATM networks in Australia, as well as six locally-based phone banking centres, with a strategic focus on offering innovative and transformational opportunities to its customers. Customer service teams assist customers with queries about their banking and help them find the right solution to meet their financial needs and goals. The Commonwealth Bank is committed to improving its customers' financial wellbeing through ongoing innovation in technology and productivity initiatives, which enables them to maintain the friendly, personal and efficient service they are renowned for.[38]

Figure 2.15 Commonwealth Bank's 'retail bank'

Examples such as this demonstrate how many aspects of IMC can provide consumers with memorable personal experiences, which are likely to be relived at a later stage and to guide subsequent behaviour.

In line with everything that we have discussed so far, it is clear that consumer behaviour principles and theories are at the heart of how IMC works. They also underpin the whole rationale of IMC.

The next section presents some empirical evidence to critically evaluate whether IMC can influence consumer behaviour, and to what extent this is actually possible in light of concrete findings and well-known patterns in what consumers do.

Empirical evidence

In evaluating assumptions and theories about how anything works, it is often best to consider the evidence. Unfortunately, as discussed in Chapter 1, marketers over the years have not been very receptive to **empirical evidence**; that is, knowledge derived from the analysis of (real) recurring trends and patterns in the most concrete aspects of consumer behaviour.

Over time, this omission resulted in knowledge that is lopsided, confused and uncritical, all of which have tended to reduce its efficacy both in academic or educational terms and in making a practical contribution to marketing.[39] In fact, studies have been conducted that suggest that high school students are as effective at predicting a marketing outcome as marketing professionals and marketing professors.[40] This is the reason why this book takes a different standpoint, and considers the link between consumer behaviour and IMC in terms of the empirical evidence, which has emerged from the theoretical principles of consumer behaviour discussed so far; yet, it is also much more factual and informative, so it is much more valuable to link to IMC's decisions and strategies.

Earlier in this chapter, it was mentioned that consumer behaviour often looks like a series of 'as-if random' occurrences determined, to a great extent, by past behaviour, which establishes purchase propensities. What we are yet to discuss is the fact that empirical evidence has revealed that this characterises not only consumer goods such as coffee or toothpaste—it also appears to hold for what should be highly involved purchases such as cars[41]; luxury goods[42]; aviation fuel contracts[43]; and pharmaceutical prescriptions by general practitioners.[44]

Years of research across many different contexts have established relevant knowledge, which has been often formalised in **empirical generalisations**[45] or **empirical laws of marketing**[46], some of which marketers do not even know exist, irrespective of their significance in explaining consumer behaviour and their relevance to IMC.

Empirical generalisations facilitate the analysis of consumer behaviour and lead to the identification of relevant insights that can be embedded in marketing strategies, such as tactics for growing the customer base or retaining existing customers. In fact, empirical knowledge can supersede theories of consumer behaviour by describing how consumers buy more clearly, and by indicating ways to prevent unnecessary marketing expenditures (especially in relation to IMC). For example, these laws demonstrate that within each product or service class consumers tend to buy from a small sub-set of preferred brands (commonly referred to as **repertoire buying**)[47] without rejecting any brand; that is, consumers allocate as-if-random (very few) occasional purchase decisions across a limited number of alternatives that are seen as considerably similar. This tendency holds across the various contexts that consumer behaviour and advertising theories prescribe. As such, empirical marketing knowledge suggests that the majority of consumer behaviour, even for what would be traditionally thought of as high-involvement purchases, is very stable and habitual.

The number of relevant empirical laws of marketing is constantly growing, thanks to ongoing scientific research gathering large sets of data capturing buying behaviour in different contexts. In this chapter, we focus on two important laws that have implications for marketing and IMC strategies and are worth considering when examining the link between consumer behaviour and IMC:

- the **Duplication of Purchase Law (DoPL)**
- the **Double Jeopardy Law (DJL)**.

The Duplication of Purchase Law (DoPL)

The DoPL demonstrates that within a certain type (category) of products or services, brands 'share' customers in line with each brand's market share (that is, the proportion of sales for a brand relative to competitors).[48] For instance, over a certain period of time (e.g. one year) the great majority of consumers purchasing toothpaste tend to buy Colgate along with other (smaller) brands such as White Glo. As mentioned earlier, this is extremely common for most low-involvement purchases such as Fast Moving Consumer Goods (FMCGs) and services that consumers access on a regular basis or via subscription (such as banking and insurance). There is also evidence that the exact same pattern characterises higher involvement contexts.

Table 2.1 shows the duplication purchases in luxury fashion brands, revealing exactly the same pattern. Specifically, the figures in the table show that 31 per cent of the consumers bought a Hugo Boss branded product. Of this 31 per cent, 49 per cent also owned Burberry, 46 per cent Prada, and so on. In each row the figures steadily decline, suggesting that these luxury brands are sharing customers in line with their market share. Exceptions to this pattern are very rare; yet, if they occur, they are commonly referred to as **market partitions** and capture 'clusters' of brands that have strong similarities; for example, in terms of the specific consumers' needs targeted.

Table 2.1 Duplication of purchase in luxury fashion brands

	% BOUGHT	HUGO BOSS	BURBERRY	PRADA	GIVENCHY	KENZO	MARC JAC.	FENDI	MOSCHINO	BALENCIAGA	BOTTEGA
Hugo Boss	31		49	46	42	44	31	27	27	12	15
Burberry	30	52		48	38	31	34	32	28	19	16
Prada	24	59	58		43	42	32	40	29	19	14
Givenchy	21	62	54	50		48	33	37	38	22	20
Kenzo	21	66	44	49	49		35	37	37	16	16
Marc Jac.	17	57	60	47	42	31		34	29	26	25
Fendi	15	55	61	63	51	37	37		35	25	24
Moschino	13	65	63	55	61	60	38	41		22	23
Balenciaga	10	39	59	49	48	34	46	39	30		39
Bottega V.	8	57	57	41	53	41	51	45	37	47	
Average	**19**	**57**	**56**	**50**	**47**	**41**	**36**	**36**	**32**	**23**	**21**

Romaniuk, J. & Sharp, B. (2016). *How Brands Grow. Part 2, Including Emerging Markets, Services and Durables, New Brands and Luxury Brands*. Melbourne: Oxford University Press.

An immediate implication of this empirical law is the fact that, by definition, the reinforcement and habit models of consumer behaviour constitute the 'norm', even in higher involvement purchases such as cars and luxury goods. Consequently, IMC tactics should be primarily aimed at stimulating awareness and trial for the brand, and at reinforcing consumers' predisposition to purchase the brand alongside other competing brands (e.g. by enhancing the brand's mental availability or encouraging point-of-sale decisions with promotional activities). Moreover, from a general strategic standpoint, the primary concern of IMC should be attracting more occasional 'buyers' in order to increase market share. In fact, when eyeballing Table 2.1 in further detail, it is evident that bigger brands take a larger share of each other brands' customers, while smaller brands do not. For example, Bottega Veneta loses more of its customers to other brands (and therefore retains fewer customers) than bigger brands such as Hugo Boss and Burberry. This is known as the Double Jeopardy Law (DJL), which is explained next.

Double Jeopardy Law (DJL)

Across many contexts and markets it has been demonstrated that brands with a small market share 'suffer twice' (hence the term 'Double Jeopardy') because they typically attract fewer customers than brands with a greater market share[49]; and these customers are also relatively less loyal, whereby brand loyalty is often expressed in terms of frequency of buying.

Table 2.2 depicts the DJL for a typical high-involvement context: banks. The table clearly highlights that as market share declines from BNZ (market leader in the context considered; that is, New Zealand) to Countrywide, so does the percentage of brand buyers (commonly referred to as 'purchase penetration') and the average frequency of use.

Table 2.2 Double Jeopardy—banks and credit cards

BANKS (NEW ZEALAND)	PENETRATION (%)	AVERAGE USAGE FREQUENCY (OVER 10 WEEKS)
BNZ	15	8.1
ANZ	13	8.1
Westpac	11	8.5
Trust Bank	9	8.5
National Bank	9	7.4
ASB	4	6.4
Countrywide	2	4.1
Average	**9**	**7.3**

Sharp et al., 2002

Exceptions to the DJL are very rare; however, if they occur they mainly fall into two 'types':

- *niche brands*—small brands that serve a small base of highly loyal customers (Vespa, for example, an iconic brand selling motor vehicles with a vintage vibe)
- *change-of-pace brands*—large brands that are purchased rather infrequently, mostly because they have reached the maturity stage in the life cycle and are selected occasionally as a result of variety seeking.

There is also empirical evidence suggesting that the DJL further extends to other relevant aspects of how a brand performs in a certain market, which is equally relevant to IMC: referring back to the ANT memory framework, consumers retain less information (fewer associations) in memory about small brands (i.e. brands with a smaller market share) relative to big brands (i.e. brands with greater market share).[50]

Therefore, similarly to the DoPL, the immediate implication of the DJL is that it explains consumer behaviour and provides insights relevant to IMC tactics; for example, in relation to the strategic importance of improving a brand's market share; the spurious nature of loyalty; and even implications in relation to the possibility of bolstering memory associations.

While there is not sufficient room in this book to get into an in-depth explanation of these two empirical marketing laws or to discuss other laws, the references provided shed light on the variety of contexts in which they appear; that is, in terms of product (and service) categories, media and countries. The overwhelming evidence clearly suggests that even in what would be considered high-involvement contexts, consumer behaviour is largely habitual. This needs to be kept in mind when developing IMC strategy and activities, especially throughout the marketing and IMC planning processes, which the next chapter discusses.

■ CHAPTER SUMMARY

In this chapter we discussed the link between IMC and the principles of consumer behaviour. In particular, we discussed the principles of the decision-making process, memory and learning, illustrating how these concepts offer a fundamental framework to inform IMC decisions and practices.

In terms of the decision-making process, we presented the cognitive model of consumer behaviour, which illustrates decision making as a series of steps. We illustrated how IMC tactics can essentially have (at least in theory) an underlying impact across all stages of consumer decision making.

We learnt that consumer decisions often fall across a continuum of problem-solving ranging from high levels of involvement and cognitive (rational) computation (e.g. house purchases) to mere habits and routines, such as decisions with little or no thinking involved (e.g. buying your morning coffee). There can also be decisions that are 'nudged' (or reinforced) by the environment (e.g. purchasing a new pair of jeans on sale). This way of looking at consumer behaviour is often referred to as the reinforcement model and challenges the effects of IMC tactics, indicating that they are most effective if deployed 'close enough' to the point of purchase. Nonetheless, in the instance of consumer decisions akin to the habit and reinforcement model, there is scope for a wide range of IMC initiatives to be used, but the strategic focus is making a certain product or service marketed mentally available.

We elaborated further on these concepts by introducing two key learning theories that closely match the different models of consumer behaviour discussed: behavioural learning theories (including classic and operant or instrumental conditioning, with the latter including positive reinforcement, negative reinforcement and punishment) and cognitive learning. To understand cognitive learning in more detail, we extended the explanation of how memory works, especially in relation to the concept of information retrieval. Doing so, we were able to highlight the importance of IMC tactics to establish and maintain a network of concepts associated with a certain brand or offering in the mind of consumers—something that can facilitate the consumer's ability to think of a certain alternative when making purchase decisions (mental availability). We explained that it is possible to facilitate this process by successfully establishing and maintaining familiar associations between the brand and inherent concepts or through facilitating the reliving of episodes of consumption that are autobiographical in nature. Both tactics can be enacted through IMC strategies.

We concluded the chapter with a series of critical reflections on the many valuable insights that empirical evidence offers to the understanding of how IMC works in relation to its likely influence of consumption. We illustrated two empirical laws of marketing: the Duplication of Purchase Law and the Double Jeopardy Law.

Case study: Understanding Dior customers

Lara Stocchi and Maxwell Winchester

As the main holding of the LVMH Moët Hennessy Louis Vuitton SE group (known as LVM), a European multinational luxury goods conglomerate, Dior is currently among the most valuable brands in the world and continues to thrive across different generations, different artistic directions and even through some of the most remarkable changes that have characterised the fashion industry in recent years. Originally positioned to cater exclusively for the taste of female consumers, over the past decades the company has extended its business quite remarkably to other markets, including men's fashion, children's fashion, cosmetics and accessories. Besides a wide range of ready-to-wear luxury items, the company maintains its status of iconic haute couture maison, trading under the name of its founder, Christian Dior. A recent change in Dior's artistic direction (championed by Italian designer and artist Maria Grazia Chiuri) has elevated the brand even further, with strong connections to important concepts of feminism, empowerment, artistry and surrealism.

Several factors embedded in the firm's strategy seem to be pivotal to its acclamation in the fast-paced and ever-changing world of fashion. First, the firm has never ceased to promote its classic designs and heritage through prestigious exhibitions all over the world. For example, the Esprit Dior exhibition features the brand's history and touches on 10 different themes: 'Paris,' 'Dior and his artist friends', 'Dior Garden', 'Dior Allure', 'Dior Atelier', 'Dior's Stars', 'Versailles: Trianon', 'Miss Dior', 'From Pink to Red' and 'J'adore'. Another exhibition is the New Look Revolution, which featured the evolution of the Bar Suit. The iconic item first appeared in Dior's earliest collection. Not only did the exhibition feature how the item has changed, but it also featured the hard work that it took to create it.

Second, Dior caters to a wide range of very different audiences through multiple social media accounts. For instance, the brand has two key Instagram accounts: Dior official (@dior) and Dior Homme (@diorhomme). The former is targeted at its main consumers, while the latter caters specifically to its male audience. Dior's Instagram strategy is a massive success. Its official Instagram (@dior) has 15 million followers and @diorhomme has 88 000 followers (statistics from 2018). It also has other accounts for makeup and fragrances and has been launching specific campaigns aimed at millennial audiences, such as the Poison Girl short film featuring celebrity Camille Rowe promoting one of Dior's youngest fragrances. Moreover, the brand has also made clever use of e-commerce opportunities offered by social media and has recently conquered Chinese consumers by selling products on WeChat through targeted events and time-bound promotions.

Third, the company has continued to maintain its status of luxury icon elevating its approach to fashion shows to the next level. This included the creation of large-scale and highly remarkable art installations at the heart of the most iconic cities in the world, such as Paris. Here, in the recent fashion seasons, iconic landmarks of the city of lights served as a backdrop to highly innovative fashion runways, blending art installations, architecture, couture and philanthropy into unforgettable and spectacular exhibitions. For example, during Paris Fashion Week in 2018, as newspapers from all over the world applauded, 'the worlds of modern art and high fashion were framed together as one unified concept', as Maria Grazia Chiuri unveiled her latest Dior couture collection as an ode to surrealism and a 'dream of fashion where there are no limits to pushing boundaries and experimenting with technique, material and form'.[51]

Staged in the Musée Rodin, transformed into a gallery for the occasion with giant ceramic casts of body parts suspended from the ceiling, a predominantly monochrome colour palette provided the basis for an offering that sought to weave the wonderfully weird twentieth-century movement into wearable art. The show also created a subtle, but very important connection to the work of Argentinian surrealist painter Leonor Fini, who held her first exhibition in Christian Dior's gallery in the 1930s and who is renowned for her portrayals of powerful women. Her work was echoed in iconic makeup and body tattoos created by milliner Stephen Jones, spelling out the new brand message 'Attitudes Spectrales'.[52]

Figure 2.16 Dior fashion show at Musée Rodin

Figure 2.17 'Dior Eyes', a VR headset that lets you see what's going on backstage at Dior events

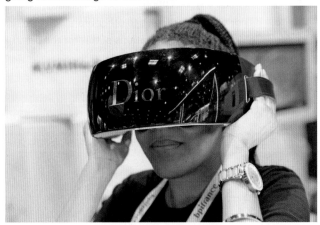

Other exclusive events and VIP balls attended by the world's elite (e.g. highly influential designers, artists, celebrities and social media personalities from all over the world) accompanied the shows, lifting the image of the brand to a global scale. Dior even created 'Dior Eyes' (a VR headset) using virtual reality to upgrade the way people see fashion by enabling them to see what is going on backstage (see Figure 2.17).

Questions

1. Discuss the overall strategy of the brand Dior in trying to influence consumers all over the world and to maintain, over the years, its status of being an iconic brand.

2. The decision to purchase luxury items most certainly entails a high level of consumer involvement, which is akin to the cognitive model of consumer behaviour. Critically evaluate the strategy that Dior is using from a social media perspective by clearly explaining whether you think it can actually influence the consumer's decision-making process and in what way.

3. This chapter illustrated the importance of facilitating mental availability by enhancing the familiarity of brands through establishing and reinforcing associations with many concepts, or through facilitating the recollection of memorable biographical experiences. Comment on the various strategies that Dior is using and indicate whether you think they can be effective at attaining these objectives.

4. In this chapter, we reflected on important empirical evidence that challenges the possibility of influencing consumer behaviour via IMC. The Duplication of Purchase Law represents one such example of relevant empirical evidence. Look at Table 2.3 below ('Simulated market statistics') and answer these questions.

   a. What main pattern is evident in Table 2.3 and what are the main implications for the Dior brand?

   b. Are there any exceptions to this main pattern?

   c. If Dior were to lose sales to other brands, which brand(s) is it most likely to lose share to? Comment on the implications of this for the brand and its current global branding and IMC strategy.

Table 2.3 Simulated market statistics

	% WHO BOUGHT	% WHO ALSO BOUGHT ...							
		REVLON	L'ORÉAL	OIL OF OLAY	ESTÉE LAUDER	CLINIQUE	ELIZABETH ARDEN	DIOR	SHISEIDO
Revlon	61		57**	68	53	53	44	35	24
L'Oréal	59	59		52	43	45	38	31	23
Oil of Olay	59	70	52		47	47	40	30	24
Estée Lauder	43	75	59	64		56	52	43	35
Clinique	39	83	69	71	63		53	49	35
Elizabeth Arden	32	84	71	74	71	65		56	34
Dior	26	84	71	69	72	73	69		44
Shiseido	19	78	71	75	80	73	58	60	
Average	**42**	**76**	**64**	**68**	**61**	**59**	**51**	**43**	**31**
Estimated sharing		*82*	*79*	*79*	*58*	*52*	*43*	*35*	*25*
Difference		*−6*	*−15*	*−12*	*+3*	*+7*	*+8*	*+9*	*+6*

**Interpreted as 57% of people who bought Revlon also bought L'Oréal

Source: Romaniuk, J. & Winchester, M.K. (2007) Prestige brands: Consumer perceptions and loyalty compared to non-prestige brands. Paper presented at the Thought Leader International Conference on Brand Management Proceedings, Birmingham, UK.

Practitioner profile: Sonia Heinrich

Marketing Manager, Cafetto

I began my career in marketing almost 10 years after graduating from high school. Initially I worked in Event Management before deciding to return to study and enrol in an Advanced Diploma of Marketing at TAFE SA. Following TAFE, I worked in an administrative role for two years for global company REHAU where I was advised that a business degree would greatly assist my career development. I decided to enrol in a Commerce degree at University of Adelaide and followed this with a trip to Melbourne seeking employment in a marketing position. I was fortunate to begin working for Finnish company KALMAR in the logistics sector where I began as a marketing coordinator and developed the role into a Brand and Communication Manager position. This role managed all events and marketing activities for the Oceania region and was integrated with the global marketing team. Working in the global organisation provided me with many opportunities to develop my marketing knowledge, including the chance to complete a program certificate at IMD business school in Switzerland. In 2017 I returned to Adelaide and began my position as Marketing Manager for Cafetto, a company established in Adelaide within the global coffee industry.

Describe your current role and the organisation you work for, and give a brief account of what you do in your role on a day-to-day basis.

I am the Marketing Manager at Cafetto, a company that specialises in manufacturing coffee machine cleaning products for the global coffee industry. The position involves strong communication skills and the ability to adapt easily to various markets and campaigns, liaising on a daily basis with various stakeholders within our company as well as external agencies and customers.

How important is Integrated Marketing Communication (IMC) to what you and your organisation do?

IMC facilitates consistent messaging and strengthens the opportunity for us to reach our target market through running the campaign across multiple channels.

What types of promotional tools do you use in your IMC campaigns? Please provide examples.

Promotional tools include email direct campaigns, advertising and editorials within industry magazines, trade show stands, social media posts, attendance and sponsorship of trade events, event creation and online advertising. These promotional tools are supported by strong, consistent imagery of our products, testimonials and interviews with industry professionals as well as a well-designed website, which we can direct traffic to through our campaigns on various channels.

What would your ideal IMC campaign look like and why?

My ideal IMC campaign would be scheduled with the opportunity to review and revise promotional tools and content prior to release to ensure that the messaging, channels and imagery is the best we can produce. There would also be an opportunity to conduct customer research to obtain insights on campaign effectiveness.

What has been your favourite IMC project to work on and did it achieve its objectives?

My favourite IMC project was during my time with KALMAR. We released a machine for industrial handling that was an industry first and the outcome of extensive customer research—therefore a very exciting product release for the industry. The release was supported with an integrated global marketing approach, adapted for each regional area. In the ANZ region I worked with industry publications to produce a series of advertisements, product reviews and editorials, and coupled this with planning and scheduling product launch events and trials. The campaign was successfully executed across both Australia and New Zealand and achieved customer enquiries and strong sales.

How do you believe an IMC campaign affects the consumer decision-making process for your particular target audience?

A good IMC campaign will achieve strong brand exposure and in turn achieve strong brand recall, which strengthens the chance of consideration during the consumer decision-making process. In B2B marketing, an IMC campaign that includes testimonials and independent product testing reviews can influence the purchase decision process as they search for credible information to support their purchasing decision, which is often a significant investment.

How has your application of IMC changed with the increase in digital marketing?

The increase in digital marketing has widened the channels, strengthened presence and shortened the lead time for campaign implementation. For a company that does not have any store presence, we rely heavily on our website and strong IMC campaigns to deliver our presence in the market place. Additionally, consumers are using digital platforms to research and weigh up the options; therefore strong, consistent digital presence is vital to be considered.

What do you believe are some of the challenges to implementing an IMC campaign?

IMC campaigns rely heavily on coordinating multiple stakeholders, platforms and deadlines, and their effectiveness is determined on the ability to successfully meet budget, obtaining concept sign-off, development of artwork, timing with industry events and feature publications and booking/submission of media. Additionally, new product development can pose challenges when creating a new product launch IMC campaign—in some instances the product may be delayed or there may be unforeseen product defects which require a change of plans or delaying of the campaign.

What advice would you offer a student studying IMC?

Develop strong communication and organisation skills to support your projects and understand where your target audience seeks product information. IMC campaigns require management of multiple internal and external stakeholder relationships. Collaborating and effectively communicating the campaign and timeline to management, sales, finance and graphic design teams will help to avoid any roadblocks. Additionally, it is beneficial to build relationships with key industry contacts including editors, event organisers and advertising sales representatives. Building relationships with these key contacts will provide opportunities to communicate IMC plans and coordinate editorial and advertising opportunities.

Key terms

Associative Network Theory (ANT) of memory

behavioural learning theories

brand equity

brand image (associations)

change-of-pace brands

classical conditioning

cognitive learning theory

cognitive model of consumer behaviour

compensatory decision-making rules

consideration set

consumer behaviour

continuum of problem solving and information processing

decision making

distinctive branding elements

Double Jeopardy Law (DJL)

Duplication of Purchase Law (DoPL)

Ehrenberg and Goodhardt's repeat purchase model

empirical evidence

empirical generalisations (empirical marketing laws)

evaluation of alternatives

evaluation of outcomes

evoked (or awareness) set

external contingencies

familiarity

habit model of consumer behaviour

hedonic factors

heuristics

inertia

information search

instrumental conditioning

involvement

learning

limited information processing

market partitions

memory

mental availability

negative reinforcement

niche brands

physical availability

positive reinforcement

problem (or need) recognition

punishment

purchase propensities

rational problem-solvers

recollection (autobiographical recollection)

reinforcement model of consumer behaviour

repertoire buying (or purchase repertoire)

universal set

utility

Revision questions

1. Outline the components of the cognitive consumer decision-making model, highlighting where the different elements of IMC might influence consumer behaviour in the model.

2. Describe the different factors that can alter (for example, shorten) the decision-making process. What are the implications of these factors from the perspective of setting IMC strategies?

3. Explain the idea of a continuum of consumer behaviour, ranging from high to low involvement, and high to low cognitive (or rational) computation. Support your answer with a range of examples that apply to you as a consumer.

4. Explain and contrast the two learning theories introduced in this chapter. Include in your answer some clear examples of IMC strategies that match these learning theories and exemplify how the theoretical principles of consumer behaviour can be used to design IMC tactics.

5. How do consumers bring back to mind brands? What can marketing and communication managers do to facilitate the process?

6. Describe the Duplication of Purchase Law and what its impact on IMC strategy might be.

7. Give an overview of the Double Jeopardy Law and the implications of this to niche branding strategies.

8. What sort of IMC tactic would you use for a low-involvement consumer decision versus a high-involvement one?

9. Think about the last time you went to a restaurant with friends. Mentally reconstruct the experience and the various details of it, such as when you went, where you went, who was there, what you ate, and so on. Now think about the next time you'll go out for a meal with friends. Do you think reliving your past experience might influence your future decision? If so, is this mental construction likely to influence your decision more or less than, for example, having a discount voucher for another restaurant?

10. Consider your recurring habits in terms of weekly supermarket shopping. Do you find yourself buying the same products over and over (mostly), and occasionally trying something else if your favourite items are not available? Have you ever bought an item because something encouraged you to do so in store? (The odds are, you answered 'yes' to these questions and so would many other consumers.)

11. The consumer decision-making process is outlined in this chapter. Draw this model on a piece of paper, and make notes as to where you think different IMC tools may work. For example, where in the process might advertising work? Where might sales promotion work?

Further reading

Evans, M., Jamal, A. & Foxall, G. (2006). *Consumer Behaviour.* John Wiley & Sons Ltd.

Graham, C., Bennett, D., Franke, K., Henfrey, C.L. & Nagy-Hamada, M. (2017). Double Jeopardy–50 years on. Reviving a forgotten tool that still predicts brand loyalty. *Australasian Marketing Journal (AMJ)*, *25*(4), 278–87.

Romaniuk, J. & Sharp, B. (2016). *How Brands Grow. Part 2: Including Emerging Markets, Services and Durables, New Brands and Luxury Brands.* Oxford University Press.

Sharp, B., Wright, M., Kennedy, R. & Nguyen, C. (2017). Viva la revolution! For evidence-based marketing we strive. *Australasian Marketing Journal (AMJ).*

Solomon, M., Russell-Bennett, R. & Previte, J. (2012). *Consumer Behaviour.* Australia: Pearson Higher Education.

Notes

1   www.adnews.com.au/campaigns/air-new-zealand-tells-aussies-there-s-a-better-way-to-fly

2   East, R., Singh, J. Wright, M. & Vanhuele, M. (2017). *Consumer Behaviour: Applications in Marketing*. London: Sage.

3   Solomon, M., Russell-Bennett, R. & Previte, J. (2012). *Consumer Behaviour*, Pearson Higher Education Australia.

4   Armstrong, G., Adam, S., Denize, S. & Kotler, P. (2014). *Principles of Marketing*. Pearson Australia.

5   Engel, J. F., Kollat, D. T. & Blackwell, R. D. (1982). *Consumer Behaviour* (4th edn). New York, NY: Hott, Rinehart & Winston; Solomon et al., op. cit.

6   Solomon et al., op. cit.

7   Nedungadi, P. (1990). Recall and consumer consideration sets: influencing choice without altering brand evaluations. *Journal of Consumer Research*, *17*(3), 263–76; Roberts, J. H. & Lattin, J. M. (1997). Consideration: review of research and prospects for future insights. Journal of Marketing Research, 406–10; Shocker, A. D., Ben-Akiva, M., Boccara, B. & Nedungadi, P. (1991). Consideration set influences on consumer decision-making and choice: issues, models, and suggestions. Marketing Letters, 2(3), 181–97.

8   Gigerenzer, G. (2004). Fast and frugal heuristics: the tools of bounded rationality. *Blackwell Handbook of Judgment and Decision Making*, 62, 88; Gigerenzer, G. & Todd, P. M. (1999). Fast and frugal heuristics: the adaptive toolbox. In *Simple Heuristics That Make Us Smart*, Oxford University Press, 3–34; Todd, P. M. (2001). Fast and frugal heuristics for environmentally bounded minds. *Bounded Rationality: The Adaptive Toolbox*, 51–70.

9   Lussier, D. A. & R. W. Olshavsky (1979). Task complexity and contingent processing in brand choice. *Journal of Consumer Research*, 6(September), 154–65; Reed, S. K. (1996). *Cognition: Theory and Applications*. Pacific Grove, Brooks/Cole Publishing.

10 Hirschman, E. C. & Holbrook, M. B. (1982). Hedonic consumption: emerging concepts, methods and propositions. *The Journal of Marketing*, 92–101.

11 Sharp, B. (2010). *How Brands Grow: What Marketers Don't Know*. Melbourne: Oxford University Press.

12 Simon, H. A. (1972). Theories of bounded rationality. *Decision and Organization*, *1*(1), 161–76.

13 East et al., op. cit.

14 East et al., op. cit.; Solomon, op. cit.

15 East et al., op. cit.

16 Ehrenberg, A. S., Uncles, M. D. & Goodhardt, G. J. (2004). Understanding brand performance measures: using Dirichlet benchmarks. *Journal of Business Research*, *57*(12), 1307–25; Sharp, B., Wright, M., Dawes, J., Driesener, C., Meyer-Waarden, L., Stocchi, L. & Stern, P. (2013). It's a Dirichlet world: modelling individuals' loyalites reveals how brands compete, grow and decline. *Journal of Advertising Research*, *52*(2), 203–13.

17 East et al., op. cit.

18 ibid.

19　Jain, K. & Srinivasan, N. (1990). An empirical assessment of multiple operationalizations of involvement. *ACR North American Advances*; Schneider, K. C. & Rodgers, W. C. (1996). An 'importance' subscale for the consumer involvement profile. *Advances in Consumer Research*, *23*(1); Zaichkowsky, J. L. (1986). Conceptualizing involvement. *Journal of Advertising*, *15*(2), 4–34.

20　Chatfield, C. & Goodhardt, G. (1975). Results concerning brand choice. *Journal of Marketing Research*, *12*(1), 110–13.

21　Yanamandram, V. & White, L. (2010). Are inertia and calculative commitment distinct constructs? An empirical study in the financial services sector. *International Journal of Bank Marketing*, *28*(7), 569–84.

22　Solomon et al., op. cit.

23　McSweeney, F. K. & Bierley, C. (1984). Recent developments in classical conditioning. *Journal of Consumer Research*, *11*(2), 619–31; Shimp, T. A. (1991). Neo-Pavlovian conditioning and its implications for consumer theory and research. *Handbook of Consumer Behavior*, 162–87.

24　Romaniuk, J. & Sharp, B. (2016). *How Brands Grow. Part 2, Including Emerging Markets, Services and Durables, New Brands And Luxury Brands*. Melbourne: Oxford University Press.

25　Christodoulides, G. & De Chernatony, L. (2010). Consumer-based brand equity conceptualization and measurement: a literature review. *International Journal of Market Research*, *52*(1), 43–66; Keller, K. L. (1993). Conceptualizing, measuring, and managing customer-based brand equity. *The Journal of Marketing*, 1–22; Yoo, B. & Donthu, N. (2001). Developing and validating a multidimensional consumer-based brand equity scale. *Journal of Business Research*, *52*(1), 1–14.

26　Nord, W. R. & Peter, J. P. (1980). A behavior modification perspective on marketing. *The Journal of Marketing*, 36–47; Solomon et al., op. cit.

27　www.peteralexander.com.au

28　ibid.

29　Anderson, J. R. (1983). A spreading activation theory of memory. *Journal of Verbal Learning and Verbal Behavior*, *22*(3), 261–95; Anderson, J. R. (1993). *Rules of the Mind*. New Jersey: Lawrence Erlbaum Associates Inc.; Anderson, J. R. (1996). The architecture of cognition, 1983. Reprint. Mahwah, NJ: Lawrence Erlbaum Associates; Collins, A. M. & Loftus, E. F. (1975). A spreading-activation theory of semantic processing. *Psychological Review*, *82*(6), 407; Teichert, T. A. & Schöntag, K. (2010). Exploring consumer knowledge structures using associative network analysis. *Psychology & Marketing*, *27*(4), 369–98.

30　Romaniuk & Sharp, op. cit.; Sharp, op. cit.

31　Anderson 1983, op. cit.; Anderson 1993, op. cit.; Anderson 1993, op. cit.; Anderson 1996, op. cit.; Anderson, J. R. & Bower, G. H. (1973a). *Human Associative Memory*. Washington: Winston & Sons; Anderson, J. R. & Bower, G. H. (1973b). *Human Associative Memory*. Washington, DC: Hemisphere Publishing Corporation; Anderson, J. R., Reder, L. & Lebiere, C. (1996). Working memory: activation limitations on retrieval. *Cognitive Psychology*, 30, 221–56; Collins & Loftus, op. cit.

32　Krishnan, H. S. (1996). Characteristics of memory associations: a consumer-based brand equity perspective. *International Journal of research in Marketing*, *13*(4), 389–405.

33　Romaniuk, J. & Sharp, B. (2004). Conceptualizing and measuring brand salience. *Marketing Theory*, *4*(4), 327–42.

34 Reder, L. M., Nhouyvanisvong, A., Schunn, C. D., Ayers, M. S., Angstadt, P. & Hiraki, K. (2000). A mechanistic account of the mirror effect for word frequency: a computational model of remember–know judgments in a continuous recognition paradigm. *Journal of Experimental Psychology: Learning, Memory, and Cognition*, *26*(2), 294; Reder, L. M., Angstadt, P., Cary, M., Erickson, M. A. & Ayers, M. S. (2002). A reexamination of stimulus-frequency effects in recognition: two mirrors for low-and high-frequency pseudowords. *Journal of Experimental Psychology: Learning, Memory, and Cognition*, *28*(1), 138.

35 Baumgartner, H., Sujan, M. & Bettman, J. R. (1992). Autobiographical memories, affect, and consumer information processing. *Journal of Consumer Psychology*, *1*(1), 53–82; Klein, S. B. (2004). The cognitive neuroscience of knowing one's self. In *The Cognitive Neurosciences* (3rd edn). Cambridge: MIT Press.

36 Braun-LaTour, K. A., LaTour, M. S., Pickrell, J. E., Loftus, E. F. & Distinguished, S. U. i. a. (2004). How and when advertising can influence memory for consumer experience. *Journal of Advertising*, *33*(4), 7–25; Sujan, M., Bettman, J. R. & Baumgartner, H. (1993). Influencing consumer judgments using autobiographical memories: a self-referencing perspective. *Journal of Marketing Research*, 422–36.

37 Stocchi, L. & Wright, M. (2016). The impact of episodic recollection on brand retrieval and purchase intention. Paper presented at the Australia and New Zealand Marketing Academy Annual Conference (ANZMAC), Christchurch, NZ.

38 www.commbank.com.au

39 Foxall, G. R. (1977). *Consumer Behaviour: A Practical Guide*. Corbridge, UK: RPA Books, p. 11.

40 Armstrong, J. S. (1991). Prediction of consumer behavior by experts and novices. *Journal of Consumer Research*, *18*, 251–56.

41 Colombo, R. et al. (2000). Diversity in analyzing brand-switching tables: The car challenge. *Canadian Journal of Marketing Research*, *19*, 23–36; Bennett, D. & Graham, C. (2010). Is loyalty driving growth for the brand in front? A two-purchase analysis of car category dynamics in Thailand. *Journal of Strategic Marketing*, *18*(7), 573–85.

42 Romaniuk & Sharp 2016, op. cit.

43 Ehrenberg, A. S. (1975). The structure of an industrial market: aviation fuel contracts. *Industrial Marketing Management*, *4*(5), 273–85; Uncles, M. D. & Ehrenberg, A. S. (1990). Industrial buying behavior: aviation fuel contracts. *International Journal of Research in Marketing*, *7*(1), 57–68.

44 Stern, P. (2002). How health managers see prescribing. *Marketing Intelligence & Planning*, *20*(2), 104–12.

45 Barwise, T. P. (1995). Good empirical generalizations. *Marketing Science*, *14*(3, Part 2 of 2), G29–G35; Bass, F. M. (1995). Empirical generalizations and marketing science: a personal view. *Marketing Science*, *14*(3), G6–G18.

46 Sharp, op. cit.

47 Sharp, B., Wright, M. & Goodhardt, G. (2002). Purchase loyalty is polarised into either repertoire or subscription patterns. *Australasian Marketing Journal*, *10*(3), 7–20; Sharp, op. cit.

48 Uncles, M., Ehrenberg, A. & Hammond, K. (1995). Patterns of buyer behavior: regularities, models, and extensions. *Marketing Science*, *14*(3); Ehrenberg, A. S. C. (1988). *Repeat-Buying: Facts, Theory and Applications*. London: Oxford University Press; Sharp, op. cit.

49 Ehrenberg, A. S., Goodhardt, G. & Barwise, T. P. (1990). Double Jeopardy revisited. *Journal of Marketing*, *54*(3), 82–91; Sharp, op. cit.; Graham, C., Bennett, D., Franke, K., Henfrey, C.L. & Nagy-Hamada, M. (2017), Double Jeopardy—50 years on. Reviving a forgotten tool that still predicts brand loyalty. *Australasian Marketing Journal (AMJ)*, *25*(4), 278–87.

50 Romaniuk, J., Bogomolova, S. & Dall'olmo Riley, F. (2012). Brand image and brand usage: is a forty-year old empirical generalization still useful? *Journal of Advertising Research*, June, 243–51.

51 www.standard.co.uk/fashion/christian-dior-paris-haute-couture-fashion-week-2018-ode-to-surrealism-a3746706.html

52 www.theguardian.com/fashion/2018/jan/22/fashion-week-image-of-the-day-surrealist-vision-christian-dior-couture

CHAPTER 3

Marketing Communication Strategy and Planning

Lara Stocchi

Airbnb: Don't just go there, live there

Airbnb is a trusted community marketplace where people can list, discover and book accommodation around the world—online or from a mobile phone or tablet. It connects people through unique travel experiences, at any price point, in more than 65 000 cities and 191 countries (2018 statistics). With world-class customer service and a growing community of users, Airbnb is the easiest way for people to monetise their extra living space, becoming an active agent in the consumption process, which has caused a dramatic change in the hospitality industry in recent years.

Figure 3.1 Airbnb's tagline reads: 'Don't just go there. Live there.'

Brian Chesky, Airbnb's co-founder and CEO says, 'the number one reason people choose to travel on Airbnb is they want to live like a local'. Accordingly, over the years Airbnb has launched features such as Neighbourhoods and Weekend Getaways, experimenting with new functionalities that moved away from the core peer-to-peer rentals business. With the recent announcement of new product features, a significant update to mobile apps and the rollout of a new global brand campaign, Airbnb is reshaping the strategic focus of the company to offer guests the best possible travel experience, matching users and their preferences with people and places that will make their trip even more memorable.

The most recent campaign by Airbnb is focusing more than ever on real experiences, using the tagline: 'Don't just go there,

Figure 3.2 Airbnb: a real home away from home

live there'. This urges people to live in the cities they travel to—not simply visit them—and feel at home even if just for a night. This is all possible, says Chesky, thanks to changes in Airbnb's technological platform, which empowers the consumer by offering new ways to discover (and book) the best and most personalised travel experiences, reclaiming the true nature of travelling. Part of the strategic challenge of building up the new campaign included planning how to marry the scale of Airbnb around the globe with the nature of the service, its functionalities, the benefits offered and the different way of communicating to consumers. Andrew Schapiro, Head of Art Department, reports that the process resulted in significant updates into the Airbnb app; for example, the 'Matching Experience' and guidebooks, which use an innovative system that understands consumer preferences in order to pair them to homes and local experiences. The process of strategic redefinition also supports the #OneLessStranger initiative to create a sense of community and belonging, promoting how small and friendly the world can be, a concept at the heart of Airbnb's corporate strategy.

Sources: http://blog.airbnb.com/belong-anywhere; www.airbnb.com/livethere?c=tumblr&af=746240; www.airbnb.com.au/about/about-us

■ INTRODUCTION

The previous Airbnb example demonstrates the high level of intricacy that binds the IMC process with strategic plans and the execution of specific marketing and communication tactics. To many organisations, a strategy represents a roadmap; that is, a more or less clear indication of where the firm is and where it should be in the future, and all the steps required to make it happen.[1]

Strategies are often formed across different layers of the organisation; for example, at the *corporate level* (the overarching strategic direction of the firm, as outlined by the top executives) and at the *business level* (the specific business plans prepared for each significant sub-division of the organisation, such as business units). The 'glue' connecting all these layers is the marketing strategy (and related plan), which typically connects the mission of a certain organisation (its purpose) with the scope of business-level strategies, thereby facilitating the realisation of the corporate strategy.[2]

The focus of this chapter is to outline and explain the most important foundations of strategy definition and marketing planning, clarifying how these connect extensively with the IMC planning process.

First, we will explain in more detail the link between an organisational strategy and the marketing strategy. Second, we will touch on the key aspects embedded in any marketing strategy. Third, we will review in detail the various components of the IMC planning process, paying particular attention to the principles of strategic brand management. In doing so, we will reflect on the most important strategic considerations linked to the establishment of different types of IMC objectives. Finally, we will consider different approaches to the definition of IMC budgets and the relative implications for the identification of suitable approaches for the implementation, control and evaluation of IMC programs.

As part of the control and evaluation of IMC programs, the focus of this chapter will be on the introduction of a range of key marketing metrics that should inform strategic decisions.

LEARNING OBJECTIVES

After reading this chapter you should be able to:

1. define the link between organisational strategy and marketing strategy
2. describe the various elements of marketing strategies and the marketing planning process
3. explain the link between the marketing plan and the IMC planning process
4. outline the various elements of the IMC plan and link it to fundamental strategic brand management tactics
5. explain the key types of IMC objectives and reflect critically on the strategic considerations that need to inform these objectives
6. critically evaluate the different IMC budgeting methods
7. critically evaluate the importance of marketing metrics in the control and evaluation of IMC programs.

The different levels of strategy

Although strategies are formed at different levels of the organisation, they are always connected and a certain degree of coordination is required to ensure that firms remain competitive and profitable while pursuing their intended objectives. As organisations become more complex and grow on a global scale, strategies adapt and evolve, becoming more detailed. Figure 3.3 depicts the different strategies that could co-exist within one organisation.

Figure 3.3 Different levels of strategy

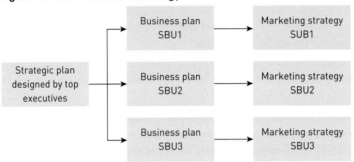

The strategic plan designed by top executives represents the **corporate strategy**, which is often executed via the realisation of multiple business plans for each **strategic business unit** or **SBU** (**business strategy**); these, in turn, require the creation of a **marketing strategy**.[3] Depending on the level of business diversification across the various SBUs, firms might require one single overarching marketing strategy *or* different ones. For example, large multinational manufacturers such as Mars embrace a number of highly diverse business units, from confectionary to pet care. While all operations and activities of the organisation will feature in an overarching corporate-level strategic plan, the various business units will each have separate business plans and relative marketing strategies. Mars Australia, in the corporate section of its website, claims: 'Whether

Figure 3.4 Key brands owned by Mars Australia

it's the simple pleasure of savouring the world's best-loved chocolate and confectionery, the warmth that a healthy and contented pet brings to your family, or the rewards that come from creating fantastic tastes in your own home, Mars is the company behind many of the enduring brands Australians and New Zealanders (or Pacific consumers) have come to know and trust'.[4] Its overarching goal of offering products of high quality and value to consumers is then applied across the main areas of pet care (e.g. Pedigree, Whiskas), chocolate (e.g. M&Ms, Mars Bars, Maltesers), food (e.g. Dolmio, Uncle Ben's) and confectionary (e.g. Wrigley and Skittles). See Figure 3.4. Each of these business units (and related brands) has specific marketing strategies, enabling the overall realisation of the Mars corporate strategy.

It is important to keep in mind that in many instances the definition of corporate strategies (and subsequent adaptations across the various SBUs) is not necessarily based on empirical evidence. In fact, many organisations rely on simplistic frameworks[5] that outline various strategic 'options' to choose from such as:

* pursuing a cost advantage—that is, trying to be the cheapest option for consumers (see IMC in Action: the success of Aldi in Australia on page 81)
* significantly narrowing the market scope—that is, pursuing a market **niche product** strategy
* striving for a high level of differentiation.

In reality, when setting a **strategy**, a 'cookie cutter' approach is never a good idea, especially because many widely used options are based on fundamentally mistaken assumptions. For example, in Chapter 2 we considered some important aspects of consumer behaviour that set clear limits to what can be feasibly pursued using IMC tactics. Table 3.1 recaps three key known facts about consumers that challenge the feasibility of widely used strategic options.

Table 3.1 Key empirical facts and relative implications for strategy and planning

KEY CONSUMER BEHAVIOUR FACTS BASED ON EMPIRICAL EVIDENCE	STRATEGIC APPROACH CHALLENGED	ALTERNATIVE APPROACH
Fact 1: Within a given product category, consumers see brands as highly substitutable and as having very similar attributes, which are somewhat expected (or prototypical).	• Differentiation strategy • Narrow market scope strategy (niche)	• Focus on *distinctiveness* to enhance mental availability (easy to 'think of', not different)
Fact 2: Within a given product category, consumers are naturally drawn towards more popular brands (higher market share) and buy these brands more frequently (Double Jeopardy). This effect is the result of popular offerings having more resources to invest in IMC that ultimately enhance their mental and physical availability.	• Differentiation strategy • Narrow market scope strategy (niche) • Cost advantage	• Focus on *distinctiveness* to enhance mental availability (easy to 'think of', not different) • Focus on enhancing physical availability (easy to find and widely available)
Fact 3: Within a given product category, consumers tend to purchase multiple offerings at the same time (repertoire buying) in a rather 'as-if random' fashion. Therefore, brands systematically share customers with competitors (Duplication of Purchase Law).	• Differentiation strategy • Narrow market scope strategy (niche) • Cost advantage	• Focus on *distinctiveness* to enhance mental availability (easy to 'think of', not different) • Focus on enhancing physical availability (easy to find and widely available)

Unfortunately, not all organisations take these simple facts into consideration and strategic management practices are usually completely estranged from the tradition of empirical research in marketing. As a result, many organisations end up pursuing strategies that work well in the mind of top executives, but do not correspond to real and well-known consumption patterns. However, some of these pitfalls can be ironed out when outlining a marketing plan and throughout the execution of the marketing strategy; they can also be managed in the context of IMC planning.

Marketing planning and strategy

On a simple level, the milestones that characterise a **marketing planning process** are:

* analysis of the market
* development of specific objectives and strategies

Figure 3.5 Milestones of the marketing planning process

- identification of suitable marketing programs and activities
- implementation, control and evaluation of marketing programs.[6]

See Figure 3.5.

The **analysis of the market** typically includes:

- *identification of the target customer*—this links to segmentation analysis and, more generally, market research activities aimed at detecting and understanding the primary recipient of what an organisation has to offer
- *analysis of competitors*—no marketing initiative can exist without a conscientious understanding of what others are currently doing and offering.

- *identification of relevant environmental and contextual factors*—to do so, firms often rely on generic frameworks to identify contextual factors likely to impact the feasibility and success of the intended marketing strategy. For example, a widely used framework is the so-called **PESTEL framework**, which considers political, economic, social, technological, ecological and legal factors likely to have impact on the marketing strategy.

The **development of marketing objectives and strategies** naturally follows the analysis of the market and concerns the identification of pathways for sustainable growth, whether within the same **target market**, into new ones or by significant business and operations expansion. To do so, firms often rely on existing frameworks, such as the **ANSOFF matrix** and the **Boston Consulting Group (BCG) matrix**.[7] You may have learnt about these frameworks in your earlier studies in marketing. Although relatively easy to understand and use, these frameworks often have several limitations because they tend to prescribe various scenarios on the basis of unrealistic assumptions.[8] For this reason, it is always advisable to develop marketing objectives and strategies on the basis of empirical evidence, such as the array of known facts about consumer behaviour discussed in Chapter 2.

Identifying and outlining **suitable marketing programs and activities** concerns the definition of the key **marketing mix strategies**; that is, strategies that relate to the product (or service), pricing and distribution strategies and all promotional strategies to be used.[9] It also comprises all IMC initiatives and processes, including all choices of the message to communicate to the target market; the media to use and the communication and/or promotional tools to deploy; and **internal marketing** strategies (that is, activities directed within the organisation to motivate and empower employees). As such, this stage represents an explicit overlap between the marketing planning process and IMC planning.

Lastly, the **implementation, control and evaluation** milestone involves:

- the concrete translation of strategy into actions
- an adequate anticipation of monitoring mechanisms and possible corrective actions
- formal activities for appraising outcomes.[10]

Organisations can engage in control and evaluation of results against objectives monthly, quarterly and/or annually, using a variety of performance indicators that will be discussed later in the chapter.

Crucially, the marketing planning process should be carried out explicitly within a firm and should be conceived as a platform for gathering the commitment and support of the organisation's top executives, as outlined in Figure 3.6.[11]

Figure 3.6 A formal marketing planning process

Source: Armstrong, J. S. (1982). The value of formal planning for strategic decisions: review of empirical research. *Strategic Management Journal, 3*(3), p. 2.

The **IMC planning process** sits at the heart of the marketing strategy and contributes greatly to the realisation of business strategies and the accomplishment of corporate strategies. Arguably, it is also the key facet of a firm's strategy and can cater for some of the issues outlined earlier, if designed on the basis of a robust understanding of consumer behaviour and empirical evidence.

The IMC planning process

For many organisations that have a well-established marketing function, the IMC planning process (see Figure 3.7) is connected to the marketing planning process in a number of ways.[12]

Figure 3.7 The IMC planning process

Market research

Both the IMC planning and the marketing planning process start with **market research**. However, the market research conducted at the beginning of the IMC planning process is primarily focused on two aspects, as follows. First, IMC planning requires *product (or service) specific research*, which is aimed at identifying the attributes and features most desired and valued as well as the benefits sought. Second, IMC planning needs *consumer specific research* to uncover reasons for buying and using, underlying psychological factors, consumer views, thoughts and feelings. In both instances, the research typically involves a mixture of different research methods, ranging from quantitative research such as surveys and experiments, to qualitative research such as consumer focus groups.

Target market

A second point of connection between the IMC planning process and the marketing plan is the identification and understanding of the **target market**; this often starts with **segmentation research**. In essence, segmentation involves the identification of groups of consumers who have similar characteristics on the basis of selected criteria such as psychographic criteria (e.g. lifestyle and patterns of consumption), the demographic and socio-economic profile of consumers, their purchase behaviour and so on. The assumption that many organisations make is that, on the basis of these factors, it is possible to identify meaningful differences across different groups of consumers and that some groups of consumers are more worthwhile serving than others (e.g. they are more 'attractive' in terms of the overall size of the market potential and the degree of competition). Accordingly, organisations typically select and target the most attractive segments, and design specific marketing programs to appeal to them. Chapter 4 discusses in greater detail the principles of segmentation and targeting. However, in this chapter, given the strong emphasis on planning and strategies, we should emphasise that this assumption is actually broadly incorrect. This is in light of empirical evidence concerning how similarly consumers behave in the market place (e.g. in terms of their tendency to be drawn towards more popular offerings) and in terms of their views and perceptions (e.g. how similar they see brands being offered within the same product or service category), which we have already touched on in this chapter.

Product and brand positioning

Following the identification and understanding of the target market, the next stage of the IMC planning process is often strongly connected with **product and brand positioning**. Product and brand positioning require a series of important strategic decisions concerning what specific 'place' to occupy in the mind of consumers.[13] Although you will learn more about these decisions in Chapter 4, for now it is important to keep in mind that these decisions are particularly important in the IMC planning process. This is due to the many implications in terms of which promotional tools to use, the core message(s) to communicate through IMC, the media to use and so on.

Strategic brand development

Another aspect that is at the heart of the IMC planning process is **strategic brand development**.[14] A relevant framework that managers can use for this is Keller's **Customer Based Brand Equity (CBBE) framework** (see Figure 3.8).[15] This framework is crucial for determining everything that needs to be done, from an IMC perspective, to build and maintain a strong brand over time. This idea is supported by a wealth of empirical research in marketing, which has demonstrated the existence of a relationship between CBBE and several key performance indicators, including sales, consumer loyalty and the financial (intangible) value of brands.[16]

From a theoretical perspective, the CBBE framework is based on the psychological principles of memory discussed in Chapter 2, such as the Associative Network Theory (ANT) of memory.[17] From a practical perspective, the CBBE framework enables managers to identify the 'building blocks' that constitute the 'DNA' of a brand, outlining objectives and metrics to be used strategically when designing IMC tactics.

Figure 3.8 Keller's Customer Based Brand Equity (CBBE) framework

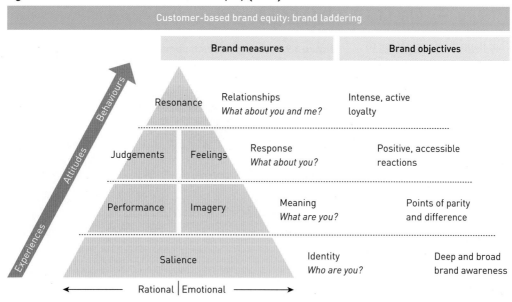

Source: www.verdegroup.com/solutions/reputation-risk.

The development of a strong brand starts with making it salient by ensuring that it has a clear identity, and that as many consumers as possible are able to recognise the brand in the market place, which is linked to the notion of **brand awareness**.[18] This first step is essential to product and brand positioning decisions, which the framework outlines as the second stage of brand building. Specifically, the CBBE framework suggests that it is essential to create and communicate **brand meaning**,[19] leveraging the brand's performance (i.e. the brand's concrete features) and perceptions and images linked to the brand (or *brand image*). This stage of brand development requires the identification and refinement of the following aspects:[20]

- *frame of reference*—that is, the target market
- *Points of Parity* (POPs)—that is, the features that the brand shares with other brands competing within the same frame of reference; these include category POPs (features that the brand must offer to serve the target market) as well as competitive POPs (features that the brand should offer to counteract competitors' PODs)
- *Points of Difference* (PODs)—that is, strong, favourable and unique features of the brand that can distinguish it from its competitors within the same frame of reference. PODs need to be desirable (i.e. consumers need to be interested in them) and deliverable (i.e. the firm and brand must actually feasibly deliver these aspects). See 'IMC in Action: Samsung Gear VR' (Samsung's new campaign for its Gear VR mobile virtual reality headset).

These aspects typically generate a response within consumers; that is, **judgments and feelings** likely to underpin the reaction to IMC initiatives, which, in turn, can lead to **brand resonance** (i.e. consumer loyalty and lasting relationships).

IMC IN ACTION: SAMSUNG GEAR VR

What happens if you refuse to listen to what 'can't be done'? Samsung believes the only way to achieve the impossible is by refusing to accept that anything is impossible: #DoWhatYouCant.

Samsung knows a thing or two about making TV commercials that go viral online, but that doesn't necessarily mean Samsung's ads are always great. However, that might change in the future. At the end of its Galaxy S8 Unpacked event, the company played an awesome TV commercial that's easily the best phone ad the company has ever made.

Figure 3.9 Samsung's ostrich commercial

Rather than taking obvious hits at Apple's iPhone, or just running through the main features of the Galaxy S8 phone, Samsung chose a different approach for this commercial: using an ostrich. And who doesn't love silly animal clips?

We've got a curious ostrich, which somehow gets stuck into a Gear VR headset that happens to play a flight simulator video of all the VR content that could be playing on the phone. The entire clip shows the ostrich's immersive Gear VR experience, and its determination to do the unthinkable after experiencing flight inside Gear VR. All the other ostriches—the ones that didn't get to play with a Gear VR—are left behind. They'll never know what flying feels like. The message is pretty clear. The Gear VR doesn't just work by itself. It needs a phone inside it—such as the Galaxy S8 that Samsung just unveiled—to help you do the unthinkable. 'We make what can't be made,' Samsung says at the end, 'so you can do what can't be done'.

Source: http://bgr.com/2017/03/29/galaxy-s8-ostrich-tv-commercial

The CBBE framework is relevant to IMC planning because it combines the *rational* and *emotional* aspects of consumption[21], thus embracing the basic principles of communication discussed in Chapter 1 and the foundations of consumer behaviour discussed in Chapter 2. Furthermore, its dynamic nature lends itself to the identification and evaluation of IMC strategies, thanks to being an ongoing strategic development tool that connects consumers' experiences, their evaluations of a certain brand (i.e. attitudes) and their purchase decisions.

Nonetheless, following through from the critique of standard business strategies mentioned earlier in the chapter, empirical evidence challenges quite markedly the idea of differentiating brands or making them somewhat 'unique', and firmly suggests that instead of aiming for differentiation, brands should aim at being highly *distinctive*.[22] This claim shares the same psychological assumptions as the CBBE framework (e.g. memory theory) but favours the use of highly recognisable brand elements (i.e. brand **distinctive assets** to ensure that a brand is mentally available)[23] as opposed to simply claiming to be in some way different from competitors. In other words, what truly sets brands apart is their mental market share; that is, the quantity and quality of concepts that consumers associate with brands.[24] Chapter 4 will elaborate more on this debate, presenting more critical reflections on brand positioning.

The strategic importance of distinctiveness over well-established business strategies revolving around differentiation is a rather new take on IMC. It also requires systematic gathering of information about consumer behaviour in the market of interest (i.e. product or service category), especially in relation to the key **strategic brand management/development** stepping-stones (e.g. brand awareness and brand image). Marketing communication managers can do this by analysing consumer survey data.[25] The analysis of this type of data sheds light on important aspects, including the brand's **mental market share**, but also the brand's current *strengths* (i.e. features to be maintained and defended through IMC activities) and *weaknesses* (i.e. features that consumers are not currently associating with the brand and that should be enhanced through IMC activities).

IMC objectives

This 'evidence-based' strategy offers a viable approach to the definition of the **IMC objectives** (see Figure 3.10), which typically include the following:

- *persuasion and communication objectives* (in line with what we discussed in Chapters 1 and 2), which include:
  - → reinforcing and influencing consumer decisions
  - → changing consumer attitudes (i.e. triggering a hierarchy of effects by tapping into cognitive, affective and conative dimensions of consumption by getting consumers to 'think', 'feel' and 'do')
  - → facilitating the correct comprehension of the advertising message and aiming for congruency between consumer values and beliefs
  - → helping advertising recall (i.e. ensuring that consumers can correctly identify the advertiser at a later stage following advertising exposure)
- *brand building objectives* (in line with the strategic brand management objectives resulting from the CBBE framework), which include:
  - → building brand awareness (i.e. maximising the consumer's ability to recognise and recall the brand)
  - → enhancing brand image (i.e. ensuring that the brand is spontaneously associated with many concepts and that the associations established are maintained fresh in the minds of consumers)
  - → mental availability (i.e. maximising the chance that a consumer will 'think of' the brand in the context of decision making)
  - → ensuring that consumers will respond positively to marketing initiatives (e.g. by including the brand in their purchase repertoire or by evaluating it more positively than other alternatives)
- *sales and economic returns objectives*, including:
  - → building and/or increasing demand
  - → increasing sales and reaching sales targets

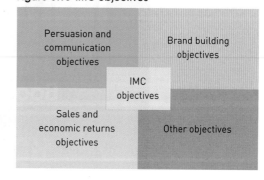

Figure 3.10 IMC objectives

Persuasion and communication objectives

Brand building objectives

IMC objectives

Sales and economic returns objectives

Other objectives

→   encouraging repeat purchase, brand loyalty and customer retention

→   increasing and/or maintaining market share and purchase penetration

• *other objectives*, which primarily concern the validation of the importance of the marketing function and IMC activities within the organisation. For example, a fundamental objective of every IMC plan should be ensuring the overall **Return on Marketing Investments (ROMI)**.[26]

Importantly, all objectives identified through the IMC planning process should be Specific, Measurable, Achievable, Relevant and Timely—**SMART objectives**—as well as coherent and synergetic with the marketing objectives and the overall strategic objectives of the organisation.[27]

Strategy considerations

Following the identification of the objectives, the next step of the IMC planning process includes a second-to-last stage, during which the organisation needs to **make concrete choices** in terms of:

1. message
2. media
3. promotional tools.

See Figure 3.11.

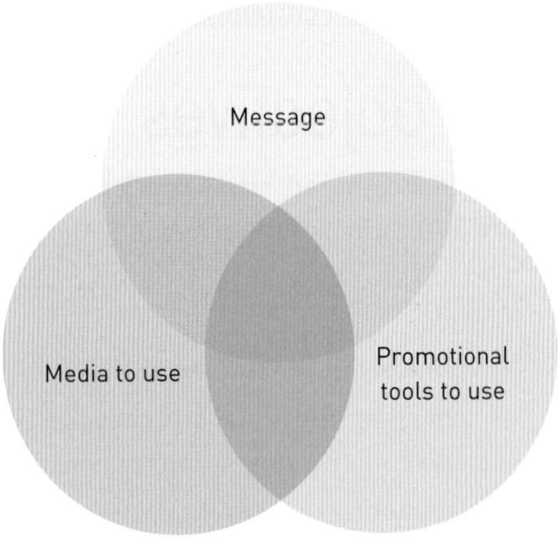

1. Strategic decisions concerning the *message* typically require choosing from three different types of message:[28]

→   *cognitive message*—aimed at clarifying consumer needs, increasing brand awareness and product (or service) knowledge; this is typically linked to **generic or pre-emptive advertising**, which has the primary goal of communicating the benefits that the product (or service) offers; see, for example, Booking.com's advertisement in Figure 3.12.

→   *affective message*—aimed at improving the brand or corporate image, and increasing brand preferences, desire and liking; this is conventionally linked to *affective advertising*, which is aimed at involving the viewer and leveraging symbolic and/or experiential aspects.

Figure 3.11 IMC choices

Message

Media to use

Promotional tools to use

Figure 3.12 Booking.com's campaign

→ *conative message*—aimed at inducing behaviour (e.g. stimulating searches, encouraging trial purchases and/or repurchases, and increasing word-of-mouth recommendations); this is typically paired with **salience advertising**, which should resonate with the positioning strategy determined earlier in the IMC planning process; see, for example, AirAsia's campaign for flights to the UK in Figure 3.13.

Figure 3.13 AirAsia's campaign for UK flights

It is important to keep in mind that there is a strong connection between the choices of message and the different theories of consumer behaviour discussed in Chapter 2. Specifically, the habit and reinforcement model of consumer behaviour typically calls for the use of a conative message, deployed to 'nudge' consumer decisions in the context of well-established repeat purchase behaviour patterns. In contrast, the cognitive theory of consumer behaviour matches more closely cognitive and/or affective messages, implying that the IMC message should influence the consumer decision-making process by providing relevant information and/or triggering emotional reactions.

2. Which *media* to use: choosing between conventional broadcast media (television and radio), print media (newspapers and magazines), digital media, owned and paid media, and social media; further details of choices concerning media are examined in Chapter 10.

3. Which *promotional tools* to use: including outlining specific strategies for each individual element of the promotional mix that the organisation intends to use (i.e. outlining an advertising strategy, a sponsorship strategy, a PR strategy, a digital marketing strategy, etc.) and putting forward strategic decisions in relation to the promotional mix as a whole, in order to embrace a holistic approach to IMC planning and strategy.

Organisations should always strive for coherence and synergy across all IMC choices, ensuring that the message chosen is executed by using the most suitable promotional tools and media. Furthermore, the strategic decisions outlined during the IMC planning process need to occur simultaneously with the identification of a budget for all IMC initiatives, as discussed in greater detail in the following section.

Setting IMC budgets

The definition of a total expenditure capacity for IMC activities yields considerable implications in terms of the promotional tools and media that the firm can afford; consequently, it has also many implications in terms of how to feasibly attain all the desired outcomes mapped in the IMC plan. However, setting IMC budgets is a rather controversial aspect of marketing and communication strategies.

Difficulties inherent to the IMC budgeting process are primarily due to the many implications related to other functions within the organisation, but also because it tends to be a somewhat 'political' process, which is often impacted by the characteristics of the management style of the organisation.[29] For example, the background of the executive managers involved in the IMC planning process can vary and does not necessary involve only marketing managers, communication managers or brand managers. Contextually, large organisations clearly dispose of greater marketing budgets whereas many small and medium organisations, as well as not-for-profit organisations, might have very limited money to spend on IMC activities. Therefore, firms use a variety of methods and approaches when setting IMC budgets, which can often not be entirely accurate or evidence-based.

On a general level, approaches for setting IMC budgets fall into two categories:

- *a **prescriptive budgeting method***, whereby management within the organisation is concerned with applying sophisticated techniques to the optimisation of expenditure level
- *the **descriptive budgeting method*** (i.e. 'rules of thumb'), which managers routinely use.[30]

While prescriptive budgeting approaches yield several benefits (e.g. they are somewhat 'evidence-based' and often lead to informed decision making), descriptive techniques are unsurprisingly common. To some extent, the reason for this disparity lies in the organisational setting in which IMC decisions are made. In other words, a substantial proportion of the variation in budget sizes and trends can be 'explained' by variations in the power of the marketing department and the emergence of political behaviour that influences the budgeting process.

On a basic level, the most widely used budgeting methods are:[31]

- *identifying a certain **percentage of sales** to be reinvested in IMC activities*. Although very common, this practice is somewhat illogical given that one of the objectives of the IMC activities is to impact sales, and given that the relationship between advertising and sales is *convex*;[32] that is, after a certain threshold, increasing investments in advertising generate diminishing returns in sales
- ***'meeting' the competition*** *(also called **competitive parity**)*. This means matching what competitors are doing and allocating a budget in line with the 'going rate' or average amount just like the rest of industry. This approach is widely used and, although logically sound, it neglects several factors such as the existence of the Double Jeopardy Law (see Chapter 2), which is known to penalise the market performance of smaller brands in several ways
- *the **affordability approach***. This involves setting a budget for IMC initiatives by considering exclusively the immediate availability of resources, with little or no consideration of other strategic factors, and no consideration of competition. Realistically, this is the method that many small organisations use
- *the **objective and task approach***. This approach includes more concrete strategic considerations and implies connecting specific IMC objectives (e.g. 'increasing brand awareness by 20 per cent for the intended target market within the next calendar year') to a pre-specified budget with the purpose of ensuring that the intended objective is attained
- ***payout planning***. With this approach managers typically establish the budget as a ratio of expenditures for IMC initiatives to sales or market share, which tends to change over time in line with the different stages of the life cycle of a product (i.e. the ratio is greater during the introduction or early stages of the life cycle and smaller when the product reaches maturity)
- ***quantitative models***. At times, managers embrace more complex budgeting techniques, which involve the use of computer simulations to model the relationship between IMC activities, sales and profits, and industry-specific factors (e.g. degree of competition). Because of the need to resort to complex statistical analyses, this approach is primarily used in larger organisations and although it may carry several benefits (e.g. accounting for industry-specific factors), it is based on assumptions that may

not be realistic. For example, the Duplication of Purchase Law (see Chapter 2) suggests that brands systematically share customers in line with their market share. Yet, quantitative models for setting advertising budgets do not consider benchmarks derivable from this law.

Empirical research that has examined issues of identifying budgets for IMC activities has recognised the existence (and recurring use) of a plethora of methods, and has suggested that managers should take into consideration **advertising elasticity**. Advertising elasticity refers to the percentage change in sales of a brand for a 1 per cent change in the level of advertising.[33] The academic literature showed that, on average, advertising elasticity is 0.10; it also showed that changes in crucial elements of the IMC plan (i.e. changes in media choices, target segments, advertising message and so on) are more likely to yield changes in sales than changes in **advertising weight** (i.e. the advertising budget).[34] Accordingly, researchers such as Wright (2009) proposed simple 'fool proof' methods for setting IMC budgets, by simply using the gross profit multiplied by the advertising elasticity.[35] Accordingly, it is reasonable to assume that a firm should spend approximately 10 per cent of its gross profit on advertising.

Successful IMC planning

So far in this chapter, we have linked IMC planning to the key layers of an organisation's strategy (i.e. corporate, business and marketing strategies) and unpacked the various stages of IMC planning, from the definition of objectives, to budget considerations. We are yet to discuss what makes an IMC plan successful.

To understand whether an IMC plan is (likely) to be successful, it is fundamental to consider the following aspects:

- Is the plan cohesive? Does it add up and does it revolve around the brand that the IMC tactics will build and maintain, while staying true to the DNA of the organisation?
- Is the plan revised and adjusted on an ongoing basis, taking into account possible changes and resorting to contingent approaches?
- Are all IMC tactics considered consistently, or is the IMC plan perhaps too skewed towards **above the line activities**, such as advertising?

While all of these questions should be considered truthfully, it could be argued that the last question is the one that requires greater reflection.

Advertising is undeniably the most prominent element of any IMC budget because it requires considerably greater monetary outlay than most **below the line activities** (e.g. direct marketing, sales promotions, SEO). Accordingly, firms that engage in IMC planning processes tend to focus on setting advertising-related objectives, budgets and decisions, leaving considerations about the other aspects of the promotional mix somewhat secondary. However, the key to successful IMC planning resides in considering the IMC as a whole and creating synergies across all IMC initiatives, as outlined in more detail in the case study at the end of this chapter on the IMC approach used for the TV show *Games of Thrones*.

Similarly, smaller organisations often tend to carry out strategic considerations for individual promotional activities (e.g. price promotions and direct marketing campaigns) and fail to embrace a more holistic approach to IMC planning.

Another fundamental consideration in relation to the success of IMC planning concerns the connection between the plan itself and the Strong vs. Weak approach to advertising, discussed in Chapter 1. As a reminder, a Strong approach to advertising implies conceiving IMC initiatives primarily to get consumers to *think*, *feel* and *do* (transforming awareness into interest, desire and action); a Weak approach to advertising plans IMC tactics to create *awareness* and encourage *trial*, or to *reinforce* behaviour. It is also important to consider the consumer behaviour principles discussed extensively in Chapter 2. Accordingly, it is fundamental to keep in mind that the success of the IMC plan will depend on the extent to which all elements in it are suitably aligned with the relevant advertising approach and consumer behaviour model. Also, the identification of the IMC objectives (i.e. choosing between persuasion and communication objectives; brand building objectives; sales and economic returns objectives; and 'other' objectives) needs to be informed by empirical marketing evidence. Above all, marketing and communication managers need to consider that in most instances (including contexts of high consumer involvement) IMC tactics should be aimed at creating *awareness* and encouraging *trial*, or *reinforcing* behaviour.

Planning using relevant marketing metrics

Imagine for a minute that you are getting ready for a fun road trip with friends. Planning the itinerary, looking at the map, shopping for snacks, coordinating with your mates on departure time, meeting point, and so on, are certainly important aspects of making this experience successful. Yet, even meticulous planning does not necessarily guarantee that you will have a fun weekend or make the most of your time away. To a great extent, working on an IMC plan is pretty much the same. If carried out robustly, it can most certainly offer some baseline reassurance for the likely positive outcome of IMC initiatives. However, it cannot automatically translate into tangible and positive results. This is why marketing communication managers should complement, as much as possible, IMC planning processes with a solid understanding of the key marketing metrics that should be monitored and benchmarked over time.

In earlier stages of your marketing studies, you may have already familiarised yourself with some marketing metrics. For convenience, in this book we recap the key metrics, which are derived from the analysis of panel data; that is, records of individual purchases made by consumers over a set period of time (e.g. a month or a year) and within a set product or service category (e.g. toothpaste). Importantly, we focus on these metrics because they can be used to infer how a certain brand performs relatively to competitors in the following ways:[36]

- *market share*—that is, the proportion of a brand's sales (in units sold, volume or dollar value) relatively to competitors
- *purchase penetration*—that is, the proportion of a brand's buyers (consumers who bought the brand at least once in the time period considered) out of the total number of potential buyers (market potential)
- *purchase frequency*—that is, the average number of times the brand was purchased by its buyers and a widely used measure of brand loyalty.

The calculation and analysis of these marketing metrics over time offers a snapshot of where the firm is at and where it wants to be. Changes in the values of these metrics can also be interpreted in conjunction with the implementation of specific IMC tactics to infer whether such initiatives returned the desired results. Importantly, these metrics constitute the basis for the creation of the wide array of empirical marketing knowledge that we are considering in this book. So, they should be interpreted in line with known facts about consumption, such as the Duplication of Purchase Law and the Double Jeopardy Law discussed in Chapter 2. 'IMC in Action: the success of Aldi in Australia' showcases the importance of considering these metrics (purchase penetration in this instance) when designing marketing strategies (more generally) and IMC tactics (more specifically).

IMC IN ACTION: THE SUCCESS OF ALDI IN AUSTRALIA

Aldi's Australian market share saw an increase of nearly 7 per cent between 2010 and 2017, with consumer numbers growing five times as quickly as those of its major competitors. Despite competitor efforts, Aldi will continue to compete aggressively in the Australian supermarket war. The discount retailer has plans to grow to 15 per cent market share by 2021, with a $700 million program to expand to over 500 stores, including major developments in Western Australia and South Australia, and an aim to compete with its rivals in fresh food offerings.

The Aldi example showcases the importance of considering key marketing metrics in the context of outlining marketing strategies and setting IMC plans (especially IMC objectives). In a country historically dominated by two 'super brands' (Coles and Woolworths), this growth is certainly remarkable.

So how did Aldi do it? Through its IMC tactics, the retailer emphasises as a key value proposition the close connection with local food producers.[37] However, this is obviously not a distinctive claim. In fact, other retailers use fairly similar positioning approaches, especially one of the two key competitors.[38] In reality, following the model already used in Europe, Aldi's success was actually driven by a very aggressive geographical extension plan, constantly increasing the number of stores to ensure robust market coverage. This strategy has caused an obvious increase in Aldi's mental physical availability, eroding market shares from Aussies' favourites simply by increasing purchase penetration.

Source: http://coriolisconsulting.com.au/supermarket-wars-aldi-approach/

When discussing the basic principles of strategic brand management earlier in this chapter, we also touched on several important 'building blocks' for brands and the concept of mental availability. As mentioned, these metrics can be examined via the acquisition of consumer survey data; that is, through the analysis of the responses gathered in questionnaires distributed online, or through other methods (e.g. phone and face-to-face).[39] Examples of the most important marketing metrics derivable from survey data include:[40]

- *brand awareness*—that is, the proportion of consumers who can name the brand when prompted with a cue (e.g. the product or service category for that brand) or when showed a visual prompt (e.g. the logo or packaging)
- ***brand image associations***—that is, the proportion of attributes consumers associate with the brand vs. its competitors, which can be translated into:
  → a calculation of the brand's mental market share[41]
  → an assessment of the brand's strengths and weaknesses (i.e. attributes systematically associated with the brand vs. attributes only seldom associated with the brand).[42]

Empirical evidence suggests that these marketing metrics follow the same underlying patterns of the metrics derived from panel data, albeit reflecting aspects of consumer behaviour more closely linked to how memory works and likely 'gaps' between memory and buying.[43] Crucially, these metrics can capture more effectively and in a timelier manner the effects of IMC tactics,[44] whereas there could be a 'lag' between an IMC initiative and its effects on sales. Consequently, these metrics constitute a fundamental ingredient of effective IMC planning.

The analysis of marketing metrics based on panel data and consumer survey data is becoming common practice in many large and medium corporations that invest resources in the systematic collection and analysis of large sets of data. In fact, research suggests that firms can gather great tangible benefits (e.g. sales and profits) and intangible benefits (e.g. brand equity and share value) from doing so. This is why this textbook assists you with your understanding of these marketing metrics and the value of empirical evidence in the context of all IMC activities.

■ CHAPTER SUMMARY

In this chapter we accompanied you on a journey across different aspects of strategy and planning, connecting IMC planning to other important aspects of strategy definition across the organisation. At the start, we clarified that in many organisations, strategies are formed at *corporate level* (the strategic direction of the organisation, as outlined by the top executives) and *business level* (specific business plans prepared for significant sub-divisions such as business units). The 'glue' connecting these layers is the *marketing strategy* (and related plan), which typically connects the mission of a certain organisation (its purpose) with business-level strategies, thus facilitating the realisation of the corporate strategy. IMC planning sits within the context of marketing strategy.

When introducing these concepts, we clarified that corporate and business strategies are often based on assumptions that are fundamentally incorrect and/or do not reflect empirical evidence concerning consumer behaviour. Therefore, we then focused on the nuts and bolts of the marketing planning process and the IMC planning, highlighting how to stay clear of misleading assumptions.

We clarified that the marketing plan outlines all decisions and actions that need to be undertaken for the realisation of the corporate and business strategies of a firm. In synthesis, we explained that the planning process includes a thorough analysis of the market; the development of specific objectives and strategies; the identification of suitable marketing programs and activities; and decisions concerning the implementation, control and evaluation of marketing programs. Decisions in regard to marketing tactics are a crucial outcome of this process and shape marketing mix decisions. This is where the marketing plan and the IMC plan overlap the most.

The IMC plan shares a great deal of information already gathered in the context of the overarching marketing plan (e.g. consumer-specific research and segmentation research), but includes more through strategic considerations of market and brand positioning. We approached this aspect by drawing upon strategic brand management principles (e.g. Keller's Customer Based Brand Equity framework). We also stressed the importance of considering empirical evidence, which emphasises the strategic importance of building mental availability for brands over conventional differentiation strategies. Accordingly, we outlined the key types of objectives of IMC: persuasion and communication objectives; brand building objectives; sales and economic returns objectives; and other objectives (e.g. ROMI). We then outlined some of the inherent difficulties in setting budgets for IMC activities, which yield implications in terms of linking planning objectives with media and tools decisions. Regardless, on a general level, organisations can use various methods, most of which are rather descriptive (i.e. mostly 'rules of thumbs') and only seldom resort to prescriptive (evidence-based) methods. Some of the most commonly used methods include percentage of sales; meet the competition; affordability method; objective and task method; payout planning; and quantitative models.

Finally, we presented a series of reflections on what makes an IMC plan effective, with an overview of the key marketing metrics that should be gathered and examined systematically, such as market share, purchase penetration, purchase frequency, brand awareness and mental availability.

Case study: *Game of Thrones*

Lara Stocchi

Game of Thrones' marketing and communication strategy deeply involves the use of social media and social media marketing. When *Game of Thrones* was first being produced, it was announced on the HBO network, which promoted the show on all of its own social media platforms. Afterwards, *Game of Thrones* opened its own social media accounts.

Figure 3.14 *Game of Thrones* logo

Figure 3.15 Spotify's *Game of Thrones* service

By creating such a cultural phenomenon, and limiting it (10 episodes per season), *Game of Thrones* created an experience where each episode is a cultural event. These 'cultural events' can be marketed on social media in very interactive ways, especially the premiere and finale of each season. This also allows for other brands, organisations and companies to integrate into their own campaigns. These campaigns create online, as well as in-person, conversation and engagement about the show. A good example is Spotify's integration of *Game of Thrones* into its service. Users were able to see which *Game of Thrones* characters they were based on their music tastes and playlists. This campaign was called 'With Whom Do You Listen?' Another example was when cast members of *Game of Thrones* surprised fans holding viewing parties with their friends. Actress Maisie Williams, who plays Arya Stark on the show, tweeted a video of the surprise. This demonstrates how the actors of the show can use their 'personal' social media pages to help promote the show.

Furthermore, the *Game of Thrones* Twitter page always promoted live tweets with fans and cast members, as well as question and answer sessions with cast members. Twitter is an effective social media platform for HBO and *Game of Thrones* because it offers an avenue for the show to disseminate bite-size posts, and a place where the show can engage and interact with its fans and viewers. *Game of Thrones* also utilises Twitter during the airing of each episode. Fans tuning into the show often share their reactions to the episode being aired in real-time.

Game of Thrones' content, characters and other elements are constantly appropriated and integrated into jokes, memes and a plethora of other promotional materials. This rehashing of content helps to amplify *Game of Thrones*' already strong presence because it gets shared through social media, friends and so on, which is why it is so powerful. This type of social media marketing is essentially giving the target audience tools that they then use. It builds a lot more credibility.

On Facebook, *Game of Thrones* has amassed more than 20 million likes. This is a huge testament to the massive, strong fan base that *Game of Thrones* has built. *Game of Thrones*' other social media platforms—such as Twitter, YouTube, and Instagram—also have huge followings. These social media platforms are currently the largest and most popular social networks, which means that the *Game of Thrones* brand can reach more people more easily. In fact, *Game of Thrones* has released countless promotional photos, trailers and videos on its social media, creating buzz, excitement and suspense.

Additionally, the show has implemented many great advertising, marketing and publicity campaigns over the years. For example, for Season 6 of *Game of Thrones*, HBO's goal was to attract a younger millennial audience. One campaign that it launched was called '#ArtTheThrone'. This campaign was executed by recruiting five rising artists to produce artwork in different mediums. Each artist recreated a scene or element from the series.

Game of Thrones also created a 'Live Concert Experience'. It got the musicians involved to live tweet the concerts, which was a good way of creating further interaction with fans. HBO also released a new promo that showcased the cast members from a variety of HBO's most popular shows. While it includes cast members from its other hit shows, such as *Girls*, HBO was able to include many of the main cast members of *Game of Thrones*.

Game of Thrones tease its fans and audience to create more mystery, intrigue and suspense. As the TV series is based on the *Game of Thrones* novels, many fans are excited about and interested in seeing what changes are made and what plot points or elements are kept the same.

Notably, a slightly different form of social media marketing is the *Game of Thrones* production blog, which offers a behind-the-scenes aspect to the show. These types of aspects to the *Game of Thrones* marketing strategy were embedded into the *Game of Thrones* social media platforms, which further generated buzz.

This level of social media engagement is necessary, especially because of the gaps between seasons. *Game of Thrones* has no shortage of epic elements, from production aspects such as the musical score, to epic plotlines (battle scenes, etc.). These are used as *Game of Thrones* jumping-off points for their promotional campaigns. In particular, when the promotional campaign involves something user- or fan-generated, or an epic event, the *Game of Thrones* brand capitalises on experiential marketing and getting users themselves to share and spread the word—similar to the word-of-mouth method of marketing.

In conclusion, *Game of Thrones* is able to captivate its audiences and fans by constantly tapping into the epic quality of the show, innovating and being creative with its promotional material and social media content.

Adapted from: Jessica Nguyen, 'How Game of Thrones Successfully Implemented Social Media into Their Various Promotional Campaigns', Medium, https://medium.com/rta902/with-the-reportedly-second-last-of-game-of-thrones-approaching-this-summer-i-thought-it-would-be-8684dfe5c64e

Questions

1. Discuss the strongest points of the overall IMC strategy that has been supporting the great success of *Game of Thrones* in building an astonishingly large base of fans and constantly increasing the size of its audience. Why is HBO's IMC strategy for the show so effective?

2. In your view, how essential is the role of spontaneous collaborations and partnerships with other brands to the success of global social media campaigns to promote *Game of Thrones*? What about the role of the cast members and other endorsers, such as celebrities?

3. What are the most distinctive aspects of the *Game of Thrones* brand, in comparison to other acclaimed TV shows owned by HBO or other companies? Why is the series successful at attracting and growing a large audience base, penetrating the industry of TV shows so broadly?

4. The case study refers to the success of *Game of Thrones* in attracting young millennials. In light of some of the aspects discussed in this chapter, you should be able to comment on this strategy. Do you think it actually reflects the audience base for this TV show? Is the franchise using any particular strategy that is likely to appeal to other demographics? If not, should it do so? Why/why not?

5. The presence of *Game of Thrones* across all the most popular social media platforms (e.g. Twitter, Facebook and Instagram) and the scope of other global IMC tactics used most certainly comes with the outlay of substantial budgets. In your view, is the success of this TV show on a global scale a good enough factor to justify the allocation of large IMC budgets and future increases in marketing investments?

6. In light of highly anticipated spin-offs of the show, can you come up with some recommendations for the likely IMC planning process and resulting strategy for HBO?

Practitioner profile: Damien White

Director of Marketing and Business Development, Dahua Technology

I am a multidisciplinary manager with senior experience across most business functions including general management, product management, product marketing, project sales, account management and marketing in companies such as UTC, Honeywell and Assa Abloy.

I've had a non-traditional trajectory into marketing, initially starting my working life as a tradesperson. From there I moved into account management and sales, while studying for my Master of Marketing and MBA at Melbourne Business School. After completing the double master degrees I worked in Shenzhen, China for five years. At one stage I worked as a product marketing manager for Honeywell and was responsible for a large group of their products across the South-East Asia region.

My current role is with Dahua Technology where I am Director of Marketing and Business Development. This has been an exciting time where we have grown a virtually unknown Chinese brand into a leading player in the Oceania market. My multidisciplinary customer-centric approach of combining marketing communication, product marketing management and leading technical support has been instrumental in the exponential 40-fold growth that our brand has achieved in only three years.

Describe your current role and the organisation you work for, and give a brief account of what you do in your role on a day-to-day basis.

My current role is with Dahua Technology as the Director of Marketing and Business Development.

Dahua Technology has its head office in Hangzhou, China, and is one of the leading manufacturers of electronic security products in the world. It is currently ranked number 2 globally for revenue in the CCTV industry.

As the Director of Marketing and Business Development my daily duties are extremely varied. On the marketing side you will see me working on both off and online marketing communication strategy, event management for exhibitions and liaising with agencies for any outsourced activities.

On the Business Development side there is also a significant amount of work that would traditionally be performed by a marketing team such as analysing the market and identifying opportunities for our products, working with teams on offline communication strategy and execution and analysing sales statistics to identify any opportunities or problems.

How important is Integrated Marketing Communication (IMC) to what you and your organisation do?

Integrated Marketing Communication is extremely important within Dahua Technology. An integrated approach is driven by marketing strategy with specific goals. It helps to align the different marketing tactics and achieve higher ROI on any marketing spend. When marketing communication is not undertaken using an integrated approach it not only affects the ROI but can also confuse the target customer as to what the actual message is.

What types of promotional tools do you use in your IMC campaigns? Please provide examples.

Dahua uses tools such as email, Facebook, Twitter, LinkedIn, websites, mobile apps with push notification functions, trade magazines, YouTube, WeChat, telemarketing, SMS and POS displays. In the B2B space that Dahua operates in I am seeing that telemarketing combined with follow-up email and SMS campaigns delivers the highest ROI of all.

What would your ideal IMC campaign look like and why?

A clear communication objective is set from the beginning. The message across all channels is consistent; online and offline interactions with target consumers are able to be tracked and then analysed through a single platform; the IMC not only integrates different marketing channels but also integrates different parts of Dahua such as marketing, sales, technical support and operations to help deliver a result that is great for the consumer. All too often I see a great marketing campaign fail because the marketing team has not had buy-in and assistance from the rest of the business.

What has been your favourite IMC project to work on and did it achieve its objectives?

I would have to say my favourite IMC during my career was when we launched Dahua Technology into the Australian market. In 2015, Dahua was virtually unknown in Australia among the professional security community. An 18-month-long IMC began in mid 2016 with the primary objective of increasing brand awareness and the secondary objective of pulling sales through our authorised distribution channel. The IMC was more successful than we could have ever imagined. Sales through our distribution channel had increased 30 fold by the end of 2017.

How do you believe an IMC campaign affects the consumer decision-making process for your particular target audience?

For Dahua in the Oceania region the message we promote in almost all of our IMC is to educate the consumer about who Dahua is, with a focus on the level of quality and the in-country support that we offer. From the consumer perspective a majority of the feedback that we receive is that they choose Dahua as they believe a relationship with Dahua is a true partnership that gives them peace of mind that they will receive exceptional support no matter how big or small their application of Dahua products is.

How has your application of IMC changed with the increase in digital marketing?

I use digital marketing techniques on a daily basis; however, I do not focus my IMC around digital. I generally find that offline tactics are far more effective in the segment we operate in. However, we can amplify the effectiveness of offline activities by using digital. One area where digital stands out for me is in building brand awareness and increasing unaided brand recall. However, when it comes to increasing revenue and customer loyalty, offline communication is the most effective way.

What do you believe are some of the challenges to implementing an IMC campaign?

The two biggest challenges that I face are, first, ensuring the organisation can deliver the brand promise I am communicating through an IMC, and second, ensuring that a consistent brand message is being communicated across all channels, both online and offline.

What advice would you offer a student studying IMC?

You will need to interact with the different parts of any organisation to ensure the brand promise you are communicating is actually what is being delivered. As the customer-facing part of marketing, IMC is extremely important as the entire organisation is relying on it to deliver the brand promise that the organisation has been working towards. Additionally, I would recommend that you not focus purely on digital—you need to learn about the offline channels that are available, as a targeted offline campaign can sometimes yield a higher ROI and deliver faster results than an online campaign in certain circumstances.

Key terms

above the line activities

advertising elasticity

advertising weight

affective advertising

affective message

affordability approach

analysis of the market

ANSOFF matrix

below the line activities

Boston Consulting Group
(BCG) matrix

brand awareness

brand building objectives

brand meaning

brand resonance

business strategy

cognitive message

competitive parity

conative message

corporate strategy

Customer Based Brand Equity
(CBBE) framework

descriptive budgeting method

distinctive assets

frame of reference

generic or pre-emptive
advertising

IMC objectives

IMC planning process

implementation, control and
evaluation

internal marketing

judgments and feelings

market research

market share

marketing mix strategies

marketing planning process

marketing strategy

mental market share

niche products

objective and task approach

payout planning

percentage of sales

PESTEL framework

points of difference

points of parity

prescriptive budgeting
method

product and brand
positioning

purchase frequency

purchase penetration

quantitative models

Return on Marketing
Investments (ROMI)

sales and economic returns
objectives

salience advertising

segmentation research

'SMART' objectives

strategy

strategic brand management/
development

strategic business unit (SBU)

target market

Revision questions

1. Outline the difference between corporate, business and marketing strategies. How are these linked?

2. Describe the key milestones of the marketing planning process.

3. What are the commonalities between the marketing planning process and the IMC planning process?

4. Discuss the importance of strategic brand management in the context of the IMC planning process and in the context of the marketing plan.

5. Illustrate Keller's Customer Based Brand Equity framework and clarify its relevance in the context of IMC plans.

6. Critically evaluate the value of strategies pursuing differentiation vis-à-vis strategies pursuing distinctiveness and mental availability.

7. Define and describe the four different types of IMC objectives that the textbook has highlighted.

8. What is the link between message, media and promotional tools decisions and the definition of budgets for IMC activities?

9. Discuss some of the most controversial aspects of setting IMC budgets within organisations.

10. Which factors should be taken into consideration when setting the objectives of an IMC plan?

11. Discuss the importance of using marketing metrics derived from consumer panel data and survey data in the context of evaluating the outcomes of an IMC plan.

12. Is it possible for organisations to make decisions about promotional tools and media use without having a comprehensive understanding of how much they can afford? Think about the instance of a new product launch: before the product is made available to the target market it is nearly impossible to make exact estimates of sales and profits. Yet, advertising and other IMC initiatives are needed in order to generate those sales and introduce the product into the market. Should managers simply 'guess' what to do?

13. Consider the soft drinks market and the various brands in it, such as Coca-Cola, Pepsi, Solo, home brands (e.g. Coles' brand) and so on. In light of the empirical evidence that we have mentioned several times in this book, which brands do you expect to have better performance in purchase penetration? What about purchase frequency: would you expect to see great differences between brands?

Further reading

Barnes, J. D., Moscove, B. J. & Rassouli, J. (1982). An objective and task media selection decision model and advertising cost formula to determine international advertising budgets. *Journal of Advertising*, *11*(4), 68–75.

Chatzipanagiotou, K., Veloutsou, C. & Christodoulides, G. (2016), Decoding the complexity of the consumer-based brand equity process. *Journal of Business Research*, *69*(11), 5479–89.

Christodoulides, G., Cadogan, J.W. & Veloutsou, C. (2015). Consumer-based brand equity measurement: lessons learned from an international study. *International Marketing Review*, *32*(3/4), 307–28.

Christodoulides, G. & de Chernatony, L. (2009). Consumer based brand equity conceptualization and measurement: a literature review. *International Journal of Marketing Research*, *52*(1) 43–66.

Corfman, K. P. & Lehmann, D. R. (1994). The prisoner's dilemma and the role of information in setting advertising budgets. *Journal of Advertising*, *23*(2), 35–48.

Ehrenberg, A., Barnard, N. & Scriven, J. (1997). Differentiation or salience. *Journal of Advertising Research*, *37*(6), 7–15.

Keller, K. L. (2010). Brand equity management in a multichannel, multimedia retail environment. *Journal of Interactive Marketing*, *24*(2), 58–70.

Keller, K. L. (2016). Reflections on customer-based brand equity: perspectives, progress, and priorities. *AMS Review*, *6*(1–2), 1–16.

Krishnan, H. S. (1996). Characteristics of memory associations: A consumer-based brand equity perspective. *International Journal of Research in Marketing*, *13*(4), 389–405.

Mitchell, L. A. (1993). An examination of methods of setting advertising budgets: practice and the literature. *European Journal of Marketing*, *27*(5), 5–21.

Nedungadi, P. & Hutchinson, J. W. (1985). The prototypicality of brands: relationship between brand awareness, preference, and usage. In E. C. Hirschman & M. B. Holbrook, (eds). *Advances in Consumer Research*, *12*. Provo, UT: Association for Consumer Research, pp. 498–503.

Percy, L. & Rossiter, J. R. (1992). A model of brand awareness and brand attitude advertising strategies. *Psychology and Marketing*, *9*(4), 263–274.

Punj, G. N. and Hillyer, C. L. (2004). A cognitive model of customer-based brand equity for frequently purchased products: Conceptual framework and empirical results. *Journal of Consumer Psychology*, *14*(1), 124–31.

Romaniuk, J., Wight, S. & Faulkner, M. (2017). Brand awareness: revisiting an old metric for a new world. *Journal of Product & Brand Management*, *26*(5), 469–76.

Notes

1   Wood, M. B. (2004). *Marketing Planning: Principles into Practice.* Prentice Hall/Financial Times.

2   ibid.

3   ibid.

4   www.mars.com/australia/en/about-us; www.mars.com/uk/en/doing-our-part/principles-in-action.

5   Porter, M. E. (2008). *Competitive Strategy: Techniques for Analyzing Industries and Competitors.* Simon and Schuster.

6   Walker, O. C. & Mullins, J. W. (2011). *Marketing Strategy: A Decision-Focused Approach.* McGraw Hill.

7   ibid.

8   Sharp, B. (2010). *How Brands Grow: What marketers Don't Know.* Melbourne: Oxford University Press.

9   Walker & Mullins, op. cit.

10 ibid.

11 Armstrong, J. S. (1982). The value of formal planning for strategic decisions: review of empirical research. *Strategic Management Journal, 3*(3), 197–211.

12 Clow, K. E. (2004). *Integrated Advertising, Promotion, and Marketing Communications.* Global Edition. Pearson Education.

13 Keller, K. L., Apéria, T. & Georgson, M. (2008). *Strategic Brand Management: A European Perspective.* Pearson Education.

14 ibid.

15 Keller, K. L. (1993). Conceptualizing, measuring, and managing customer-based brand equity. *The Journal of Marketing,* 1–22; Keller, K. L. (2001). *Building customer-based brand equity: a blueprint for creating strong brands.* Cambridge, Mass: Marketing Science Institute; Keller, K. L. (2003). Understanding brands, branding and brand equity. *Interactive Marketing, 5*(1), 7–20.

16 Romaniuk, J. & Sharp, B. (2004). Conceptualizing and measuring brand salience. *Marketing Theory, 4*(4), 327–42; Romaniuk, J. (2013). Modeling mental market share. *Journal of Business Research, 66*(2), 188–5; Romaniuk, J. & Sharp, B. (2016). *How Brands Grow. Part 2, Including Emerging Markets, Services and Durables, New Brands and Luxury Brands.* Melbourne: Oxford University Press; Stocchi, L., Driesener, C. & Nencyz-Thiel, M. (2015). Brand image and brand loyalty: do they show the same deviations from a common underlying pattern?, *Journal of Consumer Behavior, 14*(4), 317–24; Stocchi, L., Wright, M. & Driesener, C. (2016). Why familiar brands are sometimes harder to remember. *European Journal of Marketing, 50*(3/4), 621–38; Stocchi, L., Pare, V., Fuller, R. & Wright, M. (2017). The Natural Monopoly effect in brand image associations. *Australasian Marketing Journal.* doi: 10.1016/j.ausmj.2017.11.003; Stocchi, L. & Fuller, R. (2017). A comparison of brand equity strength across consumer segments and markets. *Journal of Product & Brand Management, 26*(5), 453–68.

17 Anderson, J. R. (1983). A spreading activation theory of memory. *Journal of Verbal Learning and Verbal Behavior, 22*(3), 261–95; Anderson, J. R. (1993). *Rules of the Mind.* New Jersey: Lawrence Erlbaum Associates Inc.; Anderson, J. R. (1996). *The Architecture of Cognition, 1983.* Reprint, Mahwah,

NJ: Lawrence Erlbaum Associates; Collins, A. M. & Loftus, E. F. (1975). A spreading-activation theory of semantic processing. *Psychological Review*, *82*(6), 407.

18 Hoyer, W. D. & Brown, S. P. (1990), Effects of brand awareness on choice for a common, repeat-purchase product. *Journal of Consumer Research*, *17*(2), 141–8; Nedungadi, P. (1990). Recall and consumer consideration sets: influencing choice without altering brand evaluation. *Journal of Consumer Research*, *17*(3), 263–76; Biedenbach, G. & Marell, A. (2010). The impact of customer experience on brand equity in a business-to-business services setting. *Journal of Brand Management*, *17*(6), 446–58.

19 Keller et al., op. cit.

20 ibid.

21 ibid.

22 Sharp, op. cit.; Romaniuk, op. cit.; Romaniuk & Sharp 2016, op. cit.

23 Romaniuk & Sharp 2016, op. cit.

24 Romaniuk, op. cit.

25 Driesener, C. & Romaniuk, J. (2006). Comparing methods of brand image measurement. *International Journal of Market Research*, *48*(6), 681.

26 Stewart, D. W. (2009). Marketing accountability: linking marketing actions to financial results. *Journal of Business Research*, *62*(6), 636–43.

27 Wood, op. cit.

28 Barry, T. E. & Howard, D. J. (1990). A review and critique of the hierarchy of effects in advertising. *International Journal of Advertising*, *9*(2), 121–35.

29 Clow, op. cit.

30 ibid.

31 ibid.

32 Taylor, J., Kennedy, R. & Sharp, B. (2009). Is once really enough? Making generalizations about advertising's convex sales response function. *Journal of Advertising Research*, *49*(2), 198–200.

33 Sethuraman, R., Tellis, G. J. & Briesch, R. A. (2011). How well does advertising work? Generalizations from meta-analysis of brand advertising elasticities. *Journal of Marketing Research*, *48*(3), 457–71.

34 Tellis, G. J. (2009). Generalizations about advertising effectiveness in markets. *Journal of Advertising Research*, *49*(2), 240–45.

35 Wright, M. (2009). A new theorem for optimizing the advertising budget. *Journal of Advertising Research*, *49*(2), 164–9.

36 Ehrenberg, A. S., Uncles, M. D. & Goodhardt, G. J. (2004). Understanding brand performance measures: using Dirichlet benchmarks. *Journal of Business Research*, *57*(12), 1307–25.

37 www.aldi.com.au/en/about-aldi/australian-made

38 www.woolworths.com.au/shop/discover/pick-woolies

39 Driesener & Romaniuk, op. cit.

40 Stocchi & Fuller, op. cit.

41 Romaniuk, op. cit.; Romaniuk & Sharp 2016, op. cit.

42 Romaniuk, J. & Sharp, B. (2000). Using known patterns in image data to determine brand positioning. *International Journal of Market Research*, *42*(2, Spring/Summer), 219–30.

43 Stocchi et al. 2015, op. cit.

44 Romaniuk, op. cit.

CHAPTER 4

Positioning and Objectives

Maxwell Winchester

Coca-Cola and stevia: A healthy alternative?

Tiffany Winchester

Introduction and external environment

Obesity is a major concern in Australia. With three in five Australian adults overweight and a 5 per cent increase in the number of overweight or obese adults since 1995, this trend is something to keep an eye on. While the increase in 'fat free' or 'diet' products has also increased, consumers are sceptical about their health benefits, especially when a reduction in fat may indicate an increase in sugar (consider fat-free yogurts, for example).

We all know about Coca-Cola. Chances are, you've purchased a Coke product in the past two weeks. And we know it's not good for us. The US liquid refreshment beverage market remained flat in 2013, and carbonated soft drink volumes, which constituted 43 per cent of the estimated net volume, declined for the ninth consecutive year. Why? Consumer culture is changing. Health and wellness awareness decreases our likelihood of buying a sugary drink. Both Coke and Pepsi have pledged to reduce the calorie count in their beverages by 20 per cent per person by 2025.

Coca-Cola with Stevia

With the slow-down in the soft drinks market, Coca-Cola has continued to search for a solution to the problem with its high sugar content. Introducing Coca-Cola Life. In the words of the company, Coke Life was developed in response to strong consumer demand for sweetened drinks that contain ingredients from natural origins, as well as fewer calories.

Coke Life, rebranded as Coca-Cola with Stevia in 2017, is the first new cola product launched by Coca Cola in Australia since Coke Zero in 2006. This product is sweetened with a blend of sugar and stevia. Stevia is a shrub native to South America and its leaves have been used for hundreds of years as a sweetener, often added to tea. It is about 200 times sweeter than natural sugar, has almost no kilojoules (calories) and does not raise blood sugar levels. Compared to classic Coke, it has 35 per cent less sugar and 35 per cent fewer kilojoules. For those people who are concerned about artificial sweeteners (sales of diet soda have declined at even steeper rates than their full-calorie counterparts) and want to focus on natural alternatives, stevia seems like the next best thing.

Product launch and initial response

Coke Life was first launched in South America in 2013, and currently has been released in the UK, Sweden, Argentina, Chile, Mexico, and parts of the U.S. However, there have been mixed reviews. Sales in South America have fallen short of forecasts because stevia's bitter aftertaste has turned off loyal Coke drinkers. A new formula was developed for the US and UK markets which contained a lower stevia content but obviously a higher sugar content than its South American counterpart.

The new drink was launched in Australia in April 2015. But who is the product for? A number of different views have been proposed, all from Coca-Cola.

Coca-Cola South Pacific's group marketing manager, Dianne Everett, stated that 'It doesn't replace anything else in the portfolio; it's a wonderful complement to the other three products that sit in the trademark, being Coke Classic, Diet Coke and Coke Zero'.

When Coke Zero was launched, it sold 30 million litres in its first few weeks in shops. Coke Vanilla sold 14 million litres in its first few weeks when it launched back in 2005. Compare that to Coke Life's 7 million litres in the first five weeks and one can see that repeat purchases of this product seem to be falling short of expectations.

Barry O'Connell, head of Coca Cola Amatil's (CCA) Australian non-alcoholic beverages business claimed in 2015 that Coke Life was on track to meet expectations of accounting to 1–2 per cent of Coke sales, in line with the UK sales.

Barry O'Connell told Fairfax Media that it was wrong to compare Coke Life with Zero or Vanilla, as the new drink was aimed at 'lapsed cola drinkers and low cola drinkers.'

However, CCA boss Alison Watkins of Coke Australia said that the success or otherwise of the new product is 'all about repeat [purchases] and whether it becomes an ongoing part of the repertoire.' She added that it would also be important to consider how it affects purchases of classic Coke.

Sources

https://www.coca-colajourney.com.au/faq/what-happened-to-coke-life

http://www.smh.com.au/business/retail/cocacola-life-falling-short-of-sales-expectations-20150526-gh9uhd.html

http://www.afr.com/business/retail/cola-wars-cocacola-drops-prices-in-supermarkets-20150715-gic5pc

Tiffany Winchester is a lecturer at the Monash Business School

■ INTRODUCTION

In the previous chapters, we saw models of communication, consumer behaviour and how IMC relates to marketing strategy. In this chapter, we continue the discussion by considering how IMC strategy might be developed into brand positioning and execution strategies.

LEARNING OBJECTIVES

After reading this chapter you should be able to:

1. explain alternative brand segmentation approaches
2. critique the brand positioning and salience approaches
3. debate the alternative approaches to brand positioning and distinctive assets
4. relate the concepts of brand positioning and salience to the Strong and Weak theories of marketing communication
5. explain the different execution approaches used in IMC.

Branding and IMC

Before considering brand positioning, we must consider what a brand is. The concept of branding merchandise has been around since Egyptian times, when brick makers would use symbols on bricks to identify their products.[1] In more recent centuries, cattle owners and whiskey distillers would use branding so people could recognise their products and property.[2] Branding enables consumers now, as it did then, to identify the maker of a product.

Measuring memory metrics that include brand information is important for a marketing team because it tells them what consumers think about the brand. The types of measures used include:[3]

- **brand awareness**
- brand image associations
- customer satisfaction and service quality
- **intention to buy**/future consideration of brand.

The most prominent brand measure used is **top of mind awareness**.[4] This can be prompted or unprompted. The exercise below helps us to consider top of mind awareness.

It was first noted in the 1950s that there was more to brands than just recognition of product attributes. Gardner and Levy (1955) demonstrated that feelings, ideas and attitudes were also important in brand choice.[5] Keller (1993) argues that one of the main **objectives** of any marketing program should be to improve the perceptions of the brand:[6]

> the success of a marketing program is reflected in the creation of favourable brand associations—that is, consumers believe the brand has attributes and benefits that satisfy their needs and wants such that a positive overall brand attitude is formed.

The term 'brand image' (discussed in Chapter 2) was developed to describe the image consumers had in their minds of a brand. However, the absolute definition of brand image is not clear in the literature, and the definition and measurement of it has been inconsistent for around 50 years.[7]

For the sake of efficiency and also improved accuracy, perceptions are usually gathered using simple association questions the consumer responds to—or not—regarding a brand (rather than scaling or ranking, which is rarely done).[8] For example, in the fast food category, a typical brand attribute might be 'which fast food outlet has convenient opening hours?' Consumers are then able to respond with whatever brands come to mind—McDonald's and KFC, for example.

Customer satisfaction and dissatisfaction are among the most collected brand perceptual data, even in small firms. For example, even in a boutique hotel that does not have the money for a full-blown brand image study, there will quite often be a paper-based satisfaction survey left in rooms for customers to fill out. Larger brands, on the other hand, have the financial ability to run large-scale, continuous brand image studies where a substantial sample of consumers are contacted over time to monitor changes in brand perceptions.

An important part of branding is widely accepted to be managing the brand's position to the point that it is considered a 'cornerstone of brand marketing practice'.[9] We will now consider this concept.

Brand segmentation, targeting and positioning (STP)

The concept of **brand positioning** was first discussed in 1972 in a book by Ries and Trout, *Positioning: The Battle for Your Mind*. In this book, the authors argue that to successfully stand out from its competitors, a brand must own a position in the consumer's mind that is unique from its competitors. This point of view has become commonplace in marketing literature and marketing practice.[10] To be able to position a brand, marketers must first segment their market, then select a target market. Once this has been completed, an appropriate brand position can be determined.

Brand segmentation

Market segmentation is considered a first crucial step in marketing strategy as it precedes the development of **targeting** and positioning strategies.[11]

Market segmentation, as the name suggests, involves dividing a competitive market into parts. First of all, it is acknowledged that different product offerings might be attractive to different types of consumers.[12] Further to this, it is believed that different brands will be attractive to different types of consumers too.[13]

Segmentation in principle appears quite logical. The argument that no one brand can meet the needs of all consumers leads to the logical conclusion that a company should focus on meeting the needs of a group of consumers when it has the capability to meet those needs.[14] In addition, it is thought to be more profitable to do this.[15]

As there is no shortage of material on segmentation, we will not go into much detail in this chapter apart from outlining the basics. Generally, there are four accepted variables upon which a segmentation strategy may be based:

1. *geographic segmentation*—segmenting a market based on the location of consumers
2. *demographic segmentation*—segmenting a market on variables that include age, income and gender
3. *psychographic segmentation*—segmenting a market based on psychographic variables such as attitudes and values
4. *behavioural segmentation*—segmenting a market based on behavioural variables such as the frequency of purchase.

Once the marketing team have worked out their desired segmentation strategy, they should not move forward with it until they are sure it meets the criteria for successful segmentation; namely that the segmentation strategy is:

1. *measureable*—can the segmentation variables be measured successfully?
2. *substantial*—is there a substantial group of consumers to make a segment viable?
3. *accessible*—can the segment be accessed through target marketing an IMC program to them?
4. *different*—is the segment different enough from other segments in the market?
5. *actionable*—is the segmentation strategy actionable?

This set of criteria has been widely attributed to several authors, among them Wedel and Kamakura (1998),[16] Kotler and Keller (2009),[17] Kotler (1984)[18] and Brassington and Petit (1997).[19] The fact that the criteria are so broadly cited and attributed demonstrates how widely accepted they are within the marketing profession.

Brand targeting

The second step in the STP process is targeting. Once a suitable segment has been identified, an IMC program is developed to target the segment.

The premise of targeting is that you must select appropriate media that are most likely to be consumed by the target audience. For example, if the product is a brand of women's clothing, it is logical that the IMC program would be targeted through media that are more likely to be consumed by women, such as women's magazines. If the clothing is made for younger women, then the marketing team would seek out media that targets younger women.

This concept is discussed in more detail in Chapter 10.

Brand positioning

Positioning is the final step in the STP process. For decades this process has been widely accepted as one of the most fundamental and important activities any chief marketing officer can undertake as part of their role.[20] However, this chapter will discuss positioning and Chapter 10 will consider targeting in some depth as part of the discussion on media.

Some examples of brand positions include the ideas that Volvo drivers purchase the car because the brand is positioned on safety and Mercedes Benz drivers purchase the car to reward themselves.[21]

Positioning strategies

There are a number of positioning strategies available to the marketer, including features, price/quality, use/application, product class dissociation, user, competitor, benefit and heritage/cultural symbol.

Features

The first positioning strategy is to use product or service features. The example given earlier of Volvo being positioned on 'safety' is a good example of this. Another example is Ecover's environmentally friendly house cleaning products, which are positioned on the product not being harmful to the environment. A service example is Etihad Airlines, which uses its Skytrax five-star rating to position itself as offering a better service experience than other airlines. Similarly, Hungry Jack's (the brand name the global burger chain Burger King uses in Australia) positions its burgers as 'flame grilled' and 'with no added hormones' as a way to differentiate itself from its key competitor, McDonald's.

Price/quality

The second positioning strategy is to highlight the price or quality of the product/service. While many examples of this would be brands that position on having good prices and value for money—such as the global supermarket chain Aldi—a few position on having higher quality and higher prices.

An example of this is Stella Artois, which has used the position of 'reassuringly expensive' for decades to reassure consumers a good beer is worth the extra money. Similarly, Lindt is notoriously positioned as a premium chocolate brand for gifting—in direct contrast to Cadbury chocolate, which is a mass market chocolate brand.

Use/application

Use of the product is another form of positioning strategy that can be used. An example of this is considering how cereal bars are essentially cereals but can be used differently (namely, you can take them with you rather than having to sit at the table and eat them with milk). When cereal bars were first developed and advertised, the message revolved around people who were running late but didn't have to skip breakfast because they were able to take a cereal bar with them. Similarly positioned in this way are 3M's Command Strips for damage-free hanging of various objects, including picture frames, key holders and other items.

Figure 4.1 'I Can't Believe It's Not Butter'—positioned against product class

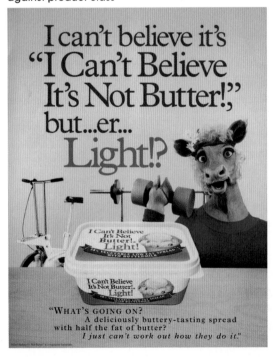

Product class dissociation

Product class dissociation is a positioning strategy that aims to separate the particular brand from other competing brands in the product category. An example of this is the brand 'I Can't Believe It's Not Butter' (see Figure 4.1).

In its advertisements, the message is always that this brand ('I Can't Believe It's Not Butter') is a margarine that is different from other margarines in that this one actually tastes like butter (which is in a different product category). In a more subtle way, M&M's recently launched chocolate blocks (see Figure 4.2) in an attempt to dissociate the brand, at least in part, from bite-size confectionery.

User

A positioning strategy that bases itself on the 'user' is one that focuses on the type of customer who uses the brand. For example, Capital One Bank in the US focused on helping smaller businesses rather than large businesses like its competitors.

Figure 4.2 M&M's new chocolate blocks

Bic 'For her' pens are specifically designed to appeal to female users of the iconic and 'commodity-like' pen, with a smaller shape (easier to hold for females) and light pastel colours (see Figure 4.3).

Competitor

Some brands position themselves against a large competitor. For decades, the positioning strategy of Avis Rent A Car has been 'Avis tries harder' because it was never the largest brand in the market (see Figure 4.4). Similarly, Microsoft Surface Pro is positioned to be a more efficient and powerful tablet than Apple's iPad.

Figure 4.3 Bic's 'For her' range

Figure 4.4 Avis positions its brand against competitors

Benefit

A product benefit can also be a positioning strategy. For example, Sensodyne toothpaste has positioned itself as being suitable for sensitive teeth when compared to other toothpaste brands in the market.

Heritage/cultural symbol

The final way a brand can position itself is on heritage. This is usually reserved for brands that have been in the marketplace a long time, but is quite popular for such brands. For example, many luxury brands position themselves on their year of establishment by stating something like 'Making watches since 1938'.

This type of positioning, however, is not just for luxury brands. Brands such as Hovis bread and Qantas highlight the heritage of the brand and the role they have played in society and people's lives.

Measuring a brand's position

Once a marketing team has worked out their desired brand position and started to communicate it to their target audience, the next challenge is to measure **brand perceptions** to see if consumers perceive the brand to have the desired position.

As discussed above, marketing teams will put in place a brand image study; this is conducted continually to monitor consumer perceptions.

From the entire set of image data, a correspondence analysis is conducted to create a positioning map.[22] Figure 4.5 shows an example of what a simplified positioning map might look like. It presents the relationship between each brand and each brand attribute. The closer in space the brand is to an attribute, the more aligned the two are. An example of this is that Subway is associated with 'healthy', so of all brands it is the most distinctively positioned on any one attribute.

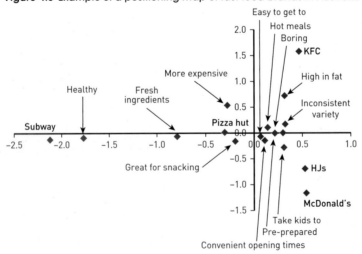

Figure 4.5 Example of a positioning map of fast food brands in Australia

A critique of brand STP

Critiquing segmentation

While extremely popular in both marketing academia and practice, empirical research in marketing has often challenged the rationale behind segmentation, especially at brand level, and in contexts where consumer behaviour is aligned with the behavioural model of decision making (see Chapter 3). While there are hundreds of thousands of papers published on how to do segmentation (a quick Google Scholar search on the topic found nearly one million results), very few studies have considered the success of segmentation or targeting at an aggregate level by reviewing consumer profiles of competitive brands.[23] The common approach is to just assume segments exist rather than examining whether they actually do.[24]

Studies that have investigated differences in consumer profiles across brands have found very little difference, suggesting no or very limited segmentation occurs in practice.[25] For example, the **brand user profile** for Coca-Cola would be fairly similar to the profile of the users of the Pepsi brand. This lack of segmentation across brands has held up consistently across several years.[26] It seems that, in practice, there has been little clear evidence of successful segmentation.

Nonetheless, many firms develop their marketing and communication strategies on the basis of specific target markets. For instance, GoPro set up a marketing strategy and IMC approach on the basis of lifestyle segmentation—trying to appeal to specific types of consumers who are younger, adventurous, social media savvy and eager to share their unique life experiences outdoors practising different sports. Yet, the company has recently adapted its strategy to also start attracting purchases from different types of consumers, being more open on what it means to be a GoPro 'hero'.

Aside from the critical evidence of segmentation, there is also a question regarding the criteria for successful segmentation discussed earlier. One of these is that the segments must be stable—yet we know from Chapter 2 that consumers generally have repertoires of brands they use. This suggests that segments are unlikely to be either unique or stable as consumers regularly use competing brands that in theory attract different kinds of consumers.

Critiquing targeting

While it may seem logical that an IMC program should be targeted at the desired segment to avoid wastage, the evidence available on the success of targeting in practice leaves a lot of questions as to whether this is possible.

The major issue that has been found is that, as with brands, consumers have repertoires of media consumption.[27] This means that profiles of viewers of different TV channels, readers of different newspapers or listeners of radio stations do not differ very much, as the same people switch between the different media channels.

Aside from the above point suggesting targeting success is unlikely, there is also the assumption that it is more profitable to tailor IMC programs to a particular target audience than to the **mass market**.[28]

This topic will be covered in more depth in Chapter 10.

Critiquing positioning

There has been limited research on the effectiveness of brand positioning; however, the empirical research conducted suggests that most attempts to position a brand are unsuccessful. An example of this is the study by Romaniuk and Sharp (2000), which removed the effects of brand size and attribute size from data to demonstrate deviations for attributes across brands.[29] For the most part, once size effects were accounted for, there was very little difference across brands.

In a presentation to the Marketing Research and Intelligence Association of Canada in 2001, Winchester and Sharp summarised the major reasons why positioning does not work. They suggested the empirical evidence available demonstrates[30]:

1. that brand perceptions are largely affected by brand usage.[31] This means that consumers tend to say positive things about brands they already use

2. that brand attributes are prototypical in that attributes that score highly for one brand also score highly for all other brands.[32] This is because attributes are related to membership of a product category[33] so consumers see all brands having that particular attribute (such as all fast food outlets being perceived to have 'convenient opening hours')

3. that individual responses to brand attributes are not stable over time, but aggregate responses are stable. When consumers respond to brand image surveys at one point in time, upon re-interview only around 50 per cent of respondents will nominate the same attribute for the same brand[34]

4. that consumers are loyal to repertoires of brands, as discussed in Chapter 2. If brand positioning were effective in the way described by the likes of Ries and Trout (2001),[35] consumers would find the brand with the most appropriate position for their needs and remain loyal to it. However, decades of research on consumer purchase patterns demonstrates this not to be the case

5. further to the above, the discussion in Chapter 2 on Duplication of Purchase Law shows us that consumers use more than one brand. It is therefore not possible that different types of people use each brand (as each person is using a number of brands). This means that while segmentation in theory may sound strategically sensible, in practice, segmentation rarely exists. The fact that different brands do not appeal to different customers makes it unlikely that any attempt to position brands would be successful. This is supported by a number of empirical studies on segmentation.[36]

The points above must be taken in the context that both segmentation and targeting strategies precede positioning and therefore both must be successful before positioning can be successful.

As can be seen from these points, empirical evidence suggests an alternative approach to brand positioning may be needed.

Alternative approaches to brand positioning and distinctive assets

It has been demonstrated that specific **brand attributes** that brands may be positioned on had no effect on loyalty to a brand, but rather the number of attributes associated with a brand was indicative of loyalty to a brand.[37] This is known as the **brand salience** approach, which has been argued by numerous authors and supported by empirical evidence.[38]

Given the lack of support for brand positioning, the realm of empirical evidence that has emerged in recent years has provided marketing and communication managers with an alternative approach. This approach suggests that consumers will not buy a brand because it is perceived as performing better than other competing brands (or that it is somewhat 'different'), but instead it will be bought because it was noticed better than other brands—that is, it was easy to 'think of' or 'mentally available' (a concept that we discussed in Chapters 1 and 2). Empirical evidence has also clarified that this can be easily attained by using **distinctive assets**—that is, highly recognisable brand elements (also discussed in Chapter 2).

If consumers who hold more 'bits' of knowledge about a brand have a higher probability of buying a brand, how do such bits of knowledge get held and recalled in memory? As discussed in Chapter 1, such bits of information are encoded through repetition to prototypical attributes for the item in question. These bits of information are then recalled by having a relevant cue triggered. Evidence suggests that it may actually not be the differentiation or positioning of a brand that leads to it being recalled by consumers, but its distinctive elements—such as the shape of packaging or the distinctive colour of a logo.[39] Such elements of a brand do not indicate any level of superior performance, but do allow the brand to be noticed and remembered.

If we consider, first, that the empirical evidence demonstrates that consumers buy from a small repertoire of brands, then it is very likely that they perceive brands are largely substitutable and perform relatively similarly. Second, consumers have a propensity to buy a brand from their repertoire on any purchase occasion, and it is the irrelevant but distinctive brand elements that are likely to make a consumer think about the brand in the purchase situation.

IMC execution

There is much emphasis in the industry on the importance of creativity, particularly in the ability of a campaign to cut through the clutter and engage consumers.

Part of the creative process is choosing an **IMC execution** for a campaign. In this part of the chapter, we consider the nine main styles of creative execution appeals. These are divided into two groups under the main headings of 'Informational appeals' and 'Emotional appeals' (see Table 4.1).[40] This is argued to be the case because advertising is said to make people feel or think.[41]

Table 4.1 The nine main styles of creative execution appeals, divided into 'informational' and 'emotional'

INFORMATIONAL APPEALS	EMOTIONAL APPEALS
Factual	Fear or shock
Slice of life	Humour
Demonstration	Sexual innuendo
Comparative	Music
	Fantasy

Informational appeals

Informational appeals (also known as 'utilitarian appeals') are appeals to the consumer that involve product information as the main communication of the campaign.[42]

Factual

A factual appeal involves communicating facts about the product or service being promoted. For example, a campaign about a car could highlight product features or fuel economy. An airline might communicate its on-time performance or safety record. This kind of appeal assumes a consumer is highly involved in the decision-making process and therefore would rely on factual information about the product or service to make a decision.

Figure 4.6 BCAA breakdown insurance slice of life ad

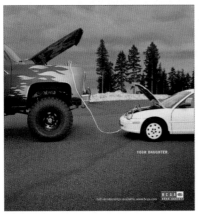

Slice of life

The slice of life appeal is literally that: an example of the product or service being used in a person's life. For instance, the British Columbia Automobile Association (BCAA) breakdown service advertisement in Figure 4.6 shows a 'slice of life' scenario of how having breakdown insurance can help your daughter.

Demonstration

An informational appeal that involves demonstration is usually some form of IMC program that demonstrates the product to the consumer. For example, many laundry powder advertisements offer a dramatisation that shows their brand of laundry powder gets dirty clothes cleaner than that of their competitors.

Another example is that advertisements for four-wheel-drive vehicles will often show the vehicle going through a muddy road to demonstrate how well the vehicle handles such conditions.

Comparative

Comparative appeals are those in which the brand is compared to competing brands in the market. In most countries there are very strict laws about whether this can be done or how it can be done. In the US, however, it is quite a common appeal tactic.

Figure 4.7 shows a Pepsi advertisement that is comparative but does not use the words 'Coca-Cola'. It is obvious that most consumers would know it was being compared to a Coca-Cola product though.

Figure 4.7 Comparative Pepsi advertisement

Emotional appeals

Emotional appeals (also known as 'value-expressive appeals') aim to get an emotional reaction out of the consumer.[43]

Fear or shock

Fear or shock emotional appeals are often used in public safety campaigns. Particularly in road safety campaigns or anti-smoking campaigns it is thought that shocking the audience or making them fear the consequences of the target behaviour will be effective.

The Transport Accident Commission (TAC) Victoria has around 20 years of award-winning fear and shock campaigns that can be found on YouTube.

Humour

A common emotional appeal is humour. Funny advertisements are widely used in advertising,[44] possibly because humour makes the advertisement more likeable. However, when an IMC campaign is running globally, it is important to acknowledge that humour is culturally bound and what is considered funny in one country may not be considered funny elsewhere.[45]

Sexual innuendo

You have probably heard the saying 'sex sells'. Sexual innuendos are common in IMC campaigns, particularly for generally male-dominated product categories.

One risk of using sexual innuendos in advertising is that consumers may be offended by it. However, in what may be a surprising result, research by Zimmermann and Dahlberg (2008)[46] suggests that young, educated women are less offended by sexual innuendos in advertising today than was the case in the past.

Music

Music, particularly in the form of jingles, can be a very effective appeal.[47] It has been suggested that pop music favoured by the 'teen' target group leads to emotional ties to brands, especially when there are few differences to distinguish between brands.[48]

Research suggests that having music in advertisements makes them more enjoyable, can increase brand recognition and increases engagement.[49] Jingles, in particular, have been found to be more effective than other music because they are brand specific so people can't associate them with anything else.[50]

Fantasy

A fantasy appeal is one in which the IMC campaign is set in a fantasy world. It could be anything from a gorilla playing drums (as was the case in the famous UK Cadbury campaign) to a family taking baths in their private jet (as was the case in a Cussons soap ad from the 1970s).

The example in Figure 4.8 is a Lavazza coffee campaign that not only plays on the word 'express' but also pictures a well-dressed model in space, drinking coffee.

Figure 4.8 Lavazza fantasy execution in coffee advertising

■ CHAPTER SUMMARY

In this chapter we presented a critical overview of the STP (segmentation, targeting and positioning) process, along with a review of the types of creative executions that are commonly used in IMC campaigns.

We identified that while the STP process is seen by most marketers as one of their most important tasks, the empirical evidence behind performing it doesn't really stack up.

We outlined alternative brand segmentation approaches including geographic, demographic, psychographic and behavioural segmentation.

Brand positioning approaches were discussed, including features, price/quality, use/application, product class dissociation, user, competitor, benefit and heritage/cultural symbol

An alternative approach to STP was presented that involves making a brand distinctive and mentally available.

Finally, we reviewed IMC execution and discussed the nine different IMC appeals that can be used.

Case study: BMW changes campaign

Tiffany Winchester and Maxwell Winchester

Introduction

BMW is one of the world's most successful premium car makers. Along with its German rival, Mercedes Benz, BMW has been successfully selling diesel-engined high-performance cars in Europe for many years.

In the US and Canada, diesel cars were very popular in the late 1970s and early 1980s with a range of Volvo and Mercedes Benz models that ranged from 2-door touring coupes to large elegant saloons. This was largely driven by the economy of diesel engines during the oil crisis of the 1970s.[51] Since the 1990s, however, in that part of the world diesel has been a dirty word. Commonly associated with cars that have underpowered, loud clanging engines that pour out black smoke, diesels lost their popularity. In addition to their loss of popularity, the highly efficient common rail direct injection engines used in Europe in the early 2000s could not be sold in either the US or Canada because the diesel fuel was not up to standard. After many years of lobbying, European carmakers celebrated the reduction in sulphur content in diesels in North America; however, they needed to get over the negative perception that diesel-engined vehicles had in that part of the world.

A campaign put together by GSD&M Idea City for BMW USA starts by showing older diesel vehicles, including large trucks and older cars that had been successful in the 1980s such as Mercedes Benz and Volvo, exaggerating their loud motors and black smoke. The advertisement showcased the 335d, a high-performance, small, four-door car with a turbocharged new-generation diesel motor growling with acceleration around a corner then passing an old diesel Volvo with ease up a hill.

The TV advertisement was complemented with print ads. While the print part of the campaign concentrated on the environmental side of lower emissions and better fuel economy, the TVC (television commercial) offered a cheeky insight into the vehicle's performance. BMW's nearest rival, Mercedes Benz, released a TVC highlighting the fact that they were the first car manufacturer to release a car with a diesel engine and that the newest Bluetec diesels are more environmentally friendly than previous diesels.

Patrick McKenna, Marketing Manager of BMW in the US, expected the campaign to bring

Figure 4.9 BMW 'Diesel gone good' advertisement

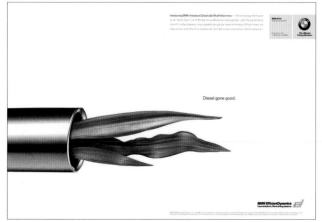

the US luxury market up to speed with the one in Europe.[52] While during the first decade of the twenty-first century more than half of the cars sold in Europe were diesel-engined, they were virtually non-existent in North America. The main point of the campaign was to reposition the perception that Americans have of diesel-engined cars.

Questions

1. What positioning strategy/strategies have BMW used in their campaign? What about Mercedes Benz?

2. What type of execution has each company used? Why do you think this is the case?

3. Do you think that BMW concentrating on the performance of its diesel cars will be more effective than concentrating on environmental credentials? Why or why not?

Sources

Parekh, R. (2012). BMW changes gears with new campaign from KBS&P. *Ad Age*.

Vranica,S. (2009). BMW Works to Clean Up Diesel's Rep. *Wall Street Journal*, http://online.wsj.com/article/SB123137437553662817.html

Practitioner profile: Vicky Kalofolias

I am a senior marketing professional with more than 26 years' experience in the beauty and fashion industry. I started my professional career as a sales manager at Oroton in 1990 and then moved to Crabtree & Evelyn in 1992. I also worked part time for several years at Gucci.

While at Crabtree & Evelyn, I progressed into various roles, from store management to buying, visual merchandising and marketing. As the company grew organically, so did my role within the organisation. A Brand Management role was created for me which encompassed managing the marketing for all sales channels at Crabtree & Evelyn, as well as graphic design, e-commerce, visual merchandising, purchasing and retail store development. This role required me to undertake a marketing course. I completed a Graduate Certificate at Holmesglen and went on to complete my Masters in Business Marketing at Swinburne University. In 2014, I took on a secondment as Global Head of Marketing for Crabtree & Evelyn for a six-month period. I returned to my role after this. In May 2018, I left my role to seek new challenges.

Describe your current role and the organisation you work for, and give a brief account of what you do in your role on a day-to-day basis.

I am currently in a two-month contract role at L'Occitane Australia, working as the Wholesale Marketing Manager. I have always admired this brand for its values as well as products and took up the opportunity to work here and experience B2B marketing at a greater level. They have also won several awards through Great Place To Work, recently being awarded 19th in 2018, so this was another reason to work with this brand.

This role entails developing monthly campaigns for wholesale channels, including department stores and pharmacies. My role also entails developing marketing strategies for hotel chains, corporate business and B2B consumers.

How important is Integrated Marketing Communication (IMC) to what you and your organisation do?

Integrated Marketing Communication is the fundamentals behind a successful campaign. I was fortunate to be able to study and work in a marketing role at the same time and was able to apply theory into practice. Understanding the importance and value IMC can bring to a marketing campaign and to the overall business objectives is key.

What types of promotional tools do you use in your IMC campaigns? Please provide examples.

As a business, IMC is applied to all launches at L'Occitane Australia. I have been fortunate to be a part of the marketing team executing an integrated campaign, on-counter launch September 2018. All marketing channel heads have worked collaboratively to form the overall plan.

For the wholesale channel, the specific tools used in a campaign include promotional offers, point-of-sale support material, visual merchandising tools, social media assets, email campaign assets, consumer sampling and training tools—several touchpoints to reach the end consumer through a B2B customer.

What would your ideal IMC campaign look like and why?

My ideal IMC campaign would begin at least six months before the product on-counter date. Understanding your consumers and their needs is crucial so that you can start marketing to each consumer segment. Planting the seeds with your long lead customers comes first, such as wholesale customers (department stores). This would be followed by long lead and traditional print media; media buying; creation of all assets; training materials for all teams; teaser sampling to end consumers; launch to short lead media and influencers; and finally the on-counter date.

Every single effort in marketing communication needs to come together to achieve campaign objectives. The goal should be to build momentum for a launch and ensure there is communication at every touch point.

What has been your favourite IMC project to work on and did it achieve its objectives?

There have been several that I have been fortunate enough to experience in my career. The current launch I am working on with the team at L'Occitane has to be a standout in terms of a current-day IMC campaign. The launch has not gone live but I am confident it will achieve its objectives.

However, my first IMC campaign was 11 years ago for the Crabtree & Evelyn India Hicks Island Living launch. This was my first foray into a successful IMC campaign. We began our IMC planning 12 months before on-counter date and started the campaign activities six months before on-counter date. We spent a great deal of time researching the market and knowing what our consumer would pay for this collection. The collection was a first … with several items priced at premium price points.

We targeted long lead media (there was no social media at the time) and we secured several stories with leading Australian fashion and lifestyle magazines. We also secured a live TV on-air *Today* show editorial segment; several magazine editorial pieces—a first of many coups—two editorial pages in *Australian Vogue*; one page in *Belle*, at the time with Neale Whitaker as editor. I still remember meeting him to discuss the launch. We also took Wendy Squires, one of Australia's leading writers, to the Bahamas and we did a photoshoot and were immersed in the inspiration of the India Hicks collection. This resulted in a ground-breaking 14-page editorial piece in *Madison*.

The press was the biggest event that my team and I had ever organised. We took over Est Restaurant at The Establishment and Peter Doyle created an amazing island-inspired menu using fresh Australian produce. The media attendance was astounding, with over 75 editors attending the event and many calling to secure their attendance. The press event was at full capacity. Our guest, India Hicks, was in attendance and enthralled the crowd. To say it was a success was an understatement: the setting, the menu, the ambience and the flowers all played a part in capturing a mood and engaging our audience. We secured many stories and worked with the editors to ensure the stories hit the stands in a timely manner. We timed the release of stories, a month beforehand and this gradually built. By the time the product was on-counter, there was so much awareness in the market about this collection.

Our wholesale channel did not miss out with pre-launch activities and communication pieces tailored to this channel.

The retail launch involved pre-sampling and direct mail pieces. We also had pre-VIP viewings for top-tier customers and they were able to secure and hold their pieces ahead of the launch. The launch was a success, with many crowds of existing and new consumers lining up to purchase this collection. It was such a success, that we ran out of stock. The premium price points were not a barrier to the consumer. This IMC campaign had covered all areas.

How do you believe an IMC campaign affects the consumer decision-making process for your particular target audience?

IMC plays a crucial part in the decision-making process. You need to know your target audience to tailor your IMC efforts for this audience in order to engage them.

How has your application of IMC changed with the increase in digital marketing?

IMC has certainly changed these past few years. Digital marketing has become a big focus, given that it is more cost effective. Digital marketing engages consumers in real time; it is more approachable and personable. Consumers are more connected and feel more like a part of a brand's community. Receiving a reply in real time from a brand via social makes a brand feel more real and personable. Brands are always online—there is no offline.

What do you believe are some of the challenges to implementing an IMC campaign?

Challenges include budget constraints and receiving finished product and tools in time for all the IMC campaign to begin. Getting stakeholder buy-in can be a challenge, particularly stakeholders from other departments.

What advice would you offer a student studying IMC?

Embrace IMC!

It is so rewarding as a marketing manager to see a product launch succeed with the efforts of an integrated campaign. Seeing all campaign activities come together to build momentum for a launch is the ultimate goal.

Key terms

behavioural segmentation   demographic segmentation   psychographic segmentation

brand attributes   geographic segmentation   segmentation

brand perception   IMC execution   targeting

brand positioning   intention to buy   top of mind awareness

brand salience   mass market

brand user profile   objectives

Revision questions

1. Outline the four segmentation approaches.
2. What are the criteria for successful segmentation?
3. What are the different strategies for positioning a brand?
4. What does empirical evidence tell us about segmentation?
5. What does empirical evidence tell us about targeting?
6. What are the arguments against brand positioning?
7. What alternatives are there to brand positioning?
8. What are the alternative IMC execution methods?
9. Refer to Chapter 2, particularly the section on cognitive and behavioural approaches to consumer behaviour. Taking these into account, what assumptions are being made about consumer behaviour when the quote from Keller (1993) in Chapter 4 (see page 99) is considered?
10. Consider a well-known brand that uses its brand positioning to drive consumer purchases. Is this brand's position unique when compared to other brands in the market? Do you imagine that it would create loyalty to the brand from target consumers?
11. Revisiting the opening vignette about Coke Life at the start of the chapter, consider the following questions:
    *   What industry does Coke operate in? Who are the competitors?
    *   Should Coke stick with its mass marketing approach, or focus more specifically on segment(s) of the market who may be more profitable? Why or why not? Discuss the pros and cons of segmentation for this product.
    *   If you recommend that they should segment, what segmentation bases would you suggest they use? Outline what the proposed segment might look like using at least 3 segmentation bases.
    *   If you argued that Coca Cola Life should be targeted at a particular segment of the market, how would you target the brand?
    *   Given what you now know about consumer behaviour, repertoires, and duplication of purchase law, what is the best strategy for Coke to use to get more people to purchase Coke Life?

- If you believe the best approach is through an STP process, justify your position. If you believe it is through the alternative distinctiveness approach, identify distinctive elements that may help your IMC campaign.

Why do you think you thought of some brands before others? As a consumer, what is notable to you about these brands?

12. Write down which brand first comes to mind (top of mind awareness) when you think of the following product categories:
    - fast food restaurants
    - supermarkets
    - cars
    - airlines.

Why do you think you thought of some brands before others? As a consumer, what is notable to you about these brands?

Further reading

Armstrong, J. S. & R. Schultz (1993). Principles involving marketing policies: an empirical assessment. *Marketing Letters*, *4*(3), 253–65.

Assael, H. & Roscoe Jr, A. M. (1976). Approaches to market segmentation analysis. *The Journal of Marketing*, *40*(4), 67–76.

Dickson, P. R. & Ginter, J. L. (1987). Market segmentation, product differentiation, and marketing strategy. *The Journal of Marketing*, April, 1–10.

DiMingo, E. (1988). The fine art of positioning. *The Journal of Business Strategy*, *9*(2), 34–8.

Ehrenberg, A. S. C., Goodhardt, G. J. et al. (1990). Double jeopardy revisited. *Journal of Marketing*, 54(July), 82–91.

Evans, F. B. (1961). The brand image myth. *Business Horizons*, 4(Fall), 19–28.

Frank, R. E., Massey, W. F. & Wind, Y. (1972). *Market Segmentation*. Prentice Hall.

Hubbard, R. & Armstrong, J. S. (1994). Replications and extensions in marketing: rarely published but quite contrary. *International Journal of Research in Marketing*, 11: 233–48.

Johnson, R. M. (1971). Market segmentation: A strategic management tool. *Journal of Marketing Research*, 8, 13–18.

Kraus, S. J. (1995). Attitudes and the prediction of behavior: a meta-analysis of the empirical literature. Personality and Social Psychology Bulletin, 21(1), 58–75.

McDonald, M. & Dunbar, I. (2004). *Market Segmentation: How to Do It, How to Profit From It*. Butterworth-Heinemann.

McPhee, W. N. (1963). *Formal Theories of Mass Behaviour*. New York: The Free Press of Glencoe.

Tolo, M., Riebe, E. et al. (2001). Explaining retail brand performance—comparing a model's predictions to informal prior knowledge. ANZMAC, Auckland New Zealand: Massey University.

Wedel, M. & Kamakura, W. A. (2012). *Market Segmentation: Conceptual and Methodological Foundations*, 8. Springer Science & Business Media.

Winchester, M. & Lees, G. (2016). An investigation of the success of targeting newspapers and efficiency of advertising in Ireland. *Journal of Promotion Management*, *22(5)*, 620–36.

Wright, M. & Klÿn, B. (1998). Environmental attitude—behaviour correlations in 21 countries. Journal of Empirical Generalisations in Marketing Science, 3, 42–60.

Notes

1 Farquhar, P. H. (1990). Managing brand equity. *Journal of Advertising Research*, *30*(4), RC7–RC12.

2 East, R. (1997). *Consumer Behaviour: Advances and Applications in Marketing.* London: Prentice Hall.

3 Sharp, B. (2017). *Marketing: Theory, Evidence, Practice.* Melbourne: Oxford University Press.

4 Holden, S. J. S. (1993). Understanding brand awareness: let me give you a c(l)ue! *Advances in Consumer Research*, *20*(1), 383–88; Hoyer, W. D. & Brown, S. P. (1990). Effects of brand awareness on choice for a common, repeat-purchase product. *Journal of Consumer Research*, *17*(2), 141–8.

5 Gardner, B.B. & Levy, S.J. (1955). The product and the brand. *Harvard Business Review*, March–April, 33–9.

6 Keller, K. L. (1993). Conceptualizing, measuring, and managing customer-based brand equity. *Journal of Marketing*, *57*(January), 5.

7 Dobni, D. & Zinkhan, G. M. (1990). In search of brand image: a foundation analysis. *Advances in Consumer Research*, *17*, 110–19; Bullmore, J. (1984). The Brand and Its Image Re-visited. *International Journal of Advertising*, *3*, 235–38.

8 Driesener, C. & Romaniuk, J. (2006). Comparing methods of brand image measurement. *International Journal of Market Research*, *48*(6), 681–98.

9 Bhat, S. & Reddy, S. K. (1998). Symbolic and functional positioning of brands. *Journal of Consumer Marketing*, *15*(1), 32.

10 Ries, A. & Trout, J. (2001). *Positioning: The Battle For Your Mind.* NY: McGraw Hill; DiMingo, E. (1988). The fine art of positioning. *The Journal of Business Strategy*, *9*(2), 34–8; Alpert, M.I. (1971). Identification of determinant attributes: a comparison of methods. *Journal of Marketing Research*, *8*(May), 184–91.

11 McDonald, M. & Dunbar, I. (1998). *Market Segmentation: How To Do It and How to Profit From It.* London: Macmillan Press Ltd.; Yankelovich, D. (1964). New criteria for market segmentation. *Harvard Business Review*, *42*, 83–90.

12 Smith, W. R. (1956). Product differentiation and market segmentation as alternative marketing strategies. *Journal of Marketing*, *20*(July), 3–8.

13 McDonald & Dunbar, op. cit.; Yankelovich, op. cit.

14 Aaker, D. A. & G. Shansby. (1982). Positioning your product. *Business Horizons*, *25*, 56–62.

15 Bock, T. & Uncles, M. (2004). A taxonomy of differences between consumers for market segmentation. *International Journal of Research in Marketing*, *19*(3), 215–24.

16 Cited in Lemon, K. N. & Mark, T. (2006). Customer lifetime value as the basis of customer segmentation. *Journal of Relationship Marketing*, *5*(2), 55–69.

17 Cited in Kazbare, L. et al. (2010). A-priori and post hoc segmentation in the design of healthy eating campaigns. *Journal of Marketing Communications*, *15*, 1–2.

18 Cited in Dibb, S. (1999). Criteria guiding segmentation implementation: Reviewing the evidence. *Journal of Strategic Marketing*, *7*(2), 107–29.

19 Cited in Rees, P. & H. Gardner (2005). Political marketing segmentation: The case of UK local government. *Journal of Nonprofit and Public Sector Marketing*, *14*(1/2), 169–84.

20 McDonald & Dunbar, op. cit.; Yankelovich, op. cit.; Yankelovich, D. & Meer, D. (2006). Rediscovering market segmentation. *Harvard Business Review*, February, 122–31.

21 Durgee, J. F. (1996). Translating values in product wants. *Journal of Advertising Research*, *36*(6), 90–100.

22 Whitlark, D. B. & Smith, S. M. (2001). Using correspondence analysis to map relationships. *Marketing Research*, *13*(3), 22–7.

23 Winchester, M. & Lees, G. (2013). Do radio stations in New Zealand target successfully? *Australasian Marketing Journal*, *21*, 52–8.

24 Uncles, M., Kennedy, R., Nenycz-Thiel, M., Singh, J. & Kwok, S. (2012). In 25 years, across 50 categories, user profiles for directly competing brands seldom differ. *Journal of Advertising Research*, June, 252–61.

25 Hammond, K., Ehrenberg, A. S. C. & Goodhardt, G. (1996). Market segmentation for competitive brands. *European Journal of Marketing*, *30*(12), 39–49; Uncles et al., op. cit.; Barwise, P. & Ehrenberg, A. (1988). *Television and Its Audience*. London: Sage; Winchester, M. & Lees 2013, op. cit.

26 Lees, G. & Winchester, M. (2014). Do customer profiles change over time? An investigation of the success of targeting consumers of Australia's top ten banks—2008 and 2011. *Journal of Financial Services Marketing*, *1*, 4–16; Anesbury, Z., Winchester, M. & Kennedy, R. (forthcoming). Brand user profiles seldom change and seldom differ. *Marketing Letters*.

27 Barwise & Ehrenberg, op. cit.; Lees, G. & Wright, M. (2013). Does the duplication of viewing law apply to radio listening? *European Journal of Marketing*, *47*(3/4), 674–85; Sharp, op. cit.

28 Wright, M. (1996). The dubious assumptions of segmentation and targeting. *Management Decision*, *34*(1), 18–24; Sharp, B. (2010). *How Brands Grow*. Melbourne: Oxford University Press.

29 Romaniuk, J. & Sharp, B. (2000). Using known patterns in image data to determine brand positioning. *International Journal of Market Research*, *42*(2), 219–30.

30 Winchester, M. & Sharp, B. (2001). Arguments against brand positioning. Presentation for MRIA conference, https://mria-arim.ca/sites/default/uploads/files/BrandPositioning.pps

31 Bird, M. & Channon, C. (1969). Brand Usage, Brand Image, and Advertising Policy—Part I. *Admap*, 6, 27–46; Bird, M. & Channon, C. (1970). Further analysis of former users brand image deviations—Part II. *Admap*, January, 28–32; Bird, M., Channon C. & Ehrenberg, A. (1970). Brand image and brand usage. *Journal of Marketing Research*, *7*(3), 307–14; 1 Bird, M. & Ehrenberg, A. S. C. (1970). Consumer attitudes and brand usage. *Journal of the Market Research Society*, *12*(4), 233–47; Riquier, C. & Sharp, B. (1997). Image Measurement and the Problem of Usage Bias. 26th EMAC Conference, Warwick Business School, U.K.: The University of Warwick; Winchester, M., Romaniuk, J. & Bogomolova, S. (2008). Positive and negative brand beliefs and brand defection/uptake. *European Journal of Marketing*, *42*(5/6), 553–70.

32 Nedungadi, P. & Hutchinson, J. W. (1985). The prototypicality of brands: Relationships with brand awareness, preference and usage. *Advances in Consumer Research*, *12*(1), 498–503.

33 Romaniuk & Sharp, op. cit.

34 Dall'Olmo Riley, F., Ehrenberg, A. S. C., Castleberry, S., Barwise, P. & Barnard, N. (1997). The variability of attitudinal repeat-rates. *International Journal of Research in Marketing*, 14(5): 437–50.

35 Ries & Trout, op. cit.

36 Hammond et al., op. cit.

37 Romaniuk, J. (2001). Brand positioning in financial services: A longitudinal test to find the best brand position. *Journal of Financial Services Marketing*, *6*(2), 111–21; Romaniuk & Sharp, op. cit.

38 Alba, J. W. & Chattopadhyay, A. (1986). Salience effects in brand recall. *Journal of Marketing Research*, *23*(4), 363–69; Ehrenberg, A., Barnard, N. & Scriven, J. (1997). Differentiation or salience. *Journal of Advertising Research*, *1*(November), 7–14; Miller, S. & Berry, L. (1998). brand salience versus brand image: two theories of advertising effectiveness. *Journal of Advertising Research*, *38*(5), 77–83; Romaniuk, J. (2003). Brand attributes—distribution outlets in the mind. *Journal of Marketing Communications*, *9*(June), 73–92.

39 Romaniuk 2001, op. cit.; Sharp 2010, op. cit.; Romaniuk & Sharp 2016, op. cit.

40 Vaughn, R. (1986). How advertising works: A planning model revisited. *Journal of advertising research*, *26*(1), 57–66.

41 ibid.

42 Johar, J. S. & Sirgy, M. J. (1991). Value-expressive versus utilitarian advertising appeals: When and why to use which appeal. *Journal of Advertising*, *20*(3), 23–33.

43 ibid.

44 Toncar, M. F. (2001). The use of humour in television advertising: Revisiting the US-UK comparison. *International Journal of Advertising*, *20*(4), 521–39.

45 ibid.

46 Zimmerman, A. & Dahlberg, J. (2008). The sexual objectification of women in advertising: A contemporary cultural perspective. *Journal of Advertising Research*, *48*(1), 71–9.

47 Wallace, W. T. (1991). Jingles in advertisements: can they improve recall? *Advances in Consumer Research*, *18*, 239–42.

48 Branthwaite, A. & Ware, R. (1997). Music in advertising. 50th ESOMAR Congress. Edinburgh.

49 ibid.; Kellaris, J. J., Cox, A. D. & Cox, D. (1993). The effect of background music on ad processing: A contingency explanation. *Journal of Marketing*, *57*(October), 114–25.

50 Romaniuk, J., Nenycz-Thiel, M., Hartnett, N. & Corsi, A. (2010). Developing memory structures for brand identity elements in packaged goods markets. Australian & NZ Marketing Academy Conference Proceedings, December 2010, Christchurch, NZ. 1–8. http://researchoutputs.unisa.edu.au/1959.8/119230

51 Veranica, (2009). BMW works to clean up diesel's rep. *Wall St Journal*, 8 January.

52 Cruipi, A. (2009). BMW pumps diesel in a big way. *Adweek*.

CHAPTER 5

Advertising

Peter Ling

Rolex brand fame

Almost everyone was talking about the Rolex 'Celebrating Cinema' 60-second commercial that ran at the 89th Academy Awards in February 2017. The film showed memorable movie clips of actors who had worn Rolex watches in movies over the decades—Marlon Brando, Charles Bronson, Gabriel Bryne, Jim Carrey, Benecio Del Toro, Fay Dunaway, Harrison Ford, Dustin Hoffman, Dennis Hopper, Terence Howard, Paul Newman, Nick Nolte, David Oyelowo, Bill Paxton, Guy Pearce, Peter Sellers, Jack Swigert and Owen Wilson. The tagline at the end was: 'It doesn't just tell time. It tells history'.[1]

The film was possible because Rolex, being a new sponsor of the 89th Academy Awards, could access the library of the Academy of Motion Picture Arts and Sciences.[2] Rolex had also produced another commercial featuring filmmaker James Cameron, who spoke about details that go into producing great movies.[3]

Cameron had also been featured in the campaign 'Every Rolex tells a story'. Other celebrities who had appeared individually in the campaign included tennis legend Roger Federer, golfer Lydia Ko, show jumping champion Steve Guerdat, alpine ski racer Lindsey Vonn, Formula 1 champion Sir Jackie Stewart, singer Michael Bublé and marine biologist Sylvia Earle.[4]

Rolex has associated with celebrities who excel in exploration, science, sports and arts, aligning with the Rolex philosophy of perfection in watchmaking. In one 1927 advertisement, Rolex featured Mercedes Gleitze, a British swimmer whose Rolex waterproof watch survived the 10-hour swim across the British Channel. The advertisement also included a direct response sales promotion blurb: 'Send for this coloured brochure, it's FREE!' (See Figure 5.1).

In 1930, Rolex advertised British racecar driver Malcolm Campbell, whose Rolex Oyster withstood 12 hours of intense vibration when he broke the world speed record. In 1953, Rolex honoured the feat of Sir Edmund Hillary and Tenzing Norgay when they conquered the

Figure 5.1 Rolex advertising in 1927

Source: www.mashable.com/2014/04/17/rolex-marketing-strategy/#rORXax.M6Pqi.

summit of Mount Everest. In 1960, oceanographer Jacques Piccard testified that the Oyster Watch was still accurate at 6.8 miles deep in the ocean.[5]

Arts-conscious Rolex has partnered, sponsored or presented various events like the Vienna Philharmonic New Year Concert and Summer Night Concert; the Salzburg Festival and its Whitsun Festival; the International Architecture Exhibition La Biennale di Venezia; and the Rolex Mentor and Protégé Arts Initiative, where masters and young artists collaborate for a year.[6] Since 1976, the Rolex Award for Enterprise recognises pioneering work in exploration, environment and applied science and technology. There is also the Young Leaders section for applicants aged 18–30 years who improve lives or advance knowledge.[7]

Rolex has started using social media with its YouTube channel for adventurous documentaries, a Facebook website to tell stories about its watches and a Pinterest website to feature Rolex and various associations with exploration, arts, sports and science.[8] Building a successful Rolex brand through advertising in diverse forms (see Figure 5.2) has created a 'grey market' of non-authorised retailers who sell at discounted prices.[9] Rolex has addressed this problem with its retail advertising to drive shoppers to official retailers who would also run co-opt advertising in different locations.[10]

Figure 5.2 Building a successful Rolex brand

■ INTRODUCTION

Advertising is like a successful actor capable of playing diverse roles. Advertising can be entertaining or boring. Sometimes, advertising communicates humour, fun, fear and sex appeal. Sometimes advertising plays a cameo role, conveys a straight monologue or provides the voice-over for a commercial. At other times, advertising as an actor takes on a different look of shape, size, colour and makeup to attract attention. Also, advertising archives tell diverse stories of history, culture, fashion, music and symbols.

Indeed, advertising—like the actor—has unique control of the creative and timely delivery of words and expressions, albeit under the eyes of the director.

So what is advertising? Who advertises? What is the history of advertising? Which media categories attract global advertisers? How is advertising created? How effective is advertising? This chapter will attempt to answer these questions.

LEARNING OBJECTIVES

After reading this chapter you should be able to:

1. explain advertising
2. discuss the various sectors of advertising
3. discuss milestones in the history of advertising
4. discuss how advertising is created
5. discuss effective advertising from the perspectives of theories, best industry practices and key research studies.

What is advertising?

Advertising practitioners once described the advertising function in 1897 and 1904 as 'salesmanship in print'.[11] That was during the days of print advertising, but advertising has gone through eras of outdoor, radio, television and the internet. These days, we also read about advertising on Google, Facebook, LinkedIn, Twitter, YouTube, blogs and various online media.

However, there has been no consensus on an acceptable definition of advertising! These are some online definitions from the American Marketing Association and from academics who have attempted to define advertising for the digital era.

Oxford Dictionaries: The activity or profession of producing advertisements for commercial products or services.[12]

Oxford Reference: A communication that is paid for by an identified sponsor with the object of promoting ideas, goods, or services.[13]

American Marketing Association: The placement of announcements and persuasive messages in time or space purchased in any of the mass media by business firms, nonprofit organizations, government agencies, and individuals who seek to inform and/or persuade members of a particular target market or audience about their products, services, organizations, or ideas.[14]

Richards & Curran, 2002, Stage 1 synthesis of textbook definitions: Advertising is a paid nonpersonal communication from an identified sponsor, using mass media to persuade or influence an audience.[15]

Richards & Curran, 2002, Stage 2 definition after feedback from a panel of practitioners: Advertising is a paid, mediated form of communication from an identifiable source, designed to persuade the receiver to take some action, now or in the future.[16]

Dahlen & Rosengren, 2016, after involving academic and industry experts: Brand-initiated communication intent on impacting people.[17]

Several key terms are frequently mentioned in the definitions. Advertising is paid communication. It is about communicating information, ideas, goods, services and organisations. The purpose is to inform, persuade, influence or impact an audience.

Although the term 'identified' is mentioned several times, there are occasions when the advertiser does not identify itself—for example, some recruitment, 'Seeking Friends' and 'Lonely Heart' advertisements in classified advertisements simply display a post box number.

The term 'mass media' is mentioned twice, but may not be relevant to individuals, home-based businesses and small businesses that advertise only in non–mass community newspapers circulated in their suburbs.

The term 'non-personal' may not be relevant in the digital age when advertising engages more interactively with younger audiences; for example, consumers interacted with Burger King's 'Subservient Chicken' in 2004 and the submissive chicken character responded to any command typed on its subservientchicken.com website.[18]

The term 'commercial' is also not accurate because advertising could be placed by individuals, non-profit organisations, government ministries as well as business firms. When there was criticism on the 'brand-initiated' description, the researchers defended themselves by responding that the term was a convenient way to cover causes, organisations and people.

There was no mention of the unique nature of advertising as paid communication. Paying for the communication gives the advertiser creative control, within regulatory standards, of the content, presentation of the message, media selection, timing and frequency of communication. Hence, advertising is a paid form of advertiser-controlled communication to an audience in any medium.

Which definition is an accurate reflection of what is advertised, who advertises, where advertising appears, how the message is advertised and so on? The next section could provide some illumination.

Who advertises?

We may see more brand advertising, but there is advertising in various sectors. This section discusses advertising by individuals, home and small businesses, professional services, government, non-profit organisations, industry marketers and brand marketers.

Individuals

Individuals advertise to announce certain news through print or online classifieds advertisements. There could be birth, birthday, graduation, wedding, divorce, death, funeral and memorial notices. Some classifieds advertisements announce selling of cars or property; garage sales; selling or buying of second-hand goods; lost/found pets or things; and seeking job opportunities.[19] I have seen notices disowning family members!

Home and small businesses

Some businesses advertise through classifieds notices about job vacancies or former staff not authorised to sell services or collect payments; restaurants and entertainment; business opportunities; and trades and services.[20] Some classifieds promote escort services and massage parlours.[21]

Australian community newspapers encourage trades and services to advertise in weekly distributed newspapers, offering categories such as air conditioning and refrigeration; bathroom renovations and kitchens; blinds, shutters and curtains; bricklayer; cabinet maker; carpet cleaning, and so on.[22]

While community newspapers also offer online classifieds, some small businesses take advantage of Google **AdWords** to advertise locally or globally, paying only when a customer clicks on the advertisement.[23]

Professional services

You may have referred to the Yellow Pages, magazines and newspapers for advertisements on professionals such as accountants, architects, dentists, doctors, engineers, lawyers, management consultants, optometrists and tax consultants.[24] Some professional services place advertising notices of bankruptcies, creditors or partnership dissolution, Sheriff sales, unclaimed money, and so on.[25] Other professional services advertise to invite the public to buy shares in initial public offerings (or IPOs).[26] There is now more advertising by professional services such as management consultancy firms who leverage their data and digital knowhow to attract more customers.[27]

Government

Governments in different countries do spend a sizeable size of money on advertising, whether on recruitment, tenders, public services, elections or innovation initiatives. For example, the Australian government has spent A$100–200 million during different budget years on its Senate voting system, asylum issues, defence force recruitment, trade agreements, advertising on domestic violence, anti-smoking and drug use.[28]

Non-profit organisations

Besides government departments, non-profit organisations sometimes run **public service advertising** to influence public behaviour and attitude on social issues.[29] Many non-profit organisations exist globally, such as United Nations International Children's Emergency Fund (UNICEF), American Red Cross and World Wildlife Fund.[30] Actor Liam Neeson and footballer David Beckham have appeared in advertising to end violence against children.[31]

The Ad Council in the US has been running public service campaigns since 1941 when it sold the idea of war bonds during the Second World War. Since then, the Ad Council has advertised security of war information, women in war jobs, wildfire prevention, American Red Cross, polio, pollution, Peace Corps, United Negro College Fund, crime prevention, drunk driving prevention, safety belt education, AIDS prevention, domestic violence, adoption from foster care, autism awareness, children's oral health, college access, foreclosure prevention assistance, gay and lesbian bullying prevention, high school equivalency-free adult education classes, emergency preparedness and veterans' mental health.[32]

In Australia, there are campaigns to encourage breast screening, bowel cancer screening, quitting smoking, young women participating in sport, stopping of violence against women, smart travel overseas, defence jobs and awareness of border protection measures.[33] Encouraging the public to quit or reduce smoking is one form of **demarketing** to decrease demand.[34]

In 2014, the International Advertising Association also launched a global public service advertising campaign, 'The Case for Advertising', to educate governments and consumers on marketing communication's contribution to economies. Several messages were communicated. First, advertising creates awareness, market demand and hence jobs. Second, advertising gives consumers the right to choose suitable brands. Third, advertising helps to fund the news brought to consumers. Fourth, advertising sponsorship of concerts, musicians and artists increases entertainment options while reducing costs. Fifth, advertising publicises better product options and motivates manufacturing innovation.[35]

Acknowledging that public service advertising is a separate category that needs to be judged differently from 'brand-led work', the Cannes Lions International Festival of Creativity has a Grand Prix for Good Awards to recognise creativity for appeals, charities, donations, equality and health messages, foundations, funds, not-for-profit art facilities, not-for-profit associations and unions, and state education.[36]

IMC IN ACTION: LONG-RUNNING PUBLIC SERVICE CAMPAIGN

Sid the Seagull appeared on Australian television screens in the summer of 1981 singing to deliver a simple message of 'Slip, Slop, Slap' to prevent skin cancer: Slip on a shirt, slop on sunscreen and slap on a hat.[37]

Melanoma skin cancer has always been a problem in Australia because of the culture of enjoying surf, sand and sun. Instead of a hard-sell serious approach, the light-hearted approach made the campaign memorable. The campaign evolved into the SunSmart program in 1988 to target various outdoor sports and audiences, including schools, kindergartens and community groups. Then, in 2005, Sid the Seagull added to 'Slip, Slop, Slap' by asking audiences to Seek shade and Slide on a pair of sunglasses.[38]

The campaign has been effective. Melanoma rates among young people dropped by 5 per cent yearly between the 1990s and 2010. However, Queensland still has the highest melanoma rate globally.[39]

The SunSmart campaign has continued to reduce cancer rates among young Australians—from 25 per 100 000 in 1996, to 14 per 100 000 in 2010 and 9.4 per 100 000 in 2016.[40]

The message has been expanded to 'Slip, Slop, Slap, Seek and Slide'.[41] See Figures 5.3 and 5.4 for the original 1981 campaign and the 2017 campaign respectively.

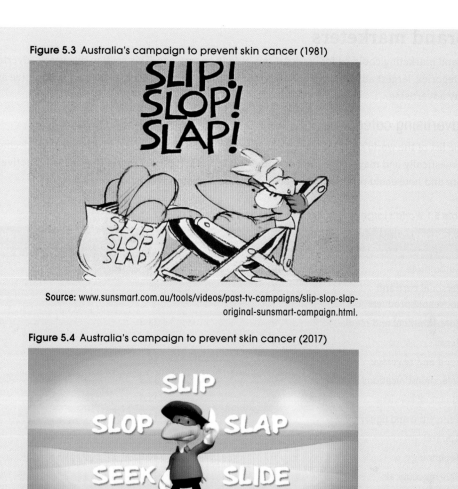

Figure 5.3 Australia's campaign to prevent skin cancer (1981)

Source: www.sunsmart.com.au/tools/videos/past-tv-campaigns/slip-slop-slap-original-sunsmart-campaign.html.

Figure 5.4 Australia's campaign to prevent skin cancer (2017)

Source: www.sunsmart.com.au/tools/videos/current-tv-campaigns/slip-slop-slap-seek-slide-sid-seagull.html.

Industry marketers

Industries also advertise without a specific brand identified in the message. Meat & Livestock Australia has been running campaigns to promote consumption of beef and lamb.[42] Australian Pork Limited, representing pork producers, has promoted bacon and ham.[43] There is also a 'Love that avocado feeling' campaign to attract consumers.[44] There used to be a 'What, no potato?' advertising campaign in Australia.[45] In the US, the 'Got Milk?' campaign ran for 20 years![46] Now even the television industry is advertising itself to persuade marketers to use television rather than Facebook and Google.[47]

Brand marketers

Brand marketing could be for corporations, goods or services. This section discusses advertising by categories, largest advertisers and other brand communication such as apology, corrective and April Fools' Day advertising.

Advertising categories

The list of the world's largest advertisers may surprise you as we often see retail advertisements domestically and may not be aware of other categories. Table 5.1 shows that the 'automotive' and 'personal care and household products' categories have the highest advertising shares.[48]

Table 5.1 World's largest advertisers by category, 2015

CATEGORY	NO. OF COMPANIES	2015 TOTAL WORLDWIDE ADVERTISING SPENDING (US$ BILLION)	SHARE OF TOP 100% SPENDING
Automotive	16	47	19.5
Personal care and household products	12	45.7	19.0
Entertainment and media	9	23.3	9.7
Retail	14	21.0	8.7
Food and beverage	9	18.5	7.7
Telecommunications	8	15.9	6.6
Financial services	7	13.5	5.6
Beer, wine and liquor	5	12.2	5.1
Apparel	4	11.3	4.7
Technology	6	10.9	4.5
Pharmaceuticals	6	10.6	4.4
Restaurants	2	5.5	2.3
Travel	2	5.1	2.1
Top 100	100	240.5	100

Source: adage.com/article/advertising/world-s-largest-advertisers/306983.

However, if you divide the category spending by the number of advertisers, you get a different picture for the average spending per advertiser in each category. The personal care and household products category spends an average US$3.8 billion on advertising, followed by automotive, apparel, restaurants, and entertainment and media. See Table 5.2.

The advertisers in the Top 100 categories are business-to-consumer (B2C) marketers of consumer products, which include fast-moving consumer goods (FMCG); convenience services like entertainment and media; shopping products like appliances, cars, furniture and television; specialty or luxury products like Rolex watches; and unsought services like life insurance. While marketers of industrial products advertise in trade and business publications, their advertising budgets are small compared to the Top 100 advertisers because these business-to-business (B2B) marketers sell to smaller groups of business buyers who purchase raw or manufactured materials; capital items like installations and accessory equipment; and operating supplies and repair or maintenance services.[49]

Table 5.2 Average advertising spend per category, 2015

CATEGORY	AVERAGE SPENDING PER ADVERTISER (US$ BILLION)
Personal care and household products	3.8
Automotive	2.9
Apparel	2.83
Restaurants	2.75
Entertainment and media	2.6
Travel	2.55
Beer, wine and liquor	2.44
Food and beverage	2.0
Telecommunications	1.99
Financial services	1.9
Technology	1.8
Pharmaceuticals	1.77
Retail	1.5

Source: adage.com/article/advertising/world-s-largest-advertisers/306983.

Largest advertisers

Based on the average spending per advertiser in each product category, it is not surprising to find personal care and household products companies occupying the top 3 for world's largest advertisers.[50] See Table 5.3.

Table 5.3 World's five largest advertisers, 2015

RANK	COMPANY	HEADQUARTERS	2015 TOTAL WORLDWIDE ADVERTISING SPENDING (US$ BILLION)
1	Procter & Gamble Co.	US	10.4
2	Unilever	Netherlands/UK	8.9
3	L'Oréal	France	8.2
4	Volkswagen	Germany	6.6
5	Comcast Corp.	US	5.9

Source: http://adage.com/article/advertising/world-s-largest-advertisers/306983/

Procter & Gamble (P&G) advertises its top brands, such as Gillette, Oral-B, Olay, Old Spice, Pampers, Pantene Pro-V and Tampax.[51] Unilever promotes its brands, such as Axe, Dove, Jif, Lipton, Lux, Magnum, Rexona and Sunsilk.[52] L'Oréal has Garnier, Lancôme, Giorgio Armani, Maybelline New York, Ralph Lauren and The Body Shop.[53]

Although there is no clear correlation between advertising spending and winning creative effectiveness awards, somehow Unilever and P&G ranked among the top 2 marketers from 2011 to 2017 in the Effie Effectiveness Index, which analyses data of winners and finalists from 40 Effie awards competitions worldwide.[54]

Other brand communication

While not indicated in the data, advertising budgets do cover brand, corporate, PR, sales promotion, sponsored events, sponsored television shows, movie product placements, direct marketing and special projects. Three types of advertising are worth noting here as these appear from time to time in advertising media: an **apology advertisement**, **corrective advertising** and April Fools' Day pranks.

Apology advertisements

You may have seen the occasional 'Apology' advertisements from local or national retailers about pricing errors. Sometimes, 'Apology' advertisements in one country are picked up by news media globally. Chipotle advertised in 61 US newspapers to apologise when 140 customers fell ill after eating at its burrito chain.[55] Samsung had full-page advertisements in US newspapers apologising for its Note 7 overheating defects and product recall.[56] Deutsche Bank AG ran full-page advertisements in the German media to apologise for company losses due to some employees' misconduct.[57] Volkswagen also ran full-page text-only advertisements in 30 US newspapers to apologise for its 2.0L VW diesel emissions issue.[58] See Figure 5.5 for Volkswagen's apology advertisement.

Figure 5.5 Volkswagen's apology advertisement

Source: www.mashable.com/2015/11/17/volkswagen-ad/#uTkMDOfXYuqx.

Corrective advertising

Sometimes, advertisers are compelled by government authorities to invest in some corrective advertising to rectify misleading or false competitive claims. Warner-Lambert had to run corrective advertising in 1977 when the US Federal Trade Commission (FTC) found false claims that Listerine cured colds. Listerine had to run a US$10 million advertising campaign specifically stating that 'Listerine will not help prevent colds or sore throats or lessen their severity'. In 1999, Novartis had to spend US$8 million over a year to state that 'Although Doan's is an effective pain reliever, there is no evidence that Doan's is more effective than other pain relievers for back pain'.[59] See Chapter 11 for more examples of corrective advertising.

April Fools' Day pranks

Each year, some well-known brands run advertising that turns out to be an April Fools' Day prank. In 2017, prank advertising included Burger King introducing a Whopper Toothpaste; Lexus offering a Lane Valet car with the technology to shove slow drivers to another lane; Jim Beam Whiskey extending into Jim Beans; Snickers selling Knickers; and KFC offering sushi in New Zealand.[60] BBC has also run some spectacular prank videos, like showing spaghetti growing on trees in Switzerland and penguins flying in the Antarctic.[61]

In summary, advertising can be by individuals, home and small businesses, professional services, government, non-profit organisations, industry marketers and brand marketers. Most advertising budgets are on brand marketing, which communicates corporations, goods and services, as well as occasional apology, corrective and prank messages. The next section on the history of advertising provides more insights on advertising practices.

History of advertising

Advertising as a paid form of communication has a long history. This section provides a short overview of advertising's history from the early centuries, covering developments in the US, the UK, Europe, Japan and Australia and ending with advertising in a digital era.

Pre-seventeenth centuries

Early paid forms of communication included fliers, posters, trademarks and visual signs. From the mid 1440s, after Johannes Gutenberg introduced the printing press, advertisers used more posters and handbills. The first English advertisement appeared in 1625 to promote a book and every subsequent advertisement integrated with news content was identified as 'Advertisement'. Subsequently, advertising agents sprang up in Paris and London in 1630 and 1659 respectively.[62]

Eighteenth and nineteenth centuries

In the US, the first newspaper advertisement—for an Oyster Bay Long Island estate—appeared in 1704 in the *Boston News-Letter*.[63] In 1814, John Haddon & Co. established an advertising agency in London. Advertising also appeared on posters on buildings, but the *Metropolitan Police Act 1839* in the UK made it illegal to post advertising notices without the property owner's permission. Eventually, artistic posters were used for advertising in the UK, France, Germany and Italy in the 1880s.

In the US, Volney Palmer set up the first US advertising agency in Philadelphia in 1843; the *New York Herald* banned display advertising in 1846 to protect small businesses that could only afford small-space notices; and N. W. Ayer started an advertising agency in Philadelphia with the first media commission system.

In London, several advertising agencies started in the 1890s, including S. H. Benson in 1893. J. Walter Thompson became the first American agency to open a London office in 1899. In Japan, advertising agencies started in the 1880s and 1890s, among them Hakuhodo. The Association of American Advertisers was formed in 1899.[64]

In Sydney, Australia, European settlers set up commercial businesses and advertised in outdoor sites, street frontages, handbills, directories, public transport and press advertising. The *Sydney Gazette* offered advertising columns to commercial firms in 1803. With more avenues for advertising, more agents sold space to advertisers and more companies printed outdoor advertising posters. One such agent was FT Wimble & Company, which operated in the 1880s as a printing company and an advertising agency. Another agent, Thomas A. Miller, eventually set up the first full-service advertising agency in 1902.[65]

Twentieth century

1900–1920

Dentsu advertising started in Japan in 1901, while US advertising pioneers such as Claude Hopkins, John E. Kennedy and Albert Lasker used the **hard-sell** rational 'reason-why' approach in the 1900s. The '**soft-sell**' approach followed thereafter, with Walter Dill Scott's 1908 book *The psychology of advertising* advocating prestige, pleasure and integrity in advertising. Helen Lansdowne, a 'reason-why' pioneer, added sex appeal and romance in 1911 to advertise Woodbury facial soap—'A skin you love to touch'—in the *Ladies' Home Journal*. In 1917, the American Association of Advertising Agencies was formed with 111 charter member agencies.[66] This was also the decade when advertisers disguised their advertisements to look like editorials, leading to the term **advertorial**.[67]

1920s

Radio became a mass communication tool, with the Netherlands, Germany, France, the UK and the US among the pioneers. Sponsored radio shows such as *The Eveready Hour* and *The Lucky Strike Show* appeared. In 1928, Unilever formed Lintas (Lever International Advertising Services) as a house agency in the UK, the Netherlands and Germany.[68]

1930s

Global media publisher Advertising Age was launched in Chicago in 1930. Radio popularity also triggered the growth of US advertising agencies such as McCann Erickson and Leo Burnett. Advertisers became a serious part of sponsored sports events, and agencies wrote and produced popular entertainment radio programs to promote their clients' products.[69]

1940s

The first television spots appeared on NBC WNBT, featuring Bulova watches on 1 July 1941.[70] The War Advertising Council started public service advertising. Advertisers turned to television-sponsored programs like *The Gillette Cavalcade of Sports*, *Kraft TV Theatre* and *The Texaco Star Theater*. Radio quiz programs were also popular.[71]

1950s

Colour broadcasting was introduced in 1953. Motivational research led by Ernest Dichter tapped into consumers' hidden desires and helped to produce advertising metaphors like 'the Marlboro Man', 'the Maidenform woman' and 'the Hathaway shirt man'. Automobiles became the largest advertised category, ahead of packaged goods and cigarettes. Advertising agencies produced television shows such as *Hallmark Hall of Fame*, *Colgate Comedy Hour* and *Goodyear TV Playhouse*. **Alternate sponsorships** also became popular, with different television sponsors each week. For example, the *What's My Line?* program had Remington Rand business machines and Stopette deodorant sponsors in separate weeks. In 1957, Vance Packard's book *The hidden persuaders* attacked advertising for its mind-control manipulation.[72]

1960s

The Interpublic Group of Companies was the first advertising conglomerate to manage competing client accounts. The creative revolution combined art and commerce, leveraging the visual impact of television and popular posters. This decade was also known as the 'image/impression' era, with self-deprecating, irreverent and humorous advertising appeals, such as Doyle Dane Bernbach's campaigns for Volkswagen: 'Think Small', 'Ugly' and 'Lemon'. There were also memorable advertising spokescharacters such as the Pillsbury Doughboy, the Maytag repairman and Ronald McDonald.[73]

1970s

This was the 'positioning' era; for example, 7 UP's 'Uncola' campaign. Computer technology provided data analyses for accountable financial and marketing decision making. There were more agency mergers and acquisitions to expand agency conglomerates. Comparative advertising increased, together with greater monitoring from industry and government review boards. Listerine and Anacin ran corrective advertising to correct claims they had made.[74]

1980s

The Omnicom Group became the world's largest advertising company through BBDO, Doyle Dane Bernbach and Needham Harper Worldwide. Martin Sorrell from the WPP Group bought J. Walter Thompson and then the Ogilvy Group. Technology development led to cable television, including CNN, in 1980; video cassette recording; remote television controls; direct-response home shopping; 30-minute **infomercials** or television advertorials; and 15-second television commercials.[75]

1990s

The internet began in 1993 with five million online users. The digital platform led to online advertorials such as Hewlett-Packard's interactive advertorial in 1996.[76] Mass media became more sophisticated, leading to specialised consultants in interactive media and database marketing; small creative niche agencies; independent media companies of agency conglomerates such as MindShare from the WPP Group; integrated marketing communication services such as advertising, public relations, sales promotion, direct response and online marketing services; and computer-generated images for advertising content.[77] Social media developed with GeoCities, Blogger, Friends Reunited, Yahoo, AOL Instant Messenger and Google.[78]

Twenty-first century

The first decade of the 2000s saw more social media appearing on the internet, also described as the 'information superhighway', with the launch of Friendster, MySpace, LinkedIn, Facebook, YouTube, Digg, Bebo, Twitter, Beacon, Bing and Tumblr. Beginning in 2010, there was the launch of Buzz, Instagram, Ping, Pinterest and Google+.[79] The term '**native advertising**' surfaced in 2011 to refer to advertising that is 'native' to the digital environment or where the advertisement blends in with the online media form, such as sponsored posts on Twitter, LinkedIn and Facebook.[80]

China has its own 'Great Firewall' to block Western social media platforms like Google, Facebook, Instagram, Twitter and WhatsApp. Its popular social media platforms include WeChat, Weibao, QZone, Youku and even LinkedIn.[81] China's version of Google is Baidu, launched in 1999.[82]

Branded storytelling through websites and web videos, or **webisodes**, became popular, with more productions of 5-minute web series providing entertainment and communication.[83] For example, BMW of North America produced *The Hire*—a series of online mini-movies—in 2001, while American Express produced webisodes in 2004 featuring comedian Jerry Seinfeld and Superman.[84] Figure 5.6 shows the opening frame of an American Express webisode of Seinfeld and his adventures with Superman.

Figure 5.6 American Express and Superman webisode

Source: www.coloribus.com/adsarchive/tv-commercials/
american-express-card-superman-524555.

Digital marketing companies then planned and tracked viral videos; for example, Digital Media Communications for its client Virgin Mobile with videos featuring rapper Busta Rhymes and singer Christina Aguilera.[85] Publications began to track most-viewed branded viral videos, including music videos like Korean entertainer Psy's 'Gangnam Style'.[86]

The digital marketing era now offers advertisers many platforms to connect with consumers via broadband households, digital video recorders, online video, video on demand, portable digital music players and mobile phones.[87]

Indeed, advertising as an actor has evolved with storytelling through posters, print media, advertorials, radio sponsored shows, television advertising and sponsored programs, infomercials, webinars and digital platforms such as native advertising. The history of advertising has also witnessed dialogues on hard-sell, soft-sell, advertising metaphors, positioning, agency conglomerates, media buying companies and integrated marketing services. The next section explores how advertising is created.

Creating advertising

Advertising stories for various private, public and not-for-profit advertisers are now in diverse media, both traditional and digital. How do the advertising cast members conceive and tell the stories in various formats? Do creative teams consider whether to adopt the Strong theory concept of persuasion or the Weak theory option of reinforcement for advertising campaigns? Similarly, do they choose between a hard-sell or soft-sell approach to advertising? Do they use more of the right brain than the left brain to create brand stories and communicate them in memorable ways? Do they focus more on the big idea and not the execution, or vice versa? This section will address these questions.

Strong/Weak or hard/soft sell?

Since earlier chapters in the book have comprehensively discussed the Strong and Weak theories of advertising, it is sufficient to say that both theories exist during the life cycle of the brand. Therefore, this section looks at the often-used terms of hard-sell and soft-sell approaches in advertising.

Hard-sell advertising rationally sells the direct benefit of using the advertised product or service. Hard-selling messages include 'Colgate cleans your breath as it cleans your teeth' and 'M&M candies melt in your mouth, not in your hand'.[88]

Soft-sell advertising emotionally and indirectly creates positive feelings, impressions and associations for the advertised brand through humour, entertainment or warmth. Examples of soft-sell messages include 'Lemon' for a Volkswagen advertisement and 'We're No. 2, we try harder' for an Avis Rent a Car advertisement.[89]

Some advertisements have a blended yin and yang approach: for example, Leo Burnett's 'Marlboro Man' advertisement in 1955 combined the soft-sell approach of featuring a macho cowboy and the hard-sell slogan 'Delivers the goods on flavor'.[90]

Some advertisers run a soft-sell approach followed by a hard-sell push depending on the economy (or for other reasons); for example, Mercedes-Benz ran television commercials reflecting status and then switched to hard-sell advertising selling safety, reliability, durability and economy.[91] On the other hand, Rolex advertisements hard-sell the endurance of its watches and soft-sell the imagery associated with high-performance celebrities in swimming, racing and exploration; its Academy Awards film was soft-selling the Rolex association with celebrity actors.

Famous advertising men Rosser Reeves and David Ogilvy were known for their respective hard-sell rational 'claim school' or 'unique selling proposition' (USP) and soft-sell emotional 'image school' or 'story appeal' during the 1950s and 1960s. However, both men believed in research to create effective advertising as 'fuel' for marketers.[92]

Left brain-right brain or whole brain?

The creative process is a whole-brain approach and not a right-brain or left-brain option since the creative right brain and the analytic left brain are connected to collaboratively solve problems.[93] According to Ned Herrmann's whole-brain research, the brain is made up of four quadrants of facts, fantasies, forms and feelings.[94] His 'balanced' creative process has six steps: Interest (left and right brains), Preparation (left brain), Incubation (right brain), Illumination (right brain), Verification (left brain) and Application (left and right brains).[95]

Herrmann's whole-brain creative process is akin to the famous model of Preparation-Incubation-Illumination-Verification by Graham Wallas in 1926.[96] The Institute of Practitioners in Advertising (IPA), in describing the advertising creation process, also indirectly reflects the Wallas and the Herrmann models. The IPA process is: from brief to research; from research to plan; from plan to execution; and from execution to analysing campaign effectiveness.[97]

A study of 21 UK agency practitioners identified 24 advertising creative process stages which they synthesised into a seven-step model: task identification, agreement of task objectives, ideation, response, internal review validation, external review validation and decision.[98]

The stages corresponded with the five-stage model of creativity researcher Amabile: Problem, Preparation, Response Generation, Response Validation and Outcome.[99]

Hence, the advertising creativity process goes through an integrated 'triple phenomenon',[100] such as the artist-jester-sage personalities and the conscious-unconscious-preconscious mental interactions.[101] The investment theory of creativity also suggests that there is a confluence of motivation, thinking styles, intellectual abilities, personality, knowledge and environment. This theory also highlights the need to take risks to buy into unpopular ideas that may eventually be popular.[102]

Big idea or execution?

In 2015, American advertising publisher Adweek inaugurated its Creative 100 to recognise 'masters of the creative idea' who engage consumers with an 'irresistible force' through clever, entertaining and fascinating content. Among the honorees were Chief Creative Officers (CCOs) from famous advertising agencies such as BBSO, Wieden + Kennedy, Young & Rubicam, Grey, and Goodby, Silverstein & Partners.[103]

The terms 'idea' and 'execution' are often used in advertising creativity. The 'idea' is the thought conveyed in the advertising, while the 'execution' refers to the tangible production details.[104] Famous adman John O'Toole described the big idea as the fresh insight that creatively connects the strategic purpose, the brand benefit and consumer desire.[105] Leo Burnett's creative approach was to look for the inherent product drama that penetrates the consumer mind; hence he created memorable advertising icons such as The Marlboro Man, Jolly Green Giant, Tony the Tiger and Pillsbury Doughboy.[106]

Big ideas have several advantages. They resonate with audiences. They are game-changers. They have buzz value. They have universal value, transcending brand, cultural and geographic and human levels. They often emerge from research into consumers' actions, thinking and feeling.[107]

While research companies and consultants do provide human insights that lead to big ideas, account planners in advertising agencies have provided a formal planning process working with creatives and clients.[108]

Account planning as a separate department in an advertising agency started in the UK through Stephen King at JWT in 1964 and Stanley Pollitt at BMP in 1968. King integrated consumer research insights into creative effective advertising while Pollitt positioned planners as the consumers' 'voice' to enrich the development of advertising. Account planning now exists in advertising agencies as well as client marketing departments and firms specialising in design, direct marketing, media and PR.[109] The Account Planning Group (APG) is the 'Home for planners and strategists' with global members and its Creative Strategy Awards.[110]

The traditional process of planners working with creatives is evolving to meet the demands of the digital age, with some agencies having planners, creatives, designers and developers working as a team to delve into human nature and consumer needs.[111]

Great ideas can be executed or communicated in various ways.[112] For example, the idea for the 'Got Milk?' campaign emerged from focus group research when a participant commented that she thought about milk only when she ran out of it.[113] The idea was executed with a milky moustache mnemonic featuring various celebrities over a period of 20 years.[114]

Although the emphasis has often been on the creative idea first, some practitioners profess that the execution is more important. Advertising Hall of Fame honoree Joe Sedelmaier—who created the Wendy's fast-food restaurant commercial 'Where's the beef?'—said that there was 'very little' idea except for the brilliant casting of the sweet old lady asking repeatedly, 'Where's the beef?'.[115]

Creative strategy consultant Alan Wolk believes that the idea is more aligned to advertising in mass media when consumers have no direct product access. He wrote that execution is more important at retail outlets such as Gap, where its display or execution of mid-price clothes stands out competitively, and Starbucks, where its idea of serving upmarket coffee is saved by its premise design and coffee aroma. Based on his experience at the Hive Awards for the Unsung Heroes of the Internet, he found that many winning entries had user-experience executions. For example, TripIt.com's idea is about organising travel plans in one place, but its website executes the message with user-convenience design. Also, Ford Mustang's idea of consumers designing their cars was executed in a cool, fun and engaging way to enable social sharing of design creations. Ultimately, execution cannot be separated from the idea and must be intrinsically integrated into the process.[116]

See the IMC in Action for examples of how campaigns have been developed through the integration of research, the idea and the execution.

Always #LikeAGirl

P&G wanted its sanitary brand Always to be relevant to young girls and to associate the brand as a supporter from puberty onwards. Research provided an insight to empower young girls, whose confidence is at its lowest during puberty.

During a development session to explore how girls would be influenced, someone had written on a paper a derogatory expression, 'Like a girl'. That triggered the idea of turning an insulting expression 'Like a girl' into a positive statement of empowerment.

The execution was an experiment to show the social impact of 'like a girl', with a video capturing interpretations of the phrase. The video started a social conversation about the phrase, which often meant vanity and weakness. The campaign #LikeAGirl rallied girls and women to embrace the phrase in amazing, meaningful and powerful ways.

Figure 5.7 #LikeAGirl

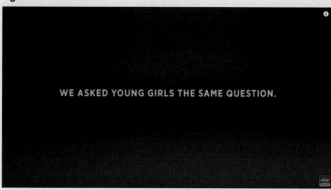

WE ASKED YOUNG GIRLS THE SAME QUESTION.

Source: www.youtube.com/watch?v=XjJQBjWYDTs.

The campaign attracted 85 million views on YouTube, changed perceptions of women and men towards the phrase, and increased brand equity by double digits. The campaign won numerous awards, including 'Creativity for Good'.[117] See the campaign via the source link in Figure 5.7.

Fearless Girl

State Street Global Advisors (SSGA) wanted to promote its SHE investment product by leveraging on research highlighting the need for more corporate women leaders. SSGA chose International Women's Day 2017 to deliver its message through the idea of a 'fearless girl' bravely facing off with Wall Street's Charging Bull icon.

The execution of the Fearless Girl idea took a lot of planning. She had to symbolise female empowerment despite her small size. She had to command a powerful presence in Wall Street. She had to create buzz for women everywhere. Using the same aesthetics and bronze material as the Charging Bull, Fearless Girl was designed as a bronze statue of a young, smiling, confident girl standing strong with chin high and hands on hips.

When Fearless Girl was launched, there was immediate social media buzz: more than one billion Twitter impressions in less than one day; 405 million Instagram impressions over six weeks; and awareness across 128 countries. The SHE fund jumped 384 per cent in trading volume within three days.[118] It reportedly gained more than US$7 million in free marketing through coverage on television and various media.[119] Fearless Girl won over the hearts of many Americans and visitors, who petitioned for the sculpture to be a permanent fixture in New York City.[120] See Figure 5.8 for the Fearless Girl campaign.

Figure 5.8 Fearless Girl

Source: https://www.youtube.com/watch?v=fADyZ2NL-xY.

Sweetie

Terre des Hommes [TDH] is a Swiss-based humanitarian organisation that works for children's rights and equitable development.[121] Amsterdam-based advertising agency Lemz worked with TDH to develop a digital social good advertising campaign that culminated in identifying 1000 paedophiles online, arrests and legal changes in several countries.

The problem was that male sexual predators seek young girls online to perform sexual acts via webcams. TDH wanted to mobilise police and politicians globally to address the problem. The research insight was that predators share identifiable information online. Wanting to go beyond online chats with a fake name, the idea was an online sting through a girl to get predators to solicit her sexually and commit a crime.

The girl was an authentic 3D Filipino girl called Sweetie. Animators, artists and production specialists created Sweetie over a year to ensure she would have the right expressions and movements on webcam. The campaign team advertised Sweetie for 10 weeks on global websites using a Filipino IP address with secure encryption.

While Sweetie interacted with online predators, the team gathered and cross-referenced the names, webcam footages and locations of 1000 predators across 71 countries. The team handed the results to Interpol, released the findings through a news conference in The Hague and live streaming, and shared online its special project documentary.

More than one billion people saw the Sweetie news. The Philippines investigated the problem and released hundreds of victims. Australia, the UK and the US jointly dismantled a network of more than 700 online predators and convicted several violators.[122] See Figure 5.9 for an image from the Sweetie campaign.

Figure 5.9 Sweetie

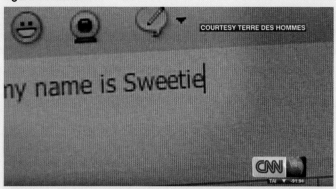

Source: www.youtube.com/watch?v=gYP2tlnr_YY.

IMC IN ACTION: SNICKERS—A BIG IDEA EXECUTED GLOBALLY

Snickers introduced its campaign 'You're not you when you're hungry' during Super Bowl 2010 and it became the number one advertisement on the USA Today's Super Bowl Ad Meter. The television commercial featured actress Betty White sluggishly trying to play football with team mates who were frustrated with her performance until she took a bite of a Snickers bar offered to her and turned into Mike, one of the regular guys. The campaign has since gone global across 80 countries with different executions.[123]

In the first year, global sales increased by nearly 16 per cent and market share jumped in 56 countries. The campaign has won various awards such as Cannes Lions, D&AD, Effies and the Institute of Practitioners in Advertising. Before the campaign started, Snickers was losing market share globally.

Snickers' company, Mars, needed a global creative strategy around a single idea that could be executed in various markets. Borrowing from Ehrenberg's marketing laws, Mars wanted a memorable idea that would increase brand fame, penetrate the market, attract more buyers, remind slag users and become the preferred brand.

Research uncovered an insight about male pack behaviour, where you have to maintain an ability to belong to a group. Connecting this insight to Snickers, the idea was that you are not yourself when you are hungry and that affects your belonging to your group. Hence, the expression was 'You're not you when you're hungry'.

The 30-second commercial featuring Betty White attracted 91 days of media coverage and was valued at about US$29 million—over 11 times more than the media investment. Betty White spread the Snickers brand fame when she appeared on television talk shows.

There was global buy-in to the idea with local market executions. Russia featured Russian ballerina Anastasia Volochkova in a basketball game. China featured Mr Bean as a fumbling Chinese fighter until he took a bite of Snickers offered to him. Australia had workmen acting 'out of sorts' until Snickers satisfied their hunger and also ran a 'Hungerithm' where 7-Eleven stores offered discounts on Snickers depending on the online mood of social postings. Puerto Rico had a DJ playing the wrong music genre because he was hungry. The UK used Twitter to showcase celebrities behaving out of character because of hunger.[124]

Various 'You're not you' commercials have appeared on the Super Bowl Commercials YouTube websites.[125] See Figure 5.10 for the Betty White campaign that started global executions around a single idea.

Figure 5.10 The Snickers campaign that started with Betty White

Source: www.youtube.com/watch?v=dbpFpjLVabA.

Advertising effectiveness

Some advertisers have expressed that half of advertising spending is wasted, possibly due to inferior product quality, non-rigorous pre-advertising testing, non-targeted media selection, inadequate measurement of advertising accountability and inability to create widespread brand fame.[126] This section reviews best industry practices and key research studies on advertising effectiveness.

Best industry practices

There are 'why' and 'how' lessons to learn from Advertising Age's selection of the Top 100 Campaigns of the 20th Century, the Top 15 Ad Campaigns of the Early 21st Century and the Cannes Creative Effectiveness Grand Prix winners since the inception of this award in 2011.

Top ad campaigns of the twentieth century

Advertising Age, the leading industry publication, had three criteria when it selected its Top 100 Campaigns of the 20th Century.[127] First, was the campaign a watershed changing advertising or popular culture? Second, did the campaign create a category or entrench the brand as number one in its category? Third, was the campaign unforgettable? Based on the three criteria, the number one campaign of the twentieth century was Volkswagen's 1959 'Think small' campaign, created by advertising agency Doyle Dane Bernbach (DDB).

The self-deprecating, disarming tone in the 'Think small' advertisement actually made the Volkswagen brand big in a US era of stylish large cars. See Figure 5.11 for the 'Think small' advertisement.

DDB was also the top agency for seven other Top 100 campaigns: 'We try harder' for Avis car rental; 'Share the fantasy' for Chanel; 'It's so simple' for Polaroid; 'You don't have to be Jewish to love Levy's Rye Bread'; 'Hey Mikey' for Life Cereal; 'The Gorilla' for American Tourister; and 'Daisy' for the Lyndon Johnson for President campaign.[128]

Top 100 Campaigns of the 20th Century featured a mix of emotional and rational appeals. Some campaigns used celebrities, metaphors, status, love, sex, religion, music, charm, candour, aspiration, humour, fear and consumer insecurities.[129] See Table 5.4 for a summary of the Top 10 campaigns from the list of 100 featured.[130]

Figure 5.11 Volkswagen's 'Think small' advertisement

Table 5.4 Ad Age's top 10 ad campaigns of the twentieth century

RANKING	CAMPAIGN	CLIENT	AGENCY	YEAR
1	'Think small'	Volkswagen	Doyle Dane Bernbach	1959
2	'The pause that refreshes'	Coca-Cola	D'Arcy Co	1929
3	'The Marlboro Man'	Marlboro	Leo Burnett Co	1955
4	'Just Do It'	Nike	Wieden & Kennedy	1988
5	'You deserve a break today'	McDonald's	Needham, Harper & Steers	1971
6	'A diamond is forever'	DeBeers	N. W. Ayer & Son	1948
7	'The Absolut Bottle'	Absolut Vodka	TBWA	1981
8	'Tastes great, less filling'	Miller Lite	McCann-Erickson Worldwide	1974
9	'Does she … or doesn't she?'	Clairol	Foote, Cone & Belding	1957
10	'We try harder'	Avis	Doyle Dane Bernbach	1963

Source: www.adage.com/article/special-report-the-advertising-century/ad-age-advertising-century-top-100-advertising-campaigns/140150.

Figure 5.12 A Dove 'Campaign for Real Beauty' advertisement

☐ grey?
☐ gorgeous?

Why can't more women feel glad to be grey?

campaignforrealbeauty.co.uk ⬥ | Dove

Top ad campaigns of the twenty-first century

Following their Top 100 Campaigns of the 20th Century, Advertising Age then selected their Top 15 Campaigns of the Early 21st Century in 2015. From a list of 50 nominees, industry judges voted and ranked the selections against the three criteria used for the Top 100 Campaigns of the 20th Century. The judges found the Top 15 broke the norm with a strong point of view.[131]

The top groundbreaking campaign was the Unilever Dove 'Campaign for Real Beauty', which changed the conversation around women's beauty by individuals, social media and news media. Since 2004, the Ogilvy-created campaign interacted with consumers, featuring real women and asking consumers whether they were fat or fit, grey or gorgeous and wrinkled or wonderful. See Figure 5.12 for one of the Dove advertisements.

The other memorable campaigns included P&G's Old Spice 'The man your man could smell like', Burger King's 'Subservient Chicken', Apple's 'Get a Mac' and P&G's 'Thank you, Mom'. See Table 5.5 for an extract of the Top 10 campaigns from the list of 15.[132]

Table 5.5 Ad Age's top 10 ad campaigns of the twenty-first century

RANKING	CLIENT CAMPAIGN & AGENCY	IDEA	AGENCY
1	Unilever Dove 'Campaign for Real Beauty'	Redefining beauty to make women feel good about themselves	Ogilvy & Mather
2	Nike+ Fuelband	Wearable calorie-burning tracker, that links to Apple devices, for fitness users who are competitive self-improvers	R/GA New York
3	BMW Films *The Hire*	Web-based series of short films about a nameless hired transporter	Fallon Worldwide
4	Procter & Gamble Old Spice repositioning	'The man your man could smell like'	Wieden & Kennedy
5	Red Bull Stratos project	'The mission to the edge of space'	Anomaly Production
6	Burger King 'Subservient Chicken'	You can order chicken sandwich any way—and command the 'submissive' chicken character to do anything	Crispin Porter & Bogusky (CP&B)
7	American Express 'Small Business Saturday'	Create a day to celebrate small business	Crispin Porter & Bogusky (CP&B)

RANKING	CLIENT CAMPAIGN & AGENCY	IDEA	AGENCY
8	Apple 'Get a Mac'	Mac vs PC 'friends' metaphor and their playful banter about Macs and PCs	TBWA/Chiat/Day
9	Procter & Gamble 'Thank you, Mom'	Honouring moms, the unsung heroes behind Olympians	Wieden & Kennedy
10	American Legacy (national public health foundation anti-smoking campaign)	'Truth'—an interactive subversive campaign against the lies of big tobacco companies via public stunts, advertising and non-conventional media channels.	Crispin Porter & Bogusky (CP&B) + Arnold Worldwide

Source: Ad Age. (2015). Top ad campaigns of the 21st century: http://adage.com/lp/top15/#winners.

What are the common advertising appeals in these top campaigns of the twenty-first century? There is emotional appeal in one form or another, such as in the Unilever and P&G campaigns, which started cultural conversations around beauty and manly scents. There are challenge, action, adventure and entertainment in the campaigns for Nike, BMW and Red Bull. The Dove, Old Spice, Burger King, American Express and American Legacy campaigns initiated engaging interactions with consumers and

the community. Short films are used to tell stories, as in the BMW films and the Nike+ Fuelband. While there is humour and rationale behind the 'Get a Mac' campaign, there is also the confrontation and factual communication that 1200 people die daily from tobacco in American Legacy's 'Body Bags' advertising (see Figure 5.13). You can view the top ad campaigns of the twenty-first century on YouTube.[133]

Figure 5.13 American Legacy's 'Body Bags' advertising

Source: www.youtube.com/watch?v=SOfJyeW3v4o.

Cannes Creative Effectiveness Grand Prix winners

The Cannes Festival of Creativity, the 'Oscars' of advertising awards, has been running its Cannes Lions awards since 1954.[134] It introduced a Creative Effectiveness category in 2011 to recognise creative campaigns that have impacted on brand equity, consumer behaviour and sales. The Creative Effectiveness category is only open to shortlisted or Lion winners from the previous year and entries are judged on strategy (25 per cent), idea (25 per cent) and results (50 per cent) to determine the Grand Prix winner.[135]

Entrants need to submit a 400-word summary and a 3000-word report covering objectives and strategy for the creative work; a description of the creative work; the effect of the creative work in the market; factors that may have impacted campaign effectiveness; the client's commercial gain from the campaign; and a reflection on how the campaign helps the understanding of effective creativity.[136]

The Grand Prix winners have come from London (twice), Amsterdam, Melbourne, Sweden and the US. See Table 5.6 for a summary of the winners.

Table 5.6 Cannes Lions Creative Effectiveness Winners, 2011–2017

YEAR	CLIENT/AGENCY	CAMPAIGN/IDEA	RESULTS
2011	PepsiCo UK, Abbott Mead Vickers BBDO London	Walkers Crisp potato chips: 'Walkers can make any sandwich more exciting, even a small English town called Sandwich'. The idea was executed through surprising celebrity events; for example, actress Pamela Anderson of *Baywatch* fame was a barmaid for a day.[137]	Sleepy Sandwich village became 'the most exciting place in Britain'. Revenue growth of 26 per cent exceeded the 15 per cent target.[138]
2012	Unilever, BBH London	Axe Excite deodorant: 'Even angels will fall'. Sexy angels fall from heaven and rip off their halos and wings for an irresistible Axe-user man.[139]	Maintained price premium and grew volume sales by about 5 per cent.[140]
2013	Heineken International, Wieden+Kennedy Amsterdam	'Surprising demonstrations of legendary behaviour' by aspiring Men of the World	Enhanced premium brand image, volume share and value share.[141]
2014	Melbourne V/Line, McCann Melbourne	A new product, 'The Guilt Trip', a pre-paid ticket bought by regional folks for loved ones in the city to visit regional Victoria.[142]	Off-peak sales increased 15 per cent against a 5 per cent target.
2015	Volvo Trucks Sweden, Forsman & Bodenfors	'Live test films': Extreme product tests in live set-up with unknown outcome.[143]	Sales increased 23 per cent for this B2B campaign.[144]
2016	John Lewis UK retailer, Adam&EveDDB London	'Give someone the Christmas they've been dreaming of': Monty the Penguin gets a penguin toy, Mabel.[145]	Single week sales of £179 million was the first time in 150-year history.[146]
2017	Art Institute of Chicago, Leo Burnett Chicago	'Van Gogh's Bedrooms': Rent a Van Gogh replica bedroom on Airbnb for US$10 a night to coincide with 12-day exhibition of Van Gogh bedroom paintings created in 1888 and 1889.	Attendance up 54 per cent, largest in 15 years; 500 million media impressions; US$6 million in earned media.[147]

The Cannes Creative Effectiveness winners had big ideas and emotional appeals. Associating the English town of Sandwich with the Walkers Crisp campaign to combine its chips with sandwiches. Exaggerating the Axe effect on female angels and the Heineken men's legendary behaviour. Touching on guilt to have city-based children returning to visit parents in their regional homes. Drawing on childhood imagination to buy a Mabel penguin for love-stuffed Monty. Tapping into masculine emotions in Volvo's B2B truck campaign. Re-engaging with Chicagoans who had stayed away from art exhibitions by inviting them to 'Let Yourself In' and experience Van Gogh's troubled world.

So, what do we learn from the Advertising Age selections of top campaigns for the twentieth and twenty-first centuries as well as the Cannes Lions Creative Effectiveness winners? There were big ideas persuasively executed emotionally in one form or another as well as some campaigns with rational appeals, such as Apple's 'Get a Mac' campaign, American Legacy's 'Body Bags' advertising and the $10-a-night stay in a Van Gogh bedroom. Advertising as an actor conveyed ideas in an emotionally engaging soft-sell manner and a humorously or forcefully hard-sell pitch.

Advertising effectiveness research

Five major research studies have analysed more than 3000 winning cases, primarily from the IPA Effectiveness Awards, Effie Awards and Cannes Lions Awards.

Binet & Field, 2007

The first research study by Binet & Field in 2007 analysed 880 case studies from the IPA Effectiveness Awards, known for its rigorous criteria, written paper submission, answers to a compulsory questionnaire and judging panel of academics and industry practitioners. The research analysed five measures of effectiveness and accountability—namely, accountability success rate from effectiveness prizes; effectiveness success rate from reported business effects like penetration, sales, share gain and profit; reported intermediate effects of brand awareness, brand image and brand equity or brand health; market share gain; and validated return on investment.

The study concluded that emotional advertising outscored rational appeals in many measures: penetration, sales, loyalty, market share and profit. The researchers also identified a profitable 'holy trinity' of brand differentiation, quality perceptions and brand fame, where the brand is talked about and becomes famous. For example, Marks & Spencer suffered from profit and image issues but created an emotional glamorous lifestyle campaign with celebrity models such as Twiggy to make the retailer famous, distinctive and reputable, thereby doubling profits. Hence, fame-building campaigns are powerful for building credible authority perceptions and category leadership.[148]

Reinartz & Saffert, 2005–2010

The researchers examined 437 television campaigns for 90 highly competitive and highly advertised fast-moving consumer goods brands in Germany. They measured perceived creativity and sales across five creativity dimensions of originality, flexibility, elaboration, synthesis and artistic value. The research methodology involved a trained panel of consumers rating each dimension on a 1 to 7 scale. The analysis showed that only 11 campaigns, five of them for colas, scored above 5 and that combinations of originality-artistic value and originality-elaboration were the most effective pairings while flexibility-elaboration and flexibility-artistic value were the least effective on sales contributions. The researchers suggested that campaigns with a higher creativity index would be more memorable and effective even with lower media budgets.[149]

Field, 2010–2011

Independent consultant Peter Field undertook research commissioned by the Institute of Practitioners in Advertising (IPA) and Thinkbox, a UK marketing organisation for commercial television, to analyse the link between creativity and effectiveness by examining the IPA Effectiveness Databank and the Gunn Report database of campaigns that had won creativity awards. In 2010, Field analysed 257 campaigns between 1998 and 2008 and then in 2011 examined 435 campaigns for the period 1994–2010. He analysed variables such as market share, sales, profit and loyalty. He reported that many creativity-awarded campaigns, especially emotionally driven television campaigns that had a lower share of media voice, were a dozen times more effective at increasing market shares of brands.[150]

Twose & Jones, 2011

These researchers analysed 251 advertisements from 92 brands that were winners in the IPA Effectiveness, Effie and Cannes Lions Awards between 1996 and 2011. The research revealed attributes of long-term brand building and short-term sales-oriented advertising. Memorable, effective brand-building advertising campaigns were more emotionally involving and enjoyable, conveying emotions such as affection, contentment, excitement, attraction, aspiration, pride or guilt. Effective brand-building campaigns also had emotionally engaging creative ideas or branding cues: for example, the Andrex Puppy, the Marlboro Cowboy and the Hovis bread delivery boy. Effective short-term persuasive advertising communicated relevant and credible news.[151]

Binet & Field, 2013

Binet & Field, described by a practitioner as 'Godfathers of advertising effectiveness',[152] followed up on their IPA research by focusing on 996 advertising effectiveness cases covering 700 brands and 83 product categories over 30 years. They continued recommending brand fame but also suggested balancing variables. First, communicate to a narrower base of consumers to enjoy earlier effects and smaller paybacks in the short term as well as a broader segment of immediate-cum-long-term prospects that would provide slower effects but big paybacks in the long term.[153]

Second, appeal to the 'head and heart' with rational product–price messages to influence short-term behavioural responses and emotional brand associations to reinforce long-term brand preferences. This means scheduling multiple advertising exposures to integrate rational sales-activation messaging to boost short-term purchases and emotional priming to grow a stronger brand for long-term volume increase. Binet considered emotional priming as marketing's 'lethal force' and 'emotional halos' to influence brand fame, brand preference, price elasticity and profit.[154]

Third, budget for sustained **share of voice** and **share of mind** advertising exposures, with about 40 per cent of budget for short-term activation channels through online, direct marketing and newspaper advertising as well as 60 per cent of spending on brand-building channels such as television, newspaper, online, outdoor, radio and cinema advertising.

Fourth, have a balanced scorecard to measure short-term sales from explicit persuasive communication and long-term business performance, price elasticity, econometrics and brand equity from implicit emotional responses and fame metrics.

Analysing the five advertising effectiveness research studies, there is consensus that creative, emotional and memorable advertising can contribute effectively to sales. Although some practitioners believe that an emotional approach should have priority to change attitude and behaviour,[155] an integrated approach is required, with short-term persuasive advertising and long-term emotional brand-building campaigns.

Overall, this section on advertising effectiveness from the perspectives of best practices and research studies reveals the need for a balanced approach. Both the Strong theory and Weak theory of advertising exist throughout the brand life cycle. Both hard-sell and soft-advertising co-exist depending on short-term and long-term goals. Both emotional and rational appeals are required collectively or separately to tell interesting brand stories to achieve advertising and marketing objectives.

■ CHAPTER SUMMARY

In this chapter we discussed the key concepts of advertising: definition, diverse advertising sectors, milestones in advertising, advertising creation and effective advertising perspectives.

We began by explaining advertising. Advertising is a paid form of advertiser-controlled communication in any medium to convey information, ideas, goods, services and organisations. Within regulatory standards, the advertiser controls content, delivery style of the message, media selection, timing and frequency of advertising.

Advertising is no longer salesmanship in print because of diverse audio, visual and digital media platforms. Most advertising is identified, but some advertisers do not reveal their identities. Mass media is often used in consumer advertising, but other advertisers may use non-mass media. Many advertisements are non-personal but advertisers do create interactive digital campaigns. Advertising is used not only by commercial companies but also by individuals, home businesses and so on.

Next was a discussion of the various sectors of advertisers. Advertisers could be individuals, home and small businesses, professional services, the government, non-profit organisations, industry marketers and brand marketers. Government and non-profit organisations often run public service advertising. Most advertising budgets are on brand marketing, which communicates corporations, goods and services as well as occasional apology, corrective and prank messages. The largest advertisers are B2C marketers, with FMCG companies such as Procter & Gamble, Unilever and L'Oréal among the world's main ones.

We then examined milestones in the history of advertising. Advertising as an actor has evolved with telling stories through posters, print media, advertorials, radio-sponsored shows, television advertising and sponsored programs, webinars and digital platforms such as native advertising. The history of advertising has also witnessed dialogues on hard-sell, soft-sell, advertising metaphors, positioning, agency conglomerates, media buying companies and integrated marketing services. The practice of creating advertising that simulates news content or the media platform has appeared in various forms such as advertorials, sponsored radio shows, specially created television shows, infomercials, webinars, online advertorials and native advertising.

Subsequently, we considered how advertising is created. Advertising could be hard-sell and/or soft-sell. Hard-sell advertising is rational while soft-sell advertising is emotional and image-oriented. The process of advertising creativity is not either a left brain or right brain function but an integration of both brain hemispheres, and mental interactions of our conscious-unconscious-preconscious minds and multiple personal attributes. Having fresh insights into the consumer often leads to brilliant ideas, which must also be brilliantly executed. Account planners, researchers and consultants help to find such fresh insights.

We concluded the chapter by reviewing effective advertising from the perspectives of best industry practices and key research studies. Industry best practices often reveal a mix of emotional and rational advertising appeals. When you analyse the top campaigns of the twentieth and early twenty-first centuries as well as the Cannes Creative Effectiveness Grand Prix awards, you will see that emotional appeals exist in one form or another in most campaigns with big ideas, including American Express and BMW films or webinars to tell stories through *Superman* and *The Hire*. Advertising as an actor could also tell stories with humour and logic, aggression and facts, angels and sex appeal, guilt and imagination, friendship and fantasy, and so on.

Research studies revealed that emotional advertising outscored rational appeals in many measures. Effective brand-building campaigns also had emotionally engaging creative ideas or branding cues such as the Andrex Puppy, the Marlboro Cowboy and the Hovis bread delivery boy. Effective short-term persuasive advertising communicated relevant news. Ultimately, a balanced approach is required: persuasive and reinforcement advertising; hard- and soft-sell advertising; short-term sales and long-term emotional brand building; and emotional and rational advertising appeals to tell interesting brand stories.

Case study: P&G successfully sponsors mums!

Peter Ling

How does a company acknowledge the mums who buy its nappies, detergents, fabric freshener, dishwashing liquid, paper towels, bath tissue, soap, shampoo, toothpaste and many other household products? Well, Procter & Gamble (P&G) launched its emotionally driven corporate campaign to say 'Thanks, Mum' during the Vancouver Winter Olympics in 2010 using two television commercials.[156]

The 'Kids' commercial showed athletically dressed children competing in winter sports, ending with the tagline 'To their moms, they'll always be kids'; logos of P&G brands Tide, Pampers, Crest, Olay, Charmin and Bounty; and a final visual: 'P&G: Proud sponsor of Moms, Proud Partner of the US Olympic Team'.[157] See Figure 5.14 to view the tagline from the 'Kids' commercial.

Figure 5.14 P&G's 'Kids' tagline

Source: https://www.youtube.com/watch?v=vKdFPowwh-I.

The second commercial, 'Never Walk Alone', showed various mums with their children during significant life moments such as childbirth, preparing for a school bus ride and nursing a bruise. One mum carries her daughter's hockey sticks and bag and another watches her daughter performing an ice-skating routine. The commercial ended with 'Thank you, Mom', followed by brand logos, P&G sponsorship of mums and a P&G partnership with the US Olympic Team.[158]

P&G extended the 'Proud sponsor of Moms' theme in several other ways in 2010. First, it set up a Thankyoumom.com microsite for athletes to send messages to their mums. Second, it established a P&G family home at the Olympic Village for US athletes and their families to use beauty, entertainment and laundry facilities. Third, it sponsored Team USA's mums to watch children compete in Vancouver. Fourth, it sponsored 25 mums to attend the Singapore 2010 Youth Olympic Games, including mums from Argentina, Australia, Canada, France, Germany, Indonesia, Korea, the Philippines, Poland, Singapore, Turkey, the UK and the US. Fifth, it organised a P&G Thank You Mom reception before the Youth Olympic Games opening ceremony.[159]

During the 2010 Youth Olympic Games, P&G widened its 'Proud sponsor of Moms' advertising to South-East Asia with two commercials. The first consisted only of words on the screen recognising mums for not missing any training sessions or competitions, for being the first to believe in their children's dreams and for seeing the Youth Olympic Games as the beginning of an Olympic journey.[160]

The second commercial represented the nurturing nature of mums, who see the future potential of their children even when they tumble as toddlers or doggy paddle as young children.[161]

Seeing the positives in thanking mums, P&G continued with its 'Proud sponsor of Moms' theme through each Olympic Games; for example, the 2011 Special Olympics World Games in Athens;[162] the 2012 London Olympic and Paralympic Games;[163] the 2013 Special Olympics in Missouri, US;[164] the 2014 Olympic Games in Sochi, Russia;[165] the 2015 Special Olympics in the US and Singapore;[166] and the 2016 Rio Olympic Games.[167]

The Special Olympics has a special meaning for P&G, which has supported the movement for nearly 40 years.[168] Since Eunice Kennedy Shriver established the Special Olympics in 1968 with a small group of athletes, the movement has expanded to about four million athletes across 170 countries.[169]

P&G commercials continued with soft-sell emotional advertising between 2011 and 2016. In 2011, P&G's commercial 'What I See' featured Special Olympics Athlete Molly Hincka happily training on the tracks, with visuals of her coping positively while growing up. The voiceover of her mum told the story of how doctors had said that Molly would never be able to walk or talk, how she never believed that of Molly and how she never 'saw the things my child couldn't do, I only imagined what she could'.[170]

In 2012, P&G had a two-minute commercial, 'Best Job', featuring mums from Beijing, London, Los Angeles and Rio de Janeiro supporting and cheering their kids throughout their athletic development.[171] The commercial showed mums doing motherly chores while their children developed, became successful Olympians and acknowledged their teary mums, with the tagline 'The hardest job in the world, is the best job in the world'.[172] A 30-second version ended with the tagline 'Behind every athlete is a loving Mum'.[173] P&G also produced and shared a series of videos through social media websites on 'Raising an Olympian', featuring mums and the development of their Olympian children.[174]

For Mother's Day 2013, P&G produced a special online video where Maria Shriver, former First Lady of California, acknowledged her mother Eunice Shriver as the 'mother of Special Olympics' who also gave her 'the gift of possibility, the gift that I could do anything that I wanted to do'.[175] In addition, P&G had a Facebook site to promote its partnership with the first Special Olympics Asia Pacific. The video had the theme 'Thank you, Mom, for supporting me on my journey' as well as a promotional message saying that P&G would donate funds to help intellectually disabled Special Olympics athletes when consumers bought P&G products from a local retailer.[176]

In 2014, a commercial called 'Pick them back up' that aired during the Sochi Olympic Winter Games showed child athletes falling, getting up, being hurt, crying, with a bandage, touching an ice pack on a sore shoulder and nursing a broken leg. The message thanked mums 'For teaching us that falling only makes us stronger'.[177]

In 2015, P&G won *PR Week*'s 'Global Campaign of the Year' for its integrated videos and commercials: the 'Raising an Olympian' series telling the stories of 28 Olympians and their mums; the 'Pick them back up' commercial; the P&G Family Home at the Olympic Village; the featuring of 17 P&G brands in 54 Olympic events; exclusive coverage in selected news media; Twitter engagement; and extensive social media followers.[178]

For Rio Olympics 2016, P&G stepped up the emotionally driven 'Thank you, Mom' message with a 'Strong' commercial. Interspersed with memories of typhoons, car crashes, stuck elevators, air turbulence, neighbourhood bullying, sexist taunts and verbal abuse, there was always a strong mum to make Olympians stronger and successful.[179]

In addition to winning the Cannes Gold and Emmy for Commercial of the Year awards, the P&G 'Thank you, Mom' commercials have consistently won the hearts of women and made them 'tear up'. 'Strong', 'Best Job' and 'Pick Them Back Up' have scored above industry norms in quantitative and qualitative surveys on attributes such as Attention, Likeability and Relevance. Viewers have expressed views such as 'most powerful', 'emotionally moving', 'inspirational' and 'very touching and motivating'.[180]

While most of the campaigns behind the 'Proud sponsor of Moms' strategy were soft-sell with emotional appeals, P&G also integrated hard-sell persuasive promotions. For example, there was the 2011 Special Olympics brandSAVER coupon book worth US$95, distributed in newspapers for redemption on P&G brands Crest, Duracell, Olay, Pampers, Pantene and Tide—with P&G making a Special Olympics donation for every redeemed coupon. There was also the 2011 sales promotion where P&G donated US$1 for every Facebook 'Like', 'Share' or 'Comment' to help send Special Olympics Team USA to Athens.[181]

Leveraging the Shriver 'gift' video, P&G offered US$1 to Special Olympics projects for every Facebook 'Share' and every retweet of 'The gift' video.[182] P&G also created a #MomsWisdom social campaign on Facebook and Twitter for the public to share their mums' wise words during the 'Thank You, Mom' Mother's Day promotion. This led to the public creating posters with messages like

Figure 5.15 P&G #MomsWisdom Mother's Day 2013 poster messages

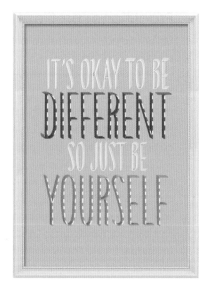

Source: http://stage.wk.com/campaign/
momswisdom.

'Release Negative Feelings' and 'It's okay to be different so just be yourself'.[183] See Figure 5.15 for examples of #MomsWisdom poster messages.

The 'Proud Sponsor of Moms' strategy has turned P&G from a large global corporation into a 'brand with a heart'. Based on its 2013 Cannes Lions Gold Titanium & Integrated Award, the campaign generated more than 76 billion media impressions; garnered 370 million Twitter interactions; attracted 74 million global social media views; increased global sales by US$500 million; enhanced retail sales by 5–20 per cent; and achieved the most success in the then-175-year history of P&G.[184]

The P&G 'heart' has also won support in India. A P&G brand, Vicks, ran a film—*Touch of Care*—to tell the true story of a transgender mum, Gauri Sawant, who has raised an orphan girl, Gayatri, against all odds. The ending featured the message, 'Everyone deserves the touch of care. Where there's care, there's family. VICKS Caring for families for generations'. The words are different from 'Proud Sponsor of Moms' or 'Thank You, Mom', but the sentiments are the same—although Gayatri may not be a future Olympian because her dream is to be a lawyer for her mum.[185]

Questions

1. How wise was P&G's strategy to thank mums?
2. How has P&G integrated soft-sell and hard-sell advertising?
3. How successful has P&G's strategy to thank mums been?
4. Besides the non-Olympian approach in P&G India's corporate video, how else could the corporation engage with its diverse consumers?

Practitioner profile: Alicia Pridgeon

Senior Lead, Advertising and Events,
Holmesglen Institute

Creative wordsmithing always came easy to me. Plus, working my way through school with a number of retail jobs meant that I was comfortable finding and talking about USPs. After completing my undergrad in communications, I originally wanted to get into corporate communications. But, being a graduate with limited real work experience, it took a while to crack the industry. (My biggest advice here is to find a course with plenty of practical components, or to just get out there and get your hands dirty—do what you have learnt!) In the meantime I managed bookstores for a few years before studying my post grad in editing and publishing, which got me into sales and marketing in academic publishing. After a few years in publishing I moved to my current role, marketing vocational and higher education. So why TAFE? Because we change lives through the transformative power of education.

Describe your current role and the organisation you work for, and give a brief account of what you do in your role on a day-to-day basis.

I work as Senior Lead, Advertising and Events at one of the largest vocational and higher education training providers in Victoria: Holmesglen Institute. In my role I develop above-the-line marketing strategies and future initiatives that align with the strategic vision of the institute. I ensure consistent brand and voice throughout all communications, as well as managing internal clients, and supporting, leading and developing small teams. My day can involve anything from being on a film shoot or media buying, to running open days or creating client briefs.

How important is Integrated Marketing Communication (IMC) to what you and your organisation do?

Being in education, we need to communicate across channels in a way that evokes trust, reliability, authority and first choice. IMC strategy is ultimately an overall brand strategy that provides overarching clarity, consistency and impact for campaigns. Think of it as a task list to achieve your goals (which in turn align to your strategy). Without this thought process you risk incohesive campaigns that fragment your voice, splintering your share of market.

What types of promotional tools do you use in your IMC campaigns? Please provide examples.

We use above-the-line advertising (including TVC, out of home, radio and print), digital advertising (Google search, display, retargeting), in-house blog content, direct marketing, events, social media, public relations, printed support materials and sales forces.

What would your ideal IMC campaign look like and why?

I love telling stories. So what I want to see in IMC is a hero concept that can be explored across mediums. I want my IMC to mean something to me, so I always ask myself 'why?'

I would show you a general story that teased a backstory (which is what you use to elaborate). I would have an establishing product (doesn't matter the medium—you can do this for all), then cut down versions to reinforce the original message but at the same time adding an additional piece of information. This works across TVC, outdoor, print and digital. The important thing is to make sure that you are telling the same story across all these platforms. Then my retargeting and direct marketing would be tailored to my target audience's interest area. The look and feel would remain the same, but I would have a style that matches them. As organisations we need to find a way to feel familiar, not foreign, to be part of the conversation and not imposing, yet at the same time achieve cut through.

What has been your favourite IMC project to work on and did it achieve its objectives?

Our most extensive and successful IMC surrounds our open days strategy. Since moving from a single open day model to up to 10 open day events per year we have increased our engagement funnel by 375 per cent. The project involved an extensive website UX revamp, integrated CRM functionality, comprehensive digital marketing and retargeting, direct marketing plans, SMS, call centre activity and above-the-line advertising.

How do you believe an IMC campaign affects the consumer decision-making process for your particular target audience?

Education can have an extended decision-making cycle ranging from months to years. As an organisation in this sector the aim is to be top-shelf recall for consumers. An effective IMC interacts with our target audience at key stages of their decision-making process, introducing and reasserting our organisation as a first choice education provider.

How has your application of IMC changed with the increase in digital marketing?

Digital marketing requires the same thought process as any other medium: you need to consider your message and creative for the market. It gives you a chance to extend your campaigns: to further qualify, to challenge thinking, to add to the conversation.

What do you believe are some of the challenges to implementing an IMC campaign?

As one of the largest vocational and higher education providers in Victoria, we offer hundreds of courses, from certificates to degrees, across numerous study areas. Our IMC needs to work together, not in isolation, and herein lie some challenges. Every study area has its own persona and every target demographic has its own consumption habits. We need to create an IMC that holistically represents what we are about at the same time as reflecting unique sub-personalities. For us the risk is reinforcing silos or stealing oxygen from one area to feed another.

What advice would you offer a student studying IMC?

Take your organisation's mission statement and turn it into a mantra (check out Guy Kawasaki for more on this). Understand your message intimately. Integrated marketing shouldn't be something that you strive for; it should be something that is innate in all you do. Ask yourself: does this activity clearly communicate my message? Does my communication directly align to my mantra? Is my mantra reflective of my organisational goals? If at any stage you're unsure or you can't answer with an emphatic yes, hit the drawing board.

Key terms

advertorial	demarketing	share of mind
AdWords	hard-sell	share of voice
alternate sponsorships	infomercials	soft-sell
apology advertisement	native advertising	webisodes
corrective advertising	public service advertising	

Revision questions

1. Why has Rolex been able to run its celebrity advertising since 1927?
2. How is advertising like an actor?
3. How have you been a user of advertising as a consumer and/or advertiser?
4. What kind of public service advertising has influenced your attitude and behaviour on social issues?
5. Why is industry advertising as important as brand advertising?
6. Which brand advertising tends to capture your attention?
7. What apology and/or corrective advertising have you seen?
8. Which development in the history of advertising has greatly impacted modern advertising?
9. How are leading advertisers engaging with consumers digitally?
10. What are your views on the hard-sell/soft-sell advertising approach?
11. What are your views on the advertising creativity process?
12. What advertising cases have you come across that deconstruct campaigns' insights, ideas, execution and results?
13. Which top campaigns of the twentieth and early twenty-first centuries and Cannes Lions Creative Effectiveness Winners impress you and why?
14. What do you learn about advertising effectiveness from the research studies?
15. What is your definition of advertising after reading through the chapter?

Further reading

A century of advertising education: http://www.aaasite.org/assets/docs/a%20century%20of%20 advertising%20education.pdf

Advertising in social media: a review of empirical evidence: http://www.tandfonline.com/doi/full/ 10.1080/02650487.2015.1021898

Advertising repetition: a meta-analysis on effective frequency in advertising: http://www.tandfonline.com/ doi/full/10.1080/00913367.2015.1018460

Content marketing primer: https://www.iab.com/wp-content/uploads/2015/07/
IABContentMarketingPrimer.pdf

Creative that sells: how advertising execution affects sales: http://www.tandfonline.com/doi/full/10.1080/
00913367.2015.1077491

Gender roles and humor in advertising: the occurrence of stereotyping in humorous and nonhumorous
advertising and its consequences for advertising effectiveness: http://www.tandfonline.com/doi/full/
10.1080/00913367.2013.857621

Going native: effects of disclosure position and language on the recognition and evaluation of online native
advertising: http://www.tandfonline.com/doi/abs/10.1080/00913367.2015.1115380

If advertising won't die, what will it be? Toward a working definition of advertising: http://www.
tandfonline.com/doi/full/10.1080/00913367.2016.1172387

Integrated marketing communication (IMC) and brand identity as critical components of brand equity
strategy: a conceptual framework and research propositions: http://www.tandfonline.com/doi/abs/
10.1080/00913367.2005.10639213

Lessons from the rich and famous: a cross-cultural comparison of celebrity endorsement in
advertising: http://www.tandfonline.com/doi/abs/10.1080/00913367.2005.10639190

Living in media and the future of advertising: http://www.tandfonline.com/doi/full/10.1080/
00913367.2016.1185983

Persuasion in advertising: when does it work and when does it not?: http://www.tandfonline.com/doi/full/
10.1080/02650487.2014.994732

Social media definitions: http://www.iab.com/wp-content/uploads/2015/12/MRC-Social-Media-
Measurement-Definitions-FINAL.pdf

The case for advertising: http://www.iaaglobal.org/YourRightToChoose.aspx

The future of advertising or whatever we're going to call it: http://www.tandfonline.com/doi/full/10.1080/
00913367.2016.1185061

The gamification of advertising: analysis and research directions of in-game advertising, advergames,
and advertising in social network games: http://www.tandfonline.com/doi/full/10.1080/
00913367.2013.774610

The native advertising playbook: https://www.iab.com/wp-content/uploads/2015/06/IAB-Native-
Advertising-Playbook2.pdf

Unlocking the power of integrated marketing communications: how integrated is your IMC
program?: http://www.tandfonline.com/doi/full/10.1080/00913367.2016.1204967

Viral advertising in social media: http://www.tandfonline.com/doi/full/10.1080/15252019.2011.10722189

Welcome to the IAB Interactive Advertising Wiki: https://wiki.iab.com/index.
    php?title=Category:Glossary&pageuntil=DVR#mw-pages

When is advertising? Comparing responses to non-traditional and traditional advertising media: http://
    www.tandfonline.com/doi/abs/10.1080/10641734.2007.10505206

Weblinks

Associations

Australian Association of National Advertisers: http://aana.com.au
Interactive Advertising Bureau: https://www.iab.com
International Advertising Association: http://www.iaaglobal.org
World Federation of Advertisers: https://www.wfanet.org

Awards

Ad Age Creativity Awards: http://adage.com/article/agency-news/finalists-ad-age-s-creativity-awards/
307928/
Australian Marketing Institute Awards for Marketing Excellence: https://e-award.com.au/2017/
amiawards/newentry/about.php
Cannes Young Design Competition: https://www.canneslions.com/competitions/young-lions-design-
competition
Cannes Young Lions Competitions: https://www.canneslions.com/competitions/young-lions-media-
competition
Young Lions Digital Competition: https://www.canneslions.com/competitions/young-lions-digital-
competition
Creative strategy awards: http://www.apg.org.uk/apgawards; http://www.communicationscouncil.org.au/
public/content/ViewCategory.aspx?id=1240
Young Cyber Competition: https://www.canneslions.com/festival/young-lions-competitions/young-
cyber-competition
Young Film Competition: https://www.canneslions.com/competitions/young-lions-film-competition
Young Marketers Competition: https://www.canneslions.com/competitions/young-lions-marketers-
competition
Young Media Competition: https://www.canneslions.com/competitions/young-lions-media-competition
Young PR Competition: https://www.canneslions.com/competitions/young-lions-pr-competition
Young Print Competition: https://www.canneslions.com/competitions/young-lions-print-competition

Advertising effectiveness awards

Campaign Brief: http://www.campaignbrief.com/wa
The Communications Council: http://www.communicationscouncil.org.au/public/content/ViewCategory.
aspx?id=315
Effie: http://www.effie.org/ideas_that_work/
Euro Effie: http://www.euro-effie.com/index.asp

IPA effectiveness awards: http://www.ipa.co.uk/effectiveness
Media Federation of Australia: http://mediafederation.org.au/mfa-awards/past-winners

Advertising creative awards

Australian Writers & Art Directors: http://www.awardonline.com/
Cannes: http://www.canneslions.com/
Clio awards: http://www.clioawards.com/
New York Festivals: http://www.newyorkfestivals.com/
The One Show: http://www.oneclub.org

Advertising resources

Adforum: https://www.adforum.com
Ads of the world: http://adsoftheworld.com/top-ads
Coloribus: https://www.coloribus.com

Journals

International Journal of Advertising: http://www.tandfonline.com/toc/rina20/current
Journal of Advertising: http://www.tandfonline.com/loi/ujoa20
Journal of Advertising Education: https://journalofadvertisingeducation.org/cumulative-index/
Journal of Advertising Research: http://www.journalofadvertisingresearch.com
Journal of Current Issues & Research in Advertising: http://www.tandfonline.com/toc/ujci20/current
Journal of Interactive Advertising: http://www.tandfonline.com/loi/ujia20

Notes

1 Daily Commercials. (2017). Rolex Celebration Cinema. https://dailycommercials.com/rolex-celebrating-cinema/

2 Doerr, E. (2017). Rolex, sponsor of the 89th Academy Awards, airs movie watch appearance montage during 2017 Oscars, 27 February. https://www.forbes.com/sites/elizabethdoerr/2017/02/27/rolex-sponsor-of-the-89th-academy-awards-airs-movie-watch-appearance-montage-during-2017-oscars/#9e7910f79bac

3 Rolex.com. (2018). Rolex and the arts: Celebrating Cinema. https://www.rolex.com/arts-and-culture/rolex-and-cinema.html

4 Rolex.com. (2018). Rolex stories: Every Rolex tells a story. https://www.rolex.com/every-rolex-tells-a-story.html

5 Epstein, E. (2014 April 18). Rolex: How a 109-year-old brand thrives in the digital age. http://mashable.com/2014/04/17/rolex-marketing-strategy/#rORXax.M6Pqi

6 Rolex.com. (2017). Rolex and the Arts. https://www.rolex.com/arts-and-culture/the-arts.html

7 Rolex Awards. (2018). About the awards. http://www.rolexawards.com/about

8 Epstein, E. (2014 April 18). Rolex: How a 109-year-old brand thrives in the digital age. http://mashable.com/2014/04/17/rolex-marketing-strategy/#rORXax.M6Pqi

9 Perman, S. (2016). Swiss watches are getting more affordable, 11 February. http://fortune.com/2016/02/11/swiss-watches-gray-market/

10 Watch Pro. (2012 June 11). Rolex rolls out ads to support authorised dealers. http://www.watchpro.com/rolex-rolls-out-ads-to-support-authorised-dealers/

11 AdAge. (2003). Hard-sell/soft-sell advertising, 15 September. http://adage.com/article/adage-encyclopedia/hard-sell-soft-sell-advertising/98687/

12 Oxford Dictionaries. (2018). Advertising. https://en.oxforddictionaries.com/definition/advertising

13 Oxford Reference. (2016). Advertising. *A dictionary of business and management* (6th edn). http://www.oxfordreference.com/view/10.1093/acref/9780199684984.001.0001/acref-9780199684984-e-164?rskey=g7xVX4&result=1

14 AMA. (2018). Dictionary—Advertising. https://www.ama.org/resources/pages/dictionary.aspx?dLetter=A

15 Richards, J. I. & Curran, C. M. (2002). Oracles on 'Advertising': Searching for a definition. *Journal of Advertising, 31*(2), 63–77.

16 Richards, J. I., & Curran, C. M. (2002). Oracles on 'Advertising': Searching for a definition. *Journal of Advertising, 31*(2), 63–77.

17 Dahlen, M., & Rosengren, S. (2016). If advertising won't die, what will it be? Toward a working definition of advertising. *Journal of Advertising, 45*(3), 334–45.

18 Morrison, M. (2014 April 27). Burger King resurrects Subservient Chicken. http://adage.com/article/news/burger-king-resurrects-subservient-chicken/292902/

19 *The Advertiser.* (2018). Classifieds. http://www.adelaidenow.com.au/classifieds

20 *Herald Sun.* (2018). Place my ad. http://www.heraldsun.com.au/classifieds/placemyad

21 Skenazy, L. (2007 June 25). Classified ads: the acceptable way to sell immigrant sex slaves. *Advertising Age, 78*(26), 21. http://adage.com/article/news/p-g-boost-ad-spending-u-s/236504/

22 LocalWA.com.au. (2018). Find a tradie in your local area. https://www.looklocalwa.com.au; *Herald Sun.* (2018). Place my ad. http://www.heraldsun.com.au/classifieds/placemyad; Advertisers.com.au. (2018). Advertise with us. https://advertisers.com.au

23 Adwords. (2018). Get your ad on Google today. https://adwords.google.com/intl/en_au/home/#?modal_active=none

24 Bloom, P. (1984 September). Effective marketing for professional services. *Harvard Business Review.* https://hbr.org/1984/09/effective-marketing-for-professional-services

25 Vic.gov.au. (2018). Victoria Government Gazette. http://www.gazette.vic.gov.au/gazette_bin/place_notice.cfm?bct=placenotice

26 Holding Redlich. (2014 July 30). Getting your IPO out there. https://www.holdingredlich.com/corporate-commercial/getting-your-ipo-out-there

27 Tadros, E. (2017 March 12). PwC bulks up as ad agencies face onslaught from services giants. *AFR Weekend.* http://www.afr.com/business/accounting/pwc-bulks-up-as-ad-agencies-face-onslaught-from-professional-services-giants-20170310-guv9ri

28 Hickman, A. (2016 December 6). Australian government spends near-record $175m on advertising. *AdNews.* http://www.adnews.com.au/news/australian-government-spends-near-record-175m-on-advertising

29 AdCouncil.org. (2017). Frequently asked questions. http://www.adcouncil.org/About-Us/Frequently-Asked-Questions#How%20do%20you%20define%20public%20service%20advertising?

30 topnonprofits.com. (2017). Top 100 nonprofits on the web. https://topnonprofits.com/lists/best-nonprofits-on-the-web/

31 Niles, C. (2013). Liam Neeson supports UNICEF anti-violence initiative. https://www.unicef.org/protection/57929_70030.html; Delahaye, J. (2016). David Beckham stars in powerful UNICEF video to end violence against children, 5 December. http://www.hellomagazine.com/celebrities/2016120535021/david-beckham-stars-in-powerful-unicef-video-to-end-violence-against-children/.

32 AdCouncil.org. (2018). Inspiring change. Improving lives. http://www.adcouncil.org

33 Australia.gov.au. (2017). Campaigns. http://www.australia.gov.au/news-and-social-media/campaigns

34 Kotler, P. & Levy, S. (1971). Demarketing, yes, demarketing. *Harvard Business Review, 49*(6), 74–80.

35 Campaign Brief. (2014). The IAA launches 'The case for advertising' global public service campaign in Sydney, 17 February. http://www.campaignbrief.com/wa/2014/02/the-iaa-launches-the-case-for.html

36 canneslions.com. (2018). Awards for Good. https://www.canneslions.com/the-awards/good

37 cancervic.org.au. (1980). Slip! Slop! Slap! http://www.sunsmart.com.au/tools/videos/past-tv-campaigns/slip-slop-slap-original-sunsmart-campaign.html

38 cancervic.org.au. (2010). SunSmart—Celebrating 30 years of protecting Victorians. https://www. youtube.com/watch?v=2jXsMFmbwPY

39 Cheer, L. (2014 May 22). Slip, slop, slap, success: Skin cancer rates plummet thanks to long-running nationwide sun safety campaign. *Daily Mail*. http://www.dailymail.co.uk/news/article-2635981/Skin-cancer-rates-plummet-thanks-long-running-sun-safety-campaign.html

40 Stokes, K. (2016 July 13). Young Australians heeding slip, slop, slap message as overall melanoma cases rise. *Herald Sun*; Cheer, L. (2014 May 22). Slip, slop, slap, success: Skin cancer rates plummet thanks to long-running nationwide sun safety campaign. *Daily Mail*. http://www.dailymail.co.uk/news/article-2635981/Skin-cancer-rates-plummet-thanks-long-running-sun-safety-campaign.html

41 sunsmart.com.au. (2017). Slip, Slop, Slap, Seek & Slide: Sid Seagull. http://www.sunsmart.com.au/tools/videos/current-tv-campaigns/slip-slop-slap-seek-slide-sid-seagull.html

42 MLA. (2017). Beef campaigns. https://www.mla.com.au/marketing-beef-and-lamb/domestic-marketing/beef-campaigns; MLA. (2017). Lamb campaigns. https://www.mla.com.au/marketing-beef-and-lamb/domestic-marketing/lamb-campaigns/

43 Australian Pork. (2018). Marketing. http://australianpork.com.au/industry-focus/marketing/

44 Australian Avocados. (2014). Australian avocados are now on TV. Love that avocado feeling. http://australianavocados.com.au/the-daily-spread/home-entertaining/australian-avocados-are-now-tv-love-avocado-feeling

45 Western Potatoes. (2003). Marketing the humble potato in Western Australia. http://www.seafooddirectionsconference.com/images/archivecontent/2003_Perth/Jim_Murphy.pdf

46 DelVecchio, G. (2014 May 12). Got Milk? Got fired: 5 valuable lessons that all executives must heed. http://www.huffingtonpost.com/gene-del-vecchio/got-milk-got-fired-5-valu_b_4938176.html

47 Battersby, L. (2016 December 1). Television industry advertising itself on television to advertising industry. http://www.smh.com.au/business/media-and-marketing/television-industry-advertising-itself-on-television-to-advertising-industry-20161130-gt1fls.html

48 Johnson, B. (2016 December 4). What you need to know about the world's largest advertisers, from Adidas to Yili. http://adage.com/article/advertising/world-s-largest-advertisers/306983/

49 Kotler, P., Brown, L., Adam, S., Burton, S., & Armstrong, G. (2007). Marketing (7th ed.). Frenchs Forrest NSW: Pearson Education Australia.

50 Johnson, B. (2016 December 4). What you need to know about the world's largest advertisers, from Adidas to Yili. http://adage.com/article/advertising/world-s-largest-advertisers/306983/

51 PG.com. (2018). Our brands. http://us.pg.com/our-brands

52 Unilever.com. (2017). Our brands. https://www.unilever.com/brands/?page=3

53 Loreal.com. (2017). L'Oréal. http://www.loreal.com

54 O'Leary, N. (2011 June 23). New Effie Effectiveness Index. http://www.adweek.com/brand-marketing/new-effie-effectiveness-index-132847; Effie Index. (2017). Most effective marketers May 2017. https://www.effieindex.com/ranking/?rt=6

55 Lorenzetti, L. (2015 December 16). Chipotle's founder just issued another very public apology. http://fortune.com/2015/12/16/chipotle-ad-apology-safety/

56 Hern, A. (2016 November 9). Samsung takes out full-page ads to apologise for Note 7 defects. https://www.theguardian.com/technology/2016/nov/08/samsung-takes-out-full-page-ads-to-apologise-for-note-7-defects

57 Andresen, T. (2017 February 6). Deutsche Bank buys ads to apologize for 'Serious Errors'. https://www.bloomberg.com/news/articles/2017-02-05/deutsche-bank-purchases-ads-to-apologize-for-serious-errors

58 Kulp, P. (2015 November 18). Volkswagen apologizes to customers in giant full-page ad with no pictures. http://mashable.com/2015/11/17/volkswagen-ad/#uTkMD0fXYuqx

59 AdAge. (2003 September 15). Corrective advertising. http://adage.com/article/adage-encyclopedia/corrective-advertising/98418/

60 Ohlheiser, A., & Selk, A. (2017). An updated (and depressing) list of all the April Fools' pranks on the Internet. https://www.washingtonpost.com/news/the-intersect/wp/2017/03/31/an-updated-and-depressing-list-of-all-the-april-fools-pranks-on-the-internet/?utm_term=.85fb085b5e8c

61 Hoaxes.org. (2014). The BBC's April Fool's Day Hoaxes. http://hoaxes.org/af_database/display/category/bbc

62 AdAge. (2003 September 15). History: Pre-19th Century. http://adage.com/article/adage-encyclopedia/history-pre-19th-century/98707/

63 AdAge. (1999 March 29). Ad Age advertising century: Timeline. http://adage.com/article/special-report-the-advertising-century/ad-age-advertising-century-timeline/143661/

64 AdAge. (2003 September 15). History: 19th Century. http://adage.com/article/adage-encyclopedia/history-19th-century/98706/

65 Crawford, R. 2008. *Advertising* [Online]. Dictionary of Sydney. http://dictionaryofsydney.org/entry/advertising

66 AdAge. (2003 September 15). History: 1910-1920. http://adage.com/article/adage-encyclopedia/history-1910-1920/99072/

67 Manalo, J. 2014 March 28. A brief history of native advertising. https://contently.com/strategist/2014/03/28/a-brief-history-of-native-advertising/

68 AdAge. (2003 September 15). History: 1920s. http://adage.com/article/adage-encyclopedia/history-1920s/98699/

69 AdAge. (2003 September 15). History: 1930s. http://adage.com/article/adage-encyclopedia/history-1930s/98700/

70 AdAge. (1999 March 29). Ad Age advertising century: Timeline. http://adage.com/article/special-report-the-advertising-century/ad-age-advertising-century-timeline/143661/

71 AdAge. (2003 September 15). History: 1940s. http://adage.com/article/adage-encyclopedia/history-1940s/98698/

72 AdAge. (2003 September 15). History: 1950s. http://adage.com/article/adage-encyclopedia/history-1950s/98701/

73 AdAge. (2003 September 15). History: 1960s. http://adage.com/article/adage-encyclopedia/history-1960s/98702/

74 AdAge. (2003 September 15). History: 1970s. http://adage.com/article/adage-encyclopedia/history-1970s/98703/

75 AdAge. (2003 September 15). History: 1980s. http://adage.com/article/adage-encyclopedia/history-1980s/98704/

76 AdAge. (1996 April 26). HP launches online advertorial. http://adage.com/article/news/hp-launches-online-advertorial/1854/

77 AdAge. (2003 September 15). History: 1990s. http://adage.com/article/adage-encyclopedia/history-1990s/98705/

78 Glenn, D. (2012 February 16). The history of social media from 1978-2012. *AdWeek*. http://www.adweek.com/digital/the-history-of-social-media-from-1978-2012-infographic/

79 Glenn, D. (2012 February 16). The history of social media from 1978-2012. *AdWeek*. http://www.adweek.com/digital/the-history-of-social-media-from-1978-2012-infographic; Bruner, R. (2016 July 16). A brief history of Instagram's fateful first day. *Time*. http://time.com/4408374/instagram-anniversary.

80 Pattison, S. (2014 April 11). Native advertising doesn't need to be rocket science. *The Guardian*. https://www.theguardian.com/media-network/media-network-blog/2014/apr/11/native-advertising-content-marketing-fred-wilson; Vinderslev, A. (2015 March 1). Native advertising definition. https://nativeadvertisinginstitute.com/blog/the-definition-of-native-advertising.

81 Aalders, D. (2016 July 25). Social media in China: The Top 5 platforms you must use. https://www.linkedin.com/pulse/social-media-china-top-5-platforms-you-must-use-daan-aalders

82 Barboza, D. (2006 September 17). The rise of Baidu (That's Chinese for Google). *The New York Times*. http://www.nytimes.com/2006/09/17/business/yourmoney/17baidu.html

83 Hampp, A. (2010). If you build a web series around it, will they come? *AdAge*. http://adage.com/article/madisonvine-digital-entertainment/branded-entertainment-brands-flock-web-series/145276/

84 Elliott, S. (2004 March 30). Seinfeld and Superman join forces again in spots for American Express, this time on the Web. *The New York Times*. http://www.nytimes.com/2004/03/30/business/media-business-advertising-seinfeld-superman-join-forces-again-spots-for.html?_r=0

85 Whitehead, J. (2004 June 7). Virgin Mobile returns to toilet for latest viral campaign. *Campaign*. http://www.campaignlive.co.uk/article/virgin-mobile-returns-toilet-latest-viral-campaign/213142

86 Learmonth, M. (2010 September 2). The Top 10 viral ads of all time. *AdAge*. http://adage.com/article/the-viral-video-chart/digital-marketing-top-10-viral-ads-time/145673; Zazzi, J. (2015 December 17). Five highly emotional ads that went viral in 2015. *Forbes*. https://www.forbes.com/sites/onmarketing/2015/12/17/five-highly-emotional-ads-that-went-viral-in-2015/#4a27da551f32; AdAge. (2017). The viral video chart. http://adage.com/section/the-viral-video-chart/674; Pardee, G. & Hubby, K. (2017 January 8). The 25 most-viewed YouTube videos of all time. *The Daily Dot*. https://www.dailydot.com/upstream/most-viewed-youtube-videos.

87   Bernoff, J. (2010, January 5). The 2000s, by the numbers. Advertising Age. http://adage.com/article/digitalnext/digital-marketing-digital-decade-numbers/141305/

88   AdAge. (2003 September 15). Hard-sell/soft-sell advertising. http://adage.com/article/adage-encyclopedia/hard-sell-soft-sell-advertising/98687/

89   AdAge. (2003 September 15). Hard-sell/soft-sell advertising. http://adage.com/article/adage-encyclopedia/hard-sell-soft-sell-advertising/98687/

90   AdAge. (1999 March 29). The Marlboro Man. http://adage.com/article/special-report-the-advertising-century/marlboro-man/140170/

91   Farhi, P. (1990 December 23). Advertising takes hard-sell approach. https://www.washingtonpost.com/archive/politics/1990/12/23/advertising-takes-hard-sell-approach/91f71108-0f3b-44aa-9b2e-980b2d17208c/?utm_term=.723d5271a901

92   Haygood, D. M. (2016). Hard sell or soft sell? The advertising philosophies and professional relations of Rosser Reeves and David Ogilvy. *American Journalism, 33*(2), 169–88.

93   Sperry, R. W. (1981). Roger W. Sperry - Nobel lecture. https://www.nobelprize.org/nobel_prizes/medicine/laureates/1981/sperry-lecture.html

94   Herrmann, N. (1996). *The whole brain business book*. New York: McGraw-Hill.

95   Herrmann, N. (2018). Is it true that creativity resides in the right hemisphere of the brain? *Scientific American*. https://www.scientificamerican.com/article/is-it-true-that-creativit/

96   Wallas, G. (1926). *The art of thought*. London: J. Cape.

97   ipa.co.uk. (2018). The advertising process. http://www.ipa.co.uk/page/the-advertising-process#.WpmjkWZL3-Z

98   Turnbull, S., & Wheeler, C. (2017). The advertising creative process: a study of UK agencies. *Journal of Marketing Communications, 23*(2), 176–94.

99   Amabile, T. M. (1996). *Creativity in context*. Colorado: Westview Press.

100   Ling, P. (2016). *Be the innovators: How to accelerate team creativity*. Melbourne: Oxford University Press.

101   Kubie, L. S. (1958). *Neurotic distortions in the creative process*. New York: University of Kansas Press.

102   Sternberg, R. J. (2006). The nature of creativity. *Creative Research Journal, 18*(1), 87–98.

103   Nudd, T. (2015 July 19). The Adweek Creative 100: America's most inventive talent in marketing, media and tech. http://www.adweek.com/brand-marketing/meet-adweeks-creative-100-americas-most-inventive-talent-marketing-media-and-tech-165993/

104   Lane, D. (2015 May 11). The difference between an idea and an execution. https://dingosbreakfast.wordpress.com/2015/05/11/the-difference-between-an-idea-and-an-execution/

105   John O'Toole. (1985). *The trouble with advertising* (2nd ed.). New York: Random House.

106   Fuel Lines. (2018). Leo Burnett still wins ad agency new business 40 years after his death. http://www.fuelingnewbusiness.com/2012/01/25/leo-burnett-still-wins-ad-agency-new-business-40-years-after-his-death/

107 Hernandez, R. (2012). Big ideas: Research can make a big difference. http://www.millwardbrown. com/docs/default-source/insight-documents/points-of-view/Millward_Brown_POV_Big_Ideas.pdf

108 Grant, I., Gilmore, C., & Crosier, K. (2003). Account planning: whose role is it anyway? *Marketing Intelligence & Planning, 21*(7), 462–72.

109 Baskin, M. (2001 Apr 3). What is account planning? (and what do account planners do exactly?). http://www.apg.org.uk/single-post/2001/04/02/What-is-Account-Planning-and-what-do-account-planners-do-exactly

110 APG. (2018). Transform your thinking. http://www.apg.org.uk

111 MacDonald, R. (2015 June). How planners and creatives can problem-solve together. https://www. thinkwithgoogle.com/intl/en-aunz/marketing-resources/content-marketing/au-how-planners-and-creatives-can-problem-solve-together/

112 Clerehan, E. (2015 March 12). What's the difference between an idea and execution? http://blog. clerehan.com/?p=216

113 Goodby, J. (2013 October 25). 20 years of 'Got Milk?'. http://www.adweek.com/creativity/20-years-got-milk-153399/

114 Huffington Post. (2017 December 6). The 31 best 'Got Milk?' ads, definitively ranked. https://www. huffingtonpost.com/2014/02/24/got-milk-ads_n_4847121.html

115 Crain, R. (2016 June 27). Why the execution of an idea is more important than the idea itself. *AdAge.* http://adage.com/article/print-edition/execution-idea-outweighs-idea/304657/

116 Wolk, A. (2010 June 28). Execution has become as important as the big idea. *AdAge.* http://adage. com/article/guest-columnists/execution-important-big-idea/144678/

117 D'&AD. (2015). Case study: Always #LikeAGirl. Retrieved from https://www.dandad.org/en/d-ad-always-like-a-girl-campaign-case-study-insights/

118 Welovead.com. (2017). Fearless Girl. http://www.welovead.com/en/works/details/bfewgpxAe

119 Richards, K. (2017 September 10). Fearless Girl stole the world's heart, but what did it do for the client's business? Retrieved from http://www.adweek.com/brand-marketing/fearless-girl-stole-the-worlds-heart-but-what-did-it-do-for-the-clients-business/

120 Bach, N. (2018). Wall Street's 'Fearless Girl' statue is getting a new home next week. http://fortune. com/2018/03/01/fearless-girl-new-york-statue-moving-location-wall-street/

121 Terre des Hommes. (2018). International Federation for children, their rights and equitable development. http://www.terredeshommes.org

122 D&AD. (2014). Case study: Sweetie. https://www.dandad.org/en/d-ad-sweetie-case-study-digital-marketing-social-good/

123 The Drum. (2016). BBDO New York creates 'You're not you when you're hungry' campaign for Snickers with Betty White. http://www.thedrum.com/news/2016/03/31/2010-bbdo-new-york-creates-youre-not-you-when-youre-hungry-campaign-snickers-with

124 Miller, J. (2016 October 26). Case study: How fame made Snickers' 'You're not you when you're hungry' campaign a success. https://www.campaignlive.co.uk/article/case-study-fame-made-snickers-youre-not-when-youre-hungry-campaign-success/1410807

125 Super Bowl Commercials. (2018). Snickers. https://www.superbowlcommercials.co/snickers/previous-campaigns; YouTube. (2018). Snickers you're not you when you're hungry. https://www.youtube.com/results?search_query=snickers+you%27re+not+you+when+you%27re+hungry.

126 Bullmore, J. (2013). Why it's time to say goodbye to IKTHTMISOAIW. *WPP Annual Report & Accounts*. http://www.wpp.com/annualreports/2013/what-we-think/why-its-time-to-say-goodbye-to-ikthtmisoaiw/

127 Garfield, B. (1999 March 29). Ad Age advertising century: The Top 100 campaigns. http://adage.com/article/special-report-the-advertising-century/ad-age-advertising-century-top-100-campaigns/140918/

128 AdAge. (1999 March 29). Ad Age advertising century: Top 100 campaigns. http://adage.com/article/special-report-the-advertising-century/ad-age-advertising-century-top-100-advertising-campaigns/140150/

129 Garfield, B. (1999 March 29). Ad Age advertising century: The Top 100 campaigns. http://adage.com/article/special-report-the-advertising-century/ad-age-advertising-century-top-100-campaigns/140918; AdAge. (1999 March 29). Ad Age advertising century: Top 100 campaigns. http://adage.com/article/special-report-the-advertising-century/ad-age-advertising-century-top-100-advertising-campaigns/140150.

130 AdAge. (1999 March 29). Ad Age advertising century: Top 100 campaigns. http://adage.com/article/special-report-the-advertising-century/ad-age-advertising-century-top-100-advertising-campaigns/140150/

131 AdAge. (2015). Top ad campaigns of the 21st century. http://adage.com/lp/top15/#intro

132 AdAge. (2015). Top ad campaigns of the 21st century. http://adage.com/lp/top15/#winners

133 www.youtube.com/watch?v=l8WiI6YeXFE&index=1&list=PLComNResqCikOu9a85YJeittwTKUudyEd

134 canneslions.com. (2018). Celebrating creativity since 1954. https://www.canneslions.com/our-awards

135 Campaign India. (2010 Oct 28). Cannes Lions launches Creative Effectiveness award. http://www.campaignindia.in/article/cannes-lions-launches-creative-effectiveness-award/412976

136 canneslions.com. (2013). Cannes Lions. https://www2.canneslions.com/resources/downloads/Rules/2013/Creative_Effectivness_2013.pdf

137 AMVBBDO. (2011). Walkers Sandwich - AMV BBDO 2011 Cannes Effectiveness Grand Prix. https://www.youtube.com/watch?v=DClOTJyVQzc

138 AdAge. (2011). Walkers: Sandwich-Cannes Creative Effectiveness Grand Prix Winner. http://creativity-online.com/work/walkers-sandwichcannes-creative-effectiveness-grand-prix-winner/23635

139 BBH. (2012). Axe Angels. https://www.youtube.com/watch?v=_ADycM5r-dY

140 Cannes Effectiveness Lions. (2012). Axe Excite: Returning to universal truths to create global hits. *WARC*.

141 Cannes Effectiveness Lions. (2013). Heineken's Legendary Journey: Justifying a premium the world over. *WARC*.

142 McCann. (2014). V/Line Guilt Trips, case study. https://www.youtube.com/watch?v=Chiy7l7D1rk

143 Best-Marketing.eu. (2015). Case study: Volvo Trucks live test series. http://www.best-marketing.eu/case-study-volvo-trucks-live-test-series/

144 Cannes Effectiveness Lions. (2015). Volvo Trucks: Live test series. *WARC*.

145 Adam&EveDDB. (2016). John Lewis-Monty The Penguin case study. https://www.youtube.com/watch?v=iwNoLKv7gnI

146 Cannes Effectiveness Lions. (2016). John Lewis: Monty's Christmas. *WARC*.

147 Wohl, J. (2016 April 7). Want to rent Van Gogh's 'Bedroom'? http://adage.com/article/creativity/art-instti/303425; Leo Burnett. (2017 June 23). Leo Burnett Chicago wins Grand Prix in Creative Effectiveness for 'Van 'Bedrooms'. http://leoburnett.com/articles/news/leo-burnett-chicago-wins-grand-prix-in-creative-effectiveness-for-van-goghs-bedrooms.

148 Binet, L., & Field, P. (2008). Overview of Marketing in the Era of Accountability. from WARC

149 Reinartz, W., & Saffert, P. (2013 June). Creativity in advertising: When it works and when it doesn't. *Harvard Business Review, 91,* 106–12.

150 Hull, J. (2011 June 9). The link between creativity and effectiveness. https://www.thinkbox.tv/Research/Thinkbox-research/The-link-between-creativity-and-effectiveness

151 Twose, D., & Jones, P. W. (2011 November). Creative effectiveness. from WARC

152 ipa.co.uk. (2015). The long and the short of it. http://www.ipa.co.uk/page/The-Long-and-the-Short-of-It-publication#.WpouoWZL1-U

153 Binet, L., & Field, P. (2013). The long and the short of it presentation. http://www.ipa.co.uk/Document/The-long-and-the-Short-of-it-presentation

154 Roland, L. (2013 June 12). The long and short of it: Measuring campaign effectiveness over time. https://www.warc.com/NewsAndOpinion/Opinion/1727

155 Nyilasy, G., & Reid, L. N. (2009). Agency practitioner theories of how advertising works. *Journal of Advertising, 38*(3), 81–96.

156 Malykhina, E. (2010). P&G Olympics push pays homage to Moms. http://www.adweek.com/brand-marketing/pg-olympics-push-pays-homage-moms-107045/

157 P&G. (2010). Kids. https://www.youtube.com/watch?v=SEnRYuqFoPg

158 P&G. (2010). Never walk alone. https://www.youtube.com/watch?v=p12RCwLVHJE

159 P&G. (2010 August 16). P&G helps moms share their kids' Olympic experiences. http://news.pg.com/blog/company-strategy/pg-helps-moms-share-their-kids-olympic-experiences

160 P&G (2010). YOG 2010 commercial. https://www.youtube.com/watch?v=bVkSGEiGluA

161 P&G (2010). YOG 2010 commercial 'Nurture'. https://www.youtube.com/watch?v=SuXAWgUEf68

162 DeVries Public Relations. (2011). Procter & Gamble brandSAVER supports Special Olympics. https://www.businesswire.com/news/home/20111227005021/en/Procter-Gamble-brandSAVER-Supports-Special-Olympics

163 Vega, T. (2012). Mothers will get the glory in P&G's campaign. http://www.nytimes.com/2012/04/17/business/media/mothers-get-the-glory-in-procter-gamble-campaign.html?mtrref=undefined&gwh=8A51669660715E56C7636B3692FA6F96&gwt=pay

164 Special Olympics. (2013). Thank you, Mom: P&G supports Special Olympics mothers. https://specialolympicsmissouri.wordpress.com/2013/05/07/thank-you-mom-pg/

165 P&G. (2013). Procter & Gamble brands unite to kick off Sochi 2014 Olympic Winter Games 'Thank You Mom' campaign by launching a series of 28 Raising an Olympian films. http://news.pg.com/press-release/pg-corporate-announcements/procter-gamble-brands-unite-kick-sochi-2014-olympic-winter-

166 Special Olympics. (2014). Procter & Gamble Company. http://www.specialolympics.org/Sponsors/Procter___Gamble.aspx; Neo, W. W. (2015). P&G and NTUC partner with Special Olympics to enable athletes to achieve their sporting dreams. http://theneodimension.com/pg-and-ntuc-partner-with-special-olympics-to-enable-athletes-to-achieve-their-sporting-dreams

167 Olympic.org. (2016). P&G supporting athletes and their families during Olympic Games Rio 2016. https://www.olympic.org/news/p-g-supporting-athletes-and-their-families-during-olympic-games-rio-2016

168 Special Olympics. (2014). Procter & Gamble Company. http://www.specialolympics.org/Sponsors/Procter___Gamble.aspx

169 Special Olympics. (2011). Procter & Gamble honors moms of Special Olympics Athletes by supporting the global movement and Special Olympics Team USA's journey to the upcoming World Games. http://specialolympics.org/Press/2011/Procter___Gamble_Honors_Moms_of_Special_Olympics_Athletes.aspx

170 P&G. (2011). What I See. https://www.youtube.com/watch?v=iXLC5Y1atC0

171 Fast Company. (2012). P&G salutes mothers in 2012 Olympics campaign. https://www.fastcompany.com/1680577/pg-salutes-mothers-in-2012-olympics-campaign

172 P&G. (2012). Best Job. https://www.youtube.com/watch?v=HO50_FZfwXs

173 P&G. (2012). Best Job P&G London 2012 Olympic Games Film-Australia. https://www.youtube.com/watch?v=4otZjR95qaY

174 Vega, T. (2012). Mothers will get the glory in P&G's campaign. http://www.nytimes.com/2012/04/17/business/media/mothers-get-the-glory-in-procter-gamble-campaign.html?mtrref=undefined&gwh=8A51669660715E56C7636B3692FA6F96&gwt=pay; P&G. (2012). Gabrielle Douglas: Raising an Olympian. https://www.youtube.com/watch?v=H2L5F41tyGw.

175 P&G. (2013). Maria and Eunice Shriver: The gift my mother gave me. https://www.youtube.com/watch?v=YjYuj4BvIsc

176 Special Olympics. (2013 May 28). Special Olympics Asia Pacific. https://www.facebook.com/soasiapacific/videos/10151959263567942/

177 https://www.youtube.com/watch?v=6Ult4t-1NoQ

178 PRWeek. (2015 March 20). Global campaign of the year 2015. http://www.prweek.com/article/1337841/global-campaign-year-2015

179 P&G. (2016). P&G 'Thank You, Mom' campaign ad: 'Strong' (Rio 2016 Olympics). https://www.youtube.com/watch?v=rdQrwBVRzEg

180 Zazzi, J. (2016 May 4). Ad of the week: P&G dazzles again with 'Thank You, Mom—Strong'. Campaign. http://www.campaignlive.com/article/ad-week-p-g-dazzles-again-thank-you-mom-strong/1393558

181 DeVries Public Relations. (2011). Procter & Gamble brandSAVER supports Special Olympics. https://www.businesswire.com/news/home/20111227005021/en/Procter-Gamble-brandSAVER-Supports-Special-Olympics

182 Special Olympics. (2013). Thank you, Mom: P&G supports Special Olympics mothers. http://stage.wk.com/campaign/momswisdom/

183 WK.com. (2013 May 6). Procter & Gamble #MOMSWISDOM. http://www.wk.com/campaign/momswisdom/from/procter__gamble

184 Welovead.com. (2013). Proud sponsor of Moms. http://www.welovead.com/en/works/details/541wnuvAh

185 P&G. (2017). Vicks—Generations of Care #TouchOfCare. https://www.youtube.com/watch?v=7zeeVEKaDLM

CHAPTER 6
Public Relations

Peter Ling

The public relations 'air' is everywhere!

On 9 March 2017, *PRWeek* named United Airlines CEO Oscar Munoz its US Communicator of the Year because of his ability to rally employees to support his United Airtime and transformation vision.[1]

On 17 March 2017, *PRWeek* announced that United Airlines also won the publication's 'Best in Public Affairs 2017' for its 'United to Cuba' bid against 12 airlines to the Department of Transportation. The bid team commissioned research, proposed flights from various US cities to benefit more travellers, communicated via various media platforms, gained support from diverse stakeholders and secured the highest percentage of flights against competitors.[2]

On 27 March 2017, United received social media outrage for banning two girls at a Denver International Airport gate for being improperly dressed in leggings.[3]

From 10 April 2017, United received a mountain of bad publicity after a passenger's video went viral (See Figure 6.1). The video showed security men from Chicago O'Hare International Airport

Figure 6.1 Injured passenger Joseph Dao, who was dragged off a United Airlines flight in 2017

forcibly dragging a passenger who had refused to give up his seat on the overbooked Flight 3411 from Chicago to Louisville. United needed to fly four employees to Louisville but no passenger took up the first offer of US$400 and then the second offer of US$800 plus accommodation to give up their seats. Then a manager selected four people through a computer. The extremely upset passenger in the video was injured during the forceful removal from the plane. Children and other passengers were also upset.[4]

Within a day, the video attracted more than 100 million views on China's Twitter equivalent, Weibo. The man had said in the video that he was being discriminated against for being Chinese. Weibo commenters called for a boycott of United Airlines. Munoz referred to the incident as 'upsetting'.[5] *PRWeek* received backlash for its award to Munoz.[6]

In subsequent statements, Munoz described the 69-year-old passenger, Joseph Dao, as 'disruptive and belligerent', later expressed 'deepest apologies' and eventually lamented being 'ashamed' by the incident. Within days, Dao sued United Airlines, online petitions clamoured for Munoz to resign and the United Airlines market value dropped by US$1 billion.

That treatment of Dao led to some positive developments. Munoz admitted that Dao's removal was 'a mistake of epic proportions'. United Airlines reached an early undisclosed financial settlement with Dao. The airline raised the payment to customers who vacate seats on overbooked flights to US$10 000 and introduced policies for better customer service.[7]

■ INTRODUCTION

Public relations, like air, is everywhere. It is present in any interaction with internal and external audiences. It is present when companies cope with employee sex scandals, employee attitude and behaviour, backlash on policies, staff walkouts, union rallies, consumer complaints, natural disasters, product tampering, product defects, questionable corporate practices and misleading marketing activities.

Just as there is clean and polluted air in our environment, there is also good and bad 'air' in public relations practice. It is good when there is positive public perception about a company's reputation and activities through staff incentives, corporate expansion, community investments, charitable work and so on.

It is bad when things go wrong in terms of actions, behaviours and comments by corporate representatives. It is also bad when public relations companies malign each other, a phenomenon known as **black PR**,[8] and when companies claim to be environmental champions when they have questionable practices, a concept known as **greenwashing**.[9]

While PR is everywhere, it is often not visible when compared to advertising. As a result, students have described public relations as 'boring'. Questions have been asked: What really is public relations? What is the history of public relations? What are the theories and communication models behind public relations? How is public relations practised and what is its relationship with marketing or marketing communication? This chapter will provide a clearer perspective on the field of public relations.

LEARNING OBJECTIVES

After reading this chapter you should be able to:

1. explain public relations
2. discuss significant influences in public relations such as communication eras, public relations pioneers and industry associations
3. discuss how theories and models of communication guide professional practice
4. discuss public relations practice in terms of functions, planning processes, media tools and codes of practice.

What is public relations?

One research study in 1975 went through a rigorous process to attempt to define public relations.[10] The researcher collected 472 definitions, synthesised them into a draft definition, had 65 practitioners provide feedback to improve or change the definition, revised the definition, sent it to the same practitioners again for comments, amended the definition, rechecked again with the practitioners and finally arrived at this definition:

> Public relations is a distinctive management function which helps establish and maintain mutual lines of communication, understanding, acceptance and cooperation between an organization and its publics; involves the management of problems or issues; helps management to keep informed on and responsive to public opinion; defines and emphasizes the responsibility of management to serve the public interest; helps management keep abreast of and effectively utilize change, serving as an early warning system to help anticipate trends; and uses research and sound and ethical communication techniques as its principal tools.[11]

Compare the definition above with definitions from other sources, namely those of PR pioneer Edward Bernays; Cutlip and Center's book *Effective Public Relations* ('the bible of public relations'); the Public Relations Society of America (PRSA); the Chartered Institute of Public Relations (CIPR) in the UK; and the Public Relations Institute of Australia (PRIA).

> **Bernays:** Public relations is applied social science. It applies an understanding of social psychology, anthropology, sociology, psychology, economics and history. If I'm advising my client, unless I know the impact of religion or ethnic background or social or economic conditions on a human being, I can't deal with the problem.[12]
>
> A public relations counsel is an applied social scientist who advises a client on the social attitudes and actions he or she must take in order to appeal to the public on which it is dependent. The practitioner ascertains, through research, the adjustment or maladjustment of the client with the public, then advises what changes in attitude and action are demanded to reach the highest point of adjustment to meet social goals.[13]
>
> **Cutlip and Center:** Public relations is the management function that establishes and maintains mutually beneficial relations between an organization and the publics on whom its success or failure depends.[14]
>
> **PRSA:** Public relations helps an organization and its publics adapt mutually to each other (1982 definition).
>
> Public relations is a strategic communication process that builds mutually beneficial relationships between organizations and their publics (2011–12 definition based on crowdsourcing and public vote).[15]
>
> **CIPR:** Public Relations is about reputation—the result of what you do, what you say and what others say about you. Public Relations is the discipline which looks after reputation, with the aim of earning understanding and support and influencing opinion and behaviour. It is the planned and sustained effort to establish and maintain goodwill and mutual understanding between an organisation and its publics.[16]
>
> **PRIA:** The deliberate, planned and sustained effort to establish and maintain mutual understanding between an organisation (or individual) and its (or their) publics.[17]

All definitions share common features. First, PR is about mutual understanding and goodwill between an organisation and its various audiences. Second, PR is about changing opinions, attitudes and actions of both the organisation and its audiences—otherwise there would be no mutually beneficial relationships. Third, PR is a strategic and sustained communication process guided by research on public opinion.

Although less often mentioned across the various definitions, PR is a management function for building and maintaining trust between an organisation and its diverse audiences. PR also requires a social-science approach to understand human attitudes and actions, advise management and clients appropriately to address issues and problems, and communicate ethically using a variety of techniques.

The next section traces the history of PR to provide a better understanding of the discipline.

History of public relations

The historical context of public relations provides a better picture of what the industry is all about. This section examines a communication timeline, PR pioneers and industry associations.

Communication timeline

The Museum of Public Relations at Baruch College in New York City has an interesting timeline of human communication and PR through the ages. The museum traces communication from the cave drawings of Dawn of the Ages (37 000–17 000 BC) through to Age of Empires, Age of Faith, Age of Print, Age of Mass Media and Age of Digital Media.[18] See Table 6.1 for a summary of the timeline and of the timeline clusters.

Table 6.1 Timeline of the different ages of communication

PERIOD	EVENT
37 000–17 000 BC—Dawn of the Ages	Cave drawings used as communication
3300 BC—Age of Empires	Egyptian hieroglyphs used to convey biographies, calculations, ideas, magical texts, prayers, royal documents, worship details
1500–1800BC—Age of Empires	Moses and Ten Commandments on stone tablets
551–479 BC—Age of Faith	Confucius communicated family values
469 BC—Age of Empires	Greek philosophers advocated the importance of public opinion
First century—Age of Faith	Saint Paul wrote 13 of 27 books in the Bible to spread the message of Christ
206 BC–220 AD—Age of Faith	Handwritten news during the Han dynasty
Third century—Age of Faith	Scholarly scrolls in the Egyptian Library of Alexandria
390–400s—Age of Faith	Saint Patrick from Ireland spread Christianity
1162-1227—Age of Faith	Genghis Khan set up horse stations for riders to receive news and spread orders
1440—Age of Print	Johannes Gutenberg developed the printing press to spread information and knowledge
1517—Age of Print	Martin Luther used his '95 theses' document to begin the Protestant Reformation
1572–1627—Age of Print	Pope Gregory XIII and his 'Propaganda' mission to spread Catholicism in non-Catholic countries
1773–Age of Print	Samuel Adams as a 'master of propaganda' opposed British monarchy through political messages and the Boston Tea Party tax protest
1776–Age of Print	The *Common Sense* pamphlet and Declaration of Independence symbolised the break from Great Britain
1829–Age of Print	Newspaper owner Amos Kendell wrote White House policy messages to re-position war hero President Andrew Jackson as an intellectual
1831–Age of Print	Abolitionists Frederick Douglass and William Lloyd Garrison published anti-slavery newspapers
Nineteenth century—Age of Mass Media	The Age of Invention produced the telegraph, **daguerreotype** photograph, telephone, phonograph, gramophone, motion picture camera, wireless telegraphy and radio communication

PERIOD	EVENT
1871—Age of Mass Media	Phineas Taylor Barnum promoted events and the travelling show
1882—Age of Mass Media	The words 'The public be damned' by railroad controller William Henry Vanderbilt triggered massive editorial coverage, speeches and cartoons
1906—Age of Mass Media	Ivy Lee issued to editors the 'Declaration of Principles' to advocate that a company should issue accurate and timely news to the press and public. Lee also helped to re-position vilified oil baron John D. Rockefeller as a philanthropist
1917—Age of Mass Media	President Woodrow Wilson's Committee on Public Information—which included George Creel, Edward Bernays and Carl Byoir—used speaking volunteers, billboards and posters to get the public to support US entry into WWI
1919—Age of Mass Media	Author and journalist Doris Fleischman wrote speeches and press releases for the firm of her husband Edward Bernays
1923—Age of Mass Media	Edward Bernays wrote *Crystallizing Public Opinion* to convey 'two-way-street' communication between a firm and its public
1927 onwards—Age of Mass Media	In-house public relations counsellors became senior corporate advisors
1930s—Age of Mass Media	The Depression led to the rise of PR
1933—Age of Mass Media	Campaigns Inc. became the first political consulting PR firm
1939—Age of Mass Media	Television was introduced
1942—Age of Mass Media	The US Office of War Information communicated war news to the public
1930s–1950s—Age of Mass Media	PR agencies sprang up after the war: Carl Byoir, Edelman and Burson-Marsteller
1950s–1970s—Age of Mass Media	Anthems, buttons, chants and posters helped in social change (e.g. 'Make love, not war')
1969—Age of Digital Media	The internet started on 29 October 1969.
1982—Age of Digital Media	The effective handling of the Tylenol capsule poisoning—through various stakeholders and media—became a benchmark for corporate responsibility and crisis communication
Twentieth century—Age of Digital Media	Integrated media emerged through advertising, marketing and PR conglomerate companies
2008—Age of Digital Media	The 2008 presidential election campaign successfully used social media as a two-way communication tool to win youth votes
2015—Age of Digital Media	*The New York Times* used virtual reality for storytelling

Source: PR Museum. (2015). Public Relations through the ages: a timeline of social movements, technology milestones and the rise of the profession.

Age of Empires

The timeline between 3300 BC and 469 BC covered Egyptian hieroglyphs, Moses and his Ten Commandments and Greek philosophers advocating the importance of public opinion.

Age of Faith

This history during 551–479 BC and 1227 AD highlighted Confucius emphasising family values; Saint Paul and his writing of 13 of 27 books in the Bible to spread the message of Jesus Christ; handwritten news during the Han Dynasty; scholarly scrolls in the Egyptian Library of Alexandria; Saint Patrick from Ireland spreading Christianity; and Genghis Khan setting up horse stations for riders to receive news and spread orders.

Age of Print

The era from 1440 to 1831 listed developments that facilitated the spread of information: Johannes Gutenberg and his printing press; Martin Luther with his '95 theses' document to begin the Protestant Reformation; Pope Gregory XIII and his 'Propaganda' mission to spread Catholicism in non-Catholic countries; Samuel Adams as a 'master of propaganda' to oppose British monarchy through political messages and the Boston Tea Party tax protest; the Common Sense pamphlet and Declaration of Independence that helped the break from Great Britain; newspaper owner Amos Kendell writing White House policy messages to re-position war hero President Andrew Jackson as an intellectual; and abolitionists Frederick Douglass and William Lloyd Garrison publishing anti-slavery newspapers.

Age of Mass Media

The period from the nineteenth century to the 1970s traced inventions and key people that started the early beginnings of professional public relations practice. The Age of Invention produced the telegraph, daguerreotype photograph, telephone, phonograph, gramophone, motion picture camera, wireless telegraphy and radio communication. Between 1871 and 1882, Phineas Taylor Barnum promoted events and the travelling show while the words 'The public be damned' by railroad controller William Henry Vanderbilt triggered massive editorial coverage, speeches and cartoons.

Key pioneers in PR were featured between 1906 and 1923. Ivy Lee issued to editors the 'Declaration of Principles' to advocate that a company should issue accurate and timely news to the press and public. Lee also helped to re-position vilified oil baron John D. Rockefeller as a philanthropist. President Woodrow Wilson's Committee on Public Information—which included George Creel, Edward Bernays and Carl Byoir—used speaking volunteers, billboards and posters to get the public to support US entry into the First World War.

While in-house public relations counsellors became senior corporate advisors from 1927, the Depression led to the rise of PR. Television was introduced in 1939 and the US Office of War Information communicated war news to the public in 1942. PR agencies sprang up after the war: Carl Byoir, Edelman and Burson-Marsteller. Between the 1950s and the 1970s, anthems, buttons, chants and posters such as 'Make love, not war' helped in social change.

This Age of Mass Media is also divided into specific eras: the Seedbed Era of 1900–1916 had Ivy Lee and President Theodore Roosevelt; the organisational attitude of 'Let the public be informed'; and defensive publicity. The First World War period of 1917–1918 included George Creel and organised promotion to promote patriotism through interest groups. The Booming Twenties Era of 1919–1929 with Edward Bernays focused on mutual understanding and promoting products. The Roosevelt and Second World War era of 1930–1945 centred on radio and social responsibility. The post-war era of 1946–1964 featured television, PRSA, consumerism and professionalism. The Period of Protest and Empowerment from 1965 to 1985 included Marshal McLuhan and his message that 'the medium is the message'.[19]

Age of Digital Media

The timeline from 1969 to 2015 showed developments that have impacted on modern PR.

The computer-linked internet started on 29 October 1969. The effective handling of the Tylenol capsule poisoning in 1982—through various stakeholders and media—became a benchmark for corporate responsibility and crisis communication. Integrated media emerged through advertising, marketing and PR conglomerate companies at the end of the twentieth century. The 2008 presidential election campaign successfully used social media as a two-way communication tool to win youth votes. *The New York Times* used virtual reality for storytelling in 2015. Another source cited the digital age and globalism era beginning from 1986, necessitating a focus on 24/7 technological engagement, social networks, mobile technology, global relationships and corporate transparency.[20]

IMC IN ACTION: TYLENOL AS THE BENCHMARK FOR CRISIS COMMUNICATION

The handling of the Tylenol product tampering crisis in 1982 has gone down in PR history as the model for crisis management and communication.

Seven people in Chicago died of cyanide-laced poisoning after they consumed Extra-Strength Tylenol capsules. News spread like wildfire and caused panic nationwide. Police with loudspeakers warned the public about Tylenol poisoning. Television networks announced the deaths from poisoning. The Food and Drug Administration cautioned consumers about consuming Tylenol capsules. Hospitals were inundated with calls and admissions on suspected poisonings.

The Tylenol brand, its firm McNeil Consumer Products and parent company Johnson & Johnson seemed to be doomed as a result of this poisoning incident. The Tylenol painkiller had a 37 per cent market share for over-the-counter sales in its category. Corporate reputation was also at stake.

Johnson & Johnson implemented a two-prong strategy with its Chairman James E. Burke involved and decisions guided by the corporation's credo, which focused on its responsibility to employees, consumers, medical professionals, communities and shareholders. In Stage 1, Johnson & Johnson planned and implemented a series of actions. It informed the public and medical professionals about the tampering. It worked with the Food and Drug Administration as well as the Chicago Police and FBI and put up a US$100 000 reward for information. It stopped Tylenol production nationally and recalled 31 million bottles of Extra-Strength Tylenol worth US$100 million. It cooperated fully with all news media, stopped Tylenol brand advertising and launched a corporate advertising campaign. The corporate advertising alerted the public to the tampering and offered consumers an exchange of its capsules for tablets.

In Stage 2, six weeks after discovery of the product tampering, McNeil Consumer Products held a sales conference to announce Tylenol's comeback. McNeil—the first pharmaceutical company to comply with Food and Drug Administration regulations—re-launched Tylenol with new tamper-resistant, triple-seal packaging. McNeil offered US$2.50-off coupons for any Tylenol product. The sales team also introduced a 25 per cent discount and presented the new Tylenol to medical professionals. Brand advertising communicated the new Tylenol packaging and special offer.

The two-stage strategy generated massive positive publicity, which helped protect the corporate reputations of McNeil and Johnson & Johnson as well as the brand image of Tylenol. Tylenol regained much of its market share within a short time![21] The link in Figure 6.2 takes you to a news report from 1982 on the Tylenol product tampering crisis.

Compared to Tylenol's professional crisis communication, other corporate disasters have received mixed reviews. Union Carbide Corporation *eventually* accepted responsibility when toxic gas leakage in its Indian Bhopal pesticide plant in 1984 killed 3800 people and many animals in the streets of Bhopal as well as creating ill-health to thousands of people exposed to the gas. Initially, Union Carbide blamed its Indian subsidiary, disgruntled employees and even extremist groups.[22]

Toyota agreed to pay the US Justice Department a US$1.2 billion fine in 2014 after it lied about the safety of its vehicle accelerators. The sticky pedal matter had started in Europe in 2008 and surfaced in the US in 2009 when a family of four died after the sudden acceleration of their Lexus. Despite recalling millions of vehicles, it was found that Toyota had misled consumers and Congress about safety issues around its sticky pedals.[23]

When Malaysian Airlines flight 370 mysteriously disappeared in 2014 on its Kuala Lumpur–Beijing route with 239 people aboard, PR experts criticised the unprofessional handling of the crisis, such as poor communication with distraught families and demanding media.[24] However, PR experts praised the airline for quick social media communication when another disaster struck in 2014, with 295 people killed when flight MH17 was reportedly shot down in Eastern Ukraine.[25]

There was 'textbook' crisis management in two other airline crashes in Asia. In 2000, Singapore Airlines' CEO Cheong Choong Kong was praised for his apology and supervision of a crisis management strategy after SQ006 took a wrong turn in bad weather on the Taipei Airport runway, burst into flames and killed 82 people.[26] When AirAsia flight QZ8501 crashed in the Indonesian Java Sea in 2015, killing 162 people, AirAsia's CEO Tony Fernandes acted swiftly and was praised for his crisis communication. He came across as compassionate, empathetic, apologetic, professional, authentic and credible.[27]

Figure 6.2 The packaging for Tylenol Extra-Strength capsules, which caused poisoning in 1982

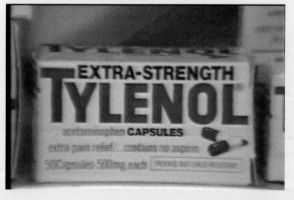

Source: www.youtube.com/watch?v=OnrhluH8-jA.

PR pioneers

Information disseminator Ivy Lee and social scientist Edward Bernays are recognised as PR pioneers during the Age of Mass Media. In this section we will talk about each of these pioneers in more detail.

Ivy Lee

Lee was a distinguished high-school orator who worked as a correspondent for New York newspapers to help fund his Princeton University studies. He later enrolled at Harvard Law School but dropped out early to be a reporter for the *New York Journal* and later for *The New York Times* and *New York World*.

From 1903, Lee switched to publicity and promotional work for the Fusion Party and the Democratic Party before setting up Parker & Lee to counsel business and industrial clients in matters such as changing public perception towards the Pennsylvania Railroad and managing the coal strike crisis at the Anthracite Coal Roads & Mines Company.

In 1916, Lee set up a new company with his brother and a former editor to handle PR for the I.R.T.'s New York subway. Over the years, Lee worked with clients such as Bethlehem Steel, Chrysler, General Mills, the Rockefeller Family, Standard Oil and United States Rubber.

While Lee provided pro bono services to charities, churches and universities and enhanced the image of his clients, he received negative publicity for his interest in Russian and German matters in the 1930s before his death, aged 57, in 1934.[28]

Nevertheless, Lee has been described as the 'other father of public relations', having introduced the 1906 Declaration of Principles as the code of ethics for the press and PR practitioners and having pioneered both the press release and crisis management.[29]

He distinguished publicity from propaganda, or 'press-agentry', by including credible information sources and focusing on honest, fact-based, interesting news that affected people's well-being. He also defined publicity as a way to express an idea, policy or organisation using advertising, articles, books, brass bands, magazines, mass meetings, moving pictures, parades and radio.[30]

Using various metaphors in a 1916 convention speech, Lee described publicity as follows:

> Publicity must not be thought of as it is by a good many as a sort of umbrella to protect you against the rain of an unpleasant public opinion.
>
> Publicity must not be regarded as a bandage to cover up a sore and enable you to get along pretty well with the real trouble still there.
>
> Publicity must, if your trouble is to be cured, be considered rather as an antiseptic which shall cleanse the very source of the trouble and reveal it to the doctor, which is the public.
>
> To change the metaphor again, publicity must not be thought of as a cloak to look well on the outside of a body deformed and diseased within.[31]

Edward Bernays

The Museum of Public Relations is a legacy of Bernays, who is known in the industry as the 'father of public relations'. At the age of 101, in 1993, he suggested the idea of a PR museum, which led to its launch in 1997, after his death in 1995 aged 103.

The museum has more than 600 books, artefacts, correspondence, photographs, displays, exhibits and digital videotapes of significant practitioners and media events over the industry's 100-year history. Among the collections are Bernays' often-cited 1923 book *Crystallizing Public Relations* and books donated by his uncle, Sigmund Freud, who had influenced Bernays' social science approach to PR practice.[32]

Born in Vienna in 1891, Bernays grew up in New York from 1892 and graduated in architecture from Cornell University in 1912. However, he became a journalist, worked on US Government propaganda projects during the First World War and started business as a PR counsellor with his wife Doris Fleischman. His 'Freudian instincts' and war-based techniques on engineering public opinion attracted clients such as US Tobacco Company, Procter & Gamble, General Electric, Time Inc., CBS, NBC and the United Fruit Company.[33]

As a PR visionary, Bernays marketed corporations and brands through surveys, facts, newsletters, media reviews, publicity guides, story themes, public events, luncheons, art shows, exhibitions, celebrity endorsements, competitions, awards and specially created products to shape public opinion for his clients.[34]

Bernays championed the licensing of the PR profession to protect clients, employers, qualified executives and the public from inept and unqualified practitioners, but the Massachusetts Joint House and Senate Committee on Government Relations rejected his proposed legislative bill in 1992 (when he was aged 100).[35]

Nevertheless, Bernays had gone down in history as the only PR executive named in *Life* magazine's 1990 special issue on 'The 100 Most Important Americans of the 20th Century'. The list included Albert Einstein, Walt Disney, Dale Carnegie, Elizabeth Arden, John Dewey, T. S. Eliot, Milton Friedman, George Gallup, Ernest Hemingway, Helen Keller, Edwin Land, Ray Kroc, Jonas Salk, Thomas Watson and the Wright brothers.[36] See the case study 'Edward Bernays' PR campaigns in the 1920s–1930s' at the end of this chapter.

Industry associations

This section briefly reviews the PR associations in the US, UK and Australia as well as the global PR body.

The US

The Public Relations Society of America (PRSA) was established in 1947 to set industry standards, develop professionals and maintain members' ethical principles. PRSA then introduced its Code of Ethics for members in 1950[37] and its Accredited Public Relations (APR) voluntary certification program in 1964. In 1998, the APR came under the administration of the Universal Accreditation Board, which then changed the oral examination to a Readiness Review and the formal examination to a computer-based process testing knowledge, skills and attitudes (KSA)—essential for a PR professional.[38]

For the Readiness Review, the candidate writes about their PR experience and preparation for APR and then discusses their competence with a Readiness Review Panel. After clearing the Readiness Review stage, the candidate takes the four-hour multiple-choice examination at a testing centre. The examination comprises six KSA categories with different weightings: researching, planning, implementing and evaluating programs (33 per cent of the examination); leading the PR function (18 per cent); managing relationships (15 per cent); applying ethics and law (13 per cent); managing issues and crisis communication (13 per cent); and understanding communication models, theories and history of the profession (8 per cent). The successful candidate is then entitled to use the APR status.[39]

The UK

The history of PR in the UK is linked to several events, organisations and people. The War Propaganda Bureau in 1914 and the Home Office with its information bureau and Department of Information provided war updates to the masses. After the First World War, Stephen Tallents hired talents in art, film and publicity at the government's Empire Marketing Board to engage with various publics to promote British trade.

Southern Railways appointed John Elliot as Director of Public Relations in 1925 and Basil Clarke set up a PR firm, Editorial Services, in 1924.

After the Second World War, a group of local government PR practitioners started the Institute of Public Relations (IPR) in 1948 and later expanded membership to include executives in central government and private sectors.[40] IPR became CIPR when it received chartered status in February 2005.[41] CIPR has an Accredited Public Relations Practitioner recognition for members of CIPR who have a CIPR diploma or a CIPR-recognised master's degree and have completed one yearly cycle of continuing professional development.[42]

Australia

The Public Relations Institute of Australia (PRIA) was established in 1949 to represent the PR industry and enforce ethical standards. It also recognises accredited degrees in Australia that meet its education framework, covering knowledge of culture and society, communication and media, and organisation and relationships; professional skills; and personal competencies.

Knowledge of culture and society includes ethics, regulations, laws and corporate social responsibility. Knowledge of communication and media comprises history, theories and principles of both communication and public relations as well as social media and digital engagement. Professional skills are writing and editing; integrated reporting; print and web publishing; design and creativity; software applications; business processes and planning; campaign and program planning; presenting and pitching; and management of events, projects, finance, clients and social media. Personal competencies include critical analysis and critical thinking; problem solving; strategic thinking; team work and independence; leadership; resilience; self-reflexivity; and career development skills.[43]

Global alliance

PRSA, CIPR and PRIA are members of the Global Alliance for Public Relations and Communication Management (GAPRCM), which officially started in 2002 to agree on global issues such as core competencies, curriculum, accreditation programs and codes of ethics. GAPRCM members spread across Africa, Asia, Europe, Latin America, North America and Oceania.[44] The seven core competencies are to:

- research, plan, implement and evaluate communication programs and projects
- apply PR/communication theories, models and practices
- apply PR/communication strategies to business goals and objectives
- manage issues and crisis communication
- uphold professional standards and practise ethical behaviour
- demonstrate communication skills such as written, oral, presentation and negotiation
- effectively manage human, financial and technological organisational resources.[45]

In summary, communication has gone through different ages, such as print, mass media and digital media. Mass communication accelerated with innovations in printing, radio, television, the internet and social media. PR pioneers such as Ivy Lee and Edward Bernays paved the way for integrated media campaigns involving publicity, marketing communication and audience engagement. Industry associations in the US, UK, Australia and globally synergised development of curriculum frameworks, practitioner competencies, social science knowledge and industry standards. Ivy Lee's metaphor of 'a good-looking cloak on a badly-diseased body' is perhaps symbolic of some companies trying to impress externally but suffering internally.

The next section explores diverse theories and models in the PR industry.

PR theories and models

The evolution of public relations over a century has contributed significant communication theories and models. This section reviews the key PR theories and models that guide practice.

Theories

Theories predict or explain happenings, while models illustrate practice and how things work. There are theories on transmission/media effects, audience, message and the PR process.[46]

Transmission/media effects theories

These include the two-step flow theory, agenda setting and framing. The **two-step flow theory** involves an opinion leader influencing the decision maker. **Agenda setting** occurs when there is a repeated focus on an issue. **Framing** is another level of agenda setting with media describing an issue or a person in certain 'frames' or attributes.

Audience theories

Some of the most-cited audience theories include the diffusion of innovation theory, situational theory of publics and the attribution theory. **Diffusion of innovation theory** is about adopting ideas or products as innovator, early adopter, early majority, late majority and laggard. **Situational theory** is contextual, where active people seek information while passive consumers are disinterested. **Attribution theory** involves attributing personal or situational factors to an event.

Message theories

Two theories are significant. The **rhetoric theory** involves persuasive communication through a role model and the emotional or logical appeal of the person's message. The **sleeper effect theory** is about a person forgetting an unreliable source but remembering and accepting the message.

PR-specific theories

Key PR theories include agenda building, excellence and relationship management. **Agenda-building theory**, which is related to agenda-setting theory, is about using information channels such as news releases, interviews and blogs to influence media interest on selected topics. **Excellence theory** relates to PR as a catalyst for organisational effectiveness. **Relationship management theory** is about PR being a strategic management function for relating with various publics.

Models

The models of communication include the traditional communication process and the four classic models of PR.[47]

Communication process

The **Shannon-Weaver Model** of Sender-Encoder-Channel-Decoder-Receiver as a communication process has been around since 1948. There is 'noise' at the Channel stage that could interfere with the message, such as historical distrust, language used, non-credible spokespersons, cultural misalignment, inappropriate media, negative opinion leaders, time available, censorship and contextual reference frames. The model has evolved to include feedback from receiver to source.[48]

Classic models of PR

Grunig and Hunt's 1984 models for PR practice are part of the excellence theory. The four models are:

- **press agentry/publicity**
- **public information**
- **two-way asymmetric**
- **two-way symmetric**.

See Table 6.2, which describes eight characteristics of the four models of PR.[49]

Table 6.2 Characteristics of the four models of PR

CHARACTERISTICS	PRESS AGENTRY/ PUBLICITY MODEL	PUBLIC INFORMATION MODEL	TWO-WAY ASYMMETRIC MODEL	TWO-WAY SYMMETRIC MODEL
Purpose	Propaganda	Information dissemination	Scientific persuasion	Mutual understanding
Communication nature	One-way: truth not essential	One-way: truth important	Two-way: imbalanced effects to influence audience to the views of the organisation	Two-way: balanced effects of both public and organisation changing attitudes or behaviour
Communication model	Source>Receiver	Source>Receiver	Source>Receiver>Feedback	Person/ Group>Person/ Group>Feedback
Historical origin	1830s–1900	1900–1920s	1920s	From 1960s
Historical figures	P. T. Barnum	Ivy Lee	Edward L. Bernays	Bernays, educators, professional leaders
Practice sectors	Promoting products, sports, theatres	Associations, business, education, government, non-profit	Business, PR firms, PR-cum-advertising firms	PR firms, large business firms
Estimated usage percentage	15%	50%	20%	15%
Media outputs	Media publicity	Press relations programs, pamphlets, magazines, consumer guidebooks, fact sheets, films, videotapes	Research findings, news features, advertising, recipes, booklets	Invitations to journalists to develop stories or have dialogue with organisational executives, invitations to educators and community leaders to forum or dialogue sessions

Source: Adapted from Grunig, J. E. & Hunt, T. (1984). *Managing Public Relations.* New York: Holt, Rinehart & Winston, pp. 21–43.

The Grunig and Hunt model estimates that half of corporate communication is on truthful information dissemination, with another 15 per cent on establishing mutual understanding. Scientific persuasion accounts for 20 per cent of communication, while propaganda forms 15 per cent of communication. One critic, online PR author David Phillips, proposed a variation of the model to align with digital tools of communication, modified the two-way asymmetric model to a **one-way asymmetric model** and provided a variety of communication tools for each model.[50] See Table 6.3.

Table 6.3 Digital era and the four models of PR

CHARACTERISTICS	PRESS AGENTRY/ PUBLICITY MODEL	PUBLIC INFORMATION MODEL	ONE-WAY ASYMMETRIC MODEL	TWO-WAY SYMMETRIC MODEL
Purpose	Propaganda	Information dissemination	Scientific persuasion	Mutual understanding
Communication tools	Static websites, FAQ page, intranet	Frequently updated websites, web advertisements, search advertising, website enabling public to send information	Blogs with comment enabled, content sharing sites, Wiki editable information, Rich Site Summary or RSS feed, online community voting	Open corporate social media sites, Twitter, interactive online community contribution

This section on communication theories and models provides a guide on media, audience, message and PR communication theories. It also highlights the traditional communication Sender-Encoder-Channel/ Noise-Decoder-Receiver model and the classic model of press agentry/publicity, public information, two-way asymmetric and two-way symmetric communication. Many media outputs or communication tools are used for propaganda, information dissemination, scientific persuasion and mutual understanding.

Public relations practice

The history of PR provides a useful context for understanding industry pioneers and the disciplinary expertise required to succeed in this industry. This section reviews the PR functions highlighted by PRSA, CIPR, PRIA and PR consultancies; the planning processes involved in PR; the media tools used to engage with diverse audiences; and the codes of practice for PR practitioners.

PR functions

A good way to gain a clearer picture of PR functions is to look at industry associations' campaign effectiveness awards and the practices of PR consultancies.

Industry associations

PRSA has been running its Silver Anvil Awards since 1944. The 13 Silver Anvil Award categories are community relations, crisis communication, events and observances, global communication, integrated communication, internal communication, investor relations, issues management, marketing, multicultural public relations, public affairs, public service and reputation/brand management. PRSA chooses the Best of Silver Anvil Award from Silver Anvil Award winners.[51]

CIPR has had Excellence Awards since 1984 across the UK, Europe and any country worldwide. Its categories include corporate and business communication, internal communication, consumer relations, public sector, corporate social responsibility, public affairs, not-for-profit, healthcare, integrated campaign, global public relations, issues or crisis management, media relations, social media and digital.[52]

PRIA has been running its awards since 1976 to cover diverse campaigns for government initiatives, advocacy and public affairs, issues management, crisis management, internal or change management, corporate communication, community relations, health, content marketing, digital and social, experiential, integrated marketing and communication, consumer, business-to-business and thought leadership.[53]

The GAPRCM COMM PRIX Awards consist of nine categories: public sector PR, non-government sector PR, business sector PR for large companies, business sector PR for small and medium companies, corporate social responsibility, internal communication, political communication, digital communication and best adaptation of international campaigns.[54]

Common PR functions across many of the industry campaign awards include marketing relations, corporate relations, internal relations, investor relations, consumer relations, business relations, community relations, industry relations, media relations and government relations. Communication across various audiences could come under strategic integrated communication.

PR consultancies

The Top 10 PR consultancies provide more details of the PR functions, describing these as practice areas and expertise. Table 6.4 reflects the practice areas of the top 10 PR firms.[55]

An analysis of the services offered by the Top 10 PR firms reveals that marketing and corporate communication are the most commonly mentioned areas of expertise, somewhat aligning to the most-mentioned categories in PR industry awards. The other common practice areas are public affairs; digital and social media; crisis, risk, issues and reputation management; management consulting; media relations; healthcare communication; and executive training. There were fewer mentions of technology communication; financial communication; employee engagement; research and insights; data security; start-up development; and multicultural engagement. Many of the functions could be described as **proactive public relations** while crisis management would be **reactive public relations**.[66]

Marketing expertise highlighted by the PR firms includes brand marketing, business marketing, consumer marketing, lifestyle marketing, market entry, partnership marketing, retail marketing, social marketing and sports marketing. Related mentions were on branded entertainment, brand experience, events and experiential campaigns, major events and sports network.

Corporate communication expertise listed by PR firms includes corporate citizenship, corporate social responsibility, strategic integration, association works, social change, litigation communication, science communication and stakeholder engagement.

CIPR distinguishes marketing communication and corporate communication. Marketing communication focuses on promoting a product or service to a market while corporate communication is strategic integrated communication for a corporation and could include corporate social responsibility, crisis management, environmental communication, financial PR and healthcare communication.[67]

In practice, marketing and corporate communication are often integrated in PR campaigns, just as in the Tylenol poisoning case mentioned in the IMC in Action mini case study. Brand and corporate marketers have increased global sponsorship spending from US$53 billion in 2013 to US$63 billion in 2017, primarily

Table 6.4 Top 10 PR firms and their practices

RANKING	AGENCY	EXPERTISE/PRACTICES
1	Edelman	Branded entertainment; B2B communication; CEO transition communications; citizenship & corporate social responsibility; consumer health & wellness; creative newsroom; crisis & risk management; data security & privacy; data visualisation; digital; employee engagement; executive coaching services; executive positioning; financial communications & capital markets; government services; health engagement; integrated advocacy; litigation communication; management consulting; market entry; media relations; multicultural engagement; public affairs; public health; reputation & trust management; science communication & visualisation; social business planning; social media marketing; stakeholder mapping & engagement; start-up development; talent services; video influencers.[56]
2	Weber Shandwick	Business marketing; consumer marketing; corporate; crisis communication & issues management; digital; financial communication; financial services; government relations; healthcare; measurement & analytics; Mediaco services in operations setup and consulting, brand content and media R&D; public affairs; technology; travel & lifestyle marketing.[57]
3	FleishmanHillard	Brand marketing; crisis management; media relations; public affairs; reputation management; research & analytics; social & innovation; strategic integration.[58]
4	Ketchum	Brand marketing; management consulting; corporate communication; social media & digital marketing.[59]
5	MSLGroup [Publicis]	Consumer; citizenship; digital & social media; employee practice; events & experiential; financial communication; healthcare; public affairs; reputation management and corporate communication; technology.[60]
6	Burson-Marsteller	Consumer and brand marketing; corporate and financial communication; digital; future perspective trend analysis; healthcare communication & market access; crisis management; major events bidding & hosting; media; public affairs; sports marketing; technology communication.[61]
7	Hill+Knowlton Strategies	Cybersecurity/data breach; partnership marketing; employee communication; brand identity; brand experience; SJR innovation consultancy; research + data insights; public affairs; Brexit Advisory; H+K EastWest consultancy; behavioural insights; training; issues + crises[62]
8	Ogilvy PR	Association works; brand marketing; content; corporate; 'Espresso' big brand services for beginning brands and new start-ups; executive branding; healthcare; media influence; OgilvyEarth sustainable business practices; Ogilvy Sports Network; public affairs; Social@Ogilvy; social change; technology; Boutique@Ogilvy retail division.[63]
9	BlueFocus	Integrated marketing services: digital marketing; public relations; mobile & traditional advertising; creative media production; media buying; social media[64]
10	Golin [Interpublic]	Consumer; corporate; digital; healthcare; multicultural; technology[65]

on sports and secondarily on entertainment, causes, arts, festivals, fairs and annual events.[68] For the Rio Olympics in 2016, Coca-Cola, Visa, Panasonic and P&G ran corporate-cum-brand communication to convey company and brand messages.[69]

The Top 10 PR consultancies position themselves as integrated communication firms. Edelman is 'a leading global communications marketing firm'.[70] Weber Shandwick is 'a leading global communications agency'.[71] FleishmanHillard helps 'clients integrate communications into their operations to achieve their business goals'.[72] Ketchum prides itself in being a global company of 'storytellers, singers, dancers, authors, advisors and counselors'.[73] MSLGroup has a 'truly holistic approach to communications'.[74] Burson-Marsteller is 'a leading global public relations and communications firm'.[75] Hill+Knowlton Strategies is 'a global public relations and integrated communication agency'.[76] Ogilvy PR 'operates at the intersection of influencer management, behavior change and narrative' and affirms that PR 'is most effective when masterfully crafted stories are grounded in social science.'[77] BlueFocus offers 'brand management services'.[78] Golin is 'an integrated agency with PR, Digital and Content'.[79]

IMC IN ACTION: DOVE CAMPAIGN FOR REAL BEAUTY

Edelman and its client Unilever won the coveted PRSA Best of Silver Anvil Award in 2006 for the Dove personal care brand campaign.

Research on 3000 women across 10 countries revealed that most women felt that media had stereotyped unattainable beauty. Using this insight, Edelman worked with Unilever to plan the Campaign for Real Beauty to widen the concept of beauty, start a conversation on real beauty and enable women to feel good about their size, shape, curves or age.

The campaign to boost self-esteem and body appreciation engaged women emotionally to increase Dove brand awareness and sales in a highly competitive market. The PR-driven campaign integrated customer marketing, retail, advertising, consumer promotion and online engagement. There was the Dove Self-Esteem fund to help young girls optimise their potential. There was an influencer campaign of two dozen women in entertainment and media who served as VIPs and brand ambassadors. There was also a partnership with American Women in Radio and Television, which magnified the national conversation.

Creative implementation was essential to deviate from featuring traditional perfect beauty and break through the media clutter of beauty and health advertising. The Dove campaign featured six models of various sizes, dressed in underwear, in billboard and print advertising. See Figure 6.3.

The campaign naturally started a national conversation in the media and on the Dove website. Talk shows such as *Oprah* and *Ellen* featured the six models. National television programs, newspapers, magazines and radio publicised the campaign. The campaign website received more than 60 000 visits during launch day and eventually had more than 1 million visitors sharing conversations on beauty and their self-esteem. The emotional engagement with women enhanced Dove's image and sales increased 600 per cent for the products advertised as part of the campaign in its initial two months.[80]

Figure 6.3 Dove's campaign for Real Beauty

Source: https://au.pinterest.com/pin/386042999282622551/

Planning processes

PRSA, CIPR, PRIA and GAPRCM have different judging criteria for their PR effectiveness awards. PRSA requires a two-page submission encompassing a four-step process of research, planning, implementation and evaluation (RPIE).[81] CIPR entries must submit within 1000 words a process with audit, measurable objectives, strategy and plan, measurement, plus results and evaluation.[82] PRIA campaign awards are judged on the brief, research, SMART (Specific, Measurable, Attainable, Relevant, Timely) objectives, target publics or key stakeholders, communication strategy, execution, budget, results and impact, measurement and evaluation, as well as standards of professional communication and ethics.[83] GAPRCM evaluates entries on how analysis of stakeholders influences the strategy, goals of the communication approach, impact of the communication work on stakeholders, lessons for other global communicators and contribution to the advancement of the profession.[84]

Other authors have suggested alternative planning processes: RACE for research, action, communication and evaluation;[85] RASE for research, adaption, strategy and evaluation;[86] ROPE for research, objectives, program and evaluation;[87] ROPES for research, objectives, program, evaluation and stewardship;[88] and ROSIE for research, objectives, strategies, implementation and evaluation.[89] No matter which PR planning model you use, there is always research, objective, strategy, implementation, evaluation and reflection for the next planning cycle (ROSIER)!

Media tools

In the past, practitioners such as Bernays used advertising, publicity and created media to communicate with their audiences. These days, some of the communication tools are described as **non-controlled media**, namely the news media that control whether to publish news that they receive from news releases, news conferences, media interviews, media forums, public blogs or social media. The news media has also been referred to as the **4th estate**, as a comparison of historical social class terms that included the '1st estate' of the clergy, the '2nd estate' of the nobility and the '3rd estate' of the common people.[90]

Other tools are classified as **controlled media**, where senders control their own communication tools such as advertising, blogs, brochures, broadcasts, podcasts, emails, special events, films, intranet, meetings, speeches, position papers, teleconferences or video conferences, and websites.[91] Controlled media could include trade shows and exhibitions, where a high percentage of visitors are empowered to buy or influence the buying of goods and services displayed.[92] Sporting sponsorships can also be a controlled channel; for example, Emirates investing more than US$320 million on golf, horse racing, soccer, tennis and Australian footy.[93]

The PESO model

Then there are practitioners who prefer the **PESO model** of paid media, earned media, shared media and owned media.[94] Paid media is not just about traditional media advertising. It also includes email marketing, social media advertising and sponsored content. Earned media is publicity through media relations. Shared media is social media. Owned media is content creation control on websites, blogs and other corporate media. See Table 6.5 for an elaboration of PESO.[95]

Table 6.5 The PESO model

Owned media	Shared media
Brand journalism	Facebook
Employee stories	Instagram
Expert content	LinkedIn
Podcasts	Pinterest
User-generated content	Twitter
Videos	YouTube
Webinars	
Paid media	**Earned media**
Advertising lead generation	Publicity through building relations with media,
Facebook sponsored posts	bloggers and influencers
Sponsored tweets	
Twitter cards	

Technology company Dell had adopted an integrated PESO model for its 2014 Dell World conference, attended by 3000 delegates. The communication team initiated a Global Technology Adoption Index (GTAI) and soon the idea involved owned media, social media, earned media and paid media. Dell's agencies worked synergistically for the conference: WPP (launch), Y&R (advertising), VML (digital) and Mediacom (media buying).[96] See Table 6.6 for Dell's PESO integration.

Table 6.6 Dell's usage of the PESO model

Owned media	Shared media
1 Launched Global Technology Adoption Index [GTAI] 3 Dell's media site Tech Page One published story 'Tech hype meets tech reality'	2 GTAI shared across LinkedIn, Twitter, Facebook #delltechindex
Paid media	**Earned media**
5 GTAI advertising in *The New York Times* 6 Paid social posts on LinkedIn and Twitter	4 PR team pitched 'Tech Hype' story to media, which resulted in news coverage across business and online tech media sites

While PESO is a memorable acronym, creator, practitioner and author Gini Dietrich prefers an OESP process; that is, owned media, then earned media, shared media and paid media.[97] Dietrich also recently suggested a variation of owned media, shared media, paid media and earned media.[98] One critic prefers aligning it with Greek storyteller Aesop, suggesting an alternative storytelling model of (A)ESOP for earned, shared, owned and paid media.[99] A research paper proposed an SOEP model of shared, owned, earned and paid media.[100]

Interestingly, the three models put paid media as the last priority. On the other hand, a global PR firm may have subconsciously indicated a preference by describing consumer media consumption as 'paid, owned, earned or shared'.[101]

Not every company would use PESO wholly in any manner. PRSA used owned media, shared media and earned media for its PR Defined initiative in 2011–2012 to find a new definition for PR. It collaborated with 12 allied organisations representing global PR practitioners and created a special blog, Public Relations Defined, for its online crowdsourcing campaign. Through its shared media blog, PRSA received 927 submissions between 21 November and 2 December 2011 and earned commentary from blogs and news media.

The PRSA Definition of the Public Relations Task Force then analysed the submissions and commentaries qualitatively and quantitatively to arrive at six definitions. PRSA's allied partners provided feedback and three definitions were chosen for practitioners to comment on online. After online commentary and further feedback from partners, PRSA refined the three definitions for voting by practitioners. From 1447 votes submitted, PRSA announced, on 2 March 2012, the winning definition: *Public relations is a strategic communication process that builds mutually beneficial relationships between organizations and their publics.*[102]

Global brands have also actively used crowdsourcing through specialist providers using shared and paid media. Companies such as Coca-Cola, Danone, Nestlé, Pepsi, Samsung, Hewlett-Packard, Ford, Nokia, Toyota, General Electric, Microsoft, Google and Johnson & Johnson have contributed to the rapid growth of crowdsourcing as shared and paid media, with prizes given to the best submitted entries for competitive ideas and created content.[103]

Whichever PESO model you prefer and however you integrate the four components, the fact is that integrated communication needs to be planned, created, shared with various audiences through diverse media tools, paid for and monitored for earned publicity and other outcomes.

Codes of practice

PRSA, CIPR, PRIA and GAPRCM have their own codes of practice. Since GAPRCM represents more than 160 000 practitioners and academics globally, this section provides a short overview of its Code of Ethics.

Its principles include objectivity, conduct and performance standards, serving a broader society beyond clients or employers and intellectual skill mastery through training and education.

Its code of professional standards covers responsible advocacy, honesty, integrity, expertise and loyalty.

Its code of practice advocates protecting and enhancing the profession; being realistic about the scope and limitations of PR; being up-to-date on ethical practices; continuous professional development; and adhering to professional ethical decision making.

Its guidelines on ethical decision making suggest the following steps:
- First, define a specific ethical issue.
- Second, identify internal or external factors that influence decision making.
- Third, identify key values such as honesty and loyalty.

- Fourth, identify affected audiences.
- Fifth, select ethical principles such as preserving communication process integrity.
- Sixth, decide and justify the decision, including advice on legal issues and caution on deceptive practices.[104]

This section reviewed the PR functions highlighted by PR associations and consultancies; the PR planning processes; the media tools used to communicate with various audiences; and the codes of practice for PR practitioners. Common PR functions incorporate diverse areas, many of which could be clustered under strategic integrated communication to engage diverse audiences. The planning processes are varied but could be ROSIER with research, objective, strategy, implementation, evaluation and reflection. Media tools are non-controlled, dependent on news media finding value in the information they receive, or controlled by the marketing and/or corporate communicator. The PESO model, which could embed crowdsourcing, is a form of strategic integrated communication to facilitate paid, earned, shared and owned media. While there are codes of practice for each association in each country, a good guide for ensuring that the PR air is not polluted by bad practices is the GAPRCM's Code of Ethics.

IMC IN ACTION: ETHICS IN PUBLIC RELATIONS

While the PR industry has often been praised or criticised for its handling of crisis communication, now and then it receives negative publicity about the ethics of some practitioners. Enron Corporation, Fuel PR and Bell Pottinger UK are some notable examples.

Enron Corporation

Energy trader and supplier Enron Corporation was a 'media darling' as it had invested in its public image through investor relations, opinion makers, lobbying staff and media relations executives. Enron 'played' many news media who had not seen through the Enron hype.[105]

Enron played up its image as the US's Most Innovative Company between 1995 and 2000 until it became bankrupt in December 2001 as a result of the 2000 recession, heavy losses in its broadband division and financial accounting irregularities such as income inflation.[106]

While employees and shareholders suffered financially from Enron's collapse, Enron executives denied any wrongdoing until facts of unethical transgressions emerged. Several top management executives were then convicted of insider trading, fraud and conspiracy. The Enron fiasco led to the introduction of the Sarbanes-Oxley Act in 2002 to ensure accurate financial reporting and accountability by public companies.[107]

Fuel PR

Fuel PR in the UK sent a 'real life' feature to Press Association about a young woman, Esme de Silva, who had suffered excessive sweating until she used the antiperspirant brand Odaban. Press Association then distributed the story to several newspapers. Unfortunately, industry publication *PRWeek* discovered that Esme was actually Leandra Cardozo, who worked for Fuel PR, the consultant for Odaban.[108]

A Fellow of the Public Relations Communications and Association (PRCA) lodged a complaint against Fuel PR. PRCA concluded that Fuel PR had breached the Professional Charter and expelled the consultancy from its membership in October 2015, removing the Fellowship honour from Fuel's Managing Director Gillian Waddell.[109]

Bell Pottinger

PRCA expelled Bell Pottinger UK in September 2017 from its membership for stirring up racial tension on behalf of its South African client, Oakbay Capital, which was owned by the Indian-born Gupta family. The Guptas, who had been attacked for political influence and financial gain from their close relationship with President Jacob Zuma, wanted Bell Pottinger to narrate 'economic emancipation' and stir debate on 'economic apartheid' in South Africa.[110]

The opposition Democratic Alliance complained to PRCA that Bell Pottinger's campaign had portrayed opponents as 'white monopoly capital' via Wikipedia, a Gupta-owned television channel, fake Twitter accounts and misleading journalism.[111]

PRCA reviewed the complaint against its Professional Charter and Public Affairs and Lobbying Code of Conduct clauses. PRCA then expelled Bell Pottinger for infringing Public Affairs and Lobbying Code of Conduct clause 13: '*A member shall not act or engage in any practice or conduct in any manner detrimental to the reputation of the Association or the profession of Public Affairs and Lobbying in general*'.[112]

The membership expulsion led to the resignation of the CEO of Bell Pottinger UK, the loss of clients and the Singapore-based Asia office breaking away under the name Klareco Communications.[113]

IMC IN ACTION: MISSING TYPE CAMPAIGN FOR BLOOD DONATION

National Health Service (NHS) Blood and Transplant in the UK used the PESO model for its National Blood Week in 2015 to address the 40 per cent decline in blood donors over a decade and to achieve 10 000 registrations of new donors. It launched a 'Missing Type' campaign to get companies and people to drop the letters A, B and O, symbolic of blood types, from their names. A television advertisement conveyed the message 'Without As, Os and Bs, we're nowhere. Help fill in the gaps. Save lives by registering as a new blood donor at Blood.co.uk'.[114]

The *Daily Mirror* dropped A and O from its masthead and published an editorial to encourage reader participation. Other national media including Buzzfeed, *Daily Telegraph*, *Mail Online*, *The Guardian*, *The Sun* and *The Times* also publicised the Missing Type campaign. There was broadcast coverage on BBC channels, Sky News and Good Morning Britain. Even Downing Street dropped its 'O' (See Figure 6.4).

More than 60 digital influencers and 1000 organisations and brands—including Allianz, Cadbury, Coca-Cola, Google, Microsoft and the Tottenham Hotspurs football team—supported the campaign.

Figure 6.4 NHS Missing Type campaign: D WNING STREET

Source: www.campaignlive.co.uk/article/campaign-big-awards-2015-gold-paul-arden-award/1369176

The campaign also included advertising and sponsored social media posts on NHS media channels. The campaign exceeded expectation, with 30 000 registrations.[115]

The 'Missing Type' campaign went international with more than 21 countries supporting it. In Singapore, the Singapore Red Cross and the Health Sciences Authority launched the campaign in August 2016 with 33 organisations participating: hospitals, government agencies, schools, universities, businesses, shopping malls and the media. Even *Today Online* dropped the 'O' from its masthead.[116]

The Australian Red Cross and Australian icons such as Australia Post, Coles, Etihad Stadium, NAB, the *Neighbours* television show, Qantas, Surf Life Saving NSW and the Sydney Opera House also joined the campaign.[117] See Figure 6.5 for Australian Red Cross #MissingType advertisement.

Figure 6.5 Tourism Australia's 'Missing Type' campaign

WITH Y_UR HELP, WE'LL FILL THE G_PS T_GETHER

#missingtype

Australian Red Cross
BLOOD SERVICE

Source: https://www.donateblood.com.au/missing-type

■ CHAPTER SUMMARY

In this chapter we dealt with key concepts around the definition of 'public relations'; significant influences in public relations; theories and models of communication that guide professional practice; and public relations practice in terms of functions, planning processes, media tools and codes of practice.

We began with an explanation of the term 'public relations'. The various definitions from Bernays, Cutlip and Center, PRSA, CIPR and PRIA share a common understanding. PR is about mutual understanding or mutually beneficial relationships between an organisation and its various audiences. It is a management responsibility crossing internal and external stakeholders. It is a strategic, planned, integrated and sustained interactive process guided by research on public opinion. It uses two-way ethical communication that leads to organisations and audiences mutually changing their attitudes and behaviours to sustain goodwill and trust. It requires practitioners with knowledge of social science, professional communication skills and ethical standards to communicate effectively with diverse audiences and cultures.

We then discussed significant influences in public relations, such as communication eras, PR pioneers and industry associations, which have gone through various ages, such as print, mass media and digital media. Mass communication accelerated through innovations in printing, radio, television, the internet and social media. PR pioneers such as information disseminator Ivy Lee and social scientist Edward Bernays paved the way for media publicity, integrated communication and audience engagement.

Industry associations in the US, UK, Australia and globally synergised development of curriculum frameworks, practitioner competencies and industry standards. PR cannot be a good-looking cloak on a diseased body. The PR air cannot be polluted with bad practices.

Next, we examined how theories and models of communication guide professional practice. Communication theories and models provide a guide for PR practice. There are communication theories on transmission/media effects, audience, message and PR processes. There is the traditional communication model of Sender-Encoder-Channel/Noise-Decoder-Receiver. The classic communication model comprises press agentry/publicity for propaganda, public information for information dissemination, two-way asymmetry for scientific persuasion and two-way symmetry for mutual understanding.

In the digital age, many media outputs or communication tools are used for propaganda, information dissemination, scientific persuasion and mutual understanding.

Finally, we considered public relations practices in terms of functions, planning processes, media tools and codes of practice. The PR 'air' is everywhere. Common PR functions include relationships with marketing, corporations, employees, investors, consumers, retailers, communities, industries, media and government. As such, PR is also present in marketing and marketing communication activities as well as in corporate actions. Many of these functions could be grouped under strategic integrated communication to engage diverse audiences. The Top 10 PR consultancies position themselves as integrated communication firms.

The planning process is varied but could be ROSIER with research, objective, strategy, implementation, evaluation and reflection. Industry awards have their own requirements to communicate their planning processes.

Media tools are non-controlled, dependent on news media finding value in the information that they receive, or controlled by the marketing and/or corporate communicator. Marketing projects such as the

Dove Campaign for Real Beauty are also PR-driven with integration of advertising, consumer promotion, customer marketing, content creation and online engagement. Therefore, marketing must be PR-oriented and PR needs to be marketing-driven too.

The PESO model used by practitioners is a form of strategic integrated communication for facilitating paid, earned, shared and owned media. Whichever order is used in PESO—for example, starting with owned media—various advertising, digital and media consultancies work synergistically to communicate PESO messages, with PR often driving the marketing message. PRSA used crowdsourcing with owned, shared and earned media to arrive at a new PR definition in 2011–2012. Many top global brands use crowdsourcing as a form of shared and paid media to obtain ideas and created content from online consumers.

While there are codes of practice for each association in each country, the Code of Ethics from GAPRCM helps to ensure that the global PR air is not polluted by bad practices such as black PR and greenwashing.

When there is a diversity of PR functions necessitating sustained interaction with various audiences through creative communication tools, PESO or otherwise, it could be 'boring' to work on advertising-only campaigns!

Case study: Edward Bernays' PR campaigns (1920s–1930s)

Peter Ling

Bernays' famous cases are featured on the Museum of Public Relations website. Some examples could serve as benchmarks or lessons for young practitioners. We will look at Ivory soap, Cheney Brothers, American Tobacco Company, Lights Golden Jubilee, General Motors, and Philco Radio and Television.

Ivory Soap

Bernays' PR work for Procter & Gamble stretched over 30 years covering community relations, crisis communication, media campaigns, product publicity and public affairs. When P&G hired him in 1923 to promote the white unperfumed Ivory soap, Bernays surveyed consumer preferences and had media publishing the survey results. He followed up with synergistic activities: household hints featuring Ivory; a Central Park soap yacht race; a girl performing group's resolution to use unscented soap for facial wash; a suggestion to Ivory-wash statues and buildings; and a children's National Soap Sculpture Competition in White Soap. The competition turned soap-hating children to Ivory lovers when they created more than 2000 artistic sculptures that went on country-wide exhibitions and generated media reports internationally. The competition ran for 25 years, facilitating P&G success through public opinion support.[118]

Cheney Brothers

Bernays turned a declining 100-year-old silk manufacturing business, Cheney Brothers New York, into a success story and a benchmark for the use of art in industry and French-style adaptation. He provided French fashion bulletins and letters for salesmen and newspaper editors. There was massive publicity when First Lady Mrs Warren Harding received a silk dress at the White House from Cheney's oldest worker and when the textile museum in Lyons, France, accepted and endorsed Cheney's silk fabric. Bernays then created an 'Art in Industry' award, with the Architectural League presenting it to Cheney's director of style Henry Creange. Bernays organised art shows in the country with Cheney silks draping French ironworks, winning praise from art critics, designers and fashion journalists. Extending French endorsement and Cheney's art leadership, Bernays had American silk displayed in the Louvre, commissioned painting with Cheney colours for store window displays, and arranged for US representation in the 1925 Paris International Exposition of Modern Decorative and Industrial Arts. Bernays' PR helped to generate sales and public acceptance of manufactured beauty.[119]

American Tobacco Company (ATC)

Women in 1920s America could attend college and work but were not permitted to smoke outdoors. ATC hired Bernays to tap the women's market for their Lucky Strike cigarettes. A psychoanalyst revealed that women regarded cigarettes as 'torches of freedom'.[120] Bernays conceived the idea of having young women smoking and parading along Fifth Avenue on Easter Sunday. His friends at

Vogue magazine helped to provide names of debutantes. His secretary signed and sent a personalised telegram message to the women:

> IN THE INTERESTS OF EQUALITY OF THE SEXES AND TO FIGHT ANOTHER SEX TABOO I AND OTHER YOUNG WOMEN WILL LIGHT ANOTHER TORCH OF FREEDOM BY SMOKING CIGARETTES WHILE STROLLING ON FIFTH AVENUE EASTER SUNDAY. WE ARE DOING THIS TO COMBAT THE SILLY PREJUDICE THAT THE CIGARETTE IS SUITABLE FOR THE HOME, THE RESTAURANT, THE TAXICAB, THE THEATER LOBBY, BUT NEVER NO NEVER FOR THE SIDEWALK. WOMEN SMOKERS AND THEIR ESCORTS WILL STROLL FROM FORTY-EIGHTH STREET TO FIFTY-FOURTH STREET ON FIFTH AVENUE BETWEEN ELEVEN-THIRTY AND ONE O'CLOCK.[121]

The same message signed by a feminist was advertised in New York newspapers. Ten women lighting 'torches of freedom' in public triggered front-page news and subsequent editorials. Women began to smoke outside in various cities.

However, ATC wanted women to buy more Lucky Strike. Since women did not like the green packaging as it clashed with their clothing, Bernays suggested making the colour neutral. When ATC rejected the idea because it had already invested heavily in advertising, Bernays countered with the idea of changing the fashion colour to green.

Since Paris had set fashion trends through costumes and décor at annual haute couture events, Bernays conceived the idea of a Green Ball in New York. He researched into the colour green and learnt that it manifested positive values, springtime, serenity and trendy French fashion lines. He then convinced the Women's Infirmary of New York that a Green Ball would benefit the hospital and the Onondaga Silk Company could lead with green style.

Onondaga staged a Green Fashions Fall Luncheon, which featured green paper menu, green food, green art and a discussion on the psychology of the colour green. It also launched a new range of green silks. There was also a focus on green in clothing, accessories, interior decoration and home furnishings. Other companies joined the green momentum with green hats, green stockings, green nail polish and green window displays. Art editors, department stores, pattern firms, radio fashion broadcasters, theatrical producers and trade media were on the green mailing list.

The Infirmary Green Ball Committee secured green dresses from Paris for US society women to model. Parisian fashion elites and the French Government supported the campaign as it was good for international trade.

Publicity on the charity green ball pulled in debutante volunteers and society editors as well as sparking Fifth Avenue window displays and magazine covers to showcase green fashions. After the successful ball, there was a green exhibition of paintings and gifts of green paper dolls. The Lucky Strike green packaging finally matched the green fashion![122] See Figure 6.6 for one of the Lucky Strike advertisements.

Light's Golden Jubilee

General Electric and Westinghouse wanted to celebrate the fiftieth anniversary of Thomas Edison's invention of incandescent light. Between May and October 1929, Bernays secured widespread publicity involving several activities. Bernays sent out stories on Edison and his invention, with the letterhead featuring President Hoover and Henry Ford as supporters of a dedication ceremony.

When the media ran stories on Edison and the dedication, US towns also planned to honour Edison. Bernays staged a Diamond Jubilee event in Atlantic City and also arranged for a fiftieth anniversary commemorative stamp and coin.

At the dedication ceremony of the Edison Institute of Technology in Michigan, US President Hoover headed a VIP list that included Henry Ford, John D. Rockefeller Jr, Madame Curie, Orville Wright and outstanding journalists. Global utility firms switched off power for a minute to honour Edison.

The well-planned Jubilee event was a PR landmark because it showed to critics and the public that PR had a positive contribution as it had engineered public consent to the idea. Therefore, there was a better understanding and respect for PR as an honourable profession through the Jubilee celebration.[123]

Figure 6.6 Freedom for women to smoke publicly in 1928

General Motors (GM)

GM hired Bernays in 1932 to promote their vehicles at the New York auto show since sales had dropped by nearly 47 per cent. Bernays' strategy embraced several areas. First, he highlighted the new cars' draft-prevention windows and value appeal to attract consumers to the show. Second, he arranged for the Metropolitan Committee on Better Transport to issue a report on the need for improved vehicle ventilation. Third, he secured 150 endorsements from famous US leaders, engineers and retailers to support the message of high quality through research and development. Fourth, he arranged for three luncheons at the show to emphasise GM technological innovation, global understanding through motoring and a survey showing business optimism and consumer confidence. GM's president and CEO Alfred P. Sloan Jr was so impressed with PR effectiveness and value over advertising that he appointed Bernays as PR counsel, a role that included training of executives at 51 GM subsidiaries.

Sloan, as the new convert to PR, wrote in the GM annual report:

> the corporation's most vital relationship is with the public. Its success depends on a current interpretation of the public's needs and viewpoints, as well as on the public's understanding of the corporation's motives in everything it does.[124]

Philco Radio and Television

Radio was associated with the Depression and lower classes. Philco hired Bernays to broaden the market, boost radio sales at a higher price and enhance profits. With the goal of launching a high-fidelity radio, Bernays surveyed music fans and learnt that radio was not reproducing music quality.

Needing to show the high-fidelity radio quality, Bernays arranged for opera star Lucrezia Bori to sing through the radio product. The invited press reported the human voice quality of Philco's product.

Bernays then developed the Radio Institute of the Audible Arts to campaign for better radio broadcasting, music and contribution to education. This led to radio being used by libraries, schools and music clubs. Philco began selling a higher priced radio product. Winning over a disinterested upper-class segment, Bernays created a black-tie event to sell the idea of specially designed radio music rooms. The affluent bought the idea.

Bernays then worked on freedom of speech in radio broadcasting. When television was introduced, Bernays arranged for Philco to demonstrate the product at Philco's Philadelphia factory. Philco became a leader in both radio and television.[125]

Questions

1. Which of the Bernays' campaigns impressed you and why?
2. What planning process did Bernays use for his campaigns?
3. What were some of the integrated communication tools that he used?
4. Would the communications tools used by Bernays about a century ago still be relevant in today's digital era?

Practitioner profile: Emily Tutt

Head of Customer Engagement and Acquisition, Australian Hearing

Emily Tutt is the Head of Customer Engagement and Acquisition at Australian Hearing, leading the traditional marketing function for Australia's largest provider of hearing services, with responsibility for consumer marketing across more than 600+ locations nationwide. Emily has rocketed through the ranks, from being the department's youngest member ever to most recently reporting directly to the Managing Director, running the company's brand and culture multimillion-dollar transformation program.

In 2017 Emily was named in B&T magazine's '30 Under 30' awards, winning the category for Marketing and as a Finalist in CXO's 2017 'Rising Stars Awards'. Emily has a Bachelor of Speech and Hearing Sciences degree from Macquarie University and a Masters of Business (Marketing) at the University of Technology, Sydney.

Over the past few years, Emily has been an Ambassador for Heart Research Australia, raising awareness of issues around heart health and raising funds for vital research.

How did your career start?

Marketing definitely wasn't on my agenda when I first finished school—in fact, I studied a Bachelor of Speech and Hearing Sciences before I realised that a career in Speech Pathology just wasn't for me. During that degree I did all my electives in Marketing and loved it; therefore I went on to study a Masters of Business, majoring in Marketing. At the age of 21 and still in full-time study, while working in retail and as a market research assistant, I wrote an email to the Marketing Executive at Australian Hearing asking for a job. Two weeks later I was offered an internship and less than five years later I am currently leading the traditional marketing team.

How important is Integrated Marketing Communication (IMC) to what you and your organisation do?

Without a doubt, incredibly important. To build competitive advantage and ultimately drive positive results to the bottom line, we need to make sure we consider all the different channels and the promotional mix so that we achieve maximum impact with our campaigns.

What types of promotional tools do you use in your IMC campaigns? Please provide examples.

The tools we use in our IMC campaigns include direct marketing, digital, social media, advertising, point-of-sale material and public relations. I am a big fan of public relations and sharing case studies within media publications. Word-of-mouth, I believe, is one of the most effective forms of marketing, and sharing these positive stories of client outcomes is more trustworthy than an advertisement in the newspaper.

What would your ideal IMC campaign look like and why?

An ideal IMC campaign would involve a lot of pre-planning to align every communication channel with the same message and call to action. For example, we send an electronic direct mail (EDM) to clients at certain times during the year and knowing when this will be sent is important to align with the campaign communication.

Additionally, planning what a good return on investment (ROI) looks like and how you will measure the success of the campaign is vital.

What has been your favourite IMC project to work on and did it achieve its objectives?

Every year we have a large IMC campaign highlighting Hearing Awareness Week. Our aim is to attract as many customers as possible to attend one of our hundreds of events held around the country. All the communication messages across the channels are aligned with the same call to action. The promotions mix includes a digital and social media focus driving customers to the campaign webpage. We accompany this with direct mail, both in the post and electronically, to customers and draw on public relations to raise awareness of events happening in local communities. We streamline our campaign point-of-sale material (posters, brochures, promotional merchandise, etc.) so that it all has a similar look and feel specific to the campaign. In addition to all these external channels, we have an internal communication plan that advises all staff of the campaign messages so that they're prepared for customer enquiries.

This flagship campaign continues to grow year-on-year, acquiring new clients and seeing the financial results to the bottom line.

How do you believe an IMC campaign affects the consumer decision-making process for your particular target audience?

In the hearing industry, it takes up to eight years for someone to be motivated enough to do something about their hearing from when they first notice they might be struggling. In comparison to the fast-moving consumer goods (FMCG) industry this is an exceptionally long time to attract a client. Therefore, with all of our IMC campaigns, we need to have as part of our objective an awareness focus, so that over time the client first becomes aware (through a number of communication channels), then stimulated to ultimately take up the campaign call to action.

How has your application of IMC changed with the increase in digital marketing?

The world is continually changing and industries need to evolve in line with global and local developments. At this point in time, rapid developments in technology and digitisation are transforming the way customers interact with organisations, and companies need to keep pace.

In the hearing industry, online retailers and international retail chains are bringing new, easy and low-cost hearing technology to the market and people are becoming increasingly comfortable with this way of shopping.

Until recently the majority of Australian Hearing clients, the over 65s, may not have necessarily felt confident with using the internet or even computers. However, the generation coming into this age group now are increasingly moving online and more tech savvy. While the digital channel may not have the return on investment that other channels have, it is important that it is part of the mix with the changing demographics and trends.

It is crucial that we embrace each new digital technology as a way to change and add to our promotion mix in how we engage our clients and operate our business, in order to maintain and improve our levels of customer loyalty and to promote our point of difference.

What do you believe are some of the challenges to implementing an IMC campaign?

An IMC campaign requires a lot of work to align all the promotional tools and messages together in harmony. Therefore, one of the worst scenarios to happen could be that the customer is ready to take the call to action from the campaign but the employees at the frontline haven't been informed about the campaign, immediately resulting in a lost lead and a negative customer experience. Don't underestimate the importance of having a strong internal communication strategy and engagement plan. It is critical that all levels of staff are aware of the campaign and what is being communicated externally so they can convert the lead.

What advice would you offer a student studying IMC?

In marketing there are lots of opportunities to go and specialise within any of the promotional mix functions of advertising, public relations, direct marketing, sales promotions, digital, social media, etc. However, carving a role as a 'generalist' marketer, in my opinion, allows you to contribute to the 'big picture' and work across all the communication channels. Trying to stay on top of current marketing trends and promotional channels as they constantly evolve and change is hugely exciting as marketers!

Finally, failure of campaigns is inevitable, especially within Integrated Marketing Communication. For example, one promotion channel may not have the ROI that the other channel(s) have, therefore we need to be resilient and learn so that we can turn those failures into future successes.

Key terms

4th estate

agenda-building theory

agenda setting

attribution theory

black PR

daguerreotype

diffusion of innovation theory

excellence theory

framing

greenwashing

non-controlled media

one-way asymmetric model

PESO model

press agentry/publicity

proactive public relations

public information

reactive public relations

relationship

    management theory

rhetoric theory

Shannon-Weaver Model

situational theory

sleeper effect theory

two-step flow theory

two-way asymmetric

two-way symmetric

Revision questions

1. Why is public relations everywhere?

2. How could United Airlines learn from Tylenol's 1982 handling of its product tampering crisis?

3. What is your own definition of public relations?

4. What knowledge and skills would be required if public relations were considered a social scientist profession?

5. How do you see the age of digital media evolving in the next few decades?

6. What can the current and/or future public relations industry learn from Edward Bernays, 'the father of PR'?

7. How can PR associations help to develop the PR industry?

8. Which communication theories and/or models play a more significant role in professional communication?

9. What are the key public relations functions in the digital era?

10. What is PR's relationship with marketing and marketing communication?

11. What planning process would you use to plan your strategic integrated communication campaigns?

12. How do you see the PESO media model being used for strategic integrated communication?

13. Why is a code of ethics important in today's digital age?

14. What did you learn from the IMC in Action mini-cases in this chapter?

Further reading

Carolyn J. S. & Becker-Olsen, K. L. (2006). Achieving marketing objectives through social sponsorships. *Journal of Marketing, 70*(4), 154–69.

Hoek, J. (2013). Sponsorship: an evaluation of management assumptions and practices. *Marketing Bulletin, 10*, 1–10.

Hoek, J. et al. (1997). Sponsorship and advertising: a comparison of their effects. *Journal of Marketing Communications, 3*(3), 21–32.

Mamic, L. I. & Almarez, I. A. (2013). How the larger corporations engage with stakeholders through Twitter. *International Journal of Market Research, 55*(6), 851–72.

Walraven, M., Bijmolt, T. H. A. & Koning, R. H. (2014). Dynamic effects of sponsoring: how sponsorship awareness develops over time. *Journal of Advertising, 43*(2), 142–54.

Weblinks

Associations

ASEAN Public Relations Network (APRN)
http://www.aseanprnetwork.org

Chartered Institute of Public Relations
https://www.cipr.co.uk

Institute of Public Relations of Singapore (IPRS)
http://iprs.org.sg

International Association of Business Communicators (IABC)
https://www.iabc.com

International Association of Exhibitions and Events (IAEE)
http://www.iaee.com

International Public Relations Association (IPRA)
https://www.ipra.org

Public Relations and Communications Association (PRCA)
https://www.prca.org.uk

Public Relations Consultants Association (PRCA)
https://www.prca.ie

Public Relations Institute of Australia (PRIA)
https://www.pria.com.au

Public Relations Society of America (PRSA)
http://www.prsa.org

The Global Alliance for Public Relations and Communication Management
http://www.globalalliancepr.org

The Public Relations Council
https://www.communicationscouncil.org.au/public/content/viewCategory.aspx?id=979

Awards

Australian Marketing Institute Awards for Marketing Excellence
https://e-award.com.au/2017/amiawards/newentry/about.php

Chartered Institute of Public Relations Excellence Awards
https://www.cipr.co.uk/content/awards-events/excellence-awards

Effie Worldwide
https://www.effie.org

Institute of Public Relations Singapore PRISM Awards
http://iprs.org.sg/prism-awards-2017

Marketing PR Awards
http://www.marketing-interactive.com/pr-awards/sea/

PR Awards Asia
http://www.prawardsasia.com

PR News Platinum Awards
http://www.prnewsonline.com/platinum-pr-awards

PR Week Awards
http://www.prweekawards.com

PR Week Global Awards
http://www.prweekglobalawards.com

Public Relations Institute of Australia Golden Target Awards
https://www.pria.com.au/eventsawards/golden-target-awards

Public Relations Society of America Awards
http://www.prsa.org/awards/

The Communications Council Award Shows
http://www.communicationscouncil.org.au/public/content/ViewCategory.aspx?id=1203

The Mumbrella ComsCon Awards
https://mumbrella.com.au/commsconawards

Journals

Asia Pacific Public Relations Journal
http://www.pria.com.au/journal

International Journal of Sports Marketing & Sponsorship
http://www.imrpublications.com/journal-landing.aspx?volno=L&no=L

Journal of Convention & Exhibition Management
http://www.tandfonline.com/toc/wzce20/.U5qLStzyQpE

Journal of Public Relations Research
http://www.tandfonline.com/toc/hprr20/.U5qHutzyQpE

Marketing Communication News
http://www.marcomm.news/tag/exhibition/

PR News
http://www.prdaily.com/Main/Home.aspx

Public Relations Journal
http://www.prsa.org/Intelligence/PRJournal/#.U5qHb9zyQpF

Public Relations Review
http://www.journals.elsevier.com/public-relations-review/

Notes

1   PRWeek. (2017). United Airlines CEO Oscar Munoz named PRWeek U.S. Communicator of the Year, 9 March. http://www.prweek.com/article/1426909/united-airlines-ceo-oscar-munoz-named-prweek-us-communicator-year

2   PRWeek. (2017). Best in Public Affairs 2017, 17 March. http://www.prweek.com/article/1427583/best-public-affairs-2017

3   Gajanan, M. (2017). United wouldn't let 2 girls on a plane because it apparently has a leggings ban. *Time,* 27 March. http://time.com/4713370/united-airlines-leggings-ban/

4   Farber, M. (2017). Video shows man being dragged off of overbooked United flight. *Fortune,* 10 April. http://fortune.com/2017/04/10/united-airlines-overbooked-flight-video/

5   Griffiths, J. & Wang, S. (2017). Man filmed being dragged off United flight causes outrage in China, 11 April. http://edition.cnn.com/2017/04/11/asia/united-passenger-dragged-off-china-reaction/index.html?iid=EL

6   Calfas, J. (2017). 'This didn't age well.' *PRWeek* gets backlash for naming United CEO Communicator of the Year. *Fortune,* April 11. http://fortune.com/2017/04/10/united-airlines-ceo-prweek/

7   Banks, S. (2017). United Airlines CEO admits removing passenger David Dao was a 'mistake of epic proportions, 3 May. http://www.independent.co.uk/news/world/americas/united-airlines-latest-david-dao-passenger-forcible-removal-chief-executive-officer-oscar-munoz-a7714466.html

8   Yu, S. (2014). How firms are using 'black PR' to tear down their rivals, 4 January. http://www.scmp.com/business/china-business/article/1396461/how-firms-are-using-black-pr-tear-down-their-rivals

9   Watson, B. (2016). The troubling evolution of corporate greenwashing, 21 August. https://www.theguardian.com/sustainable-business/2016/aug/20/greenwashing-environmentalism-lies-companies

10 Harlow, R. F. (1976). Building a Public Relations definition. *Public Relations Review, 2*(4), 34–42.

11 Harlow, R. F. (1976). Building a Public Relations definition. *Public Relations Review, 2*(4), 36.

12 Fry, S. L. (1991). A conversation with Edward L. Bernays. *Public Relations Journal, 47*(11), 31–3.

13 Bernays, E. L. (1992). The case for PR licensing. http://prvisionaries.com/bernays/bernays_1990.html

14 Broom, G. M. (2009). *Cutlip & Center's Effective Public Relations* (10th edn). Upper Saddle River, NJ: Prentice Hall.

15 PRSA. (2018). About Public Relations. http://apps.prsa.org/AboutPRSA/PublicRelationsDefined/

16 CIPR. (2018). What is PR? https://www.cipr.co.uk/content/careers-advice/what-pr

17 PRIA. (2018). About Public Relations. https://www.pria.com.au/aboutus/what-is-public-relations/

18 PR Museum. (2015). Public Relations through the ages: a timeline of social movements, technology milestones and the rise of the profession. http://www.prmuseum.org/pr-timeline/

19 Broom, G. M. (2013). *Cutlip and Center's Effective Public Relations* (11th edn). New York: Pearson.

20 Broom, G. M. (2013). *Cutlip and Center's Effective Public Relations* (11th edn). New York: Pearson.

21 Kaplan, T. (2005). The Tylenol crisis: how effective public relations saved Johnson & Johnson. http://195.130.87.21:8080/dspace/handle/123456789/111; Knight, J. (1982). Tylenol's maker shows how

to respond to crisis, 11 October. https://www.washingtonpost.com/archive/business/1982/10/11/tylenols-maker-shows-how-to-respond-to-crisis/bc8df898-3fcf-443f-bc2f-e6fbd639a5a3/?utm_term=.885d7cbf0e34; Lewin, T. (1982). Tylenol posts an apparent recovery, 25 December. http://www.nytimes.com/1982/12/25/business/tylenol-posts-an-apparent-recovery.html.

22 Broughton, E. (2005). The Bhopal disaster and its aftermath: a review. *Environmental Health, 4*(6).

23 Douglas, D. & Fletcher, M. A. (2014). Toyota reaches $1.2 billion settlement to end probe of accelerator problems. https://www.washingtonpost.com/business/economy/toyota-reaches-12-billion-settlement-to-end-criminal-probe/2014/03/19/5738a3c4-af69-11e3-9627-c65021d6d572_story.html?utm_term=.eb04c039004f

24 Mintz, Z. (2014). A disastrous void: Why the MH370 public response failed. http://www.ibtimes.com/disastrous-void-why-mh370-public-response-failed-1598774

25 Washkuch, F., Bradley, D. & Stein, L. (2014). Crisis experts: Malaysia Airlines had to respond where news is breaking—on Twitter. https://www.prweek.com/article/1304142/crisis-experts-malaysia-airlines-respond-news-breaking-twitter

26 Shameen, A. (2000). After the crash. http://edition.cnn.com/ASIANOW/asiaweek/magazine/2000/1117/biz.airlines.html

27 Associated Press. (2015). AirAsia boss Tony Fernandes lauded for crisis management. http://newsinfo.inquirer.net/662083/airasia-boss-tony-fernandes-lauded-for-crisis-management

28 Hiebert, R. E. (1966). *Courtier to the crowd: The story of Ivy Lee and the development of Public Relations.* Ames, Iowa: Iowa State University Press.

29 Bulldog Reporter. (2017). Museum of Public Relations to unveil newly discovered artifacts from the archives of Ivy Lee, 29 March. https://www.bulldogreporter.com/museum-of-public-relations-to-unveil-newly-discovered-artifacts-fromt-the-archives-of-ivy-lee/

30 Lee, I. L. (1925). *Publicity: Some of the things it is and is not.* http://memory.loc.gov/cgi-bin/ampage?collId=cool&itemLink=r?ammem/coolbib:@field(AUTHOR+@band(Lee,+Ivy+Ledbetter,+1877+1934.+))&hdl=amrlg:lg51:0001

31 Lee, I. L. (1916). Publicity as applied to public service corporations. Publicity: *Some of the things it is and is not.* New York: Industries Publishing Company, p. 44.

32 Carufel, R. (2015). PR pioneers: World's only museum of public relations keeps 100 year history alive and accessible, 23 April. https://www.bulldogreporter.com/pr-pioneers-worlds-only-museum-of-public-relations-keeps-100-years-of-p/

33 Solender, T. J. (1995). Obituary: Edward Bernays, 22 March. http://www.independent.co.uk/news/people/obituaryedward-bernays-1612237.html

34 The Museum of Public Relations. (2018). Edward Bernays. http://prvisionaries.com/bernays/bernays_1915.html

35 The Museum of Public Relations. (2018). 1992: The case for PR licensing. http://prvisionaries.com/bernays/bernays_1990.html

36 *Life* magazine. (1990). The 100 Most Important Americans of the 20th Century/Special Issue, Fall.

37 Frause, B. & Frankel, J. S. (2008). What role should PRSA play in establishing practice standards for the Public Relations profession? http://apps.prsa.org/AboutPRSA/Ethics/documents/PRSA_StrategicDialogFinal.pdf

38 PRSA. (2014). Happy 50th to the APR: Celebrting Accreditation's Golden Anniversary. Retrieved from http://apps.prsa.org/Intelligence/Tactics/Articles/view/10589/1091/Happy_50th_to_the_APR_Celebrating_Accreditation_s#.WQ61plfsGOo

39 PRSA. (2017). *Study guide for the examination for Accreditation in Public Relations Eras of public relations history.* http://www.praccreditation.org/resources/documents/apr-study-guide.pdf

40 Waddington, S. (2014). CIPR President presents 'A brief history of the CIPR: the route to professionalism', 3 July. http://newsroom.cipr.co.uk/cipr-president-presents-a-brief-history-of-the-cipr-the-route-to-professionalism

41 CIPR. (2016). Lead Public Relations at the CIPR. http://newsroom.cipr.co.uk/lead-public-relations-at-the-cipr/

42 CIPR. (2017). Accredited practitioners. https://www.cipr.co.uk/accredited

43 PRIA. (2013). Professionalism and standards. https://www.pria.com.au/documents/item/6427

44 Global Alliance PR. (2016). Global Alliance history. http://www.globalalliancepr.usi.ch/website/page/global-alliance-history

45 Global Alliance PR. (2007). Core competencies for professional credentials in Public Relations/Communications. http://www.globalalliancepr.usi.ch/website/sites/default/files/nolie/Download/Appendix2-Credentials-matrix-consultation-.final.oct.pdf

46 PRAccreditation.org. (2017). Understanding communication theories, models and the history of the profession. *APR Study Guide*, 112-119. Retrieved from http://www.praccreditation.org/resources/documents/apr-study-guide.pdf

47 PRAccreditation.org. (2017). Communication models. *APR Study Guide*, 120–4. http://www.praccreditation.org/resources/documents/apr-study-guide.pdf

48 Chandler, D. & Munday, R. (2011). *A dictionary of media and communication* (2nd edn). Oxford University Press.

49 Grunig, J. E. & Hunt, T. (1984). *Managing Public Relations*. New York: Holt, Rinehart & Winston.

50 Phillips, D. (2009). A Grunigian view of modern PR, 9 January. http://leverwealth.blogspot.com.au/2009/01/grunigian-view-of-modern-pr.html

51 PRSA. (2017). Silver Anvil Awards. http://apps.prsa.org/awards/silveranvil/silveranvilenter/documents/sa17.pdf

52 CIPR. (2016). CIPR Excellence Awards 2016 winners revealed, 9 June. http://newsroom.cipr.co.uk/cipr-excellence-awards-2016-winners-revealed/

53 PRIA. (2017). Celebrating 41 years of recognising excellence in public relations, 17 May. https://www.pria.com.au/eventsawards/golden-target-awards

54 Global Alliance PR. (2017). Global Alliance members' awards. http://www.globalalliancepr.org/member-awards/

55 The Holmes Report. (2017). Global Top 250 PR agency ranking 2017. https://www.holmesreport.com/ranking-and-data/global-pr-agency-rankings/2017-pr-agency-rankings/top-250

56 Edelman. (2018). Expertise. http://www.edelman.com/what-we-do/expertise/

57 Weber Shandwick. (2016). What we do. https://www.webershandwick.com/what-we-do/practices/government-relations

58 FleishmanHillard. (2018). Practices & sectors. http://fleishmanhillard.com/expertise/

59 Ketchum. (2018). Ketchum expertise. https://www.ketchum.com/expertise

60 MSL. (2017). Expertise. https://mslgroup.com/expertise

61 Burson-Marsteller. (2018). Capabilities. http://www.burson-marsteller.com/what-we-do/capabilities/

62 Hill+Knowlton Strategies. (2018). Our Expertise. http://www.hkstrategies.com/global/en/our-expertise/

63 Ogilvy Public Relations. (2018). Expertise. https://www.ogilvypr.com/expertise/

64 PR Newswire. (2017). BlueFocus Communication Group announces 2016 revenue of RMB12.3 billion, becoming the first China-based marketing company to earn over RMB 10 billion in annual revenue. https://www.prnewswire.com/news-releases/bluefocus-communication-group-announces-2016-revenue-of-rmb-123-billion-becoming-the-first-china-based-marketing-company-to-earn-over-rmb-10-billion-in-annual-revenue-300451309.html

65 Golin. (2018). About us. http://golin.com/about-us/

66 PRSA. (2018). Glossary terms. https://www.prsa.org/about/about-pr/glossary-of-terms/

67 CIPR. (2018). PR dictionary. https://www.cipr.co.uk/content/policy-resources/students/cipr-students/careers-advice/pr-dictionary

68 Sponsorship.com. (2017). Sponsorship spending forecast: Continued growth around the world. http://www.sponsorship.com/iegsr/2017/01/04/Sponsorship-Spending-Forecast--Continued-Growth-Ar.aspx

69 Burrell, I. (2016). Rio 2016: How sponsors Coca-Cola, Visa, P&G and Panasonic are telling their stories, 20 July. http://www.prweek.com/article/1402209/rio-2016-sponsors-coca-cola-visa-p-g-panasonic-telling-stories

70 Edelman. (2018). About Edelman. http://www.edelman.com/who-we-are/about-us/

71 Weber Shandwick. (2018). We are engaging always. http://www.webershandwick.com

72 FleishmanHillard. (2018). About FleishmanHillard. http://fleishmanhillard.com/about/

73 Ketchum. (2018). Quick facts about Ketchum. https://www.ketchum.com/quick-facts

74 MSL. (2017). We're a global public relations and integrated communications partner. https://mslgroup.com/about

75 Burson-Marsteller. (2018). We are a leading global public relations and communications firm. https://www.burson-marsteller.com/who-we-are/we-are-a-leading-global-public-relations-and-communications-firm/

76 Hill+Knowlton Strategies. (2018). About us. http://www.hkstrategies.com/global/en/about/

77 Ogilvypr.com. (2018). Ogilvy Public Relations. https://www.ogilvypr.com

78 Reuters.com. (2018). BlueFocus Communication Group Co Ltd. https://www.reuters.com/finance/stocks/overview/300058.SZ

79 Golin. (2018). About us. http://golin.com/about-us/

80 BusinessWire. (2006). PRSA announces 2006 Best of Silver Anvil Award Winner; 'Dove campaign for real beauty receives top honors at annual PR event, 9 June. http://www.businesswire.com/news/home/20060609005490/en/PRSA-Announces-2006-Silver-Anvil-Award-Winner; Simmons, T. (2006). Real women, real results: A look at Dove's best of Silver Anvil-winning campaign, 8 August. http://apps.prsa.org/searchresults/view/471/105/Real_women_real_results_A_look_at_Dove_s_best_of_S#.WSZW0VfsGOp.

81 PRAccreditation.org. (2017). The four-step process. http://www.praccreditation.org/resources/documents/APRSG-Planning.pdf

82 CIPR. (2011). Research, planning & measurement toolkit. https://www.cipr.co.uk/sites/default/files/Measurement%20March%202011_members.pdf

83 PRIA. (2017). The criteria, 16 May. https://www.pria.com.au/eventsawards/2017-golden-target-awards-information/the-criteria

84 Global Alliance PR. (2018). COMM PRIX Awards. http://www.globalalliancepr.org/entry-guidelines-comm-prix-awards/

85 Marston, J. E. (1963). *The nature of public relations*. New York: McGraw-Hill.

86 Kendall, R. (1996). Public relations campaign strategies: Planning for implementation. (2nd edn). Pearson.

87 Hendrix, J. A. & Hayes, D. C. (Eds.). (2009). *Public Relations Cases* (8th edn). Boston, MA: Wadsworth Cengage Learning.

88 Kelly, K. S. (2001). ROPES: A model of the fund-raising process. In J. M. Greenfield (ed.), *The nonprofit handbook: Fundraising*. New York: John Wiley & Son, 96–116.

89 Crifasi, S. C. (2000). Everything's Coming Up Rosie. *Public Relations Tactics, 7*(9), 34–7.

90 The Free Dictionary. (2018). Estate of the realm. http://www.thefreedictionary.com/estate+of+the+realm

91 PRAccreditation.org. (2017). Definitions. Retrieved from http://www.praccreditation.org/resources/documents/apr-study-guide.pdf

92 EEAA. (2018). The marketing power of exhibitions. https://eeaa.com.au/what-we-do/our-campaigns/the-marketing-power-of-exhibitions/

93 Hawthorne, M. (2015). Emirates bets on $17m on sport advertising spend, 31 January. http://www.smh.com.au/business/media-and-marketing/emirates-bets-on-17m-on-sport-advertising-spend-20150129-131r2y.html

94 Dietrich, G. (2015). Why your PR team should embrace the PESO model. https://www.americanexpress.com/us/small-business/openforum/articles/pr-needs-embrace-peso-model/

95 Dietrich, G. (2015 March 23). PR Pros must embrace the PESO model. Retrieved from http://spinsucks.com/communication/pr-pros-must-embrace-the-peso-model/

96   Iliff, R. (2014). Why PR is embracing the PESO model, 5 December. http://mashable.com/2014/12/
      05/public-relations-industry/#cmdoiv_66OqO

97   Dietrich, G. (2017). The challenges and solutions of the PESO Model, 14 March. http://spinsucks.com/
      communication/peso-model-challenges-solutions/

98   Sutton, P. (2017). Why the PESO model is the future of digital marketing, 21 April. http://paulsutton.
      co/2017/04/21/peso-model-future-digital-marketing/

99   Sanders, A. (2017). The problem with PESO. https://prfortoday.com/2017/01/31/the-problem-with-
      peso/

100   Macnamara, J., Lwin, M., Adi, A. & Zerfass, A. (2016). 'PESO' media strategy shifts to
      'SOEP': Opportunities and ethical dilemmas. *Public Relations Review, 42*(3), 377–85.

101   Elliott, S. (2013). The new look of Public Relations, 28 April. *The New York Times.*
      http://www.nytimes.com/2013/04/29/business/media/fleishmanhillard-rebrands-itself-with-a-21st-
      century-focus.html?_r=3&

102   PRSA. (2012). Public Relations defined: A modern definition for the new era of public relations, 11
      April. http://prdefinition.prsa.org

103   Eyeka.com. (2017). The state of crowdsourcing in 2016. https://en.eyeka.com/resources/
      reports?download=cs_report_2016.pdf

104   Global Alliance PR. (2016). Code of Ethics. https://static1.squarespace.com/static/
      561d0274e4b0601b7c814ca9/t/56c201e11d07c00b66443b47/1455555043172/GA+Code+of+Ethics.pdf

105   Anderson, K. (2002). How Enron played the media. http://news.bbc.co.uk/2/hi/business/1817445.
      stm

106   Investopedia.com. (2018). Enron scandal: The fall of a Wall Street darling. https://www.investopedia.
      com/updates/enron-scandal-summary/

107   Bowen, S. (2007). Ethics and Public Relations. https://instituteforpr.org/ethics-and-public-relations/

108   Rogers, D. (2015). 'Sweaty-gate' leaves a bad smell for PRs and journalists. http://www.independent.
      co.uk/voices/comment/sweaty-gate-leaves-a-bad-smell-for-prs-and-journalists-10478969.html

109   PRCA. (2015). The Public Relations Consultants Association terminates the membership of Fuel PR
      International, 12 October. http://news.prca.org.uk/the-public-relations-consultants-association-
      terminates-the-membership-of-fuel-pr-international/

110   John, T. (2017). The British PR firm disgraced by a South African racism scandal, 5 September. http://
      time.com/4926830/bell-pottinger-jacob-zuma-guptas-racism-scandal/

111   Cave, A. (2017). Deal that undid Bell Pottinger: inside story of the South Africa scandal, 5 September.
      https://www.theguardian.com/media/2017/sep/05/bell-pottingersouth-africa-pr-firm

112   PRCA. (2017). PRCA announces expulsion of Bell Pottinger, 5 September. http://news.prca.org.uk/
      prca-announces-expulsion-of-bell-pottinger/

113   Tay, V. (2017). Bell Pottinger Asia name change: good PR move for a distressed PR firm?
      http://www.marketing-interactive.com/bell-pottinger-asia-name-change-good-pr-move-for-a-
      distressed-pr-firm/

114 Farey-Jones, D. (2016). NHS' 'Missing type' blood appeal is back with international campaign, 16 August. http://www.campaignlive.co.uk/article/nhs-missing-type-blood-appeal-back-international-campaign/1405719

115 Harrington, K. (2016). The PESO Model: Changing the world - one PR campaign at a time, 23 November. http://spinsucks.com/communication/peso-model-blood-week-pr-campaign/

116 TodayOnline. (2016). #MissingTypeSG campaign launched to highlight need for more blood donors, 16 August. http://www.todayonline.com/singapore/missingtypesg-campaign-launched-highlight-need-more-blood-donors

117 Wolfe, N. (2016). What does the world have against the letters A, B and O? 18 August. http://www.news.com.au/lifestyle/health/what-does-the-world-have-against-the-letters-a-b-and-o/news-story/e24cd4176dee8ec20c4ac1144fcbac2d

118 The Museum of Public Relations. (2017). 1923 Soap and art. http://prvisionaries.com/bernays/bernays_1923.html

119 The Museum of Public Relations. (2017). 1924 Recognition through collaboration: Art in industry. http://prvisionaries.com/bernays/bernays_1924.html

120 The Museum of Public Relations. (2017). 1929 Torches of freedom. http://prvisionaries.com/bernays/bernays_1929.html

121 Bernays, E. (1965). *Biography of an idea: memoirs of public relations counsel Edward. L. Bernays.* New York: Simon and Schuster, p. 387.

122 Bernays, E. (1965). *Biography of an idea: memoirs of public relations counsel Edward. L. Bernays.* New York: Simon and Schuster.

123 The Museum of Public Relations. (2017). 1929 Light's Golden Jubilee. http://prvisionaries.com/bernays/bernays_1929a.html

124 The Museum of Public Relations. (2017). 1932 General Motors: Value and sales appeal. http://prvisionaries.com/bernays/bernays_1932.html

125 The Museum of Public Relations. (2017). 1939 Philco Radio and Television. http://prvisionaries.com/bernays/bernays_1939.html

CHAPTER 7

Direct Marketing

May O. Lwin

Délifrance Singapore: Savouring great deals

Délifrance is an international bakery that serves French-style baked goods in more than 50 countries. In Singapore, Délifrance views itself as the epitome of French bakeries, specialising in baked goods such as baguettes, feuilletés and viennoiseries. It also prides itself on its croissants.

Figure 7.1 Daily Délifrance coupons

In conjunction with its 34 years in Singapore, Délifrance launched 'daily Délifrance coupons' (see Figure 7.1)—an initiative to make a targeted marketing effort with its consumers after the festive periods. The marketing aim was primarily to encourage continuous consumer spending post the festive Chinese New Year period in January. This direct marketing campaign targeted existing Délifrance customers and potential new customers.

The coupons, which featured value-added meal sets and daily specials, were launched in the month of February to encourage continuous consumer spending. These coupons were distributed to recipients via direct mailers in both traditional physical and digital ways. Traditional direct mailers were disseminated to get the coupons into the hands of consumers at homes and offices. Meanwhile, Délifrance leveraged digital media to enable itself to obtain a wider reach, along with giving customers an opt-in response option.

When putting the coupon deal together, each deal was carefully considered in terms of what would be most desirable to customers. The goal was for customers to keep them in their wallets and mobile phones for redemption at Délifrance outlets. Délifrance had also leveraged social media and the strength of food bloggers to promote its products.

The direct mailer not only aimed to target and reward existing customers during slower periods to draw continuous support, it also aimed to draw new customers through the use of the mailer. The campaign ran over four months, surpassing its targeted incremental sales figure of 12 per cent.

Aside from the use of direct marketing, Délifrance has looked towards engaging in continuous upgrades in product innovation, new products, concepts and flavours. This has evolved to cater to new customers and stay ahead of the game. The brand has also developed products such as oriental-flavoured feuilletés, Asian-inspired sandwiches and lava croissants.

■ INTRODUCTION

Marketing communication is shifting towards businesses and advertisers reaching out to consumers directly. In direct marketing (DM), marketers forgo the use of mass media such as television and newspapers to directly communicate with consumers. The advent of various new media platforms, from websites to emails to social media, has exponentially enhanced direct marketing channels across the world.

Direct advertising (DA) is a subset of direct marketing where advertising provides a mechanism for consumers to respond directly to the message from the marketer—although not utilising a media platform, this is still known as the advertisement. Again, digital media has widened the potential response platforms and mechanisms, which allows marketers to directly communicate to the consumers.

In this chapter we will examine these important topics, but first we will look at the meaning and history of the term 'direct marketing' and examine the considerations in developing direct marketing materials and content.

LEARNING OBJECTIVES

After reading this chapter you should be able to:

1. explain why direct marketing is a powerful IMC tool that is gaining favour
2. discuss how databases are used in direct marketing
3. describe types of direct marketing strategies typically utilised by marketers
4. discuss the various types of direct marketing channels
5. explain and differentiate between direct marketing and direct response advertising.

What is direct marketing?

What is **direct marketing** and why run direct marketing activities when there are many other IMC tools available? This section discusses definitions of direct marketing; provides information regarding the scope and efficacy of direct marketing; and explains why direct marketing is such an important consideration in the IMC strategy of many products and services.

Direct marketing typically refers to marketing activities that involve direct communication and interaction between the marketer and the consumer. Compared to other forms of marketing and promotions, direct marketing lacks a middle intermediary, typically a media platform where advertising space is purchased, such as on television or in print magazines.

Nevertheless, there are a variety of definitions, including:

> **AMA:** 1. (retailing definition) A form of nonstore retailing in which customers are exposed to merchandise through an impersonal medium and then purchase the merchandise by telephone or mail. 2. (channels of distribution definition) The total of activities by which the seller, in effecting the exchange of goods and services with the buyer, directs efforts to a target audience using one or more media (direct selling, direct mail, telemarketing, direct-action advertising, catalog selling, cable selling, etc.) for the purpose of soliciting a response by phone, mail, or personal visit from a prospect or customer.[1]

Wiki: Direct marketing is a form of advertising which allows businesses and nonprofit organizations to communicate directly to customers through a variety of media including cell phone text messaging, email, websites, online adverts, database marketing, fliers, catalog distribution, promotional letters and targeted television, newspaper and magazine advertisements as well as outdoor advertising. Among practitioners, it is also known as direct response.[2]

Business dictionary: Contacting and influencing carefully chosen prospects with means such as telemarketing and direct mail advertising.[3]

Direct marketing offers a number of benefits to businesses, chief among which is the ability to gauge audience response to the efforts of the marketer using directly quantifiable assessments of response, purchase patterns, repurchases, referrals and so on. Such information provides a timely assessment of campaign reach, purchase behaviours and loyalty markers. This allows for the appropriate selection and adaptation of direct marketing tools based on efficacy measures.

Direct marketers can use a variety of direct marketing channels including direct mail, online communication (e.g. email, websites, social media) and **telemarketing**. **Direct-response advertising** is also one form of direct marketing.

Direct marketing is a major marketing tool used globally, with businesses as wide ranging as hotels and tourism, retail and the financial sectors having traditionally depended heavily in their IMC mix on reaching both existing and new customers in this way. Today, with the evolution of the digital platforms and data systems, direct marketing has become an indispensable tool in almost all sectors of business. Even niche sectors such as education and charitable organisations—which used to depend on traditional advertising and direct selling—are now utilising direct marketing as a primary component in their marketing efforts.

History of direct marketing

The origin of direct marketing can be tracked back to Benjamin Franklin, who used direct mail to market *Poor Richard's Almanac* throughout the outlying American colonies from 1732. Direct mail continued to grow with the creation of the Montgomery Ward catalogue in 1872 and the Sears catalogue in 1888.[4] These mass mailers were popular as many rural communities in the US lived far away from stores.

Historically, direct marketing marketers also favoured using catalogue and mail drops in target neighbourhoods to generate much of the traffic into stores. A typical direct marketing example in traditional media are the cards, or tear-outs, found in almost all magazines. *The New Yorker*, for instance, uses both floating and tear-out coupons inside its magazines to self-promote and generate subscriptions with an attractive $1 an issue offer. Each card is a complete mailer in itself and includes business reply mail information (see Figure 7.2).

As media technology advanced, telemarketing and broadcast direct advertising moved into the direct marketing space, offering broad coverage and decent responses. More recently, the internet has offered unparalleled opportunities to target and reach vast numbers of users.

Each channel provides structure for sales transactions. One of the major reasons why direct marketing has gained popularity is that sales and responses arising from direct marketing campaigns are typically measurable and traceable to marketer efforts. Direct marketing additionally gained popularity in cities among people who are time-challenged when it comes to shopping and wish to shop without leaving the comfort of their homes or offices.

Figure 7.2 Coupon inserts reach readers in *The New Yorker*

The business of direct marketing

Direct marketing is offered by advertising agencies, independent direct marketing agencies, printing houses and database management firms, in silo or in collaborative formats. Advertising agencies that specialise in advertising either have a department or a sub-company that focuses on direct response marketing.

Direct marketing can also be handled by independent agencies specialising in direct response marketing. The function is offered by firms that specialise in supplying printing and mailing to lists of customers. There are also service firms that offer back-end functions such as **fulfilment** and delivery of orders received.

Databases and direct marketing

Databases have become an indispensable tool in direct marketing. They are repositories of existing customers or potential customers and provide rich data from which to segment the target market and develop strategies to reach the desired segment. It is imperative for a database to produce up-to-date information and, as such, the data must be constantly and diligently managed and updated. Databases also allow for further macro-level information, such as trends over time.

The capabilities of marketing databases include:

- managing customer personal identifiers including names and contact information (members or client lists)
- identifying and managing prospects (prospects lists, which may be self-sourced or purchased)
- integrating and assessing crossover between two or more lists
- storing and analysing results of direct marketing efforts
- storing and then measuring purchasing performance over time or across groups
- filtering various target groups (e.g. selecting by region or age)
- providing longitudinal response profiles.

Two types of **databases** are normally used in direct marketing: the customer database and the potential customer database. With concerns of privacy and data theft becoming more prevalent, most large organisations manage their own customer databases with in-house experts. Such in-house databases are derived from customer information, and may include personal information such as personal identifiers (e.g. identity cards and mobile phone numbers). Take for instance direct mail from Macy's for its annual summer sale brochure, which consists of heavily discounted items in the store. Macy's sends this to all its customers in its database in the week leading up to the sale. Not only are the regular customers informed of the sales items, they are offered an additional 20–25 per cent off on the entire purchase if they use the two coupons on the cover.

The potential customer databases can be generated by marketers (e.g. by collecting responses to lead-generating direct advertising) or purchased from external parties. These are sold by commercial database firms, which market various types of lists, or databases of **prospects** based on various demographic, geographic and even psychographic parameters. Generally, quality lists provide up-to-date information with powerful details such as ownership of certain products. In the Macy's example above, Macy's reached out to potential customers through tie-ups with newspapers with desired demographics, such as *The New York Times*. Subscribers to *The New York Times* in the greater New York City area are also invited to the Macy's sale using the same brochure, which is inserted into the newspaper.

While **database marketing** has been prevalent in the US, many companies across Asia and Australia now deploy database marketing, often with the aid of database software programs. Across this region, the main sectors that are managing databases include travel and tourism, finance and insurance, supermarkets and large retail chains, luxury products and high-value products such as cars.

Hotels, for instance, typically have loyalty programs for their clients and issue loyalty cards. When a guest stays at one of the partner hotels, the system adds the item-by-item list of guest purchases to existing customer information.

Singapore Airlines is a major airline that strategically uses its database of loyal customers. The company's KrisFlyer loyalty program members in top tiers such as the PPS Club and KrisFlyer Gold are highly valuable.[5] They are identified, signed-up and enjoy various benefits in the air and on the ground, such as the opportunity to use the airline's premium lounges before and between flights. The powerful database is used to target various types of travellers and develop strategies to enhance future marketing activities to each segment.

The airline has used customer feedback to give members additional incentives the more they travel in premium classes with Singapore Airlines and its sister companies SilkAir and Scoot. This includes perks such as double KrisFlyer miles and redemption discounts as well as one-class cabin upgrades for flights.[6]

An organisation's use of database marketing of its customers typically follows these steps:

- *Phase 1:* a preliminary collection of customer information. For Singapore Airlines this might be at the time of purchasing a ticket, or when completing details opting into its program on the airline's website
- *Phase 2:* the marketer uses the data and undertakes analyses such as segmentation, clustering, forecasting and trend representations
- *Phase 3:* the knowledge from the database is used to address specific marketing objectives
- *Phase 4:* the database is refined and updated continually through corrections and amendments. Data may be shared with partners for cross-selling joint advertising promotions.

Similar to advertising, the major industry players are the marketers, agencies (which specialise in direct marketing) and consumers. Nowadays almost all major agencies offer expertise in online direct marketing platforms and are able to integrate direct marketing execution with overall IMC strategies.

Direct-marketing strategies

Direct marketing involves the use of existing data or marketing research to influence strategy—as well as database development—to better target customers.

One major weakness of direct marketing is that the tool has sometimes been limited in suitability for mass marketing efforts. As a result, in major marketing campaigns, direct marketing needs to be integrated together with other tools. However, for targeted campaigns, especially where databases are available, direct marketing is particularly efficient. Direct marketing enables marketers to continually assess and calculate the effectiveness of offers made in direct marketing campaigns. By using devices such as tracking email responses, printed codes or calls made to telephone numbers, offers that yield good results can be used to modify poor responses. Such accurate quantifications and modifications are invaluable in successful IMC strategies.

There are a number of steps in the process of direct marketing. These include objective setting, choice of medium and offer, database selection and fulfilment of offers/customer service. Depending on the direct marketing task, all or some of these steps can be activated.

Setting an objective

All direct-marketing campaigns commence with the objective starting point. With the enhancement of data tracking technologies, the types of objectives have become numerous and varied:

- *Generation of leads or traffic:* this refers to the motivation of users to a particular consumer-centred locale, be it physical (retail or location-based) or virtual (online entities such as websites).
- *Behavioural objectives:* this refers to actual behavioural numerics such as enhancing the number of visitors to an event or achieving sales targets, time duration or even comparative percentages.

For example, a new suburban restaurant might utilise a direct-marketing program to assist in its launch by targeting new customers in the neighbourhood. However, this base objective can be further streamlined to include information such as targeting different types of customers for lunch versus dinner; weekdays and weekends; food orders; and so on.

Direct-marketing strategies that can be utilised to achieve these objectives include direct-response advertising, online websites, direct mail and emails. The restaurant can develop a direct mailer that can be physically dropped or posted to the homes in the neighbourhood. Such a mailer can offer a discount coupon for dining on days of the week when the restaurant is particularly in need of patrons. Such an offer can be repeated on the website for online users searching for restaurants in this neighbourhood to widen the prospect base.

Selecting a medium

Direct marketers can consider a variety of media to reach consumers directly. Typical direct marketing channels are known as 'controlled media', where the direct marketer has a good amount of control regarding who the recipients of the messages are. These media include online and social media platforms, email, catalogues, telemarketing and direct mail. Through a combined effort with database management, marketers can target the consumers and tailor messages to specific audiences. In contrast, direct advertising can utilise all forms of media similar to advertising (e.g. print, broadcast, internet and other media such as outdoor media).

Selecting an offer

The direct-marketing offer typically includes information about the product or service and highlights the terms of sale. Most of the time, a sales promotion is included (see Chapter 8) to incentivise the purchase. An attractive direct marketing offer would ideally involve the consumer identifying a call to action that is supported by some kind of benefits to action. For the offer to be effective in inducing behaviour, it should meet the needs of the target market. For instance, a hotel that wants to enhance food and beverage spending by its guests might offer coupons with a free drink. A car sales team may offer free servicing for new car owners in the first year.

Such matching of offer incentives needs to be carefully strategised to enhance the response rate, often through research and feedback analysis, to satisfy the needs of the consumer. Offers often include the price, related costs such as tax and shipping, and elective product features.

Selecting a message

The selection and crafting of direct marketing messages is an important element of direct marketing. It needs to clearly articulate the offer and present the product or service being offered in persuasive terms to match the needs of the target segment. The direct marketing message also needs to match the medium, with print formats such as newspapers typically offering suitable space for lengthy (and often wordy), visually complex messages. Outdoor media such as train station boards, when used as direct marketing, need much more succinct information by way of a key offer incorporating response devices such as QR codes, which are an easy response mechanism.

Automobile company Nissan added a QR code sticker on each window of its 2012 line-up vehicles to deliver information about the car and its visual gallery, showcase accessories, product reviews, incentive offers, how to request a quote, dealer addresses and location, and—most importantly—how to join its mailing list.[7]

Historically, direct marketing messages have tended to be long and detailed to provide all the basic information needed for the reader/viewer to achieve the decision to make the sales transaction.

Consequently, these messages provided information including price, warranty, availability and so on and were considered **one-step offers**. However, with digital media offering comprehensive websites detailing the products, two **(two-step offer)** or more steps can be involved in the offer designed to move interested consumers to undertake the next course of action. Such action can involve, for instance, going to the website to gain further information, or signing up for a sales representative to call back.

An example of a relatively extensive direct marketing message is the Citroën campaign in Singapore where the car brand endeavours to tie to the concept of comfort in a collaborative effort with the Ikea retail chain by targeting Ikea customers. As customers leave an Ikea showroom they are offered a free ride to wherever they are going in a 'masked' or unbranded Citroën car.[8]

Citroën's campaign, titled 'The Most Comfortable Test Drive', allows customers to judge the C4 Picasso's level of comfort based solely on their experience rather than any preconceived notions they might have.

Test drive cars are 'masked' to cover up brand logos on the exterior and the steering wheel. Accompanied by a Citroën sales representative, consumers can then choose to drive themselves or be driven to their preferred location. Thereafter, shoppers are asked to rate their comfort experience and guess the brand of the car before having it revealed to them by a Citroën sales representative.

Managing customer relationships

The management of customers through assessing behaviour is an important facet of database marketing. Termed **customer relationship management (CRM)**, it involves the analysis of the relationship between an organisation and each of its customers through various types of data analytics, often aided by software. This enables marketers to attain a better understanding of customer characteristics and transactions, leading to better strategies and improved services throughout the customer's lifeline. The organisation can also utilise this knowledge to target new customers and identify problematic relationships.

Many companies utilise CRM in an attempt to improve customer relationships and services. The Hilton Hotels chain, for example, makes sure that customer service and satisfaction are important cornerstones of each customer relationship. Every stay in a hotel is followed up with a service feedback survey to ensure that the customer's experience is a highly satisfactory one. Each customer's needs and preferences are also recorded so that customisation, such as room and linen preferences, is considered for future bookings and stays.

The concept of CRM is linked to the notion of long-term loyalty by the customer through various life stages where relevant. The Hilton Hotels chain sees each customer as a potential client not just in the current context but in a variety of life stages and responsibilities. For instance, a young sales executive who travels regularly to various regional destinations would be considered as a potential hotel client in many arenas of relevance at the present time and in the future. He could be organising a conference for his company next year. On a personal level, he might be planning a wedding within the next two years so he is also a target for Hilton's banquet sales. This could be accompanied by a honeymoon in the resort city of Bali, which again is an opportunity for the hotel. In the mid and longer term future, there will be more business trips and holidays, perhaps with children.

The measurement of how much business Hilton may gain from this sales executive in his entire lifetime is called **lifetime customer value (LCV)**. LCV estimates the total purchase volume over time from the client/customer or the entire segment/group. This approximation is useful for marketers in deciding how much to spend in terms of direct marketing and other IMC activities to obtain and retain the customer.

Responding to and fulfilling orders

While various facets of IMC can have objectives ranging from generating awareness to creating knowledge, the purpose of direct marketing is to generate consumer responses. This includes active behaviours such as purchases or attendance at a demonstration or asking for further information. Direct marketing encourages behaviour with a clear offer providing a quick means for purchase.

Responding to an order involves back-end functions by the sales team, on various platforms, which could be made in person, via manual mail orders or on digital systems. The easy link to a toll-free customer telephone service and payment mechanisms such as credit cards are critical at the point of purchase. The offer is then immediately moved to the stage of **fulfilment**, where the product or service is delivered or made available to the customer.

In the Hilton Hotel example, the booking pages of the hotel's website allow for various payment options, including booking a room, holding this booking and then paying only after a stipulated period of time.[9] Similarly, the 'shopping cart' pages of online service providers such as Qantas Airways are populated with all forms of easy payment options, including credit cards, PayPal and debit cards.

In case customers have any questions, direct links to customer service hotlines, chat services and options, including getting the customer service personnel to call the customer, are provided. Furthermore, cancellation and refund policies are clearly spelt out to provide ease of mind. These enable the customer to overcome psychological barriers at the point of booking and payment.

Direct marketing platforms

In this section we will examine the various types of direct marketing channels available to marketers, beginning with direct marketing on an online platform, which is currently the fastest growing direct marketing channel.

Online media

The online platform has transformed direct marketing strategies and capabilities substantially.

First, the internet has provided an added platform to mount the materials that previously went into traditional direct mail into the digital domain. Many companies that used to rely on sending mailers to their customer bases now utilise the internet solely or in combination with other online media channels.

Second, the internet has enabled a level of customisation that was otherwise unthinkable just a decade ago. Marketing entities can now customise messages to a fine level such that each communication can be tailored not just to individual names and addresses but to combinations of specific needs and preferences.

The Disney organisation utilises its database of the thousands of visitors to theme parks to customise visitor offerings. When planning a trip to one of the theme parks, the Disneyworld.com member services enables visitors to customise not just the various Disney theme park offerings (e.g. Orlando's Magic Kingdom, or Disney's Hollywood Studios), it also recommends hotels and peripheral services such as dining to meet the consumer's group profile and precise wishes, designed specifically around age and past behaviours.

Third, the evolution of social media and search engines has allowed for online advertisements to match what internet users are seeking or referring to.

In that space, direct-response advertising plays a prominent role as the consumer seeking a product or service is given incentives/offers in a well-timed manner. Take for example a magazine which offers readers an opportunity to subscribe at discounted rates. The cover of the magazine for any particular issue is replicated in the advertisement that appears at the back of the magazine, with an attractive offer for an annual subscription. Readers are urged to go to the website link provided to subscribe.

In the past two decades, email marketing to both new prospects and existing customers has grown in parallel to the decline in postal mail marketing. With the proliferation of emails and other forms of communication on social media, marketers have been criticised for generating unwanted emails (called 'spam') and communication.

An approach called **permission marketing** has been introduced in response to this, whereby customers receive an opportunity to 'opt-in' to a notification service from a company.

Email as a direct marketing tool has become so prevalent that even sectors that have traditionally depended on postal mail have now made email their main communication and marketing channel for existing customers.

One of the most common users of direct marketing is the financial sector. Consumer banks such as ANZ now routinely use the email platform to interact with monthly statements, bank product offers and other updates. This leads to a typical interaction of a few emails per month to customers.

Figure 7.3 A seasonal catalogue for *Gardener's Edge*

Catalogues

Catalogues are direct marketing promotional material with multiple pages showcasing the marketers' range of merchandise. Although larger retailers have traditionally complemented their instore sales with catalogues, paper catalogues are declining in demand with more consumers turning to online websites. The online version of the catalogue provides not just the static visuals of the 2D format but also opportunities for more sophisticated visualising, for instance from different angles, and close-up.

A major catalogue marketer, Victoria's Secret, incorporates in its website the products in its physical catalogue and offers links to its annual fashion show when the show is streamed.[10]

In both the paper and digital space, specialty catalogues for various sports, gourmet and ethnic foods, and hobbies have seen a rise, especially in the US. *Gardener's Edge*, a leading gardening catalogue in the US, seasonally adjusts both its offerings and discount schemes to the seasonal behaviour of gardeners across the US (see Figure 7.3).

Figure 7.4 The annual IKEA catalogue

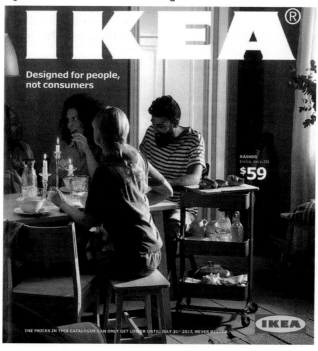

For retailers with large or numerous stores, the catalogue can serve the dual purpose of direct sales orders or driving customers to the store. It was with the latter purpose that Swedish furniture retailer IKEA prints its annual catalogue and floods entire countries with it. The catalogue is highly successful and has been known to be kept by families as a reference book for the entire year (see Figure 7.4).

Direct mail

Direct mail refers to promotional messages in print for a product or service delivered by postal mail. These include leaflets, brochures and letters with a return envelope dropped in mailboxes.

The cost and reliability of direct mail differs from country to country, but in most places, direct mail can be sent via the post office in bulk.

Direct mail has advantages and disadvantages, some of which are similar to catalogues. Table 7.1 summarises these and suggests how advertisers can use direct mail most effectively.

Direct mail literally lands directly in the hands and personal physical space of customers. Direct mail also provides an opportunity for creative 3D products to be mounted as promotional messages. Traditional direct mailers typically include an outer envelope; a letter, flyer or brochure; and sometimes a reply card with a return envelope. More creative mail can come in the form of fold-out cards, paper bags or even sample products.

Table 7.1 Advantages and disadvantages of catalogues and direct mail

ADVANTAGES	DISADVANTAGES
Targeted: can be directed at specific market segments	**Perceptions:** negative; viewed as junk mail by many recipients
Engages attention: can employ high-quality design and visuals creatively (including 3D formats)	**Costs:** cost per thousand of catalogues is higher than mass media
Complete information: extensive product information and comparisons	**Response rate:** response is relatively low at 2 to 4 per cent
Convenience: offer easy purchase options	**Database management:** databases must be constantly updated
Flexible formats: offer a variety of formats and provide enough space	
Engages attention: attract readers' attention and engages with readers	
Personalisation: databases make it possible to personalise direct mail across a number of consumer characteristics, purchase history and demographics such as age	
Ease of response: build in various feedback mechanisms for the recipients	
Reaches wide populations: can reach audiences who are inaccessible by other media (e.g. non digitally savvy)	

TIPS FOR CREATING EFFECTIVE DIRECT MAIL

- Grab the attention of the targeted prospect with the outer covering or envelope.
- Show the consumer why they need it.
- Reassure the buyer by pre-empting and answering questions.
- Provide critical information about the product's usefulness.
- Inspire confidence and minimise risk, and establish that the company is reputable.
- Make it easy to buy, order, call and make a payment.
- Use incentives to encourage a fast response.

Since the creative elements are important in attracting the recipient to open and read further (or throw away) the mail, the design of the mail package is of utmost importance. The outer envelope, for instance, can communicate the offer or tease the reader to open the package.

Some direct-mail devices are made up of an envelope and a letter. The letter usually explains the details of the offer, and may refer to other inserts such as a sales brochure and response device, sometimes with a pre-paid envelope.

The major consideration in a direct-mail package involves the creation of message elements to maximise response. Direct marketers have found that creativity directly leads to enhanced responses and more sophisticated direct marketing efforts endeavour to create messages that go beyond typical mail.

Telemarketing

At the end of the last century, **telemarketing**—where consumers are contacted via phone—rose in prominence. Telephone campaigns often provided returns on investment that surpassed mass advertising.

There are two types of telemarketing: inbound and outbound. Incoming or **inbound telemarketing calls** originate with the customer, who is responding to an advertisement, for instance. These require telemarketing teams of trained experts, often with various language abilities, to answer questions and take orders. The inbound call is often a very important step in order/purchase finalisation.

The other type, **outbound telemarketing calls**, are made by organisations initiating calls to customers or the public and are usually not welcome by consumers. There are numerous news of scammers and other types of phone callers who have succeeded in cheating consumers.

In response to nuisance concerns in telemarketing, many countries have a 'Do Not Call' Registry where the consumer has the right to list telephone numbers they do not wish to be contacted at. The Federal Trade Commission in the US also enacted the Telemarketing Sales Rule (TSR), which restricts such things as calling time and disclosure. This is discussed further in Chapter 11.

With these issues being prevalent, telemarketing use needs to be carefully managed. For outbound use, the message must be simple and compelling (e.g. an invitation to a neighbourhood launch event for a new store opening). For inbound calls, the telemarketers must be well trained and empowered to assist with any form of order taking.

Direct advertising

Direct advertising (DA) or direct-response advertising is a form of direct marketing. It utilises a blend of formats, from the traditional advertising elements to unique components of direct advertising that involve direct communication between the consumer and the advertiser, incorporating a call to action. For instance, direct advertising for a jeweller can include traditional elements such as copy, visual and brand message in a magazine print format, and at the same time incorporate key features such as an order coupon, a link to an online website to place an order and a bar scan for a mobile phone.

Such direct advertising features supplement traditional advertising by enabling the marketer to build traffic to a desired direct marketing channel (e.g. a website) and concurrently help to drive desired direct marketing goals such as sales or sign-ups.

More than four decades ago, the legendary 'father of advertising' David Ogilvy called direct advertising his 'secret weapon' in new product introductions and wrote that direct advertising is feasible for both high-end and value items. This was showcased in one of the earliest direct advertisings of an advertising agency at the time (see Figure 7.5)[11]

Figure 7.5 David Ogilvy's direct advertisement for an advertising agency

Source: http://swiped.co/file/how-direct-response-advertising-ad-by-david-ogilvy

Today's direct advertising still aims to realise an objective built around consumer action—such as calling a hotline, purchasing a product or visiting a retail outlet—as a tangible result of the direct advertising. Direct-response advertising employs mass media in the process. While most advertising aims to create a recall or an attitude change, direct advertising's ultimate objective is sales. In that respect, direct advertising can be seen to be expensive for advertisers, with the final 'cost' calculations often depending on response rate. However, the effective targeting of customers makes direct advertising an important IMC tool.

Following are the key platforms for direct advertising.

Direct advertising on the internet

Direct marketers utilising the multimedia channels have seized the opportunity to expand myriad direct advertising activities on the e-commerce platform.

Direct advertising opportunities abound with the online links just a click away—for example, customised emails and pop-up ads—to recent shoppers by almost every online entity ranging from Amazon.com to Walmart Online[12] and CDNow.[13]

In the recent era, internet entities such as Google and Facebook have utilised search habits and activities such as emails to target customers. This practice has not been without controversy regarding privacy.[14] However, with the evolution of these practices, it is clear that the web provides numerous and unique opportunities for one-to-one or personalised marketing.

Internet-based direct advertising offers numerous benefits, such as digital 'sampling' (e.g. in clips of movies), active browsing, access to reviews and price comparisons.

Direct-marketing strategies on the internet nowadays need to consider social media platforms where consumers have a greater say and control. Many new techniques are experimental as the media space continues to evolve and offer exciting new methods for promoting products and services online.

Online business think-tanks such as Business Insider offer insights into some popular platforms. Table 7.2 offers a summary of some popular social-media platforms.

Direct advertising on print media

Print media has traditionally been one of the most commonly used media for direct advertising. Ads in the print media are an established practice that continues to yield opportunities for an effective direct response. Direct advertising in print usually calls to action information (e.g. to ask for a new car brochure and test drive) or to purchase using payment mechanism.

Direct advertising in print is typically deployed in newspapers and magazines and is therefore time intensive in terms of the response. With newspapers, the exposure and response lasts one day, while magazines can have a much longer readership cycle. So response devices such as coupons, email addresses, weblinks, hotlines or toll-free numbers and order forms need to fit into the readership cycle.

Print media, especially magazines, order various response mechanisms including tear-out cards or inserts. Such devices make it easy for customers to respond. The idea is to make it as easy as possible for the reader to take action.

Direct advertising on broadcast media

Direct advertising on broadcast uses television and radio. Television, whether on public networks or cable, offers a particularly effective medium for products that require demonstrations, such as exercise equipment, kitchen utensils and gardening tools.

Table 7.2 Summary of three popular social media platforms

FACEBOOK
• Large number of active users (approximately 1.11 billion users, which was an exponential growth from merely 100 million users in 2008)[15]
• Large amount of data on users so advertisers can better target them
• Users go to Facebook to interact with friends and family and do not like intrusions from companies. Friends' and family's recommended products on Facebook, and company links are useful for prospects to learn about products, discover new uses, find discounts, and share all this with their friends
• Can make more brand impressions than other media
• Offers the potential to reach a much larger audience at a much lower cost every day of the week
• While Facebook limits ad sizes to very small spaces, good marketers can make effective use of the space allotted with concise headlines

TWITTER
• Has a total of 554 million registered users
• Currently listed as one of the top 10 most visited sites[16]
• Limits users to 140 characters.
• Accounts for much less Web traffic than Facebook and other social media
• Users tend to be influential
• Can easily be linked to other social media sites, such as Facebook, so Tweets can automatically appear on Facebook simultaneously
• Has proven to be very effective in responding to complaints, rumours and factual mistakes for damage control and to provide better customer service

YOUTUBE
• Provides a useful platform for **rich media** content
• Provides a place for companies large and small to reach their target audience without paying the high 'real estate' costs of commercial TV channels
• Videos can be shared, and if they go viral, the number of viewers that actually watch the commercial can rival and even surpass TV audiences
• Viewers can play the videos over and over again as well as share them with even larger networks of viewers enabling advertisers to make more brand impressions and greater sales

Source: adapted from http://www.businessinsider.com/the-exploding-importance-of-direct-marketing-2013-

These are found in infomercial off-prime time slots, sometimes going by names such as 'sell-a-vision' QVC and the Home Shopping Network mediums for advertising to broadly targeted groups. A direct-response commercial can be short (30 seconds) or in the form of a longer infomercial format (up to 30 minutes) with the necessary information such as a 1800 phone number or Web address for the consumer to request information or make a purchase.

Direct-response television advertising used to offer off-prime-time infomercials that pitched for unique home and self-help products. These offerings have nowadays diversified into fashion and lifestyle and are becoming more general in appeal with the integration of other direct marketing efforts.

Radio direct advertising can offer a sense of urgency based on its immediacy and local context of the station. It is a relatively easy and cheap medium for mounting a direct advertising campaign as the direct advertising can be in a simple format announced by the station personnel. For example, retailers use radio to announce sales and promotions happening on a particular day to encourage traffic to the event at the store.

Integrated direct marketing

Direct marketing was one of the first spheres of marketing communication that implemented an integrated approach to customer outreach that uses two or more direct communication tools together (e.g. telemarketing followed by an email). Instead of treating each medium separately, databases offer companies opportunities to reach audiences from multiple touch points. **Integrated direct marketing (direct marketing)** is proposed as 'a systematic method of getting close to your best current potential customers.'[17]

Integrated direct-marketing campaigns pursue the attainment of various synchronised mediums at the right point in time to achieve outcomes. Direct marketing can enhance its power through the integration not just within direct channels but with non-direct channels.

Companies with effective campaigns have linked product packaging and off-line media to social and online media. For instance, direct mail and direct response advertising on print media should provide links to social media, and vice versa. With many companies embracing social media users to 'like' or 'follow' them on social media, social media efforts need to be linked to off-line and other direct marketing efforts, synergising marketing and brand strategies. Such efforts can enhance response generation from a particular percentage on a single medium alone.

A successful example involves Coach USA, which offers sale coupons on numerous platforms and links direct sales efforts with social media efforts to drive in-store traffic during major sales events. These simple coupons are disbursed on the website to generate excitement, be shared with friends to widen the campaign reach, and for downloading—with the customers who visit the stores being rewarded with additional discounts at the retail premises (see Figure 7.6).

Marketers such as Coach have found that obtaining traffic and contact information of the people downloading coupons is worth more than the costs of the offerings, and adds valuable contact information to their database.

To ensure that direct-marketing messages and advertising messages often reinforce one another, major agencies now offer the two functions—and often many more, such as content generation and sales promotion—as part of their services. This leads to greater coordination of the clients' marketing communication programs.

Figure 7.6 Coach sales coupons

Pei Wen Wong and May Lwin

Changes in consumer shopping habits and increased mobile internet penetration rates have created opportunities for businesses and brands to market directly to consumers, sometimes without investing a single advertising dollar. With clever social media content marketing strategies and a mobile phone, marketers can create quick and efficient content for their customers.

Hock Siong & Co., a small–medium enterprise in Singapore dealing in used goods and upcycled furniture started its Facebook page in 2011 because it was free. Today, its social media platforms are primarily used in the brand's direct marketing strategies to generate sales interest and convert online browsing to retail traffic in-store.

Tucked away in a quiet industrial estate warehouse that is not easily accessible, Hock Siong & Co. is enjoying enormous crowds on a particularly hot and humid summer weekend. The customers who are die-hard fans had rushed down to the sprawling, non-air-conditioned warehouse after watching the weekly 11 am Facebook Live broadcast of 'Walkie-Hockie', a regular content pillar on Hock Siong & Co.'s content calendar, where the owner's daughter gives online fans a 360-degree tour of what's available, without them having to set foot in the store. The content produced is shot on a mobile phone. While the quality is not TV-commercial worthy, it has proven to be useful content for customers. The host also adopts a friendly and casual tone throughout, making audiences feel like she is introducing the store to a friend.

On this particular weekend, a shipment of bulk purchase from a retail store that has closed down attracted many customers. Shimmery glassware, colourful cushions, outdoor dining sets and lounge sofas were sold within hours after 'Walkie-Hockie' was aired. Since Hock Siong & Co. does not allow reservations, customers will rush to the warehouse upon seeing an item they like on the live-stream.

As the owner notes, marketing second-hand, refurbished or almost-new items in a warehouse without air-conditioning takes twice the effort in a retail climate that favours low prices from China's biggest shopping website, Taobao.com, over bricks and mortar's high prices. Inventory is unpredictable and not every item is perfect. With direct marketing on social media platforms, Hock Siong & Co. is able to see whether 'Walkie-Hockie' attracts a live audience and gauge the sales-conversion rates from online viewing to in-store purchases every weekend. Originally aired at 2 pm when it started, data insights on Facebook have prompted them to try different timings to capture the most views from their target audience. Social media also allows its close to 40 000 fan base to share content with non-fans allowing a wider reach in potential customers. The exponential reach is an advantage over traditional catalogue or direct marketing drops.

Indeed, 'Walkie-Hockie' has created an environment of treasure hunting, turning its business challenge into an advantage and strengthening customer relations. The organic reach for its social media posts is at least 25 per cent of its fan base, which is much higher than the amplified reach for many name brands.[18]

The art of using direct marketing in the IMC strategy continues to offer extensive opportunities for marketers as technology advances. Direct marketing should constantly be considered among the strategic IMC tools as it offers marketers a chance to combine creative opportunities with insightful data analytics and quick feedback.

Pei Wen Wong is a lecturer at Nanyang Technological University

■ CHAPTER SUMMARY

In this chapter we considered the key concepts of direct marketing: as well as direct-marketing's sub-component, direct advertising.

First we explained why direct marketing is a powerful IMC tool that is gaining favour. It is now a major marketing tool globally, with businesses as wide ranging as hotels and tourism, retail and the financial sectors using it to their benefit and with the evolution of the digital network, direct marketing has become an indispensable tool in almost all sectors of business.

Next we described two general types of direct marketing objectives: generation of leads, or traffic, and behavioural objectives.

We then examined the use of databases in direct marketing and the two types of databases normally used in direct marketing: the customer database and the potential customer database.

We explained and differentiated between direct marketing and direct-response advertising. Direct marketing is a form of IMC that allows businesses to communicate directly to customers through a variety of media. Direct-response advertising is a form of direct marketing. It utilises a blend of formats from traditional advertising elements to unique components of direct advertising that involve a direct communication between the consumer and the advertiser.

We concluded the chapter by recognising the various types of direct marketing channels—including online media, catalogues, direct mail, telemarketing, direct advertising and integrated direct marketing—and their integration.

Direct marketing links well to the channels of communication and can deliver messaging using multiple sources that reinforce one another.

Case study: Delightful direct campaign for the Arts Centre

Background

Seeing a live performance can change the course of a child's life and career. But if you live far away from a theatre—or you don't have much money—it's hard to get the opportunity to see a show.

To give as many Victorian primary and secondary students access to as many live performances as possible, Arts Centre Melbourne set up the First Call Fund. Since 2008, the First Call Fund has enabled thousands of Victorian students (and their teachers) to experience the performing arts at Arts Centre Melbourne, many for the first time. This inspiring program is funded through the generosity of donors.

Figure 7.7 *Sally Sees Her First Show* children's book

Objectives

The objective of the 'Sally's First Show' campaign, developed by OgilvyOne, Melbourne was to increase donations by about 23 per cent on the previous year, while mailing to a smaller audience.

Strategy

Ogilvy's insight was simple: the audience (people on Arts Centre Melbourne's mailing list) want to share their passion for the performing arts with others. So the key message was that a donation to the First Call Fund would bring children closer to the performing arts. It allowed art lovers to feel they were contributing to the arts and inspiring a new generation of patrons and performers. The communication was delivered entirely by mail—a single pack sent to 12 000 recipients.

With five natural disasters in quick succession (floods in Victoria, floods and a cyclone in Queensland, a tsunami in Japan and an earthquake in Christchurch), the campaign team recognised that the market was tired of bleak or distressing pleas for help, so they took an opposite approach to cut through with something positive and upbeat. They knew the target market was passionate about the arts, so a charming children's book was created to dramatise the benefit of the First Call Fund.

Based on a number of real-life case study examples, the buoyant creative told a story of a student, Sally, who has the opportunity to experience a performance at Arts Centre Melbourne for the first time. The book begins with drama-loving Sally holding dances and concerts and puppet shows for herself in her small country town. Having no exposure to the arts, her friends aren't interested in joining in. But a magical trip to Arts Centre Melbourne changes all that and soon everyone wants to be part of Sally's act.

Because it didn't feel like a piece of advertising, this piece thoroughly engaged the recipients. In fact, many of them wrote back to Arts Centre Melbourne praising the book.

Execution

OgilvyOne Melbourne developed a direct mail pack and follow-up postcard to be sent to the Arts Centre Melbourne database to drive donations. The follow-up postcard was sent a week later to those recipients that had not yet donated to the fund. The messaging was tailored to past and new donors.

The cover included a personalised thank-you message with the donor's name where the author's name would usually appear. A personalised letter was included on the inside cover, and the donation form on the back was pre-populated with the recipient's information to make it easier for them to donate.

The book itself was a thing of beauty. It involved handcrafted typography, 10 bespoke illustrations and graphic manipulation of textures to really make it feel like a proper children's book. The paper was slightly textured too, to make it more tactile.

Results

The pack achieved an 88 per cent increase on the donation increase target and 132 per cent increase on the previous year.

Response rates increased 232 per cent year on year and the average donation amount increased by 106 per cent.

Of course, with a project like this, it's not just about percentages and dollar figures. Judith Isherwood, chief executive, Arts Centre Melbourne says, 'As a result of donations received from this campaign, an extra 3500 children will be able to visit Arts Centre Melbourne and engage with our programs and activities.'

Additionally, the campaign won a number of industry awards:

- 2011 ADMA Bronze for Flat Mail,
- 2011 ADMA Silver for Art Direction Craft,
- 2011 Caples Bronze for Direct Mail, Flat,
- 2011 Mobius Gold for Copywriting,
- 2011 Mobius Silver for Art Direction,
- 2011 Mobius Best of Show for Direct,
- 2012 ECHO Bronze for Not for Profit, and
- 2012 ECHO Gold Mailbox Award (USPS).

Questions

1. What elements of the Arts Centre direct mail campaign do you think contributed to the success of this campaign?

2. Why do you think the Arts Centre decided to use a direct mail approach in this campaign?

3. Other than direct mail, what other forms of direct marketing could the Arts Centre consider deploying for this campaign?

Adapted from and originally published 5 March 2013 on the Marketing Magazine website: https://www.marketingmag.com.au/hubs-c/delightful-direct-campaign-for-the-arts-centre/.

Practitioner profile: Stephanie Swain

I never planned for a career in marketing. After graduating from a Creative Arts degree, I wanted to apply my passion for writing to a career in publishing. I got my first full-time job as a sales and marketing assistant at Oxford University Press (OUP) to get a foot in the door, thinking I'd then move into a publishing or editorial position. Well, I fell in love with marketing and found it really suited my professional strengths: creativity, harnessing new technology and building organisational systems and processes. I progressed up through a range of marketing roles at OUP, where I honed my skills in digital marketing, copywriting, data analysis and product development. After five years, I was looking for a new challenge and took on a newly created marketing position with Monash University.

Describe your current role and the organisation you work for, and give a brief account of what you do in your role on a day-to-day basis.

I'm a marketing projects coordinator in the Faculty of Medicine, Nursing and Health Sciences at Monash University. I'm part of a small, dynamic marketing team responsible for servicing Monash's largest research faculty. Our work focuses on three key pillars: student recruitment, research promotion and enterprise opportunities. I work across a range of marketing projects but tend to focus on content creation, reporting and innovative technology. This can be anything from coordinating a photoshoot in one of our labs to reporting on our social media performance to testing augmented reality apps. No two days are the same. It's fast-paced and challenging, but it's rewarding to know that the work I'm doing plays a part in creating a healthier world.

How important is Integrated Marketing Communication (IMC) to what you and your organisation do?

IMC is extremely important to what we do at Monash. I'm part of a small team with a large portfolio (we are the university's largest research faculty), so we need to utilise our time and resources strategically. Using IMC means we are more efficient. We can invest in quality visual content and spend time crafting excellent copy, then use this across all of our channels, rather than reinventing the wheel or having to come up with new messaging each time.

What types of promotional tools do you use in your IMC campaigns? Please provide examples.

Our promotional tools include:

- digital marketing with SEO and SEM, email marketing and automation for lead nurturing
- social media—we manage Faculty Twitter and Instagram accounts, where we create, share and repost campaign content

- direct marketing through EDM (electronic direct mail) and targeted print mailouts. We also use Monash newsletters as a way to directly connect with key groups such as school counsellors and overseas education agents
- advertising—if the campaign is future-student focused, we favour digital and social media advertising (such as Facebook or Twitter) or sponsored posts
- event marketing—we make sure our campaign messaging is incorporated into major events such as Open Day or Change of Preference.

What has been your favourite IMC project to work on and did it achieve its objectives?

My favourite IMC project to work on was 'Immerse Yourself in the Monash Experience', a virtual reality campaign for Monash Medicine, Nursing and Health Sciences in 2016. We wanted to harness this exciting technology to give prospective interstate and international students the opportunity to experience what it's like to study here. Our team produced a guided 360-degree tour of our key learning facilities, enabling students anywhere in the world to step inside our anatomy lab or watch a paramedic simulation in action. We produced Monash-branded Google cardboards to complement the experience, which were mailed out to education agents, career counsellors and international students with pending offers. Our campaign was supported by a custom-built VR website, social media content for Twitter, Facebook and Youku, articles in Monash newsletters and hands-on training with our student recruitment team.

It's definitely one of my professional highlights as this project was the first of its kind at Monash so we experienced the challenges of trialling new technology, but also reaped the rewards of being innovative in the market. As a result, we had high engagement with the campaign on social media and our website, and our international student conversion rate increased. This campaign was shortlisted for an Australian Marketing Institute Excellence Award.

How do you believe an IMC campaign affects the consumer decision-making process for your particular target audience?

Choosing a university is a big decision. Over the course of two years, a student will have multiple touchpoints with us throughout their decision-making journey. Because of this, it's important that all elements of our marketing—whether that be an EDM, a course guide, our website or one of our Facebook ads—all tell a consistent story and have a recognisable look-and-feel. IMC helps prospective medicine, nursing and allied health science students get to know what Monash stands for, and what sets us apart and builds trust in us as a brand. It means they can feel confident in making the decision to study their degree here.

How has your application of IMC changed with the increase in digital marketing?

Digital marketing has definitely increased the opportunities for delivering our message with new tools, channels and technologies. On the flipside, it means we need to be across more elements within any one campaign to ensure they're all aligned. A change I've noticed is that while digital marketing brings us closer to our customers, it makes the feedback loop shorter and more public so we find out quickly if a campaign isn't working, or if the messaging doesn't hit the mark and needs to be reworked.

What do you believe are some of the challenges of implementing an IMC campaign?

The volume of content needed can be challenging. You need a strong content plan and personally I've found a style and tone of voice guide to be invaluable. Our team also uses a content calendar and channels document, so we can make sure that any new campaigns are covered across all of the marketing channels available to us.

Another challenge we've found is that being part of such a large organisation it can take time to get everyone on board with a new IMC campaign and roll out integrated messaging across all channels. To keep everyone on the same page during a campaign, we use internal communication tools such as Workplace, as well as regular face-to-face meetings or conference calls that bring everyone together.

What advice would you offer a student studying IMC?

I would say:

- Take advantage of internships or work industry learning projects while you're studying. These are great opportunities to put your classroom theory into practice and experience real executions of IMC.
- Keep an eye on emerging trends in technology—think about how new tools or platforms such as AI or Chatbots could be harnessed as part of an IMC campaign.
- Read industry publications and blogs and listen to marketing podcasts. I love *Marketing* magazine for a deep-dive into some of the most innovative campaigns in the market and advice from marketers to watch.

Key terms

catalogue

customer relationship
    management (CRM)

database marketing

direct mail

direct marketing

direct-response advertising

fulfilment

inbound telemarketing call

integrated direct marketing
    (direct marketing)

lifetime customer value (LCV)

outbound telemarketing call

permission marketing

prospects

telemarketing

Revision questions

1. Why is direct-response marketing gaining tremendous popularity?
2. What are the major advantages and disadvantages of the various direct-response media?
3. Direct mail is sometimes seen as 'junk' mail. Say you are designing a mailer for a local grocery store. What can you do to make your mailer attain better receptivity and response?
4. Suppose you are in a service organisation raising funds for charity. How would you develop a program to promote campus fundraising among students? What direct-marketing channels would you consider for your campaign?
5. Of the insights offered by David Ogilvy historically (see page 231), which do you think is most relevant today in the age of online media?
6. Browse the Whole Foods website (www.wholefoodsmarket) and identify the direct marketing strategies utilised. Which do you think are most effective and why?

Further reading

Bird, D. (2007). *Commonsense Direct Marketing*, (5th edn). Glasgow: Bell & Bain.

Nash, E. (1995), *Direct Marketing: Strategy, Planning, Execution*. McGraw Hill.

Pradeep K. Korgaonkar, Karson, E. J. & Akaah, I. (1997). Direct marketing advertising: the assents, the dissents, and the ambivalents, *Journal of Advertising Research*, September/October, 41–5.

Rieck, D. (2001). 10 basics for writing better letters. *Direct Marketing*, *63*(12), 52–3, 62.

Tippen, M. (1996). Building customer loyalty through quality telemarketing. *Direct Marketing*, September, 14–15.

Weblinks

Associations

American Catalog Mailers Association
https://catalogmailers.org/

ASEAN Public Relations Network (APRN)
http://www.aseanprnetwork.org

Association for Data-Driven Marketing and Advertising
https://www.adirect marketing a.com.au/

Data and Marketing Association
https://thedirect marketing a.org/

Direct Marketing Association (UK)
https://direct marketing a.org.uk/

Direct Marketing Association of Canada
http://www.directmac.org/

Direct Marketing Association of Singapore
http://www.direct marketing as.org/

eMarketing Association
http://www.emarketingassociation.com/

Internet Marketing Association
http://imanetwork.org/

National Mail Order Association
http://www.nmoa.org/

Web Marketing Association
http://www.webmarketingassociation.org/wma/

Awards

AC&E Awards
https://www.adirect marketing a.com.au/events/2017/acandeawards?utm_source=Adirect marketing A&utm_medium=Homepage&utm_campaign=ACEentries

Australian Marketing Institute Awards for Marketing Excellence
https://e-award.com.au/2017/amiawards/newentry/about.php

Effie Worldwide
https://www.effie.org

Internet Advertising Competition
http://www.iacaward.org/iac/

Web Awards Competition
http://www.webaward.org/

Journals

Direct Marketing: An International Journal
http://www.emeraldinsight.com/journal/direct marketing ij

Journal of Direct Marketing
http://www.sciencedirect.com/science/journal/08920591

Marketing Communication News
http://www.marcomm.news/tag/exhibition/

Resources

Marketing Association of New Zealand, Direct Marketing resources, templates and guides
https://www.marketing.org.nz/Resources/Direct_Marketing

Notes

1 www.ama.org/resources/Pages/Dictionary.aspx?dLetter=D

2 https://en.wikipedia.org/wiki/Direct_marketing

3 www.businessdictionary.com/definition/direct-marketing.html

4 www.businessinsider.com/the-exploding-importance-of-direct-marketing-2013-11/?IR=T

5 www.marketing-interactive.com/sia-bolsters-krisflyer-loyalty-programme-after-customer-feedback

6 www.marketing-interactive.com/sia-bolsters-krisflyer-loyalty-programme-after-customer-feedback

7 www.autoguide.com/auto-news/2011/08/nissan-launches-quick-response-code-campaign-for-all-of-its-2012-vehicles.html

8 www.marketing-interactive.com/cycle-carriage-partners-with-ikea-for-masked-test-drive-campaign/

9 www3.hilton.com/en/index.html

10 www.victoriassecret.com

11 http://swiped.co/file/how-direct-response-advertising-ad-by-david-ogilvy

12 www.wal-mart.com

13 http://www.cdnow.com

14 www.independent.ie/business/technology/google-will-stop-reading-your-emails-to-target-you-with-adverts-35860624.html

15 Brain, S. (2017a). Facebook statistics: http://www.statisticbrain.com/facebook-statistics/

16 Brain, S. (2017b). Twitter statistics: http://www.statisticbrain.com/twitter-statistics/

17 McFadden, F. R. & Hoffer, J. A. (1985). Data Base Management. Menlo Park, CA: Benjamin/Cummings, 3.

18 Find Hock Siong & Co. on Facebook (https://www.facebook.com/hocksiongco/) and Instagram, (https://www.instagram.com/hocksiong/)

CHAPTER 8

Sales Promotions

Peter Ling

Exciting sales promotions

Supermarkets offer incentives to shoppers every day to increase sales of household essentials. These promotions are often price discounts, value packs or product sampling. There's nothing creatively exciting about such sales promotions as consumers tend to take for granted that supermarkets need to offer daily incentives in a highly competitive market.

Now and then, there is excitement in sales promotion during special sports events, such as incentives aligned with the Olympics, Soccer World Cup and the Australian Open. There is also excitement when a much-awaited movie is launched with various brand tie-ups.

Take for example the movie launch of *Star Wars: The Force Awakens* by Lucasfilm, a subsidiary of The Walt Disney Company. Several companies joined together in the **cross-promotion** campaign in 2015 to promote their products as well as the movie, including General Mills, Lego, CoverGirl, Nestlé and Facebook.[1]

General Mills introduced special collectable cereal packs, such as its Honey Nut Cheerios featuring BuzzBee dressed as Darth Vader.[2] Lego offered specially made characters such as a Jedi Master, Princess Leia and C-3PO.[3] CoverGirl had its galactic looks and Star Wars Limited Edition Colorlicious Lipsticks.[4] Nestlé created five Star Wars-themed Coffee-Mate collectable coffee-creamer bottles, including new flavours Darth Vader espresso chocolate and Chewbacca spiced latté.[5] Facebook set up a Star Wars page and inserted a lightsabre to the user's profile picture for a week as an incentive whenever the user Liked the page. There were more than 18 million Likes on the Facebook Star Wars page.[6]

Star Wars also had 'May the 4th' day deals in 2016 featuring other sales promotion tie-ups with brands such as Toys 'R' Us, Hasbro, Amazon, Walmart, Target, Uniqlo, Hallmark and New Zealand Mint.[7]

■ INTRODUCTION

Consumers like receiving sales promotion incentives, whether at a local bakery, a restaurant chain or an online store. A local baker could run an end-of-day special offer to clear unsold goods, with only nearby shoppers being aware because of shop signs. A restaurant chain may advertise a festive discount in mass media to attract more customers. An online store's discounts may be promoted through its website, social media and email marketing. As you can see, sales promotion does not operate in isolation but in collaboration with other tools of marketing communication.

However, sales promotion as a marketing tool is like a double-edged sword with favourable and unfavourable consequences. On the plus side, the marketing activity could generate positive earned publicity, increase sales, enhance brand equity and win the support of various stakeholders such as the sales force, retailers and consumers. The negative side of sales promotion could impact marketing operations, sour the relationship with retailers or consumers, attract negative viral comments and damage brand reputation.

In this chapter we address the common questions raised on sales promotion: What is sales promotion? Why run sales promotion activities? How different are sales promotion incentives for different stakeholders such as the sales force, business buyers and consumers? What diverse incentives are used to attract consumers? What exciting sales promotions can marketers run besides the usual unexciting price-offs? What are the challenges facing the sales promotion industry? In this chapter we will attempt to answer these questions.

LEARNING OBJECTIVES

After reading this chapter you should be able to:

1. explain sales promotion and objectives for the sales force, retailers and consumers
2. distinguish between incentives for the sales force and business buyers
3. discuss the various types of consumer sales promotion incentives
4. discuss some exciting sales promotion examples
5. discuss challenges in sales promotion.

What is sales promotion?

What is sales promotion and why run sales promotion activities? This section discusses definitions of sales promotion and then looks at sales objectives targeting the sales force, business buyers and consumers. In layman terms, sales promotion means a marketing activity that promotes sales. However, six sources reveal different definitions, some inaccurately conveying the concept of sales promotion:

> ... activities or techniques intended to create consumer demand for a product or service.[8]

> The use of publicizing methods other than paid advertising to promote a product or service etc.[9]

> ... activities and devices designed to create goodwill and sell a product; *especially*: selling activities (as use of displays, sampling, demonstrations, fashion shows, contests, coupons, premiums, and special sales) that supplement advertising and personal selling, coordinate them, and make them effective.[10]

… the methods or techniques for creating public acceptance of or interest in a product, usually in addition to standard merchandising techniques, as advertising or personal selling, and generally consisting of the offer of free samples, gifts made to a purchaser, or the like.[11]

The media and nonmedia marketing pressure applied for a predetermined, limited period of time at the level of consumer, retailer, or wholesaler in order to stimulate trial, increase consumer demand, or improve product availability.[12]

Sales promotion is one level or type of marketing aimed either at the consumer or at the distribution channel (in the form of sales-incentives). It is used to introduce new product, clear out inventories, attract traffic, and to lift sales temporarily.[13]

There are three central messages from the six different definitions:

- Sales promotion is about increasing sales through creating awareness, goodwill and distribution of goods and services.
- Sales promotion involves different stakeholders such as retailers and consumers.
- Sales promotion selling or incentive activities are promoted through various channels such as advertising, publicity and selling activities.

However, a misconception needs to be addressed. Webster's *New World College Dictionary* defines sales promotion as 'publicizing methods *other than paid advertising*'. This is an inaccurate definition. While sales promotion is usually communicated through point of sale signage, major sales offers are also advertised through various media such as television, print media and outdoor posters.

The concept of sales promotion can be better understood when put in the context of the communication model of source, audience, message and media:

- *Source:* the marketer attempting to build sales or brand image
- *Audience:* a varied lot comprising the sales force, business buyers and consumers
- *Message:* the selling incentive to urge immediate purchase of the goods or services
- *Media:* the channels communicating the message.

So, a more appropriate definition of sales promotion would be: *Sales promotion is a marketer's selling activity aimed at various stakeholders and communicated through various media channels to incentivise immediate actions.*

Sales objectives

This section looks at the immediate actions or sales objectives for the sales force, retailers and consumers.

Objectives for the sales force

Effective sales come from skilled, knowledgeable and motivated sales people in **business-to-business (B2B)** and selected **business-to-consumer (B2C)** sales.

In B2B, the sales force sells to business buyers who purchase **industrial goods and services** such as capital items, materials and parts, and supplies and services for their companies to produce other goods and services for government offices, not-for-profit organisations, businesses and individuals. Capital items would be building installation and office accessory equipment. Materials and parts cover raw materials (e.g. farm animals, iron ore) and manufactured materials (e.g. milk, steel). Supplies and services are operating supplies (e.g. paper) and maintenance-repair items (e.g. paint) offered to various buyers.[14]

Some sales forces in B2B sell to businesses that market **consumer goods and services**, such as convenience products of services and non-durable, fast-moving consumer goods; durable products of communication devices, household items, cars and bicycles; specialty branded products; and unsought services such as funeral services and blood donation.[15]

B2B sales forces need to secure new customers, convert sales leads and sell specific items or obtain larger orders from existing customers.[16] Some sales force personnel could be 'hunters' tracking potential customers, or 'farmers' focusing on current customers.[17]

In certain B2C categories, there would be more need for sales personnel in retail outlets that sell durable products, specialty-brand products and unsought services. These sales personnel would be required to sell to casual shoppers and consumers pulled by advertising or referrals.

Objectives for retailers

Marketers incentivise retailers to sell more of their products and support promotional activities.[18] Consequently, marketers would provide incentives to retailers to achieve three objectives:

- stock up on the products, especially for new product launches and any promotional campaigns
- display the products visibly so that shoppers could easily see the products and the offers
- promote the products instore and through advertising media such as newspapers and television.

Objectives for consumers

Marketers have various reasons to incentivise consumers: try the new product or a related product, buy again, purchase more volume or bigger packs, patronise on certain days or times of the day, buy as gifts, and buy during festive or sports events.[19]

Summarising this section, sales promotion is a marketer's selling activity aimed at various stakeholders and communicated through various media channels to incentivise immediate actions. The immediate actions or sales objectives desired by the marketer would vary depending on the stakeholders. A B2B sales force needs to secure new customers, convert sales leads, sell specific items or obtain larger orders. A B2C sales force in retail outlets such as durable goods would need to convert drop-in consumers. Marketers incentivise retailers to sell more of their products and support promotional activities. Marketers also incentivise consumers to act in different ways.

The next section discusses sales promotion incentives for a company's sales force, business buyers and consumers.

Incentives for the sales force

The sales force would also need to be incentivised to increase sales in B2B and selected B2C product categories. Incentives include incentive pay, sales contest and incentive travel.

Incentive pay

Apart from salary, a company could provide the sales force with **incentive pay** such as commission or a percentage of sales.[20] There could also be a bonus for a sales person who exceeds sales expectations.[21]

One *Harvard Business Review* report indicated that B2B companies in the US spend three times more on sales force compensation than on advertising. Some businesses offer quarterly rather than yearly bonuses. Other companies celebrate sales successes with leasing for Porsches or VIP tickets to sports events.[22]

Another report suggested providing commission on gross revenue or sales profitability; bonuses over shorter periods to motivate low sales performers; and a combination of salary, commission and bonuses when sales goals are achieved.[23]

Sales contest

A short-term **sales contest** incentive for the sales force provides financial and non-financial motivation such as cash prizes and achievement recognition.[24] Competition formats could be sales person versus past performance, current goal, other sales colleagues or sales teams.[25]

In Singapore, life insurance companies often advertise their top performers using full page advertisements.[26] This has the benefit of giving pride to the top achievers, spurring others to move up the award categories and providing consumers with some possible names to contact if they are in the market for life insurance. In Australia, the Financial Services Council has Life Insurance Awards to recognise the Young Achiever of the Year; Industry Mentor Awards; and Industry Leader Awards.[27] Danish pharmaceutical company Novo Nordisk introduced a virtual five-day program, 'Welcome to Club V', to engage its 2000 sales force to launch its Victoza non-insulin medication product. The virtual nightclub motivated the sales force to gain awards through individual competitions, team contests and certifications while learning about the new drug.[28]

Incentive travel

Sales people could also receive **incentive travel** holidays for exceeding targets.[29] The incentive travel could be a family holiday, a golf vacation or attending international conferences.

The US non-cash incentive market alone grew from US$27 billion in 2000 to US$90 billion in 2016, with US$14 billion recorded for incentive travel and US$76 billion invested in award points, gift cards, merchandise and rewards for sales personnel, general employees, retailers and customers.[30]

A UK study revealed that incentive travel enhances employee appreciation, management interaction, company trust and corporate loyalty. Consequently, incentive travel has been increasing in companies such as Peugeot, Citroën, Telecoms, NuSkin, NCH Europe and BMW.[31] German carmaker BMW appointed event company Zibrant to deliver five global incentives to Cape Town, Finland, Shamwari Game Reserve and Vietnam.[32]

Overall, some sales force personnel may prefer financial incentives, while other employees may gain greater satisfaction from non-financial peer recognition.[33]

Incentives for business buyers

This section looks at incentives from industrial sellers to business buyers who purchase industrial goods and services or consumer goods and services.

Industrial goods and services

McDonald's or KFC would undertake the following when setting up a new branch: renting or buying a retail space; installing various types of equipment in the restaurant; having regular supplies of food products and paper supplies. If you are the central corporate buyer for the retail giant, what would help determine who you buy from? Would it be quantity discount, credit terms, quality testing of products, free training for staff to use machines, speedy product delivery or efficient after sales service for equipment?

A McKinsey report indicated that business buyers are looking for value-added services, such as inexpensive and simple transactions, customised solutions, use of data analytics to predict consumer behaviour and boost sales, more responsive sales service, more sales force time, risk sharing agreements and accessible technical expertise or virtual specialists to service customers.[34]

Consumer goods and services

Now, assume that you are selling convenience goods to retailers. What incentives could you offer the supermarket chain buyers to stock up on your goods, display them, promote them and continue replenishing stocks to ensure they are never out of stock? This is known as the **push strategy**; that is, pushing from the supplier to wholesalers/retailers to consumers. In contrast, the **pull strategy** pulls consumers to stores to buy goods to make retailers purchase from suppliers.[35] See Table 8.1 for some push strategy incentives that could be offered to supermarkets, such as allowances for advertising, displays and bulk buying.[36]

Many of the push strategy incentives fall under the category of 'allowance'; for example, allowance for advertising, bulk purchase, free product and display. Marketers such as Red Bull, Coca-Cola, Pepsi, Nestlé, Nescafé, Cadbury, Kit Kat, Snickers, Toblerone, Heinz, Johnnie Walker, Duracell, Pampers and Dove provide retailers with unique displays to increase consumer attention and sales.[37] Since the nineteenth century, Coca-Cola has been providing retailers with posters and display decorations to enhance brand awareness.[38]

Table 8.1 Push strategy incentives

INCENTIVE	DESCRIPTION
Accelerated purchase	An incentive to fast-purchase goods before the normal purchase cycle
Advertising allowance	An incentive for the retailer to advertise the supplier's product
Buying allowance	A discount incentive based on bulk purchasing a product
Count and recount promotion	An incentive given based on quantity sold after a pre-/post-inventory period
Dating	An incentive to pay for a product purchase over a period of time
Dealer loader	An extra deal is loaded for a special display or product promotion
Dealer tie-in	An incentive for the retailer to tie-in with the supplier through store display, cooperative advertising, contests and featuring of the product in the store's advertising
Display allowance	An incentive to display the product in a special place in the store such as an end-aisle spot
Factory pack	Multiple packaging by the supplier as a value pack of one or several products
Free merchandise	A free product for purchasing a minimum quantity from the supplier or to offer as samples to consumers
Incentive travel	A holiday reward to retail staff for exceeding sales targets
Push money	An incentive to retail sales people to push sales of a supplier's brand
Seasonal discount	A discount for retailers who order seasonal products in advance

Incentives for business buyers vary depend on whether the purchases are industrial or consumer goods and services. Industrial buyers may prefer incentives such as inexpensive transactions, quantity discounts, credit terms, quality testing of products, customised solutions, risk sharing, free training, speedy product delivery, access to technical expertise and efficient after-sales service. Retail buyers of consumer goods and services may prefer various forms of 'push strategy' allowances for advertising and display and to be assured of 'pull strategy' incentives to motivate consumers to buy their stocked goods and services.

Incentives for consumers

While suppliers such as Coca-Cola Amatil in Australia push their products to retailers, marketers also need a pull strategy to create demand among consumers and encourage them to buy or request the products from retailers.

From your own personal experiences, you may have been pulled by incentives such as free trials, buying a second pair of jeans at half price or a free holiday. See Table 8.2 for a description of various pull strategy incentives.[39]

Delayed or immediate incentives

Many of the sales promotion incentives in Table 8.2 offer immediate benefit to consumers while other incentives are only enjoyed later. Immediate incentives include price-offs, twin packs, buy one get one free, scratch and win, sampling and premiums. McDonald's has a different way of branding their immediate incentives: All-Day Breakfast, which offers consumers breakfast value throughout the day; and McPick2, where customers can pick two items for $2 from a menu selection.[46]

Delayed incentives are tickets to a future event, frequent flyer or credit card usage points that can be redeemed for prizes, coupons or vouchers to be used by a certain date, sweepstakes for a future lucky draw and contest results after the closing date.

Incentives could also be classified as rational monetary sales promotion with a functional benefit or emotional non-monetary sales promotion that also generates greater positive brand associations. A rational incentive could be a 15 per cent discount on Ferrero Rocher. An emotional incentive could be the opportunity to look good in a gift of a pair of earrings if you collect three bar codes plus the chance to win a prize in a sweepstake. Research found that monetary sales promotion offers align with utilitarian products while non-monetary incentives could be used for both hedonic and utilitarian products.[47]

IMC IN ACTION: KFC CHIZZA

KFC in Singapore launched in February 2017 with 'Chizza', a chicken fillet with pizza toppings such as mozzarella cheese, pineapple chunks, chicken ham and pizza sauce.

KFC had introduced Chizza in the Philippines in 2015 and then launched it in India, Japan, Korea, Taiwan and Thailand.[48]

Appealing to chicken and pizza lovers, KFC introduced a Chizza Meal of Chizza, French fries and Pepsi at S$7.50 while a Chizza Box of Chizza, drumsticks, whipped potato, potato winders and Pepsi was offered at S$9.50.[49] KFC also produced a video on the making of its Chizza.

Table 8.2 Pull strategy incentives

INCENTIVE	DESCRIPTION
Bonus pack	A special package like a value pack, twin pack or deal merchandise where the consumer receives more of the product at a lower price per unit. Sometimes a smaller pack is included, such as a small unit of a mouthwash or a hair gel
Bounce back offer	An offer included in a purchased product to sell another product or more of the same product[40]
Buy one get one free	An incentive where the second same product is free
Club plan selling	Like 'Member Get Member' where a current member receives prizes or discounts for introducing another member
Contest	A promotion where consumers use a skill to qualify for a prize. A contest could also help to enhance the brand image
Coupon	A printed or digital offer for a price reduction. It could be a co-op coupon featuring several sellers, an in-store coupon valid only at a specific retail chain or a specialty distributed coupon on the back of a cashier's receipt.[41] It could also be in a **free-standing insert**, which is a pre-printed catalogue of coupons inserted in a magazine or newspaper[42]
Courtesy days	A privilege provided to selective consumers to buy special-offer goods before they are advertised to the public[43]
Cross-ruff	Using a non-competitive product to distribute a sample or coupon
Cross selling	Selling related products at a retail outlet; for example, at fast food outlets when the counter person suggests additional items such as dessert when you buy a burger
Free sample	Common in supermarkets (free sampling of a new drink or product) and in department stores (free perfume sachet)
Frequent shopper program	A form of continuity plan or loyalty program where consumers redeem points for products or enjoy free products after loyalty cards are stamped over a period of time
Game	This involves collecting and matching symbols to win a prize
Multiple-unit packaging	Another form of value pack such as a six-pack of beer to encourage volume purchase[44]
Odd-even pricing	Odd pricing ends with an odd number, e.g. $3.99. Even pricing ends with a round number, e.g. $5.00
Premium	A gift offered as an incentive. It could be an in-pack premium (placed inside a pack), an on-pack premium (attached to the product or product package) or a near-pack premium (a large gift placed near the display, e.g. near the cashier)[45]
Price-off offer	A common rebate or discount incentive
Refund	Some retailers offer a free refund of the product purchased if the purchaser is not satisfied within a certain time period
Sweepstake	A promotion where chance rather than skill determines winners of prizes

Appropriateness of incentives

Would pull incentives apply to all consumer goods and services? It would be interesting for you to analyse whether the incentives listed could be applied to consumer goods and services such as convenience products, durables or shopping products, specialty products and unsought services.[50] See Table 8.3.

Table 8.3 Sales promotion incentives for various consumer goods and services

INCENTIVES	CONVENIENCE PRODUCTS		DURABLES OR SHOPPING PRODUCTS	SPECIALTY PRODUCTS	UNSOUGHT SERVICES
	NON-DURABLES, E.G. FAST MOVING CONSUMER GOODS	SERVICES, E.G. MOBILE CONNECTION, NEWS, ENTERTAINMENT, FINANCE, HEALTH, TRAVEL	APPLIANCES, CARS, FURNITURE, CLOTHES	LUXURY ITEMS, E.G. DIAMONDS, ROLEX	LIFE INSURANCE, BLOOD DONATION, FUNERAL SERVICES
Bonus pack					
Bounce back offer					
Buy one get one free					
Club plan selling					
Contest					
Coupon					
Courtesy days					
Cross-ruff					
Cross selling					
Free sample					
Frequent shopper program					
Game					
Multiple-unit packaging					
Odd-even pricing					
Premium					
Price-off offer					
Refund					
Sweepstake					

I once flashed two slides, one after another, in one of my classes. The first slide showed popular consumer incentives and some students voiced their personal favourites. See Table 8.4.

Table 8.4 Popular consumer incentives—students' favourites

POPULAR INCENTIVES	STUDENTS' FAVOURITES
Free trial	✓
$20 off	
Early bird special	
Buy 1 get 1 free	
Free travel bag	✓
Win a holiday prize	✓
Loyalty program	

Table 8.5 Popular consumer incentives—funeral services?

POPULAR INCENTIVES	FUNERAL SERVICES
Free trial	
$20 off	
Early bird special	
Buy 1 get 1 free	
Free travel bag	
Win a holiday prize	
Loyalty program	

The second slide (See Table 8.5) showed the same consumer incentives but this time the right-hand column featured funeral services. The students joked about which incentives to offer!

The lesson that students took away was: not all incentives can be applied across all consumer products. A funeral services company may give a price discount for booking an early bird special but would not be able to provide many other incentives.

Visiting the website of a regularly advertised funeral services provider in Australia, White Lady Funerals, there is no explicit 'Early Bird Special' offer. The only incentive message under 'Preplan a funeral' is a comparison of 'Prepaid vs Funeral Insurance Calculator', where a prepaid funeral plan could cost A$6000 versus A$30 246 in funeral insurance premiums over 24 years.[51]

There are lots more sales promotion 'pull strategy' incentives aimed at consumers. Some are immediate incentives where the benefit is instant, such as price offers. Some are delayed incentives where the benefit would be enjoyed much later, such as accumulating frequent flyer or credit card points to exchange for a reward at a future date. Some incentives offer a rational functional benefit while other incentives provide a non-monetary or emotional benefit that also generates positive brand association. Ultimately, some sales promotion incentives are appropriate only for certain goods and services.

Exciting sales promotions

Supermarket daily sales promotion offers such as price-offs and special packs tend to be expected and unexciting. There are opportunities for marketers to benefit diverse stakeholders through exciting sales promotion campaigns that tie in with social causes, movie launches, television reality shows, global sports competitions or specially created events.

Social causes

Some incentives involve an intrinsic, inner-directed element, such as buying a product knowing that its purchase will benefit a charity cause. For example, when you buy a RED product, the manufacturer contributes a certain percentage of the profit to the Global Fund to help fight against the deadly virus Acquired Immune Deficiency Syndrome (AIDS).

Since celebrities Bono and Bobby Shriver started the RED concept in 2006, corporate partners have contributed more than US$465 million to help fight AIDS. Partners include Apple, Bank of America, Beats by Dr Dre, Belvedere Vodka, Coca-Cola, Gap, Sales Force, SAP, Starbucks and Telcel & Claro. Apple has contributed more than US$100 million through sales of its special RED line of cases for iPod, iPad and iPhone. Gap has contributed more than US$10 million through sales of its apparel products branded with the Gap(RED) logo and statements such as FI(RED) UP, INC(RED)IBLE, and INSPI(RED).[52] See Figure 8.1, which shows an iPhone 7 Plus (RED).

Figure 8.1 iPhone 7 Plus (RED)

Movie launches

When Disney UK launched the movie *Beauty and the Beast* in March 2017, seven marketers became partners to join the global promotional blitz and gain positive associations for their brands. The marketers were Unilever, Procter & Gamble, Sony, Comparethemarket.com, HomeAway Rentals, the Hamptons International estate agent chain and Latest in Beauty.[53]

Unilever's Persil detergent brand had a special on-pack promotion with a £5 Disney shopping voucher.[54] P&G ran a sweepstake with a New York holiday prize with purchases of its Olay Moisturiser.[55] Sony Mobile offered customers of its Xperia smartphone and tablet a 'Disney's Beauty and the Beast Bundle' of ringtone, phone theme and a six-month DisneyLife entertainment subscription.[56]

Comparethemarket.com offered its Meerkat Movies customers a two-for-one tickets incentive to see *Beauty and the Beast*.[57] Hamptons International offered three ways of entering a 'Paris Prize Draw': booking a market appraisal, participating in its online data entry survey and first place winner of its free 'Draw Your Happily Ever After' competition.[58] Latest in Beauty curated a limited edition of The Beauty Box and The Beast Box of beauty and grooming products (see Figure 8.2).[59]

Figure 8.2 The Beast Box Limited Edition grooming products

Source: https://www.latestinbeauty.com/beauty-and-the-beast

Television reality shows

The Voice Australia also attracted the interest of consumers and marketers. Channel 9 and ITV Studios invited consumers to register to be part of the studio audience, with successful applicants obtaining free tickets.[60]

Cadbury tied up with *The Voice* in 2015 for several events. First was a competition, 'Snap Your Selfie', where consumers posed with their favourite Cadbury bar and answered the question 'Why your favourite Cadbury Bar brings you Joy' for the chance of winning ticket prizes to *The Voice Australia*'s grand finale. Second was for consumers to visit a Big W store to take photographs in *The Voice* Coach Chairs and upload messages on Instagram. Third was a promotion with Woolworths, where consumers spent $5 or more on Cadbury products to have a chance of winning one of 5000 $20-dollar iTunes vouchers instantly and one of three VIP experiences with *The Voice* judge Jessie J. The VIP experiences included attending a private performance, tickets to the grand finale, and flights and accommodation for the winner and three friends.

Cadbury's promotion with *The Voice* helped to increase brand likeability from 14 per cent to 27 per cent (especially with positive associations of celebrating and sharing joyful moments), medium bar sales by 19 per cent, and sales increased by 53 per cent at a Woolworths store through a staff incentive program.[61]

Global sports competitions

Global events such as the Olympics and World Cup Soccer attract global brands as sponsors, which then run sales promotion campaigns. Sweepstakes, special edition products and experiential events are popular sales promotion incentives.

During the 2016 Rio Olympics, Coca-Cola, Panasonic, Visa, Citi, Nissan, Milk Life and 24 Hour Fitness ran sweepstakes; Samsung, Omega, Nike, Chobani and Hershey introduced special edition products; Samsung, Visa and Kellogg's provided experiential events; McDonald's, GE and BP offered free product or discounts; and Bridgestone rewarded top employees with incentive travel to the US Olympic Committee Training Center. See Table 8.6 for a summary of the Rio Olympics sales promotion campaigns.

During World Cup 2014, partners and sponsors of the Fédération Internationale de Football Association (FIFA) also promoted sweepstakes, product prizes, limited edition products and incentives for various stakeholders. Adidas, Hyundai, Sony, Visa, Emirates, McDonald's, Oi Telecommunications, Kia and Budweiser offered World Cup holiday trips to winners.

Table 8.6 Rio Olympics Sales Promotion

SPONSORS	SALES PROMOTION INCENTIVES
Coca-Cola	Sweepstake: buy any Coke product, register purchase for chance to win one of three trips to the Rio 2016 Games plus a lucky draw of $1000 Visa Gift Cards daily[62]
Panasonic	Raffle draw to win one of four trips to Rio Games[63]
Visa	Chance for Visa card users to win a Rio Games trip for two plus five VIP Lounges for Visa Chase United Card members[64]
Citi	Chance for Citi Visa card users to win Rio Games Opening Ceremony trip for two[65]
Nissan	Test-drive the new Nissan Kicks and stand a chance to win a car or tickets to Rio[66]
Milk Life	Chance to win 1000 prizes plus $1 off next purchase[67]
24 Hour Fitness	Sweepstake to win Rio Games trip[68]
Samsung	Special Edition Olympic Games Galaxy S7 Edge mobile phone plus 85 hours of virtual reality programming to owners of Samsung Galaxy and Samsung Gear VR[69]
Omega	Special Edition Rio 2016 Omega watch[70]
Nike	Unlimited Olympic Collection, Then & Now Collection[71]
Chobani	Limited edition yogurt flavours[72]
Hershey	Special edition red, white and blue packaging[73]
Kellogg	Opportunity for consumers to experience sports virtually[74]
McDonald's	100 specially selected children from 18 countries participated in the Opening Ceremony, athlete meetings and sports events. Free food in its Olympic Village restaurant for athletes and their families.[75]
Procter & Gamble	Free grooming and beauty treatments for athletes and families at P&G's Family Home at the Olympics through P&G brands Cover Girl, Gillette, Head & Shoulders, Olay and Pantene[76]
GE	A free drone daily to anyone who submitted a question at the Drone Week live broadcast[77]
BP	Refuelling aircraft within 20 minutes and discounted fuel offer[78]
Bridgestone	Top employees gained trip to US Olympic Committee Training Center[79]

While Budweiser acknowledged grassroots football heroes and McDonald's treated children, fans and employees to World Cup experiences, Kia sent leaders of soccer organisations, grassroots soccer winning teams, children and global top dealers. Budweiser, Johnson & Johnson and Coca-Cola also produced limited edition products for their World Cup promotion while Castrol gave away prizes such as Sony, Adidas and Castrol-branded soccer balls. See Table 8.7 for sales promotion incentives by FIFA partners and Figure 8.3 for an example of Budweiser's World Cup promotion.[80]

Reviewing the global sales promotion campaigns of partners and sponsors of the Olympics and the World Cup, the favourite incentives are sweepstakes, special edition products, experiential events and free products. Since these global events are held every four years, marketers optimise their partnerships or sponsorships by not only promoting to consumers but to employees, retailers, children and community leaders as well.

Table 8.7 FIFA World Cup sales promotion

SPONSORS	SALES PROMOTION INCENTIVES
Adidas	Chant Challenge for a chance to win World Cup trip for two[81]
Hyundai	Coin slogans for each national team bus and lucky winner gets trip for two to World Cup[82]
Sony	Fans submitted videos on home teams for opportunities to win World Cup trips[83]
Visa	Sweepstakes to win trip to World Cup final[84]
Emirates	14 pairs of World Cup final tickets to Emirates Skywards loyalty program members[85]
McDonald's	VIP holiday to World Cup for children, fans and McDonald's employees. Also, Fantasy Football Game with Kia, Adidas and McDonald's prizes.[86]
Oi Telecommunications	Buy one of 14 service bundles for a lucky draw of tickets to World Cup matches.
Kia	Free trips to the World Cup for soccer organisations, grassroots soccer winning team, children as Kia Mascot Friends and Global Top Dealer Contest for 32 Kia dealers[87]
Budweiser	Trip to Rio for grassroots football heroes who have impacted on communities or teammates. Also, limited edition trophy-look gold aluminium bottles[88]
Johnson & Johnson	Buy Listerine and get a limited edition World Cup rinse cup. Also, buy three Band-Aid products to receive Band-Aid World Cup collectable tin[89]
Coca-Cola	Collect augmented reality app for users to create Facebook avatars and messages. Also, limited edition collection of 20 mini bottles[90]
Castrol	Best predictions of matches win prizes such as Sony and Adidas products. Also, buy five quarts of Castrol products to win Castrol-branded soccer ball[91]

Figure 8.3 Budweiser World Cup promotion

Specially created events

Besides sponsoring major global sports events, marketers also specially create their own events, such as the long-running Pillsbury Bake-Off Contest.

The Pillsbury contest started in 1949 as the Grand National Recipe and Baking Contest to celebrate the eightieth anniversary of the Pillsbury brand, but was renamed after media referred to it as a Bake-Off. The first winner won US$50 000, but the grand prize money increased to US$1 million in 1996.[92]

The contest challenged US cooks to submit original recipes using fewer than seven Pillsbury ingredients and needing a maximum of 30 minutes to prepare. The judging process is rigorous. First, a panel of independent judges reviews each eligible entry submitted. Second, the Pillsbury Bake-Off Test Kitchens selects the best recipes for actual preparation.[93] Third, the top 100 finalists prepare their food creations with ingredients supplied by Pillsbury in GE ovens set up at the bake-off venue.[94] Fourth, another panel of 12 judges in four categories assesses the creations of the 100 finalists on creativity, taste, appearance and crowd appeal to pick the winner of each category.[95]

While the judging panel of category winners collectively selected the grand prize winner in previous years, the process changed for the forty-seventh contest in 2014 to allow public voting to help select the $1 million grand prize winner from the four best recipes: Amazing Doable Dinners, Savory Snacks & Sides, Simply Sweet Treats and Weekend Breakfast Wows. The judges' points accounted for 55 per cent while the public's online voting made up the other 45 per cent. There were also other sponsor awards worth US$5000 each, such as the GE Imagination at Work Award, the Jif Peanut Butter Award, the Crisco is Cooking Award, the Eagle Brand Signature Recipe Award, the Pillsbury Gluten Free Award, the Pillsbury Clever Twist Award, the Watkins Vanilla Award and the Reynolds Baking Magic Award.[96]

This long-running Pillsbury Bake-Off Contest has benefited various corporate stakeholders via pull and push strategies. General Mills gained more consumer awareness for its brands Pillsbury, Haagen-Dazs, Yoplait, Betty Crocker and Green Giant. Sponsors such as the following gained publicity: GE Appliances; JM Smucker for its brands Jif peanut butter, Crisco oils and Eagle Brand sweetened condensed milk; Reynolds Consumer Products for its brands Reynolds Wrap® Aluminum Foil and Reynolds Parchment Paper; JR Watkins for its Watkins Spice and Extract range of baking products; and Pyrex for its glassware products.[97]

Obviously, contest participants had a mixture of intrinsic and extrinsic motivation. There is the intrinsic motivation of challenging yourself to submit eligible recipes and to be among the top 100 out of thousands of entries. There is the extrinsic motivation of being a special award winner, a category winner or a grand prize winner and there is the publicity of being interviewed by the media and having your recipe featured on the Pillsbury Bake-Off Contest website.[98] Here is a summary of the Pillsbury contest within the communication model.

- *Source:* Pillsbury & sponsors
- *Audience:* amateur cooks, judging agency, home economists and judges, online voters
- *Message:* challenge, fame and cash
- *Media:* website and recipes, news media, televised bake-off.

As you can see, exciting sales promotions that benefit various stakeholders are possible through social causes, movie launches, television reality shows, global sports competitions or specially created events. In a social-cause promotion, your purchase could help fight a community problem such as AIDS. When Disney UK launched the movie *Beauty and the Beast*, marketing collaborators sold special products and gained positive brand associations. During the 2016 Rio Olympics and World Cup 2014, consumers benefited from limited edition products, experiential events and sweepstake holiday prizes while top employees, retailers and community leaders enjoyed incentive travel to Brazil. The specially created Pillsbury Bake-Off event provided the intrinsic motivation of challenging yourself and the extrinsic motivation of being a special award, category or grand prize winner.

Challenges in sales promotion

Sales promotion practice and research have revealed several challenges facing the industry. This section discusses key issues of sales promotion, specifically deceptive pricing, coupon redemption, PR impact and sales promotion effectiveness.

Deceptive pricing

Deceptive pricing results from false claims made about factory prices, special sales or two for the price of one offers.[99] The Australian Competition & Consumer Commission website on 'False or misleading claims' provides examples of deceptive pricing: a jewellery retailer that never sold a watch for $200 but advertises it as 'Was $200. Now $100'; a product is not free if some payment is required; a competitive price comparison is misleading if the other price is from a different geographical market; and an advertised total price is deceptive if a customer must pay for something else.[100]

Consumer Affairs Victoria also has a website for 'Misleading or deceptive conduct': it is misleading, for example, for a department store to promote '25 per cent off all clothing' and '15 to 40 per cent off housewares' when the advertisement's small print excludes certain clothing and houseware items.[101]

Related to deceptive pricing is the practice of 'bait advertising' or 'bait and switch'. This is when a retailer advertises an offer to pull consumers but pushes a higher priced item.[102] Sometimes, the advertised offer is not available or limited in stock. It is not deceptive pricing if the retailer clearly states that the offer has limited stock or is only available for a limited period.[103]

Retailers need to be transparent about pricing. There have been lawsuits against retailers for deceptive pricing luring shoppers into believing they are receiving huge bargains. In 2015, Michael Kors paid US$4.88 million to settle a US lawsuit on deceptive pricing.[104]

Coupon redemption

A common feature of sales promotion coupons is the need to redeem the offer at a retail or redemption outlet. The redemption rate or percentage of total coupons redeemed varies.[105] It could be as high as 38 per cent for coupons from free-standing inserts, 20 per cent from a cross-ruff offer or 4 per cent from a direct mail coupon. Many shoppers do not redeem coupons because of fast expiry dates, inappropriate products, misplaced coupons, non-digital coupons, conditions of buying other items or stringent redemption rules.[106]

This could lead to 'misredemption', where there is an improper claim due to non-compliance with rules, deadlines and eligibility.[107] There is also the issue of coupon fraud, an illegal way of redeeming coupons.[108]

Taking a different approach towards retailers and consumers, Groupon works with one million merchants in 15 countries to sell more than one billion special-offer coupons—or 'Groupons'—to 53 million customers who have to date saved a total of US$20 billion.[109] The company started in 2008 in Chicago in the US, and by 2010 had spread to various US cities and international markets.[110] Groupon launched in Australia in 2011 and since then has worked with 16 000 merchants to sell more than 15 million special-offer vouchers to five million members for goods and services such as automotive, bars, beauty and spas, electronics, entertainment, grocery, fashion, food and drink, health and fitness, home improvement, jewellery and watches, kids toys and nursery, personal services, and sports and outdoor equipment.[111]

PR impact

Some sales promotion campaigns enhance the brand reputation, such as sweepstakes that send children, a sales force and dealers to sporting events. However, some sales promotion sweepstakes and volume purchases turn sour. This section features two sales promotion fiascos that practically devalued the brands: Pepsi in the Philippines and Hoover in the UK.

Pepsi's Number Fever

Pepsi's bottle cap promotion in the Philippines in 1992 turned into a disaster. Consumers bombed Pepsi factories, burnt 30 Pepsi trucks, issued death threats against Pepsi executives and filed thousands of fraud cases against Pepsi. Five people died from grenade attacks. The massive negative media publicity fuelled by anti-Pepsi groups destroyed Pepsi's reputation.

The original thinking was strategic: increase Pepsi sales to counter Coca-Cola's market leadership in the Philippines. The big idea was to offer one million Philippine pesos, about US$40 000 then, to consumers with Pepsi bottle caps having three digits that matched the officially announced numbers. Pepsi sales soared by 40 per cent after the February 1992 launch of Number Fever, with 17 people winning one million pesos each. Pepsi extended the 12-week promotion by another five weeks because of the overwhelming success.

Then disaster struck. The number announced on 25 May 1992 was 349. Unfortunately, this was an error. There were more than 800 000 bottle caps with the digits 349. Pepsi refused to pay the millions of pesos to holders of these bottle caps. Faced with public wrath and negative media coverage, Pepsi decided to offer US$20 to each holder of a bottle cap with the digits 349. Instead of a budget of US$2 million in prizes, Pepsi paid US$10 million to 500 000 consumers. The lost reputation was incalculable.[112]

Hoover free flights fiasco

The famous Hoover vacuum cleaner brand in the UK ran a sales promotion campaign in 1992 that became known as the Hoover free flights fiasco.

The objective was to clear Hoover stocks in warehouses. The idea was simple: buy a Hoover vacuum cleaner worth a minimum £100 and receive two free return air tickets worth £600 to Europe or the US.[113] See Figure 8.5 for examples of Hoover's free flights advertising campaign.

Figure 8.4 Hoover's free flights advertising

Source: www.campaignlive.co.uk/article/history-advertising-no-141-hoovers-free-flights-voucher/1356868

The outcome was a disaster when Hoover gained £30 million in sales but spent £50 million on air tickets and had its reputation destroyed.[114]

What happened?

First, the sales projection was flawed. Hoover executives had estimated that only a small percentage of customers would redeem the free flight vouchers and eventually fly. However, the bargain offer had turned Hoover from a conservative brand to a highly popular one.

Second, over-ambitious Hoover executives had started with the free flight to Europe offer but soon after added the US flight incentive instead of waiting for the Europe offer to finish and evaluating the outcome. The two offers further increased demand for Hoover products, with consumers buying products for the free flights and giving away vacuum cleaners as wedding presents or advertising to resell them.

Third, the unexpected demand turned into a logistical nightmare. Hoover tried to keep up with increased demand for its products by working a seven-day schedule. Some products were faulty. One customer was so incensed with a Hoover employee calling him 'stupid' for believing in the offer that he hijacked the employee's van!

Fourth, many customers waited and waited for their free flight vouchers. One customer, Harry Cichy, set up a Hoover holiday pressure group. Customers complained about Hoover restricting redemptions to one per household and restricting travel to certain dates and from certain airports.

Fifth, there was negative media publicity on customer complaints and the flight redemption process. Some retailers withdrew the flight offers because they were worried about Hoover's ability to deliver on the free flights. As a result, Hoover's US owner fired three top British bosses, pledged £20 million to guarantee the free flights and even chartered entire planes to fulfil the promise. Although 540 000 people had applied for the promotion of a free flight offer, only one-third received tickets!

Hoover had spent millions destroying its good name! The company closed its UK factories and sold its UK branch to Italian company Candy.[115] Once bestowed with a Royal Warrant for being a supplier to the Royal household, Hoover was eventually removed from the list in 2004.[116] Industry experts concluded that the offer should have been one free flight with every purchase of £200 and Hoover should have embedded a promotion risk management plan.

Both the Pepsi and Hoover sales promotion fiascos suggest that there should be rigorous planning and logistics in implementing campaigns as well as the involvement of PR experts to address any possible issue, risk or crisis.

Sales promotion effectiveness

There is **double jeopardy** in sales promotion. Two perspectives are worth noting. The perspective put forward by Hammond and Ehrenberg is that small brands always lose out to big brands by having fewer customers who buy less often.[117] A study of 175 cases from four countries reported that price-related promotions for fast-moving consumer goods tend to reach few buyers, attract past rather than new customers and hence do not increase future sales.[118]

The Jones perspective is that there is reduced profit of increased sales through expensive sales promotion in the short term and no increase in repeat purchase or brand image in the long term after the promotion to 'bribe' retailers and consumers.[119]

While discounting may cheapen brands,[120] it would depend on product categories. Is the brand image of Aldi, Coles or Woolworths cheapened when they offer daily discounts and value packs? After all, these brands do run exciting sales promotion and image advertising to make consumers feel good about them; for example, Woolworths with its Rio Olympics limited edition gold coin promotion[121] and its image advertising campaigns 'Fresh Food People'[122], 'How do you grow a champion?'[123] and 'That's why I pick Woolies'.[124]

Some consumers are highly prone towards non-price or price promotions such as coupons and rebates.[125] While some consumers are attracted by utilitarian benefits such as savings and product quality, other consumers prefer non-monetary promotions that provide hedonic benefits such as entertainment and value expression.[126]

Other researchers have reported on short-term and long-term gains of different types of sales promotion. Price promotion can influence some users to increase buying. Sampling combined with discount coupons can increase trials while instant-win incentives do influence repeat purchases. Constant price promotion can harm a brand if there is no brand-building advertising. Non-price promotion has less immediate impact on sales but can enhance brand value and consumer loyalty.[127]

One study based on 61 advertised sales promotions and 17 000 consumer interviews revealed that coupons and discounts may not enhance the brand or build consumer loyalty. However, promotions can enhance brands if the incentives provide exciting, value-added 'wow' deals such as contests, games and rewards; emotional fun pursuits such as 'Dream Home' promotions; and challenging promotions that make consumers feel smart and valued.[128]

The success of sweepstakes, coupons or price reductions depend on cultural, economic, family, legal, religious and social factors in different countries. For example, consumers' familiarity with coupons; family attitudes towards using coupons; social embarrassment from using coupons; price-consciousness of coupon users; and availability of coupons.[129]

One study in Hong Kong discovered that discounting, coupons and offering a free product with purchases were most effective in accelerating stockpiling and quantity purchases, while sweepstakes and games were ineffective in triggering consumer response.[130] A study in New Zealand recommended selective sampling to ensure that target consumers would actually get the samples, try the product and subsequently buy the sampled brand.[131]

In Indonesia, an emotionally oriented promotion helped to increase overall sales of premium-priced Pampers nappies by 550 per cent during a 2010 campaign in a highly competitive market driven by gift and price promotions. Following thematic advertising showing blissfully asleep babies in Pampers nappies, the company challenged parents to submit photographs of their happily sleeping babies at selected supermarkets.

Parents submitted 5000 photographs of their sleeping babies, which were pinned on a 100-metre 'Wall of Sleep' that eventually broke the local version of the Guinness World Records. Together with celebrity parents' testimonials, free symposiums on sleeping habits and baby development, limited edition Pampers pillow cases and lullaby CDs, the promotion secured massive publicity for the brand.[132]

Effective sales promotion types depend on many factors. Consumers group sales promotion incentives differently from retailers and manufacturers, categorising them as savings, convenience, learning, cultural connectivity and trust. Savings are basic or exciting deals and fun ways to win; convenience includes time savers such as in-car shopping and home delivery; learning covers first-hand experiences through sampling and in-store demonstration; cultural connectivity supports local sourcing and fair trade; and trust is about reducing risks via free shipping, return policy, money-back guarantee and warranty.[133]

Indeed, there are many challenges in sales promotion and this section has reviewed a few issues to provoke your interest to investigate further. There are challenges of deceptive pricing and the need for transparent pricing; coupon misredemption or fraud; PR impact that is positive (e.g. promotions that send various stakeholders to sporting events) or negative (e.g. Pepsi Fever and Hoover free flights); as well as short-term and long-term sales promotion effectiveness in terms of bottom-line and brand reputation.

IMC IN ACTION: NEWS CORP AUSTRALIA

News Corp Australia has facilitated childhood literacy and parental bonding while promoting its newspapers such as *The Daily Telegraph* and *The Sunday Telegraph*. In 2014, News Corp discovered through its Newspoll research about the value of parents reading to children, with more than 70 per cent of parents highlighting parental bonding and developing children's imagination as well as language skills. In early 2014, it offered the popular Mr Men and Little Miss book collections.[134]

Also in 2014, News Corp encouraged readers to collect 14 David Attenborough DVD series in 14 days at a special price of A$2.50 each. The result? Consumers bought 3.4 million DVDs and News Corp had an incremental audience of 100 000 additional readers.[135]

In 2015, consumers who bought its *Courier Mail* and *Sunday Mail* newspapers at A$2.70 received Disney's Read to Me Storybooks and CDs such as *Snow White and the Seven Dwarves*. The promotion was publicised through advertising in the newspapers as well as on television, and in outdoor and social media advertising.[136]

In 2016, New Corp offered 14 Hasbro board games such as Monopoly, Twister and Guess Who? with purchases of its newspapers at participating supermarkets and newsagencies.[137] It also ran a 'Raise a Reader' campaign for parents to buy books by Dr Seuss, such as *The Cat in the Hat*. Such promotions added value to News Corp newspapers, increased circulation by 8 to 10 per cent and slowed down print circulation decline in the face of digital publishing.[138]

In 2017, News Corp launched a set of 14 books from children's author Roald Dahl, with the first book and collector's case free upon purchase of its newspapers and subsequent books priced at A$2.60 over the two weeks of the promotion. News Corp also donated 10 000 books to The Smith Family education-oriented charity for disadvantaged children.[139]

Not all News Corp promotions focus on childhood literacy. During the 2015 Centenary of the ANZAC Campaign, News Corp collaborated with the Royal Australian Mint to sell a 14-piece coin collection at newsagencies. The coins also told ANZAC First World War stories of bravery, courage, endurance and mateship.[140]

■ CHAPTER SUMMARY

In this chapter we covered key concepts on the definition of 'sales promotion'; sales objectives for the sales force, retailers and consumers; incentives for the sales force and business buyers; various incentives for consumers; exciting sales promotions that benefit diverse stakeholders; and challenges in sales promotion.

First we explained sales promotion and objectives for the sales force, retailers and consumers. Sales promotion is a marketer's selling activity aimed at various stakeholders and communicated through various media channels to incentivise immediate actions. The immediate actions or sales objectives desired by the marketer would vary depending on the stakeholders. B2B sales forces need to secure new customers, convert sales leads, sell specific items or obtain larger orders. B2C sales forces in retail outlets such as durable goods would need to convert drop-in consumers. Marketers incentivise retailers to sell more of their products and support promotional activities. Marketers also incentivise consumers to act in different ways.

Next we distinguished between incentives for the sales force and business buyers. Incentives for business buyers vary depending on whether the purchases are industrial or consumer goods and services. Industrial buyers may prefer incentives such as inexpensive transactions, quantity discounts, credit terms, quality testing of products, customised solutions, risk sharing, free training, speedy product delivery, access to technical expertise and efficient after-sales service. Retail buyers of consumer goods and services may prefer various forms of 'push strategy' allowances for advertising and display and to be assured of 'pull strategy' incentives.

We then examined various types of consumer sales promotion incentives. There are lots more sales promotion 'pull strategy' incentives aimed at consumers. Some are immediate incentives where the benefit is instant, such as price offers. Some are delayed incentives where the benefit would be enjoyed much later, such as accumulating frequent flyer or credit card points to exchange for a reward at a future date. Some incentives offer a rational functional benefit while other incentives provide a non-monetary or emotional benefit that also generates positive brand association. Not all sales promotion incentives are appropriate for all goods and services; for example, you would not offer 'buy one get one free' for a funeral service marketer.

Following this, we considered some exciting sales promotion examples in this chapter. Exciting sales promotion is possible through social causes, movie launches, television reality shows, global sports competitions or specially created events. In a social cause promotion, your purchase could help fight a community problem such as AIDS.

Finally, we discussed challenges in sales promotion. There are many challenges in sales promotion and this section mentioned a few issues to provoke your interest to investigate further. There is a great need for rigorous planning and logistics, often involving PR experts, to ensure that sales promotions do not destroy brand reputation.

Case study: Inciting consumer feedback

Peter Ling

It seems that fast food chains are keen to obtain consumer feedback on their purchases. Here are three examples of how KFC, Hungry Jack's and McDonald's obtain feedback and then provide incentives for your survey response. See which promotion is most attractive in terms of the incentive and redemption processes.

KFC

When you purchase a KFC food item, the top of your receipt reads:

> FREE PEPSI & CHIPS!! Min. spend of $4.95 applies. See back for details on how to redeem. Write your validation code here.

The back of the receipt reads:

Feedback has its rewards.

1. Visit kfcfeedback.com.au anytime within the next 3 days.
2. Fill out the survey and receive a great offer to redeem online or instore.

   Once you visit the KFC feedback website, the following pages appear:[141]

1. Guest experience survey introduction page, which describes the use of cookies for data collection.
2. Welcome page, where you type in details from the receipt such as store number, date of visit, time of visit and order number.

   When you click 'Start', the following pages appear with questions (which may vary depending on your satisfaction level):

1. Please select your order type:
   Dine In/Take Away/Delivery/Drive Thru
2. How did you place your order?
   Online/Over the phone/Mobile App/Kiosk/At the counter/Drive thru speaker/window
3. Please rate your overall satisfaction with your experience at this KFC:
   Highly Satisfied/Satisfied/Neither Satisfied nor Dissatisfied/Dissatisfied/Highly Dissatisfied
4. Please rate your satisfaction with:
   → The cleanliness of the restaurant
   → The friendliness of the employees
   → The taste of your food
   → The accuracy of your order
   → The speed of service
   → The overall value for the price you paid
   Highly Satisfied/Satisfied/Neither Satisfied nor Dissatisfied/Dissatisfied/Highly Dissatisfied

5. Which menu item had the biggest impact on your taste of food rating?

6. Which of the following describes why you were not satisfied with the cleanliness of the restaurant?

7. Did you experience a problem during your visit?
   Yes/No

8. Based on this visit, what is the likelihood that you will:
   → Recommend this KFC to others in the next 30 days?
   → Return to this KFC in the next 30 days?
   Highly Likely/Likely/Somewhat Likely/Not Very Likely/Not at All Likely

9. Please tell us why you were Not Highly Satisfied with your experience at this KFC? Be as specific as you would like.

10. Would you like to recognise someone for great service or great food so we can share with our team?
    Yes/No

    Thank you for your feedback. We have just a few more questions.

11. Including this visit, how many times have you visited this KFC in the past 30 days?
    One/Two/Three/Four or more

12. Was this your first visit to this KFC?
    Yes/No

13. Did you order the Shaker Salad?
    Yes/No

14. Did a manager/staff member tell you about the survey?
    Yes/No

    These final questions are for classification only.
    Please indicate your gender:
    Female/Male/Prefer not to answer
    Please indicate your age:
    Under 18/18–24/25–34/35–49/50–64/65 and over/Prefer not to answer

15. Would you be interested in signing up to receive periodic emails or mailings regarding promotions, news and special offers from KFC?
    Yes/No

Thank You! Please write the following validation code on your receipt ... We appreciate your input and hope you will visit KFC again very soon.

Hungry Jack's

The introduction page of the website 'My Hungry Jack's Experience Satisfaction Survey' carries the same information about cookies and data collection as the KFC Guest Experience Survey website. The welcome page asks for the survey code from the receipt plus the time of visit to the outlet.

Once you click 'Start', the following questions appear in subsequent website pages:[142]

1. Please choose your order type:
   Dine-In/Take Away

2. How many people in your party?
   Just yourself/2 people/3 people/4 or more people

3. Please rate your overall satisfaction with your experience at this Hungry Jack's restaurant:
   Highly Satisfied/Satisfied/Neither Satisfied Or Dissatisfied/Dissatisfied/Highly Dissatisfied

4. Please rate your satisfaction with …
   → The speed of service
   → The quality of your food
   → The friendliness of our staff
   → The exterior cleanliness of the restaurant
   → The temperature of your food
   Highly Satisfied/Satisfied/Neither Satisfied Or Dissatisfied/Dissatisfied/Highly Dissatisfied

5. Please rate your satisfaction with …
   → The appearance of the people who work for the restaurant; that is being neat and clean
   → The accuracy of the order you received
   → The atmosphere or ambience of the restaurant
   → The interior cleanliness of the restaurant
   → The ease of placing your order
   Highly Satisfied/Satisfied/Neither Satisfied Or Dissatisfied/Dissatisfied/Highly Dissatisfied

6. The value for the money:
   Highly Satisfied/Satisfied/Neither satisfied or dissatisfied/Dissatisfied/Highly Dissatisfied

7. Please rate your satisfaction with …
   The French fries you ordered. If you did not order French fries, select NA.
   Highly Satisfied/Satisfied/Neither Satisfied Or Dissatisfied/Dissatisfied/Highly Dissatisfied/NA

8. Did you encounter any problems with your Hungry Jack's experience?
   Yes/No

9. Based on this experience, how likely are you to…
   → Recommend this Hungry Jack's restaurant to a close friend or relative?
   → Order from this Hungry Jack's restaurant within the next month?
   Highly Likely/Likely/Somewhat Likely/Not Very Likely/Not at All Likely

10. Please indicate how much you agree or disagree with the following statements:
    → The design of this Hungry Jack's made me want to visit
    → The design of this Hungry Jack's is appealing
    → Hungry Jack's is a brand for people like me

> → Hungry Jack's always has something for me regardless of time, budget and appetite
>
> → This Hungry Jack's is a place where everyone feels welcome
>
> *Strongly Agree/Agree/Neither Agree Nor Disagree/Disagree/Strongly Disagree*

11. Please indicate how much you agree or disagree with the following statements:

    → Hungry Jack's is one of my favourite fast food restaurants

    → Hungry Jack's menu offers a good range of menu options

    → Hungry Jack's is becoming more popular

    Strongly Agree/Agree/Neither Agree Nor Disagree/Disagree/Strongly Disagree

12. Please tell us in three or more sentences why you were *Not Highly Satisfied* with your Hungry Jack's experience

13. Which of the following menu items did you order for yourself on this visit? (Check all that apply)

14. Which of the following side items or desserts did you order for yourself on this visit? (Check all that apply)

15. How many times have you ordered from any Hungry Jack's location in the past month?
    1 time/2 times/3 times/4 times/5 or more times

16. What best describes your reason for visiting Hungry Jacks?
    Had a voucher/A celebration, such as a birthday/A recommendation from a friend or family member/A previous positive experience/The convenient hours/To try an advertised item/The type of food offered/ Some other reason

17. Which fast food hamburger restaurant do your order from most often?
    McDonald's/Hungry Jack's/Red Rooster/Chicken Treat/Oporto

    These final questions are for classification purposes only.

18. Please indicate your gender/Please indicate your age/Please indicate your annual household income

19. In order for us to better understand and serve our customers, please enter your zip/postal code below.

    Thank you for completing the survey. Hungry Jack's would like to invite you to come back and visit our restaurants. Do not forget to present the offer that appears on your ticket in your next visit. You must write the following code on your ticket …

    Thank you for your participation.

McDonald's

A McDonald's receipt draws attention to your purchase: How was your experience? www.macc.as/ feedback. Help us be mac-nificent!

When you visit the feedback website, McDonald's highlights the message 'Tell us how we went, and get a treat—by signing into MyMacca's. You can choose from: free small fries with any purchase available after 10.30 am; free 10 pack chicken McBites with any purchase available after 10.30 am; or free soft serve cone with any purchase.[143]

When you click 'Get started', the following pages appear with questions:

1. Which Macca's did you visit?
   Enter restaurant number/postcode/suburb

2. Where did you order from?
   Counter/Kiosk/Drive Thru/McCafé

3. What time did you visit us?
   Breakfast/Lunch/Dinner/Late Night

4. When did you visit us?
   Today/Yesterday/Other

5. Based on this visit, rate your overall satisfaction with your experience:
   Highly Satisfied/Satisfied/Neither satisfied or dissatisfied/Dissatisfied/Highly Dissatisfied

6. How satisfied were you with the quality of your meal?
   Highly Satisfied/Satisfied/Neither Satisfied or Dissatisfied/Dissatisfied/Highly Dissatisfied

7. How satisfied were you with the friendliness of your experience?
   Highly Satisfied/Satisfied/Neither Satisfied or Dissatisfied/Dissatisfied/Highly Dissatisfied

8. Did we get your order right?
   Yes/No

9. How satisfied were you with the speed of service?
   Highly Satisfied/Satisfied/Neither Satisfied or Dissatisfied/Dissatisfied/Highly Dissatisfied

10. How satisfied were you with the cleanliness of the restaurant?
    Highly Satisfied/Satisfied/Neither Satisfied or Dissatisfied/Dissatisfied/Highly Dissatisfied

11. How likely are you to recommend this Macca's to family or friends?
    10 Highly likely ... 1 Unlikely

    If you click '10' or '9' on the above, this dialogue box appears: WOW! We're glad you loved your restaurant experience. Who or what deserves the credit?

    If you click '8' or '7', this dialogue box appears:

    So close to gold. How could we be a perfect 10?

    If you click '6' to '1', this dialogue box appears:

    Oops, looks like we slipped up somewhere. How could we improve? Would you like to be contacted by this Macca's? *Yes/No*

Before you click 'Submit', you need to verify 'I'm not a robot' or the message comes on 'Please verify that you are not a robot'.

When you click on 'I'm not a robot', another dialogue box appears: 'Select all images with a store front/Verify'. And then another dialogue box appears: 'Select all squares with street signs/Verify'. And then another dialogue box appears: 'Select all images with a house/Verify'. And then another dialogue box appears: 'Select all images with street numbers/Verify'. If you are not frustrated at this stage, you click 'Submit'!

When you finally 'Submit', you receive the message 'Thanks for your feedback. Which Macca's offer would you like to receive? You can choose from free small fries, free 10 pack chicken McBites or a free soft serve cone. When you click on your choice, the message appears: Sign into MyMacca's—to receive your treat. Or you can create an account.

When you have completed your registration with name, email, postcode and password, you receive this message:

'Congratulations! Your mymacca's account is now active! This username and password will get you into everything McDonald's, including McDelivery, mymacca's and Monopoly. Enjoy!'

When you sign in with your email address and password, the Choose Offer page appears with the three options and your first name, last name and email address. Then you have to click on the following before clicking on 'Submit':

'I agree to receiving information, promotions & offers from McDonald's, including electronically.

I've read & agree to the Terms & Conditions and Privacy Collection Statement and confirm that I am 18+ or 14+ and have parent/guardian consent.'

I clicked on the second box, and *finally* this message appears: 'Great choice!'

'We'll email a coupon for your tasty treat in the next few days—keep a look out for it.'

'In the meantime, check out the mymacca's™ hub for more chances to have your say and be rewarded by McDonald's.'

Questions

1. Which of the three feedback methods and their consumer incentives appeals to you most?
2. How could Hungry Jack's improve its feedback incentive?
3. How could McDonald's improve its feedback incentive process?

Practitioner profile: Christopher Villani

General Manager of Marketing, Brand and Insights, Foodland Supermarkets Australia

As far back as I can remember I have always wanted to be a marketer. While in high school, I took a keen interest in media studies. I should point out that this was three years before *Mad Men* hit Australian screens and transformed advertising into an (even more) attractive profession. What drew me to the discipline was the creative manner in which one needs to communicate with a mass audience across multiple mediums. At the time, I was under the impression that marketing was simply advertising. It was not until I studied marketing at university that I learnt it was so much more. Graduating with a degree in marketing and communication from the University of South Australia (and its renowned Ehrenberg-Bass Institute), my marketing career to date has seen me work around Australia on multiple campaigns for national and international brands.

Please describe your current role and the organisation you work for, and give a brief account of what you do in your role on a day-to-day basis.

I am currently the General Manager of Marketing, Brand and Insights at Foodland Supermarkets Australia. This is just a fancy (some might say wanky) way of saying I am responsible for understanding and communicating with customers. Foodland Supermarkets are a network of supermarkets operating in South Australia under the 'Foodland' banner. Our 100 plus supermarkets are all independently owned and operated, ensuring they can best cater to their communities' needs (that is to say, no two stores are alike). Competing against some of Australia's (and the world's) leading retailers as a state-based brand has its challenges, but is rewarding. As the General Manager of Marketing, Brand and Insights (still sounds wanky), I am in control of the brand's advertising, communications, media, sponsorships, public relations and consumer insights. As a result of this diverse range of tasks, no two days are ever alike. One day, I might be planning the next advertising campaign and media schedule, the next I could be talking about opportunities with a new sponsor and planning point-of-sale material.

How important is Integrated Marketing Communication (IMC) to what you and your organisation do?

Integrated Marketing Communication (IMC) is the keystone of my marketing strategy. Without the ability to utilise IMC, building and refreshing brand memory structures diminishes. Without these memory structures, coming to mind in a buying situation is compromised. Additionally, consistency is key when trying to tell a unified message about your brand.

What types of promotional tools do you use in your IMC campaigns? Please provide examples.

As a grocery retailer, the good old-fashioned catalogue is a weekly production. In addition to this catalogue, television and radio ads are produced that reinforce not only the brand message but the promotions found within the catalogue. Adding to this dynamic ecosystem (wanky marketing lingo) is the fact that point of sale needs to be tied up at store level. For example, Foodland may have a carbonated soft drink on promotion for the week. This promotion is communicated in the catalogue (using a visual cue), on television (both visual and audial), radio (audial) and at store with point of sale (visual). These communications, although using different cues (visual and/or audial), need to convey the same message across all mediums.

What would your ideal IMC campaign look like and why?

My ideal IMC campaign will be one that is well planned out, flexible yet consistent. At the start of any campaign or strategy, it is vital to plant the flag. That is to say, you need to answer key questions: where do you want the brand/campaign to go? How will you get there? Do I have an exit strategy and contingency plan? How adaptable is the campaign? In addition to having concrete answers to these questions, writing a supurb (not good!) brief to one's creative team is vital. Any IMC campaign needs to be creative so it can cut through all of the advertising clutter, in addition to being well branded. No point in having great creative that cannot be attributed back to you and vice versa.

What has been your favourite IMC project to work on and did it achieve its objectives?

I have been fortunate to work on multiple IMC projects in my marketing career. The one that stands out the most is my involvement with Foodland's 2015 Great Food Lives Here campaign. This was the first campaign that I was in charge of (no pressure, Villani). Faced with ever-increasing retail competition and a plethora of advertising which, at the time, focused solely on a price proposition, Foodland needed to be distinctive and cut through the clutter. After examining our business and consumer trends, it was decided that we would take the fight away from the typical 'cheap price' communications and focus on the quality offer that each Foodland store is known for.

Objectives for the campaign were to, holistically, increase penetration, and also to create a well-branded and likable ad. Through incorporation of the campaign into TVC, radio, online, press, outdoor, catalogue and point of sale, Great Food Lives Here not only achieved all its intended targets, it actually surpassed many of the industry benchmarks. In addition, store penetration is up, and tracking the ads' performance has seen year-on-year growths in recognition, branded correctly and likability metrics. A large component of this succuss was a clearly defined IMC strategy.

How do you believe an IMC campaign affects the consumer decision-making process for your particular target audience?

With any brand, communication consistency is key. The starting point for any IMC campaign should be accurate and informative research (as boring as it sounds, its actually quite fun). Research will give invaluable insight into *WHO* is your customer, *WHEN* and *HOW* they buy, as well as the distinctive elements of your brand. With these insights in mind, one can truly begin to shape an IMC campaign to influence consumer behaviour. However, while the aforementioned insights will be unique to each organisation, some principles of consumer behaviour must be incorporated into all IMC campaigns regardless of industry, budget or offer. They hold true across all industries I have ever worked in and across every country. Specifically they are:

1. Consistency of message
2. Being well branded
3. Being distinctive
4. Reaching as many potential category customers as possible .

How has your application of IMC changed with the increase in digital marketing?

The increase of digital platforms has given marketers more (and often creative) ways to reach customers. However, the rise in digital media has also brought with it some complexities. A marketer's media mix now needs to (at the very least) consider the use of digital for IMC. Adapting already existing creative to this platform can prove to be difficult (been there, had the hissy fits). The trade-off is that when it does go right, truly great creative can be produced on digital platforms. However, take heed of my experiences: many marketers in the industry are finding that digital offerings are growing more rapidly than research into its actual effectiveness. Many brands are learning this the hard way and have been over-investing their IMC campaigns into digital.

What do you believe are some of the challenges to implementing an IMC campaign?

The largest challenge is creating well-branded and distinctive creative that cuts through. Getting both is difficult and needs to be a constant negotiation between brand managers and creative agencies (fisticuffs are common). There is a fine line between science and art and getting this right will set up a successful IMC campaign. Additionally, adapting said creative to multiple mediums can be more challenging than first appears. With each medium comes a new set of 'rules' on how to effectively use each one. For example, radio is purely audio, outdoor is visual, while both television and online can be both. Ensuring campaign creative is flexible to meet all of these needs is a challenge. However, this challenge is a non-negotiable. Lastly, set clearly defined and realistic goals for the campaign.

What advice would you offer a student studying IMC?

To every student studying IMC, I say this: 'enjoy it' (cliché, right? Hear me out). IMC should be the keystone for most brand communication strategies. Having an inside-out viewpoint is a skill all marketers should have. IMC can teach you how to do this effectively through demonstrating how one can look within your brand, your category it operates in, your customers (both current and potential) and the mediums at your disposal. I also recommend better understanding principles of other related disciplines. I'm specifically talking about consumer behaviour and psychology, media planning and commerce. Being able to share the cup of knowledge across multiple disciplines will complement your knowledge of IMC.

Key terms

accelerated purchase	courtesy days	incentive travel
advertising allowance	cross-ruff	industrial goods and services
bonus pack	cross selling	multiple-unit packaging
bounce back offer	dating	odd-even pricing
business-to-business (B2B)	dealer loader	premium
business-to-consumer (B2C)	dealer tie-in	price-off offer
buy one get one free	display allowance	pull strategy
buying allowance	factory pack	push money
count and recount promotion	free merchandise	push strategy
club plan selling	free sample	refund
consumer goods and services	frequent shopper program	sales contest
contest	game	seasonal discount
coupon	incentive pay	sweepstake

Revision questions

1. What is your own definition of sales promotion after reading this chapter?
2. What are similarities and differences in objectives for the sales force, retailers and consumers?
3. If you were starting as a sales person selling B2B or B2C household appliances, which incentives would appeal to you and why?
4. If you were a business buyer purchasing goods and services for your chain of retail outlets, what sales promotion incentives would you prefer and why?
5. Distinguish between push and pull strategies.
6. Which pull strategy incentives appeal to you and why?
7. Do you prefer delayed and/or immediate sales promotion incentives and why?
8. If you were planning a sales promotion campaign for a luxury brand, which incentives would you use and why?
9. Which exciting sales promotion campaign have you come across?
10. What are popular sales promotion incentives during global sports events?
11. What is your personal experience with a retailer's deceptive pricing or coupon redemption process?
12. What other sales promotion fiasco have you come across, besides the Pepsi Fever and Hoover Free Flight fiascos highlighted in this chapter?
13. What other successful sales promotion campaigns have you come across?
14. Discuss whether sales promotion cheapens or enhances a brand.

Further reading

Coursera Sales Promotion: https://www.coursera.org/learn/integrated-marketing-communications/lecture/muX5p/sales-promotions

Effective sales promotion lessons for today: a review of twenty years of Marketing Science Institute-sponsored research: http://www.msi.org/reports/effective-sales-promotion-lessons-for-today-a-review-of-twenty-years-of-mar/

Examining the role of advertising and sales promotions in brand equity creation: http://www.sciencedirect.com/science/article/pii/S0148296311002669

Getting the most out of advertising and promotion: https://hbr.org/1990/05/getting-the-most-out-of-advertising-and-promotion

JC Penney adds sales promotion back into the marketing mix: http://adage.com/article/news/jc-penney-adds-sales-promotion-back-marketing-mix/239476/

Long-term profitability: advertising versus sales promotion: https://www.warc.com/fulltext/Recession/54683.htm

Loyalty programs and their impact on repeat-purchase loyalty patterns: a replication and extension: http://www.sciencedirect.com/science/article/pii/S0167811697000220

P&G will keep hiking ad spend amid soft sales: http://adage.com/article/cmo-strategy/pg-hiking-ad-spend/303731/

Promotions not so special anymore: http://www.nielsen.com/au/en/insights/news/2014/promotions-not-so-special-anymore.html

Sales impact of displaying alcoholic and non-alcoholic beverages in end-of-aisle locations: http://www.sciencedirect.com/science/article/pii/S0277953614001361

Sales promotion: https://www.inc.com/encyclopedia/sales-promotion.html

Sales promotion FAQs: http://www.marketingdonut.co.uk/customer-care/sales-promotions-faqs

Sales promotion in Asia: successful strategies for Singapore and Malaysia: http://www.emeraldinsight.com/doi/abs/10.1108/13555851311290939

Six trade promotion tips—why less can be more: http://www.nielsen.com/us/en/insights/news/2010/six-trade-promotion-tips-why-less-can-be-more.html

Supermarket promotions at lowest level for 11 years: http://www.nielsen.com/uk/en/press-room/2017/supermarket-promotions-at-lowest-level-for-11-years.html

Supermarkets face inquiry into 'rip-offs': http://www.telegraph.co.uk/news/shopping-and-consumer-news/11551351/Supermarkets-face-inquiry-into-rip-offs.html

The double jeopardy of sales promotions: https://hbr.org/1990/09/the-double-jeopardy-of-sales-promotions

The science that makes us spend more in supermarkets, and feel good while we do it: https://theconversation.com/the-science-that-makes-us-spend-more-in-supermarkets-and-feel-good-while-we-do-it-23857

To discount or not to discount? That is the question: https://www.forbes.com/sites/steveolenski/2017/01/16/to-discount-or-not-to-discount-that-is-the-question/#70eab3384314

WARC on competitions, contests, giveaways: https://www.warc.com/Search/promotions/Competitions,%20contests,%20giveaways?Sort=ContentDate%7c1&DVals=4294615787+4294615754+4294638086&RecordsPerPage=25

WARC on promotions: https://www.warc.com/topics/media-channels/promotions

WARC on sales promotion: https://www.warc.com/Search/promotions/Sales%20promotion?Sort=ContentDate%7c1&DVals=4294615787+4294615754+4294951686&RecordsPerPage=25

Why your sales force needs smarter incentives: http://review.chicagobooth.edu/strategy/2016/article/why-your-sales-force-needs-smarter-incentives

Weblinks

Publications

Advertising and marketing by *The New York Times*
https://www.nytimes.com/topic/subject/advertising-and-marketing

Consumer Behaviour articles by *The New York Times*
https://www.nytimes.com/topic/subject/consumer-behavior

Journal of Promotion Management
http://www.tandfonline.com/loi/wjpm20?open=23&year=2017&repitition=0#vol_23_2017

Sales promotion associations

American Marketing Association (AMA)
https://www.ama.org/resources/pages/dictionary.aspx?dLetter=A

Australasian Promotional Marketing Association (APMA)
http://www.communicationscouncil.org.au/public/content/ViewCategory.aspx?id=1006

Australasian Promotional Products Association (APPA)
http://www.appa.com.au

Promotional Products Association International (PPAI) USA
http://www.ppai.org

Sales Promotion Executives Association (SPEA) USA
http://www.mcei.lu/history

The Association of Promotional Marketing Consultants (APMC) Europe
http://apmc.ie/europe/

The Institute of Promotional Marketing [IPM] UK
https://www.theipm.org.uk

Sales promotion effectiveness awards

Cannes Lions Promo & Activation Winners
http://www.canneslionsarchive.com/winners/entries/cannes-lions/promo-and-activation/

Cannes Lions Promo & Activation Winners—Man Boobs
http://www.canneslionsarchive.com/winners/entry/766503/manboobs

Cannes Lions Winners
http://www.canneslionsarchive.com/winners/categories/cannes-lions

IPA Effectiveness Awards UK
http://www.ipa.co.uk/ease

Mobile marketing
http://mobilemarketingmagazine.com/awards-preview-effective-sales-promotion-campaign-2016-john-lewis-amstel-tesco-one-stop-schwartz-textlocal-guide-dogs/

Reggie Awards (for best marketing campaigns)
https://www.reggieawards.org/a

Super Reggie Award—Baby Stroller Test-Ride by Contours
https://www.youtube.com/watch?v=1BzNpfZp9U0

Regulatory sites

Advertising, promotion and sales practices
https://www.commerce.wa.gov.au/consumer-protection/advertising-promotion-and-sales-practices

Advertising Standards Authority UK
https://www.asa.org.uk/type/non_broadcast/code_section/03.html

Australian Competition & Consumer Commission—misleading or deceptive conduct
https://www.accc.gov.au/publications/advertising-selling/advertising-and-selling-guide/avoid-misleading-or-deceptive-claims-or-conduct/misleading-or-deceptive-conduct

Australian Competition & Consumer Commission ScamWatch website
https://www.scamwatch.gov.au

Business Queensland
https://www.business.qld.gov.au/running-business/marketing-sales/marketing-promotion/marketing-basics/promotional-activities

Consumer Affairs Victoria
https://www.consumer.vic.gov.au/shopping/advertising-and-promotions/misleading-or-deceptive-conduct

Federal Trade Commission—deceptive pricing
https://www.ftc.gov/enforcement/rules/rulemaking-regulatory-reform-proceedings/deceptive-pricing

Notes

1   Schwindt, O. (2015). Star Wars' mania awakens The Sales Force: Here are the movie's weirdest brand cross-promotions. http://www.ibtimes.com/star-wars-mania-awakens-sales-force-here-are-movies-weirdest-brand-cross-promotions-2226511

2   Hunt, K. (2015). These are the droids you're looking for. http://blog.generalmills.com/2015/10/these-are-the-droids-youre-looking-for/

3   Lego. (2016). Characters. https://www.lego.com/en-us/starwars/characters/luminara-unduli-73ae2f21510a4bc2b76e459310d715cb

4   McDougall, A. (2015). May the force be with … Max Factor and CoverGirl. *Cosmetics Design*. http://www.cosmeticsdesign-europe.com/Brand-Innovation/P-G-brands-collaborate-with-Lucasfilm-for-Star-Wars-promo-campaign

5   Dairy Foods. (2015). Nestlé's Coffee-mate releases limited-edition Star Wars-themed creamer bottles. http://www.dairyfoods.com/articles/91469-nestls-coffee-mate-releases-limited-edition-star-wars-themed-creamer-bottles

6   Facebook. (2015). Star Wars. https://www.facebook.com/pg/StarWars.UK/likes/?ref=page_internal

7   Star Wars. (2016). Star Wars Day 2016 Deals! http://www.starwars.com/news/star-wars-day-2016-deals

8   Collins. (2017). Sales promotion. https://www.collinsdictionary.com/dictionary/english/sales-promotion#sales-promotion__1

9   *Webster's New World College Dictionary*. (2010). Sales promotion. http://www.yourdictionary.com/sales-promotion#websters

10 Merriam-Webster. (2017). Sales promotion. https://www.merriam-webster.com/dictionary/sales%20promotion

11 Dictionary.com. (2017). Sales promotion. http://www.dictionary.com/browse/sales-promotion

12 AMA. (2017). Dictionary—Sales Promotion. https://www.ama.org/resources/Pages/Dictionary.aspx?dLetter=S

13 Inc. (2017). Sales Promotion. http://www.inc.com/encyclopedia/sales-promotion.html

14 AMA. (2017). Dictionary—Industrial products. https://www.ama.org/resources/pages/dictionary.aspx?dLetter=I

15 Kotler, P. T. & Keller, K. L. (2016). *Marketing Management* (15th edn). New York: Pearson.

16 AMA. (2017). Dictionary—Sales. https://www.ama.org/resources/pages/dictionary.aspx?dLetter=S

17 Hancock, M., Hatami, H. & Rayan, S. (2011). Using your sales force to jump-start growth. *McKinsey Quarterly*, April.

18 AMA. (2017). Dictionary—Trade sales promotion. https://www.ama.org/resources/Pages/Dictionary.aspx?dLetter=T

19 AMA. (2017). Dictionary—Consumer Sales Promotion. https://www.ama.org/resources/pages/dictionary.aspx?dLetter=C

20 AMA. (2017). Dictionary—Incentive pay. https://www.ama.org/resources/Pages/Dictionary. aspx?dLetter=I#incentive+and+incentive+plan

21 AMA. (2017). Dictionary—Bonus. https://www.ama.org/resources/Pages/Dictionary. aspx?dLetter=B#bonus

22 Steenburgh, T. & Ahearne, M. (2012). Motivating sales people: What really works. *Harvard Business Review*, July–August.

23 Chung, D. J. (2015). How to really motivate salespeople. *Harvard Business Review*. https://hbr.org/2015/04/how-to-really-motivate-salespeople

24 AMA. (2017). Dictionary—Sales contest. https://www.ama.org/resources/Pages/Dictionary. aspx?dLetter=S

25 Boudinet, J. (2016). How to use contests to inspire your Millennial workforce. Salesforce, 28 September. https://www.salesforce.com/blog/2016/09/use-contests-inspire-millennial-workforce.html

26 Great Eastern. (2017). Congratulations to our Great Eastern Life Achievers Club 2016 Qualifiers. https://www.greateasternlife.com/sg/en/careers/distribution-representative/achievers-club-qualifiers.html

27 William-Smith, H. (2017). FSC recognises life insurance industry at awards night. *Money Management,* 30 March. http://www.moneymanagement.com.au/news/financial-planning/fsc-recognises-life-insurance-industry-awards-night

28 Casison, J. (2011). The right remedy: a sales incentive case study. *Incentive*, 7 June. http://www. incentivemag.com/article.aspx?id=7268

29 AMA. (2017). Dictionary—Incentive travel. https://www.ama.org/resources/Pages/Dictionary. aspx?dLetter=I#incentive+compensation+and+straight+salary+plan

30 Jakobson, L. (2016). $90 billion spent annually on non-cash incentives. *Incentive*. http://www. incentivemag.com/News/Industry/Incentive-Federation-$90-Billion-Market-Size/

31 Harwood, S. (2015). Incentive travel report: brands buying into staff rewards. *Conference & Incentive Travel,* 18 November.

32 Cernik, L. (2016). BMW selects Zibrant for incentive programmes. *Conference & Incentive Travel,* 27 October.

33 Dizik, A. (2016). Why your sales force needs smarter incentives, 25 May. http://review.chicagobooth. edu/strategy/2016/article/why-your-sales-force-needs-smarter-incentives

34 Davie, C., Stephenson, T. & ValdiviesoDeUster, M. (2010). Three trends in business-to-business sales, May. http://www.mckinsey.com/business-functions/marketing-and-sales/our-insights/three-trends-in-business-to-business-sales

35 AMA. (2017). Dictionary—Push strategy. https://www.ama.org/resources/Pages/Dictionary. aspx?dLetter=P

36 AMA. (2017). Dictionary—Trade sales promotion. https://www.ama.org/resources/Pages/Dictionary. aspx?dLetter=T

37 Pinterest. (2017). Explore store fridges, push strategy and more! https://au.pinterest.com/pin/389279961511743718/

38   Feloni, R. (2015). 7 brilliant strategies Coca-Cola used to become one of the world's most recognisable brands. *Business Insider Australia,* 14 June.

39   AMA. (2017). Dictionary—Consumer sales promotion. https://www.ama.org/resources/pages/dictionary.aspx?dLetter=C

40   AMA. (2017). Dictionary—Bounce back offer. https://www.ama.org/resources/Pages/Dictionary.aspx?dLetter=B#bonus

41   AMA. (2017). Dictionary—Coupon. https://www.ama.org/resources/pages/dictionary.aspx?dLetter=C#consumer+sales+promotion

42   AMA. (2017). Dictionary—Free standing insert. https://www.ama.org/resources/pages/dictionary.aspx?dLetter=F

43   AMA. (2017). Dictionary—Courtesy Days. https://www.ama.org/resources/pages/dictionary.aspx?dLetter=C#coupon

44   AMA. (2017). Dictionary—Multiple-unit pricing. https://www.ama.org/resources/pages/dictionary.aspx?dLetter=M

45   AMA. (2017). Dictionary—Premium. https://www.ama.org/resources/pages/dictionary.aspx?dLetter=P#premium

46   Peterson, H. (2016). McDonald's fixed customers' top two complaints—and sales are soaring. *Business Insider Australia,* 23 April.

47   Palazón-Vidal, M. & Delgado-Ballester, E. (2005). Sales promotions effects on consumer-based brand equity. *International Journal of Market Research, 47*(2), 179–204.

48   HuiZhen. (2017). KFC's fried chicken pizza finally in Singapore. *Asiaone,* 7 February.

49   Tan, C. (2017). KFC Chizza: Fried Chicken & Pizza mashup comes to Singapore—is it as good as it looks? https://sethlui.com/kfc-chizza-singapore/

50   Kotler, P. T. & Keller, K. L. (2016). *Marketing Management* (15th edn). New York: Pearson.

51   White Lady Funerals. (2016). Prepaid vs funeral insurance calculator. http://www.whiteladyfunerals.com.au/preplan-a-funeral/funeral-calculator

52   Red.org. (2017). Our proud partners. https://red.org/our-partners/

53   Gwynn, S. (2017). Disney partners with Unilever, P&G and Sony for Beauty and the Beast launch. *Campaign.* http://www.campaignlive.co.uk/article/disney-partners-unilever-p-g-sony-beauty-beast-launch/1426026

54   Convenience Store. (2017). Persil partners Disney's Beauty and the Beast. https://www.conveniencestore.co.uk/products/persil-partners-disneys-beauty-and-the-beast/549581.article

55   Olay. (2017). Olay TTE Beauty and the Beast Prize Draw Ts and Cs. http://www.olay.co.uk/en-gb/olay-coupons/beauty-and-the-beast-competition

56   Campaigns. (2017). Sony promotion: Disney's Beauty and the Beast Bundle Offer. https://campaigns.sonymobile.com/tc/o2promotion/

57   comparethemarket.com. (2017). Meerkat Movies Disney's Beauty and the Beast. https://www.comparethemarket.com/meerkat-movies/beauty-and-the-beast/

58 Hamptons International. (2017). Win a family trip to Paris. https://www.hamptons.co.uk/beautyandthebeast/

59 Latest In Beauty. (2017). Discover the limited edition Beauty Boxes. https://www.latestinbeauty.com/beauty-and-the-beast

60 ITV Studios. (2017). *The Voice Australia* Series 6—Audience FAQs. http://onair.thatstheticket.com.au/library/audience/thevoice_2017/faq.pdf

61 Nine Entertainment Co. (2015). *The Voice* Cadbury Integration Case Study July 2015. http://prod.static9.net.au/_/media/network/nineentertainmentco/pdf-downloads/the-voice--cadburycase-study.pdf

62 IEG. (2016). Rio 2016 sponsor profile: Top sponsor Coca-Cola. http://www.sponsorship.com/Latest-Thinking/Rio-2016-Olympic-Sponsorship-Insights/Coca-Cola.aspx

63 IEG. (2016). Rio 2016 sponsor profile: top sponsor Panasonic. http://www.sponsorship.com/Latest-Thinking/Rio-2016-Olympic-Sponsorship-Insights/Panasonic.aspx

64 IEG. (2016). Rio 2016 sponsor profile: top sponsor Visa. http://www.sponsorship.com/Latest-Thinking/Rio-2016-Olympic-Sponsorship-Insights/Visa.aspx

65 IEG. (2016). Rio 2016 sponsor profile: USOC sponsor Citi. http://www.sponsorship.com/Latest-Thinking/Rio-2016-Olympic-Sponsorship-Insights/Citi.aspx

66 IEG. (2016). Rio 2016 sponsor profile: Rio 2016 Organising Committee Sponsor—Nissan. http://www.sponsorship.com/Latest-Thinking/Rio-2016-Olympic-Sponsorship-Insights/Nissan.aspx

67 IEG. (2016). Rio 2016 sponsor profile: USOC sponsor Milk Life. http://www.sponsorship.com/Latest-Thinking/Rio-2016-Olympic-Sponsorship-Insights/Milk-Life.aspx

68 IEG. (2016). Rio 2016 sponsor profile: USOC sponsor—24 Hour Fitness. http://www.sponsorship.com/Latest-Thinking/Rio-2016-Olympic-Sponsorship-Insights/24-Hour-Fitness.aspx

69 IEG. (2016). Rio 2016 sponsor profile: top sponsor Samsung. http://www.sponsorship.com/Latest-Thinking/Rio-2016-Olympic-Sponsorship-Insights/Samsung.aspx

70 IEG. (2016). Rio 2016 sponsor profile: top sponsor Omega. http://www.sponsorship.com/Latest-Thinking/Rio-2016-Olympic-Sponsorship-Insights/Omega.aspx

71 IEG. (2016). Rio 2016 sponsor profile: USOC sponsor Nike. Retrieved from http://www.sponsorship.com/Latest-Thinking/Rio-2016-Olympic-Sponsorship-Insights/Nike.aspx

72 IEG. (2016). Rio 2016 sponsor profile: USOC sponsor Chobani. http://www.sponsorship.com/Latest-Thinking/Rio-2016-Olympic-Sponsorship-Insights/Chobani.aspx

73 IEG. (2016). Rio 2016 sponsor profile: USOC sponsor Hershey. http://www.sponsorship.com/Latest-Thinking/Rio-2016-Olympic-Sponsorship-Insights/Hershey.aspx

74 IEG. (2016). Rio 2016 sponsor profile: USOC sponsor Kellogg. http://www.sponsorship.com/Latest-Thinking/Rio-2016-Olympic-Sponsorship-Insights/Kellogg.aspx

75 IEG. (2016). Rio 2016 sponsor profile: top sponsor—McDonald's. http://www.sponsorship.com/Latest-Thinking/Rio-2016-Olympic-Sponsorship-Insights/McDonald-s.aspx

76 Cosmetics Business. (2016). P&G offers Rio 2016 Olympic athletes free treatments, 8 August. https://www.cosmeticsbusiness.com/news/article_page/PG_offers_Rio_2016_Olympic_athletes_free_treatments/120159

77 IEG. (2016). Rio 2016 sponsor profile: Top sponsor GE. http://www.sponsorship.com/Latest-Thinking/Rio-2016-Olympic-Sponsorship-Insights/GE.aspx

78 IEG. (2016). Rio 2016 sponsor profile: USOC sponsor—BP. http://www.sponsorship.com/Latest-Thinking/Rio-2016-Olympic-Sponsorship-Insights/BP.aspx

79 IEG. (2016). Rio 2016 sponsor profile: Top sponsor Bridgestone. http://www.sponsorship.com/Latest-Thinking/Rio-2016-Olympic-Sponsorship-Insights/Bridgestone.aspx

80 Campaign Brief. (2014). Coca-Cola launches new 2014 FIFA World Cup promotion + campaign with Woolies via Ogilvy, 18 March. http://www.campaignbrief.com/2014/03/coca-cola-launches-new-2014-fi.html

81 IEG. (2014). World Cup 2014 Sponsor Profile: FIFA Partner-Adidas. http://www.sponsorship.com/Latest-Thinking/2014-FIFA-World-Cup-Brazil-Sponsorship-Insights/Adidas.aspx

82 IEG. (2014). World Cup 2014 Sponsor Profile: FIFA Partner-Hyundai. http://www.sponsorship.com/Latest-Thinking/2014-FIFA-World-Cup-Brazil-Sponsorship-Insights/Hyundai.aspx

83 IEG. (2014). World Cup 2014 Sponsor Profile: FIFA Partner-Sony. http://www.sponsorship.com/Latest-Thinking/2014-FIFA-World-Cup-Brazil-Sponsorship-Insights/Sony.aspx

84 IEG. (2014). World Cup 2014 Sponsor Profile: FIFA Partner-Visa. http://www.sponsorship.com/Latest-Thinking/2014-FIFA-World-Cup-Brazil-Sponsorship-Insights/Visa.aspx

85 IEG. (2014). World Cup 2014 Sponsor Profile: FIFA Partner-Emirates. http://www.sponsorship.com/Latest-Thinking/2014-FIFA-World-Cup-Brazil-Sponsorship-Insights/Emirates.aspx

86 FIFA. (2014). McDonald's 2014 FIFA World Cup Player Escort Program. http://www.fifa.com/marketinghighlights/brazil2014/World-Cup-Sponsors/McDonalds/index.htm

87 IEG. (2014). World Cup 2014 Sponsor Profile: FIFA Partner-Kia. http://www.sponsorship.com/Latest-Thinking/2014-FIFA-World-Cup-Brazil-Sponsorship-Insights/Kia.aspx

88 EG. (2014). World Cup 2014 Sponsor Profile: World Cup Sponsor-Budweiser. http://www.sponsorship.com/Latest-Thinking/2014-FIFA-World-Cup-Brazil-Sponsorship-Insights/Budweiser.aspx

89 IEG. (2014). World Cup 2014 Sponsor Profile: World Cup Sponsor-Johnson & Johnson. http://www.sponsorship.com/Latest-Thinking/2014-FIFA-World-Cup-Brazil-Sponsorship-Insights/Johnson---Johnson.aspx

90 IEG. (2014). World Cup 2014 Sponsor Profile: FIFA Partner-Coca-Cola. http://www.sponsorship.com/Latest-Thinking/2014-FIFA-World-Cup-Brazil-Sponsorship-Insights/Coca-Cola.aspx

91 IEG. (2014). World Cup 2014 Sponsor Profile: World Cup Sponsor-Castrol. http://www.sponsorship.com/Latest-Thinking/2014-FIFA-World-Cup-Brazil-Sponsorship-Insights/Castrol.aspx

92 Grauschopf, S. (2016). The Pillsbury Bake-Off Content: an American Icon. https://www.thebalance.com/pillsbury-bake-off-contest-896870

93   Grauschopf, S. (2016). The Pillsbury Bake-Off Content: an American Icon. https://www.thebalance. com/pillsbury-bake-off-contest-896870

94   Denn, R. (2013). What makes a Pillsbury Bake-Off winner? We talk with a judge. http://blogs. seattletimes.com/allyoucaneat/2013/11/14/what-makes-a-pillsbury-bake-off-winner-we-talk-with-a-judge/

95   Klein, M. (2012). I was a Pillsbury Bake-Off judge. http://www.philly.com/philly/food/20120404_ Somewhere_between_the_Thai_Chicken_Subs_and_the_Indonesian_NO_HEAD_SPECIFIED.html

96   PRNewswire. (2014). 47th Pillsbury Bake-Off Contest announces four recipes vying for $1 million grand prize. http://www.prnewswire.com/news-releases/47th-pillsbury-bake-off-contest-announces-four-recipes-vying-for-1-million-grand-prize-281433171.html

97   PRNewswire. (2014). 47th Pillsbury Bake-Off Contest announces four recipes vying for $1 million grand prize. http://www.prnewswire.com/news-relcases/47th-pillsbury-bake-off-contest-announces-four-recipes-vying-for-1-million-grand-prize-281433171.html

98   Pillsbury. (2017). Pillsbury Bake-Off. https://www.pillsbury.com/our-makers/bake-off-contest

99   AMA. (2017). Dictionary—Deceptive pricing. https://www.ama.org/resources/pages/dictionary. aspx?dLetter=D

100   ACCC. (2017). Misleading claims & advertising. https://www.accc.gov.au/consumers/misleading-claims-advertising

101   Consumer Affairs Victoria. (2017). Misleading or deceptive conduct. https://www.consumer.vic.gov. au/shopping/advertising-and-promotions/misleading-or-deceptive-conduct

102   AMA. (2017). Dictionary—Bait and switch. https://www.ama.org/resources/pages/dictionary. aspx?dLetter=B

103   ACCC. (2017). Misleading claims & advertising. https://www.accc.gov.au/consumers/misleading-claims-advertising

104   Stempel, J. (2015 June 12). Michael Kors settles U.S. lawsuit alleging deceptive price tags. http:// www.reuters.com/article/us-michaelkors-settlement-idUSKBN0OS2AU20150612

105   AMA. (2017). Dictionary—Redemption rate. https://www.ama.org/resources/pages/dictionary. aspx?dLetter=R#redemption+rate

106   INMAR. (2016). Promotion industry trends: a year in review. http://go.inmar.com/rs/134-NXN-082/ images/Inmar-Promotion-Industry-Trends-A-Year-In-Review.pdf

107   AMA. (2017). Dictionary—Misredemption. https://www.ama.org/resources/pages/dictionary. aspx?dLetter=M

108   AMA. (2017). Dictionary—Coupon fraud. https://www.ama.org/resources/pages/dictionary. aspx?dLetter=C

109   Groupon. (2017). Groupon: We are building the daily habit for local commerce. http://files. shareholder.com/downloads/AMDA-E2NTR/4344241613x0x934037/AC787026-C11F-4CC2-B15E-568BC780B57F/Q4_2016_Groupon_Public_Fact_Sheet.pdf

110   Groupon. (2018). The history of Groupon. https://www.groupon.com/merchant/article/the-history-of-groupon

111 Groupon. (2018). About us. https://www.groupon.com.au/merchant/about-us

112 Drogin, B. (1993). Pepsi-Cola uncaps a lottery nightmare—Bombings, threats follow contest with too many winners, 26 July. http://community.seattletimes.nwsource.com/archive/?date=19930726&slug=1712840

113 Campaigns. (2015). History of advertising: No 141: Hoover's free-flights voucher, 23 July. http://www.campaignlive.co.uk/article/history-advertising-no-141-hoovers-free-flights-voucher/1356868

114 Stevenson, T. (1998 14 August). Great financial disasters of our time: The Hoover fiasco. *Independent*. Retrieved from http://www.independent.co.uk/life-style/great-financial-disasters-of-our-time-the-hoover-fiasco-1171711.html

115 BBC. (2013). Business nightmares: Hoover free flights fiasco documentary. https://www.youtube.com/watch?v=CGVe2l0baoI

116 Rainey, S. (2012). Has the Royal Warrant lost its lustre? *The Telegraph*, 25 October.

117 Ehrenberg, A. S. C., Goodhardt, G. J. & Barwise, T. P. (1990). Double jeopardy revisited. *Journal of Marketing, 54*(3), 82–91.

118 Hammond, K. & Ehrenberg, A. (2001). The case against price-related promotions. *Admap Magazine,* June, p. 418.

119 Jones, J. P. (1990 September-October). The double jeopardy of sales promotions. *Harvard Business Review*. Retrieved from https://hbr.org/1990/09/the-double-jeopardy-of-sales-promotions

120 Capps, B. (2005). Everyone an employee as GM spawns copycats. *Advertising Age,* 5 September.

121 ramint.gov.au. (2016). Woolworths shoppers win gold with exclusive Olympic coin launch. https://www.ramint.gov.au/publications/woolworths-shoppers-win-gold-exclusive-olympic-coin-launch

122 Ward, M. (2014). Woolworths brings back 'Fresh Food People' positioning in first brand campaign from Leo Burnett, 11 August. https://mumbrella.com.au/woolworths-brings-back-fresh-food-people-positioning-brand-campaign-leo-burnett-243805

123 Ward, M. (2016). Woolworths asks 'how do you grow a champion?' in Olympics ad, 8 August. https://mumbrella.com.au/woolworths-asks-grow-champion-olympics-tv-ad-386342

124 Canning, S. (2016). 'It's all about the customer: Woolworths top marketers on its new brand campaign, 13 July. https://mumbrella.com.au/woolies-marketer-says-refresh-380223

125 Lichtenstein, D. R., Burton, S. & Netemeyer, R. G. (1997). An examination of deal proneness across sales promotion types: a consumer segmentation perspective. *Journal of Retailing, 73*(2), 283–97.

126 Chandon, P., Wansink, B., & Laurent, G. (2000). A benefit congruency framework of sales promotion effectiveness. *Journal of Marketing, 64*(4), 65-81.

127 White, R. (2002). Best practice sales promotion and the brand. *Admap Magazine,* July, p. 430.

128 Precourt, G. (2016). The art of persuasion along the customer journey. *WARC Event Reports, ANA Brand Activation Conference,* April.

129 Huff, L. C. & Alder, D. L. (1998). An investigation of consumer response to sales promotions in developing markets—a three-country analysis, *Journal of Advertising Research, 38*(3), 47–56.

130 Yi-Zheng, S., Ka-Man, C. & Prendergast, G. (2005). Behavioural response to sales promotion tools. *International Journal of Advertising, 24*(4), 469–89.

131 McGuinness, D., Gendall, P. & Mathew, S. (1992). The effect of product sampling on product trial, purchase and conversion. *International Journal of Advertising, 11*(1), 83–92.

132 Coloribus.com. (2010). Pampers: Record breaking 'Wall of Sleep'. https://www.coloribus.com/adsarchive/promo-casestudy/pampers-record-breaking-wall-of-sleep-16570855/

133 Foley, C., Kuhn, D. & Harris, E. (2017). Rethinking short-term persuasion: a proposed approach for marketers—a holistic examination of brand incentives' effectiveness to drive short-term sales. *Journal of Advertising Research, 57*(2), 190–206.

134 Ward, M. (2014). News Corp want to encourage reading in children with Mr Men books promotion. *Mumbrella*. https://mumbrella.com.au/news-corp-want-encourage-reading-children-mr-men-little-miss-books-promotion-204927

135 Christensen, N. (2015). News Corp marketing boss: 'sales promotions are slowing print circulation declines'. *Mumbrella*. https://mumbrella.com.au/news-corp-marketing-boss-sales-promotions-are-slowing-print-circulation-declines-292637

136 Ward, M. (2014). News Corp want to encourage reading in children with Mr Men books promotion. *Mumbrella*. https://mumbrella.com.au/news-corp-want-encourage-reading-children-mr-men-little-miss-books-promotion-204927

137 Ward, M. (2016). News Corp's Damian Eales says retail offers have helped slow newspaper circulation decline. *Mumbrella*. https://mumbrella.com.au/news-corp-hasbro-damian-eales-newspapers-402013

138 Davidson, D. (2016). News Corp relaunches reader offers campaign with children's books. *The Australian*. http://www.theaustralian.com.au/business/media/news-corp-relaunches-reader-offers-campaign-with-childrens-books/news-story/6a599808191e1a241c5bb7d059993ec3

139 News Corp Australia. (2017). News Corp Australia offers squifflingly good reads for Aussie kids. http://www.newscorpaustralia.com/news/%E2%80%8B%E2%80%8Bnews-corp-australia-offers-squifflingly-good-reads-aussie-kids

140 News Corp Australia. (2015). News Corp Australia, Westpac and Legacy unite to keep ANZAC flame burning. http://www.newscorpaustralia.com/news/news-corp-australia-westpac-and-legacy-unite-keep-anzac-flame-burning

141 https://u.kfcvisit.com/aus

142 https://www.myhjexperience.com

143 https://mcdonalds.com.au/feedback

CHAPTER 9

Electronic and Social Media (ESM)

Wonsun Shin and Hyunjin Kang

The consumer journey in the 21st century

Imagine that you need to buy a new laptop. You might begin with a Google or Amazon search, typing in a few keywords such as 'laptop for college students', 'laptops under $1000' or 'laptop deals'. According to a survey of 1000 US consumers, the majority of purchase decisions begin with a Google or Amazon search.[1] After the initial online search, you might want to know what other consumers think about laptops in the market by reading online reviews on Amazon or other consumer review sites such as CNET. The Pew Research Center reports that about eight out of ten US adults read online customer reviews before purchasing items for the first time, and that around two-thirds of those who read online reviews believe online reviews generally give accurate information about the products.[2] After reading product reviews, you might ask your Facebook friends and Twitter followers about a few laptops you have in mind, and your friends and followers might make recommendations for you. A survey conducted by Nielson confirms that eight out of ten global consumers trust the recommendations of friends and family.[3]

By conducting searches on Google and Amazon, reading consumer reviews and discussing options with social media friends, you have narrowed your choices to a handful of options. Now it's time to make a purchase decision. You might want to visit a couple of real stores to see how those laptops look and feel. You can ask a sales person a few questions about the products and deals at their stores. Of course, you might make a purchase at the store, but you might also come home and buy a laptop from a merchandiser's website or another online vendor using a desktop computer or smartphone if you find better deals available only online. You might also use shopping apps such as BuyVia, ShopSavvy and Amazon Price Check to make the purchase.

Buying, of course, is not the end of the consumer journey. After purchasing a laptop, you might want to contact the merchandiser to ask some questions about the laptop's functions via live chats on a brand website or social media channel. The merchandiser might also send you a welcome email with discount coupons for laptop accessories. This post-purchase experience will affect your feelings about the laptop and its merchandiser, and you might share your brand experiences and feelings with other consumers through social networking sites, the laptop brand's social media channels or consumer review sites.

OXFORD UNIVERSITY PRESS

Compared to the journey that consumers used to undertake in the twentieth century, the consumer journey in the twenty-first century is much more complicated, involving multiple channels and a multitude of information sources. Consumers leave their digital footprints in various places, and at every step of the consumer journey—before, during and after a purchase. They also often engage in numerous digital platforms, actively share their brand experiences and rely on other consumers, not advertisers, to make decisions. How should marketers understand and map the new consumer journey? What are the opportunities and challenges that shape the *marketers'* journey?

■ INTRODUCTION

The emergence of the Web and social media has brought about significant changes in how marketers create and deliver their messages and how consumers respond to them. Marketers now have a wider range of media platforms than ever to communicate with consumers, thereby cultivating relationships with them.

However, new media present marketers with distinct challenges. Consumers are empowered with easy access to an array of information sources and interactive communication tools. Using those sources and tools, they share product information with peer consumers and 'pull' the information that is relevant to their current contexts while actively avoiding irrelevant marketing messages. So the traditional one-way 'push' model does not seem to be a viable option for marketers who want to appeal to digital consumers.

In order to deal with consumers' growing demands for relevant messages and to cope with consumer resistance to the advertising clutter, marketers should be equipped with an in-depth understanding of the changing media environment and new consumer trends. For marketing practitioners, therefore, the important questions to consider are: How have media users and the media landscape changed over the past few decades? How should marketers use the emerging media as marketing communication tools? How do consumers respond to the new forms of marketing communication? What are the social implications of those changes?

In this chapter we will present an advanced understanding of the contemporary electronic and social media landscape by tracing the emergence of the new generation of digital media, examining the growing structural integration of digital marketing tools and discussing issues associated with current digital marketing practices.

LEARNING OBJECTIVES

After reading this chapter you should be able to:

1. describe a paradigm shift in marketing communication
2. explain how digital and social media shape consumer behaviours
3. discuss different electronic and social media options for IMC
4. discuss challenges that marketers face due to emerging media
5. discuss future developments in electronic and social media as IMC tools.

A paradigm shift in marketing communication

Before the introduction of mass communication tools, people relied only on interpersonal communication with their friends, family members and neighbours to acquire information about goods and services. Then traditional mass media such as newspapers, magazines, radio and television emerged. Those were the main tools for marketers to promote their products and services—until the mid-1990s, when the internet was introduced and 'the Web', 'the information highway,' and 'digital revolution' became buzz words.

Web 1.0, 2.0 and 3.0

When the internet emerged as a communication tool, its function and look were not significantly different from how traditional print media operate, providing one-way communication tools with limited interaction with users. This generation of the internet is often referred to as **Web 1.0**, or 'read-only' web, as the internet user's experience was limited to reading information presented to them.[4] Typical examples of Web 1.0 marketing tools include static brand websites containing information without user interaction features and static banner ads displayed on those websites. Hyperlinks embedded in static websites enabled users to move around, between and across content, providing some degree of **interactivity**. However, **interactivity** in the Web 1.0 context was quite limited as very little information flowed from recipients back to information producers.

Despite the obvious shortcomings, the advent of Web 1.0 can be viewed as a revolutionary paradigm shift. Before Web 1.0, a marketing message delivered through a traditional media platform typically reached a limited group of consumers within a limited geographic boundary during a certain period of time. Web 1.0 overcame this restriction, as information published on the Web could be assessed by anyone with internet access at any time, 24 hours a day, 7 days a week. In short, it launched the **information age**.

AT&T's **banner advertising** (Figure 9.1) is considered the world's first online banner advertisement. This advertisement appeared on Hotwired.com on 27 October 1994.[5] Clicking the advertisement took the user to a website created by AT&T. However, the advertisement itself did not have any interactive features such as pull-downs, animations or expandability. This banner advertisement was very similar to a traditional print advertisement in that it was displayed along with independent information without any user interaction functions (other than being clickable), which was typical for online ads in the Web 1.0 era.

Figure 9.1 The world's first banner advertisement

Source: http://mashable.com/2013/08/09/first-banner-ad/#NM8stKPQTiqU

The true revolution began with the birth of **Web 2.0**. Web 2.0 is also known as the 'read-write' web since it enables users to be message producers as well as message recipients. It generally refers to developments in internet- and web-based technology that are characterised by interactivity, user control, collaboration and sharing.[6] Key Web 2.0 tools and services include blogs, wikis, **user-generated content**, social networking sites such as Facebook and Twitter, and video sharing sites such as YouTube.[7] These tools have become increasingly popular among Web users. Figure 9.2 illustrates the growth of social networking site users between 2005 and 2015 in the US.

Web 2.0 technologies have enhanced user interaction and two-way communication between marketers and consumers. Consumers expect to have more control over the information that is available to them and how that information is created and shared.[8] They also actively participate in branding

Figure 9.2 Social networking site usage in the US: 2005–2015

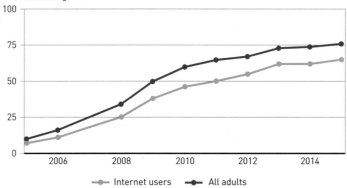

% of all American adults and internet-using adults who use at least one social networking site

Source: Pew Research Center 2015, Social Media Usage: 2005–2015, www.pewinternet.org/2015/10/08/social-networking-usage-2005-2015/

and marketing activities, as well as creating and sharing user-generated content, which is considered as an important component of IMC (See 'IMC in Action: The Doritos "Crash the Super Bowl" campaign' for a case study on a user-generated content campaign). The distinction between message senders and message recipients has become unclear in the Web 2.0 era, as anyone can create and distribute content through various types of networks.

IMC IN ACTION: THE DORITOS 'CRASH THE SUPER BOWL' CAMPAIGN⁹

In early 2006, Andrew Robinson at Marketing Arm pitched an idea to Frito-Lay: **crowdsourcing** consumers to create commercials to be aired during the following year's Super Bowl. When the idea of investing US$2 million in consumer-generated advertising was shared for the first time, it was considered radical and risky, and thus met resistance within the organisation. Frito-Lay nevertheless decided to go for the stunt and launched its first user-generated ad campaign, 'Crash the Super Bowl,' inviting consumers to create 30-second commercials for Doritos products. A total of 1065 consumers submitted their user-generated content to Frito-Lay's contest site, crashthesuperbowl. com. Five finalists' consumer-made advertisements were displayed on the contest site for one month, and the public was invited to vote for the best one. The advertisement that received the most votes, 'Live the Flavor', was aired during the 2007 Super Bowl (see Figure 9.3). This advertisement was the first user-generated advertisement ever aired in Super Bowl history, and it became the most liked advertisement of the 2007 Super Bowl. Given the fact that social media was not a widely known concept for consumers and that Facebook was limited to college students in 2007, the concepts of crowdsourcing and user-generated advertising campaigns were considered innovative and even revolutionary.

Figure 9.3 Doritos' 'Live the Flavor' Super Bowl 2007 advertisement

Source: www.nytimes.com/2007/01/26/business/media/26adco.html

Frito-Lay continued to invite consumers to its user-generated campaign every year until the brand announced the end of the 10-year campaign in 2016. The last campaign received 4500 submissions from 28 countries.

This user-generated campaign is viewed as a breakthrough in the world of marketing communication, garnering tremendous publicity and enhancing the brand's value. Its advertisements claimed the top five rankings on USA Today's Ad Meter every year and contributed to the brand's growth from a brand value of $1.54 billion in 2006 to $2.2 billion in 2015. Encouraged by Frito-Lay's success, many other brands have adopted crowdsourcing campaigns. Starbucks invites the public to provide new ideas for the brand via 'My Starbucks Idea'. Ben & Jerry's launched a global campaign 'Do the World a Flavor' in 2009, asking consumers to create new flavours for the brand, and received 100 000 submissions in total. Now, user-generated content is a popular marketing tool as it tends to generate greater memorability for and greater trust in brands.

The next phase of the Web evolution is referred to as **Web 3.0**. Although there is no widely accepted definition of Web 3.0, it generally refers to the Web that links, integrates and analyses various sets of data collected through multiple platforms to summarise and transform a large amount of information into knowledge.[10] That is, the system (Web, computer or device)—not humans—generates knowledge and wisdom. For this reason, it is also referred to as the 'read-write-execute' Web. Before Web 3.0, it was 'users' who would execute information searches using Google or other search engines to find a famous local restaurant, a good book or a song to lift their mood. This typically involves multiple information searches and comparisons, sometimes requiring much time and effort of consumers. With Web 3.0, the machine—either an internet site, a smartphone app and/or a cloud computing system—does the users' job, offering personalised suggestions based on a wide range of information available about the users collected from different information sources. The types of user information include their prior purchases, information search histories, preferences and current location and time. The growth of big data and tracking strategies is expected to further enhance the utility of Web 3.0 to provide consumers with added value.

How digital and social media shape consumer behaviour

The evolution of the Web and digital technology has substantially influenced consumers' expectations of marketers. Primarily, consumers have become active processors who increasingly demand two-way communication and timely feedback from marketers. They are multitaskers, engaging in multiple media activities concurrently, immersing themselves in the sea of information and exposing themselves to various forms of marketing communication.

As illustrated at the beginning of the chapter, a wide range of electronic and social media allow consumers to become smart and informed shoppers. They may begin with their consumer journeys through in-store browsing to try out the product and then decide to purchase online after finding better deals available on the web (**showrooming**). They can also start with online browsing, reading consumer reviews and garnering their friends' opinions, and then go to a physical store, touch and test the product, and make an in-store purchase (**webrooming**). A good understanding of how consumers pull information and make purchase decisions across multiple channels has become imperative for marketing communication practitioners.

Consumers also demand more relevant and personalised communication that matches up with their current priority and context.[11] In addition, they heavily rely on the networks of their friends and acquaintances to acquire product information and learn about the marketplace. According to the Nielson Global Survey of Trust in Advertising, more than eight out of ten consumers in the world trust **word-of-mouth** recommendations from people they know. On the other hand, only three to four out of ten consumers trust online banner advertisements (42%) and mobile text advertisements (36%). Table 9.1 presents consumers' trust in different advertising formats by region.

Overall, the evolving Web and digital technology has resulted in a significant paradigm shift in communication. Before the age of Web 2.0, the dominant communication paradigm was one-way, marketer-to-consumer communication. In general, consumers were more like passive recipients of information disseminated by marketers, and marketers pushed information to consumers through mass media. Now, the dominant paradigm of marketing communication through the internet and social media is two-way, bi-directional communication where the distinction between information creators and recipients is blurred. Consumers are active processors, engaging in information research through multiple media platforms and pulling the information that is directly relevant to their current needs and situations. Figure 9.4 summarises these paradigm shifts.

In response to the new consumer demands and expectations, marketers now pay greater attention to user interaction, relationship building and customisation through various interactive communication platforms, ranging from brand websites, display advertisements, and native advertising to social media and **mobile marketing**. These tools have become the essential components of effective IMC campaigns. The next section discusses some of the major electronic and social media options that are widely used by contemporary marketers.

Table 9.1 Percentage of respondents who trust advertising format by region

	Asia-Pacific	Europe	Africa/Middle East	Latin America	North America
Recommendations from people I know	85%	78%	85%	88%	82%
Branded websites	78%	54%	76%	75%	61%
Editorial content, such as newspaper articles	71%	52%	71%	74%	63%
Consumer opinions posted online	70%	60%	71%	63%	66%
Ads on TV	68%	45%	70%	72%	63%
Brand sponsorships	67%	43%	73%	70%	57%
Ads in newspapers	63%	44%	69%	72%	65%
Ads in magazines	62%	43%	65%	70%	62%
Billboards and other outdoor advertising	60%	40%	64%	63%	57%
Emails I signed up for	60%	41%	59%	65%	64%
TV program product placements	60%	35%	64%	64%	53%
Ads before movies	59%	38%	57%	62%	56%
Ads on radio	54%	41%	62%	68%	60%
Online video ads	53%	33%	55%	52%	47%
Ads on mobile devices	50%	26%	49%	48%	39%
Ads on social networks	50%	32%	57%	54%	42%
Ads served in search engine results	50%	36%	52%	58%	49%
Online banner ads	48%	27%	49%	46%	41%
Text ads on mobile phones	42%	22%	41%	39%	37%

Source: Nielson 2015. *Global Trust in Advertising*, www.nielsen.com/content/dam/nielsenglobal/apac/docs/reports/2015/nielsen-global-trust-in-advertising-report-september-2015.pdf

Figure 9.4 New communication paradigm

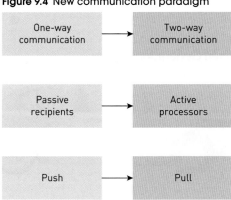

ESM marketing communication options

In this section, we will look at the various electronic and social media options that can be incorporated into IMC campaigns, which include brand websites, display advertising, native advertising, social media marketing and mobile marketing.

Brand websites

Brand websites are arguably the first frontier of digital and interactive marketing. Marketers use brand websites as advertising and branding channels, and relationship building tools. Earlier versions of websites (Web 1.0) functioned like print media, also called **brochureware**. Information dissemination was mostly unidirectional, from marketers to consumers, without providing consumers with feedback loops.

With the growth of digital technology and the emergence of Web 2.0, brand websites have transformed to interactive marketing communication platforms. Now many brand websites increasingly incorporate user interaction features such as online forms for inquiries, online live chats with customer sales representatives, and message boards where consumers can leave comments, enabling them to provide their own input. They also serve as information dissemination tools, providing a multitude of information on the brand's offerings with various options that allow consumers to share information with others.

For example, Adobe Australia fulfils users' desire for both information and engagement through various informational and interactive features.[12] The website is designed to promote a wide range of Adobe products and provides detailed information for each product using step-by-step interactive walkthroughs and videos. Its links to community forums enable users to interact with experts and peer users. The website also has links to social networking sites, including Facebook, Twitter, Instagram and LinkedIn. Its online live chat lets consumers talk to experts to solve their technical problems.

However, research suggests that many companies still use their brand websites mainly for one-way rather than two-way communication. A group of researchers content-analysed 100 top global brands' websites in 2012 and found that information-dissemination features were more prevalent than user engagement features on those websites.[13] The researchers suggested that marketers should take advantage of the potential of brand websites as conversation and relationship-building tools, given that interactivity and user engagement lead to positive business outcomes. Take a look at BMW's website, which won the

Figure 9.5 BMW's website

Webby Award for the best car/car culture site in 2018 (Figure 9.5). Browse the website and see how this website fulfils consumers' needs for information and engagement.

Display advertising

Display advertising refers to various forms of advertisements that contain text, images, videos and audio that are 'displayed' on the pages of websites.[14] Marketers can use display advertising to increase brand awareness, deliver brand messages and generate responses from consumers.

Banner advertising is the earliest form of display advertising. It typically refers to a static or animated image that comes with standardised shapes and sizes under a number of names, including leaderboard, half page, large rectangle and skyscraper.[15] With advanced graphic technology, traditional banner advertising has progressed to **rich media**, which refers to a broader range of internet advertising that exhibits dynamic motion or audio powered by Java or Flash.[16] Rich media takes diverse forms and sizes and is located in various positions on websites. Examples include expandable banners, page peelbacks, floating advertisements, full-page takeovers, pop-ups and pushdowns. Research shows that dynamic rich media with video are more effective than static banner advertising in increasing brand awareness and purchase intentions.[17]

Pop-ups, also known as **interstitials**, are possibly the most controversial form of display advertising.[18] Interstitials are full- or partial-page texts and images that appear in the transition between two content pages. Interstitials are often considered intrusive and irritating as they tend to force exposure to advertisements before visitors can continue on their content path. Although forced exposure may attract users' attention and thereby potentially enhance brand awareness, the distraction can result in negative attitudes towards the advertised brands.[19]

Digital video advertising is another form of display advertising, referring to advertisements that appear before, during or after digital video content. Currently, digital video advertising is one of the most popular and lucrative forms of display advertising. According to the Interactive Advertising Bureau (IAB), advertisers spent more than $10 million on digital video in 2016, primarily due to its high return on investment (ROI).[20] According to a survey conducted by BrightRoll, 72 per cent of 120 responding advertising agencies in the US said digital video advertising is more effective than television.[21] The survey respondents rated *completed views*, *conversion*, and *brand lift* as the most important success metrics for digital video campaigns.

Native advertising

New forms of media and marketing tools have created more advertising clutter as consumers are exposed to a substantial amount of marketing communication messages via a number of digital media platforms. This has led consumers to increasingly avoid and ignore marketing communication messages. As the aforementioned Nielson Global Survey of Trust in Advertising indicates, consumers also tend to be sceptical about traditional, overt forms of display advertising, including online banner advertisements and digital video advertisements. To cope with consumers' scepticism towards advertising and to break through the clutter, many marketers are now paying greater attention to native advertising.

As we learnt in Chapter 5, native advertising refers to paid advertising that takes the specific form and appearance of editorial content so that the advertisements look like the content surrounding them. Native advertising is similar to traditional forms of display advertising in that both are paid and displayed on websites. However, the former is less overt than the latter, which blends into the content and surroundings. Given that traditional overt display advertising is becoming less effective, with average **click-through rates** lower than 0.2 per cent,[22] covert advertising such as native advertising has become a more feasible option for marketers. Research shows that consumers are more likely to view, share and click native advertising than traditional banner advertisements because the former is considered less intrusive and more relevant.[23]

The Interactive Advertising Bureau (IAB) classifies native advertising into six categories.

Figure 9.6 In-feed unit on BuzzFeed

1. *in-feed units:* advertising content is placed within a website's content feed to make it look like normal content written by the publisher (e.g. BuzzFeed's sponsored articles—see Figure 9.6)

2. *aid search units:* promoted listings that appear at the top of customers' organic search results

3. *ecommendation widgets:* widgets that consumers encounter at the end of a web publisher's article, which often comes with such headings as 'recommended for you', 'you may also like' and 'you may have missed'.

4. *promotional listings:* listings featured on e-commerce sites, not content-based sites, to promote sponsored products

Source: Business Insider 2015. www.businessinsider.com.au/buzzfeed-native-advertising-is-paying-off-2015-8?r=US&IR=T

5. *in-ad with native element units:* advertisements that look like typical display advertising but are contextually relevant to the publisher's content (e.g. a banner advertisement promoting a shampoo product displayed on a beauty community page)

6. *custom/'can't be contained':* native advertising that does not fit any of the formats above.

According to BI Intelligence, native display advertising, which includes social native and native advertisements in-feed on publisher websites, will drive 74 per cent of the total US display advertising revenue by 2021.[24] Social platforms such as Facebook, Twitter and Instagram generate most of the revenue from native advertising, and this trend is expected to continue through 2021.

However, native advertising is also viewed as a deceptive and misleading practice. Charles R. Taylor, editor of the *International Journal of Advertising*, called native advertising 'a black sheep of the marketing family' as it does not conform to the typical ethical boundary of the field.[25] Native advertising blurs the line between advertising and content, and it typically does not clearly disclose that the message is indeed a sponsored advertisement. Such practices may lower consumers' persuasion knowledge, thereby leading them to be less critical about advertisers' persuasive intent.

Social media marketing

Social media is defined as 'a group of internet-based applications that build on the ideological and technological foundations of Web 2.0, and that allow the creation and exchange of user generated contents'.[26] This suggests that user-generated contents and interactions are central to social media. However, it is also important to note that technological features that facilitate user interactions vary across different types of social media platforms. Table 9.2 presents a classification of social media based on levels of self-presentation and media richness. As the table shows, social media ranges from blogs and Wikipedia that provide simple features (i.e. writing and reading), to Second Life, which is based on virtual reality enhanced by much more sophisticated technology.

Table 9.2 Classification of social media by media richness and self-presentation

		MEDIA RICHNESS		
		LOW	MEDIUM	HIGH
Self-presentation	High	Blogs	Social networking sites (e.g. Facebook)	Virtual social worlds (e.g. Second Life)
	Low	Collaborative projects (Wikipedia)	Content communities (e.g. YouTube)	Virtual game worlds (e.g. World of Warcraft)

Source: Kaplan, A. M. & Haenlein, M. 2010. Users of the world, unite! The challenges and opportunities of Social Media. *Business Horizons, 53*(1), 59–68.

Social media has become a major communication platform where consumers acquire a variety of information and interact with one another. The number of social media users reached a total of 2.8 billion worldwide in 2016; Facebook is the most popular social media platform with 1871 million active users, followed by WhatsApp (1000 million) and YouTube (1000 million) (see Figure 9.7).[27] Average users spend around 2 hours and 19 minutes on social media platforms per day.[28] For many brands, social media have become a necessity, not an option, to communicate with their target audience.

In the previous chapters, we discussed the traditional marketing communication environment in which marketing messages are owned and managed by companies or organisations. In the social media environment, however, brand-related information and content are often co-created, revised and transmitted through interactions among consumers connected via networks. In this environment, marketers are less likely to achieve desirable business outcomes if they try to over-control the information shared and discussed among social media users or to simply view social media as an information dissemination tool.

Figure 9.7 Number of active users of key social media platforms

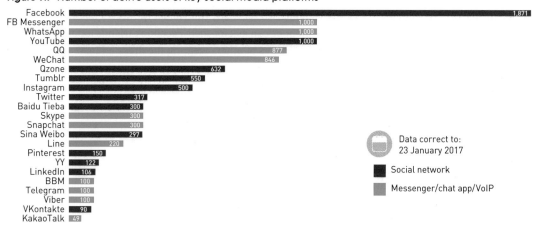

Source: https://wearesocial.com/sg/blog/2017/01/digital-in-2017-global-overview

To fully exploit the potential of social media as a marketing communication tool, marketers should use social media as a strategic platform to communicate and cultivate relationships with current and potential customers.

Marketers should also understand that those who follow a brand through social media are more likely to engage with the brand than those who do not follow the brand. When followers acquire information on a company or brand of interest, they are more likely to share the information and discuss it with their social media peers. Therefore, the success of **social media marketing** largely depends on whether the marketing content shared through social media can generate positive **social buzz** among interested consumers. This highlights the importance of understanding information flows between and among consumers and brand followers. If the content is interesting enough to social media users, it will be shared with vast audiences who are connected to each other through the networks. Marketing costs can decrease remarkably if marketers are able to utilise social media effectively.

The global brand Nike, for instance, has about 28 million followers on Facebook, and more than 7 million followers on Twitter. Most of the posts shared on Nike's Facebook page are designed to ignite discussions among its followers. When Kevin Durant became an NBA world champion as a member of the Golden State Warriors basketball team in June 2017, Nike created and posted video footage of Durant with the comment, 'Debate This. @KDTrey5 is now a world champion. #NikeBasketball' on both Facebook and Twitter. Within two days, this post acquired about 29 thousand likes, more than 1200 comments and 12 000 shares on Facebook. On Twitter, the post was shared more than 40 000 times, and received 54 000 reactions and 1500 replies.

Marketers can also use social media to gain consumers' insights by analysing their sentiments about the brand by tracking and monitoring content shared in social media. Various intelligent software programs such as brandwatch[29] and Google Analytics[30] help organisations monitor and analyse what consumers say about brands and companies in social media. By using such analytic tools, social media marketers can acquire a deeper understanding of consumers and more accurate diagnoses of current consumer sentiments regarding their branding and marketing activities.

When combined with mobile technology, the power of social media soars, because mobile devices enable social media users to be connected to their social networks at any time and anywhere. For example, using a social media app on a smartphone, a clothing shopper can ask for their Facebook friends' opinions about a dress in a fitting room at the store and search for images of others wearing the dress on Instagram.

'IMC in Action: the Gillette Venus "Tag the Weather" campaign' presents a real-life example of how social media can be used to connect with customers.

IMC IN ACTION: THE GILLETTE VENUS 'TAG THE WEATHER' CAMPAIGN[31]

Gillette Venus is the leading brand of women's razor worldwide. However, there was a major challenge for Gillette in the Swedish market—the weather. Sweden has cold and dark winters that normally last about 5 months in every year. The problem was that unit sales of Venus razors plummets during the long winter in Sweden.

To tackle this situation, Gillette connected the Venus brand to its target audience (women aged 18 to 35) by tapping into their normal daily social media and mobile behaviours via photo sharing and commenting, instead of telling them to shave often during the winter. To achieve this, Gillette Venus developed a reward-based campaign utilising social media. In this campaign, they encouraged young Swedish women to post photos and comments about the winter weather in Sweden on Instagram. When weather photos uploaded on Instagram, they were given a 'bad weather score' based on historical weather data of the same location and date. Collaborating with e-retailers, uploaders could use the bad weather scores to get discounts on Venus ProSkin. An online gallery created for this campaign displayed all the winter photos shared during the campaign, and 14 finalists picked by famous fashion bloggers were invited for a trip to Miami, in Florida, US.

This campaign was hugely successful. During the campaign, more than 5800 photos were uploaded on Instagram, reaching approximately 444 500 Gillette Venus users. More than 90 per cent of all Swedish women aged 18 to 35 have been reached via Facebook and Instagram through the campaign. As a result, online sales of blades increased by more than double, and unit sales of promoted products in the campaign soared by more than 570 per cent (see Figure 9.8).

Figure 9.8 Gillette Venus 'Tag the Weather' campaign in Sweden

Source: http://saatchi.se/en/case/venus-tag-weather/

Mobile marketing

Along with social media, mobile technology has dramatically changed how consumers consume, utilise and share information. In a store, for example, many consumers no longer rely on sales people to obtain information about products, as they can search for information about the products via their mobile devices. They can also compare prices and offerings of other outlets before making final purchase decisions, which has resulted in intensified competition across numerous industries. Overall, the emergence of mobile technologies provides ample opportunities as well as various challenges to marketers.

According to eMarketer, 58.7 per cent of the global population owns and uses mobile devices, a figure that is expected to grow to 62.6 per cent by 2020 (see Figure 9.9). Furthermore, about 40 per cent of total web pages are viewed on mobile phones.[32] In response to this trend, marketers now devote significant effort and resources to communicating with consumers through mobile devices. In the US, spending on mobile-based advertising has risen sharply, whereas spending on desktop-based advertising is continually decreasing.[33] It is evident that current marketing communication strategies should be geared towards consistently connected consumers using an array of mobile devices.

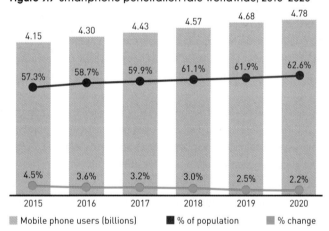

Figure 9.9 Smartphone penetration rate worldwide, 2015–2020

Source: www.emarketer.com/Article/Mobile-Phone-Smartphone-Usage-Varies-Globally/1014738

Currently, there is a wide range of mobile marketing options, including:

- *short message service (SMS):* a service for sending text messages on a mobile phone system
- *multimedia message service (MMS):* a service for sending messages that include multimedia content on a mobile phone system
- *push notification:* a message that pops up on a mobile device
- *mobile application (app):* application software designed to run on a mobile device
- *mobile display advertising:* advertising messages displayed on mobile websites or in apps
- *Quick Response (QR) code:* a two-dimensional barcode used to provide easy access to information through mobile devices
- *location-based advertising (LBA):* targeting consumers with location-specific advertising on their mobile devices using GPS, Wi-Fi or users entering locations into the devices.

Although various forms of mobile marketing exist, the Mobile Marketing Association defines mobile marketing as 'a set of practices that enables organizations to communicate and engage with their audience in an interactive and relevant manner through any mobile device or network'.[34] As the definition indicates, the key to successful mobile marketing lies in *interactivity* and *relevance*, which also applies to effective social media marketing. As discussed earlier, today's consumers demand personalised services and content that is highly relevant to their needs. Consumer-focused mobile marketing enabled by mobile technology provides consumers with unique brand experiences and added value. Mobile marketing campaigns built on deeper emotional connections with consumers and providing relevant offerings will lead to more successful IMC campaigns than those that focus primarily on general mobile behaviours, such as search or video viewing.[35]

In addition, location tracking features embedded in mobile devices provide mobile marketers with ample opportunities to connect with individual target consumers. **Location intelligence** allows for precise targeting by utilising real-time data acquired from individual consumers' activities using mobile devices. Mobile ads can target consumers nearby or at stores, thereby influencing every step of the consumer journey, from advertising exposure to purchase. Some of the location-based mobile marketing tips that marketers can incorporate into their IMC campaign are as follows (see also Figure 9.10).[36]

- *Geo-targeting* detects consumers' location using IP addresses and provides information based on their locations, such as advertisements or promotion offers. Location data can be combined with other data about individual consumers' demographic characteristics (e.g. gender or age) or preferences. For example, when a regular customer of Starbucks approaches a Starbucks restaurant in a certain location, Starbucks can send a push notification to the customer's smartphone about special promotions at that restaurant.

- *Geofencing* targets a broader audience, as it is about setting a 'fence' to target people in a certain area. When geofencing is used, marketers capture all of the people in the given zone. For example, when a new McDonald's restaurant is established, McDonald's can provide digital coupons to all the people in the nearby area to increase awareness and stimulate business.

- *Beaconing* utilises Bluetooth technologies to capture individual consumers' very specifically targeted locations (e.g. the specific aisle in a supermarket). For example, an advertising message from Heinz can be sent to those who have spent more than 20 seconds in the sauce aisle at a large supermarket.

Figure 9.10 Geo-targeting, geofencing and beaconing

Geo-targeting	Geofencing	Beaconing

IMC IN ACTION: BAND-AID'S 'MAGIC VISION' AUGMENTED REALITY MOBILE APP[37]

In April 2012, Band-Aid adhesive bandage sales were down by 3.9 per cent. The main factor explaining these sluggish sales was that consumers were increasingly switching to cheaper options—store brand bandages. To tackle this challenge, Band-Aid's urgent aim was to find a unique brand selling point.

The main target audience of adhesive bandage brands, including Band-Aid, is households with accident-prone children. The marketers focused on the fact that wound-care occasions are emotional for both children and adults with children. 'We like to think about Band-Aid as the magic healing brand. Mum puts the Band-Aid on and seals it with a kiss,' Hugh Dineen, a vice president of Band-Aid's parent company Johnson & Johnson said.

Drawing upon this insight, they wanted parents to use Band-Aid bandages to create an emotional bond with their children during wound-care situations. Towards this end, Band-Aid, collaborating with JWT New York, developed an **augmented reality** mobile app, named MagicVision™ featuring the Muppets of Disney. When a Muppets Band-Aid applied on a kid's wounded part is scanned with the Magic Vision app, the kid can swing Kermit, who sings and plays banjo, by swinging the mobile phone (see Figure 9.11). Also using the app, the kids can take photos with Miss Piggy and interact with Gonzo's stunts by touching the mobile screen.

As a result of this campaign, the Magic Vision app prompted 76 per cent of all participants to revisit and reuse the app, reached 80 per cent of its target audience by generating earned media, and contributed to a 12.6 per cent increase in unit sales.

Figure 9.11 Band-Aid's Magic Vision campaign

Source: www.nytimes.com/2012/05/23/business/media/band-aids-and-muppets-soothe-childs-scrapes.html

Challenges in electronic and social media

The evolution of technology, especially social media and mobile technologies, provides marketers with rich and new opportunities to communicate their messages and achieve their marketing objectives. Current brand marketers can no longer avoid 'going digital', 'going social media' and 'going mobile' because these approaches provide clear advantages that have substantially altered consumer experiences with brands. However, there are several issues marketers need to consider when incorporating ESM into their IMC strategies.

First, consumers are multi-device users, moving across different devices for consistent connections and a seamless consumer experience. For this reason, marketers should design multi-screen strategies to cater to consumers' needs in different circumstances at different steps of the consumer journey. It is advisable for marketers to design a marketing strategy that focuses on different devices at different times of the day. For example, many consumers spend substantial time commuting in the morning. Therefore, small mobile devices such as smartphones are more likely to be used by consumers in the morning than desktops or tablets, making smartphones more viable marketing communication options at that time of the day. When consumers are at work during the day, they are more likely to be using desktop computers. It was also shown that tablets are the most popular device used during the evening, as consumers tend to use tablets while relaxing at home (see Figure 9.12).

Figure 9.12 Daily usage of multi screens

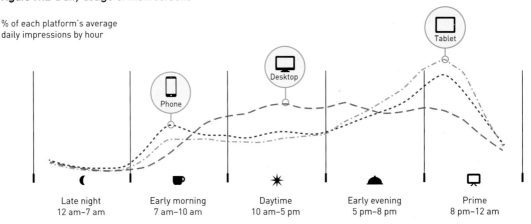

Source: www.smartinsights.com/mobile-marketing/mobile-marketing-analytics/
mobile-marketing-statistics/attachment/2017-mobile-use-through-day/

Another significant challenge in ESM marketing is the privacy issue. Web 2.0 and 3.0 marketing are rapidly moving towards precise targeting and **personalisation**. However, personalisation represents two sides of a coin. While many consumers may find personalised marketing content useful, personalisation has also raised significant privacy concerns.[38] Research shows that 80 per cent of social media users are concerned that their personal data can be unknowingly collected and used by third parties such as advertisers. The research also demonstrates that privacy is the top concern among users of mobile apps. Specifically, more than half of mobile app users responded that they had decided not to install an app on their phones because of privacy concerns.[39] A general suggestion for marketers is to make targeted marketing using digital technologies something useful and relevant to users, but not in a creepy way. To do so, it is important to enable consumers to manage their privacy on their digital devices.

The next challenge of using ESM for IMC strategy is that regulations and policies related to online, social and mobile marketing are continually changing because technology is evolving so rapidly. Therefore, marketers need to consistently and carefully consider whether any of the marketing practices using digital media unlawfully invade any aspects of consumer privacy, infringe on intellectual property, create discrimination and defamation, or conflict with content ownership laws.[40] In the US alone, there are more than 10 000 regulations and rules pertaining to digital communication, and they vary remarkably by industry and circumstance. Therefore, firms need to have experts in digital communication laws in order to protect against potential legal problems associated with their ESM practices.[41]

Finally, it should be noted that incorporating social media into IMC raises an important question: 'How should we measure the return on investment (ROI)?' As many companies and organisations incorporate social media into their IMC mix, measuring the ROI of social media marketing is increasingly important. CEOs and CFOs now often require their marketing teams to provide concrete evidence of expected ROI before allocating budgets for social media campaigns.[42] However, it seems that the majority of marketers are not confident in the accuracy of their social media marketing ROI measurements. A survey of 750 marketing professionals showed that 88 per cent feel that they do not measure the effectiveness of social media campaigns accurately.[43]

In fact, measuring social media ROI can be extremely difficult because marketers must measure ROI from cross-channel consumer journeys that include both social media and non-social media channels.[44] Scholars emphasise that the most important step of measuring ROI is deciding the key objective of the given social media campaign and how to measure the outcome. For example, if the objective is brand awareness, the number of unique visits or the search ranking can be measured to assess ROI. If the key objective is brand engagement, the number of followers or comments can be measured.[45] Table 9.3 shows the various metrics for social media that marketers can use based on various social media applications and key objectives.

Additionally, while ESM can appear to be more efficient in terms of ROI, it can be less effective in certain contexts. For instance, an increasing number of marketers engage in **behavioural targeting**, monitoring and tracking consumers' online behaviour and delivering individually targeted advertising messages using the collected data. If consumers look up a hotel on TripAdvisor, they will receive targeted advertisements for hotels in that location constantly thereafter on Facebook. Targeted messages inferred from the consumer's online behaviour can be considered more relevant and effective. However, it is quite possible that the consumer has already booked a room through Trivago, so the advertising messages presented on Facebook become irrelevant and the money spent on behavioural targeting is wasted.

Emerging trends

The previous sections of this chapter examined the paradigm shifts in communication (Web 1.0, 2.0, and 3.0), some widely used ESM options (brand websites, display advertising, native advertising, social media marketing and mobile marketing), and key issues associated with those ESM tools (multi-screen media planning, consumer privacy and ROI in social media).

Next, we'll ask what lies in the future of marketing communication. This section examines three key emerging trends in ESM—big data, the **Internet of Things (IoT)** and virtual reality (VR)—as marketing communication tools and examines the promise and the concerns that they present.

Big data and data-driven marketing

As discussed earlier, consumers demand more relevant and personalised marketing messages because personalised messages provide information of value regarding their most specific interests. Deeper knowledge of consumers' perceptions and behaviours has thus become imperative for marketers dealing with informed and tech-savvy consumers. Following this pattern, an increasing number of marketers have adopted sophisticated data analytic techniques to build richer and more complex consumer databases, also known as **big data**.[46] Big data refers to a large amount of data that requires machine-based technologies

Table 9.3 Relevant metrics for social media applications, organised by key social media objectives

Social media application	Brand awareness	Brand engagement	Word of mouth
Blogs	• number of unique visits • number of return visits • number of times bookmarked • search ranking	• number of members • number of RSS feed subscribers • number of comments • amount of user-generated content • average length of time on site • number of responses to polls, contests, surveys	• number of references to blog in other media (online/offline) • number of reblogs • number of times badge displayed on other sites • number of 'likes'
Microblogging (e.g. Twitter)	• number of tweets about the brand • valence of tweets +/– • number of followers	• number of followers • number of @ replies	• number of retweets
Cocreation (e.g. NIKEiD)	• number of visits	• number of creation attempts	• number of references to project in other media (online/offline)
Social bookmarking (e.g. Flickr)	• number of tags	• number of followers	• number of additional taggers
Forums and discussion boards (e.g. Google Groups)	• number of page views • number of visits • valence of posted content +/–	• number of relevant topics/threads • number of individual replies • number of sign-ups	• incoming links • citations in other sites • tagging in social bookmarking • offline references to the forum or its members • in private communities: number of pieces of content (photos, discussions, videos); chatter pointing to the community outside of its gates • number of 'likes'
Product reviews (e.g. Amazon)	• number of reviews posted • valence of reviews • number and valence of other users' responses to reviews (+/–) • number of wish list adds • number of times product included in users' lists (i.e. Listmania! on Amazon.com)	• length of reviews • relevance of reviews • valence of other users' ratings of reviews (i.e. how many found a particular review helpful) • number of wish list adds • overall number of reviewer rating scores entered • average reviewer rating score	• number of reviews posted • valence of reviews • number and valence of other users' responses to reviews (+/–) • number of references to reviews in other sites • number of visits to review site page • number of times product included in users' lists (i.e. Listmania! on Amazon.com)
Social networks (e.g. Bebo, Facebook, LinkedIn)	• number of members/fans • number of installs of applications • number of impressions • number of bookmarks • number of reviews/ratings and valence +/–	• number of comments • number of active users • number of 'likes' on friends' feeds • number of user-generated items (photos, threads, replies) • usage metrics of applications/widgets • impressions-to-interactions ratio • rate of activity (how often members personalise profiles, bios, links, etc.)	• frequency of appearances in timeline of friends • number of posts on wall • number of reposts/shares • number of responses to friend referral invites
Video and photosharing (e.g. Flickr, YouTube)	• number of views of video/photo • valence of video/photo ratings +/–	• number of replies • number of page views • number of comments • number of subscribers	• number of embeddings • number of incoming links • number of references in mock-ups or derived work • number of times republished in other social media and offline • number of 'likes'

Source: Hoffman, D. L. & Fodor, M. (2010). Can you measure the ROI of your social media marketing?
Sloan Management Review, 52(1), 41–9.

to be fully analysed.[47] It is characterised not only by massive volume, but also by the velocity, variety and complexity of information. Information consisting of big data can come from a wide range of sources and channels, including customer surveys, retail transactions, loyalty card information, mobile location, online and social media activities, and content generated and uploaded by consumers.

Sources of big data provide marketers with important advantages. They help marketers gain greater insights into consumers, not just about who they are, but where they are, what they do, how they make consumption decisions, and what influences their consumption behaviours. Based on insights gained from big data, marketers can optimise various aspects of marketing programs, including price strategies and marketing communication messages, and channel strategies. Big data can also be used for creative and media planning. For example, Warner Brothers Home Entertainment aggregated big data from more than 30 data sources, including digital log files, social media exposure, and individual-level exposure to television and out-of-home advertising, to develop effective creative and targeting strategies to promote its new movie *Pan*. The dataset allowed the marketing team to reach the most interested target audience groups with specific creatives using a customised media mix.[48]

However, big data does not always generate positive outcomes, and building big data can be considered a daunting task. First, marketers need to know what data they should collect. Excessive amounts of consumer information exist, but not all data will provide marketers with precise insights into their target consumers. Thus, marketers should determine the right types of information to collect and identify the right information sources. Second, marketers should be equipped with the knowledge and tools to analyse, aggregate, combine and interpret the data in order to draw relevant insights. Finally, marketers should understand how to convert the data-based insights into concrete actions in order to create an impact.[49]

Due to the emergence of the 'Internet of Things' (IoT), both the complexity and the volume of big data are expected to increase exponentially. Before the IoT, big data were generated primarily from information, activities and interactions of humans. Now, however, big data also includes data generated from smart devices that can communicate not only with humans but also with other smart devices. The next section discusses how the IoT may change marketing environments and strategies.

The Internet of Things

As consumers use multiple screens, engaging in multitasking using multiple devices, the focus of media planning will also shift to an approach associated with multimedia consumption.[50] Therefore, marketing practices will increasingly exploit consumers' omnipresent internet connection, also known as the **Internet of Things (IoT)**. IoT is defined as 'a system of interrelated computing devices, mechanical and digital machines, objects, animals or people that are provided with unique identifiers and the ability to transfer data over a network without requiring human-to-human or human-to-computer interaction'.[51]

Consumer IoT includes such devices as wearable gadgets (e.g. Fitbit), smart homes (e.g. Nest Thermostat), technology-based home devices and applications (e.g. Philips' Hue) and personal health trackers. Those devices sense and collect our behaviour and send the data back to the companies that created the devices, and the companies send us content through the devices. These internet-connected devices make abundant consumer data available to marketers, helping marketers understand consumer preferences and behaviours, reach consumers with targeted messages and personalised offerings and, consequently, improve the consumer experience. This will further strengthen a firm's relationship with its consumers.

IoT is still in a stage of relative infancy at this point. However, BI Intelligence estimates that 34 billion devices will be connected to the internet by 2020, leaping from 10 billion in 2015.[52] Consumers will be increasingly willing to adopt IoT devices in the near future. Further, the potential of IoT appears to be endless for marketers, enabling them to analyse consumers' buying habits and their interactions with the devices, to offer real-time services, and to cultivate quite personal relationships with consumers.[53]

Consumers' real-time information collected and delivered through the interactive devices will help communication practitioners develop relevant and targeted advertising messages that suit those consumers' current needs and contexts. One of the best examples of this is the potential for medical monitoring in the future using devices such as Fitbit. A consumer's health could potentially be monitored via basic medical monitoring enabling the consumer to take preventative actions well before encountering any serious health problems.

IoT also presents marketers with some challenges. Consumers *personally* own those devices, and, as such, their use of IoT is likely to be viewed as a personal activity. Hence, if unsolicited advertising messages are delivered through those personal IoT devices, the messages may be considered intrusive and irrelevant.[54] In this context, marketers must carefully assess their target consumers' needs and deliver contextually relevant and experientially unobtrusive messages in order to be perceived as useful and valuable by consumers. The focus should be on providing added value rather than hard-selling.[55] Another concern associated with IoT is consumer privacy. IoT requires consumer information, and while the information can be used to provide added value and customised services, many consumers are not aware of the types and amount of data collected through IoT and how those data are used.[56] In addition, some IoT devices transmit user data without proper protection, making consumers vulnerable to privacy risks.[57]

Virtual reality

Virtual reality (VR) is one of the latest and most promising technologies adopted by marketers. According to the Merriam-Webster dictionary, VR is defined as 'an artificial environment which is experienced through sensory stimuli (such as sights and sounds) provided by a computer and in which one's actions partially determine what happens in the environment'.[58] When it is used as a marketing tool, VR allows consumers to have immersive brand experiences by visualising how the brands will work and fit into a real or aspirational lifestyle. Marketers can also utilise VR to convey compelling brand stories (e.g. TOM's virtual giving trip[59]) and guide consumers to understand a product and experience it (e.g. Lexus Virtual Reality[60]).

Despite the great potential of VR in terms of user engagement, brand building and relationship cultivation, the high cost of VR equipment and production is considered a major stumbling block at this stage. However, consumer spending on VR entertainment is expected to grow. VR headset usage is expected to leap from 4 million in 2015 to 81 million in 2020.[61] As more players jump into the VR market, it is expected to become more affordable in the near future.

IMC IN ACTION: MARRIOTT'S VR CAMPAIGN, 'THE TELEPORTER'[62]

In 2014, Marriott Hotels installed two virtual reality booths in New York City. They looked like telephone booths but were equipped with Oculus Rift headsets, wireless headphones, scent dispensers, heaters and other devices to create sensations of 'exotic honeymoon destinations' (Figure 9.13). Putting on the headset, users were 'teleported' to Hawaiian beaches or downtown London for 100 seconds, feeling the texture of the ground on their feet, the moist breeze and the warmth.

In 2015, Marriott stepped forward by introducing an in-room virtual reality travel experience called 'VRoom Service'. Hotel guests can request a VRoom service to get a Samsung Gear VR

Figure 9.13 Marriott's 'Teleporter' booths

headset and headphone in their rooms (Figure 9.14). Using the VR set, guests are taken to a unique destination and follow a traveller, hearing the traveller's story about the importance of travelling. As Matthew Carroll, the vice-president of Marriott Hotels puts it, 'VRoom combines storytelling with technology, two things that are important to next generation travellers'.

Marriott's integration of VR into its marketing campaigns enabled Marriott to uniquely position itself as an innovative brand, helping the company to stand out in the market clutter.

Figure 9.14 A Marriott Hotels VRoom set

■ CHAPTER SUMMARY

This chapter has explained how the development of ESM changed consumer needs and behaviours as well as the ways marketers communicate with consumers. We learnt about the paradigm shifts that have occurred in marketing communications due to the evolution of digital technologies; key electronic and social media options that can now be used in contemporary marketing communication practices; challenges and critiques of new marketing communication practices incorporating electronic and social media marketing; and the future of digital and social marketing.

First, we described paradigm shifts in marketing communication due to the evolution of media technologies. During the early stage of internet adoption (Web 1.0), the usage of the Web for marketing communication was limited to one-way communication. However, Web 2.0 brought about the true evolution in that it has enabled consumers to actively participate in marketing communication processes through social media and user-generated content. Web 3.0 refers to the Web that incorporates advanced data analytic intelligence. In this paradigm, marketers can provide consumers with highly relevant and personalised communication using big data.

We then explained the role of digital and social media in IMC. In general, due to the introduction of electronic and social media, the paradigm of marketing communication has shifted from one-way communication to two-way communication. Before the introduction of EMS, consumers were passive recipients of marketing messages disseminated through mass media. However, with EMS, consumers became active creators and disseminators of information; this is important because they trust word-of-mouth recommendations more than advertisements directly from marketers.

Next we discussed different electronic and social media options. Below are some of the major electronic and social media options widely used in contemporary marketing practices.

- brand websites
- display advertising
- native advertising
- social media marketing
- mobile marketing.

We followed this with a critique of the current electronic and social media marketing communication practices. While ESM provides new and rich opportunities for marketing communication, we outlined the issues to consider in incorporating ESM components into an IMC strategy.

Finally, we touched on the likely future developments in electronic and social media. Big data, the Internet of Things (IoT), and virtual reality (VR) represent three key emerging trends in ESM that are expected to have significant impacts on the future of marketing communication. Big data and IoT will enable marketers to gain more sophisticated and deeper insights into consumer interests, thereby helping them to develop highly effective and personalised communication strategies. VR can be included in an IMC mix to create a unique and immersive experience with a brand or a product.

Case study: Marketing to digital kids[63]

Wonsun Shin and Hyunjin Kang

Marketers pay close attention to young consumers for many reasons. First, with declining birth rates, smaller family sizes and an increasing number of dual-income households, today's kids tend to become autonomous and influential consumers at an earlier age than previous generations. Additionally, as influencers, children substantially affect the purchase and consumption decisions of adult family members (e.g. their parents). Kids are also capable of using various persuasion techniques, from begging and pestering to bargaining and negotiating with their parents in order to pursue their consumption desires.

For marketers targeting young consumers, new media offer unprecedented opportunities. Children and teenagers have access to numerous forms of screen media,[64] and they spend substantial time engaging in multiple media activities.[65] Australian teenagers use a range of devices, including computers (91 per cent), mobile phones (78 per cent) and tablets (39 per cent) to access the internet, and half of them access the internet with two different devices.[66] In Singapore, nine-years-olds spend more than 24 hours a week, or about three and a half hours daily, on electronic devices.[67] As they do so, children and teenagers are exposed to a wide range of advertising messages, including TV commercials, online advertising and mobile marketing.[68] Marketers actively harness new media platforms to reach and appeal to young consumers.

1 Cradle-to-grave marketing: ToyToyota's 'Backseat Driver' (2011)[69]

Marketers recognise that children today represent the adult consumers of tomorrow. Some marketers specifically target kids with the hope that they will become loyal consumers of their companies'

products for life. This strategy is called *cradle-to-grave marketing*. Toyota, a Japanese car brand, sees the potential to tap into young consumer segments in precisely this way.

In 2011, ToyToyota, a toy brand from Toyota, launched a mobile game app called 'Backseat Driver.' Once children launch the application in an actual car, their virtual car in the app drives along with the real car. This iPhone app[70] enables children to enjoy driving from the backseat of the car by

Figure 9.15 ToyToyota's Backseat Driver app

using the phone's GPS to track the road ahead. Actual landmarks, buildings and stores appear on the virtual route, and if the children make the correct turns and collect objects along the road as the car advances, they can earn points and use them to customise their virtual car. Kids can share their customised cars and travel routes on Twitter. The applications were downloaded more than 100 000 times, and the brand enjoyed global publicity as a result.

2 Targeting kids and parents: Target's 'Holiday Wish List' (2014)[71]

Target, a US-based discount store retailer, wanted to transform traditional wish-list print catalogues into a multichannel wish-list experience. This campaign, called 'Holiday Wish List', is a dual-target campaign, targeting two different but related consumer segments: kids—digital natives, who are already familiar with mobile devices and technologies—and their millennial parents, who are budget-sensitive and highly mobile.

The brand launched a game-like mobile app where kids were invited to Target' 'Toy Factory' and could build their wish lists for the holiday season and send the lists to Santa. The virtual factory featured 3D-animated rooms, user-generated avatar characters, drag-and-drop wish lists and a letter to Santa. The app also included an augmented reality function for in-store wish-list making. Parents could access their children's wish lists and share them with their friends and family. When a friend or family member purchased items on the lists, the lists were automatically updated. The applications were downloaded about 75 000 times, more than 100 000 wish lists were created, and more than one million page visits were generated to Target.com.

Figure 9.16 Target's 'Holiday Wish List' app

Source: Target Facebook www.facebook.com/target/photos/a.1275428081 19.106243.8103318119/10152879789308120

3 Engaging with teen consumers using social influencers and multimedia: Coca-Cola's '#ThatsGold' campaign (2016)[72]

For the 2016 Rio Olympics, Coca-Cola launched a global IMC campaign, '#ThatsGold'. The goal of the campaign was to encourage teenagers and millennials aged 13 to 20 to share their 'gold moments'. As Coca-Cola's Vice-President of Global Creative said: 'Gold is a feeling anyone can taste … from passing an exam, to getting your Dad's car keys for the first time, to celebrating a friend's birthday—anything can be a gold moment as long as it's spontaneous and authentic … They can happen every day and all around the world'. This multiplatform campaign reached consumers in 50 countries and incorporated television and print advertisements, social media such as Facebook and Instagram, torch-bearing events and global social influencers.

The campaign began with a series of TV commercials and print advertisements (see Figure 9.17) featuring famous Olympic athletes from 23 countries and their golden medal moments. The TV commercials ended with the tagline, 'Gold is a feeling anyone can taste'. The footage of those advertisements was also posted on the brand's digital media platforms, encouraging consumers to spread the word and share their own golden moments through social media. The brand also sponsored the Olympics' Torch Relay, featuring its presence in 320 cities around the world.

The highlight of this campaign was its use of social influencers. To spread '#ThatsGold' across the world, and more importantly, to appeal to teenagers and millennials, the brand partnered with

Figure 9.17 #That'sGold's print advertisement

Source: www.adweek.com/brand-marketing/coca-cola-celebrates-gold-medal-moments-campaign-rio-olympics-172485/

young social influencers from different countries who had massive social media audiences, including Australian singer/songwriter Cody Simpson, Radio Disney host Alli Simpson, British YouTube star Jake Boys, and Brazilian social media personality Lucas Rangel. According to the Coca-Cola Company, these social influencers were selected based on the size of their global audience, their love of Coca-Cola and their passion for the Olympic Games. The selected social influencers produced and distributed their Olympic Game experiences using the official hashtag #ThatsGold through their own social media platforms such as Facebook, Instagram, Twitter and Snapchat, as well as the brand's owned media channels. They also participated in the brand's branding activities during the Olympics. For instance, two of the social influencers, Cody and Alli Simpson, who are siblings from Australia, carried the Olympic torch in Rio (Figure 9.18). Alli Simpson shared this moment with her 1.7 million Instagram, 1.5 million Twitter and 1.1 million Facebook followers. The story was also covered by local and international news. The full story and her posting can be found on the brand's website[73].

The campaign was successful. According to *Campaign US*, the campaign reached its target group of 13 to 20-year-olds, encouraging them to engage in brand conversation using social influencers and various digital and social media platforms. This campaign also helped the brand achieve the most mentioned Olympic Advertiser spot in 2016.

Figure 9.18 Australian social influencers Cody and Alli Simpson carried the Olympic torches

As these three cases illustrate, digital media can be very effective in reaching and appealing to young consumers. Current marketing practices targeting young consumers using digital media, however, have also raised concerns among parents and consumer advocate groups. In many cases, the line between promotional messages and non-commercial content often blurs, lowering children's persuasion knowledge and making them vulnerable to the persuasive intention of marketers. For instance, branded environments provided by online, social and mobile media, such as kid-friendly websites and virtual worlds, often blend commercial and non-commercial content. This practice is less likely to activate cognitive defence mechanisms in children.

In addition, some marketers try to collect personal information from children. In social media environments, 'sharing' and disclosing' have become social norms, making young consumers less critical about privacy issues.

Older consumers, such as teenagers and young adults, may be less vulnerable to such influences. However, research shows that the use of consumption-related social networking sites among young adults is positively associated with materialistic values.[74] That is, young consumers' exposure to marketing messages on social media can lead them to be more materialistic, which studies have shown to be negatively associated with the feeling of happiness.

Questions

1. What do you think about cradle-to-grave marketing?
2. Why do some marketers target both children and parents?
3. Do you think marketers should take different approaches to appeal to different groups of young consumers (e.g. children vs. teenagers)? How would you utilise different ESM platforms to target different age groups and why?
4. What can marketers do to tackle the social and ethical issues related to digital marketing directed at children?

Case study: Hashtag #12banner – How to Develop a Supercharged Social Media Campaign

Sven Tuzovic

The Super Bowl is one of the most televised sporting events in the world. Over the last decade it has become almost as famous for its commercials as the game itself. During the broadcast of the Super Bowl some of the world's biggest brands pay huge amounts (a 30-second advertisement costs up to US $5 million) to reach a large audience of more than 110 million viewers nationwide. In 2014, the Seahawks, a professional American football franchise based in Seattle, qualified for Super Bowl XLIII in New York City. So how does a local Seattle-based insurance company seize the global Super Bowl opportunity and create a highly engaged and viral social media marketing campaign, generating massive buzz and earning national media coverage? … By dreaming big and acting fast.

The Company

PEMCO Insurance Company is a regional insurance company based in Seattle, Washington. Founded in 1949, the company provides auto, home, and boat insurance coverage to customers in the northwest states of Washington and Oregon. The acronym PEMCO stands for 'Public Employees Mutual Insurance Company.' The company which is owned by the policy holders has won the prestigious J.D. Power Award for 'Highest Customer Satisfaction among Auto Insurers in the Northwest Region' for six straight years. Major competitors of PEMCO include Allstate, GEICO, Progressive, Nationwide, State Farm Insurance, and Liberty Mutual Insurance. For more than a decade PEMCO has been known for understanding the personalities of its local audience and creating quirky, yet memorable marketing campaigns. In 2007, PEMCO launched a lighthearted marketing theme ('We're A Lot Like You. A Little Different') highlighting unique Northwestern personality types. The goal was to connect local Northwest values to PEMCO that could not be matched by its national competitors. The company created 'Northwest Profiles Trading Cards' to be used in guerilla marketing efforts and local events. PEMCO's special microsite now features more than 70 different profiles, encouraging consumers to upload photos of their friends and neighbors and suggesting their own Northwest Type.

The Opportunity

In football the term '12th Man' (or 12th player) is commonly used to refer to the fans. During the 2013 NFL season, fan enthusiasm for the Seahawks grew to new record heights. Flags with the number 12 were flying all over the city of Seattle, including the Space Needle, Starbucks headquarters, construction cranes, and houses and offices. Furthermore, the Seahawks 12th Man set twice the Guinness World Record in 2013 for the loudest stadium during a sporting event (reaching more than 137 decibels). As a longtime Seahawks partner, PEMCO was highly aware of how passionate its audience is about the Seattle Seahawks. For example, its Northwest Profile #12 has been dedicated to the "Supercharged Seahawks Fan" encouraging fans for several seasons to showcase their team spirit. When the Seahawks qualified for the Super Bowl, PEMCO knew it had a one-time marketing opportunity: to tap into the passion and energy of the team's vocal fans and to get the brand name out on a global stage.

The Supercharged Campaign

PEMCO decided to act BIG, literally. They conceived the idea to fly a giant 100 x 40 foot '12' flag with 12,000 signatures of Seahawks fans over New York City and the Super Bowl venue, the MetLife Stadium. But PEMCO had only a few days to solve a number of technical and logistical challenges. Recognizing the limitations of time and geography, PEMCO offered fans the option to either sign the banner in person at a dozen different signing events or to submit their signature digitally. To support the signature collection landing pages were designed that were mobile friendly and responsive regardless of the device. PEMCO also had to spread the word, and it relied on both its strong online presence and the effective use of social media (including Facebook, Twitter, and Instagram). Moreover, the event team established an associated hashtag (#12banner) on social media sites.

The Results

The results of this campaign were remarkable. PEMCO collected more than 15,000 signatures in five days. Within hours of the launch, the hashtag #12banner was trending on Twitter in Seattle. On Instagram the picture of the banner flying above the Statue of Liberty received 30,000 likes. In addition to the word of mouth effects, PEMCO earned vast media coverage from both local and national TV, radio, newspapers and numerous blogs. Overall, the campaign led to more than one million social impressions, an earned reach of 16 500 000, earned media value of $105 000, and an increase in website visitors of 600%. In summary, PEMCO gained national awareness while winning the hearts of consumers in its local target market. All this without spending a ridiculous amount of money for a single 30-second Super Bowl ad.

Conclusion

How was PEMCO able to achieve this success? First, PEMCO's culture is conducive to 'dream big' and act quickly ('Ready, Fire, Aim, Adjust'). Second, the company has a strong foundation of customer knowledge which allowed PEMCO to effectively engage its audience. And third, PEMCO has successfully implemented an integrated strategy of its marketing communication, including in-person events, social media, public relations, and mobile marketing. The company knows how to use multiple channels and to sync them in the most effective manner. And in 2014, PEMCO did it all over again, even bigger, with 48 000 signatures and 24 000 photos from all over the world.

Questions

1. Explain the different types of technical and logistical challenges that PEMCO faced in creating and executing this campaign.
2. Explain how PEMCO was able to engage with its audience and collect more than 15 000 signatures in less than a week.

....

References

Cohen, S. (2014, January 24), "Huge banner, fan signatures to fly over Seattle Seahawks in Super Bowl," Seattle PI, https://blog.seattlepi.com/football/2014/01/24/huge-banner-fan-signatures-to-fly-over-seattle-seahawks-in-super-bowl/

Drosendahl, G. (2014, February 24), "Seattle Seahawks win Super Bowl in a rout on February 2, 2014," HistoryLink.org Essay 10730, http://historylink.org/File/10730

Hunt, J. (2018), "PEMCO Insurance Company Review," The Balance, https://www.thebalance.com/pemco-insurance-company-review-1969904

Morris, H. (2014), "WOMMortunity: The Power of 12," WOMMA, https://womma.org/wommortunity-the-power-of-12/

PEMCO (2018), "Six-Cess! PEMCO Insurance wins J.D. Power Award for the sixth year in a row," PR Newswire, https://www.prnewswire.com/news-releases/six-cess-pemco-insurance-wins-jd-power-award-for-the-sixth-year-in-a-row-300674161.html.

Tuzovic, S. and Brooks, R. (2013), "'I Love PEMCO' – Creating Conversation Worthy Buzz in the Insurance Industry with Word of Mouth Marketing," in Dienstleistungsmanagement und Social Media. Potenziale, Strategien und Instrumente. Forum Dienstleistungsmanagement, by Manfred Bruhn and Karsten Hadwich (Eds.), Springer Gabler, Wiesbaden, 593-610.

Wax Marketing (2015), "IMC Campaign of the Month: PEMCO's #12," Wax Marketing Blog, https://www.waxmarketing.com/imc-campaign-of-the-month-pemcos-12/

Dr Sven Tuzovic is Senior Lecturer of Marketing at QUT Business School, Brisbane

Case study: When I grow up, I want to be 'Instafamous'

Lara Stocchi

Once upon a time there was a beautiful princess, who met a handsome prince. The princess wore custom-made haute couture gowns and designer handbags. She went on glamorous trips across the world with her prince, who was a talented singer and songwriter. The princess and the prince were loved by many people, and did many great things. For example, the princess had her own fashion label and worked endlessly on many business projects. The prince was a respected TV personality who made music his life. One fine day, they decided to get married and brands rushed to celebrate with them their special day, which they shared with the all the people who followed them in a beautiful palace called Instagram. It was a joyous day filled with love and they then lived happily ever after.

Figure 9.19 Chiara Ferragni and Fedez

Source: https://www.instagram.com/p/BnMVJUNHHpX/?utm_source=ig_
embed&utm_campaign=embed_loading_state_control

This modern fairy tale is, in fact, a colourful description of the chronicles of Chiara Ferragni, an Italian web influencer and entrepreneur who has quickly become an international fashion icon, starting from her blog called 'The Blond Salad' and thanks to several ongoing collaborations with many global brands. In September 2018, Chiara married musician Fedez (at birth, Federico Leonardo Lucia) in a dreamlike setting in the beautiful Sicilian town of Noto. Chiara and Federico are truly 'Instagram royalty' and reach millions of people globally (on Instagram, Chiara has over 15 million followers and Federico has more than 7 million followers). Their beautiful wedding involved countless collaborations with prestigious brands, including the likes of Lancôme, Dior, Prada, Alberta Ferretti and Alitalia. Online analytics by specialised companies such as LaunchMetrics (see https://www.launchmetrics.com/resources/blog/

chiara-ferragni-fedez-wedding) mentioned that their wedding, a three-day event that was publicised primarily through the hashtag #TheFerragnez, generated significant media impact and sparked millions of interactions worth approximately $36 million. The high-calibre brands involved benefited greatly from the event, obtaining incredible buzz and online engagement on a global scale. For example, the luxury brand Dior tallied 5.6 million interactions worth $5.2 million, 30% of which was estimated to originate from Chiara's posts of her two custom-made Dior wedding gowns. As LaunchMetrics reports, these figures were comparatively greater than the results obtained by brands involved in the actual royal wedding of HRH Prince Harry earlier in 2018.

This modern fairy tale must sound very familiar to the marketers of this decade, who would be courting and worshipping web influencers and fighting for them (literally) to secure multiple (paid) 'advertising channels' that did not exist 12 or six months ago. Non-media connectors, social media or web influencers, social media celebrities and people like the metaphorical 'royal' couple of Chiara Ferragni and Fedez are often labelled in different ways. There have also been attempts to discern nuances of influence, distinguishing between mega-influencers (celebrities), macro-influencers (social media celebrities, bloggers, thought leaders etc.), everyday or micro-influencers and ordinary brand advocates – see below. Regardless, consensus is starting to emerge around the fact that influencers represent a very common 'new' and very direct advertising and branding channel. This is in spite of the fact that a career as a full-time influencer is most certainly on the list of jobs that did not exist 10 years ago.

Figure 9.20 The Pyramid of Influence

Source: https://starngage.com/influencer-marketing-australia/

With the rapid growth of a variety of social media platforms, where information and content sharing can occur seamlessly and independently from traditional broadcast media (TV or press), it would be naïve to experience any sense of surprise in relation to the increasing relevance and prominence of influencers as a method to attain marketing communications' objectives. Arguably, besides the obvious advantages in terms of reaching wide audiences globally and facilitating a high degree of engagement, a key reason why leveraging influencers in the context of digital marketing strategies is the unique 'cocktail' of endorsement, product placement, PR and sponsorship. Unlike non-digital media and, to a great extent, even unlike many opportunities that the Web 2.0 has offered so far, there is no plot twist. There is only an army of followers consuming a disproportionate amount of digital content constantly, every day of their lives.

While you are reading this case study, the odds are you have already scrolled endlessly through your social media feeds on your smart device, more than once. A lot of the content we access and peruse is, in fact, markedly branded one way or another. It is also no longer presented to us exclusively by people that we know. In most instances, we access this content through people who we do not know personally, but we follow on social media and the web for a variety of reasons. The endorsement of brands and products by these people is in itself a powerful way to acquire information, which makes the transferring of a marketing message more straightforward then in conventional media. At the same time, we witness the lifestyles of influencers as portrayed by their choices of brands, their entrepreneurial and artistic ventures and even their daily habits. This often turns into a vicarious experience, which at the very least should spark some perceptions, inevitably feeding into the beliefs that we have as consumers.

Brands that establish collaborations and partnerships with influencers are unsurprisingly making the most of this unique way to reach many consumers. In fact, brands might also enjoy greater opportunities for targeting, by simply observing and scouring down the digital persona of the influencers that they choose to collaborate with. At the same time, the world of web and social analytics is able to return some evaluations of the impact of campaigns run through social media quite easily, linking results also with other aspects of digital marketing strategies and leading to a much-desired holistic campaign assessment. The recipe seems to work for brands of different calibre, as the results mentioned earlier for global luxury brand Dior would suggest.

Questions

1. On the basis of the content of this brief case study, do you think that influencers could be a 'new' way to gain control over the diffusion of a marketing message for the purpose of strategic brand development?

2. Imagine that you are the brand manager for an online retailer selling casual and smart clothes at affordable prices, targeting younger consumers. Do some research on social media platforms and find at least two influencers who could be good ambassadors for your retailer. Why did you pick these two influencers? How would you outline the collaboration with them – i.e. what would you ask them to do and what would you offer in return?

3. Would you argue that collaborations with influencers should be high on the agenda of branding and communication strategies for all sorts of organisations?

4. Can you think of any potential pitfall or risk in including collaborations with influencers in the context of a digital marketing strategy?

5. The case study refers to influencers as 'advertising channels'. To what extent is this true and, in contrast, to what extent is this also likely to be untrue?

Practitioner profile: Reese Masita

Social Media Queen, Social Media Machine

Reese Masita is the Social Media Queen at Social Media Machine, having previously studied political science and international business at Brigham Young University in Hawaii. With an extensive and diverse background, Reese has held roles in corporate, community and not-for-profit organisations. Reese is a determined strategist who is committed to empowering change by influencing strong values that deepen audience connections.

Reese is deeply passionate about social media and is dedicated to helping businesses develop, manage and measure social media programs, monitor their online reputation and develop sustainable brands in an ever increasingly complex media landscape. Reese has successfully created social communities through developing strong vision and purpose, linked with an exceptional ability to tell compelling stories about brands.

Describe your current role and your organisation, and give a brief account of what you do in your role on a day-to-day basis.

As one of the founders, I helped create Social Media Machine with the vision of helping businesses build, engage and amplify the social media presence of their brands. My role extends across every aspect of the agency from managing social media marketing campaigns and activities, including developing relevant content topics to reach the company's target customers; creating, curating and managing all published content to account management; business development; and providing guidance to the team.

How important is Integrated Marketing Communication (IMC) to what you and your organisation do?

Every brand requires a blueprint outlining its overarching strategies and ultimate purpose. The plan is a vital element in outlining where the business positions itself, how it communicates, how it represents itself, what its products and services are and what differentiates it from others in the market place. Having a clear vision ensures that we have an effective marketing roadmap to implement on social media.

What types of promotional tools do you use in your IMC campaigns? Please provide examples.

Being solely focused on social media we develop campaigns around business objectives and vanity metrics, such as 'Like', 'Follow', 'Engagement', 'Share', 'Register' and 'Book now' campaigns and so on. We use social advertising to achieve KPIs based on the premise of being where the customers are. By posting fresh content online, the aim is to help businesses grow through consistency, on brand visibility, effective ad setup, execution and optimisation. If customers like a business, they will buy from and stay loyal to the business.

What would your ideal social media campaign look like and why?

It would be a carefully developed plan that is specific and fits into the overall IMC and social media strategy to improve on a brand's existing social voice and style. It thoroughly understands existing followers, includes budget and identifies the metrics that are used to measure the success and return on investment of the campaign. It has clearly defined goals, whether it's brand awareness, driving more traffic to websites, inspiring visitor loyalty or improving conversion rates. It has cross-channel promotion opportunities as part of IMC where the efforts of social media are supported on a number of other channels and touch points. While this makes it difficult to measure the overall success, the outcomes are aimed at the ultimate goals with achievable KPIs to determine output.

What has been your favourite social media campaign to work on and did it achieve its objectives?

We had a flagship event to promote to an enthusiastic and highly engaged audience. It was a major sporting event with elite athletes participating from all over the world. The opportunity to promote our client was hugely successful to the extent where its reach and coverage went worldwide and made for a 'totally amped' style of social media promotion. The information about the athletes was drip fed to the followers via social media and the audience 'lapped' it up. The engagement statistics for the event went through the roof, brand awareness was phenomenal and traffic was driven to a landing page that was especially created for the event. The campaign exceeded its objectives and the event was a huge success.

What impact do you think a social media campaign has on word-of-mouth and how does this affect the consumer decision-making process?

Social media marketing is akin to word-of-mouth marketing on steroids. By facilitating social interactions between businesses and customers, loyal customers create brand awareness for the business through 'social proof'. Consumers believe recommendations from friends and family over all forms of advertising because of trust. With the advent of interactive and social media platforms the patterns, forums and opportunities for word-of-mouth have evolved completely, enabling conversations to have broader reach and influence. These changes have created more impactful ways for businesses to leverage the power of word-of-mouth for marketing purposes by creating social communities around brands.

Which social media platforms do you believe are most effective at creating a social buzz? Please provide examples.

Facebook has become the world's biggest virtual shopping centre. With over 2 billion users and 1.32 billion daily active users it is the most effective 'buzz starter' by far. Twitter is becoming more and better utilised for blasting out promotions and other media. With its short and succinct style it facilitates witty conversations about brands and direct access from consumer to business and vice versa. Instagram is still best used as a brand-building tool if a business can build its following by providing beautiful images or videos. However, if you plan to use it as a marketing tool, it requires a highly strategic plan to fully capitalise.

What are some of the challenges you face in social media marketing?

The continuing decline of organic reach

To keep users on the medium and engaged, social channels use algorithms to boost or weed out posts, in order to only display the content that is relevant, performing well and potentially most interesting to the user. Facebook is pay-for-play for businesses, brands and public figures which can be frustrating for marketers trying to build and maintain organic growth.

Creating an effective cross-channel strategy

Multichannel strategies can be challenging because each channel has its own format and tone that dictates how your content should fit. Understanding the target audience for each channel and modifying appropriate content presence is innate with challenges because campaigns that perform well on one social media platform may not on another.

Proving ROI

An eternal challenge for social media marketers is how to quantify and prove the value of what they do for their client. Vanity metrics are not enough and it is a constant challenge to social marketers to deliver on business goals. Measuring and proving ROI, or determining which specific customer behaviour contributed to a conversion is difficult. Vanity metrics can be considered not valuable if they don't link directly to revenue, even though it represents a significant increase in brand awareness.

What advice would you offer a student studying IMC on incorporating social media into a campaign?

Social media is a vital marketing and communication channel as well as a valuable source of collating customer intel and data. Social media should be integrated into your IMC plan in the following ways:

1. *Use social media for market research.* An IMC plan should include a qualitative and quantitative market research section. These sections provide information about who your target audience is and offer guidance on strategy and tactics.

2. *Use social media to drive public relations.* Speed and relevance on topical issues is key in PR, and with social media you are able to get a comment out within minutes of news breaking.

3 *Use social media to advertise.* Advertising has changed dramatically in the past five years. In the short amount of time social media advertising has been around, it has proven to be the best 'bang' for advertising buck by being the cheapest and most effective method of reaching out to and engaging with the intended audience. With the ability to specifically target your audience, easily measure your social media advertising reach, and quickly make changes to your ads, it's no surprise that advertising on social media is taking an ever-increasing chunk of the advertising pie.

4. *Use social media analytics to report on your IMC plan.* There are plenty of ways you can report on your IMC plan, but with the rise of social media analytics tools, it's important to include the data found in these platforms. Pull data on how many people you reached, how many people went to your website via your social media content, with an ability to predict and understand the kind of communication that resonates with your audience.

Key terms

augmented reality (AR)	interactivity	social media marketing
banner advertising	Internet of Things (IoT)	user-generated content
behavioural targeting	interstitial	Virtual Reality (VR)
big data	location intelligence	Web 1.0
brochureware	mobile marketing	Web 2.0
click-through rate	rich media	Web 3.0
crowdsourcing	personalisation	webrooming
digital video advertising	showrooming	word of mouth
display advertising	social buzz	
information age	social media	

Revision questions

1. What are the key differences between Web 1.0 and Web 2.0?
2. How would you describe consumers in the twenty-first century? How are they different from consumers 30 years ago?
3. What makes a successful user-generated content campaign? Find a few examples of user-generated content campaigns and identify factors associated with their success.
4. How can marketers harness Web 3.0 technologies and the Internet of Things (IoT) to achieve different marketing objectives?
5. What makes a good brand website and why? Describe an 'ideal' brand website.
6. Have you come across creative and/or effective display advertisements? Describe the advertisements and explain why you think they are creative/effective.
7. Critics argue that native advertising can fool consumers by blurring the line between advertising and non-commercial content, concealing the persuasive intent and consequently lowering consumers' defences and persuasion knowledge. Do you agree with this argument? Why? Why not?
8. Do you remember any social media marketing practices? What kinds of practices are effective/not effective? Why?
9. Do you think social media and mobile marketing can completely replace marketing communication through mass media? Why or why not?
10. What are the benefits of mobile marketing for a) marketers and b) consumers?
11. What are the key challenges in current online, social and mobile marketing practices? What would you do to overcome those challenges?

12. What is virtual reality (VR)? How can it be used in IMC campaigns? How do you see the future of VR over the next 10 years?

13. Suppose you have to introduce a new brand to a foreign market, where almost no one knows your company and the brand. Also, imagine you have to launch a crowdsourcing campaign for a well-known brand in your country, targeting consumers who already know your brand. How would you use various electronic and social media in each situation? What would be your objectives and metrics for ROI?

Further reading

Boyd, D. & Ellison, N. B. (2007). Social network sites: definition, history, and scholarship. *Journal of Computer-Mediated Communication, 13*(1), pp. 210–30.

Gouillart, F. (2012). Co-creation: the real social-media revolution, *Harvard Business Review*. https://hbr.org/2012/12/co-creation-the-real-social-me

Hanna R., Rohm, A. & Crittenden, V. L. (2011). We're all connected: the power of the social media ecosystem. *Business Horizons, 54*(3), 265–73.

Hoffman, D. L. & Fodor, M. (2010). Can you measure the ROI of your social media marketing?, *Sloan Management Review, 52*(1), 41–9.

Kumar, V. & Gupta S. (2016). Conceptualizing the evolution and future of advertising, *Journal of Advertising, 45*(3), 302–17.

Metzger, M. J. (2007). Communication privacy management in electronic commerce, *Journal of Computer-Mediated Communication, 12*(2), 335–61.

Rudman, R. & Bruwer, R. (2016). Defining Web 3.0: opportunities and challenges, *The Electronic Library, 34*(1), 132–54.

Wojdynki, B. W. & Evans, N. (2016). Going native: Effects of disclosure position and language on the recognition and evaluation of online native advertising, *Journal of Advertising, 45*(2), 157–68.

Weblinks

Associations

Association for Data-driven Marketing and Advertising (ADMA): https://www.adma.com.au/

Australian Association of Social Marketing (AASM): http://www.aasm.org.au/

Global Virtual Reality Association: https://www.gvra.com/

Interactive Advertising Bureau (IAB): https://www.iab.com/

Interactive Advertising Bureau (IAB) Australia: https://www.iabaustralia.com.au/

Mobile Marketing Association (MMA): http://www.mmaglobal.com/

Web Marketing Association (WMA): http://www.webmarketingassociation.org/wma/

Awards

Cannes Lions International Festival of Creativity: https://www.canneslions.com/

Effie Awards: https://www.effie.org/

IAB Mixx Awards: http://mixxawards.iab.com/

The Advertising Research Foundation (ARF) David Ogilvy Awards: https://thearf.org/2017-arf-david-ogilvy-awards/

The Facebook Awards: https://www.facebookawards.com/

The Internet Advertising Competition Awards: http://www.iacaward.org/iac/

The Mashies Awards: http://mashable.com/mashies/

The Webby Awards: http://www.webbyawards.com/

Academic journals

Business Horizon: https://www.journals.elsevier.com/business-horizons

Computers in Human Behavior: https://www.journals.elsevier.com/computers-in-human-behavior

Cyberpsychology, Behavior, and Social Networking: http://www.liebertpub.com/overview/cyberpsychology-behavior-and-social-networking/10/

International Journal of Mobile Communications: http://www.inderscience.com/jhome.php?jcode=IJMC

Journal of Broadcasting and Electronic Media: http://www.tandfonline.com/loi/hbem20

Journal of Interactive Advertising: http://www.tandfonline.com/loi/ujia20

Journal of Interactive Marketing: https://www.journals.elsevier.com/journal-of-interactive-marketing/

Mobile Media & Communication: https://au.sagepub.com/en-gb/oce/journal/mobile-media-communication

New Media & Society: http://journals.sagepub.com/home/nms

Trade magazines/ESM industry news

Advertising Age Digital Marketing News: http://adage.com/channel/digital/20

Advertising Age Viral Video Chart: http://adage.com/section/the-viral-video-chart/674

Adweek—Digital: http://www.adweek.com/tag/Digital/

Campaign Asia: http://www.campaignasia.com/

eMarketer: https://www.emarketer.com/

Marketing Land: http://marketingland.com/

Mashable: http://mashable.com/

Media Post: https://www.mediapost.com/

Pew Research Center—Internet & Technology: http://www.pewinternet.org/

Social Media Today: http://www.socialmediatoday.com/

Techcrunch: https://techcrunch.com/

We Are Social: https://wearesocial.com/

Regulatory sites

Australian Communications and Media Authority—Staying Safe Online: http://www.acma.gov.au/Citizen/Internet/esecurity/Staying-safe-online

Australian Competition & Consumer Commission—Social Media: https://www.accc.gov.au/business/advertising-promoting-your-business/social-media

Australian Competition and Consumer Act 2010: http://www.austlii.edu.au/au/legis/cth/consol_act/caca2010265/

Office of Australian Information Commissioner—Mobile Privacy: A better practice guide for mobile app developers: https://www.oaic.gov.au/agencies-and-organisations/guides/guide-for-mobile-app-developers

Notes

1 Power Review. (2016). New study finds that retailers and brands can leverage reviews to compete with Amazon and Search. www.powerreviews.com/blog/new-study-finds-that-retailers-and-brands-can-leverage-reviews-to-compete-with-amazon-and-search/

2 Smith, A. & Anderson, M. (2016). Pew Research Center Online Shopping and E-Commerce: Online Reviews www.pewinternet.org/2016/12/19/online-reviews/

3 Nielson. (2015). Global trust in advertising. www.nielsen.com/content/dam/nielsenglobal/apac/docs/reports/2015/nielsen-global-trust-in-advertising-report-september-2015.pdf

4 Aghaei, S., Nematbakhsh, M. A. & Farsani, H. K. (2012). Evolution of the World Wide Web: from Web 1.0 to Web 4.0. *International Journal of Web & Sematic Technology*, 3, 1–10.

5 Wasserman, T. (2013). This is the world's first banner ad. http://mashable.com/2013/08/09/first-banner-ad/#NM8stKPQTiqU

6 Tuten, T. L. (2008). Advertising 2.0: Social media marketing in a Web 2.0 world. Westport, CT, Praeger.

7 Aghaei et al., op. cit.; Gangadharatla, H. (2012). Social media and advertising theory. In E. T. S. L. Rodgers (ed.). *Advertising Theory*. New York: Routkedge.

8 Tuten, op. cit.

9 Schultz, E. J. (2007). How 'Crash the Super Bowl' Changed Advertising, http://adage.com/article/special-report-super-bowl/crash-super-bowl-changed-advertising/301966/; AdAge. (2007). Doritos—Live the Flavor, http://adage.com/videos/doritos-live-the-flavor/577; Pepsico. (2015). Doritos Brand Announces Semifinalist Ads in the Final 'Crash the Super Bowl' Contest, www.pepsico.com/live/pressrelease/doritos-brand-announces-semifinalist-ads-in-the-final-crash-the-super-bowl-conte12012015

10 Rudman, R. & Bruwer, R. (2016). Defining Web 3.0: opportunities and challenges. *The Electronic Library*, 34, 132–54.

11 Kumar, V. & Gupta, S. (2016). Conceptualizing the evolution and future of advertising. *Journal of Advertising*, 45, 302–17.

12 www.adobe.com/au

13 Shin, W., Pang, A. & Kim, H. J. (2015). Building relationships through integrated online media: global organizations' use of brand web sites, Facebook, and Twitter. *Journal of Business and Technical Communication*, 29, 184–220.

14 Interactive Advertising Bureau. (2015). Display & mobile advertising creative format guidelines. www.iab.com/wp-content/uploads/2015/11/IAB_Display_Mobile_Creative_Guidelines_HTML5_2015.pdf

15 Interactive Advertising Bureau. (n.d.). IAB guidelines—universal ad package (UAP). www.iab.com/guidelines/universal-ad-package

16 Li, H. & Leckenby, J. D. (2007). Examining the effectiveness of internet advertising formats. In D. W. Schumann & E. Thorson, (eds). *Internet Advertising*. Mahwah, New Jersey: LEA.

17 Spalding, L., Cole, S. & Fayer, A. (2009). How rich-media video technology boosts branding goals: Different online advertising formats drive different brand-performance metrics. *Journal of Advertising Research*, 49, 285–92.

18 Li & Leckenby, op. cit.

19 ibid.

20 Interactive Advertising Bureau. (2016). 2016 IAB Video Ad Spend Study. www.iab.com/wp-content/uploads/2016/04/2016-IAB-Video-Ad-Spend-Study.pdf

21 Gesenhues, A. (2015). Online Vs. TV: 72% Of Agencies Say Online Video Ads Are As Effective—Or More Effective—Than TV. http://marketingland.com/online-vs-tv-72-agencies-say-online-video-ads-effective-effective-tv-survey-118854

22 Marketing Land. (2016). Native advertising, the new marketing workhorse. http://marketingland.com/native-advertising-new-marketing-workhorse-197856

23 ibid.; Okenski, S. (2015). 6 Types Of Native Advertising And How Each Can Benefit Your Business. www.forbes.com/sites/steveolenski/2015/11/12/6-types-of-native-advertising-and-how-each-can-benefit-your-business/#125315ed4455

24 Boland, M. (2016). Native Ads Will Drive 74% of All Ad Revenue by 2012. www.businessinsider.com/the-native-ad-report-forecasts-2016-5?r=US&IR=T&IR=T

25 Taylor, C. R. (2017). Native advertising: The black sheet of the marketing family. *International Journal of Advertising*, 36, 207–09.

26 Kaplan, A. M. & Haenlein, M. 2010. Users of the world, unite! The challenges and opportunities of Social Media. *Business Horizons*, 53, 59–68.

27 We Are Social. (2017). Digital in 2017: Global Overview. https://wearesocial.com/sg/blog/2017/01/digital-in-2017-global-overview

28 Globalwebindex. (2017). GWI Social: GlobalWebIndex's Quarterly Report on the latest trends in social networking. http://insight.globalwebindex.net/hubfs/Reports/Social-Q1-2017/GWI-Social-Summary-Q1-2017.pdf?t=1498055538457

29 www.brandwatch.com

30 analytics.google.com

31 Coloribus. (n.d.). Tag the weather, www.coloribus.com/adsarchive/directmarketing/gillette-venus-tag-the-weather-18485705/

32 We Are Social, op. cit.

33 Emarketer. (2015). Mobile Will Account for 72% of US Digital Ad Spend by 2019. www.emarketer.com/Article/Mobile-Will-Account-72-of-US-Digital-Ad-Spend-by-2019/1012258

34 Mobile Marketing Association. (n.d.). MMA Glossary: Mobile Marketing. www.mmaglobal.com/wiki/mma-glossary

35 Mobile Marketing Association 2016, op. cit.

36 Leonardi, L. (2016). When to choose geofencing, geo-targeting, or beaconing for your location marketing. *Relate: The Digital Mag for Marketing from Appboy*; Jones, M. (2016). 3 Ways Location-Based Marketing Is Shaping Retail in 2016. *Forbes*.

37 Newman, A. A. (2012). Band-Aids and muppets aim to soothe child's scrapes. *The New York Times*, www.nytimes.com/2012/05/23/business/media/band-aids-and-muppets-soothe-childs-scrapes.html; Effie

Worldwide. (2013). Band-Aid Brand: BAND-AID Magic Vision Augmented Reality App, www.effie.org/case_studies/case/2226; Video: https://www.youtube.com/watch?v=FE2I6G2_ogkp download

38   Metzger, M. J. (2007). Communication privacy management in electronic commerce. *Journal of Computer-Mediated Communication*, 12, 335–61.

39   Boyles, J. L., Smith, A. & Madden, M. (2012). Privacy and Data Management on Mobile Devices. www.pewinternet.org/2012/09/05/privacy-and-data-management-on-mobile-devices

40   Belbey, J. (2015). Protect Your Firm from the 12 Risks of Social Media. *Forbes*.

41   ibid.

42   Hoffman, D. L. & Fodor, M. (2010). Can you measure the ROI of your social media marketing? *Sloan Management Review*, 52, 41–9.

43   Enright-Schulz, J. (2015). Adobe Social White Paper: Guide to Showing Social ROI. https://offers.adobe.com/content/dam/offer-manager/en/na/marketing/Social%20PDFs/50618_social_ROI_whitepaper_ue_v2.pdf

44   ibid.

45   Hoffman & Fodor, op. cit.

46   Kumar & Gupta, op. cit.

47   Kaye, K. (2013). Data defined: What is 'big data' anyway? http://adage.com/article/dataworks/data-defined-big-data/239144/

48   Advertising Research Foundation. (2016). The ARF David Ogilvy Award: Big data decision drive lifecycle marketing. (Brand: Warner Bros. PAN).

49   Kumar & Gupta, op. cit.

50   ibid.

51   IoT Agenda, I. (n.d). Definition: Internet of Things (IoT). https://internetofthingsagenda.techtarget.com/definition/Internet-of-Things-IoT

52   Greenough, J. (2016). How the 'Interent of Things' will impact consumers, business, and governments in 2016 and beyond. http://www.businessinsider.com/how-the-internet-of-things-market-will-grow-2014-10?IR=T

53   I-Scoop. (n.d.). The Internet of Things in marketing: the integrated marketing opportunity. www.i-scoop.eu/internet-of-things-guide/internet-things-marketing/

54   Kumar & Gupta, op. cit.

55   ibid.

56   Bannan, C. (2016). The IoT Threat to Privacy. https://techcrunch.com/2016/08/14/the-iot-threat-to-privacy/

57   Risen, T. (2016). The privacy, security risks of the Internet of Things. www.usnews.com/news/articles/2016-01-22/the-privacy-security-risks-of-the-internet-of-things

58   Merriam-Wester. (n.d.). Virtual reality. https://www.merriam-webster.com/dictionary/virtual%20reality

59   https://with.in/watch/toms-virtual-giving-trip/

60 https://www.lexus.eu/vr/

61 Business Wire. (2016). Consumer Spending on Virtual Reality Entertainment to Hit $3.3 Billion by 2020, IHS Markit Says. www.businesswire.com/news/home/20161006005521/en/Consumer-Spending-Virtual-Reality-Entertainment-Hit-3.3

62 Marriott International News Center. (2015). Marriott Hotels introduces the first ever in-room virtual reality travel experience 2015, www.news.marriott.com/2015/09/marriott-hotels-introduces-the-first-ever-in-room-virtual-reality-travel-experience/; Wasserman T. (2014). Marriott can 'Teleport' you to Hawaii or London via Oculus Rift, http://mashable.com/2014/09/18/marriott-oculus/#70a52_SyTmqV

63 Ho H., Shin W., Lwin M. O. (2017). Social networking site use and materialistic values among youth: The safeguarding role of the parent–child relationship and self-regulation. *Communication Research*.

64 Common Sense Media. (2013). Zero to eight: children's media use in America 2013. Common Sense Media. Prakken Publications, Inc.

65 Wakefield, J. (2015). Children spend six hours or more a day on screens. BBC News. www.bbc.com/news/technology-32067158

66 Australian Communications and Media Authority. (2016). Aussie Teens and Kids Online. www.acma.gov.au/theACMA/engage-blogs/engage-blogs/Research-snapshots/Aussie-teens-and-kids-online

67 Yang, C. (2017). 12-year-olds in Singapore spend 6½ hours daily on electronic devices: Survey. *Strait Times*.

68 Federal Trade Commission. (2013). Mobile privacy disclosures: Building trust through transparency. www.ftc.gov/reports/mobile-privacy-disclosures-building-trust-through-transparency-federal-trade-commission; Wilcox, B. L., Kunkel, D., Cantor, J., Dowrick, P., Linn, S. & Palmer, E. (2004). Report of the APA Task Force on Advertising and Children. American Psychological Association.

69 Diaz, A.-C. (2011). Behind the world: Toyota Backseat Driver. AdAge (21 July), https://adage.com/article/behind-the-work/work-toytoyota-backseat-driver/228846/

70 https://itunes.apple.com/us/app/backseat-driver-toyota/id433843799?mt=8

71 Mobile Marketing Association. (n.d.). Target: Target Holiday Wish List. www.mmaglobal.com/case-study-hub/case_studies/view/36712

72 Moye, J. (2016). #ThatsGold: Get the Scoop on Coke's Global Campaign for the Rio 2016 Olympic Games: Coca-Cola Company, www.coca-colacompany.com/stories/thatsgold-get-the-scoop-on-coke-s-global-campaign-for-the-rio-2016-olympic-games; Coca-Cola Company. (2016). 'Coca-Cola Goes for Gold in Rio 2016 Olympic Games with Global #ThatsGold Campaign' (press release), 13 July; Priselac, M. (2016). Social media stars bring #ThatsGold Olympic moments to Coca-Cola fans 2016, http://www.coca-colacompany.com/stories/fans-experience-thatsgold-olympic-moments-through-coca-cola; Liffreing, I. (2016). How Coca-Cola targeted teens during the 2016 Olympic Games (Campaign US), http://www.campaignlive.com/article/coca-cola-targeted-teens-during-2016-olympic-games/1406187

73 www.coca-colacompany.com/coca-cola-unbottled/thatsgold-moment-cody-and-alli-simpson-carry-olympic-torch-in-rio

74 Ho, H., Shin, W. & Lwin, M. O. (2017). Social networking site use and materialistic values among youth: the safeguarding role of the parent-child relationship and self-regulation. *Communication Research*.

CHAPTER 10

Media Decisions

Maxwell Winchester

Media planning for a disruption in university education

For decades, concerns have been raised about the quality and relevance of learning environments within universities, yet little has been done to change the tertiary education system globally.[1]

In 2018, Victoria University in Melbourne, Australia, implemented a first in Australian university teaching by offering courses in one-month blocks. Rather than attending four classes over a 12-week semester, with a schedule of classes spread out over an entire week, students would undertake one subject at a time for four weeks, taking three, three-hour workshops every week.

The benefit to students of this model of teaching are clear. Students only have to focus on one subject area at a time and only have to turn up to university three times a week, meaning they have much more spare time to study and take on part-time work. In addition, classes are held as workshops of up to 40 students rather than traditional lectures and tutorials, meaning students have a more engaging learning environment.

This block model of teaching delivery is only offered by a handful of universities worldwide, and had never been offered in such a large university before. 'It is a change that is unique in Australia,' noted the university's Pro Vice-Chancellor of Learning and Innovation.

Such a disruption in the traditional university teaching model required communication.

The message needed to communicate the benefits of the block teaching model, including:

* turning up to university only three times a week for three-hour classes
* taking one subject at a time
* attending smaller class sizes with more student support.

Figure 10.1 Victoria University advertisement

The message to the target audience was clear. But how to communicate with them?

A marketer has many options when it comes to choosing which media platform to use to communicate with the chosen target audience. The target audience in this case was school leavers, who are considered pretty tech savvy. So is the best option to communicate with social and digital media such as Facebook and Instagram or on websites? In this chapter, we will consider alternative options and revisit this question.

■ INTRODUCTION

As we saw in the case study on Victoria University, once an IMC campaign has been developed, a decision on the medium of communication needs to be made. For the most part, in this chapter we will concentrate on mass and digital media as these are the most popular forms of media used by marketers.

Once a campaign has been developed, the job of a marketing communication team is to place the campaign somewhere where it will be seen by the target audience. There are many options in media: from television to radio; web page advertisements to social media platforms; and newspapers to magazines.

A large amount of money is spent by marketers on buying space for advertising, so an understanding of media is paramount. Generally, a marketing manager in a larger organisation will employ a **media agency** to buy media space in a range of outlets. The different types of media available are known as media channels, media vehicles or media outlets.

In the previous chapters, we learnt about how to develop suitable messages using different IMC platforms: from direct marketing to digital media, and from television advertising to sales promotions. But if we choose to use media to communicate our message, what is the most appropriate media to use? That depends on a number of factors.

In this chapter, we will consider these factors and the different media outlets, and consider how media is consumed by people.

LEARNING OBJECTIVES

After reading this chapter you should be able to:

1. describe the different media channels and evaluate the benefits of each
2. differentiate between mass media and digital media
3. articulate the impact of the duplication of viewing law as applied to media usage
4. debate the ability to target markets with media, using evidence
5. apply targeting efficiency to media usage data.

Mass media

Referring to Chapter 1 briefly, you will remember that a linear model of communication was presented. In the centre of the model, the medium of communication was fundamental to how the sender would send a message to the receiver. While in the context of interpersonal communication the medium might be verbal speech, in the context of IMC the medium is in effect one of the forms of media that marketers use, such as newspapers or radio.

When we think of mass media, we think of it as a fairly recent phenomenon, given television has only been around for the past 50 odd years and radio for another 50 years prior to that. However, **mass media** has been with us for centuries—the first printing press was available in the 1400s.[2] While advertising already existed quite some time ago, marketing as a concept is much more recent. Table 10.1 gives a brief overview of mass media's benefits and disadvantages, while more depth is offered on each form of traditional mass media—including broadcast, print and outdoor—in the following paragraphs.

Table 10.1 Mass media benefits and disadvantages

	MEDIUM					
	TELEVISION	**RADIO**	**NEWSPAPERS**	**MAGAZINES**	**OOH**	**DIGITAL**
Mass market coverage	☑	☒	☑	☒	☑	☒
Specific target	☒	☑	☒	☑	☒	☑
High absolute cost	☑	☒	☑	☑	☑	☒
Low absolute cost	☒	☑	☒	☒	☒	☑
Low cost per exposure	☑	☑	☑	☒	☑	☑
Complex creative	☑	☒	☒	☑	☒	☑
Multidimensional	☑	☒	☒	☒	☒	☑

Broadcast media

Broadcast media can be divided into two major categories: television and radio. These offer the benefit of large audiences at low cost per exposure. Most people have access to a radio and a television, even in developing countries.

As you are likely a consumer of television, you will know that one reason it is attractive to marketers is that it allows visual and auditory messages to be sent, which can give life to the message. Research into the public's trust of different media indicates that while **digital media** is gaining trust among consumers, television is still one of the most trusted media.[3]

While consumers are now using multiple screens in their homes (such as tablets and mobile phones) much of what is watched is content that would have traditionally been watched on the family television set.[4] Even today, more than 80 per cent of video watching still takes place on television sets.[5]

Radio, on the other hand, is more passive, and is often referred to as the 'half-heard' medium.[6] That's because we often listen to the radio in the background while doing something else, whereas when radio was a new technology entire families used to sit around the 'wireless' to listen to their favourite radio shows.

Advertising in broadcast media is usually sold under the name 'spot'. A **spot** can be 15, 30 or even 60 seconds. The cost of spots changes throughout the day, in that they are more expensive when more people are listening/watching and less expensive when fewer people are listening/watching. For television, peak tends to be between 7 pm and 10 pm, while radio's peak tends to be commute traffic hours when people are more likely to listen to it in their cars.[7] Not surprisingly, buying media space at these peak times is far more expensive than at off-peak times.

Print media

Print media is media that is printed on a press. The major forms of print media are newspapers and magazines.

While there is still a demand for print media, sales of advertising in printed magazines and newspapers are decreasing,[8] which is likely due to their reducing circulations. Table 10.2 shows the reduction in **circulation** Year on Year (YoY change) for each major Australian daily newspaper in its printed form.

Table 10.2 Circulation of major Australian daily printed newspapers and YoY change

PUBLICATION	CIRCULATION SEPT 2016	YOY CHANGE (%)
Herald Sun	317 517	−5.3
The Daily Telegraph	233 857	−7.1
The Weekend Australian	220 945	−1.2
Courier Mail	144 788	−7.0
The Advertiser	120 854	−4.8
The Australian	97 854	−4.8
The Sydney Morning Herald	95 733	−8.7
The Age	87 979	−9.3

Table 10.2 makes the case pretty clearly that printed newspapers are reducing in circulation markedly. However, what this table does not tell us is whether people are not reading newspapers at all, or whether they are switching to digital versions of the same newspapers. Table 10.3 presents circulations of digital versions (where available) of newspapers.

Table 10.3 Circulation of digital major Australian daily newspapers with YoY change

PUBLICATION	CIRCULATION SEPT 2016	YOY CHANGE (%)
Herald Sun	75 067	+18.0
The Daily Telegraph	N/A	N/A
The Weekend Australian	80 845	+10.4
Courier Mail	N/A	N/A
The Advertiser	N/A	N/A
The Australian	80 722	+10.4
The Sydney Morning Herald	N/A	N/A
The Age	N/A	N/A

As we can see in Table 10.3, digital versions are experiencing dramatic increases in circulation for those newspapers that are offering them. The evidence across platforms suggests that readers being lost from printed circulation are simply moving to digital rather than being lost as newspaper readers altogether, and that some titles, such as *The Daily Telegraph* and the *Herald Sun*, are actually growing in circulation.[9]

This example of data is a reminder of two things. First, that we should not look at data in isolation and conclude anything about an industry. Second, it challenges us to consider whether we can say newspaper as a medium is dying if it is simply moving to a new platform (from print to digital). After all, from a consumption point of view, the contents would not be very different for a user.

Magazines are another form of print media, most known for the high reproduction quality of advertisements and their well-targeted audiences. For example, there are golfing magazines for target audiences who like to golf, surfing magazines for those who like to surf and crocheting magazines for those who like to crochet. Advertising space is sold in such magazines as being highly targeted to those who are interested or passionate in the topic area of the magazine.

The evidence for circulation of magazines mirrors that of newspapers. If we consider printed versions alone, it appears that circulations are in decline. However, if we consider multiplatform circulation across printed and digital, there is a mixed message. Some magazines (such as *Australian Gourmet Traveller*) are dramatically losing circulation across both platforms (possibly because they do not offer a digital option), while others (such as *Elle*) are dramatically increasing their circulation.[10]

Print media is usually sold according to rates listed on a **rate card**, which outlines the cost of advertising in a particular space and the target audience of the particular title. Newspaper space is generally sold by the column centimetre, unless you are buying a quarter, half or full page. Figure 10.2 presents a rate card from *The Age* newspaper in Melbourne, Australia.

Figure 10.2 Rate card from Melbourne's *Age* newspaper

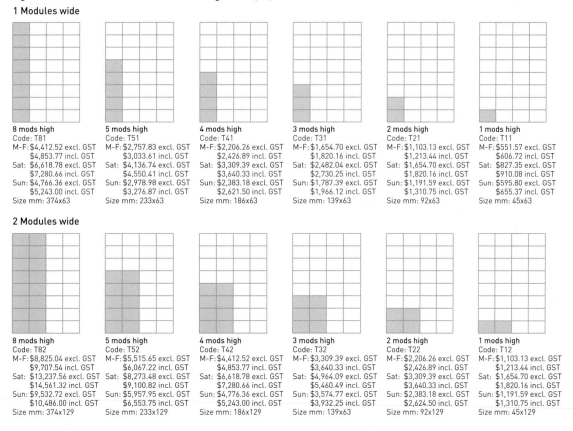

1 Modules wide

8 mods high	5 mods high	4 mods high	3 mods high	2 mods high	1 mods high
Code: T81	Code: T51	Code: T41	Code: T31	Code: T21	Code: T11
M-F: $4,412.52 excl. GST	M-F: $2,757.83 excl. GST	M-F: $2,206.26 excl. GST	M-F: $1,654.70 excl. GST	M-F: $1,103.13 excl. GST	M-F: $551.57 excl. GST
$4,853.77 incl. GST	$3,033.61 incl. GST	$2,426.89 incl. GST	$1,820.16 incl. GST	$1,213.44 incl. GST	$606.72 incl. GST
Sat: $6,618.78 excl. GST	Sat: $4,136.74 excl. GST	Sat: $3,309.39 excl. GST	Sat: $2,482.04 excl. GST	Sat: $1,654.70 excl. GST	Sat: $827.35 excl. GST
$7,280.66 incl. GST	$4,550.41 incl. GST	$3,640.33 incl. GST	$2,730.25 incl. GST	$1,820.16 incl. GST	$910.08 incl. GST
Sun: $4,766.36 excl. GST	Sun: $2,978.98 excl. GST	Sun: $2,383.18 excl. GST	Sun: $1,787.39 excl. GST	Sun: $1,191.59 excl. GST	Sun: $595.80 excl. GST
$5,243.00 incl. GST	$3,276.87 incl. GST	$2,621.50 incl. GST	$1,966.12 incl. GST	$1,310.75 incl. GST	$655.37 incl. GST
Size mm: 374x63	Size mm: 233x63	Size mm: 186x63	Size mm: 139x63	Size mm: 92x63	Size mm: 45x63

2 Modules wide

8 mods high	5 mods high	4 mods high	3 mods high	2 mods high	1 mods high
Code: T82	Code: T52	Code: T42	Code: T32	Code: T22	Code: T12
M-F: $8,825.04 excl. GST	M-F: $5,515.65 excl. GST	M-F: $4,412.52 excl. GST	M-F: $3,309.39 excl. GST	M-F: $2,206.26 excl. GST	M-F: $1,103.13 excl. GST
$9,707.54 incl. GST	$6,067.22 incl. GST	$4,853.77 incl. GST	$3,640.33 incl. GST	$2,426.89 incl. GST	$1,213.44 incl. GST
Sat: $13,237.56 excl. GST	Sat: $8,273.48 excl. GST	Sat: $6,618.78 excl. GST	Sat: $4,964.09 excl. GST	Sat: $3,309.39 excl. GST	Sat: $1,654.70 excl. GST
$14,561.32 incl. GST	$9,100.82 incl. GST	$7,280.66 incl. GST	$5,460.49 incl. GST	$3,640.33 incl. GST	$1,820.16 incl. GST
Sun: $9,532.72 excl. GST	Sun: $5,957.95 excl. GST	Sun: $4,776.36 excl. GST	Sun: $3,574.77 excl. GST	Sun: $2,383.18 excl. GST	Sun: $1,191.59 excl. GST
$10,486.00 incl. GST	$6,553.75 incl. GST	$5,243.00 incl. GST	$3,932.25 incl. GST	$2,624.50 incl. GST	$1,310.75 incl. GST
Size mm: 374x129	Size mm: 233x129	Size mm: 186x129	Size mm: 139x63	Size mm: 92x129	Size mm: 45x129

As you can see from Figure 10.2 the rates for each module change depending on which day of the week the space is being bought for.

In addition, rate cards for newspapers and magazines give some indication of the demographic profile of readers of the publication. Figure 10.3 shows the rate card for the *Cape Times* newspaper in South Africa, which includes reader profiles.

Figure 10.3 Rate card for South Africa's *Cape Times* newspaper

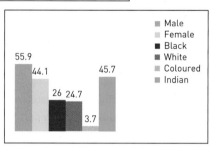

Cape Times **average issue readers in profile**

→ Cape Times has 261,000 average issue readers 82% of whom live within the Cape Peninsula

→ Circulation: 37,948 (ABC: Apr–Jun 2012)

→ Die Burger has 122,000 readers in the Cape Town metro area compared with 214,000 for Cape Times

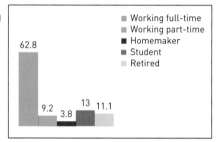

→ Cape Times is Cape Town's dominant and definitive morning daily publication servicing the needs of the upmarket reader, with an emphasis on corporate news and providing in-depth coverage of current issues

→ Business Report is an integral part of the Cape Times package and provides invaluable information and analysis for the business person

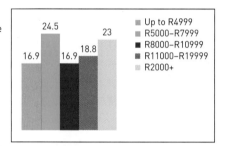

→ 63% of Cape Times readers are employed while 75% have a matric or higher education

→ 37% of Cape Times readers fall within LSM 8–10 and 36% are to be found in the recently expanded LSM groups 11–14

→ Cape Times reaches both English and Afrikaans speakers as well as upmarket African readers:

• 51% English
• 28% Afrikaans
• 15% Xhosa

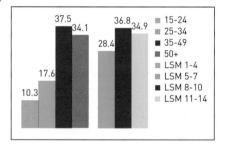

→ Cape Times readers are computer literate with 48% accessing the internet during any given week

As you can see in Figure 10.3, rate cards typically have demographic information on them; very few of them tend to have other segmentation data, such as attitudes and psychographics. This leaves us to question the value of segmenting on anything other than demographics, since most mass media rate cards sell space based on demographics only.[11]

Out Of Home (OOH)/outdoor

Out Of Home (OOH)/outdoor advertising can take a number of forms. Many of us are familiar with billboards on the sides of buildings or on the sides of motorways, but outdoor advertising is much more extensive than this.

Aside from billboards, there are a number of other types of outdoor advertising. Some very creative examples include bus shelters, painted pavements and vehicles (some examples are shown in Figure 10.4).

Figure 10.4 Examples of transit advertising (left) and own vehicle advertising

The obvious disadvantage of outdoor advertising is that it is something consumers only get a glimpse of because they are passing by rather than engaging with it. However, acknowledging this, there are strategies to ensure that consumers recall the brand advertised at a later time. These include using a logo, a short headline and/or a product picture.[12]

On the other hand, the advantages to outdoor advertising are that in many cases there is a high repeat exposure to the advertisement. Think of an advertisement on a major arterial road going into a city. Generally, the same people will pass the advertisement day after day on the way to work. Although the **reach** would only be to those who drove down the particular road, the **frequency** with which the consumers see the advertisement would be quite high as there would be a lot of repeat usage of that road for most people. This is similar to advertising on public transport. Many people catch the same bus or train to work daily and could be exposed to the same advertisement many times in a month.

Digital media

In the previous section we reviewed traditional mass media. Over the past two decades, a new form of media has emerged, known as digital or interactive media. A detailed look at social media is provided in Chapter 9. In this chapter, we consider social and digital media from a media mix perspective. This platform can be divided into six major subtypes:

1. web based
2. social-media based
3. email
4. SMS
5. apps
6. YouTube.

Web based

Web-based advertising was the first interactive media available. Initially it involved advertisements on banners on websites, but more recently it has evolved into using cookies to track browsing behaviour, followed by behavioural targeting.

Behavioural targeting involves using previously visited commercial websites in advertisements on other websites to encourage purchases. In Figure 10.5, for example, you can see the person browsing has visited the BBC News website, and has been exposed to a banner advertisement from Trivago, the travel agency, after previously visiting Trivago for a hotel room earlier that day.

Figure 10.5 Example of behavioural targeting

In addition to behavioural targeting, search engine optimisation (SEO) is another commonly used way of getting consumers to your website. It involves working out what the most common search terms for your website would be. For example, if you were a travel agency, common words you would want to optimise might include 'flight', 'hotel', 'holiday' and so on. The search engine Google, enables marketers to access Google Analytics, which can give insights into what the most commonly used search terms are.

Another aspect that must be considered in web-based media is that privacy laws are now being tightened in many countries, meaning the use of cookies must be proactively agreed to by consumers.

Although web-based media was the original digital platform, this medium is becoming less popular very quickly. Barnard (2017) indicates that this medium has the largest reduction in expenditure of many media available.[13]

Social media

Social media includes sites such as Facebook, Instagram and Twitter.

Facebook is the most popular social-media platform, and relative to other media, quite cheap, which makes it popular as an advertising platform for small businesses. Facebook uses many complex algorithms to target advertisements at users by analysing their use of the program. Tracking what users like, what they read and what they comment on is thought to be a good indicator of what products they may be interested in.

Instagram is a pictorial-based social media platform. Companies use it to send targeted advertisements, and also pay popular Instagrammers to promote their products. Like Facebook, Instagram offers good value-for-money rates for small businesses. But it's not just small businesses. An example of a global company that used Instagram as a major part of its campaign was Mercedes Benz at the launch of its CLA model.[14] In this campaign it gave a new CLA to five top Instagram photographers to take on a road trip and take photos of the new car. The photographer with the highest number of likes at the end of the road trip got to keep the car.

Email

In the first few years of email in the 1990s, it was a very popular way to promote a brand. These days, however, unsolicited emails are likely to end up in a 'junk' mailbox and even those that make it into the user's mailbox are likely to be deleted if they are not relevant to the consumer at that point in time. Combining this with privacy laws, which are becoming ever tighter in many parts of the world, keeping customer lists can only be done with the explicit permission of the consumer. This means that only customers with a real interest in your brand are likely to be willing to be kept on your list of customers.

Apps

Apps are applications that consumers can use on their smartphones or computer. While the obvious ones such as Instagram and Facebook have already been discussed, there are other apps that have been designed specifically to be part of an IMC campaign. An example of this is given in 'IMC in Action: AAMI Smart Plates'.

IMC IN ACTION: AAMI SMART PLATES

The state of Victoria, Australia, has been internationally recognised for the emphasis it places on road safety. The Transport Accident Commission has won many awards for its shock advertising campaigns over the past 20 years.

AAMI, a motor insurance company, developed a clever social marketing program that would not only have the potential to improve the safety of young drivers, but also improve its brand profile.

In the state of Victoria, young drivers must first sit for a test for their learner's permit at the age of 16. After that, aside from being trained by a professional for some of their learning, they must keep a log of their driving hours.

AAMI developed an app called 'Smart Plates', which enables learner drivers to digitally log their driving hours, along with who the supervisor is and the route taken for each trip. The app also encourages safe driving behaviour by blocking phone calls and gives safety tips.[15]

The campaign was supported with outdoor advertising, a TV commercial (TVC)[16] and cinema advertising.

Questions

1. What benefit would such an app bring to an insurer like AAMI?
2. What would be the benefit of complementing the app with other media vehicles such as television and outdoor advertising?

YouTube

YouTube is a popular video distribution site available on the Web or as an app. Whether it should be considered a form of TV viewing is something to consider since effectively it is not a medium on its own, but a way of viewing TV-like content.

The difference with YouTube is that it enables anyone to open an account and make their own video content. An example of a very successful use of YouTube is highlighted in the case study, 'IMC in Action: Dumb Ways To Die'.

Some have claimed that YouTube can be used to make a campaign viral. While this is possible (as you will see in the case study) it is in fact very rare.[17]

IMC IN ACTION: DUMB WAYS TO DIE

Safety around trains and railway stations was a concern for Melbourne Metro. To address this, they approached the McCann Erikson advertising agency to develop a campaign to highlight the dangers of being near trains and to encourage people to behave safely around railway tracks. The campaign was launched in November 2012.[18]

The agency developed what has been labelled as the most successful public service campaign in history, winning Best Campaign of the Decade in the Asia Pacific Tambuli Awards, and 28 Lions and Five Grand Prix awards, making it the most awarded campaign in history at Cannes.[19] Aside from having around 60 million YouTube hits, the campaign also achieved number 1 free app not just in Australia, but also the US, UK, Canada and Germany.[20] Part of the campaign's success is said to be the fact that it features a catchy song, which was in the iTunes charts in 28 countries and peaked at number 3 in Hong Kong.[21]

A YouTube video case study of the campaign is available at www.youtube.com/watch?v=v75CvUz58tk.

While there is no doubt that the campaign itself has been an amazing success story globally, there have been questions as to whether it actually had any effect on behaviour around railway tracks.[22]

Questions

1. Why do you think this campaign was considered the most successful public service campaign in history?
2. Although the self-promoted case study suggests a decrease of dangerous behaviour around railway tracks and trains, there has been criticism that incidents have not actually reduced in number by very much. How is it possible that such a successful campaign could not also have a significant reduction in risk-taking behaviour?

Media planning

Media planning is best described as answering the following question: 'What are the best means of delivering advertisements to prospective purchasers of my brand or service?'[23]

Media planning takes into account three factors: reach, frequency and the number of advertising cycles annually.[24]

Determining the most appropriate media vehicles will be dependent on a number of factors, which include:

1. *reach*—the proportion of the target audience that has been exposed to the campaign at least once
2. *frequency (or average frequency)*—on average, how many times a member of the target audience was exposed to the campaign
3. *budget*—the biggest influencer of what media will be used in a campaign. For example, small businesses do not have the funds to produce or run a TVC. However, if you have the capital to do it, TVCs offer good value for money when considered on a reach and frequency basis. CPM (cost per mille) is a commonly used measure that enables marketers to get an idea of the cost per thousand reach a particular spot has achieved[25]
4. *selectivity and wastage*—some marketers are only concerned about communicating with their target audience: any advertising outside of that is considered wastage. Some media vehicles are thought to be better at attracting specific segments of the market; however, as we will see later in the chapter there are some flaws with this assumption. CPM can be used to give the marketer an idea of how much of their advertising is 'wasted'
5. *advertising avoidance*—some consumers avoid advertising and are very hard to communicate with. For example, an airline that is trying to communicate with heavy travellers can find it very difficult to find media they will consume
6. *engagement, context and consumer relevance*—the media chosen may not be one that the target audience engages with. For example, while a luxury watch brand may be able to communicate with more consumers in a large circulation tabloid newspaper, it is thought that consumers will perceive this as an inappropriate place to advertise it, making the advertisement less effective. A contextual example is that an advertisement that appears just prior to the buying situation may increase the salience of the brand just prior to the purchase, which may increase the probability that the brand is bought.
7. *other qualitative considerations*—a contentious area within advertising is the importance of creative. Some argue that the creative in advertising can't be measured by CPM or **ratings** measures, as it is the qualitative aspects of the advertisement that have an exponential effect on the advertisement's retention and engagement.[26] There have been long-standing battles from those in creative, who argue that only creative sells, while at the same time often criticising research that might be critical of the effectiveness of their creativity.[27]

As an example of how the above concepts are regarded, marketers need to consider whether it is better to use their budgets to increase the number of times an advertisement is seen (frequency) or increase the number of consumers who see the advertisement (reach). Research suggests it is better to spend budget to reach consumers more than once, but the response is convex, so at some point consumers become saturated and there is no extra benefit of them seeing the advertisement again.[28] Around one to three exposures per week is said to be optimal for established brands.[29] More importantly, however, it is suggested that consumers are more likely to buy a brand if they have seen an advertisement for that brand in the previous week, highlighting the importance of recency.[30] The idea is that for Fast Moving Consumer Goods (FMCG) categories in particular, marketers never know who in the household will buy, nor when in the week they will buy, so they plan their media to be seen by as many consumers as possible, as often as possible.[31]

Scheduling is managed in a way to attain the best reach and frequency for marketers' particular target audience and their decision-making process. Figure 10.6 pictorially summarises the different media scheduling options.[32]

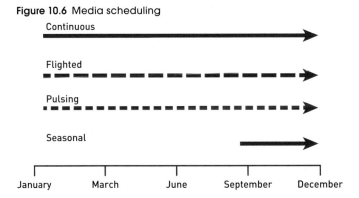

Figure 10.6 Media scheduling

Source: Adapted from Dahlén, M., Lange, F. & Smith, T. (2010). *Marketing Communications: A Brand Narrative Approach.* Chichester: Wiley & Sons, Figure 13.5.

Different product categories and different target markets have different optimum scheduling plans. For example, promotions for snow gear are best scheduled in autumn, just prior to the ski season, while soft drinks are more likely to be scheduled in either a continuous or flighted manner.

One obvious issue is that marketers do not have uncapped budgets, so the challenge is how to ensure reach and recency within the media schedule. Given this, rather than a continuous burst of media, flighted or pulsing is often chosen to increase the chance a consumer sees advertising just before the purchase occasion.[33]

Now that the issues surrounding media planning have been considered briefly, the question is, how can things such as reach and frequency be measured to ensure a campaign has been successfully targeted to the correct audience? Generally, marketers use ratings providers to assess which consumers were exposed to which campaigns.

The ratings process

The majority of IMC campaigns outline a target audience that the marketer wishes to communicate with. To understand the success of the implementation of any media plan, we need to understand how ratings of different media are determined.

It is important to understand the metrics being used when discussing target audience measurement. For example, the circulation of a newspaper may not reflect the number of people who read it, so marketers should be more interested in how many people saw the advertisement than how many people paid for a newspaper.

Companies such as Nielsen or Gallup (or Roy Morgan Research in Australasia) provide ratings of media to help marketers understand what media is being consumed by whom.

IMC IN ACTION: MEDIA PLAN FOR FIRST YEAR MODEL

Given you've had an overview of different media options and scheduling, develop a brief plan for how you would select and schedule media for Victoria University's block model teaching promotions.

In your plan, justify why you have selected the media you have selected and also consider why you would schedule the campaign in the way you have. Consideration might be given to when students select their universities and when they start thinking about which courses they want to apply to do (keeping in mind that in Australia, university starts in February each year, and students generally start selection of university courses in around August of the previous year).

Market research agencies collect media data from consumers, which is generally single source (in that they can track one particular consumer's brand purchases with media consumption across many media vehicles). The data is often collected from a panel of consumers.

Generally, the media data is matched with consumer demographic profiles.[34] For example, the market research agency compiles its sample of respondents who watched a particular TV show or listened to the radio at a certain time of day. It provides a demographic analysis of this sample, and projects it out to the general population to make estimates of the demographics of people who watched a show or listened to a particular segment.

In terms of TV watching, a panel of consumers is given set top boxes for their TV set, which monitors their watching behaviour and matches this with which TV shows were aired at the time.[35] More recently, however, with the advent of on-demand television, new technologies had to be developed to match consumers with which TV shows they watched. Digital picture matching is one of the technologies used.

Matching consumers with their behaviour is much easier on a platform such as Facebook, as the data is already matched with the advertising viewed.

Is traditional media dead?

While it is fashionable to suggest that consumers now consume more digital media than **traditional media**, the evidence may surprise you.[36] Some people may consider watching streaming television (known affectionately as T-Me) on their laptop or smartphone as digital media consumption. But is it really? Realistically, the way we consume television has changed, in that more than half of viewing is now on-demand and less than half of viewing is now traditional broadcast television.[37] But if you are watching a popular TV series, either way is still really television. For example, if we consider T-Me watching to be a form of TV consumption, in Australia consumption of this format increased from 16.6 hours per week in 2014 to 17.2 hours per week in 2015.[38]

This is consistent with worldwide media statistics, which show not only is television the most interacted-with media (at 174 minutes per day in 2016), but consumers still spend significantly more time watching television than they do on the internet (122 minutes per day).[39] However, consistent with the discussion above on engagement time, adspend for each medium also demonstrates that most advertising spend across media is television. Figure 10.7 demonstrates this.

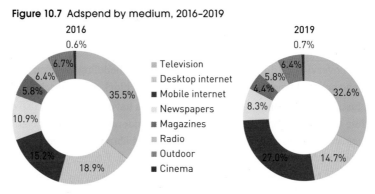

Figure 10.7 Adspend by medium, 2016–2019

Source: Barnard, J. (2017). Advertising Expenditure Forecasts, March. www. publicismedia.de/wp-content/uploads/2017/03/2017-03-27-aef-executive-summary.pdf

It needs to be acknowledged, however, that minutes watching television has been declining over the past six years, and at the same time minutes spent on the internet has been increasing over the same period worldwide.[40] Figure 10.8 is consistent with this in that it demonstrates advertising spend growth is greatest in mobile internet. An interesting surprise may be, however, that desktop internet has seen the largest reduction in advertising spend of any media. Another surprise may be that all of television, radio, outdoor and cinema continue to grow, suggesting that traditional media is far from dead.

Figure 10.8 Growth in adspend by medium

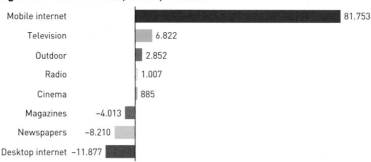

Source: Barnard, J. (2017). Advertising Expenditure Forecasts, March. www.publicismedia. de/wp-content/uploads/2017/03/2017-03-27-aef-executive-summary.pdf

It is worth remembering that digital media is not the first disruptive technology in media, and history shows us that the new media developed does not replace previous media. For example, radio did not completely replace newspapers, and television did not completely replace radio.[41] It is likely, therefore, that digital media will become another media that consumers will use in conjunction with other media.

Before writing off traditional media, it is worth considering not just the growth rates but also the penetration of traditional media. For example, Figure 10.9 shows the penetration of radio in a number of countries in 2015.

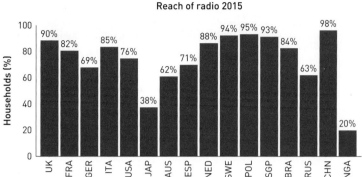

Figure 10.9 Radio penetration across countries, 2015

Source: Ofcom. (2016). The Communications Market Report, Figure 5.12, https://www.
ofcom.org.uk/__data/assets/pdf_file/0026/95642/ICMR-Full.pdf

As illustrated in Figure 10.9, in the majority of countries considered, the majority of the population is reached using radio as a medium.

This suggests that our time is well spent considering both the growing digital media and traditional mass media platforms. This is consistent with the Integrated Marketing Communication concept that different media should be used in a complementary manner, with consistent messaging throughout.

Media buying, targeting and consumption

When considering how marketers buy media, it is imperative that we consider known patterns of consumer behaviour and media consumption behaviour. Fortunately, there are laws that relate to how media consumption occurs and consumer behaviour (discussed in Chapter 2), underpinned by decades of research. In this last section of the chapter we will consider these.

Media duplication

In the discussion of the Duplication of Purchase Law (DoPL) in Chapter 2, evidence suggested that consumers use more than one brand in short periods of time (known as a brand repertoire). This has been noted in radio listening.[42] In fact, the consequence of this pattern of purchase, the Double Jeopardy Law, was first noted when William McPhee observed listening patterns of radio listeners.[43] The DoPL has been observed in TV viewing for decades.[44]

Table 10.4 shows us that that the same consumers of media are using different competing media outlets. This also means that there are unlikely to be large differences in consumer profile across media outlets, as the same people are using the different outlets. For example, evidence shows that the profile of listeners to one radio station do not differ greatly from that of listeners to other radio stations; and readers of one newspaper are not dissimilar from those of another competing newspaper.[45]

In addition to **media duplication** across different media outlets at different points in time, evidence also suggests that consumers have been duplicating across different media at the same time for quite some time (such as using a tablet while watching television).[46]

Table 10.4 Duplication of reading in women's magazines in New Zealand

	% READ	WOMAN'S DAY (NZ)	NEW ZEALAND WOMAN'S WEEKLY WEEKLY	WOMEN'S WEEKLY NZ EDITION WEEKLY NZ ED	NEW IDEA (NZ)	THAT'S LIFE	NEXT
				% WHO ALSO READ ...			
Woman's Day (NZ)	4	*	43	24	35	17	10
New Zealand Woman's Weekly	3	57	*	29	34	17	11
Women's Weekly NZ Edition	3	37	34	*	20	9	23
New Idea (NZ)	2	73	55	28	*	22	14
That's Life	2	47	34	15	28	*	6
Next	1	33	27	49	22	7	*

Source: Roy Morgan Research

Targeting heavy or high-value buyers

It is quite common in the marketing profession to believe it is efficient to target heavy buyers of a category. While this may at first glance seem an efficient use of a limited advertising budget, there are good reasons to rethink this strategy.

Figure 10.10 Kellogg's Special K buyers buying X times per annum

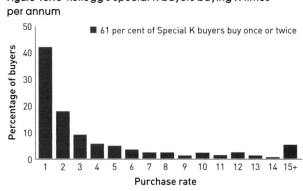

Source: Sharp, B. (2017). *Marketing: Theory, Evidence, Practice.* Oxford University Press: Melbourne, p. 46.

Consider Figure 10.10, which demonstrates a well-established pattern of consumer purchasing behaviour, the Negative Binomial Distribution (NBD).[47]

As demonstrated in Figure 10.10 even in what would be considered a big brand in a regularly purchased Fast Moving Consumer Goods (FMCG) product category, most customers buy the brand less than twice per year. There are very few customers buying it 15 or more times per year. Is it wise to focus your IMC efforts on this small group of people who buy 15+ times per year?

First, heavy buyers are already heavy buyers of the product category and will share their buying across a repertoire of brands (in line with the Duplication of Purchase Law) and will be slightly more loyal to the largest brand in their repertoire (in line with the Double Jeopardy Law). Getting a customer who already buys a lot from a product category to buy more in reality is not very likely, so reminding them about your brand (which they already are quite familiar with), while being an efficient method of spending your budget, may not actually be very effective.[48] Contrary to popular belief, the evidence suggests that heavy buyers are the least loyal buyers, simply due to them having more opportunities (as in purchase occasions) to use another brand.[49] Perhaps most importantly, brand growth does not come from retention of existing customers, but acquisition of customers in line with the brand's current NBD distribution (in that the brand will acquire many light customers and very few customers).[50] This evidence in particular indicates that targeting heavy users may be more efficient (in that your advertising targets those who are most likely to buy your brand), but less effective (in that to grow your brand, you need to attract those not currently using your brand, or light buyers).

If all of a media budget is spent in interactive media, there is an issue as to which types of consumers you will most likely target. For example, in the behavioural targeting scenario of Trivago being advertised on the BBC News website in Figure 10.5, the consumer would have already visited Trivago. While this is an efficient use of media spend to perhaps remind someone to go back to Trivago and complete their transaction for a hotel room, does it do anything to get a non-user of Trivago to the site? Much interactive media works like this. It tends to focus on heavier users and those who are already interested in your brand. For example, social media sites such as Facebook and Instagram rely on people to 'like' or 'follow' the brand. Traditional advertising follows an NBD pattern, in that a lot of consumers who are not users of a brand are exposed, while very few heavy users are exposed. On the contrary, social media sites tend to expose a lot of heavy users to a brand's advertising, while exposing very few non-users.[51] However, as already discussed above, this is efficient but not effective as it ignores those who are not aware of your brand or not familiar with your brand. As we have seen in the evidence presented, non-users and light users are extremely important in brand growth.

Aside from interactive media, it is tempting for marketers even in traditional media to focus on highly targeted media in order for their media spend to be efficient. As an example, marketers promoting golfing equipment may suggest advertising on a specialist golf channel on pay TV, rather than on a more mainstream channel on terrestrial TV.

Consider Figure 10.11, which illustrates the proportion of take-up of Pay TV by country.

Figure 10.11 Take up of Pay TV

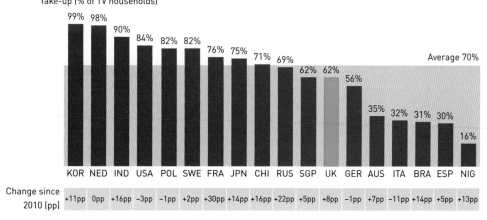

Source: Ofcom. (2016). The Communications Market Report, Figure 4.19, https://www.ofcom.org.uk/__data/assets/pdf_file/0026/95642/ICMR-Full.pdf

As can be seen in Figure 10.11, in many countries only advertising on Pay TV channels would miss a large proportion of the population. In addition to this, knowing the duplication patterns discussed earlier, anyone watching Pay TV is likely on average to watch larger, terrestrial channels more frequently (the DJ effect). For example, by advertising golfing equipment on a specialised golfing channel on Pay TV, not only would a marketer be missing a large portion of the market, but even those reached would be reached with less frequency than if the marketer advertised on a mainstream free-to-air channel.

The above discussion then raises the question as to how effective it is to target.

■ CHAPTER SUMMARY

In this chapter we presented an overview of how marketers use different media when communicating with their target audiences.

We outlined the different media channels and evaluated the benefits of each. A range of different media channels were presented, from traditional media such as television, radio and print, to digital media such as Facebook, Instagram and YouTube. Readers were encouraged to evaluate the benefits and disadvantages of each.

We differentiated between mass media and digital media. An overview of traditional mass media such as television, radio and print was given, along with an overview of common digital media platforms. This was followed by a critical analysis of how consumers use media.

Next we articulated the impact of the duplication of viewing law as applied to media usage. This knowledge enables readers to consider what the effects of duplication of media usage are on how media strategy should be developed.

This was followed by a debate on the ability to target market with media using evidence. Target marketing as a concept was challenged, particularly with the evidence of duplication of media usage. The efficiency of target marketing through particular media outlets is challenged in the case study at the end of the chapter.

Lastly, we applied an understanding of targeting efficiency to media usage data. In particular, the case study at the end of the chapter allows a critical evaluation of common beliefs about targeting efficiency using niche media outlets aimed at specific audiences.

Case study: Targeting a high-value segment[52]

Maxwell Winchester

Introduction

For decades segmentation has been seen as a key strategic activity for marketers.[53] Researchers have argued it is a crucial part of marketing strategy as it is the basis upon which targeting and positioning strategy is developed.[54] While there have been ample papers supporting the concept of segmentation over the past 50 or so years, it has come to your attention that actually implementing a segmentation and targeting strategy successfully is much less supported by empirical research.[55] There have been concerns raised about the ability to successfully implement a segmentation program,[56] whether segmentation can practically work in a market,[57] or whether segments do in fact exist in markets[58] or remain stable over time if they are found.[59] Further to the research presented in this chapter, there have also been questions about the validity of targeting.[60]

Being able to identify distinct segments of consumers in media is of particular importance in the Segmentation, Targeting and Positioning (STP) process, as it allows other marketers to target their messages effectively through advertising in the right media. Aside from this obvious issue, authors who are experts on the strategic management of print media outlets make their case clear on the importance of segmentation and targeting of particular print media to distinct audiences.[61] As a particular example, Conrad Fink states: 'No newspaper will succeed if it is distributed indiscriminately … Target marketing is required'.[62] Such target marketing not only allows for a strong strategy, but it is said to increase profitability more than using a mass-market strategy.[63] In practice, however, successful segment identification and targeting in media has been challenged.[64]

Your task: Claimed vs. actual target audiences in South African newspapers

You have been hired as a marketing communications expert for BMW dealers nationally across South Africa. You have been advised that the target market for their dealerships are consumers in the high LSM[65] segment and they want your help in determining the best national weekly publication in which to advertise the new 5 Series model due for release in a few months.

Some newspaper titles in the market do not appear to target any particular segment,[66] while others make specific claims about the readers they target.[67] Rate cards for the major daily weekly newspapers available across South Africa are presented in Table 10.5.

Before continuing, answer Question 1 at the end of the case study.

You have obtained advertising rates from rate cards for each publication. Table 10.6 highlights the standard advertising rates for weekly editions.

Table 10.5 Average circulation of competing major national South African weekly newspaper titles

	OWNER	ESTIMATED READERSHIP* (ROUNDED)	PROFILE
Sunday Times	Avusa	3.6m	No clear target profile stated
Sunday Sun	Media 24	2.6m	No clear target profile stated
City Press	Media 24	1.9m	No clear target profile stated
Sunday World	Avusa	1.6m	Targets black readers
Rapport	Media 24	1.3m	High LSM—77% in LSM 7–10
Mail & Guardian	M&G Media	0.4m	Highly educated, top LSM, young
Sondag	Media 24	0.2m	No clear target profile stated
Sunday Independent	INC	0.07m	Higher income

Sources: **Dowey** 2013, **Mail & Guardian Media** 2013, **Media 24** 2013, **Media Club South Africa** 2013, **Soccer Laduma** 2013, **Times Media** 2013[68]

Table 10.6 Advertising rates for common format advertisements in leading national South African newspapers

	B&W COL CM	FULL COLOUR COL CM
Sunday Times	R627.00	R999.00
Sunday Sun	R157.00	R208.00
City Press	R265.00	R374.00
Sunday World	R139.00	R189.00
Rapport	R413.00	R630.00
Mail & Guardian	R296.00	R307.00
Sondag	R 67.00	R 90.00
Sunday Independent	R164.21	R262.74

Note: The rates above were gathered from each newspaper's published rate cards.

Source: Dowey, J. (2013). *The Future of Media*; http://www.omd.co.za/media_facts/ FOM029_Blueprint_OMD_mediafacts2013.pdf.

Now answer Question 2 at the end of the case study.

The BMW dealerships are not happy with settling for what the publications claim as their target and they want you to conduct an analysis of each publication's audience. The details of this analysis are set out below.

1.   **Method**

The data used in this case were collected through the AMPS readership survey in 2012.[69] The data were collected by consultancy Eighty20 under contract.[70] Around 25 000 respondents over 15 years of age are interviewed per year on a rolling quarterly average using a strata sample across South Africa.[71]

The reader profiles for a number of demographic variables were calculated, and then compared to the mean by calculating a deviation from the 'average' reader. This analysis is similar to that used by Kennedy and Ehrenberg (2001) where they simply contrasted the different profiles of the various brands in each product category.[72] They did this by comparing each brand's profile against the profile of the average brand in that industry. This is a simple but effective process for identifying deviations from average readers.

2. **Results**

    Table 10.7 indicates the circulation and proportions of high LSM readers for each publication. Now answer Questions 3 and 4 below.

Table 10.7 Readership and LSM readership for national newspapers in South Africa

	ESTIMATED READERSHIP (000S)	ESTIMATED LSM 8–10 READERS (000S)
Sunday Times	3688	1918 (52%)
Sunday Sun	2601	754 (29%)
City Press	1863	671 (36%)
Sunday World	1577	615 (39%)
Rapport	1320	844 (64%)
Mail & Guardian	425	276 (65%)
Sondag	160	85 (53%)
Sunday Independent	67	42 (63%)

Questions

1. From the information in Table 10.5, which publications would you advise BMW dealers to advertise in and why?

2. Could the information in Table 10.6 lead to a revision of your answer in Question 1? Why?

3. From the information in Table 10.7, which publication would you now recommend to the dealers? Has your answer changed since answering the previous questions? If so, why?

4. Do you have any observations to make about the accuracy of claimed targets by publications?

Sources

McDonald, C. (1995). What do we know about advertising response functions? *Admap* (April), 1995.

The Age, (2018). Living the learning: Victoria University's new model for first-year students. The Age. http://paidcontent.theage.com.au/victoria-university/first-year-victoria-university/article/living-learning-victoria-universitys-new-model-first-year-students/

Victoria University, (2016). 2016 Annual Report. https://www.vu.edu.au/sites/default/files/vu-2016-annual-report.pdf.

Practitioner profile: Michael Laps

Co-Founder and Strategy Director, Yoghurt Digital

Michael is Co-Founder and Strategy Director at Yoghurt Digital, a digital marketing agency specialising in user behaviour research, customer data analysis and all things search.

After graduating from Monash University with a business degree and a double-major in marketing and management, Michael went on to work in the client services and strategy teams at both traditional advertising and digital agencies. Over the past 10 years, he has been privileged to design, build and execute digital strategies for household names such as ANZ Bank, H&R Block and Converse.

Michael is also a guest-lecturer at the University of NSW and was recently named the winner of the Australian Marketing Institute's 'Future Marketing Leader' award.

Describe your current role and the organisation you work for, and give a brief account of what you do in your role on a day-to-day basis.

I currently lead the strategy and client services teams at Yoghurt Digital, the agency I co-founded in July 2014. Having said that, as a co-founder I wear many hats and my responsibilities are varied and broad.

On a day-to-day basis I spend my time doing the very thing that I'm most passionate about: designing, developing and implementing digital strategies. As the Strategy Director, my role is not just to service our existing client base, but to inspire other companies to collaborate with Yoghurt Digital on their digital strategies.

Yoghurt Digital is unique in that in doesn't just aim to drive additional website traffic or general brand awareness, but rather has a focus on converting that traffic and awareness into a tangible result: more enquiries, more sales, more customers, more revenue. The key to this is understanding the end consumer, their pain points and their behavioural patterns and preferences.

Because of our agency's approach, I'm perpetually learning and developing, which as a strategist, allows me to continue to broaden and simultaneously sharpen skills in interesting and engaging ways.

How important is Integrated Marketing Communication (IMC) to what you and your organisation do?

Although we're a digital agency and our scope is traditionally focused on online channels, there's an expectation from our clients to collaborate with their other agencies, suppliers and internal teams to ensure there's a clear, unified and targeted message across all of the marketing channels. So for us, IMC is critical to our strategy development and ability to be effective as an agency.

There are more marketing channels now than ever before, so it's easy to have disjointed campaigns that leave customers unclear and confused about your product or service. Even under the umbrella of 'digital' there are a multitude of channels—organic search, paid search, display advertising, affiliates and social media, just to name a few. And while digital is in many cases starting to take up a larger percentage of the overall channel strategy, it still needs to integrate with more traditional efforts like TV, radio, print, PR, activations and guerrilla marketing tactics.

In order for us to drive the most effective result possible for our clients, we have to have a cohesive strategy not just among the online channels, but between the online and offline channels too.

What types of promotional tools do you use in your IMC campaigns? Please provide examples.
We have a variety of digital promotional tools we use. We use search engine optimisation (SEO), content strategy and blogging from an organic perspective. Then we also have biddable media channels like search, display, remarketing, shopping, affiliates, social media and video. Finally, we also leverage user behaviour research and customer insights to develop A/B testing strategies and user experience (UX) improvements to help convert website traffic into actual bottom-line revenue.

What would your ideal IMC campaign look like and why?
My ideal IMC campaign would be a blend of traditional channels driving a strong brand awareness piece, with digital channels driving acquisition.

One of the fantastic things about digital channels is how trackable and measurable performance is. From an optimisation perspective, it's easier to demonstrate the impact of the little tactical adjustments you can make along the way that drive continuous growth and improvement. But brand awareness is a critical component to driving traffic in the first place.

Particularly in sectors that are particularly highly competitive—like fast fashion, financial services and insurance—I always like to see more creative activations and out-of-the-box advertising linked to a well-thought-out digital strategy.

Some of the best examples of this are Koala Mattress and Frank Body, both of whom have generated incredible brand cut-through in congested industries by combining creative, tongue-in-cheek advertising methods with a powerful digital presence.

How do you believe an IMC campaign affects the consumer decision-making process for your particular target audience?
If an IMC campaign is done correctly, then it should start with a deep understanding of the various consumer persona profiles the campaign will be targeting, including demographics, psychographics, behavioural patterns and major pain points. This is how tailored communication and channel strategies that drive genuine engagement and performance are developed.

In theory, if you follow this process then you should be able to increase brand awareness, improve message recognition and generate additional sales by addressing consumers' needs. It allows you to rise above the white noise of the marketing world and speak to the consumer on a one-to-one level.

If you look at the various stages of the conversion funnel—awareness, interest, consideration, conversion, retention—an IMC campaign can affect consumer decision making at every step of the funnel. It should move consumers through each stage of the funnel by continuing to re-enforce, regardless of channel, how a company's product or service will solve their pain point.

How has your application of IMC changed with the increase in digital marketing?

On a personal level, it hasn't really changed too much. The vast majority of my career has been spent in the digital space, so I've had a front-row seat to the evolution of digital marketing and its dramatic increase in prevalence.

The most important facet of this shift that's affected my application of IMC is the consistent growth of additional online channels to include in the mix. Google, Bing, YouTube, Facebook, Instagram … the list goes on. Each of them have their own ad serving platforms and sub-channels, so there's always something new to be learning and exploring as a part of your digital strategy (and broader marketing strategy).

What this means in practical terms is that you have more channels to consider and to manage. While some might find this daunting, I think it makes being a marketer more exciting than ever before. You can have more targeted messaging and a channel strategy that's completely tailored to your end consumer, so while you technically have more hurdles from a message management perspective, you can also achieve significantly more cut-through by speaking to your customers at the right time using the right channel with the right message.

What do you believe are some of the challenges to implementing an IMC campaign?

IMC campaigns aren't limited to your traditional marketing channels, but are rather all-encompassing from a brand communication perspective. This can make things tricky because it requires alignment not just from an internal marketing team in isolation, but from an organisational perspective.

As an example, depending on how fragmented a company's internal structure might be, there could be separate departments for marketing, PR, digital, brand, product, sales, distribution and fulfilment. That's a lot of teams, a lot of opinions and a lot of conflicting interests to navigate. So how do you get everyone into the same room and agreeing on a cohesive company-wide integrated marketing campaign when everyone has a different set of KPIs and their own initiatives to take care of?

An IMC campaign operates on the premise that if every channel works together seamlessly their sum will be greater than their parts, meaning that if you're trying to roll out an IMC campaign you need to have excellent stakeholder management abilities. You need each of these teams to agree on and buy into the overarching strategy; otherwise you're going to end up with a fragmented message that doesn't translate across all channels.

To make things even more complicated, if you have a big roster of agencies that service different areas of a company, then you need to ensure they're also collaborating and developing consistent messages and targeting across their respective remits. This can often be as difficult—if not more difficult—than internal turf wars.

IMC campaigns tend to be easier to execute at smaller, more agile companies where there's less red tape and power struggles. The larger the company, the bigger the respective teams, the more noticeable the departmental siloes, the less likely an IMC campaign is possible. That isn't to say that it's impossible: it just means more work and an experienced, effective and collaborative management team.

What advice would you offer a student studying IMC?

The best advice I can offer is to become a T-shaped marketer.

Being 'T-shaped' is a term that's grown in prevalence over recent years, particularly in the digital space, although it's equally applicable in traditional marketing. The term T-shaped is used in reference to a marketer who has a basic understanding of many disciplines while also being an expert in a particular subject matter.

Consider this: in today's day and age a marketer's objective is frequently to make the website the focal point for all marketing campaigns, found easily through digital channels and tactfully structured to guide consumers through an effective sales funnel. With that in mind, understanding how each digital channel works and, even more importantly, *how they work together,* is an incredibly valuable skillset. Marketers need to know when, where and how to communicate with consumers.

The marketing landscape is changing, with the days of siloed online and offline marketing tactics now long gone. So with more touch points being required than ever before, being a T-shaped marketer will give you the best possible opportunity to consistently build successful, integrated marketing plans.

Key terms

broadcast media	media agency	ratings
circulation	media duplication	reach
digital media	Out Of Home (OOH)/outdoor advertising	scheduling
frequency		spot
mass media	print media	traditional media
	rate card	

Revision questions

1. What is the difference between traditional and digital media?
2. What are the benefits and disadvantages of radio compared with newspapers and television?
3. What is the Duplication of Viewing Law? What are the implications for target marketing?
4. What is a rate card and what is its purpose to a marketer?
5. Traditional media is often considered 'dead men walking' by 'experts' in the industry such as Steve Bulmer of Microsoft. Do you agree with this? Should all of a media budget be only placed in digital platforms? What are the benefits or disadvantages of doing so?
6. Is more advertising money placed into digital or traditional media in recent years?
7. Is all traditional media declining in spend and share while all digital media is increasing?
8. What is one of the limitations of using a media plan that only includes digital media?
9. At the beginning of the chapter, we discussed the communication of Victoria University's new teaching model to school leavers. In your opinion, would using TV or radio advertising be a good media choice? Why? Why not?
10. Can you think of any limitations to only being able to contact customers who are already quite interested in your brand?

Further reading

Barker, B. (2014). Media planning: Measuring the distance between theory and practice. *Academy of Marketing*, 7–10 July. Bournemouth, UK.

Cheong, Y. (2014). The state of research on media planning, buying, and selling. *The Handbook of International Advertising Research*, 111–23.

Herman, E. S. & Chomsky, N. (2010). *Manufacturing Consent: The Political Economy Of The Mass Media*. Random House.

Hoffman, D. L. & Fodor, M. (2010). Can you measure the ROI of your social media marketing? *MIT Sloan Management Review*, *52*(1), 41.

Jugenheimer, D. W., Sheehan, K. & Kelley, L. D. (2015). *Advertising Media Planning: A Brand Management Approach*. Routledge.

Nelson-Field, K. & Riebe, E. (2011). The impact of media fragmentation on audience targeting: An empirical generalisation approach. *Journal of Marketing Communications*, *17*(01), 51–67.

Nelson-Field, K., Riebe, E. & Sharp, B. (2013). More mutter about clutter: Extending empirical generalizations to Facebook. *Journal of Advertising Research*, *53*(2), 186–91.

Wimmer, R. D. & Dominick, J. R. (2013). *Mass Media Research*. Cengage learning.

Notes

1 Dawkins, P. & Solomonides, I. (2017). Sequential single-unit blocks pave the pathway to academic success. *The Age*, 10 May.

2 McLuhan, M. (2011). *The Gutenberg Galaxy: The Making of Typographic Man*. University of Toronto Press.

3 Perry, M. (2015). It's a trust thing: Australian's learning to place more trust in digital advertising. www.nielsen.com/au/en/insights/news/2015/its-a-trust-thing.html

4 Pfeiffer, D., Fern, M., Wright, D. & Johnson, C. (2016). Australian Multi-Screen Report Q1. www.oztam.com.au/documents/Other/Australian%20Multi%20Screen%20Report%20Q1%202016%20FINAL.pdf

5 ibid.

6 Armstrong, G. & Kotler, P. (2003). *Marketing: An Introduction*. Prentice Hall.

7 Austin, A. Barnard, J. & Hutchcon, N. (2016). Media Consumption Forecasts 2016. Zenith Media.

8 Barnard, J. (2017). Advertising Expenditure Forecasts, March. www.publicismedia.de/wp-content/uploads/2017/03/2017-03-27-aef-executive-summary.pdf

9 Roy Morgan Research (2017a). Newspaper Cross-Platform Audience: 12 months to June 2017. www.roymorgan.com/industries/media/readership/cross-platform-audiences-newspapers

10 Roy Morgan Research (2017b). Magazine Cross-Platform Audience: 12 months to June 2017. www.roymorgan.com/industries/media/readership/cross-platform-audiences-magazines

11 Winchester, M. & Lees, G. (2016). An investigation of the success of targeting newspapers and efficiency in advertising expenditure in Ireland. *Journal of Promotions Management*, *22*(5), 620–36.

12 van Meurs, L. & Aristoff, M. (2009). Split-second recognition: what makes outdoor advertising work? *Journal of Advertising Research*, *49*(1), 82–92.

13 Barnard, op. cit.

14 Bojovic, Z. (2013). Mercedes uses Instagram to launch #Untamed CLA campaign. *Branding Mag*. www.brandingmag.com/2013/04/08/mercedes-untamed-instagram-campaign

15 Canning, S. (2017). AAMI offers digital logbook with Smart Plates phone app. Mumbrella. https://mumbrella.com.au/aami-offers-digital-logbook-with-smart-plates-phone-app-430148

16 www.youtube.com/watch?v=fQK7BtukFg0

17 Nelson-Field, K. (2013). *The Science of Sharing*. Oxford University Press: Melbourne.

18 Ice, B. (2016). 'Dumb ways to die' named best campaign of the decade at Tambuli Awards. *Marketing Magazine*. www.marketingmag.com.au/news-c/dumb-ways-die-named-best-campaign-decade-tambuli-awards

19 ibid.

20 Pathak, S. (2013). How music propelled the most popular campaign of the year: McCann's 'Dumb Ways to Die'. Ad Age. http://adage.com/article/special-report-music-and-marketing/numbers-mccann-s-dumb-ways-die-campaign/244455

21 ibid.

22 Ward, S. (2015). Has Dumb Ways to Die been effective? Mumbrella. https://mumbrella.com.au/dumb-ways-die-stopped-dumb-behaviour-around-trains-270751

23 Barron, R. & Scissors, J. Z. (2010). *Advertising Media Planning* (7th edn). New York: McGraw Hill, p. 3.

24 Rossiter, J. & Danaher, P. (2011). *Advanced Media Planning*. New York: Springer Science & Business Media.

25 Lloyd, D. W. & Clancy, K. J. (1991). CPMs versus CPMIs: Implications for media planning. *Journal of Advertising Research*, *31*(4), 34–44.

26 Green, L. (2006). The creative multiplier. *Advertising works*, *15*, 3.

27 Chong, M. (2006). How do advertising creative directors perceive research? *International Journal of Advertising*, *25*(3), 361–80.

28 Taylor, J., Kennedy, R. & Sharp, B. (2009). Is once really enough? Making generalizations about advertising's convex sales response function. *Journal of Advertising Research*, June, 198–200.

29 Tellis, Gerard J., (1997). Effective frequency: one exposure or three factors? *Journal of Advertising Research*, July–August, pp. 75–80.

30 Ephron, op. cit.

31 Ephron, E. (2006). *Media planning—from Recency to Engagement*. Hyderabad: ICFAI University Press.

32 Dahlén, M., Lange, F. & Smith, T. (2010). *Marketing Communications: A Brand Narrative Approach*. Chichester: Wiley & Sons.

33 Ephron, op. cit.

34 Winchester, M. & Lees, G. (2013). Do radio stations in New Zealand target successfully? *Australasian Marketing Journal*, 21, 52–8; Rossiter & Danaher, op. cit.

35 Rossiter & Danaher, op. cit.

36 Barron & Scissors, op. cit.

37 Alcorn, N. Harding, C. & Johnson, S. (2015). Media Consumer Survey 2015. Deloitte.

38 ibid.

39 Austin et al., op. cit.

40 ibid.

41 McDonald, C. & Scott, J. (2007). A brief history of advertising. *The Sage Handbook of Advertising*, London, Sage, 17–34.

42 Lees, G. & Wright, M. (2013). Does the Duplication of Viewing Law Apply to Radio Listening? *European Journal of Marketing*, *47*(3/4), 674–85; South African Audience Research Foundation. (2013). South African Audience Research Foundation. http://saarf.co.za/.

43 McPhee, W. N. (1963). *Formal Theories of Mass Behaviour*. New York: The Free Press of Glencoe.

44 Goodhardt, G. J. & Ehrenberg, A. S. C. (1969). Duplication of television viewing between and within channels. *Journal of Marketing Research*, *6*(May), 169–78; South African Audience Research Foundation, op. cit.

45 Winchester & Lees 2013, op cit.; Winchester, M. & Lees 2016, op. cit.

46 Pilotta, J. J., Schultz, D. E., Drenik, G. & Rist, P. (2004). Simultaneous media usage: a critical consumer orientation to media planning. *Journal of Consumer Behaviour*, *3*, 285–92. doi:10.1002/cb.141

47 Ehrenberg, A. S. C. (1968). The practical meaning and usefulness of the NBD/LSD theory of repeat-buying. *Applied Statistics*, *17*(1), 17–32; Ehrenberg, A. S. C., Uncles, M. & Goodhardt, G. (2004). Understanding brand performance measures: using Dirichlet benchmarks. *Journal of Business Research*, *57*(12), 1307–25.

48 Romaniuk, J. & Sharp, B. (2016). *How Brands Grow Part 2: Including Emerging Markets, Services, Durables, New and Luxury Brands*. Oxford University Press. Melbourne.

49 Sharp, B. (2010). *How Brands Grow: What Marketers Don't Know*. Oxford University Press: Melbourne.

50 Riebe, E., Wright, M, Stern, P & Sharp, B. (2014). How to grow a brand: Retain or acquire customers? *Journal of Business Research*, *67*(5), 990–7; Romaniuk & Sharp, op. cit.

51 Nelson-Field, K., Riebe, E. & Sharp, B. (2012). What's not to like: Can a Facebook fan base give a brand the advertising reach it needs? *Journal of Advertising Research*, June, 262–9.

52 The ideas presented in this case are based on a paper presented at the 2012 Australian & New Zealand Marketing Academy Conference. The author wishes to thank in particular Prof. Byron Sharp of the Ehrenberg-Bass Institute for Marketing Science for his comments and feedback.

53 Smith, W. R. (1956). Product Differentiation and Market Segmentation as Alternative Marketing Strategies. *Journal of Marketing*, *20* (July), 3–8; Yankelovich, D. (1964). New Criteria for Market Segmentation. *Harvard Business Review*, *42*, 83–90; Wind, Y. (1978). Issues and advances in segmentation research. *Journal of Marketing Research*, *15*(August), 317–37; Dickson, P. R. & Ginter, J. L. (1987). Market segmentation, product differentiation, and marketing strategy. *Journal of Marketing*, *51*(April), 1–10; McDonald, M. & Dunbar, I. (1998). *Market segmentation: how to do it and how to profit from it*. London: Macmillan Press Ltd.

54 Yankelovich, op. cit.; McDonald & Dunbar, op. cit.

55 Smith, op. cit.; Yankelovich, op. cit.; Wind, op. cit.; Dickson & Ginter, op. cit.; McDonald & Dunbar, op. cit.

56 Dibb, S. & Simkin, L. (1994). Implementation problems in industrial market segmentation. *Industrial Marketing Management*, *23*(1), 55–63.

57 Danneels, E. (1996). Market Segmentation: Normative Model Versus Business Reality. *European Journal of Marketing*, *30*(6), 36–51.

58 Hammond, K., Ehrenberg, A. S. C. and Goodhardt, G. J. (1996). Market segmentation for competitive brands. *European Journal of Marketing*, *30*(12), 39–49; Kennedy, R. & Ehrenberg, A. (2001). Competing Retailers Generally Have the Same Sorts of Shoppers. *Journal of Marketing Communications*, *7*(1), 19–26.

59 Esslemont, D. H. B. & Ward, T. (1989). The stability of segmentation solutions in a commercial survey. *New Zealand Journal of Business*, *10*, 89–95; Hoek, J., Gendall, P. and Esslemont, D. (1993). Market segmentation: A search for the holy grail? *Asia-Australia Marketing Journal*, *1*(1), 41–6.

60 Wright, M. & D. Esslemont (1994). The logical limitations of target marketing. *Marketing Bulletin*, *5*: 133–20; Wright, M. (1996). The dubious assumptions of segmentation and targeting. *Management Decision*, *34*(1), 18–24.

61 Thompson, R. S. (1989). Circulation versus advertiser appeal in the newspaper industry: An empirical investigation. *The Journal of Industrial Economics*, *37*(3): 259–71; Wilkinson, G. (1993). Factors affecting newspaper sales. *European Journal of Marketing*, *6*(2), 107–16; Attaway-Fink, B. (2005). Market-driven journalism: Creating special sections to meet reader interests. *Communication Management, 9*(2), 145–54; Mullainathan, S. & Shleifer, A. (2005). The market for news. *The American Economic Review*, *95*(4), 1031–53; Buratto, A., Grosset, L. & Viscolani, B. (2006). Avertising channel selection in a segmented market. *Automatica*, *42*, 1343–47.

62 Fink, C. C. (1988). *Strategic Newspaper Management*. New York, Random House, p. 129.

63 ibid.

64 Winchester & Lees 2013, op cit.

65 The Living Standard Measure, a measure of social class, consists of calculating a score based on 29 measures that include education, income and occupation, and geographic location of the respondents; for example, Truter, I. (2007). An overview of the Living Standards Measurement. *SA Pharmaceutical Journal,* October, 52–4. Although there are 10 LSM categories, it is accepted that they can be broken down into three: 1–4, 5–7 and 8–10. Martins, J. H. (2006). Household cash expenditure by Living Standards Measure group. *Journal of Family Ecology and Consumer Sciences, 34,* 1–9.

66 Times Media. (2013). Times Media Group. http://www.timesmedia.co.za/wp-content/uploads/2011/05/TMG-Overview-Feb-2013FINAL.pdf.

67 Mail & Guardian Media. (2013). Mail & Guardian Advertising. http://mg.co.za/page/advertising-1/; Media 24. (2013). Media 24 Newspapers. http://www.media24.com/en/newspapers.

68 Dowey, J. (2013). The Future of Media. http://www.omd.co.za/media_facts/FOM029_Blueprint_OMD_mediafacts2013.pdf; Media 24; Media Club South Africa. (2013). The press in South Africa. http://www.mediaclubsouthafrica.com/index.php?option=com_content&view=article&id=73%3. Mail & Guardian Media, op. cit.; Media 24, op. cit.; Soccer Laduma. (2013). Advertise Soccer Laduma. http://www.soccerladuma.co.za/page/advertise; Times Media, op. cit.

69 South African Audience Research Foundation, op. cit.

70 ibid.

71 ibid.

72 Kennedy, R. & Ehrenberg, A. (2001). There is no brand segmentation. *Marketing Insights*, *Marketing Research*, *13*(1), 4–7.

CHAPTER 11

Responsible Marketing Communication

Peter Ling

Hall of Fame and Hall of Shame

'The Parents' Voice' is an Australian online community of 5000 parents who decide whether food marketers should be awarded the Hall of Fame or the Hall of Shame. 'The Parents' Voice' has the support of the Bluearth health promotion charity, Cancer Council Australia, Diabetes Victoria, VicHealth and the YMCA.

Hall of Fame winners are marketers who creatively promote healthy consumption. Winners since 2005 have included the Federal Government, the Australian Bananas industry, Woolworths Supermarkets, McCain Foods, Sanitarium Weetbix and Cricket Australia.[1]

Figure 11.1 Australian Bananas' energy snack advertisement

The Federal Government promoted the 'Go for 2+5' campaign to encourage consumption of two fruits and five vegetables daily. Australian Bananas communicated bananas as 'Nature's Energy Snack' (see Figure 11.1).

Woolworths Supermarkets advertised its 'Fresh Food Kids' and celebrity Jamie Oliver's 'Garden Collectibles' range of stickers educating children on food origins and benefits. McCain Foods launched its School Veggie Patches program by providing seeds and equipment to help schools start vegetable gardens and teach students about the origins of vegetables.

Sanitarium Weetbix positioned its breakfast cereal as the official breakfast of the Australian Socceroos. Cricket Australia encouraged the public to play cricket in their backyard.

The Hall of Shame Award for Pester Power goes to marketers whose campaigns spur kids to nag for unhealthy products. Recipients of this Shame Award have included McDonald's (six times), Kellogg's (three times), Nestlé, Coles Supermarkets and Coca-Cola Australia.[2]

McDonald's has been 'shamed' for its Happy Meal promotions enticing children with sales promotions offering toys such as Action Man, My Little Pony and Kung Fu Panda. Kellogg's gained the Shame Award for marketing its LCM Bar as 'cool' and 'making kids popular at school'. Nestlé's Shame Award was for encouraging children to make repeat purchases to win in its Wonka Chocolate Golden Ticket promotion.

Coles and Coca-Cola received the Shame Award for using emotional appeals to increase the purchase of unhealthy goods. Coles offered teenage girls tickets to a performance of the boy band One Direction, partnering with Coca-Cola, Cadbury and Pringles.[3] Coca-Cola conveyed brotherly playful interactions to promote its soft drink, with the younger brother who idolises his older cola-drinking sibling finally tasting the feeling of the brand.[4] Since 25 per cent of Australian kids are obese or overweight, Parents' Voice felt that Coca-Cola Australia had used 'shameful marketing techniques'.[5]

■ INTRODUCTION

Parents have a responsibility to look after the welfare of their children. For this reason, parents praise companies that market responsibly and shame firms that seem to be irresponsible in marketing to impressionable children and teenagers.

The Parents' Voice Hall of Shame is only one channel for highlighting what seems to be irresponsible marketing to children by some marketers. CHOICE, Australia's consumer advocacy group, has also been giving out Shonky Awards since 2006 to marketers for false advertising, faulty products, misleading claims and poor service.[6] The Advertising Standards Bureau in Australia, and equivalent self-regulatory authorities in other countries, have also compiled lists of the most complained-about advertisements over the decades, with one report alone identifying 700 complaints against the Advanced Medical Institute for three advertisements on 'longer lasting sex'.[7]

As a result, questions have been asked about protecting diverse consumers as well as marketers. Which regulatory frameworks guide responsible marketing communication? What legislative laws prevent deceptive marketing? What codes of practice ensure responsible integrated marketing communication across diverse media platforms and delivery formats? What product-specific industry codes direct responsible marketing communication of various goods and services? What are the industry association codes and guidelines for best practices in marketing communication? As part of the theme of responsibility, which is conveyed by industry regulatory bodies and leading marketing companies, this chapter will address these questions.

LEARNING OBJECTIVES

After reading this chapter you should be able to:

1. discuss the regulatory frameworks that guide responsible marketing communication
2. describe the general laws pertaining to deceptive marketing
3. discuss media-specific regulatory codes of practice for diverse media platforms
4. discuss delivery-specific industry codes of practice for different media formats
5. discuss product-specific industry codes for responsible marketing communication of various goods and services
6. discuss industry-association codes and guidelines that govern standards in marketing communication.

Regulatory frameworks

Detailed information on industry and product regulations is very useful for students and practitioners. It is beyond the scope of this chapter to compare specific regulatory codes of countries other than Australia, which is where this book is published. Using the frameworks in this chapter, readers should be able to search for equivalent codes in their respective countries.

Before looking at the specifics of government and industry regulatory codes, it is essential to review the various conceptual models discussed in research and practice. This section reviews the frameworks of:

*   the International Chamber of Commerce (ICC)
*   researchers, particularly Braithwaite and Ayres, who have influenced the regulatory models of government and industry authorities
*   the European Advertising Standards Alliance (EASA)
*   the Australian Association of National Advertisers (AANA).

The International Chamber of Commerce (ICC)

The ICC started in 1919 as a global business organisation and launched the International Court of Arbitration in 1923.[8] It then issued its first advertising code in 1937, extended the self-regulatory framework several times over the years, broadened its name to the ICC Code on Marketing and Advertising Practice in 2006, and then revised it to the ICC Consolidated Code of Advertising and Marketing Communication Practice in 2011.[9]

The latest Consolidated ICC code is a benchmark for many government and industry bodies, comprising topics such as sales promotion; sponsorship, direct marketing and direct selling; advertising and marketing using digital interactive media; environmental claims in marketing communication; market and social research; food and beverage communication; and responsible environmental, food and beverage communication.[10]

The ICC has always advocated responsible **self-regulation** for its six million members in 130 countries in regions spanning Africa, the Americas, the Asia–Pacific, Europe and the Middle East.[11] It represented 'responsible creativity and communication' in 1937 and its current consolidated code advocates responsible marketing and commercial communication in various forms but does not cover corporate news releases, media statements and annual reports.[12]

Many global marketers have embedded responsibility into their marketing policies. The Coca-Cola Company has a responsible marketing policy and aligns its marketing approach to the ICC's code and principles of responsible marketing communication.[13] Unilever's marketing communication principles also comply with laws in local countries and the ICC Responsible Food and Beverage Marketing Communication framework.[14] The Nestlé Marketing Communication to Children Policy supports ICC activities and the World Health Organization's recommendations on marketing of foods and beverages to children.[15] Procter & Gamble, Microsoft, Publicis Group advertising agency, the World Federation of Advertisers, the European Advertising Standards Alliance, the Canadian Code of Advertising Standards and the Australian Advertising Standards Bureau also support the ICC Code.[16]

ICC supporters in the food and non-alcoholic beverage industry have formed the International Food & Beverage Alliance (IFBA) to commit to responsible marketing and advertising to children. IFBA members include The Coca-Cola Company, Danone, Ferrero, General Mills, Grupo Bimbo, The Kellogg Company, Mars, McDonald's, Mondelez International, Nestlé, PepsiCo and Unilever. IFBA also has a global policy on marketing communication to children, which is guided by global public health principles of the United Nations and the World Health Organization.

The IFBA's framework for responsible marketing communication (see Figure 11.2) comprises five levels: three bottom tiers on the 'how' of marketing techniques and two rungs of the 'what' of advertised products. The 'how' levels are national/regional regulatory frameworks; national self-regulatory frameworks; and industry-wide self-regulatory codes for food marketing that align with the ICC Consolidated Code on Advertising and Marketing Communication Practice and the ICC Framework for Responsible Food and Non-alcoholic Beverage Marketing Communication. The 'what' levels are individual corporate food marketing principles and best practice through pledge programs to improve marketing to children.[17]

Figure 11.2 The IFBA's framework for responsible marketing communication

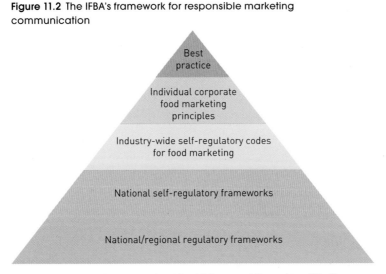

Source: IFBA. (2017). International Food & Beverage Alliance. https://ifballiance.org.

Researchers

Several researchers have written on ethics or moral conduct in marketing. There is a common research thread, with theories and frameworks covering individual specific behaviour and its impact on society. One study on the general theory of marketing ethics highlighted personal experiences and environmental variables such as culture, industry and organisation.[18] Another study on decision making on ethical issues in advertising focused on social and cultural environments with factors such as the individual, corporate policy and professional codes.[19]

John Braithwaite, a prominent regulatory researcher, recommended in his 1985 book *To punish or persuade* a regulatory response hierarchy covering four levels: self-regulation, **enforced self-regulation**, government **command regulation** with punishment discretion, and also command regulation with non-discretionary or mandatory punishment. The latter two levels could form one level of government command regulation with discretionary and non-discretionary punishment. While the research was based on coal-mining safety in the US, the UK, Australia, France, Belgium and Japan, the model of persuasion/punishment has served as a benchmark for many regulatory agencies.[20] See Figure 11.3 and the synthesis that follows.

Self-regulation

This is like private enforcement, where a company or industry sets acceptable standards of practice and an internal compliance group punishes deviations from the rules. While the government has a vision for desired practices, the industry trade association and its members would need to implement voluntary self-regulations and withdraw membership status from non-compliant members; for example, striking a doctor or lawyer from its professional register for unprofessional practices. Corporate headquarters of association members also need to see the merits of compliance and the demerits of non-compliance and to have internal systems to censor or punish non-complying managers.

Figure 11.3 Braithwaite's enforcement pyramid

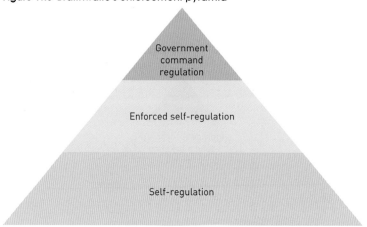

Source: Adapted from Braithwaite, J. (1985). *To punish or persuade.* Albany, NY: State
University of New York Press.

Enforced self-regulation

This is a form of public enforcement where a company or industry privately writes a set of compliance rules for the regulatory authority to publicly modify or ratify to satisfy government guidelines. While there is corporate or industry ownership in framing and writing the rules to meet government policy, the regulatory body plays an active role to verify the rules, ensure an independent internal compliance group, monitor performance and prosecute offenders. Companies tend to choose internal compliance rather than risk public censure.

Government command regulation

This is where the government writes detailed compliance rules and punishes offenders. The threat of punitive government actions could be a trigger for local offices to demand extra resourcing from corporate headquarters to ensure compliance with written government commands. There could be discretionary informal warnings for minor offences or non-discretionary mandatory punishment for serious offences. There could be financial penalties for each offence and criminal punishment of imprisonment and fines.

Braithwaite concluded that there could be a mix of enforcement strategies. It is more resource-demanding to have a regime of government command regulation. While it is beneficial for companies and industry associations to have their self-regulatory private enforcement strategies, the 'rotten apples' in business often necessitate **enforced self-regulation** and/or government command regulation.

In the US, the Federal Trade Commission (FTC) has its own inter-connected consumer protection pyramid. Law enforcement is at the peak while education and self-regulation form both sides of the broad bottom level of the pyramid. Law enforcement punishes violators and educates businesses as well as consumers to prevent similar behaviour. Consumer education is through publicity materials—including informing children about how to buy video games and toys—and partnerships of corporations, consumer organisations, industry bodies and government agencies. Business education also involves collaborative efforts with media to stop deceptive advertising. Self-regulation is through the Council of Better Business Bureau and its national advertising division, which monitors advertising, mediates on consumer or competitor complaints about misleading advertising, publicises its decisions and directs non-compliant advertisers to FTC to enforce action.[21] See Figure 11.4 for FTC's consumer protection pyramid.

Ayres & Braithwaite

In 1992, Ayres and Braithwaite published a book titled *Responsive regulation* and commented that 'The trick of successful regulation is to establish a synergy between punishment and persuasion'.[22]

In another enforcement pyramid model, they proposed a wider base of persuasion to achieve compliance, failing which there are other levels of enforcement such as a warning letter, civil monetary penalty, criminal prosecution, licence suspension and licence revocation.[23] See Figure 11.5.

Ayres and Braithwaite's regulatory theory has influenced several Australian authorities, such as the Australian Competition and Consumer Commission (ACCC), the Australian Securities & Investments Commission (ASIC), the Therapeutic Goods Administration (TGA) and the Australian Communications and Media Authority (ACMA).

Figure 11.4 FTC's consumer protection pyramid

Source: www.ftc.gov/images/transparency-1-ftc-pyramid

Figure 11.5 Ayres & Braithwaite's enforcement pyramid

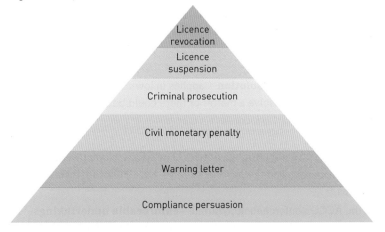

Source: Ayres, I. & Braithwaite, J. (1992). *Responsive regulation: transcending the deregulation debate.* New York: Oxford University Press, p. 35.

The ACCC's enforcement pyramid

The ACCC, an independent statutory authority that protects consumers and promotes fair competition, is like a two-sided coin with competition law on one side and consumer protection law on the other side. ACCC adapted Braithwaite's pyramid from its four levels in 2004 to six levels: education, advice and persuasion; voluntary industry self-regulation codes and schemes; administrative resolution; **infringement notices**; Section 87 settlement enforceable undertakings; and court cases (see Figure 11.6).[24]

The bottom level is ACCC's prevention strategy, which aims to facilitate compliance of the Trade Practices Act through education, advice and persuasion. The ACCC informs trade, commerce and consumers of their rights and responsibilities through its website, publications, electronic bulletins, emails,

Figure 11.6 ACCC's enforcement pyramid

media publicity, public events and information centre. There is also a consultative process through the Small Business Advisory Group, the Consumer Consultative Committee, an industry consultative committee and the Franchising Advisory Panel.

The second level—voluntary industry self-regulation or voluntary compliance—puts the onus on industry, businesses, chief executives and directors to form internal compliance processes and procedures for staff to comply with the law as part of corporate culture and practice. There could also be industry codes of conduct. At this level, it is essential for corporate leaders to work collaboratively with the ACCC.

The third level—**administrative resolution**—applies in low-risk situations. A trader may commit via correspondence to the ACCC to resolve a matter or there could be a signed agreement on resolution conditions, such as stopping corporate misconduct, compensating victims and taking measures to prevent misconduct re-occurrence.

The fourth level is a formal sanction through notices. The ACCC is empowered through the Australian Consumer Law and the *Competition and Consumer Act 2010* to issue **substantiation**, **infringement** and **public warning notices**.[25]

The fifth level of the ACCC's enforcement pyramid—**enforceable undertakings**—is interventionist, with individuals or companies publicly agreeing to accept responsibility for breaching the law, agreeing on a negotiated settlement to redress consumer loss or suffering and improving trade compliance processes and culture.

The sixth level involves court cases being employed when there is repeat illegal business conduct, when an unlawful action affects many consumers and when certain industries are misbehaving with regard to compliance. Legal action could include injunctions on current conduct, corrective advertising, financial compensation for affected businesses or consumers, compliance training programs, pecuniary fines or criminal convictions.

Although the ACCC enforcements and court cases deter potential and recurrent offenders, this process is obviously time-consuming and resource-sapping. So, prevention is better than a cure. There needs to be closer collaboration between the ACCC, industry and companies to achieve voluntary persuasion on codes of conduct and protect consumers in a fair, competitive marketplace. Nevertheless, it is comforting for consumers and companies to know that there are laws to protect them.

ASIC's regulatory compliance

ASIC also has six levels of enforcement for the financial markets industry: the first five levels of action are punitive, protective, preservative, corrective and compensatory; the bottom level is negotiated resolution. ASIC acknowledged that Ayres and Braithwaite's regulatory theory has influenced Australia's corporate law. In 1993, ASIC introduced civil penalties for corporate directors and officers who contravene their statutory duties.[26] More details on ASIC's enforcement is available in its 2014 performance report.[27]

TGA's compliance pyramid

Three models of four, five and six levels of persuasion and punishment have been associated with the TGA. A 2005 submission paper from the Foundation for Advertising Research featured Braithwaite's framework of four levels: self-regulation; enforced self-regulation; command regulation with discretionary punishment; and command regulation with non-discretionary punishment.[28] The TGA featured the Ayres and Braithwaite model in 2012 in its 'Advertising regulatory framework' report.[29] In another 2012 report, 'The TGA regulatory framework', the TGA featured a compliance pyramid of five levels: regulated entity communication and management; pharmacovigilance audit and testing; recall, suspension and advertising; civil penalties; and criminal penalties.[30]

ACMA's compliance pyramid

The ACMA is the independent statutory body that governs the media and communication industry with compliance and enforcement frameworks of different levels dated 2011 and 2014.

In a 2011 compliance pyramid, the ACMA model comprised education and outreach at the base followed by informal engagement on potential breaches; formal warnings; directions to comply; infringement notices; and Federal Court proceedings.[31] The 2014 model shows four levels: encouraging voluntary compliance; informal resolution; **administrative action**; and civil and criminal action (see Figure 11.7).[32]

Voluntary compliance

The ACMA's goal is to educate the community on regulatory requirements, empower voluntary compliance and therefore minimise enforcement intervention. Community education is done through advisory committees, consultations, discussions, guidance publications, investigation reports and seminars. The ACMA also facilitates industry self-regulatory and co-regulatory compliance codes of practice.

Informal resolution

The ACMA would contact the non-compliant person or company to resolve a minor non-compliant issue and would accept a written commitment on compliance resolution.

Administrative, civil and criminal actions

When an informal resolution is not appropriate or effective, the ACMA uses an administrative process such as issuing a formal warning and infringement penalty notice. It could also seek court-enforceable undertakings and amend, suspend or cancel licences and accreditations.

The ACMA may commence proceedings to seek civil penalties or criminal prosecution.

Figure 11.7 ACMA's enforcement pyramid

Source: ACMA.gov.au. (2014). ACMA compliance and enforcement policy, March.
http://www.acma.gov.au/theACMA/About/Corporate/Structure-and-contacts/the-acma-
overview-acma.

The EASA

The European Advertising Standards Alliance also has a four-level compliance pyramid. It was a normal pyramid framework in 2014 with a legal framework at the base followed by cross-industry self-regulation system, sector-specific codes and internal company codes.[33]

However, in 2017 the EASA converted this to an inverted pyramid (see Figure 11.8).[34]

Figure 11.8 EASA's inverted enforcement pyramid

Source: www.easa-alliance.org/ad-standards/what-are-ad-standards/regulatory-
framework.

The EASA promotes responsible advertising through 41 organisations across 25 countries, from Austria to the UK. It celebrated its twenty-fifth anniversary in 2017.[35] The EASA set up a network of international self-regulatory organisations in 2008 and followed up in 2016 with the establishment of the International Council for Advertising Self-regulation (ICAS) through founding members of self-regulatory organisations in the Asia–Pacific region, the Americas and Europe as well as the World Federation of Advertisers (WFA).[36] The WFA represents marketers globally and includes among its members the AANA.

The AANA

The Australian Association of National Advertisers, representing Australian advertisers since 1928, has an 'onion' regulatory framework. With five levels, the core focuses on the AANA's Code of Ethics and subsequent layers illustrate product-specific industry codes, specific media delivery codes, broad media co-regulatory codes and the highest level of legislation.[37] See Figure 11.9.

Figure 11.9 AANA's regulatory guide

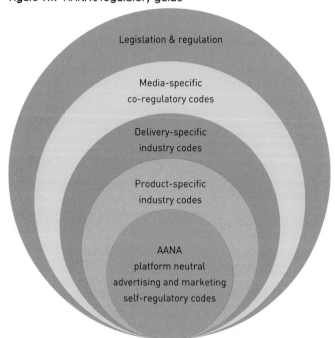

Source: http://aana.com.au/self-regulation/advertising-regulatory-guide/.

Whether you prefer to work from the outer layer to the inner layer or vice versa, the AANA framework provides a holistic picture of what to anticipate at each level. The AANA obviously suggests starting at the core of its Code of Ethics as this applies generally to any medium or product.

This section on regulatory frameworks has uncovered various models with three to six levels of persuasion and punishment. The ICC Consolidated Code of Advertising and Marketing Communication Practice covers regulatory codes for various marketing communication tools. The ICC-aligned framework of IFBA has five tiers of the 'how' and 'what' of responsible marketing and advertising to children, advocating national or regional regulatory frameworks, national self-regulatory frameworks, industry-wide self-regulatory codes, individual corporate principles and best practices. Braithwaite started with four levels: self-regulation, enforced self-regulation, and government command regulation with discretionary and non-discretionary punishment. The FTC has three levels: education, self-regulation and law enforcement. Ayres and Braithwaite then introduced a framework with six levels encompassing compliance persuasion up to licence revocation. Australian legislative enforcement authorities such as the ACCC, ASIC, TGA and ACMA have been influenced by Ayres and Braithwaite's philosophy to adopt four to six levels of their regulatory frameworks. The EASA and AANA have frameworks of four and five levels respectively.

In reviewing the various regulatory models, the IFBA, ACCC and the EASA frameworks specifically indicate the role of individual corporate food marketing principles, internal company compliance processes and codes of conduct. The IFBA framework covers the 'how' and 'what' of responsible marketing; the ACCC framework is like a two-sided coin of persuasion/punishment; and the EASA model is like a trinity of legal, industry and corporate stakeholders. Hence, the ideal regulatory framework obviously needs to have a legal framework to set the boundaries; self-regulatory systems across industries, goods and services and media to establish desired best practices; and internal company codes that become corporate values and culture for responsible marketing and communication.

The next few sections provide more insights on the five levels of the AANA's 'onion' framework:

- legislation and enforcement
- media-specific codes
- delivery-specific industry codes
- product specific industry codes
- AANA codes.

IMC IN ACTION: CORRECTING MISLEADING MARKETING CLAIMS

There are many examples of corrective advertising cases. This IMC in Action highlights some of these cases over the years: Listerine, Ribena, Bayer, Skechers and Volkswagen.

Listerine

In 1977, the Federal Trade Commission ordered Warner-Lambert to spend US$10 million over 18 months to correct 40 years of misleading advertising claiming that its Listerine mouthwash could kill germs and was a remedy for sore throats and colds. The FTC-specified advertisement stated that 'Listerine will not help prevent colds or sore throats or lessen their severity'.[38]

Ribena

This was an interesting case of two 14-year-old New Zealand girls shaming Ribena. For a 2004 school project to prove that cheaper drink brands had less vitamin C and were less healthy, the girls tested the vitamin C content of Ribena's Ready to Drink and its rivals several times each. The girls discovered that the Ribena brand lacked vitamin C content although its packaging claimed '7 mg of Vitamin C per 100 ml'.

When GlaxoSmithKline (GSK), Ribena's owner, did not comment on the girls' findings, New Zealand's 'Fair Go' consumer affairs television program highlighted its project findings and then the government watchdog, the Commerce Commission, investigated the claims. The commission took GSK to court for breaching the Fair Trading Act. The Auckland District Court penalised GSK NZ$217 500 and mandated corrective advertising. In March 2007, GSK amended the vitamin C claim on its packaging and advertising.[39]

Bayer

Bayer Healthcare Pharmaceuticals spent US$20 million on corrective advertising for its Yaz oral birth control pill. Complying with the 2009 enforcement laid down by the Food and Drug Administration and attorney generals of 27 US states, Bayer had to advertise that Yaz would not cure premenstrual syndrome or pimples, as had been claimed, and had to submit Yaz advertisements for approval over a period of six years.[40]

Skechers

In 2012, Skechers USA agreed to pay the Federal Trade Commission (FTC) $40 million for charges of deceiving consumers that its Shape-ups shoes could assist customers to shed weight and tone muscles in their abdomen, buttocks and legs. Since Skechers had also made unfounded claims for its Resistance Runner, Toners and Tone-ups shoes, FTC also alerted buyers that they could be eligible for refunds.[41]

Volkswagen

In 2016, German automaker Volkswagen AG agreed to a US$14.7 billion settlement for allegedly cheating emissions tests and deceiving consumers on their 2.0 litre diesel vehicles. The settlement included a buyback and lease termination for 500 000 US 2009-to-2015-model diesel vehicles; compensating customers; and spending $4.7 billion on green vehicle technology and pollution mitigation. The FTC settlement case website cited several legislative authorities—including the Environmental Protection Agency, the California Air Resources Board and California's 'Unfair Competition' law—involved in bringing a case against Volkswagen.[42] In 2017, the ACCC also took action in the Federal Court against Volkswagen AG and its subsidiaries Audi AG and Audi Australia for misleading representations in diesel vehicle emission claims between 2011 and 2015.[43]

Legislation and enforcement

This section reviews the enforcement authorities in Australia: the Australian Competition & Consumer Commission (ACCC), the Australian Communications and Media Authority (ACMA), the Australian Securities & Investments Commission (ASIC), the Office of the Australian Information Commissioner (OAIC) and the Therapeutic Goods Administration (TGA).[44] See Table 11.1 for a synthesis of the legislative authorities and their enforcement scope, followed by an overview of the legislative acts that are relevant to the marketing communication industry.

Table 11.1 Australian legislation and enforcement authorities

LEGISLATION	ENFORCEMENT AUTHORITIES
Competition and Consumer Act 2010 (formerly the *Trade Practices Act 1974*) Australian Consumer Law 2011	The Australian Competition & Consumer Commission (ACCC) is an independent statutory body that promotes business competition and fair trading, protects consumers and ensures that industry conduct codes protect small businesses.[45]
Broadcasting Services Act 1992 *Radiocommunications Act 1992* *Spam Act 2003* *Do Not Call Register Act 2006* *Telecommunications Act 1997* *Telecommunications (Consumer Protection and Service Standards) Act 1999* *Interactive Gambling Act 2001*	The Australian Communications and Media Authority (ACMA) is a statutory body that regulates broadcasting, the internet, radio communications and telecommunications. ACMA started in July 2005 through the merger of the Australian Broadcasting Authority and the Australian Communications Authority.[46]
Australian Securities and Investments Commission Act 2001 *Corporations Act 2001* *National Consumer Credit Protection Act 2009*	The Australian Securities & Investments Commission (ASIC) is an independent body that regulates consumer credit, financial markets and financial services firms.[47]
Privacy Act 1988 *Freedom of Information Act 1982* *Australian Information Commissioner Act 2010*	The Office of the Australian Information Commissioner (OAIC) is an independent body that regulates functions of privacy, freedom of information and government information policy.[48]
Therapeutic Goods Act 1989	The Therapeutic Goods Administration (TGA) administers the Therapeutic Goods Advertising Code 2015 to ensure that products making therapeutic claims are on the Australian Register of Therapeutic Goods and their advertising in broadcast, print and display media have advertisement permits from the Australian Self-Medication Industry or the Complementary Healthcare Council.[49]

The ACCC & enforcement

The *Competition and Consumer Act 2010*

This Act promotes fair competition, consumer protection and healthy relationships between consumers, retailers, wholesalers and suppliers. The Act covers industry codes, price monitoring, anti-competitive practices, product safety and product labelling. Section 2 of the Act includes the Australian Consumer Law and issues of misleading conduct, unfair practices, product safety and manufacturers' liabilities, product warranties and country of origin information.[50]

Some of the projects handled under Australian Consumer Law include travelling con men, Indigenous consumer protection, environmental claims, unfair contract terms, consumer guarantees, extended warranties, testimonials, country of origin labelling on food, Was/Now pricing, cash-back schemes, romance fraud scams, **property spruikers** or promoters, rent-to-buy schemes, training providers, the travel industry, credit card chargebacks, music festivals and most complained about businesses.[51]

The ACCC penalises non-compliance of a **substantiation notice** with a penalty of $1080 for an individual or $5400 for a body corporate. This penalty could increase to $3000 for an individual or $16 500 for a body corporate through a court order. There could also be an infringement notice penalty for providing misleading or false information. This could lead to a penalty of $1800 for an individual and $9000 for a corporation. Penalties could be $108 000 for a listed corporation.[52] See IMC Action for ACCC's case against the pain-relief Nurofen brand.

IMC IN ACTION: NUROFEN PENALISED FOR MISLEADING CLAIMS

Nurofen packaged and marketed a specific range of products for back pain, period pain, migraine pain and tension headache on its website between 2011 and 2015 (see Figure 11.10). The ACCC found that each specific product contained the same ibuprofen lysine 342 mg ingredient and was priced higher than comparable pain relievers when it was not formulated for a specific pain treatment.

Figure 11.10 Nurofen's range of pain products

In March 2015, the ACCC initiated Federal Court proceedings against Nurofen's owner, Reckitt Benckiser, for making misleading claims about its Nurofen Specific Pain product range.[53] In December 2015, the Federal Court found that Nurofen had made misleading specific pain claims and ordered Reckitt to comply with several enforcements: remove the Specific Pain range from shelves within three months; publish corrective notices on its website and newspapers; and pay the ACCC's legal costs.[54]

The ACCC wanted Reckitt to be penalised $6 million for breaching the Australian Consumer Law. In April 2016, the Federal Court ordered Reckitt to pay a $1.7 million penalty.[55] In May 2016, ACCC appealed the decision as Reckitt had sold nearly six million units of the product range in 8500 retail outlets.[56] In December 2016, the Full Federal Court upheld ACCC's appeal and ordered Reckitt to pay a $6 million penalty. Reckitt tried to appeal but the High Court dismissed the appeal in April 2017.[57]

At the same time, consumers, through Bannister Law, launched a class action lawsuit in February 2016 for damages and refunds.[58] As Reckitt had made $45 million in revenue from the Special Pain range over four years, it agreed in July 2017 to pay $3.5 million compensation to consumers, with Bannister Law directing customers who had bought the products between 1 January 2011 and 31 December 2015 to register for claims on a special website, nurofenclassaction.com.au/register.[59]

The ACMA & enforcement

The ACMA regulates the four converging networks of broadcasting, the internet, radio telecommunications and telecommunications. The networks include two national radio and television broadcasters; 50 commercial television and 270 commercial radio licences; 80 community television and 300 community radio licences; 2500 subscription television licences; 600 internet service providers; more than 200 Voice

Over Internet Protocol (VOIP) providers for broadband internet phone calls; 170 licensed telecommunication carriers; and more than 155 000 radio communication licences.[60]

The ACMA also registers radio and television industry codes of practice covering subscription narrowcast radio, commercial radio, community radio broadcasting, open narrowcasting, commercial television, community television, subscription broadcast television, subscription narrowcast television and open narrowcast television.[61]

The ACMA manages compliance and enforcement under several acts covering broadcasting, radio communication, telecommunication, spam, the Do Not Call Register and interactive gambling.[62] Under the *Spam Act 2003*, the ACMA could act through formal warnings, enforceable undertakings, infringement notices and Federal Court cases. Infringement notice penalties could be A$6800, A$21 600 or A$110 000.[63]

Also under the *Spam Act 2003*, ACMA administers the eMarketing Code of Practice involving Australian commercial electronic communication.[64] Similarly, the *Do Not Call Register Act 2006* empowers ACMA to penalise fax marketers, researchers and telemarketers if they breach the Act. Infringement penalties could be A$110 000 daily and court action penalties could be A$220 000 daily.[65]

The ACMA's website publishes infringement notices. For example, the Federal Court ordered Getaway Escapes Pty Limited and its director to pay $325 000 penalties for breaching the Telemarketing & Research Industry Standard and the Do Not Call Register Act between 2013 and 2014.[66] Upside.Digital e-marketing company paid $39 600 in infringement notices for breaching the *Spam Act 2003*.[67]

ASIC & enforcement

Under the *National Consumer Credit Protection Act 2009*, ASIC is empowered to issue substantiation notices, public warning notices and infringement notices. It can seek a legal injunction to stop an offending company from continuing with questionable advertising.[68]

ASIC has penalised companies for misleading advertising. National Australia Bank paid $40 800 for four infringement notices on misleading advertising of its UBank home loan product.[69] Online Capital Markets Pty Ltd paid $30 600 for misleading emails and online advertisements that claimed quick significant profits and monthly income from high-risk derivative trading and margin foreign exchange.[70] Capital Debt Solutions Australia Pty Ltd paid a $10 800 infringement fine for falsely claiming online that they were 'Government approved' and 'trusted and recommended by more than 6000 Australians'.[71]

The OAIC & enforcement

The *Privacy Act 1988* enables the Office of the Australian Information Commissioner to seek enforceable undertakings, injunctions or civil penalties (up to A$340 000 for individuals and A$1.7 million for corporations).[72] For example, OAIC and ACMA found Telstra had breached privacy laws as the information of 15 777 customers was made available online between February 2012 and May 2013.[73]

The TGA & enforcement

Guided by the *Therapeutic Goods Act 1989*, the TGA may seek market removal of a product and impose civil/criminal penalties for deliberate non-compliance. The TGA has a complaints resolution panel that recommends advertisement amendments, and withdrawal and correction of misleading claims.[74] TGA's website on 'Court action' also shows cases of companies and individuals being fined for various breaches of the Therapeutic Goods Act.[75]

In summary, the ACCC, ACMA, ASIC, OAIC and TGA enforce many legislative acts to protect consumers and fair trading across various media channels and products or services. There could be substantiation requests, formal warnings, enforcement undertakings, infringement notices, court cases, legal injunctions and financial penalties against offenders.

Marketers who are more familiar with the various laws and enforcement authorities would be better equipped to conduct their businesses more responsibly and effectively. Further information is available on 'Legal obligations of marketing', which covers advertising, competitions, signage, direct marketing, the Do Not Call Register, spam, privacy, brochures, **bill posting**, spruiking, pricing regulations, intellectual property and international relations.[76]

Media-specific codes

As the previous section indicated, the ACMA registers some radio and television platform industry codes of practice. This section looks at codes of practice for media platforms such as **free-to-air TV**, **subscription TV**, commercial radio, the internet, print and other media.

Some of the codes have been developed in consultation with media bodies such as free TV Australia, the Australian Subscription Television and Radio Association (ASTRA), Commercial Radio Australia and the Australian Community Television Alliance. Table 11.2 features the media platforms and the co-created or co-regulatory codes.

Table 11.2 Media-specific co-regulatory codes

MEDIA PLATFORMS	CO-REGULATORY CODES OF PRACTICE
Free-to-air TV	Commercial Television Industry Code of Practice 2015 of Free TV Australia, described also as Free TV Code, and registered with ACMA[77] Children's Television Standards 2009 by ACMA[78]
Subscription TV	Australian Subscription Television and Radio Association (ASTRA) Codes of Practice with ACMA consultation and AANA compliance: Subscription Broadcast Television Codes of Practice 2013; Subscription Narrowcast Television Codes of Practice 2013; Subscription Narrowcast Radio Codes of Practice 2013; and Guidelines for the Classification of Films 2012.[79]
Commercial radio	Commercial Radio Code of Practice 2017 by Commercial Radio Australia, registered by ACMA and complying with AANA codes.[80]
Internet, print and other media	Community Television Broadcasting Codes of Practice 2011 from Australian Community Television Alliance.[81] Community Radio Broadcasting Codes of Practice 2008.[82] Advertising in any media platform must also comply with AANA Codes.[83]

Complaints

Complaints about breaching codes are handled in a variety of ways. Complaints about free-to-air TV are sent to Free TV Australia, which directs the complaint to a specific broadcaster. ACMA could also be involved if the complainant is dissatisfied with the broadcaster's response. Television networks are involved when there is a breach of an ASTRA code. Similarly, a radio station would receive a complaint that breaches the Commercial Radio Code.

Advertising on subscription TV, commercial radio, digital and print media must also comply with AANA codes related to ethics, children, food and beverages, environment and wagering.

The Advertising Standards Board handles complaints about advertising on Free TV, subscription TV, commercial radio, print, the internet and various media.[84]

IMC IN ACTION: 'ROYAL PRANK' RADIO BROADCAST

A nurse allegedly committed suicide after a prank call on 4 December 2012 from two radio broadcasters at the 2DayFM radio station in Sydney.

The Duchess of Cambridge was in King Edward VII Hospital being treated for morning sickness when Mel Greig and Michael Christian from 2DayFM pretended to be the Queen of England and Prince Charles. Nurse Jacintha Saldanha transferred the call to her colleague, who updated the pranksters on the Duchess' condition.

Mel and Michael had recorded the conversation and subsequently, unsuccessfully, called the nurses again to obtain permission to broadcast the content. The station went ahead with the broadcast a few hours after the prank call despite not obtaining consent.

Three days later, colleagues found Jacintha dead in the nurses' apartment with three handwritten notes referring to the hoax call, the hospital and her funeral arrangements.[85]

The note on the hoax put the blame on the broadcasters: 'Radio Australians Mel Greig and Michael Christian responsible'. Massive global negative publicity erupted. Both Greig and Christian apologised and 2DayFM offered $500 000 in compensation to the family.[86]

ACMA investigated the incident under the *Broadcasting Services Act 1992*. Between 2013 and 2015, ACMA and 2DayFM fought the case in the Federal Court, the Full Federal Court and the High Court, which eventually found in favour of ACMA on 4 March 2015.

ACMA reported that 2DayFM had breached several clauses of the Code, particularly related to broadcasting without consent and treating participants in an exploitative and demeaning manner. 2DayFM agreed to enforcement action. First, it would broadcast a special three-hour program on media ethics and create awareness of anxiety, bullying and depression. Second, it would require employees to undergo training on legal and ethical obligations. Third, it would comply with a licence condition that stipulated informing a person or obtaining consent before broadcasting.[87]

Delivery-specific industry codes

Different media delivery formats such as outdoor, email, native advertising and testimonials also have advertising regulatory codes, guidelines and principles; for example, the Outdoor Media Association (OMA), the Association for Data-Driven Marketing & Advertising (ADMA), the Australian Digital Advertising Alliance (ADAA) and the Interactive Advertising Bureau (IAB).[88] See Table 11.3 for the codes of practice of different media delivery methods, with some industries adhering to multiple codes.

Outdoor advertising

Outdoor or **out-of-home advertising** could be in roadside, transport or retail environments. Roadside advertising could involve bicycle stations, billboards, bus or tram shelters, external panels of buses and

Table 11.3 Delivery-specific industry codes

DELIVERY METHODS	CODES, GUIDELINES & PRINCIPLES
Outdoor advertising	Outdoor Media Association (OMA) Code of Ethics. OMA members also adhere to industry codes of practice:[89]
Direct marketing	Association for Data-Driven Marketing & Advertising (ADMA) Code of Practice.[90]
Digital platforms	Australian Best Practice Guideline for Online Behavioural Advertising from the Australian Digital Advertising Alliance (ADAA). Members include Australian Association of National Advertising (AANA), Australian Direct Marketing Association (ADMA), Google, Interactive Advertising Bureau (IAB) in Australia, Media Federation of Australia (MFA), Microsoft, Network Ten Digital, NineMSN, Telstra Advertising Network, The Communications Council and Yahoo!7.[91]
Native advertising, online testimonials	Native Advertising Principles from AANA and IAB Australia to manage editorial-lookalike content.[92]

trams, free-standing panels, kiosks, phone booths and public toilets. Transport advertising could be on airport externals or internals, bus or tram internals, bus interchanges, rail concourses or platforms and train externals. Retail advertising could appear in cafés, convenience stores, medical centres, office buildings and lifts, petrol stations, shopping centres and universities.[93] Complaints are directed to the Advertising Standards Bureau, which has upheld varying numbers of complaints over the years.[94]

Direct marketing

The ADMA's Code of Practice stresses that the consumer is the hero and members need to abide by the principles of responsibility, honesty, transparency, fairness, choice and safety. For example, the ADMA's principle of using data responsibly encourages members to collect, use, store and maintain data that comply with regulatory guidelines. The principle also advocates non-excessive and non-intrusive marketing to 'vulnerable consumers'. The principle of transparency specifies that members need to be upfront about collecting personal data, such as the who, why and how of data collection.[95]

Digital advertising

Australia's Interactive Advertising Bureau (IAB) also believes in a collaborative effort to regulate digital advertising practices through federal laws, state government authorities and self-regulation. Its 2015 digital advertising policy and regulation guide cites the Australian Competition and Consumer Commission, the Australian Consumer Law, the *Competition and Consumer Act 2010*, the *Spam Act 2003*, the *Privacy Act 1988*, the Australian Communications and Media Authority, the Office of the Australian Information Commissioner, the various codes of the Australian Association of National Advertisers and the self-regulatory process of the Australian Digital Advertising Alliance.[96]

The IAB's regulatory guidelines also highlight seven principles for **online behavioural advertising**— or its alternative term, **interest-based advertising**. The seven principles are personal information, website operator, user choice, keeping data secure, sensitive segmentation to children, educating users on data issues, and being accountable to regulatory compliance.[97]

Native advertising

The IAB has also worked with the Australian Association of National Advertisers to develop principles for native advertising or advertorial-type online advertising in blogs, branded content or product placement.[98]

The principles mandate distinguishing visibly the paid content from the editorial environment and adhering to the codes of the AANA.[99]

Since consumers seek reviews of services and goods to help with buying decisions, the ACCC has established guidelines for online reviews to prevent fraudulent practices on review platforms—which include special review websites and blogs—namely:

- Review platforms must be open about commercial relationships between the platforms, reviewers and reviewed companies.
- Review platforms must not publish deceptive reviews; for example, a writer being paid to write a review without using the product; a product user who is literally paid to write an exaggerated review; or a business or competitor writing the review itself.
- Review platforms must not mislead consumers by selectively editing out negative comments.

A review platform could be fined for misleading testimonials; for example, Citymove removalists paid a $6600 infringement fee in 2011 when online reviews by 'genuine' consumers were misleading.[100]

Product-specific industry codes

There are also advertising regulatory guides for specific product categories such as vehicles, alcohol, children's food and beverage, therapeutics and weight management. See Table 11.4.

Table 11.4 Product-specific industry codes

PRODUCT CATEGORIES	INDUSTRY CODES
Vehicle	Federal Chamber of Automotive Industries (FCAI) Voluntary Code of Practice for Motor Vehicle Advertising.[101]
Alcohol	Responsible Alcohol Marketing Code from the Alcohol Beverages Advertising Code (ABAC) Scheme.[102]
Children's food/beverage and Quick-Service Restaurants (QSR)	Australian Food & Grocery Council (AFGC) Responsible Children's Marketing Initiative and AFGC Quick-Service Restaurant Initiative.[103]
Therapeutic products	Therapeutic Goods Advertising Code 2015 from the Therapeutic Goods Advertising Code Council (TGACC).[104]
Weight management	Weight Management Code of Practice 2016 from Weight Management Council Australia (WMCA).[105]

Code focus

The FCAI guides advertisers on standards for featuring messages and images on road safety. The ABAC ensures responsible alcohol marketing through advertorials, brand advertising, brand extensions to non-alcohol categories, digital communication, marketing collaterals, packaging and product names, point of sale items, retailer advertising and sales competitions.

The AFGC manages two initiatives on children's food and beverage advertising. The TGACC facilitates responsible marketing of therapeutic goods and non-deceptive advertising to consumers. WMCA's code ensures accurate and truthful marketing in terms of pricing, needs and benefits of weight management services or products.

Non-compliance

The Advertising Standards Board manages complaints related to advertising of vehicles, alcohol, children's food and beverages and fast-food restaurants.[106] TGACC's complaints resolution panel receives online submissions of complaints about therapeutic advertising and determines actions for breaches of the advertising code.[107]

The AANA's codes

Previous sections on media-specific and delivery-specific codes have mentioned AANA and the Advertising Standards Bureau. This section discusses the various codes and guidelines that form the self-regulatory framework. See Table 11.5 for an overview of the AANA's self-regulatory framework and then a discussion on the Advertising Standards Bureau.

Table 11.5 The AANA's codes and guidelines

CODES & GUIDELINES	SELF-REGULATION FOCUS
Code of Ethics 2012	This code focuses on responsible marketing to consumers, society and competitors[108]
Code for Advertising & Marketing Communications to Children 2014	Standards include factual presentation, appropriate media placement, sexualisation, safety, social values, parental authority, qualifying statements, competitions, popular personalities, premiums, alcohol, privacy, and food and beverages[109]
Food & Beverages Advertising & Marketing Communications Code 2009	Code highlights that advertising must be honest, must not encourage excess consumption, must distinguish between commercial content and news content, must not imply that the advertised product would provide physical, psychological or social advantage and must not urge children to pester parents to buy the advertised product[110]
Environmental Claims in Advertising & Marketing Code 2009	Claims must be truthful, substantiated and relevant[111]
Wagering Advertising & Marketing Communication Code 2015	This code applies to betting on greyhound, harness and horse races; competitive electronic gaming; fantasy teams, royal baby names, novelty events or award winners[112]
Best Practice Guideline: Responsible Marketing Communications in the Digital Space 2015	This 'digital marcomms' guide applies to blogs and microblogs, brand websites, instant messaging, livecasting, mobile and web applications, online advertising, online gaming, podcasts, RSS feeds, social networking, social news websites, video and photo sharing and wikis[113]
Clearly Distinguishable Advertising Best Practice Guideline 2017	This guideline applies when a marketer has reasonable content control when promoting a service or product to consumers[114]

The Advertising Standards Bureau (ASB)

The ASB is a non-government body, established in 1975, that serves as the secretariat for the Advertising Claims Board and the Advertising Standards Board.[115] As the ASB administers various industry and product-specific codes of practice at the self-regulation level, this section looks at how it facilitates resolutions of complaints of advertising in Australia across consumers, advertisers and media.

The ASB administers the AANA codes and best practice guidelines as well as the FCAI Motor Vehicle Code and AFGC codes concerning children's marketing and the Quick Service Restaurant industry. The ASB also handles advertising complaints related to free-to-air TV, subscription TV and commercial radio.[116]

The ASB reviews hundreds of complaints yearly to decide whether they breach the AANA's Code of Ethics and other codes on marketing communication of food, beverages, children's products and services, motor vehicle advertising and environmental claims.

Only written complaints by facsimile, post or online will be accepted. The ASB then writes to the advertiser and requests a written response to the complaint. The ASB Board reviews complaints during its twice-a-month meetings or via teleconference for urgent issues. The Board determines whether each complaint should be upheld or dismissed depending on whether there is a breach of any initiative or code under its jurisdiction.

The ASB notifies the advertiser of the Board's determination within 48 hours. For complaints that are upheld, the advertiser responds within five days about removing or amending the offending advertisement. The ASB then releases the final case report to the complainant and the public. If the advertiser does not comply with the Board's decision to amend or discontinue the offending advertisement, the ASB notifies the media owner or even a government authority.

The advertiser may request an independent review if a complaint is upheld. Likewise, the complainants could request a review if the Board dismisses the complaints.[117]

Most complained-about ads

The ASB publishes a yearly list of the '10 most complained about ads'. For 2016 and 2017, Ultra Tune Australia received the most complaints but ASB dismissed the cases except for one advertisement in 2016.[118] [119]
See Table 11.6 for the top 10 most complained-about advertisements for 2016 and 2017.

Table 11.6 The ASB's top 10 most complained-about advertisements, 2016 and 2017

YEAR	ADVERTISERS	DETERMINATION
2017	Ultra Tune: TV, 'Muffler' (359 complaints)	Dismissed
	Youfoodz: TV, 'forkin' (304 complaints)	**Upheld**
	Youfoodz: TV, 'forkin' (232 complaints)	**Upheld**
	Sportsbet: TV, drug cheat Ben Johnson (202 complaints)	**Upheld**
	Neds: TV, 'Telemarketing' (186 complaints)	Dismissed
	Meat & Livestock: TV, 'Leaders' (144 complaints)	Dismissed
	Neds: TV, 'Tradesmen' (139 complaints)	**Upheld**
	Industry Super Fund: TV, 'Hen House' (126 complaints)	Dismissed
	AAMI: TV, Ship Creek' (96 complaints)	Dismissed
	iSelect: TV, 'Different partners' (72 complaints)	Dismissed
2016	Ultra Tune: TV, 'We're into rubber' (418 complaints)	Dismissed
	Meat & Livestock: TV, 'Boomerang' (376 complaints)	Dismissed
	BCF: TV, camping & fishing as 'BCFing Fun' (248 complaints)	Dismissed
	Meat & Livestock: TV, 'Boomerang' (241 complaints)	Dismissed
	Ultra Tune: TV, car on train tracks (208 complaints)	**Upheld**
	Meat & Livestock: TV, 'Boomerang' (130 complaints)	Dismissed
	Ultra Tune: TV, car dangling on cliff (113 complaints)	Dismissed
	Roadshow Film: TV, horror movie (82 complaints)	**Upheld**
	Medibank Private: TV, family groups (66 complaints)	Dismissed
	Honey Birdette: Poster, woman in underwear (59 complaints)	**Upheld**[120]

For 2017, ASB received more than 6300 complaints, with nearly 1860 complaints related to the top 10 categories. The 'Top 10' complained-about advertisements in 2016 received nearly 2000 complaints out of a total of 5000 complaints received overall. Many complaints, whether from consumers or competitors, are dismissed for various reasons, such as the issues had previously been considered and consistently dismissed; they are not a concern to the broad community; or the complaints are incorrect about content.[121]

The ASB upheld complaints on four advertisements in 2017 because of issues of language, the Wagering Code and health-cum-safety. In 2016, the ASB determined that three 'Top 10' ads breached the AANA Code of Ethics by discriminating against women, degrading women and portraying violence:

1. A free-to-air Ultra Tune television commercial featured two women in a car stuck on train tracks. The message was to use Ultra Tune's auto service centres to 'avoid unexpected situations'. ASB determined that the advertisement, which received 208 complaints, was discriminating, degrading and exploitative, therefore breaching several sections of the AANA code.

2. A free-to-air advertisement for a horror movie by advertiser Roadshow Film Distributors received 82 complaints and was found to breach Section 2.3 of the Code (on violence).

3. A window poster by Honey Birdette showing a woman in revealing underwear, with 59 complaints, breached several sections of the Code by portraying sex, sexuality and nudity; discriminating; and exploiting and degrading.[122]

Most-upheld cases

A search on the ASB website uncovered several brands that had several 'upheld' decisions over the years. Advanced Medical Institute (AMI) had 19 upheld (see the case study at the end of this chapter);[123] Unilever had 11 spread across Lynx, Paddle Pop, Rexona and Lipton Iced Tea;[124] McDonald's had 10;[125] Coca-Cola had nine;[126] and Holden and Nissan had eight each.[127] [128] These upheld cases indicate non-compliance of regulatory codes on sexual portrayal, food and beverages, and vehicle advertising.

Both McDonald's and Coca-Cola had about 100 cases of complaints determined as 'dismissed' by the Board between 1998 and 2017.[129] [130]

The ASB upheld complaints about McDonald's advertising in various media that breached the Quick Service Restaurant Initiative related to nutrition criteria; for example, advertising that did not convey healthier choices; food vouchers given to children at a basketball competition and playground; and television advertising using animated characters that did not encourage physical activity.[131]

The ASB also upheld complaints directed at advertising of Coca-Cola Amatil (SPC Fruit Jelly) and Coca-Cola South Pacific (Fanta, Coca-Cola, Coca-Cola Zero and Mother). For example, Fanta advertising did not represent a healthier option; the Coca-Cola Zero 'Break-Up' advertisement featuring sexy women was inappropriate for a television time slot viewed also by children; another Coca-Cola Zero advertisement featuring a youth surfing on a bus roof had contravened the ethics code on safety; and the Mother 'Swat' advertisement portrayed unacceptable violence.[132]

Summarising this section: the AANA has its self-regulatory framework with the ASB administering best practice guidelines and marketing communication codes covering ethics, as well as segments such as children, food and beverage, Quick Service Restaurants, environmental claims, wagering and vehicle advertising. The ASB reviews hundreds of complaints annually to uphold or dismiss public complaints on advertising across various media, including subscription TV and commercial radio.

■ CHAPTER SUMMARY

In this chapter we explained key concepts of responsible marketing communication regarding regulatory theory; general laws pertaining to deceptive marketing and communication; regulatory codes for advertising in media platforms, delivery formats and product-specific categories; industry-specific codes and the role of the Advertising Standards Bureau.

First, we discussed the regulatory frameworks that guide responsible marketing communication. While there are many regulatory models, two in particular have influenced the marketing and communication industry globally. The International Chamber of Commerce, with six million members in 130 countries, introduced the first advertising code in 1937 and now has a Consolidated Code of Advertising and Marketing Communication Practice that serves as a benchmark for government and industry bodies.

The other influential model is by researchers Ayres and Braithwaite, whose regulatory theory of persuasion and punishment has influenced, in one way or another, the compliance and enforcement pyramids of government authorities.

Next, we described the general laws pertaining to deceptive marketing communication. The enforcement of laws in Australia pertaining to marketing communication rests with the Australian Competition & Consumer Commission (ACCC), the Australian Communications and Media Authority (ACMA), the Australian Securities & Investments Commission (ASIC), the Office of the Australian Information Commissioner (OAIC) and the Therapeutic Goods Administration (TGA).

There are penalties for non-compliance of laws pertaining to marketing communication.

We then considered media-specific regulatory codes of practice for diverse media platforms. There are media-specific co-regulatory codes of practice developed by media owners in consultation with the Australian Communications and Media Authority (ACMA) and the Australian Association of National Advertisers (AANA). There are codes of practice for free-to-air TV, subscription television, commercial radio, the internet, print and other media. The Advertising Standards Bureau (ASB) also handles complaints for advertising over various media platforms.

Following this, we examined delivery-specific industry codes of practice for different media formats. There are industry codes of practice governing specific media delivery through outdoor advertising, direct marketing, digital platforms, native advertising and online testimonials.

We followed this with a discussion on the product-specific industry codes for responsible marketing communication of various goods and services. There are advertising regulatory guides for specific product categories such as vehicle, alcohol, children's food and beverage, therapeutics and weight management.

Finally, we reviewed industry-association codes and guidelines that govern standards in marketing communication. The Australian Association of National Advertisers (AANA), formed in 1928, has its Code of Ethics 2012, product-specific and audience-specific regulatory codes and best practice guidelines.

The ASB is the secretariat for the two industry, non-government bodies of the Advertising Standards Board and the Advertising Claims Board. The ASB was set up in 1975 to administer the AANA's code and best practice guidelines as well as the product-specific and audience-specific codes of ethics. The ASB receives written complaints about advertising, arranges for the Board to review and determine whether advertisements breach AANA codes, and upholds or dismisses complaints.

Case study: AMI—'serial offender'

Peter Ling

An advertiser that consumers frequently complained about was Advanced Medical Institute (AMI), a marketer of a nasal delivery system to address premature ejaculations. AMI has been described as a 'serial offender' for its message of 'longer lasting sex'.[133]

ASB decisions

A search on the Advertising Standards Board's website showed that there were 102 case reports on AMI between 2001 and 2016: 83 'dismissed' and 19 'upheld'.[134] [135]

In one 2007 case, ASB had dismissed complaints for an AMI billboard message 'Want longer lasting sex?' but later upheld its decision in 2008 because community attitudes had changed towards the blatant, bold and big billboard advertising that could be exposed to children across Australia.[136]

The 19 'upheld' ASB decisions between 2006 and 2015 were for complaints on AMI advertising over radio (nine cases), on television (five cases), outdoors (four cases) and in print media (two cases).

The 19 'upheld' cases had breached five sections of the AANA Code of Ethics, in particular Sections 2.1, 2.3, 2.4, 2.5 and 2.6. Section 2.1 touches on vilification of men; Section 2.3 deals with inappropriate sex portrayal for children; Section 2.4 is about sensitive treatment of sex, sexuality and nudity; Section 2.5 is on the use of appropriate language; and Section 2.6 is about prevailing community standards.[137]

Table 11.7 ASB cases against the Advanced Medical Institute, 2006–2015

YEAR	ADVERTISEMENT	BREACH	AMI RESPONSE
2006	Radio ad through the day on premature ejaculation: 'AMI'S nasal delivery technology will turn you from a gun-jumping doodle into a marathon man' [ASB Ref#137b/06]	Section 2.3 of Advertiser Code of Ethics: inappropriate sex portrayal for children	Ad had stopped[138]
2006	Radio ad through the day on premature ejaculation: 'Nasal delivery technology can turn "ugh" into "Aaaahhh"' [ASB Ref#137d/06]	Section 2.3 of Advertiser Code of Ethics: inappropriate sex portrayal for children	Ad had stopped[139]
2008	Radio ad through the day: 'Great sex. This Valentine's Day thousands of Australian women are going to get great sex' [ASB Ref#49/08]	Section 2.3 of Advertiser Code of Ethics: inappropriate sex portrayal for children	Ad discontinued[140]

YEAR	ADVERTISEMENT	BREACH	AMI RESPONSE
2008	Outdoor: 'Want longer lasting sex?' [ASB Ref#278/08]	Section 2.3 of Advertiser Code of Ethics: 'treatment of sex in advertising would be unacceptable to the community'	'The advertiser will replace all 120 billboards by 12 September'.[141]
2009	Radio ad through the day: 'Great sex … Valentine's Day' [ASB Ref#118/09]	Section 2.3 of Advertiser Code of Ethics: inappropriate sex portrayal for children Section 2.1 of Advertiser Code of Ethics: 'discriminate against or vilify men who suffered from premature ejaculation' Section 2.6: 'contrary to prevailing community standards on men's health'	Ad discontinued.[142]
2009	TV ad in mature timezones: Police officers as bedroom police clocking a man's 'speed' in bed 'at one minute, thirty seconds' [ASB Ref#167/09]	Section 2.1 of Advertiser Code of Ethics: 'discriminate against or vilify men who suffered from premature ejaculation' Section 2.6: 'contrary to prevailing community standards on men's health'	Ad ceased.[143]
2009	Radio ad: 'if you want a love session that lasts longer than it takes to cook noodles' [ASB Ref#170/09]	Section 2.1 of Advertiser Code of Ethics: 'discriminate against or vilify men who suffered from premature ejaculation' Section 2.3: 'not sensitive to the relevant audience' Section 2.6: 'contrary to prevailing community standards on men's health'	Ad ceased.[144]
2009	Print ad in TV guide section: 'Performing at your PEAK' [ASB Ref#219/09]	Section 2.3: 'did not treat sex, sexuality or nudity with sensitivity to the relevant audience'	Advertiser unhappy with ASB ruling 'to restrict AMI from publishing the advertisement in any print media'.[145]

YEAR	ADVERTISEMENT	BREACH	AMI RESPONSE
2009	TV: 'Having trouble maintaining a good erection' [ASB Ref#418/09]	Section 2.1: 'discriminate against or vilify men who suffered from premature ejaculation' Section 2.3: did not depict sex and sexuality with sensitivity to the relevant audience'	Ad removed.[146]
2009	Yellow Envelope monthly publication: 'Want longer lasting sex' [ASB Ref#414/09]	Section 2.3: 'not sensitive to the relevant audience'	Compliance with the next issue.[147]
2010	TV ad showing track race and simulating sex with dolls: 'Coming first doesn't always mean you're a winner' [ASB Ref#0315/10]	Section 2.3: 'did not depict sex and sexuality with sensitivity to the relevant audience'	Ad removed.[148]
2010	Billboard: 'Be a man and hold your load' [ASB Ref#0464/10]	Section 2.1: discriminate against or vilify men who suffered from premature ejaculation' Section 2.4: 'did not treat the issue of sex, sexuality and nudity with sensitivity to the relevant audience' Section 2.5: 'not appropriate language to use' Section 2.3: 'treatment of sex in advertising would be unacceptable to the community'	Complied to remove billboard.[149]
2012	Transport: Car message 'Want longer lasting sex' [ASB Ref#0350/12]	Section 2.4: 'did not treat the issue of sex with sensitivity to the relevant audience' Section 2.5: 'did not use language that was appropriate'	Advertiser as an interim solution covered 'Sex' with sticker: 'censored'.[150]

YEAR	ADVERTISEMENT	BREACH	AMI RESPONSE
2013	Billboard: 'Making love. Make it bigger & last longer' [ASB Ref#0272/13]	Section 2.4: 'did not treat the issue of sex, sexuality and nudity with sensitivity to the relevant audience' Section 2.5: 'language is not appropriate for a broad audience that would include children'	Advertiser 'in the process of changing the billboards back to the earlier approved version'.[151]
2014	TV showing women unhappy with premature ejaculation problem of their partners and shouting on balconies [ASB Ref#0343/14]	Section 2.1: 'discriminate against or vilify men who suffered from premature ejaculation'	Ad replaced.[152]
2014	TV: 3 couples in bed, women yell from balcony [ASB Ref#0476/14]	Section 2.1: 'discriminate against or vilify men who suffered from premature ejaculation'.	Ad discontinued.[153]
2014	Radio: 'moan, moan, moan' [ASB Ref#0513/14]	Section 2.4: 'did not treat the issue of sex with sensitivity to the relevant audience'.	Ad discontinued.[154]
2015	Radio ad on AMI oral strips: 'average sex or mind-blowing sex' [ASB Ref#0304/15]	Section 2.4: 'did not treat the issue of sex with sensitivity to the relevant audience'. Section 2.5: did not use language that was appropriate'.	Ad discontinued.[155]
2015	Radio: 'longest lasting bedroom session' [ASB Ref #0482/15]	Section 2.5: did not use language that was appropriate'.	Ad discontinued.[156]

Table 11.7 lists the ASB cases against the Advanced Medical Institute: the non-compliant advertisements, the breaches and the advertiser's response to the ASB determination.

While the AMI had complied with the ASB's 'upheld' decisions by stopping, discontinuing or replacing the offending advertisements, it cheekily covered up the word 'Sex' with 'Censored' for its 120 billboards in 2008! The AMI did the same thing in 2012 as an interim solution for its car sticker advertisement. See Figure 11.11 for the 'Censored' billboard.

ACCC's enforcement

The AMI has also been penalised by the ACCC. In 2002, the ACCC took legal action against the AMI for contravening certain sections of the *Trade Practices Act 1974* through its 2001–2002 advertising guaranteeing erection results. Based on a Federal Court order, AMI undertook to refund money to patients who had found the treatment ineffective.[157]

In 2004, the ACCC took court action against the AMI, its advertising agent and a celebrity for an untrue newspaper advertisement claiming 'TV's Star's amazing CONFESSION!'[158] The celebrity,

Figure 11.11 The AMI's 'Censored' billboard

entertainer Ian Turpie, admitted that the advertising claim was misleading.[159] In 2006, the Federal Court found AMI's misleading advertising had breached Section 52 of the *Trade Practices Act 1974*.[160]

In 2010, the ACCC initiated Federal Court proceedings against the AMI for 'unconscionable conduct' in promoting its program through unclear communication of refund conditions and inappropriate diagnosis-cum-treatment of male sexual dysfunction.[161] As a result, the Federal Court in April 2015 found AMI had been unconscionable in using unfair tactics and contract terms to target men with premature ejaculation or erectile dysfunction problems. The Federal Court ordered the AMI, its owner-operator NRM Corporation and NRM Trading to compensate patients identified in the proceedings, restrain from certain practices and run corrective advertising.[162]

However, in August 2015, the ACCC took contempt action against the AMI, NRM Corporation and NRM Trading, alleging a breach of court orders through the AMI website and advertising on television and radio.[163] In July 2016, the Full Court dismissed NRM's appeal against the unconscionable conduct finding.[164] This led to a Federal Court decision in December 2016 to fine AMI's owners $350 000 for contempt of court.[165]

The ACCC had found AMI's conduct 'amongst the worst behavior we have seen'. Besides misleading advertising, AMI's salespeople had claimed that non-AMI treatment could lead to psychological impotence, penis shrinkage, prostate cancer or stroke.[166] [167]

....

Questions

1. How has the AMI been a serial offender?
2. Which sections of the AANA Code of Ethics has AMI breached over the years?
3. How has the ACCC penalised the AMI?

Practitioner profile: Chloe Neo

Managing Director, OMD Singapore and President,
Association of Accredited Advertising Agents Singapore

Chloe's career to date spans across media consultancy and training,
business management, and agency leadership roles in Singapore,
APAC, and China. Chloe believes and invests in a strong agency
culture for innovation and effectiveness that enables the OMD team
to empower their clients to make Better Decisions, Faster.

In 2016, OMD Singapore made the WARC 100's Top Media
Agencies in the world. In 2017, OMD Singapore's work on
McDonald's won a Media Lions Silver and was recognised by
the Gunn Report as the top global campaign. In the same year,
OMD was awarded Media Agency of the Year as well as Digital
Performance Agency of the Year in the Singapore Media Awards (SMA). In 2018, OMD bagged
the most SMA Brand Awards for validated brand and business impact delivered through effective
marketing campaigns.

As a Singapore-born and bred media professional, Chloe is proud to put Singapore on the world
map for advertising.

**Describe your current role, the organisation you work for, and a brief description of what you
do in your role on a day-to-day basis.**

My role at OMD is to enable our people to empower our clients to make Better Decisions, Faster.
A lot of my time is spent conversing and connecting with people, primarily our agency talent, clients,
and industry partners to uncover new opportunities. I'm constantly working with my team and
partners, looking at how we can better our people, product, and processes to deliver for our agency,
our people, and our clients' growth ambitions, from talent development and retention, innovation
and thought leadership to driving business returns.

**How important is Integrated Marketing Communication (IMC) to what you and your
organisation do?**

At OMD, we believe in better end-to-end consumer experiences that create more valued and valuable
relationships between people and brands. Technologies, platforms, and tools that allow us to uncover
meaningful audience insights and deliver complete and relevant engagement are strategic levers for
the manifestation of our planning philosophy.

What types of promotional tools do you use in your IMC campaigns? Please provide examples.

Along with the advancement and integration of data and technologies, we now leverage a people-
based precision marketing platform that connects our people, our data assets, and our analytics
offering to deliver more relevant and personalised messages to the right audience in the right place at
the right time.

Today, the type of IMC activation is largely driven by audience insights through data signals and further enabled by Artificial Intelligence (AI) activation for dynamic marketing.

Increasingly, we enhance our marketing with AI. The programmatic platform is a common example of machine learning and optimisation via connected platforms.

There's marketing with new product and marketing tools created by leveraging AI, such as AR, mixed reality or chatbots.

In time, we could be marketing with AI as technology replaces some of the human decision-making process.

What would your ideal IMC campaign look like and why?

My ideal IMC campaign is one that drives human creativity with the new powerful toolset provided by data and technologies.

With modern technologies, there are greater opportunities for brands to leverage AI services that deliver meaningful personalised and real-time customer engagement and communication as the consumer moves through their personal consumer journey and decision-making process, making a consumer-centric approach ever more important. Focusing on any IMC technology or tool alone is wrong; it is about understanding the application of people and machines together – *Artful* Intelligence.

What has been your favourite IMC project to work on and did it achieve its objectives?

It has to be the McDelivery Capacity Based Advertising – ranked best in the world by Gunn Media 100 and winner of a Silver Lion at Cannes 2017, to name a few among the many local and international awards, accolades, and recognition the campaign has received.

OMD Singapore was tasked with making McDelivery stand out amongst growing competition like Deliveroo and Uber Eats, whose growth has been rooted in mastery of the addressable age. The campaign, which was a global first for any brand in any category, demonstrated the smart use of real-time data to create an agile ad-delivery system. A real-time data feed (API) was set up in McDonald's delivery management system, to access customer delivery wait time by neighbourhood. Using a custom-built code, restaurants were then categorised as high, medium, or low capacity in real time as demand fluctuated. By linking real-time McDonald's customer delivery wait times, processing them, and then pushing them dynamically into paid activation, a dynamic marketing strategy that is based on live restaurant data was created.

The result – maximised media cost efficiency and managed consumer expectations of delivery time through tailored messages, mapping real-time restaurant data against paid marketing spends. It started with a digital focus but was scalable across platforms that could be connected to the live API.

How do you believe an IMC campaign affects the consumer decision making process for your particular target audience?

Leveraging modern technologies, IMC is now measurable and validated to have a clear impact on the consumer, pushing them further down the purchase funnel and encouraging post-purchase engagement.

At the very foundation, there's machine learning. Then there are less developed forms of Artificial Intelligence, although probably the ones we hear more about in the news, like robotics, such as smart vacuums, self-driving vehicles, and ecosystems bridging multiple devices and information sources to make increasingly informed decisions about our consumption behaviours, homes, or cities.

With the connected ecosystem and IMC platforms, we can smartly deploy AI services across platforms to deliver meaningful personalised and real-time customer engagement and communication, impacting the consumer's decision-making process as they move through their personal consumer journey.

How has your application of IMC changed with the increase in digital marketing?

Artificial Intelligence (AI) is now beginning to have a transformative effect on virtually every industry sector including the application of IMC.

Huge investment in AI technologies

Globally tech giants spent an estimated $20 billion to $30 billion on AI in 2016. There has also been a 14X increase in the number of active AI start-ups since 2000.

AI technologies are maturing

By 2020, 85 per cent of customer interactions will be managed without a human.

AI offers new channels to engage with consumers

Smart speaker adoption is now outpacing that of smartphones. The global chatbot market is expected to reach $1.23 billion by 2025. By 2020, 50 per cent of searches will be image or voice-based.

AI technologies are changing how brands and people can interact with each other. AI is becoming a media channel in its own right, allowing us to reach niche audiences with increased personalisation.

AI is able to process, categorise, and identify patterns in data better than humans, making it a breeze to decide which assets can be reused and delivered at the right time, in the right place, to the right audience.

AI has huge transformational abilities – from driverless cars to transcendent retail.

With all these clear benefits and value creation possibilities, it's not surprising to see Artificial Intelligence changing the face of marketing.

What do you believe are some of the challenges to implementing an IMC campaign?

A real challenge in implementing IMC is the over-leverage of data and technologies in this modern world of marketing, and the need to ensure responsible use of data for personalised marketing.

Machines are good at processing mammoth amounts of data and crystallising information in seconds to inform the IMC deployment and influence the human decision-making process. However, data and technologies are commodities we master, but human creativity is what differentiates and connects brands to people.

Nowadays, too many marketing conversations are focused on lower funnel measurements and results. While it's great to have business accountability, an over-weighted focus on last touch attribution would potentially see a more efficient IMC approach that delivers on the immediate short-term goals such as business performance and conversions but compromises on strategic brand metrics that enhance consumer experiences.

We need to have a sensible view of IMC, balancing short-term priorities with longer term strategic brand vision.

Conversely, vast amounts of personal data are collected through marketing activation, and subsequently ingested and used for smarter, data-led IMC. With the trend towards data-driven marketing comes growing concerns from individuals about how their personal data is being used. While there are legislation and regulatory laws such the Personal Data Protection Act and General Data Protection Regulation (EU) that govern the use of personal data, brands should exercise and maintain good data governance to maintain consumers' trust while balancing effective IMC.

What advice would you offer a student studying IMC?

In the world of marketing and communication, we can draw our insights and marketing efficiency from data and technology but above all – there's empathy.

Empathy is what connects people, and brands with their consumers.

Empathy is what makes us truly human.

As marketers and advertising professionals, while we have our heads in the data, we should also keep our eyes and hearts open to the real world.

Key terms

administrative action

administrative resolution

bill posting

command regulation

enforceable undertakings

enforced self-regulation

free-to-air TV

infringement notice

interest-based advertising

online behavioural advertising

out-of-home advertising

property spruikers

public warning notices

self-regulation

subscription TV

substantiation notice

Revision questions

1. How would Hall of Fame, Hall of Shame and Shonkey Awards encourage or discourage marketers to be more responsible to consumers?

2. What is significant about the ICC Consolidated Code of Advertising and Marketing Communication Practice?

3. How significant is the Braithwaite and/or Ayres & Braithwaite regulatory theory?

4. Which version of the regulatory pyramid would you adopt or adapt to suit your marketing communication practice?

5. Why is it important to be aware of the laws and enforcement authorities pertaining to marketing communication?

6. How would court-ordered financial penalties and/or corrective advertising serve to make marketers more responsible?

7. What media-specific enforcements have you come across?

8. Why are there specific codes of practice for media delivery formats?

9. Why are there specific industry codes pertaining to marketing communication of vehicles, alcohol, children's food and beverage, Quick Service Restaurants, therapeutic products and weight management?

10. Why are there self-regulatory codes on environmental claims, wagering and communication in the digital space?

11. Which advertisements have you complained about or which 'most complained about' advertisements have you come across?

12. What are your views on 'serial offenders' in the 'most complained-about' advertising cases?

13. What are your views on marketers who have responsible marketing communication policies, yet have had advertising complaints upheld against them?

Further reading

Beard, F. K. (2008). How products and advertising offend customers. *Journal of Advertising Research, 48*(1): 13–21.

Hoek, J. & Sheppard, W. (1990). Stereotyping in Advertisements Viewed by Children. *Marketing Bulletin, 1*: 7–12.

Lindgreen, A. et. al. (2009). Corporate social responsibility: an empirical investigation of US organizations. *Journal of Business Ethics, 85*: 303–23.

Marketing communications and corporate social responsibility (CSR): marriage of convenience or shotgun wedding? https://www.jstor.org/stable/40294986?seq=1#page_scan_tab_contents

Self-regulation is a success but it must be guarded: http://adage.com/article/editorials/regulation-advertising-industry-guarded/149209/

Weblinks

40 years self-regulation meeting community standards in advertising: https://adstandards.com.au/sites/default/files/40_year_self-regulation_meeting_community_standards_in_advertising_web.pdf

Advertising and marketing law: http://www.podlegal.com.au/learning-centre/articles/

Advertising and selling guide: https://www.accc.gov.au/publications/advertising-selling

Advertising self-regulation in Asia and Australasia: http://afaaglobal.org/index.php/advertising-self-regulation-in-asia-and-australasia/?uid=5&mod=document

Advertising Self-Regulatory Council (US): http://www.asrcreviews.org

Advertising Standards Bureau: codes and initiatives: https://adstandards.com.au/codes-and-cases/codes-and-initiatives

Advertising Standards Bureau: standards board cases: https://adstandards.com.au/cases

Association for data-driven marketing & advertising (ADMA) code of practice: https://www.adma.com.au/sites/default/files/CODE_QandA.pdf

Australian Association of National Advertisers: http://aana.com.au/self-regulation/advertising-regulatory-guide/

Australian Communication & Media Authority: regulatory responsibility: http://www.acma.gov.au/theACMA/About/Corporate/Responsibilities/regulation-responsibilities-acma

Australian Competition & Consumer Commission: advertising & promoting your business: https://www.accc.gov.au/business/advertising-promoting-your-business

Best Practice for the Responsible Marketing of Alcohol Beverages in Digital Marketing: http://www.abac.org.au/wp-content/uploads/2013/11/Best-Practice-in-Digital-and-Social-Media-November-2013.pdf

Codes Centre for advertising & marketing: http://www.codescentre.com

European Alliance of Communication Agencies: Self-regulation: http://eaca.eu/self-regulation/

Guide to Media and Content Regulation in Asia Pacific: http://www.commsalliance.com.au/__data/assets/pdf_file/0016/42136/Guide-to-Media-and-Content-Regulation-in-Asia-Pacific.pdf

ICC International Code of Direct Selling: http://www.codescentre.com/media/13182/685%20ICC%20International%20Code%20of%20Direct%20Selling%20Code_FINAL%20with%20covers.pdf

ICC Resource Guide for Self-regulation of Online Behavioural Advertising (OBA): http://www.codescentre.com/media/1338/654%20OBA%20Resource%20Guide_%20final%20(1).pdf

ICC/ESOMAR International Code on Market and Social Research: http://www.codescentre.com/media/2070/ICCESOMAR_Code_English.pdf

Industry self-regulation: Role and use in supporting consumer interests [OECD]: http://www.oecd.org/officialdocuments/publicdisplaydocumentpdf/?cote=DSTI/CP(2014)4/FINAL&docLanguage=En

International Chamber of Commerce: Advertising and Marketing Communication Practice Consolidated ICC Code: http://www.codescentre.com/media/2083/660%20consolidated%20icc%20code_2011_final%20with%20covers.pdf

Marketing and advertising: The law (UK): https://www.gov.uk/marketing-advertising-law/overview

OECD Industry self-regulation: Role and use in supporting consumer interests: http://www.oecd.org/officialdocuments/publicdisplaydocumentpdf/?cote=DSTI/CP(2014)4/FINAL&docLanguage=En

Parents' Choice Fame & Shame: https://parentsvoice.org.au/campaigns/fame-shame/

Responsible Children's Marketing Initiative: http://www.communicationscouncil.org.au/public/content/ViewCategory.aspx?id=890

Shonkys [Australia]: https://www.choice.com.au/shonky-awards

Singapore Code of Advertising Practice: https://asas.org.sg/code

Notes

1   Parents' Voice. (2017). Hall of Fame. https://parentsvoice.org.au/campaigns/hall-fame/

2   Parents' Voice. (2017). Hall of Shame. https://parentsvoice.org.au/campaigns/hall-shame/

3   VicHealth. (2013 Nov 26). Coles and One Direction hit the wrong note for parents. Retrieved from https://www.vichealth.vic.gov.au/media-and-resources/media-releases/coles-and-one-direction-hit-the-wrong-note-for-parents

4   Parents' Voice. (2017). Fame and Shame 2016. http://parentsvoice.org.au/campaigns/fame-shame/

5   Berry, S. (2016). Shamed: the junk food ads judged to mislead children the most. *The Sydney Morning Herald,* 6 December.

6   Choice. (2017). Hall of Shame. https://www.choice.com.au/shonky-awards/hall-of-shame

7   Hammond, M. (2012). Most complained-about ads of the past decade revealed, 11 January. http://www.smartcompany.com.au/startupsmart/news-analysis/local/most-complained-about-ads-of-past-decade-revealed/

8   ICC. (2017). The International Chamber of Commerce history at a glance. https://iccwbo.org/about-us/who-we-are/history/

9   ICC. (2009). Self-regulation and advertising: surviving the global challenges ahead. https://iccwbo.org/media-wall/news-speeches/self-regulation-and-advertising-surviving-the-global-challenges-ahead; ICC. (2011). About us: ICC and the Code. http://www.codescentre.com/about-us/icc-and-the-code.aspx.

10 ICC. (2017). Advertising and Marketing Communication Practice (Consolidated ICC Code). https://iccwbo.org/publication/advertising-and-marketing-communication-practice-consolidated-icc-code/

11 ICC. (2017). Global network. https://iccwbo.org/about-us/global-network/

12 ICC. (2011). Advertising and Marketing Communication Practice Consolidated ICC Code. http://www.codescentre.com/media/2083/660%20consolidated%20icc%20code_2011_final%20with%20covers.pdf

13 Coca-Colacompany.com. (2016). Responsible Marketing, 20 September. Retrieved from http://www.coca-colacompany.com/stories/responsible-marketing

14 Unilever.com. (2014). Unilever marketing and advertising principles for responsible food and beverage marketing, October. https://www.unilever.com/Images/unilever-marketing-and-advertising-principles-for-responsible-food-and-beverage-marketing-octover-2014_tcm244-409845_en.pdf

15 Nestle.com. (2018). Nestlé Marketing Communication to Children Policy, January. http://www.nestle.com/asset-library/documents/library/documents/corporate_social_responsibility/nestle-marketing-communication-children-policy.pdf

16 ICC. (2014). ICC contributes to APEC capacity building on ad standards, 8 August. https://iccwbo.org/media-wall/news-speeches/icc-contributes-to-apec-capacity-building-on-ad-standards/

17 IFBA. (2017). International Food & Beverage Alliance. https://ifballiance.org

18 Hunt, S. D. & Vitell, S. (1986). A general theory of marketing ethics. *Journal of Macromarketing, 6*(1), 5–16.

19 Ferrell, O. C. & Gresham, L. G. (1985). A contingency framework for understanding ethical decision making in marketing. *Journal of Marketing, 49*(3), 87–96.

20 Braithwaite, J. (1985). *To punish or persuade.* Albany, NY: State University of New York Press.

21 Starek, R. B. (1997). *The consumer protection pyramid: education, self-regulation, and law enforcement.* Paper presented at The Korea Consumer Festival '97, Seoul, Republic of Korea. https://www.ftc.gov/public-statements/1997/12/consumer-protection-pyramid-education-self-regulation-law-enforcement

22 Ayres, I. & Braithwaite, J. (1992). *Responsive regulation: transcending the deregulation debate.* New York: Oxford University Press, p. 25.

23 Ayres, I. & Braithwaite, J. (1992). *Responsive regulation: transcending the deregulation debate.* New York: Oxford University Press, p. 35.

24 Sylvan, L. (2004). Australia's competition and consumer law: ensuring compliance and enforcing the law, 16 February. https://www.accc.gov.au/system/files/Australias%20competition%20and%20consumer%20law%20ensuring%20compliance%20and%20enforcing%20the%20law.pdf; ACCC.gov.au. (2017). Compliance & enforcement policy. https://www.accc.gov.au/about-us/australian-competition-consumer-commission/compliance-enforcement-policy

25 ACCC.gov.au. (2013). ACCC powers to issue infringement, substantiation and public warning notices. https://www.accc.gov.au/system/files/707_Business%20Snapshot_ACCC%20powers%20to%20issue%20notices_FA_2015.pdf

26 aph.gov.au. (2014). Chapter 4 Regulatory theories and their application to ASIC,. http://www.aph.gov.au/Parliamentary_Business/Committees/Senate/Economics/ASIC/Final_Report/c04

27 aph.gov.au. (2014). Final report: performance of the Australian Securities and Investments Commission, 26 June. http://www.aph.gov.au/Parliamentary_Business/Committees/Senate/Economics/ASIC/Final_Report/index

28 TGA.gov.au. (2005). Submission on TGA consultation paper 'Regulating the advertising of therapeutic goods to the general public' by the Foundation for Advertising Research, 1 February. https://www.tga.gov.au/sites/default/files/consult-advertising-ris-130531-submission-far.pdf

29 TGA.gov.au. (2012). Advertising regulatory framework. https://www.tga.gov.au/sites/default/files/advertising-framework-120529.pdf

30 TGA.gov.au. (2012). The TGA regulatory framework, May. https://www.tga.gov.au/sites/default/files/tga-regulatory-framework-130626.pdf

31 ACMA.gov.au. (2011). Reconnecting the customer: Final public inquiry report, September. http://www.acma.gov.au/~/media/Consumer%20Interests/Report/pdf/Reconnecting%20the%20Customerfinal%20public%20inquiry%20report.PDF

32 ACMA.gov.au. (2014). ACMA compliance and enforcement policy, March. http://www.acma.gov.au/theACMA/About/Corporate/Structure-and-contacts/the-acma-overview-acma

33 EASA. (2014). From law to self-regulation. http://mddb.apec.org/Documents/2014/CTI/WKSP4/14_cti_wksp4_011.pdf

34 EASA. (2017). The regulatory framework. http://www.easa-alliance.org/ad-standards/what-are-ad-standards/regulatory-framework

35   EASA. (2017). EASA 25 Years. http://www.easa-alliance.org/about-easa/anniversary

36   EASA. (2016). ICAS. http://www.easa-alliance.org/about-easa/structure/ICAS

37   AANA.com.au. (2017). Advertising regulatory guide. http://aana.com.au/self-regulation/advertising-regulatory-guide/

38   AdAge.com. (2003). Corrective advertising, 15 September. http://adage.com/article/adage-encyclopedia/corrective-advertising/98418/

39   Williams, A. (2007). Ribena pays £80,000 fine for NZ misleading ad charges, 27 April. http://marketinglaw.osborneclarke.com/retailing/ribena-pays-80000-fine-for-nz-misleading-ad-charges/

40   Singer, N. (2009). A birth control pill that promised too much, 10 February. http://www.nytimes.com/2009/02/11/business/11pill.html?mcubz=0

41   FTC.gov. (2012 May 16). Skechers will pay $40 million to settle FTC charges that it deceived consumers with ads for 'Toning Shoes'. https://www.ftc.gov/news-events/press-releases/2012/05/skechers-will-pay-40-million-settle-ftc-charges-it-deceived

42   FTC.gov. (2016). Volkswagen to spend up to $14.7 billion to settle allegations of cheating emissions tests and deceiving customers on 2.0 Liter diesel vehicles, 28 June. https://www.ftc.gov/news-events/press-releases/2016/06/volkswagen-spend-147-billion-settle-allegations-cheating

43   ACCC.gov.au. (2017). ACCC takes action against Audi over diesel emission claims, 8 March. https://www.accc.gov.au/media-release/accc-takes-action-against-audi-over-diesel-emission-claims

44   AANA.com.au. (2017). Legislation and regulation: advertising regulatory guide. http://aana.com.au/content/uploads/2015/09/BLUE-6.-Legislation-and-Regulation2.pdf

45   ACCC.gov.au. (2017). Australian Competition & Consumer Commission. https://www.accc.gov.au/about-us/australian-competition-consumer-commission; ACCC.gov.au. (2017). Consumer rights & guarantees. https://www.accc.gov.au/consumers/consumer-rights-guarantees.

46   ACMA.gov.au. (2017). Introduction to the ACMA. http://www.acma.gov.au/theACMA/About/The-ACMA-story; ALRC.gov.au. (2017). 16. Enforcing classification laws: enforcement under the Broadcasting Services Act. http://www.alrc.gov.au/publications/16-enforcing-classification-laws/enforcement-under-broadcasting-services-act#_ftn14; Donotcall.gov.au. (2017). About the Do Not Call register. https://www.donotcall.gov.au/home/about-the-do-not-call-register; ACMA.gov.au. (2015). Service provider obligations. http://www.acma.gov.au/Industry/Telco/Carriers-and-service-providers/Licensing/service-provider-obligations-licence-fees-and-levies-i-acma

47   ASIC.gov.au. (2017). Our role. http://asic.gov.au/about-asic/what-we-do/our-role; ASIC.gov.au. (2017). Laws we administer. http://asic.gov.au/about-asic/what-we-do/laws-we-administer.

48   OAIC. (2017). About us. https://www.oaic.gov.au/about-us/

49   TGACC. (2017). Frequently Asked Questions. http://www.tgacc.com.au/faq.cfm

50   ACCC.gov.au. (2017). Legislation. https://www.accc.gov.au/about-us/australian-competition-consumer-commission/legislation

51   ACCC.gov.au. (2017). Current ACL national compliance projects. http://consumerlaw.gov.au/the-australian-consumer-law/acl-national-projects/

52   ACCC.gov.au. (2013). ACCC powers to issue infringement, substantiation and public warning notices. https://www.accc.gov.au/system/files/707_Business%20Snapshot_ACCC%20powers%20to%20 issue%20notices_FA_2015.pdf

53   ACCC.gov.au. (2015). ACCC targets alleged false and misleading Nurofen claims, 5 March. https:// www.accc.gov.au/media-release/accc-targets-alleged-false-and-misleading-nurofen-claims

54   ACCC.gov.au. (2015). Court finds Nurofen made misleading Specific Pain claims, 14 December. https:// www.accc.gov.au/media-release/court-finds-nurofen-made-misleading-specific-pain-claims

55   ACCC.gov.au. (2016). Reckitt Benckiser ordered to pay $1.7 million in penalties for misleading conduct regarding Nurofen specific pain products, 29 April. https://www.accc.gov.au/media-release/reckitt-benckiser-ordered-to-pay-17-million-in-penalties-for-misleading-conduct-regarding-nurofen-specific-pain-products

56   ACCC.gov.au. (2016). ACCC appeals $1.7m penalty against Reckitt Benckiser for misleading Nurofen representations, 23 May. https://www.accc.gov.au/media-release/accc-appeals-17m-penalty-against-reckitt-benckiser-for-misleading-nurofen-representations

57   ACCC.gov.au. (2016). Full Federal Court orders $6 million penalty for Nurofen Specific Pain products, 16 December. https://www.accc.gov.au/media-release/full-federal-court-orders-6-million-penalty-for-nurofen-specific-pain-products

58   Papadakis, M. (2016). Reckitt Benckiser faces class action over misleading drug claims, 29 February. http://www.afr.com/business/legal/reckitt-benckiser-faces-class-action-over-misleading-drug-claims-20160229-gn6c67

59   Armitage, R. (2017). Nurofen to pay $3.5 million compensation to customers who bought 'misleading' pain relief, 3 August. http://www.abc.net.au/news/2017-08-03/nurofen-offers-3.5-million-compensation-to-customers/8770910; BannisterLaw. (2017). Register, 31 July. http://nurofenclassaction.com.au/register.

60   Chapman, C. (2013). Connected citizens: a regulatory strategy. http://www.acma.gov.au/theACMA/About/The-ACMA-story/Connected-regulation/broadband-for-all

61   ACMA.gov.au (2017). Register of broadcasting codes & schemes index. http://www.acma.gov.au/theACMA/About/The-ACMA-story/Regulating/broadcasting-codes-schemes-index-radio-content-regulation-i-acma.

62   ACMA.gov.au. (2014). ACMA compliance and enforcement policy. Retrieved from http://www.acma.gov.au/theACMA/About/Corporate/Structure-and-contacts/the-acma-overview-acma

63   ACMA.gov.au. (2017). Spam: enforcement actions. http://www.acma.gov.au/Citizen/Internet/Complaints/Spam-complaints/spam-enforcement-actions

64   ACMA. (2005). Australian eMarketing Code of Practice. https://www.acma.gov.au/-/media/Unsolicited-Communications-Compliance/Regulation/pdf/Australian-EMarketing-Code-of-Practice.pdf

65   Donotcall.gov.au. (2017). Compliance and breaches. https://www.donotcall.gov.au/industry/industry-overview/compliance-and-breaches/

66 ACMA.gov.au. (2016 June 15). Federal Court orders Getaway Escapes and its Director to pay penalties totalling $325,000. Retrieved from http://www.acma.gov.au/Industry/Marketers/Do-not-call-register/How-to-comply-with-the-Do-Not-Call-Register/federal-court-orders-getaway-escapes-and-its-director-to-pay-penalties-totalling-$325000

67 ACMA.gov.au. (2017). Upside.Digital sees a $39,600 downside for breaching the Spam Act, 12 July. Retrieved http://www.acma.gov.au/Industry/Marketers/Anti-Spam/Ensuring-you-dont-spam/upside-digital-sees-a-39600-downside-for-breaching-the-spam-act

68 AANA.com.au. (2017). Legislation and regulation: advertising regulatory guide. http://aana.com.au/content/uploads/2015/09/BLUE-6.-Legislation-and-Regulation2.pdf

69 ASIC.gov.au. (2014). 14-235MR NAB pays $40,800 penalty for misleading UBank advertisements, 17 September. http://asic.gov.au/about-asic/media-centre/find-a-media-release/2014-releases/14-235mr-nab-pays-40-800-penalty-for-misleading-ubank-advertisements/

70 ASIC.gov.au. (2015). 15-321MR OCM pays $30,600 penalty for misleading advertising, 3 November. http://asic.gov.au/about-asic/media-centre/find-a-media-release/2015-releases/15-321mr-ocm-pays-30-600-penalty-for-misleading-advertising/

71 ASIC.gov.au. (2017). 17-130MR ASIC crackdown on misleading advertising by debt management firms, 3 May. http://asic.gov.au/about-asic/media-centre/find-a-media-release/2017-releases/17-130mr-asic-crackdown-on-misleading-advertising-by-debt-management-firms/

72 OAIC.gov.au. (2017). Data breach notification: a guide to handling personal information security breaches. https://www.oaic.gov.au/agencies-and-organisations/guides/data-breach-notification-a-guide-to-handling-personal-information-security-breaches

73 OAIC.gov.au. (2014). Telstra breaches privacy of 15,775 customers, March. https://www.oaic.gov.au/media-and-speeches/media-releases/telstra-breaches-privacy-of-15-775-customers

74 TGA.gov.au. (2012). TGA regulatory framework. https://www.tga.gov.au/tga-regulatory-framework

75 TGA.gov.au. (2016). Court action. https://www.tga.gov.au/court-action

76 Business.gov.au. (2017). Legal obligations of marketing, 6 June. https://www.business.gov.au/info/plan-and-start/develop-your-business-plans/marketing/legal-obligations-of-marketing

77 ACMA.gov.au. (2015). The ACMA registers new Commercial Television Industry Code of Practice, 10 November. http://www.acma.gov.au/Industry/Broadcast/Television/TV-content-regulation/the-acma-registers-new-commercial-television-industry-code-of-practice

78 ACMA.gov.au. (2014). Children's Television Standards 2009. http://www.acma.gov.au/~/media/Diversity%20Localism%20and%20Accessibility/Advice/pdf/childrens_tv_standards_2009%20pdf.pdf

79 ASTRA.org.au. (2017). Codes of Practice. https://www.astra.org.au/advocacy/codes-of-practice

80 ACMA.gov.au. (2017 March 9). ACMA registers new Commercial Radio Industry Code of Practice. http://www.acma.gov.au/Industry/Broadcast/Radio/Radio-content-regulation/acma-registers-new-commercial-radio-industry-code-of-practice

81 ACMA.gov.au. (2011). Community Television Broadcasting Codes of Practice. http://www.acma.gov.au/~/media/Community%20Broadcasting%20and%20Safeguards/Regulation/pdf/Community%20Television%20Broadcasting%20Codes%20of%20Practice.PDF

82 ACMA.gov.au. (2008). Community Radio Broadcasting Codes of Practice. http://www.acma.gov.au/~/media/Community%20Broadcasting%20and%20Safeguards/Regulation/pdf/Community%20Radio%20Broadcasting%20Codes%20of%20Practice.PDF

83 AANA.com.au (2017). "AANA media-specific co-regulatory codes." from http://aana.com.au/content/uploads/2015/09/BLUE-5.-Media-Specific-Industry-Codes.pdf

84 AANA.com.au (2017). "AANA media-specific co-regulatory codes." from http://aana.com.au/content/uploads/2015/09/BLUE-5.-Media-Specific-Industry-Codes.pdf.

85 Laville, S. & Davies, C. (2012). Jacintha Saldanha suicide note criticised hospital staff, 14 December. https://www.theguardian.com/world/2012/dec/13/jacintha-saldanha-suicide-notes

86 Miranda, C. (2014). 2Day FM radio royal prank in spotlight again at inquest into British nurse Jacintha Saldanha's death, 10 September. http://www.news.com.au/world/2day-fm-radio-royal-prank-in-spotlight-again-at-inquest-into-british-nurse-jacintha-saldanhas-death/news-story/2b550bf818e82658cdad42256c0860e0

87 ACMA.gov.au. (2015). 2DayFM 'Royal Prank' broadcast, 28 October. http://www.acma.gov.au/theACMA/Newsroom/Newsroom/Media-releases/2dayfm-royal-prank-broadcast

88 AANA.com.au (2017). Delivery-specific industry codes. http://aana.com.au/content/uploads/2015/12/BLUE-4.-Delivery-Specific-Industry-Codes-1.pdf

89 OMA.org.au. (2017). Outdoor Media Association Code of Ethics. http://oma.org.au/__data/assets/pdf_file/0019/10855/Code_of_Ethics_2016.pdf

90 ADMA.com.au. (2015). The ADMA Code of Practice. https://www.adma.com.au/sites/default/files/ADMA-Code-of-Practice-01.pdf

91 ADAA. (2017). About ADAA. http://www.youronlinechoices.com.au/about-adaa/

92 IAB Australia. (2015). IAB and AANA launch Native Advertising Principles. https://www.iabaustralia.com.au/news-and-updates/iab-press-releases/item/22-iab-press-releases/2016-iab-and-aana-launch-native-advertising-principles

93 OMA.org.au (2017). Using Out-of-Home (OOH). http://www.oma.org.au/using-ooh

94 OMA.org.au (2017). Complaints. http://www.oma.org.au/regulation-and-community/advertising-content-and-self-regulation/complaints

95 ADMA.com.au (2015). The ADMA Code of Practice. https://www.adma.com.au/sites/default/files/ADMA-Code-of-Practice-1-Sept-2015.pdf

96 IAB (2015). Australian Digital Advertising Policy and Regulation Guide 2015. https://www.iabaustralia.com.au/guidelines-and-best-practice/guidelines-best-practice/item/3-guidelines-and-best-practice/1958-australian-digital-advertising-policy-and-regulation-guide-2015

97 IAB (2015). Australian Digital Advertising Policy and Regulation Guide 2015. https://www.iabaustralia.com.au/guidelines-and-best-practice/guidelines-best-practice/item/3-guidelines-and-best-practice/1958-australian-digital-advertising-policy-and-regulation-guide-2015.

98 AANA.com.au (2017). Delivery-specific industry codes. http://aana.com.au/content/uploads/2015/12/BLUE-4.-Delivery-Specific-Industry-Codes-1.pdf

99   IAB (2015). Native Advertising Principles: IAB and AANA, November. https://www.iabaustralia.com.au/regulatory-affairs/iab-policy-and-guidelines/item/43-iab-policy-and-guidelines/2015-native-advertising-principles-iab-and-aana-nov-2015

100 ACCC.gov.au (2013). What you need to know about: Online reviews—a guide for business and review platforms. https://www.accc.gov.au/system/files/Online%20reviews—a%20guide%20for%20business%20and%20review%20platforms.pdf.

101 FCAI.com.au. (2007). Voluntary Code of Practice for Motor Vehicle Advertising. https://www.fcai.com.au/news/codes-of-practice/index/year/all/month/all/publication/9

102 ABAC.org.au. (2014). ABAC Responsible Alcohol Marketing Code. http://www.abac.org.au/wp-content/uploads/2014/06/ABAC-Responsible-Alcohol-Marketing-Code-30-4-14.pdf

103 AFGC. (2014). Advertising to children. https://www.afgc.org.au/our-expertise/health-nutrition-and-scientific-affairs/advertising-to-children/

104 TGACC (2015). Therapeutic Goods Advertising Code 2015. http://www.tgacc.com.au/code_gloss_files/Therapeutic_Goods_Advertising_Code_2015.pdf

105 WeightCouncil.org. (2016). Weight Management Code of Practice. http://www.weightcouncil.org/industry/weight-management-code-of-practice.htm

106 AANA.com.au (2017). Product-specific industry codes. http://aana.com.au/content/uploads/2015/09/BLUE-3.-Product-Specific-Industry-Codes.pdf

107 GA.gov.au (2017). Decisions in relation to complaints about advertisements (sorted by date). https://www.tga.gov.au/decisions-relation-complaints-about-advertisements-sorted-date

108 AANA.com.au. (2014). AANA Code of Ethics. http://aana.com.au/content/uploads/2014/05/AANA-Code-of-Ethics.pdf

109 AANA.com.au. (2014). AANA Code for Advertising & Marketing Communications to Children. http://aana.com.au/content/uploads/2014/05/AANA-Code-For-Marketing-Advertising-Communications-To-Children.pdf

110 AANA.com.au. (2014). AANA Food & Beverages Advertising & Marketing Communications Code. http://aana.com.au/content/uploads/2014/05/AANA-Food-Beverages-Advertising-Marketing-Communications-Code.pdf

111 AANA.com.au. (2014). AANA Environmental claims in Advertising & Marketing Code. http://aana.com.au/content/uploads/2014/05/AANA-Environmental-Claims-in-Advertising-Marketing-Code.pdf

112 AANA.com.au. (2016). AANA Wagering Advertising & Marketing Communication Code. http://aana.com.au/content/uploads/2016/05/Wagering_Advertising_Marketing_Communications_Code_PracticeNote-1.pdf

113 AANA.com.au. (2015). AANA Best Practice Guideline: Responsible marketing communications in the digital space. http://aana.com.au/content/uploads/2015/06/AANA_Best_Practice_Guide_Marketing_Digital_Space-030615.pdf

114 AANA.com.au. (2017). AANA Clearly Distinguishable Advertising Best Practice Guideline. http://aana.com.au/content/uploads/2017/02/AANA_Clearly-Distinguishable-Advertising-Best-Practice-Guideline.pdf

115 AdStandards.com.au. (2017). Frequently Asked Questions. https://adstandards.com.au/frequently-asked-questions

116 AdStandards.com.au. (2017). Codes and Initiatives. https://adstandards.com.au/codes-and-cases/codes-and-initiatives

117 AdStandards.com.au. (2017). Information for consumers. https://adstandards.com.au/information-consumers

118 AdStandards.com.au. (2016). 2016—Most complained about ads, 13 December. https://adstandards.com.au/media-releases/2016-most-complained-about-ads

119 AdStandards.com.au. (2017). 2017—Most complained about ads, 18 December. https://adstandards.com.au/media-releases/2017-most-complained-about-ads

120 AdStandards.com.au. (2016). 2016—Most complained about ads, 13 December. https://adstandards.com.au/media-releases/2016-most-complained-about-ads

121 AdStandards.com.au. (2018). Consistently dismissed complaints. https://adstandards.com.au/complaint-process/acceptance-complaints/consistently-dismissed-cases

122 AdStandards.com.au. (2016). 2016 - Most complained about ads, 13 December. https://adstandards.com.au/media-releases/2016-most-complained-about-ads

123 Adstandards.com.au. (2017). Standards Board cases: Advanced Medical Institute 'Upheld-Modified or Discontinued'. https://adstandards.com.au/cases?keywords=Advanced+Medical+Institute&fromDate%5Bdate%5D=&toDate%5Bdate%5D=&media=&category=&determination=Upheld-M&grouping=Determination&op=Search

124 Adstandards.com.au. (2017). Standards Board cases: Unilever 'Upheld-Modified or Discontinued'. https://adstandards.com.au/cases?keywords=Unilever&fromDate%5Bdate%5D=&toDate%5Bdate%5D=&media=&category=&determination=Upheld-M&grouping=Determination&op=Search

125 Adstandards.com.au. (2017). Standards Board cases: McDonald's 'Upheld-Modified or Discontinued'. https://adstandards.com.au/cases?keywords=McDonald%27s&fromDate%5Bdate%5D=&toDate%5Bdate%5D=&media=&category=&determination=Upheld-M&grouping=Determination&op=Search

126 Adstandards.com.au. (2017). Standards Board cases: Coca-Cola 'Upheld-Modified or Discontinued'. https://adstandards.com.au/cases?keywords=Coca-Cola&fromDate%5Bdate%5D=&toDate%5Bdate%5D=&media=&category=&determination=Upheld-M&grouping=Determination&op=Search

127 Adstandards.com.au. (2017). Standards Board cases: Holden 'Upheld-Modified or Discontinued'. https://adstandards.com.au/cases?keywords=Holden&fromDate%5Bdate%5D=&toDate%5Bdate%5D=&media=&category=&determination=Upheld-M&grouping=Determination&op=Search

128 Adstandards.com.au. (2017). Standards Board cases: Nissan 'Upheld-Modified or Discontinued'. https://adstandards.com.au/cases?keywords=Nissan&fromDate%5Bdate%5D=&toDate%5Bdate%5D=&media=&category=&determination=Upheld-M&grouping=Determination&op=Search

129 Adstandards.com.au. (2017). Standards Board cases: McDonald's 'Dismissed'. https://adstandards. com.au/cases?keywords=McDonald%27s&fromDate%5Bdate% 5D=&toDate%5Bdate%5D=&media=&category=&determination= Dismissed&grouping=Determination&op=Search

130 Adstandards.com.au. (2017). Standards Board cases: Coca-Cola 'Dismissed'. https://adstandards .com.au/cases?keywords=Coca-Cola&fromDate%5Bdate%5D=&toDate%5Bdate%5D=&media= &category=&determination=Dismissed&grouping=Determination&op=Search

131 Adstandards.com.au. (2017). Standards Board Cases: McDonald's 'Upheld-Modified or Discontinued'. https://adstandards.com.au/cases?keywords=McDonald%27s&fromDate% 5Bdate%5D=&toDate%5Bdate%5D=&media=&category=&determination=Upheld-M&grouping= Determination&op=Search

132 Adstandards.com.au. (2017). Standards Board cases: Coca-Cola 'Upheld-Modified or Discontinued'. https://adstandards.com.au/cases?keywords=Coca-Cola&fromDate%5Bdate%5D=&toDate%5Bdate %5D=&media=&category=&determination=Upheld-M&grouping=Determination&op=Search

133 Reynolds, M. (2013). AMI ads banned by ad watchdog again, 10 September. *Mumbrella*. https:// mumbrella.com.au/ad-standards-board-pulls-billboard-promoting-longer-lasting-sex-177469

134 ASB (2017). Standards Board cases : Advanced Medical Institute-Dismissed. https://adstandards. com.au/cases?keywords=Advanced+Medical+Institute&fromDate%5Bdate%5D=&to Date%5Bdate%5D=&media=&category=&determination=Dismissed&grouping= Determination&op=Search

135 ASB (2017). Standards Board cases: Advanced Medical Institute-Upheld. https://adstandards.com.au/cases?keywords=Advanced+Medical+Institute& fromDate%5Bdate%5D=&toDate%5Bdate%5D=&media=&category=& determination=Upheld-M&grouping=Determination&op=Search

136 AdNews.com.au. (2008). ASB backflips over racy ad, August 22. http://www.adnews. com.au/03FB6768-D98B-4067-813DA41C881D99AC

137 ASB (2017). "Standards Board cases - Advanced Medical Institute-Upheld." from https://adstandards.com.au/cases?keywords=Advanced+Medical+ Institute&fromDate%5Bdate%5D=&toDate%5Bdate%5D=&media=&category =&determination=Upheld-M&grouping=Determination&op=Search

138 Adstandards.com.au. (2006). Case report 173b/06 Advanced Medical Institute (not yet/doodle), 9 May. https://adstandards.com.au/cases?keywords=Advanced+Medical+ Institute&fromDate%5Bdate%50D=&toDate%5Bdate%5D=&media=&category=& determination=Upheld-M&grouping=Determination&op=Search

139 Adstandards.com.au. (2006). Case report 173d/06 Advanced Medical Institute (special cuddles), 9 May. https://adstandards.com.au/cases?keywords=Advanced+Medical+Institute&fromDate% 5Bdate%5D=&toDate%5Bdate%5D=&media=&category=&determination=Upheld-M&grouping =Determination&op=Search

140   Adstandards.com.au. (2008). Case report 49/08 Advanced Medical Institute (Valentine's Day), 12 March. https://adstandards.com.au/cases?keywords=Advanced+Medical+Institute&fromDate%5Bdate%5D=&toDate%5Bdate%5D=&media=&category=&determination=Upheld-M&grouping=Determination&op=Search

141   Adstandards.com.au. (2008). Case report 278/08 Advanced Medical Institute (Outdoor), 13 August. https://adstandards.com.au/cases?keywords=Advanced+Medical+Institute&fromDate%5Bdate%5D=&toDate%5Bdate%5D=&media=&category=&determination=Upheld-M&grouping=Determination&op=Search

142   Adstandards.com.au. (2009). Case report 118/09 Advanced Medical Institute (Valentine's Day), 14 May. https://adstandards.com.au/cases?keywords=Advanced+Medical+Institute&fromDate%5Bdate%5D=&toDate%5Bdate%5D=&media=&category=&determination=Upheld-M&grouping=Determination&op=Search

143   Adstandards.com.au. (2009 May 14). Case report 167/09 Advanced Medical Institute (bedroom police). Retrieved from https://adstandards.com.au/cases?keywords=Advanced+Medical+Institute&fromDate%5Bdate%5D=&toDate%5Bdate%5D=&media=&category=&determination=Upheld-M&grouping=Determination&op=Search

144   Adstandards.com.au. (2009). Case report 170/09 Advanced Medical Institute (noodles), 14 May. https://adstandards.com.au/cases?keywords=Advanced+Medical+Institute&fromDate%5Bdate%5D=&toDate%5Bdate%5D=&media=&category=&determination=Upheld-M&grouping=Determination&op=Search

145   Adstandards.com.au. (2009). Case report 219/09 Advanced Medical Institute (Peak), 10 June. https://adstandards.com.au/cases?keywords=Advanced+Medical+Institute&fromDate%5Bdate%5D=&toDate%5Bdate%5D=&media=&category=&determination=Upheld-M&grouping=Determination&op=Search

146   Adstandards.com.au. (2009). Case report 418/09 Advanced Medical Institute (Is that it?), 23 September. https://adstandards.com.au/cases?keywords=Advanced+Medical+Institute&fromDate%5Bdate%5D=&toDate%5Bdate%5D=&media=&category=&determination=Upheld-M&grouping=Determination&op=Search

147   Adstandards.com.au. (2009). Case report 414/09 Advanced Medical Institute (Mail), 16 September. https://adstandards.com.au/cases?keywords=Advanced+Medical+Institute&fromDate%5Bdate%5D=&toDate%5Bdate%5D=&media=&category=&determination=Upheld-M&grouping=Determination&op=Search

148   Adstandards.com.au. (2010). Case report 0315/10 Advanced Medical Institute (Track race), 28 July. https://adstandards.com.au/cases?keywords=Advanced+Medical+Institute&fromDate%5Bdate%5D=&toDate%5Bdate%5D=&media=&category=&determination=Upheld-M&grouping=Determination&op=Search

149   Adstandards.com.au. (2010). Case report 0464/10 Advanced Medical Institute (Hold your load), 24 November. https://adstandards.com.au/cases?keywords=Advanced+Medical+Institute&fromDate%5Bdate%5D=&toDate%5Bdate%5D=&media=&category=&determination=Upheld-M&grouping=Determination&op=Search

150 Adstandards.com.au. (2012). Case report 0350/12 Advanced Medical Institute (Transport), 22 August. https://adstandards.com.au/cases?keywords=Advanced+Medical+Institute&fromDate%5Bdate%5D=&toDate%5Bdate%5D=&media=&category=&determination=Upheld-M&grouping=Determination&op=Search

151 Adstandards.com.au. (2013). Case report 0272/13 Advanced Medical Institute (Making love), 14 August. https://adstandards.com.au/cases?keywords=Advanced+Medical+Institute&fromDate%5Bdate%5D=&toDate%5Bdate%5D=&media=&category=&determination=Upheld-M&grouping=Determination&op=Search

152 Adstandards.com.au. (2014). Case report 0343/14 Advanced Medical Institute (Unhappy women), 10 September 10. https://adstandards.com.au/cases?keywords=Advanced+Medical+Institute&fromDate%5Bdate%5D=&toDate%5Bdate%5D=&media=&category=&determination=Upheld-M&grouping=Determination&op=Search

153 Adstandards.com.au. (2014). Case report 0476/14 Advanced Medical Institute (3 couples), 26 November. https://adstandards.com.au/cases?keywords=Advanced+Medical+Institute&fromDate%5Bdate%5D=&toDate%5Bdate%5D=&media=&category=&determination=Upheld-M&grouping=Determination&op=Search

154 Adstandards.com.au. (2014). Case report 0513/14 Advanced Medical Institute (Moan), 10 December. https://adstandards.com.au/cases?keywords=Advanced+Medical+Institute&fromDate%5Bdate%5D=&toDate%5Bdate%5D=&media=&category=&determination=Upheld-M&grouping=Determination&op=Search

155 Adstandards.com.au. (2015). Case report 0304/15 Advanced Medical Institute (mind-blowing sex), 12 August. https://adstandards.com.au/cases?keywords=Advanced+Medical+Institute&fromDate%5Bdate%5D=&toDate%5Bdate%5D=&media=&category=&determination=Upheld-M&grouping=Determination&op=Search

156 Adstandards.com.au. (2015). Case report 0482/15 Advanced Medical Institute (longest lasting), 9 December. https://adstandards.com.au/cases?keywords=Advanced+Medical+Institute&fromDate%5Bdate%5D=&toDate%5Bdate%5D=&media=&category=&determination=Upheld-M&grouping=Determination&op=Search

157 ACCC.gov.au. (2004). Advanced Medical Institute Pty Limited, February 26. http://registers.accc.gov.au/content/index.phtml/itemId/510678

158 ACCC.gov.au. (2004). ACCC takes court action against Advanced Medical Institute, publicist and TV star for alleged misleading claims, 20 July. https://www.accc.gov.au/media-release/accc-takes-court-action-against-advanced-medical-institute-publicist-and-tv-star-for

159 Gordon, J. (2004). Turpie admits ad misleading. *The Age,* 21 July.

160 ACCC.gov.au. (2006). Federal Court declares Advanced Medical Institute's advertising 'misleading', 17 August. https://www.accc.gov.au/media-release/federal-court-declares-advanced-medical-institutes-advertising-misleading

161 ACCC.gov.au. (2010). ACCC alleges unconscionable conduct in promotion and supply of men's sexual dysfunction treatment program, 23 December. https://www.accc.gov.au/media-release/accc-alleges-unconscionable-conduct-in-promotion-and-supply-of-mens-sexual-dysfunction

162 ACCC.gov.au. (2015). Federal Court finds Advanced Medical Institute engaged in unconscionable conduct, 22 April. https://www.accc.gov.au/media-release/federal-court-finds-advanced-medical-institute-engaged-in-unconscionable-conduct

163 CCC.gov.au. (2015). ACCC takes contempt action against Advanced Medical Institute, 24 August. https://www.accc.gov.au/media-release/accc-takes-contempt-action-against-advanced-medical-institute

164 ACCC.gov.au. (2016). Full Court upholds unconscionable conduct finding against AMI, 22 July. https://www.accc.gov.au/media-release/full-court-upholds-unconscionable-conduct-finding-against-ami

165 ACCC.gov.au. (2016). Advanced Medical Institute owners fined $350,000 for contempt of court, 2 December. https://www.accc.gov.au/media-release/advanced-medical-institute-owners-fined-350000-for-contempt-of-court

166 Rolfe, J. (2016). Advanced Medical Institute which sells 'longer lasting sex' faces premature end, 18 August. http://www.dailytelegraph.com.au/news/opinion/public-defender/advanced-medical-institute-which-sells-longer-lasting-sex-faces-premature-end/news-story/425f607a2ed66d40432c79acb7fb7bf6

167 Robb, K. (2015). Federal Court slams Advanced Medical Institute for putting the hard word on erectile dysfunction patients, 23 April. http://www.smartcompany.com.au/business-advice/legal/federal-court-slams-advanced-medical-institute-for-putting-the-hard-word-on-erectile-dysfunction-patients/

GLOSSARY

4th estate
News media as the '4th estate', as a comparison of historical social class terms that included the '1st estate' of the clergy, the '2nd estate' of the nobility and the '3rd estate' of the common people.

above-the-line activities
IMC tactics that involve the use of mass media to promote brands and reach out to the target consumers (also referred to as 'one-to-many'). These include conventional broadcast media such as television and radio, print, the internet and related earned media.

accelerated purchase
An incentive to fast-purchase goods before the normal purchase cycle.

administrative action
The third level of the ACMA compliance pyramid, which involves issuing of a formal warning and infringement penalty notice.

administrative resolution
The third level of the ACCC enforcement pyramid applies in low-risk situations, with a company agreeing to resolve a matter.

advertising allowance
An incentive for the retailer to advertise the supplier's product.

advertising elasticity
The percentage change in sales of a brand for a 1 per cent change in the level of advertising. The academic literature showed that, on average, advertising elasticity is 0.10.

advertising weight
The level of advertising budget that an organisation has set.

advertorial
An advertisement disguised to look like an editorial.

AdWords
Google online advertisements where an advertiser pays only when a customer clicks on the advertisement.

affective advertising
Advertising that has the primary goal of involving the viewer and leveraging symbolic and/or experiential aspects.

affective message
An advertising message aimed at improving a brand's image (or the corporate image), increasing brand preferences, desire and liking, which typically results in affective advertising.

affordability approach
Methods according to which organisations set their budget purely on the basis of what they can afford, with no consideration of any other factor.

agenda-building theory
A PR-specific theory related to agenda setting, this is about using information channels such as news releases, interviews and blogs to influence media interest on selected topics.

agenda setting
Part of the transmission/media effects theories, agenda setting occurs when there is a repeated focus on an issue.

alternate sponsorships
A popular sponsorship format in the 1950s where there were different TV sponsors each week for the same TV show.

analysis of the market
A key milestone of the marketing planning process, which includes the identification of the target customer, the analysis of competitors and the identification of relevant environmental and contextual factors.

ANSOFF matrix
A framework that depicts different marketing objectives and strategies, which organisations can pursue, crossing over critical dimensions such as the product (new vs. existing) and the target market (new vs. existing).

apology advertisement
An advertisement by an advertiser apologising for a pricing error or product flaw.

Associative Network Theory (ANT) of memory

Psychological theory describing how individuals process information related to products and services; and how this information is accessed to carry out cognitive tasks (e.g. when a purchase decision needs to be made).

attitudes

Lasting evaluations (positive or negative) of an object (e.g. a brand or product), which include a cognitive, affective and conative dimension (i.e. attitudes underpin thoughts, feelings and actions or behaviours of consumers).

attribution theory

An audience theory, attribution theory involves attributing personal or situational factors to an event.

augmented reality (AR)

A technology that modifies a user's view of the real world with a computer-generated image.

banner advertising

A static or animated advertisement placed on a website that comes with standardised shapes and sizes.

behavioural learning theories

Theories that assume that learning occurs in the form of a quasi-default response to the environment (includes classical and instrumental conditioning).

behavioural segmentation

Segmenting consumers on how they behave, such as frequency of purchasing a product category or their loyalty patterns.

behavioural targeting

A digital targeting method used by advertisers that tracks and compiles consumers' online behaviour using cookies and other tracking tools.

below-the-line activities

IMC tactics aimed at 'one-to-one' communication with the target consumers, such as the distribution of pamphlets, handbills, stickers, promotions, brochures placed at point of sale, on the roads through banners and placards. It could also involve product demos and samplings at busy places such as malls and market places or residential complexes.

big data

Large amounts of data that require machine-based technologies to reveal patterns, trends and associations.

bill posting

Placing notices or posters on walls.

black PR

A phenomenon whereby public relations companies malign each other.

bonus pack

A special package like a value pack, twin pack or deal merchandise where the consumer receives more of the product at a lower price per unit.

Boston Consulting Group (BCG) matrix

A framework that depicts different marketing objectives and strategies that SBUs can pursue, (i.e. choosing between the critical decisions of 'investing', 'holding', 'harvesting' or 'divesting').

bounce back offer

An offer in a product to sell another product or more of the same product.

brand attributes

Qualities that brands are believed to have by a group of consumers. Similar to brand perceptions.

brand awareness

The consumers' ability to recognise and recall a brand.

brand-building objectives

IMC objectives concerning strategic brand management outcomes, such as brand awareness, brand image, mental availability and positive response to marketing initiatives.

brand equity

The intangible value of a brand resulting from strategic brand development.

brand image

The concepts that consumers associate with brands (also known as associations).

brand meaning

The combination of a brand's performance (concrete features) and a brand's imagery (perceptions and images).

brand perception

Beliefs that consumers hold about a brand. For example, consumers may believe a brand of fast food has convenient opening hours.

brand resonance
Ultimate outcome of strategic brand development, often expressed in terms of customer loyalty and lasting customer relationships.

brand salience
Knowledge of a brand in a consumer's mind—in particular it often refers to the neural network associated with a brand

brand user profile
Once a market has been segmented, the group of users should have a distinct profile that makes it possible to target them. For example, a new energy drink may be targeted at brand users who are younger and male.

broadcast media
Media that is broadcast from a place using radio frequency or digital networks. Radio and television are the two best known examples.

brochureware
Websites or webpages produced by converting a company's printed marketing or advertising materials into an internet format.

business strategy
A specific business plan prepared for a significant sub-division of the organisation, such as a Strategic Business Unit (SBU).

business-to-business (B2B)
When a business sells goods and services to another business.

business-to-consumer (B2C)
When a business sells goods and services to consumers.

buy one get one free
An incentive where the second same product is free.

buying allowance
A discount incentive based on bulk purchase of a product.

catalogues
Direct marketing promotional material with multiple pages showcasing the marketers' range of merchandise.

central route
When persuasion occurs by means of understanding a key argument or proposition presented through the IMC, resulting in a lasting change in attitudes

(consumer motivation, opportunity and ability to process the IMC message are high).

change-of-pace brands
Exception to the Double Jeopardy Law (DJL)—that is, large brands that are purchased rather infrequently, mostly because they have reached the maturity stage in their life cycle and are bought on occasion as a result of variety-seeking.

circulation
The number of sales that print media makes. For example, a newspaper with a circulation of 400 000 is a newspaper that sold 400 000 copies. This is not necessarily indicative of the number of readers, which is usually much higher due to pass-along effects.

classical conditioning
A behavioural learning theory that assumes that repeated exposure to a stimulus will induce a certain outcome behaviour (behavioural response).

click-through rate
The percentage of individuals viewing a web page who click on a specific advertisement that appears on the page.

club plan selling
Like Member Get Member, where a current member receives prizes or discounts for introducing another member.

cognitive learning theory
A theory that assumes that learning occurs as a result of complex reasoning.

cognitive message
An advertising message aimed at clarifying consumer needs, increasing brand awareness and product (or service) knowledge, which typically results in generic or pre-emptive advertising.

cognitive model of consumer behaviour
A model (or theory) of consumer behaviour that considers consumers as rational problem-solvers and describes decision making as a series of subsequent stages.

command regulation
Where the government writes detailed compliance rules and punishes offenders.

compensatory decision-making rules
A heuristic according to which the decision-maker will not compare all alternatives and their features in

detail; rather, the decision-maker will resort to simpler approaches, such as always buying the cheapest alternative.

competitive parity

Budgeting method whereby an organisation sets a budget in line with the rest of the competition within the same market or industry (also called 'meeting the competition').

conative message

An advertising message aimed at inducing behaviour (e.g. stimulating search, encouraging trial purchase and/or repurchase, increasing word-of-mouth recommendation) that typically results in salience advertising.

consideration set

In the context of decision making, it refers to the alternatives that meet more closely the needs of the decision-maker.

consumer behaviour

An applied social science that focuses on understanding all processes involved in how individuals select, access, buy, use and dispose of all sorts of goods and services.

consumer goods and services

Goods and services bought by consumers.

contest

A promotion where consumers use a skill to qualify for a prize.

continuum of problem solving and information processing

Spectrum of different levels of 'intensity' and complexity of the decision-making process, ranging from low to high problem solving (and information processing), thus capturing the three different models of consumer behaviour (cognitive, reinforcement and habit).

corporate strategy

The overarching strategic definition of the organisation, as outlined by the top executives.

corrective advertising

A series of advertisements by an advertiser to correct a misleading claim, as mandated by government authorities.

count and recount promotion

An incentive given based on quantity sold after a pre/post inventory period.

coupon

A printed or digital offer for a price reduction.

courtesy days

A privilege provided to special consumers to buy goods before they are promoted to the public.

cross-ruff

Using a non-competitive product to distribute a sample or coupon.

cross selling

Selling related products at a retail outlet.

crowdsourcing

The practice of obtaining needed services, ideas or content by soliciting contributions from a large group of consumers.

Customer Based Brand Equity (CBBE) framework

A framework developed by Kevin Keller that organisations can use to identify the 'building blocks' that constitute the 'DNA' of a brand, outlining objectives and metrics to be used strategically for the purpose of brand management/brand development.

customer relationship management (CRM)

Practices and strategies used to manage business relationships with customers, assisting in customer retention and driving sales over time

daguerreotype

An early photographic process using mercury vapour and an iodine-sensitised silver plate.

database marketing

A form of direct marketing using databases of customers or potential customers to generate strategies for promotion.

dating

An incentive to pay for a product purchase over a period.

dealer loader

An extra deal is loaded for a special display or product promotion.

dealer tie-in

An incentive for the retailer to tie in with the supplier through store display, cooperative advertising, contests and featuring of the product in the store's advertising.

decision making

A series of sub-sequent stages according to which consumers first become aware of a certain need; then seek information and alternatives likely to meet this need; compare and evaluate these alternatives; and ultimately reach a concluding decision, which provides feedback for future reference.

demarketing
Marketing to decrease demand, such as to quit or reduce smoking.

demographic segmentation
Segmenting consumers on demographic bases, including age, income, education level and gender.

descriptive budgeting method
'Rule of thumbs' (not based on evidence) that managers use to set budgets.

diffusion of innovation theory
An audience theory about adopting ideas or products as innovator, early adopter, early majority, late majority and laggard.

digital media
Media generally accessed through an electronic device such as a computer, smartphone or tablet. Examples include Facebook, Instagram, Snapchat and Twitter.

digital video advertising
Online display advertising that appears before, during or after a variety of digital video content.

direct mail
Promotional messages in print for a product or service delivered by postal mail.

direct marketing (DM)
A form of IMC where marketers communicate directly to customers through various media.

direct-response advertising
A type of direct marketing using advertisements to generate a response from consumers.

display advertising
Various forms of advertisements containing text, images, videos and audios that are displayed on websites.

display allowance
Incentive to display the product at a special place in the store such as an end-aisle spot.

distinctive assets
Highly distinctive brand elements, such as logos, taglines, characters and jingles.

distinctive branding elements
Highly distinctive brand elements, such as logos, taglines, characters and jingles (also known as 'distinctive assets').

Double Jeopardy Law (DJL)
An empirical marketing law according to which brands with a smaller market share are penalised 'twice'—that is, they have fewer customers who are also slightly less loyal than brands with a greater market share.

dual route
When persuasion occurs by means of understanding a key argument or proposition presented through the IMC as well as picking up peripheral cues, resulting in an ongoing (continuum) change in attitudes (consumer motivation, opportunity and ability to process the IMC message are moderate or medium).

Duplication of Purchase Law (DoPL)
Empirical marketing law according to which brands competing within the same product (or service) class (or category) will typically share their customers in line with the brands' market share.

Ehrenberg and Goodhardt's repeat purchase model
Formalised theory of buying behaviour that considers purchase decisions as a series of as-if-random occurrences largely determined by past behaviour; it also considers marketing stimuli's primary role in terms of 'nudging' otherwise pre-established purchase propensities (chances to buy).

empirical evidence
Knowledge derived from the analysis of (real) recurring trends and patterns in consumer purchases, as observed in data and/or factual documentation.

empirical generalisations (empirical marketing laws)
Theories of consumer behaviour that have been established through the analysis of relevant empirical evidence.

enforceable undertakings
Interventions of an enforcement authority to get individuals or companies to publicly agree to accept responsibility for breaching the law, agree on a negotiated settlement to redress consumer loss or suffering and improve trade compliance processes and culture.

enforced self-regulation
Public enforcement where a company or industry privately writes a set of compliance rules for the regulatory authority to publicly modify or ratify to satisfy government guidelines.

evaluation of alternatives
Stage of the decision-making process during which an individual compares and appraises alternatives on the basis of their perceived worth (or value).

evaluation of outcomes
Stage of the decision-making process that follows the decision (choice) and provides feedback and/or future reference, possibly leading to outcomes such as customer retention and loyalty.

evoked (or awareness) set
In the context of decision making, it refers to the alternatives that the decision maker is aware of.

excellence theory
A PR-specific theory that relates PR to organisational effectiveness.

external contingencies
Factors that are out of the direct control of marketers, and yet are likely to influence the decision-making process, such as physical availability (availability of a certain offer at the point of sale).

factory pack
Multiple packaging by supplier as a value pack of one product or several products.

familiarity
The strength of the information retained in memory and how easily it can come to mind following cue-based activation.

frame of reference
The target market where a certain brand intends to compete.

framing
Part of the transmission/media effects theories where there is another level of agenda setting with media describing an issue or a person in certain 'frames' or attributes.

free merchandise
A free product for purchasing a minimum quantity from the supplier or to offer as samples to consumers.

free sample
Common in supermarkets (free sampling of a new drink or product) and department stores (free perfume sachet).

free-to-air TV
Television transmitted without a fee to the viewer.

frequency
The number of times on average that a target group was exposed to a campaign.

frequent shopper program
A form of continuity plan or loyalty program where consumers redeem points for products or enjoy free products after loyalty cards are stamped over a period.

fulfilment
Refers to deliverance of goods and services as requested and purchased by the customer.

game
This involves collecting and matching symbols to win a prize.

generic or pre-emptive advertising
Advertising that has the primary goal of communicating the benefits that the product (or service) offers.

geographic segmentation
Segmenting consumers on the basis of where they live.

greenwashing
Occurs when companies claim to be environment champions when they have questionable practices.

habit model of consumer behaviour
A model of consumer behaviour that considers decision making as the outcome of very little or no cognitive effort (thinking) at all, and as the outcome of people's routines (or 'default' behaviour).

hard-sell
A rational persuasive approach to sell the direct benefit of using the advertised item.

hedonic factors
Feelings and emotions that may play a role in the decision-making process.

hedonism
Taking into consideration consumers' emotions and even playing with emotions in marketing

communication to attract consumers to a brand.
A good example of this is luxury brands.

heuristics
Mental shortcuts or 'rules of thumbs' that individuals
may use to simplify decision making.

IMC
Integrated Marketing Communication. The idea that all
communication to consumers should be integrated and
consistent.

IMC execution
The appeal that a particular message takes—for
example, humour, fantasy or rational.

IMC objectives
A series of crucial objectives that underpin IMC tactics,
including persuasion and communication objectives;
brand-building objectives; sales and economic returns
objectives; and other objectives.

IMC planning process
The process according to which an organisation makes
a series of concrete choices concerning the IMC (e.g.
message, media and tools) and establishes a budget to
support such choices. It starts with market research
and the identification of a target market; it then
includes product and brand positioning outlining, and
the definition of IMX objectives (i.e. persuasion and
communication objectives; brand-building objectives;
sales and economic return objectives).

implementation, control and evaluation
Milestones of the marketing planning process that
imply the translation of strategy into actions, an
adequate anticipation of monitoring mechanisms and
possible corrective actions, as well as formal activities
for appraising outcomes.

incentive pay
An incentive such as commission or a percentage
of sale.

inbound telemarketing call
A call that originates with the customer, who is
responding to an advertisement, for instance.

incentive travel
A holiday reward to retail or sales staff for exceeding
sales targets.

industrial goods and services
Goods and services used to produce other goods and
services

inertia
An instance where an individual has little or no
motivation to think about products, marketing
communication or making a decision.

infomercials
A form of hard-sell advertorial on television, popular in
direct-response advertising.

information age
A time when large amounts of information are widely
available to many people, primarily through computer
technology.

information search
Stage of the decision-making process during which an
individual engages in the quest for information across
different sources, some of which are internal (memory)
and some of which are external (environment).

infringement notice
Notice issued from an enforcement authority when
there is a contravention of the Australian Consumer
Law, such as unfair practices, product information,
product safety, non-compliance to substantiation
notices and providing misleading or false information
when responding to substantiation notices.

instrumental conditioning
Behavioural learning theory, which presumes the
use of specific approaches to trigger a behavioural
response, as individuals instinctively engage in
behaviours that produce positive outcomes and
avoid the ones that yield negative outcomes (includes
positive reinforcement, negative reinforcement and
punishment).

integrated direct marketing (IDM)
An approach to creating a unified consumer
experience with the brand/enterprise via facets of
direct marketing on various media.

intention to buy
A measure researchers use to establish that a
consumer is likely to buy a brand in the future.

interactivity
The process of two people or things working together
and influencing each other.

interest-based advertising
Advertising based on a consumer's interests as
determined by the consumer's online activities. Similar
to online behavioural advertising.

internal marketing
Activities directed within the organisation to motivate and empower employees.

Internet of Things (IoT)
Inter-networking of devices, vehicles, buildings and other items embedded with electronics, software, sensors, actuators and network connectivity that enable those objects to collect and exchange data.

interstitial
Full- or partial-page advertising text and images that appear in the transition between two content pages.

involvement
The personal relevance of a certain object, such as a product or service, a brand, a piece of information or a decision.

judgments and feelings
Consumers' reactions to marketing initiatives.

learning
How individuals decode reality, making sense of large amounts of stimuli.

lifetime customer value (LCV)
A projection to estimate a customer's monetary worth to a business after factoring in the value of the relationship with a customer over time.

limited information processing
Decisions performed without following a formalised decision-making process.

location intelligence
A technology that tracks, stores and analyses consumer behaviours based on individual consumers' location data.

long-term store
Also known as 'long term memory'. Said to be almost infinite, this is where memories are held once rehearsed.

market partitions
Exceptions to the Duplication of Purchase Law (DoPL)—that is, 'clusters' of brands that share their customer bases with one another more intensively (and irrespective of their market share) because of strong similarities in terms of the consumers' needs that they target.

market research
In the context of IMC planning, market research primarily refers to research that is product (or service) specific (aimed at identifying attributes and features that consumers value and desire) and consumer specific (aimed at uncovering the reasons for buying and using).

market share
The proportion of a brand's sales (in units sold, volume or dollar value) relative to competitors.

marketing mix strategies
Strategies in relation to the product (or service), pricing, distribution and promotional tactics that an organisation uses.

marketing planning process
The process of outlining all the decisions and actions that need to be undertaken for the realisation of the corporate, business and marketing strategies.

marketing strategy
The 'glue' that connects the mission of a certain organisation (its purpose) with the scopes of business-level strategies, thus facilitating the realisation of the corporate strategy.

mass market
The whole market rather than just a segment.

mass media
Media that has a wide coverage of the population and is not specifically targeted at any group.

media agency
A company that buys media space and then sells it to either advertising agencies or companies wishing to place advertisements.

media duplication
That consumers tend to not only use one media outlet, but will duplicate across many. This occurs not just across different platforms (so someone who watches a television on one day may also go onto Facebook), but also within a media outlet (a consumer who listens to a classical radio station may also listen to a pop station the same day).

memory
The 'place' where individuals store, retain, process and access information.

mental availability
Whether a brand is easily retrievable from a consumer's mind.

mental market share
The quantity and quality of concepts that consumers associate with brands.

mobile marketing
A set of practices that enables organisations to communicate and engage with their audience in an interactive and relevant manner through any mobile device or network.

multiple-unit packaging
A form of value pack used to encourage volume purchase.

native advertising
Paid advertising that takes the specific form and appearance of editorial content to blend into its surrounding.

negative reinforcement
An instrumental learning approach that implies removing something negative to trigger a certain outcome/behaviour (e.g. waiving fees to encourage service subscription).

niche brands
Exception to the Double Jeopardy Law (DJL)—that is, small brands that serve a small base of highly loyal customers, satisfying their specific needs.

niche product
A highly specialised offering directed to a narrow and specific segment.

non-controlled media
Media that is not controlled by the source—for example, the news media that control whether to publish news that they receive from news releases, news conferences, media interviews, media forums, public blogs or social media.

objective and task approach
A budgeting method according to which an organisation sets a budget in alignment with specific marketing or IMC objectives for the purpose of ensuring that the objective will be met.

objectives
Things that an IMC program will try to achieve or things that an organisation will try to achieve.

odd–even pricing
Odd pricing ends with an odd number (e.g. $3.99). Even pricing ends with a round number (e.g. $5.00).

one-way asymmetric model
A scientific persuasion communication model that includes blogs with comment enabled, content sharing sites, Wiki editable information, Rich Site Summary or RSS Feed and online community voting.

online behavioural advertising
Tracking a consumer's activities online and then targeting to meet the consumer's interests.

outbound telemarketing call
Where an organisation initiates calls to customers or the public.

Out-Of-Home (OOH)/outdoor advertising
Advertising that is outdoors in public places such as in roadside (e.g. billboards), transport and retail environments. It can, however, also include many other creative types of advertising in public places.

payout planning
A budgeting method according to which the organisation identifies a ratio of expenditures for IMC initiatives to sales or market share, depending on the life cycle.

percentage of sales
A budgeting method that implies identifying how much an organisation can spend on IMC initiatives as a percentage of the organisation's sales.

peripheral route
When persuasion occurs by means of remembering only peripheral cues presented through the IMC (e.g. a jingle used in a TV ad), resulting only in a temporary change in attitudes (consumer motivation, opportunity and ability to process the IMC message are low).

permission marketing
Delivering relevant messages to people who opt to get them.

personalisation
An adaptive system-initiated activity that provides users with tailored web interfaces by learning each user's preferences or interests.

persuasion
A permanent change in an individual's attitude, resulting from their ability to process focal as

well as peripheral information linked to a central argument (e.g. the brand being advertised and its characteristics).

PESO model
An integrated communication practice of using paid media, earned media, shared media and owned media.

PESTEL framework
A framework that organisations can use for the identification of relevant environmental and contextual factors (i.e. political, economic, social, technological, ecological and legal factors that may be relevant to understanding the context in which the organisation operates).

physical availability
Availability of a certain offer (e.g. product, service or brand) at the point of sale.

points of difference
Strong, favourable and unique features of a brand that distinguish it from other brands within the same frame of reference (target market).

points of parity
Features that a brand shares with other brands within the same frame of reference (target market).

positive reinforcement
An instrumental learning approach that implies the provision of a reward to trigger a certain outcome/ behaviour (e.g. free sample to encourage product trial).

premium
A gift offered as an incentive.

prescriptive budgeting method
Budgeting methods based on sophisticated techniques aimed at optimising expenditure levels and resources.

press agentry/publicity
A propaganda communication model that is one-way and where truth is not important.

price-off offer
A common rebate or discount incentive.

print media
Media that is printed, such as newspapers and magazines.

proactive public relations
Many of the PR functions could be described as proactive and strategically planned for.

problem (or need) recognition
A stage of the decision-making process during which an individual becomes aware of the existence of a gap between a desired status and their current status.

product and brand positioning
Strategic decisions aimed at identifying and establishing a specific 'place' to occupy in the mind of consumers.

property spruikers
Property investment promoters through seminars, training and materials.

psychographic segmentation
Segmenting consumers on psychographic measures such as personality and values.

public information
An information dissemination model that is one-way but where truth is important.

public service advertising
Advertising to influence public behaviour and attitudes on social issues.

public warning notices
Notices from enforcement authorities to alert consumers about scams, unsafe products, etc.

pull strategy
A marketing activity to pull consumers to stores to buy goods to make retailers purchase from suppliers.

punishment
An instrumental learning approach that implies presenting something negative to trigger a certain outcome/behaviour (e.g. surcharges to discourage credit card use).

purchase frequency
The average number of times the brand was purchased by its buyers and a widely used measure of brand loyalty.

purchase penetration
The proportion of a brand's buyers (consumers who bought the brand at least once in the time period considered) out of the total number of potential buyers (market potential).

purchase propensies
Chances to buy something again in the near future, given the number of times that it occurred in the past.

push money
Incentive to retail sales people to push sales of the supplier's brand.

push strategy
A marketing activity to push from the supplier to wholesalers/retailers.

quantitative models
Complex budgeting techniques that involve computer simulations of relationships between IMC expenditures, sales and profit, and industry-specific factors.

rate card
A card marketers use to understand the pricing of a magazine's advertising space and the target market that can be reached through it.

ratings
A measure of how many consumers watched a particular TV show or listened to a radio station at a particular time. TV shows often are cited as having ratings that can be interpreted as a percentage of the population who watched them.

rational problem-solvers
Individuals who outweigh perceived losses and benefits (in line with the economic notion of utility) and run decisions by considering the value that each alternative yields.

reach
A figure that tells a marketer how many of the target group were exposed to a campaign.

reactive public relations
PR that reacts to situations, such when a crisis occurs.

recollection (autobiographical recollection)
Reliving (in one's memory) of episodes that are autobiographical in nature, including vivid images of the episodes and specific spatial/temporal details.

refund
Some retailers offer a free refund of the product purchased if not satisfied within a certain time period.

rehearsal
The repetition of a memory, which if rehearsed enough will be encoded into the long-term store.

reinforcement model of consumer behaviour
A model of consumer behaviour that considers decision making primarily as the consumer's response to stimuli and the influence of past behaviour.

relationship management theory
A PR-specific theory about PR being a strategic management function to relate with various publics.

repertoire buying (or purchase repertoire)
In the context of decision-making, it refers to the alternatives that the decision-maker has previously purchased.

retrieval
The process of retrieving information from the long-term store into working memory.

Return on Marketing Investments (ROMI)
A way of capturing the worthiness and remuneration of marketing investments, linking economic returns to marketing expenditures.

rhetoric theory
A message theory that involves persuasive communication through a role model and the emotional or logical appeal of the person's message.

rich media
A broader range of internet advertising that exhibits dynamic motion or audio powered by Java or flash.

sales and economic returns objectives
IMC objectives concerning demand, sales, loyalty and retention, market share and purchase penetration.

sales contest
Incentive for the sales force through competition such as sales performance against other sales colleagues or sales teams.

salience advertising
Advertising that resonates with the product and brand positioning strategy.

scheduling
Over time how advertising is placed.

seasonal discount
A discount for retailers who order seasonal products in advance.

segmentation
Dividing buyers of a product category into groups on some characteristic.

segmentation research
Research that leads to the identification of groups of consumers with similar characteristics, on the basis of selected criteria such as psychographic variables

(e.g. lifestyle and consumption), demographic profile or purchase behaviour.

self-regulation
Private enforcement where a company or industry sets acceptable standards of practice and an internal compliance group punishes deviations from the rules.

sensory store
The first place any information that enters the brain arrives.

Shannon-Weaver Model
A communication model of Sender-Encoder-Channel/Noise-Decoder-Receiver.

share of mind
Top of mind awareness for a brand or its advertising.

share of voice
Share of a brand's advertising spending compared to competitors in the same product category.

showrooming
A shopping process that begins with in-store browsing and ends with online purchase.

situational theory
An audience theory that is contextual, where active people seek information while passive consumers are disinterested.

sleeper effect theory
A message theory where a person forgets an unreliable source but remembers and accepts the message.

'SMART' objectives
Objectives featured in a strategy should be specific, measurable, achievable, relevant and timely.

social buzz
Emotion, excitement and anticipation about the original marketing message created by interaction of consumers of a brand, product or service.

social media
A group of internet-based applications that build on the ideological and technological foundations of Web 2.0 and allow the creation and exchange of user-generated contents.

social media marketing
The attempt to use social media to achieve marketing objectives.

soft-sell
An emotional and indirect approach that creates positive feelings, impressions and associations for the advertised brand through humour, entertainment etc.

spot
A time-related space that is bought for advertising on television or radio, commonly in increments of 15, 30 and 60 seconds.

strategic brand management/development
A series of considerations and strategic decisions aimed at determining what needs to be done, from an IMC perspective, to build and maintain over time a strong brand.

Strategic Business Unit (SBU)
A significant sub-division of the organisation.

strategy
A more or less clear indication of where the firm is and where it should be in the future, and all the steps required to make it happen.

strength of memory associations (familiarity)
The strength of the information retained in memory and how easily it can come to mind following cue-based activation.

Strong theory
A theory that assumes IMC persuades people to buy a brand by changing their attitudes.

subscription TV
Pay TV through a special receiver.

substantiation notice
These notices from enforcement authorities seek to secure information or documentation to support a publicised claim, such as advertising 'Was/Now'.

sweepstake
A promotion where chance rather than skill determines winners of prizes.

target market
A group of consumers showing similar characteristics that is worth pursuing, in light of its size (market potential) and attractiveness (competitive appeal).

targeting
Once a market is segmented, the targeting process is the strategic decision to focus promotional efforts on one particular segment of consumers.

telemarketing

The marketing of goods or services via telephone calls to potential customers.

top of mind brand awareness

When the consumer can recall a brand without being prompted.

traditional media

Non-digital media such as television, radio, print and cinema.

two-step flow theory

A transmission/media effects theory that involves an opinion leader influencing the decision maker.

two-way asymmetric

A two-way scientific persuasion communication model that has imbalanced effects to influence audience to the views of the organisation.

two-way symmetric

A two-way mutual understanding communication model that has balanced effects of both public and organisation changing attitudes or behaviour.

universal set

In the context of decision making, it refers to all the alternatives available to the decision maker.

user-generated content (UGC)

Any form of content created by consumers or end-users of a system or service.

utility

The worth (or value) of each alternative within a set of alternatives that an individual compares in the context of decision making.

Virtual Reality (VR)

A computer technology that uses headsets, sometimes in combination with physical spaces or multi-projected environments, to generate realistic images, sounds and other sensations that stimulate a user's physical presence in a virtual or imaginary environment.

Weak theory

A theory that assumes IMC slowly builds salience for a brand, and this increases the probability that people will purchase it.

Web 1.0

Read-only web in which users' experience is limited to reading information presented to them.

Web 2.0

Read-write web where the link between information producers and consumers is blurred and is characterised by interactivity, user control, collaboration and sharing.

Web 3.0

Read-write-execute web in which the system (Web, computer or device), not humans, links, integrates and analyses various sets of data collected through multiple platforms to summarise a large amount of information into knowledge and wisdom.

webisodes

Web videos or films that are cheaper to run on the internet than television.

webrooming

A shopping process that begins with online browsing and ends with in-store purchase.

word of mouth

Act of exchanging marketing information among consumers.

working memory store

Also known as 'short-term memory'. This is where information arrives in the brain after the sensory store and before the long-term store. It is said to be able to handle 7±2 items of information.

INDEX

2DayFM radio station, 'Royal Prank' broadcast   388
2XU brand   3–4
4th estate   191

AAMI Smart Plates app   347
above the line activities   79
accelerated purchase   254
administrative resolution   378, 379
Advanced Medical Institute Pty Limited, misleading advertising   395–9
advertising   123–71
   as component of IMC   8
   categories of   130–1
   creating   136–42
   defining   125–6
   effectiveness   142–9
   history   133–6
Advertising Age
   Top 15 Campaigns of the Early 21st Century   144–5
   Top 100 Campaigns of the 20th Century   142–3
advertising allowance   254
advertising elasticity   79
Advertising Standards Bureau (ASB)   391–3, 395–9
advertising weight   79
advertorials   134
Adweek Creative 100   137–8
affective advertising   76
affordability approach   78
agenda-building theory   185
agenda setting   185
Air New Zealand #BetterWayToFly campaign   35
Airbnb 'Don't just go there, live there' campaign   65–6
alcohol advertising regulation   390
Aldi, success in Australia   81
alternate sponsorships   134
American Express webisodes   135–6
American Legacy, 'Body Bags' campaign   145
American Tobacco Company, Bernays campaigns for   200–1
analysis of the market   70
ANSOFF matrix   70
apology advertisements   132
application, brand positioning by   102
apps, advertising in   347
   see also online media

April Fools' Day pranks   133
Arts Centre Melbourne 'Sally's First Show' campaign   237–8
associations *see* professional associations
Associative Network Theory of memory (ANT)   46
attitudes   13–14
attribution theory   185
audience theories   185
augmented reality (AR)   309
Australian Association of National Advertisers, regulatory framework   381, 391
Australian Communications and Media Authority (ACMA)   379–80, 385–6
Australian Competition and Consumer Commission (ACCC)
   legal powers of   384–5
   regulatory framework   377–9
Australian Securities and Investments Commission (ASIC)
   enforcement role   386
   regulatory framework   379
awards
   as an incentive   253
   Asia Pacific Tambuli Awards   348
   Australian Web Awards   25
   Cannes Lion Awards   148
   CIPR Excellence Awards   188
   Creative Strategy Awards   138
   Effie Awards   148
   for advertising   159
   for direct marketing   244
   for electronic and social media   332
   for public relations   209
   for sales promotion   282
   GAPRCM COMM PRIX Awards   188
   Grand Prix for Good Awards   128
   IPA Effectiveness Awards   147–8
   Melbourne Design Awards   25
   public relations   209
   Shonky Awards   373
   Silver Anvil Awards   187
awareness set   38

'Backseat Driver' campaign, Toyota   317–18
Band-Aids 'Magic Vision' app   309

banner advertising   296, 302
Bayer Healthcare Pharmaceuticals, misleading
advertising   383
beaconing   308
behavioural learning theories   43
behavioural segmentation   100
behavioural targeting   311
behaviourist models of consumer behaviour
39–40
Bell Pottinger, misleading campaigns   195
below the line activities   79
benefit, brand positioning by   104
Bernays, Edward   182–3, 200–3
best industry practices   142–3
#BetterWayToFly campaign, Air New Zealand   35
big data   311–13
big ideas   137–8
bill posting   387
black PR   175
blood donations, 'Missing Type' campaign   195–6
BMW
    'Diesel gone good' campaign   111–12
    newspaper advertising by   357–9
'Body Bags' campaign, American Legacy   145
bonus pack   256
Boston Consulting Group (BCG) matrix   70
bounce back offer   256–7
Braithwaite, John   375
brand websites   301–2
branding, IMC and   99–100
brands
    attributes   106
    awareness of   73, 99
    brand building objectives   75
    brand equity   43
    image   45, 81
    indirect promotion   131–2
    marketing   130–3
    meaning   73
    perceptions of   104
    positioning   97–121, 101–7
    resonance   73
    salience   106
    segmentation by   72, 100, 105–7
    targeting by   100–1, 105, 354–5
    user profiles   105
broadcast media   232–3, 341
brochureware   301
Brown Brothers 'Colourful Conversations'

campaign   22–5
budgets for marketing   77–8
business-to-business sales (B2B)   251
business-to-consumer sales (B2C)   251
buy one get one free   256–7
buying allowance   254

'Campaign for Real Beauty', Unilever Dove
144, 190–1
Cannes Creative Effectiveness Grand Prix   145–7
Cape Times newspaper, readership profile   344
catalogue marketing   228–9
'Celebrating Cinema' campaign, Rolex   123–4
central route to persuasion   16
Chartered Institute of Public Relations (CIPR)
Excellence Awards   188
Cheney Brothers New York   200
children
    childhood literacy campaigns   268
    online marketing to   317–20, 324–6
    regulations on advertising to   390
'Chizza' campaign, KFC   255
CHOICE magazine Shonky Awards   373
circulation numbers   341–2
classical conditioning   43
click-through rates   303
club plan selling   256–7
Coca-Cola
    #ThatsGold campaign   318–20
    Hall of Shame awards   372
    use of Stevia by   97–8
codes of practice in public relations   193–4
cognitive learning theory   43
cognitive message   76
cognitive models of consumer behaviour   37
'Colourful Conversations' campaign, Brown
Brothers   22–5
command regulation   375
commercial radio   387
Commonwealth Bank of Australia, retail bank
campaign   47
communication models   9–10, 185–6
communication timeline   177–9
comparative appeals   108
Comparethemarket.com 'Meerkat' campaign   42
compensatory decision-making rules   39
Competition and Consumer Act 2010 (Cth)   384–5
competitive parity method   78
competitor, brand positioning by   103

complaints mechanisms   387–8, 392–3
conative message   77
consideration set   38
Consolidated ICC Code   374
consultancies in public relations   188
consumer behaviour   35–63, 252, 299–301
consumer goods and services
    buyer incentives   254–8
    defining   252
    feedback from   270–5, 387–8, 392–3
contests   256–7
continuum of problem solving and information processing   39
controlled media   191
corporate strategy   68
corrective advertising   132
count and recount promotion   254
coupons   256–7, 264
courtesy days   256–7
cradle-to-grave marketing   317
'Crash the Super Bowl' campaign, Doritos   297–8
Creative 100 awards   137–8
crisis communication   180–1
cross-promotions   249
cross-ruff   256–7
cross selling   256–7
cultural symbolism, brand positioning by   104
Customer Based Brand Equity (CBBE) framework   72
customer relationship management (CRM)   226

data-driven marketing   223–4, 311–13
dating incentive   254
dealer loader   254
dealer tie-in   254
deceptive pricing   264
decision-making   37
Declaration of Principles   182
Délifrance Singapore, direct marketing   219
delivery-specific industry codes of conduct   388–90
demarketing   128
demographic segmentation   100
demonstration appeals   108
descriptive budgeting method   78
'Diesel gone good' campaign, BMW   111–12
diffusion of innovation theory   185
digital media see online media
digital video advertising   302
Dior, customers of   52–4

direct advertising   231–4
direct mail marketing   229–30
direct marketing   219–46
    as component of IMC   8
    definitions   220–1
    history   221–2
    platforms   227
    regulatory framework   389
    strategy   224–7
display advertising   302–3
display allowance   254
distinctive assets   74, 106–7
distinctive branding elements   43
'Don't just go there, live there' campaign, Airbnb   65–6
Doritos 'Crash the Super Bowl' campaign   297–8
Double Jeopardy Law (DJL)   50–1, 266–7
dual route to persuasion   16
'Dumb Ways to Die' campaign, Melbourne Metro   348
Duplication of Purchase Law (DoPL)   49–50

earned media   192
Ehrenberg and Goodhard repeat purchase model   40
Elaboration Likelihood Model   15, 17
electronic media see online media
email advertising   347
    see also online media
emotional appeals   108–9
empirical evidence for marketing theory   48–51
empirical generalisations   48
empirical laws of marketing   48
enforceable undertakings   378
enforced self-regulation   375
enforcement of sanctions   383–4
Enron Corporation, misleading campaigns   194
ethics   194–5, 371–418
European Advertising Standards Alliance (EAS)   380
evaluation of alternatives   38
evaluation of outcomes   38
evoked set   38
excellence theory   185
exciting sales promotions   258–9
execution of IMC   107
external contingencies   39

factory pack   254
factual appeals   107–8
familiarity   47

fantasy, campaigns based on   109
fast food industry   270–5, 390
Fast Moving Consumer Goods (FMCG)   350
fear, campaigns based on   109
'Fearless Girl' campaign, State Street Global
Advisors   139–40
features, brand positioning by   101–2
Ferragni, Chiara   324–6
First Call Fund, Arts Centre Melbourne   237–8
framing   185
Franklin, Benjamin   221
free flights offer, Hoover vacuum cleaners   265–6
free merchandise   254
free samples   256–7
free-standing inserts   256–7
free-to-air TV   387
frequency, OOH advertising   345
frequent shopper programs   256–7
Fuel PR, misleading campaigns   194–5
fulfilment of direct orders   222, 227

game-based marketing   256–7
Game of Thrones, marketing of   83–5
GAPRCM COMM PRIX Awards   188
Gear VR campaign, Samsung   74
General Electric, Bernays campaigns   202
General Motors, Bernays campaigns   202–3
generic advertising   76
geo-targeting   308
geofencing   308
geographic segmentation   100
Gillette 'Tag the Weather' campaign   306
Global Alliance for Public Relations and
Communication Management   184
global sports competitions   260–2
glossary   420–32
governments
    advertising by   127–8
    regulation by   375–6
greenwashing   175
Groupon   264

habit model of consumer behaviour   41–2
Hall of Shame awards   372
hard-sell approach   134, 136–7
Hashtag12 banner, PEMCO Insurance Company   321–2
heavy buyers, targeting   354–5
hedonic factors   39

hedonism   17
Heinrich, Sonia   55–7
heritage, brand positioning by   104
heuristics   39
high-value buyers, targeting   354–5, 357–9
Hock Siong & Co, upcycled furniture sales   235
Holiday Wish List app, Target   318
Home Businesses, advertising by   127
Hoover vacuum cleaners, free flights offer   265–6
humour, campaigns based on   109
Hungry Jack's, eliciting customer feedback   271–3

IKEA catalogue marketing   *229*
IMC *see* Integrated Marketing Communication
implementation, control and evaluation milestone   70
inbound telemarketing calls   231
incentives
    for business buyers   253–4
    for consumers   254–8
    for sales force   252–3
    incentive pay   252–3
    incentive travel   253–4
individuals, advertising by   126–7
industrial goods and services   251, 253–4
industry associations *see* professional associations
industry marketing   129
inertia   42
infomercials   135
information age   296
information search   38
informational appeals   107–8
infringement notices   377–8
Instagram, Chiara Ferragni on   324–6
Institute of Practitioners in Advertising, advertising
creation model   137
instrumental conditioning   43
integrated direct marketing (IDM)   234
Integrated Marketing Communication (IMC)
    branding and   99
    budgeting for   77–8
    consumer behaviour theories and   37–9
    execution of   107
    introduction to   5–34
    marketing and   5–6
    objectives for   75–6
    planning for marketing   6–7, 65–94, 349–51
    responsible communication in   371–418
    strategy and planning   65–94

intention to buy   99
interactivity   296
interest-based advertising   389
internal marketing   70
International Chamber of Commerce, regulatory framework   374–5
International Food & Beverage Alliance, regulatory framework   374
internet *see* online media
Internet of Things (IoT)   311, 313–14
interstitials   302
involvement   41
IPA Effectiveness Awards   147–8
Ivory soap, Bernays campaigns for   200

Johnson & Johnson, Tylenol product tampering crisis   180–1
journals
    advertising   160
    direct marketing   244–5
    public relations   210
judgments and feelings   73

Kalofolias, Vicky   113–15
Katies, newsletter content   *16*
KFC
    'Chizza' campaign   255
    eliciting customer feedback   270–1

Laps, Michael   360–3
largest advertisers   131
Lavazza, fantasy campaign   *109*
learning theories   37, 43–8
Lee, Ivy   182
left-brain advertising   137
legislation   383–4
lifetime customer value (LCV)   226
'Like a Girl' campaign, Proctor & Gamble   139
limited information processing   39
Listerine, misleading advertising   382
'Live the Flavor' advertisement, Doritos   297–8
location-based advertising   307–8
location intelligence   308
long-term store   11–12
Lucasfilm, cross-promotion campaigns   249

Magic Vision app, Band-Aids   309
market partitions   49
market research   71
market share   80

marketing *see* advertising; brands; direct marketing; Integrated Marketing Communication (IMC); online media
marketing metrics   80–2
marketing mix strategies   70
marketing strategy   68
Marriott 'The Teleporter' campaign   314–15
Mars Australia marketing strategy   68
Masita, Reese   327–9
mass market   105
mass media   179–80, 340–7
McDonalds, eliciting customer feedback   273–5
McNeil Consumer Products, Tylenol product tampering crisis   180–1
measuring brand perception   104
media
    codes of conduct specific to   387–8
    decisions about   339–69
    duplication in   353–4
    for direct marketing   225
    public relations tools   191–3
    purchasing   353
    see also names of media
media agencies   340
media effects theories   185
Meerkat campaign, Comparethemarket.com   42
Melbourne Metro   348
memory processing
    behaviour dependent on   37
    in consumers   45–8
    in IMC   13
    models of   10–11
mental availability   7
mental market share   74
message theories   185
Miller's Law   11–12
Missing Type campaign, National Health Service (UK)   195–6
mobile marketing   299, 307
movie launches   259–60
multi-screen use   310
multiple-unit packaging   256–7
Museum of Public Relations   182–3
music, campaigns based on   109

National Health Service (UK), Missing Type campaign   195–6
native advertising   135, 303–4, 389–90
need recognition   38

negative binomial distribution (NBD)   354–5
negative reinforcement   43
Neilsen Global Survey of Trust in Advertising
299–300
Neo, Chloe   400–3
New Yorker, direct marketing   *222*
News Corp Australia, Promotional offers   268
newspapers, online vs print versions   342
niche products   69
non-compliance with advertising codes   391
non-controlled media   191
non-profit organisations, advertising by   127–8
Number Fever campaign, Pepsi-Cola   265
Nurofen, misleading advertising   385

objectives of a marketing program   97–121, 224–5
odd-even pricing   256–7
Office of the Australian Information
Commissioner   386
one-step offers   226
one-way asymmetric model   186
online behavioural advertising   389
online media   293–337
    advertising in   345–8
    as component of IMC   9
    direct advertising   232
    direct marketing   227–8
    newspapers shifting to   343
    public relations   180
    regulatory framework   389
    trust in   341
    Web 1.0   296
    Web 2.0   296
    Web 3.0   298
    web based advertising   346
    webisodes   135
    webrooming   299
    see also social media
Orger, Sloane   26–8
Out Of Home advertising   345, 388–9
outbound telemarketing calls   231
outdoor advertising   345, 388–9
owned media   192

paid media   192
'Parents' Voice' community, Hall of Fame/Shame
awards   371–2
Pay TV, take-up by country   355
payout planning   78

PEMCO Insurance Company, Hashtag12 banner   321–2
Pepsi-Cola Number Fever campaign   265
percentage of sales method   78
peripheral route to persuasion   16
permission marketing   228
personal selling, as component of IMC   9
personalisation of online media   310
persuasion   7, 13–14
PESO model   191–2
PEST/EL analysis   6, 70
Peter Alexander Sleepwear   45
Philco Radio and Television, Bernays campaigns
for   203
physical availability   39
Pillsbury Bake-Off Contest   263–4
planning for marketing
    defining   6–7
    IMC process   71–5
    media use planning   349–51
    strategy and planning   65–94
platforms for direct marketing   227–8
points of difference   73
points of parity   73
positioning *see* brands
positive reinforcement   43
pre-emptive advertising   76
premium   256–7
Preparation-Incubation-Illumination-Verification
model   137
prescriptive budgeting method   78
press agentry model   186
price-off offer   102, 256–7
Pridgeon, Alicia   154–6
print media   179, 232, 341–2
proactive public relations   188
problem recognition   38
Procter & Gamble Unilever
    Bernays campaigns for   200
    'Like a Girl' campaign   139
    'Thanks, Mum' campaign   148–53
product and brand positioning   72
product class dissociation   102
product-specific industry codes   390–1
professional associations
    for advertising   159
    for direct marketing   243–4
    for electronic and social media   331–2
    for public relations   183, 187–9, 208–9

professional services, advertising by   127

property spruikers   384

prospects, in direct marketing   223

PRWeek awards to United Airlines   173–4

psychographic segmentation   100

public information model   186

public relations   173–217

   as component of IMC   8

   campaign impact   265

   defining   175–6

   ethics in   194–5

   functions of   187–98

   history of   176–84

   journals in   210

   professional associations   183, 187–9, 208–9

   theories and models   185–7

Public Relations Institute of Australia, public relations awards   188

Public Relations Society of America (PRSA), Silver Anvil Awards   187–8

public service advertising   127–8

public warning notices   378

publicity model   186

pull strategy   254

punishment   43

purchase frequency   80

purchase penetration   80

purchase propensities   40

purchase repertoire   38

push money   254

push strategy   254

quality, brand positioning by   102

quantitative models for budgeting   78

Quick Response (QR) codes   307

rate cards   343

ratings measures   349–51

rational problem-solvers   37

reach of OOH advertising   345

reactive public relations   188

reality shows   260

Reckitt Benckiser, misleading advertising   385

refunds   256–7

regulatory frameworks   373–83

rehearsal   11

reinforcement model of consumer behaviour   40–1

relationship management theory   185

repeat purchase model   40

repertoire buying   48

researchers into ethics   375

responsible marketing communication   371–418

responsive regulation   377

retail bank campaign, Commonwealth Bank of Australia   47

retailers, objectives for   252

retrieval from memory   12–13

Return on Marketing Investments (ROMI)   76

rhetoric theory   185

Ribena, misleading advertising   382–3

rich media   302

right-brain advertising   137

Rolex Celebrating Cinema campaign   123–4

'Royal Prank' broadcast, 2DayFM radio station   388

sales and economic returns objectives   75

sales contests   253

Sales Force, objectives and incentives   251–3

sales promotions   249–90

   as component of IMC   8

   challenges in   264–8

   defining   250–1

salience advertising   77

'Sally's First Show' campaign, Arts Centre Melbourne   237–8

Samsung, Gear VR campaign   74

scheduling marketing   350

seasonal discount   254

segmentation *see* brands

self-regulation   374–6

sensory store   11

sexual innuendo, campaigns based on   109

Shannon–Weaver model of communication   185

share of mind   148

share of voice   148

shared media   192

shock, campaigns based on   109

Shonky Awards, CHOICE magazine   373

showrooming   299

situational theory   185

Skechers US, misleading advertising   383

sleeper effect theory   185

slice of life appeals   108

small businesses, advertising by   127

SMART objectives   76

Smart Plates app, AAMI   347

Snickers, 'You're not you when you're hungry' campaign   141–2

social media 293–337
    advertising on 346–7
    marketing on 304
    popular platforms 233
    social buzz 305
    upcycled furniture sales 235
    see also online media
soft-sell approach 134, 136–7
South Africa, newspaper advertising in 357–9
specially created events 263
sponsorship, as component of IMC 9
sports
    2XU sportswear 3–4
    Global sports competitions 260–2
spots on broadcast media 341
State Street Global Advisors, Fearless Girl
campaign 139–40
stevia with Coca-Cola 97–8
strategic brand management/development 72–5
Strategic Business Unit (SBU) 68
strategy for marketing 65–94
    considerations in 76–7
    direct marketing 224–7
strong theory of IMC 18–19, 136–7
subscription TV 387
substantiation notices 378, 385
SunSmart campaign 128–9
Swain, Stephanie 240–2
sweepstake 256–8
Sweetie campaign, Terre des Hommes 140–1
SWOT analysis 6

Tag the Weather campaign, Gillette 306
Target, Holiday Wish List app 318
target market 70, 72
    see also brands
targeting *see* brands
telemarketing 231
television reality shows 260
Telstra Thrive On campaign 14–15
Terre des Hommes Sweetie campaign 140–1
'Thanks, Mum' campaign, Procter & Gamble
Unilever 148–53
#ThatsGold campaign, Coca-Cola Amatil 318–20
The New Yorker, direct marketing *222*
'The Parents' Voice' community, Hall of Fame/Shame
awards 371–2
'The Teleporter' campaign, Marriott 314–15
Therapeutic Goods Administration 379, 386

therapeutic products, regulations on advertising 390
Thrive On campaign, Telstra 14–15
Top 10 PR consultancies 188–90
Top 15 Campaigns of the Early 21st Century 144–5
Top 100 Campaigns of the 20th Century 142–3
top of mind brand awareness 99
Toyota, Backseat Driver campaign 317–18
traditional communication models 9–10
traditional media, future of 351–3
transmission theories 185
trust in advertising 299–300
Tutt, Emily 204–6
two-step flow theory 185
two-step offers 226
two-way asymmetric model 186
two-way symmetric model 186
Tylenol product tampering crisis 180–1

Unilever Dove 'Campaign for Real Beauty' 144, 190–1
United Airlines, negative publicity 173–4
upcycled furniture sales, social media platforms 235
use, brand positioning by 102
user-generated content 296
users, brand positioning by 102–3
utility theory 37

value-expressive appeals 108–9
vehicle advertising regulation 390
Victoria University, block teaching model 339
Villani, Christopher 276–8
virtual reality (VR) 314–15
Volkswagen
    cheats emissions tests 383
    Think Small campaign 143

weak theory of IMC 18–20, 136–7
Web 1.0 296
Web 2.0 296
Web 3.0 298
web-based advertising *see* online media
weight management products 390
Westinghouse, Bernays campaigns for 202
White, Damien 86–8
whole-brain advertising 137
women's magazines, media duplication in 354
word-of-mouth recommendation 299
working memory store 11

'You're not you when you're hungry' campaign,
Snickers 141–2
YouTube advertising 348